Topographical Names and Protection of Linguistic Minorities

SCHRIFTEN
zum internationalen und zum öffentlichen
RECHT

Herausgegeben von Gilbert Gornig

Band 99

PETER LANG
Frankfurt am Main · Berlin · Bern · Bruxelles · New York · Oxford · Wien

Giuseppe de Vergottini
Valeria Piergigli
(eds.)

Topographical Names and Protection of Linguistic Minorities

PETER LANG
Internationaler Verlag der Wissenschaften

Bibliographic Information published by the Deutsche Nationalbibliothek
The Deutsche Nationalbibliothek lists this publication in the Deutsche Nationalbibliografie; detailed bibliographic data is available in the internet at http://dnb.d-nb.de.

This publication was financially supported
by Coordinamento Adriatico
and by Centro di Documentazione Multimediale
della Cultura Giuliana Istriana
Fiumana e Dalmata – Trieste.

Coordinamento Adriatico

www.arcipelagoadriatico.it

ISSN 0943-173X
ISBN 978-3-631-60976-7

www.peterlang.de

Contents

Authors

Lidija R. Basta Fleiner, Former Professor of Constitutional Law, University of Fribourg (Switzerland); Permanent Visiting Professor University of Belgrade (Serbia)

Antonella Benazzo, Associate Professor of Public Comparative Law, University of Padova (Italy)

Carlo Casonato, Professor of Comparative Constitutional Law, University of Trento (Italy)

Guglielmo Cevolin, Lecturer of Public Law, University of Udine (Italy)

Sergiu Constantin, Researcher, European Academy of Bolzano/Bozen (Italy)

Giuseppe de Vergottini, Emeritus Professor of Constitutional Law, University of Bologna (Italy)

Orsolya Farkas, Contract Professor of Labour Law, Free University of Bolzano/Bozen (Italy)

Thomas Fleiner, Emeritus Professor of Constitutional and Administrative Law, University of Fribourg (Switzerland)

Daniela Giaimo, Scholar of the bilingual toponomastics of Alto Adige, author of an undergraduate thesis and research for the Italian National Council of Research developed at the Linguistics Department, University of Padova (Italy), under Prof. Giovanni Battista Pellegrini

Peter Hilpold, Professor of International Law, European Law and Comparative Law, University of Innsbruck (Austria)

Dewi Llŷr Jones, Lecturer in Public Law, Bangor University Law School, Wales (United Kingdom)

Boris Krivokapić, Professor of Public International Law and Human Rights, Megatrend University of Belgrade (Serbia)

Susanna Mancini, Associate Professor of Public Comparative Law, University of Bologna (Italy); Adjunct Professor of International Law, SAIS Johns Hopkins University BC

Carlo Alberto Mastrelli, Emeritus Professor of Glottology and Germanic Philology, University of Florence (Italy)

Francesco Palermo, Associate Professor of Public Comparative Law, University of Verona (Italy); Director of the Institute for Studies on Federalism and Regionalism, European Academy of Bolzano/Bozen (Italy)

Valeria Piergigli, Professor of Public Law, University of Siena (Italy)

Giovanni Poggeschi, Associate Professor of Public Comaparative Law, University of Salento (Italy)

Davide Rossi, Lecturer of History of Medieval and Modern Law, University of Trieste (Italy)

Foreword

In a period such as the present, characterised by the crisis of state sovereignty, the breakdown of economic and cultural barriers, and irreversible pressure to delocalise vital activities and interests, fulfilment of which often escapes the spatial dimension of single States, the protection of personal and cultural identity means rethinking the local dimension and rediscovering a sense of belonging to places that often contain the historical memory and values of their stable communities. Globalisation and localisation are not antithetical but rather correlated processes: evolution of the concept of territoriality and the risk of levelling and sameness (of values, culture and so forth) make it necessary to reconsider and valorise local belonging and diversity.

Despite these changes, the boundaries drawn by geography and history remain: national borders are often redefined as a result of wars, territorial claims, struggles for self-determination and independence, more or less peaceful annexations and secessions. Today these phenomena not only have a large psychological impact on local populations, but often determine profound cultural and social transformations.

In a global context that reveals the loss of traditional coordinates (States, territory, sovereignty) and at the same time the impossibility of letting them go, exterior symbols that manifest and hand down the cultural and territorial identity of certain individuals and communities take on special meaning, perhaps more so than in the past. In the symbolic store of communities specifically characterized with respect to the rest of the population, such as linguistic and cultural minorities, *toponyms*, or the names of public places, enable community members to express their identity and will to preserve their cultural heritage. Among the positive measures for protecting members of linguistic minorities, guarantee of the right to use a minority language in toponomastics is certainly one of the first and major manifestations of sensitivity that public authorities – state and local – can show, especially towards "autochthonous" communities, namely, communities historically settled on certain geographical areas.

However, history shows that changes in sovereignty and state borders as a result of conflicts, as well as the rise and fall of political regimes in different parts of the planet, often forcibly divide local populations and/or artificially modify the names of places. At all latitudes, such measures arise from the political need to impose apparent homogeneity of culture and language, according to the model of the nation-State that does not tolerate exceptions to the supremacy of its founding values. Moreover, in the last century, the methods of brutal simplification used by various autocracies led, among other things, to different expression of place names with every ideological upheaval or modification of national linguistic policy.

At first sight it may therefore seem that attribution of place names is merely an internal question of States, often connected to the alternation of state power and the holders of sovereignty. However, since the middle of last century, the international community has concerned itself with this topic, albeit with prudence and respect for the choices of States. The topic involves technical profiles of particular complexity, when the territories or localities to be renamed evoke membership of communities with minority languages and culture. Indeed, in these cases, the objective of "standardization" of geographic names at national and international level ensures clear communication, which in turn serves socioeconomic development as well as minority identity rights.

In consideration of the specificity and multidisciplinary character of the subject, the research contained in this volume includes contributions by linguists, glottologists and historians, as well as papers on strictly legal topics. The latter consider the evolution and the regulation of toponomastics, with particular attention to European legislation concerning communities, distinguished from the rest of a national population by linguistic and cultural traits that they want to preserve, also by conservation or restoration of traditional place names. In a comparative perspective, the topic of protection and valorisation of minorities through traditional toponyms in areas of autochthonous settlement involves (albeit by different approaches) all pluralistic and plurilingual legal systems. In principle, it forms part of the promotional model variably adopted for the protection of linguistic minorities.

Despite the widespread willingness (at least in terms of intentions and formal commitment) of public powers to restore historical denominations, the right to use traditional place names is often assigned minor rank in the hierarchy of minority protection measures. This realization prompts research into the cultural, political and legal reasons for such attitudes and into ways of overcoming approaches only apparently in favour of recovery of traditional toponomastics and legal protection of linguistic minorities, but which prove ineffective or are contradicted when implemented. Emblematically, in some cases, public powers decide not to implement at all the provisions concerning the traditional place names.

This volume is conceived in an attempt to understand these mechanisms, of which there has not yet been any full legal analysis; in that perspective, it brings together some of the most significant examples of toponomastic regulation. By historical-legal study and a comparative view, it is hoped to contribute to the development of a mature and conscious approach to the topic of protection of minority identity through the maintenance and valorisation of place names, which not only express and epitomise the symbolic and cultural heritage of the communities involved, but of humanity in general.

This research is an initiative of the association *Coordinamento Adriatico* and its publication was made possible by the generosity of the *Centro di documentazione multimediale della cultura giuliana istriana fiumana e dalmata (Trieste)*.

Giuseppe de Vergottini
Valeria Piergigli

First Part
Linguistic and historical framework: general issues

Toponomastics and its partitions

Carlo Alberto Mastrelli

Summary

1. Denomination of places and toponomastics

Toponomastics is an eminently linguistic discipline concerned with the denomination of places and related problems. The term *toponomastics* is often seen as equivalent to *toponymy*, but it is preferable to use the latter term simply to indicate collection of a *corpus* of toponyms and reserve the former for the systematic scientific study of the different *corpora* and single toponyms.

In other languages, the terms *toponomastics* and *toponymy* (also *toponomatology*, *toponomasiology*, *place-name study*) are as follows:

French	*toponomastique* / *toponymie*
Spanish	*toponomástica* / *toponimia*
Italian	*toponomàstica* / *toponimìa*
German	*Toponomastik*, *Ortsnamenkunde*, *Ortsnamenforschung* / *Toponymie*, *Toponymik*, *Ortsnamenschatz*, *Ortsnamenbestand*
Russian	*toponomastika*, *toponomatologija* / *toponimija*, *toponimika*
Polish	*toponomastyka* / *toponimia*
Slovene	*toponomastika* / *toponímika*, *krajevno imenoslovje*
Serbo-Croatian	*toponomàstika* / *toponìmija*
Romanian	*toponomástică* / *toponimíă*

Toponomastics/toponymy and *anthroponomastics/anthroponymy*[1] are included in the superordinate concept of *onomastics*[2]*/name-study* which is the discipline concerned with the study of all proper names of the various determinate linguistic systems. Nouns are generally the linguistic units that evoke general semantic categories and are therefore known as *common nouns* or *appellatives*; but nouns can also be used for indicative purposes and therefore be individualizing. Thus it happens that with use, the significative function of the denomination of a place, person etc. fades and its indicative or deictic function increases. In the sentence "In Florence there is a river called Arno", the noun *river* expresses a categorical function in the undifferentiated class of "water courses" and is therefore considered a common noun or appellative, whereas Arno is a proper noun because it is now only used to indicate that particular river that flows through Florence. Similarly, in the sentence "Paul is my nephew", Paul is a proper noun used in this statement to indicate a single individual in the category "(my) nephews".

One can therefore say that "proper nouns" are nothing but nouns where the individual aspect prevails over the categorical aspect. Since the transition from common noun to proper noun is gradual and almost imperceptible, it is extremely difficult to understand, for example, when the "denomination of a place" becomes a "toponym".

Let us consider the case of a "railway station" (situated in a certain area); as long as we are dealing with a building equipped for the stopping and passage of trains, we understand it as a simple denomination adequate for the function of "station" and "railway". The situation begins to change when its function is modified with the suppression of rail traffic, and the change is even more marked when the station building is altered or destroyed. However, the place where there was once a station will usually continue to be called "station", since the aspect indicative of place has cancelled the semantic function of the word *station*: the indication *station square* or *station street* may remain but the *station* is no longer there.

---

1 This term is mainly used to refer to names of persons (but that branch would normally be called *anthroponomastics* and *anthroponymy*, study of personal names, keeping anthroponym separate from theonyms, ethnonyms, zoonyms, etc.): see French *anthroponomastique/ anthroponymie*; Spanish [*antroponomástica*]/*antroponimia*; Italian *antroponomastica/ antroponimia*; German *Anthroponomastik / Anthroponymie / Personennamenkunde*; Russian *antroponimika/antroponimija*; Polish *antroponimia*; Slovenian *antroponomastika*; Serbo-Croatian *antroponomastika*; Romanian *antroponomástică / antroponimíă*.

2 French *onomastique*; Spanish *onomástica*; Italian *onomastica*; German *Onomastik, Namenkunde*; Russian *onomástika*; Polish *onomastyka*; Slovenian *onomástika, onomatológija, imenoslovje*; Serbo-Croatian *onomástika, imenoslovlje*; Romanian *onomástică*.

Something even more drastic can occur when the word used for the denomination of the place leaves the semantic or lexical system of a language: in various towns there were "Post Hotels"; many no longer exist but where they do the name may remain: when they were built they were given that name because they were where carriages for travellers and luggage stopped; but today the word *post* is not longer used with that particular connotation.

Another example: many places in Italy are called *Luco* or *Lugo;* these forms were derived from the Latin *lucus* "sacred wood" which is now almost completely absent from Italian and dialects. As we have seen, denominations of places tend to lose their transparency of meaning and become increasingly opaque; when place names become opaque (or if their lexical use becomes opaque)[3] we speak of "proper nouns of place", "place names" or "toponyms"[4]. It is easy to guess that it is impossible to establish an exact demarcation line separating the denomination of places from toponyms: there is no demarcation but rather a transition between poles, with a gradual transition from common noun to proper noun[5].

Methodological non-rigidity makes it possible to conceive "*toponymy*" not as a closed and rigid *corpus* steeped in the past but as a compact but variable system open to modernity and the future[6]. Thus one should never forget that before appearing as a monadic entity in its own right, a toponym was the normal and natural denomination of a place.

2. Etymology and the motivation for toponyms

Since toponyms are deictically attached to the places that justified their denominations, they often survive the turmoil of historical events, so that even in the absence of written documents, they reveal linguistic processes or even changes in language not otherwise certified. It is because of this conservatorship that they attracted the attention of linguists as early as the beginning of the XIX century, as a source that could fill the gaps of documentary information.

3 Consider the name of the town *Città di Castello*: although it contains lexical elements still used as common nouns, in this case they are frozen in the definition of a precise local situation, as it were. It is no longer analyzed as a description of the place, but rather as a "proper noun".

4 English *toponym, place-name*; Italian *topònimo*, or *nome di luogo*; French *toponyme, nom de lieu*; Spanish *topónimo, nombre de lugar*; German *Toponym, Ortsname*; Russian *topónim*; Polish *toponimikon, nazwa miejscowósci*; Slovenian *toponim, krajevno ime*; Serbo-Croatian *toponim, mjesno ime, ime mjesta*; Romanian *toponím.*

5 The opposite is also possible (deonomastic): return to a common noun from a proper noun.

6 The "toponomastic heritage" is too often intended in a restrictive and identity-making sense.

However, their interest was largely instrumental because toponyms were studied essentially for the historical reconstruction of linguistic events, rather than to understand the *ratio* of the place name itself. Briefly, toponomastics were used largely to discover and characterize the most ancient linguistic *facies* of a region, to understand the phonetic and morphological changes of toponyms and to obtain an etymological interpretation[7].

Without doubt, rediscovery of the etymology of a toponym is the most onerous part of the research, but it is also important to follow all the processes of alteration and modification that may have accompanied it in its chronology; and above all it is to be hoped that this not only reveals a toponym's etymological *ratio* but also its motivation.

An example: the denomination *Campi del Diavolo* was discovered in toponomastic research of the municipality of Sambuca Pistoiese[8]. The etymological *ratio* of this toponym is evident: *campi* is the plural of *campo* from the Latin *campus* (field) and *diavolo* comes from the Greek-Latin *diabolus* (devil). This word is widely used in toponomastics to indicate dreadful places (where only the devil could reign). Places known as *Fosso del diavolo* and *Ponte del diavolo* also exist in the same municipality[9], but the motivation for *Campi del diavolo* was demonstrated to be different because "*diavolo*" was the nickname of the owner[10].

It is therefore clear that to obtain valid results in the field of toponomastics, not only linguists and dialectologists are needed, but also scholars in other disciplines must take part in the research: geographers, archaeologists, topographers, epigraphers, numismatic specialists, palaeographers, philologists and above all historians in many sectors. Political history is not enough: fundamental contributions can be made for example by administrative, economic, agricultural, industrial and church history, and the possible contributions of the natural

---

7 This is why the first toponomastic collections were ordered by etymology; see for example the volumes: *Toponomastica delle valli del Serchio e della Lima* (Turin, Loescher 1898 [Quinta dispensa dei Supplementi periodici all'*Archivio glottologico italiano* di G. I. Ascoli]) and *Toponomastica della Valle dell'Arno* (Rome, Tipografia dei Lincei 1919) by Silvio Pieri (1856–1936). Only since Carlo Battisti (1882–1975) have place names begun to be illustrated per se and as such, and listed *singulatim* in alphabetical order, municipality by municipality; see his *Dizionario Toponomastico Atesino* first published in 1936.

8 *Dizionario toponomastico del comune di Sambuca Pistoiese*, ed. Natale Rauty, with introduction by Carlo Alberto Mastrelli, Pistoia, 1993, pp. 58–59.

9 Cfr. *Ibid.*, pages 103 and 145 respectively. With regard to that particular bridge, according to local legend the architect accepted the devil's help to finish it in a day, under the condition that if it was finished on time, the devil would take the soul of the first person to it. That night, the architect organized for a dog to cross the bridge first, foiling the demon.

10 Thus the place name should not be written *Campi del diavolo*, but *Campi del Diavolo* with a capital.

sciences (mineralogy, zoology, botany, etc.) cannot be ignored. Every scientific discipline can contribute to toponomastic research, not only to illustrate the origin of place names but also their history and even their final decline.

All these competences are even more necessary now that we are beginning to understand that toponomastics is no longer a cultural and competitive pass-time of scholars, but a subject of first order in the arduous enterprise of "regional planning".

3. Physical and human toponymy

Because of the complexity of toponymy/toponomastics, attemps have been and can be attempted to identify different sectors of research that generally coincide with the same fields of geography. In fact *physical geography* and *human geography* could match *physical* and *human toponymy*. Thus physical toponymy would concern all names of natural places and be divided into: geotoponymy, phytotoponymy and zootoponymy.

Geotoponymy concerns the denomination of places according to their physical nature; *geonyms* are terms such as *mountain, hill, plain, valley, rock, stone, river* and *stream*. Further divisions could be *hydronymy*[11], that refers to water bodies (*sea, lake, marsh*) and water courses (*river, stream, brook*)[12], and *oronymy* would be concerned with names of reliefs (*mountains, hills, hillocks*), while *choronymy* would concern denominations of regions[13].

Phytotoponymy would collect and study all toponyms derived from plants[14] and *zootoponymy* those derived from animals: obviously these two branches correspond to *phytogeography* and *zoogeography*, respectively, and together to *biogeography*.

This differentiation of terminology is not merely for the sake of creating categories, but also to use a cultural approach and methodological tools appropriate for the onomastic and geographic categories. A watercourse and a mountain peak exploit physical space differently. Humans have always needed water and considered it important to live near a water body or watercourse. It is therefore not surprising that not only large rivers but also brooks generally have

---

11 Corresponding to the term *hydrogeography*.

12 The terms used here are *thalassonymy* and *limnonymy*, which match the geographical terms *thalassography/oceanography*, *limnology*, *potamology*, *glaciology*, albeit not always reversibly or one-to-one.

13 Corresponding to the term *chorography*.

14 The category of phytonyms can be further divided, for example, into *dendronymy* (the phytonymy of trees).

a proper name. Nor is it surprising that many hydronyms have a prehistoric origin and transmit messages from languages and cultures that became extinct thousands or hundreds of years ago (*Arno, Po, Tevere*, etc.). The names of mountains are different: some have always characterized regions by virtue of their imposing or majestic character and can boast names that go back to antiquity (*Alpi, Appennini, Falterona*, etc.), but many peaks were named quite late, when humans appropriated them (*Monte Pisanino, Alpe-Tre Potenze, Libro Aperto*) or made them some sort of reference.

Just as *physical toponomastics* go with *physical geography*, *human toponomastics,* understood as a branch concerned with place names regarding the various spaces where humans settled and carry or carried on a particular activity[15], go with *human geography.* It is easy to see that this is an extremely rich bank of data and questions regarding an enormous variety of historical-cultural events, affecting the lives of generations of humans and accompanying them through time and in the organization of space.

4. Stratification and historical nature of toponyms

Proceeding in decreasing order, we first encounter the denominations of peoples and States under the constraints of history. Some nations received their names from the people or peoples that live or lived in them[16]: *Spain* acquired its name from the *Hispani*, one of the Iberian populations that lived there before the Roman conquest. *France* got its name from the *Franks* who were a Germanic population that occupied the already Romanized land that the Romans called *Gaul*, maintaining the name of the Celtic population (the *Gauls*) that lived there before the Roman conquest. *England* continues the name of one of the Germanic populations, the *Angles*, who occupied it when the Romans withdrew[17].

---

15 All the terms capture a typical aspect of the situation being classified, but certainly not everything about it. This relative nature of nomenclature must always be borne in mind, especially when two terms are matched: it has long been known that all geography can only be human, because the subject of geography is humans, who inevitably condition and appropriate even purely physical aspects. Thus the binary terminology does not denominate two opposing categories, but identifies a polarity with relative differences ranging from plus to minus.

16 The category of names of peoples is defined *ethnonymy.*

17 The second element of *Inghilterra*, *-terra*, can be considered the Latin equivalent of the Germanic term *-land*, which has prevailed (*Groenlandia* = green land, *Finlandia* = land of the Finns, *Olanda* = low land [also known as the *Low Countries*], etc.).

The names of States may also be clearly artificial: see the cases of ex-Czechoslovakia (Czechs + Slovaks) and ex-Yugoslavia (meaning southern Slavia) or the United States of America and ex-Soviet Union[18].

The definition of borders is important in the study of the names of States and administrative regions. The events of history often profoundly modify borders, though the denomination may be apparently linear. Today, the name *Germany* is understood as the name of a nation originating by default, because since when Latin was used, the term *Germani* has referred to all speakers of Germanic languages, not only those today included in the denomination *Germania.* For Italians, those populations speak and write *tedesco* and curiously the inhabitants of Germany are therefore known as *tedeschi* although *tedesco* is also spoken by the Swiss of certain cantons, Austrians, etc.[19]

The name *Italy* originated in the opposite manner, because *Italia* was the name (of Oscan origin) of the southern tip of what is now Calabria: only with Octavian (Augustus) in 42 BC was it extended to the whole peninsula as far as the Alps. Today *Calabria* is a Tyrrhenian region owing its name to the *Calabri* people, but in classical times this denomination designated the Salento peninsula and Calabria was called *Bruttium,* only being named *Calabria* after the Byzantine denomination.

Another example: *Tirolo* originally indicated a cisalpine castle of Venosta with a vast county that extended over the Alps. When this county came under Austria at the end of 1300, a tripartite region was formed: *Nord-Tirol*, *Ost-Tirol* e *Süd-Tirol*. When *Süd-Tirol* came under Italy at the end of the first world war, its previous Napoleonic and Mazzinian name *Alto Adige* was restored[20].

Another chapter regards the names of cities, towns and villages, for which the term *poleonyms* is used. Like for hydronyms, among poleonyms, those of large

---

18 For example the name *Helvetic Confederation* also used for *Switzerland* alludes to the name of one of the peoples that lived there (*Helveti*) and is the basis of the abbreviation CH.

19 In Italian, this dilemma emerges when one has to speak simultaneously of the people of Austria and Germany, usually solved by using the terms *austriaci* and *germanici* (not *tedeschi* because both are "tedeschi").

20 Many French names refer to the disposition of watercourses (*Haute-Garonne, Haute-Loire, Haut-Rhin, Bas-Rhin*), mountains (*Hautes-Alpes* ~ *Basses-Alpes, Hautes-Pyrénées* ~ *Basses-Pyrénées*) or regions (*Haute-Savoie, Haute-Auvergne* ~ *Basse-Auvergne*), favouring pure geographical objectivity over the relativity of historical events and ethnic contrasts. For Italian sensibility, the term *Sud-Tirolo* is reductive because *Tirolo* was originally an exclusively Venostan name (the true and only Tirolo) and moreover the Italian language does not like combinations of consonants such as *-d* + *t-*: it does not mind *sud-africano*, *sud-americano*, but not **sud-tedesco*, **nord-pugliese* and the like, and therefore not *Sud-Tirolo* (in the press, *sudtirolese* is often used to indicate a German-speaking citizen of Alto Adige, while *altoatesino* is used for Italian-speaking citizens).

cities have proved to be the most solid and firm. Their linguistic motivation can be sought in prehistory or at least protohistoric times: peoples and cultures that often disappeared without leaving a trace come to mind. Names like *Cagliari* (= Latin *Carales*), *Sòlanto* (= Lat. *Soluntum*), *Taranto* (= Lat. *Tarentum*), are unfathomable.

Certain names were modified spontaneously within a given linguistic system (see the case of *Firenze*, that descends from the Latin *Florentia*[21] in the locative case *Florenti-ae*), or by a transformation determined by passage from one language to another (the Greek *Akragas –antos* became the Latin *Agrigentum*[22], which in turn became *Girgenti*[23] mediated by the Arab language.

It also happened that certain changes were not by chance but purposeful: the case of *Benevento* is famous. This Irpinian city was originally called *Maluentum*; when the Romans conquered it in the III century BC, they changed the initial part of the name thinking it corresponded to the Latin *malus* "bad". The name became *Beneuentum,* but the Romans did not know that "mal" was not *mal(us)* but "mountain" (see Albanian *mal-i* "the mountain").

In other cases, names have been misunderstood and changed radically in passages between different cultural and linguistic layers. The Sican city of *Enna* came to be called *castrum Ennae* but with the coming of the Arabs, the second part was interpreted as *Yanni* "Giovanni" and arabized to *Qaṣr Yānnih* and thence to a Latinism *Castrum Ioannis* (year 1091) which became *Castrogiovanni*: only in 1927 was the ancient name *Enna* restored.

5. Categories and classification of toponyms

Of course many Italian poleonyms are still semantically transparent, being prevalently Latin, though the original meaning no longer matches the current one: *bastia, borgo, camera, capanna, casa/casale, castello, castiglione, castro, civita, colonia, corte, magione, maso, ospedale, ospizio, paese, palazzo, rocca, sala, terra, torre, vico, villa*[24]. More related to work environments are toponyms derived from *bagno, canova, casèra, cella, cellaria, cisterna, granza, pila, piscina, pozzo, stabbio, stalla, taverna, tézza* e soprattutto da *calcara, fabbrica,*

---

21 This was the name of the Latin colony founded on the banks of the Arno, in contrast to the Etruscan hill settlement of *Fiesole* (Lat. *Faesulae* < Etr. *Vipsul*).

22 This form seems remodelled on the Latin word *ager, agri* "field".

23 In 1927 the current form *Agrigento* was restored from the Latin; this is not an isolated occurrence, see e.g. *Centùripe* (EN) for *Centorbi* (1863), *Enna* for *Castrogiovanni* (1927), *Ièsolo* (VE) for *Cavazuccherina* (1930).

24 *Bastia, borgo* and *sala* are of Germanic origin.

fabbro, ferrara, folliera, forno, lateraia/laterina, mácina, opera, organo, pistrino, rota, salaria/salina, torchio, trapéto, etc. Roads and means of transport are of course significant, giving rise to toponyms such as *bivio, calata, carro, compito, levata, palanca, passo, pausa/pausatoio, quadrivio, ricetto, règia, ruga, salebra, strada, traghetto, via*, etc.; likewise signs marking the borders of a private or public possession: *confinio, finale, limine, limite, termine*, etc., and the Germanisms **snaida* and **wiffa*. A special role is played by names of religious origin, or *hagiotoponyms*, such as: *abbazia/badia, altare, ancona, canonica, cappella, chiesa, immagine, monaco, monastero, pieve*, etc. with all their titles of Christ, Mary and saints.

Names related to pastoral activities (e.g. *armentaria, attegia, berbicaria, caprile, cavea, fetaria, musile, ovile, porcile, stazzo*), and above all agriculture, are other important categories. Among the latter, so-called *praedialities*, or toponyms inspired by the name of the landowner, have a major role[25]. Praedialities cover a large proportion of arable land: in Italy, Etruscan (especially in Tuscany)[26], Gallic (especially in northern Italy) and Latin (all of the peninsula and the islands) names can be found. These praedialities may directly reflect the name of the owner (e.g.: *Agno* < ANNIUS, *Candeggia* < CANDILIUS, *Doglio* < DOLLIUS, *Fagno* < FANNIUS, *Lari* < LARIUS, *Samprogno* < SEMPRONIUS, *Tricarico* < TRICARIUS, etc.), but in most cases they come from derivatives ending in *-acum/-aca* (of Gallic origin) or *-ānum/-āna* (of Latin origin)[27]; e.g. *Borzano* and *Borzago* < ABURCIUS, *Migliano* and *Lumiago* < AEMILIUS, *Dolciano* and *Dolzago* < DULCIUS, etc., *Gallerano* < GALERIUS, *Marciano* < MARCIUS, *Pontignano* < PONTINIUS, *Savigliano* < SABELLIUS, *Valeriana* < VALERIUS, etc. Other praedialities date back to the end of the Roman Empire, or have Gothic or Lombard origin ending in *–engo/-enga*; e.g. *Barengo* < *Baro*, *Bollendo* < *Bōlo*, *Gottolengo* < *Gauto +-ila*, *Massalengo* < *Mazzo +-ila*, *Rosenga* < *Rauso*, *Valdinga* < *Waldō*, etc.

The great mass of praedialities covers so much land and is complemented by a myriad of toponyms like a sort of connective tissue. This abundant toponymy of secondary importance underlies the contrast expressed by the pair of terms

---

25 The importance of the research and study of anthroponyms is evident.

26 This "facies" is not easy to recognize but is usually detected when a toponym ending in *-na* (*-ina/-enna*) is proparoxytone and in an area once occupied by Etruscans (e.g. *Ántina* < Etr. *Antinal*, *Ávena* < Etr. *Avenal*, *Cucina* < Etr. *Ceicna*, *Pártina* < Etr. *Parthanaś*, *Rósina* < Etr. *Rusna*, etc.).

27 There may also be endings in *-īcus/-īca* (especially in Veneto), such as *Bottenigo, Carniga, Formeniga, Marteniga*, etc., or in *-asius*, such as *Tignés* < TINIUS, *Torés* < TORIUS, etc., or in *-ate*, come *Abbiate* < AVIUS, *Bugnate* < BUNIUS, Cairate < CARIUS, etc.

microtoponymy and *macrotoponymy (minor name – major name)*[28]. An attempt to find the reasons for a distinction between the two terms was again unsuccessful: it proved to be a simple polarity for practical, and certainly not theoretical, reasons[29].

6. Urban toponymy and hodonymy

The practical reasons are often related to the mapping of toponyms, but the recent development of cartography on very detailed scales enables the inclusion of a great number of so-called microtoponyms and what has been called *urban toponomastics* but is more properly called *hodonymy/hodonomastics (hodonym, route name)*[30]. Interest in hodonomastics as a branch of toponomastics is recent, although street directories of cities have existed for a long time. Here I pay particular attention to this problem and establish some criteria for classification.

It was possible to speak simply of urban toponomastics when the names of the various parts of a town or city arose spontaneously and were maintained in indicative use of its various elements (for example the squares or streets of the town hall, a church, the post office, school, hospital, White Horse Inn, etc.); but as towns grew, councils had to officialise the names of streets and squares and

---

28 Corresponding to:

French	*microtoponymie ~ macrotoponymie*
Spanish	*microtoponimia ~ macrotoponimia*
Italian	*microtoponimia ~ macrotoponimia*
German	*Mikrotoponymie ~ Makrotoponymie*
Russian	*mikrotoponimija ~ makrotoponimija*
Polish	*mikrotoponimia ~ makrotoponimia*
Slovenian	*mikrotoponímika ~ makrotoponímika*
Serbo-Croatian	*mikrotoponìmija ~ makrotoponìmija*
Romanian	*microtoponimiă ~ macrotoponimiă*

29 It was thought to make an effective distinction in cartography, calling *microtoponyms* those that are not included on maps; but the possibility of including toponyms depends on the scale of the map and today with digital cartography this exclusively practical criterion no longer subsists. As well, what may seem a microtoponym today, may seem different tomorrow due to a change in social or historical conditions.

30 Corresponding to:

French	*(h)odonymie (hodonyme, nom de voie)*
Spanish	*odonimia (odónimo, nombre de estrada)*
Italian	*odonimia/odonomastica* (*odonimo*)
German	*Hodonymie (Hodonym, Strassenname)*

give new names in order to plan and to manage the population registry[31]. I think one should use the name *homonymy* only for those street names that were approved by a special act and keep the term urban toponymy (or street toponymy) for all names, used and traditional, but not officialised by act of council. For example, like in most cities, the names of the bridges of Florence (*ponte alla Carraia, ponte della Vittoria, ponte alle Grazie, ponte a Santa Trìnita*) are not listed in the official street directory because there are not usually houses or shops on them[32]. Names like *Venezia* in Livorno, *Vaticano* in Trento and *Le Cure* in Florence are therefore not hodonyms but urban toponyms.

However, today things have changed because the new road code provides that every area of public circulation has to have an official name, irrespective of whether or not there are street numbers. Councils therefore have to begin to be more heedful of the problems involved in correct *hodonymy*, especially in fast developing towns that grow beyond the ancient walls or a previous consolidated limit of the built up area.

In new urbanized areas, criteria for assigning new names should be in harmony with and respect the old and new[33]. Thus if a town extends into the surrounding land it is appropriate to recover previous toponyms in the hodonymy and assign names that have a reference to cultural reality and to the roles of the new buildings.

During the Unification of Italy, names appropriate for the period were given by reference to famous people (e.g. *Giuseppe Mazzini, Vittorio Emanuele II, Giuseppe Garibaldi, Camillo Benso di Cavour*, etc.) or ideals (*Unità, Nazione, Risorgimento,* etc.) or battles (*Goito, Villafranca, Solferino*, etc.) or "rebel" cities (*Trento, Trieste*, etc.), and the names are truly in agreement with the architecture of the buildings of those streets and squares. However, in later decades – especially after the second world war – names of ideologically contrary sign often correctly or incorrectly cancelled street names, causing great difficulty and social discomfort. So much so that many administrations have opted for "neutral", non-triumphant denominations (see frequent use of *Caduti, Martiri,*

---

31 Among other things, it should be borne in mind that a road may have variants in use or even more than one name according to what one is looking for: for example *Via di San Matteo* or *del Sole* or *della scuola*.

32 Today, it is no longer enough to officially name places of residence: names are required for all areas of public circulation. There will therefore be an increasing demand for names for bridges, gardens, roundabouts, underpasses, overpasses, ring roads, etc.

33 So far there is no dedicated rule, except the prohibition of naming streets after a person who died less than 10 years ago. It was recently specified that hodonyms can only be changed to reinstate a previously used name and that names that could cause confusion due to synonymy cannot be used (e.g. *Via dei monti*, *Via Vincenzo Monti*, *Via dei Monti*).

Vittime, etc.). Besides, where expansion is great, systemic names have been used (e.g. names of poets, writers, politicians, historians, scientists, artists, sculptors, architects, musicians, etc.), often even going to extremes with encyclopaedic nomenclature (fish, birds, etc.) and completely losing sight of the correlation with the architectural style of the area and the culture of the time.

The divergence between hodonymic processes and toponymic tradition has become too great. It is therefore necessary to restore balance in the management of cultural approaches of the society and the consequent territorial denominations.

7. Cartography and the official nature of toponyms

Let us now look at the problem of the "officialness" of toponyms, which has become somewhat disquieting in the last few decades for two reasons: the anxious search for the identity-making roots of communities and moves for autonomy within Italy. In such situations, toponyms are no longer elements of culture but symbols of "other" culture and politics.

Proceeding with a certain order, the officialness of a toponym does not reside in the toponym itself but in public recognition. The names of administrative units (regions, provinces and municipalities) are official in the highest degree because they are recognized by state laws. Toponyms included in the cartography of the Istituto Geografico Militare are official in a different sense, and likewise the toponymy of railway and postal directories (and the like). However, their officialness tends to pertain to the things themselves, rather than being absolute.

The problem of the more or less official nature of toponyms is compounded by the question of form, that is the phonetic, graphic and morphological aspect that a toponym may and must have if it is to be valid.

When Italian unity was achieved in the early 1900s, there was not the slightest doubt that the language of the new nation was to be Italian and resources were spent in that direction, endeavouring to completely Italianize all toponyms. However, since the second world war (i.e. since the middle of last century) the myth of the political, administrative and therefore also linguistic unity of the country underwent a crisis. The attention paid to shaky dialects was not so much interest as a generically anti-Italian or anti-unitary impulse. So it happened that in northern Italy, especially in Lombardy and Veneto, people wanted road signs indicating *Bergamo* replaced with *Bèrghem*, *Varese* with *Varès*, *Venezia* with *Venèssia* (in local writing *Venexia*), etc.

These exhibitionist whims seem to have passed but uncertainty and difficult remain, especially in the new regional cartography and even hodonymy, where vacillation between dialectization and Italianization is evident. The toponymy and hodonymy of maps and street directories risk being compiled in a schizoid manner.

The current search for "identity-making roots" tends to favour dialectal forms under the mistaken impression that they are indigenous or primitive. This trend is compounded by the older and more romantic tendency to mythologize oral (dialectal) forms as popular and therefore more democratic. Between the two, the dialectal or dialectized form is taken to be the truly and genuinely "correct" form and therefore the only valid one. Actually, examination of toponymic forms has to go deeper and be freed of assumptions and ideological bias. In so doing, it is necessary to consider that a toponym refers to a point in space. This point reflects historical and linguistic conditions but a proposed denomination interacts with the community that comes together at that point.

It is therefore inevitable that toponyms be guaranteed all their history and fungibility: even if in the end the choice tends to simplify, the whole historical, linguistic and social spectrum of a toponym must be borne in mind. Returning to the case of *Bergamo*, for example, it is true that today the local population says *Bèrghem* when speaking in dialect, but at the roots of this form there is another name, the Latin *Bergomum,* and the Italian *Bergamo* is certainly closer to it than the dialectal *Bèrghem*. Thus *Bergamo* is closer to the myth of "identity-making roots" and is conceivably also more democratic, being the form more known to Italians and foreigners.

Another example: the Bolognese would not dream of changing how *Bologna* is written, even if they usually pronounce it with the strong phonetic features of their dialect, nor do they think that Bologna (from the Gallic Latin *Bononia*) should be changed to the more ancient original Etruscan name *Felsina*. However, they do not eschew the adjective *felsíneo* instead of *bolognese* in literary and even sporting use.

Another example: the manner in which *Pejo*[34], *Thiene* and *Rho* are written is consolidated and even if it is common to see *Pejo* written *Peio*, no-one would dare drop the absurd *h* from *Thiene* and *Rho*. These spellings are not even etymological but only "historical"[35].

---

34 The *j* is an old Italian spelling to indicate a consonant as distinct from a vowel: see for example the case *Jugoslavia* where the *J* persists, also because this spelling is used in Serbo-Croatian: *Jugoslavija*.

35 The spelling of *Rho* could be considered etymological at a time when it was mistakenly believed (XVIII century: *Raude*) that it had something to do with the Greek *Rhodos* "Rhodes".

In toponyms, this phonetic/graphic (and even morphological) diffraction spectrum may vary in breadth. In Tuscany for example, the names *Firenze, Grosseto, Lucca, Pisa, Pistoia* and *Siena* have not undergone alterations but *Arezzo, Livorno* and *Prato* have become *Rézzo*, *Liólno* and *Prao* in spoken usage. Nevertheless it is clear that updating these names according to current use is out of the question.

8. Bilingualism and translatability of toponyms

With the above considerations, we touched another important question that regards the terminological contraposition between *endonym* and *exonym*[36]. This terminological division is mainly introduced when dealing with toponyms that have different form or expression depending on the language used: *endonym* is used for toponyms within their linguistic area and *exonym* for a different form used in a language outside that area. Thus the English endonym *London* corresponds to the Italian exonym *Londra* and the Spanish and French exonyms *Londres*.

This distinction can be useful from certain points of view, but if it becomes absolute it is incongruous and absurd (like all other terminological contrapositions). Consider the case of the Italian exonym *Parigi* of the French *Paris*, but the German *Paris* is not the same as the endonym *Paris* because it is phonetically and tonically different, though written in the same way. In German *Paris* is pronounced *páris*, whereas in French it is pronounced *parí*.

In usage, every language reacts freely, according to its linguistic, cultural, historical and social conditions. In Italy, despite distance-related difficulties, there was once a much higher rate of exonymity. *Berlino, Colonia, Monaco, Vienna* and *Zurigo* are still more common than *Berlin, Köln, München, Wien* and *Zürich*, but use of *Aidelberga, Augusta, Gottinga, Tubinga* and *Ulma* has become rarer than *Heidelberg, Augsburg, Göttingen, Tübingen* and *Ulm*. Certain difficulties are evident: with regard to the toponyms *Praha* and *Brno* Italians still say *Praga* but have forgotten the exonym *Bruna,* despite the almost insuperable phonetic difficulty of the endonym *Brno.*

Thus a polar correlation, rather than outright opposition, can also be recognized in the contraposition of *endonym* and *exonym*. Those who stress this

---

36 Corresponding to:

French	*endonyme ~ exonyme*
Italian	*endonimo ~ esonimo*
German	*Endonym ~ Exonym*

contraposition do so largely because they uphold the inviolability and untranslatability of toponyms, overriding even semantic considerations. Despite statutory requirements of bilingual toponymy, for example, some hold that in Alto Adige the local German names are exclusive and cannot be translated. This is illustrated by many cases, such as the German *Verschneid* which was coupled with the Italian *Frassineto*. Now it is sustained that *Frassineto* is spurious and should be eliminated as an "exonym". *Verschneid* is certainly a Germanization of a proto-Ladin form **Frasnedo* (< Lat. *Fraxin-ētum* 'bosco di frassini' "forest of ash = *Fraxinus*") and therefore *Verschneid* is the true "exonym". Clearly the Italian *Frassineto* is only apparently "exonymous" because the Italian form recovers the "etymological *ratio*" even better than the proto-Ladin.
In conclusion, it can be said that like all other disciplines, toponomastics needs to refine its methods of investigation and recognize the opportunity and even necessity of providing further inner repartitions. However, because it is not a discipline concerned solely with rediscovering and reconstructing the past, but is also a basis for present and future regional planning, it is in need of synthesis to produce socially useful, functional and above all fair results.

Bibliography

1) General works

Akin S. (ed.), *Noms et re-noms. – La dénomination des personnes, des populations, des langues et des territoires*, Rouen, 1999.

Althaus H.P., Henne H., Wiegand H.E. (eds.), *Lexikon der germanistischen Linguistik*, Tübingen, 1980^2.

Eichler E., Hilty G., Löffler H., Steger H., Zgusta L. (eds.), *Namenforschung – Ein internationales Handbuch zur Onomastik*, 3 vols., Berlin – New York, 1995.

Lexikon der romanistischen Linguistik, vol. III, Tübingen, 1989.

Migliorini Br., *Onomastica*, in *Enciclopedia italiana*, vol. XXV, Rome, Treccani, 1935 (reprinted 1939).

Olivieri D., *Toponomastica*, in *Enciclopedia italiana*, vol. XXIV, Rome, Treccani, 1937 (reprinted 1949).

Italian

Various Authors, *Dizionario di toponomastica. – Storia e significato dei nomi geografici italiani*, Turin, 1990.

Pellegrini G. B., *Toponomastica italiana*, Milan, 1990.

French
Baylon Chr., Fabre P., *Les noms de lieux et de personnes*, Paris, 1982.
Dauzat A., *Les noms de lieux. Origine et évolution*, Paris, 1947^{5}.
Dauzat A., *La toponimie française*, Paris, 1960^{2}.
Longnon A., *Les noms de lieu de la France*, Paris, 1929 (reprinted 1979).
Nègre E., *Les noms de lieux en France*, Paris, 1977^{2}.
Rostaing C., *Les noms de lieux*, Paris, 1964.
Vincent A., *Toponymie de la France* , Bruxelles, 1937 (reprinted 1984).

German
Bach A., *Deutsche Namenkunde*, 3 vols., Heidelberg, 1978.
Bauer G., *Namenkunde des Deutschen*, Berne – Frankfurt – New York, 1985.

Spanish
Llorente A., *Toponimia y Historia*, Granada, 1969–1970.
Llorente A., *Los topónimos españoles y su significado*, Salamanca, 1980.

2) Terminology

Achmanova O. S., *Slovar' linguističeskich terminov*, Moscow, 1966.
Beccaria G.L. (dir.), *Dizionario di linguistica e di filologia, metrica e retorica*, Turin, 1984.
Cardona G. R., *Dizionario di linguistica*, Rome, 1988.
Carreter F. L., *Diccionario de terminos filológicos*, Madrid, 1953, 1963^{2}, 1968^{4} (reprinted 1984).
Constantinescu-Dobridor Gh., *Mic dicţionar de terminologie linguistică*, Bucarest, 1980.
Dubois J. et alii, *Dictionnaire de linguistique*, Paris 1973 (It. Edition, Bologna, 1979).
Ducrot O.,Todorov T., *Dictionnaire encyclopédique des sciences du langage*, Paris, 1972.
Gołąb Zb., Heinz A., Polański K., *Słownik terminologii językoznawczej*, Warsaw, 1968.
Hartmann R. R. K., Stork F. C., *Dictionary of Language and Linguistics*, London, 1972 (reprinted 1973).
Marouzeau J., *Lexique de la terminologie linguistique*, Paris, 1933, 1951^{3}.
Mounin G., *Dictionnaire de la linguistique*, Paris, 1974.
Simeon R., *Enciklopedÿski rječnik longuističkih naziva*, 2 vols., Zagabria, 1969.

Stammerjohann H. (ed.), *Handbuch der Linguistik*, Munich, 1975.
Witkowski K., *Grundbegriffe der Namenkunde*, Berlin, 1964.

3) Cartography

Arca S., *Normative internazionali di nomi geografici*, in *Atlante dei tipi geografici*, Florence, Istituto Geografico Militare, 2004[3.]
Cantile A., *Norme topografiche nazionali, ibid.*
Linee guida per la normalizzazione dei nomi geografici ad uso degli editori di cartografia ed altri editori, Florence, Istituto Geografico Militare, 2004.

4) Hodonomastics

Le città leggibili – La toponomastica urbana fra passato e presente (*Proceedings of Conference held in Foligno, 11–13/12/2003, Perugia, Deputazione di Storia Patria per l'Umbria*), Perugia, 2004.
Mastrelli C.A. (ed.), *Odonomastica – Criteri e normative sulle denominazioni stradali* (*Proceedings of Conference held in Trento, 25/9/2002*), Trento, Provincia Autonoma di Trento, 2005.

5) Periodicals

Onoma – Journal of the International Council of Onomastic Sciences, Leuven, 1950.
Caffarelli E. (dir.), *Rivista Italiana di Onomastica*, Rome, 1994.

6) Consultation

Granucci F., *Prontuario bibliografico di toponomastica italiana*, Florence, 1988.
Onoma – Bullettin d'information et de bibliographie, Leuven, 1950–1993.
Bibliographie linguistique, Utrecht – Brussels, 1939.

The history of place names in Alto Adige/Südtirol: origin, development and sources of Italian toponomastics in the Burgraviato area of Merano and in Val Venosta in relation to German diction

Daniela Giaimo

Dedicated to the memory of Prof. Giovanni Battista Pellegrini who contributed his extraordinary and passionate knowledge of toponomastics to Italian culture.

Summary

1. In the footsteps of Rome (and before)

In Alto Adige, four linguistic strata (pre-Latin, Latin, German and Italian) reflect a long history, which has left interesting signs in the Burgraviato area of Merano and in Val Venosta. Already in the Neolithic age, and perhaps even before, humans settled near the estuary of the Passirio river (in the Merano basin) and in Val Venosta. In the pre-Roman era we find a considerable number of local names that demonstrate stable settlement around Merano. In the municipalities of the Burgraviato alone, we have the following pre-Latin names, which we report in Italian-German bilingual form: *Caines-Kuens, Cermes-Tscherms, Marlengo-Marling*, *Nalles-Nals*, *Naturno-Naturns, Parcines-Partschins, Tesimo-Thisens,* and the better known *Tirolo-Tirol* (8 of the 26 place names). In Venosta we have *Ciardes-Tschars* (which forms a single municipality with *Castelbello/ Kastelbell*), *Glorenza-Glurns, Lasa-Laas, Malles Venosta-Mals, Martello-Martell, Senales-Schnals, Silandro-Schlanders, Sluderno-Schluderns, Stelvio-Stilfs* and *Tubre-Taufers* (10 of the 13 municipalities; 14 considering *Ciardes-Tschars* separately). The main valley of the Adige river and the Valle Monastero, with its Bronze-Age tracks leading into the pre-Alps, were inhabited in pre-Latin times; archaeological material from that period has also been found in Stelvio and Gomagoi.

The campaign of Druze and Tiberius in 15 BC opened a route to the central Alps to the Romans. This penetration was made possible by the "Via Claudia Augusta" (46–47 AD) that climbed the Adige from Maia (near Merano) into Val Venosta, by a "Via Strata" (until 1357 *Vistrad,* today *Pfistrad*) that continued from Val Passiria to Mt. Giovo, then descended from the pass to Vipiteno, and by the mule track of Brennero. The Roman conquest of the central Alps led to the foundation of the province *Raetia et Vindelicia* that joined part of the upper Adige with the upper basin of the Rhine, the Inn and the Danube plain.

There are even evident reminders of extensive Roman colonization from Merano to Bolzano. This area has about sixty place names ending in *-anum* derived from Latin or Italic personal names (e.g. the municipality *Appiano-Eppan, < Lat. Appianum* denoting land belonging to *Appius*, *Andriano-Andrian <Lat. Andrianum,* that of *Andrius*), that demonstrate land subdivision under the Latins, conceivable only by extensive expropriation and a regular Roman colonization plan. The density of the new settlement and the fact that the names of the settlers were almost exclusively Latin sustain the hypothesis that these are toponomastic traces of a "veteran colony" established to guard new borders.

The archaeological findings confirm this hypothesis. *Castelfeder* in Egna municipality (south of Bolzano) is a Roman *Castellum Vetus.* Another camp, *Castrum Maiense,* created to protect the station of *Maia* near Merano, is also Roman and still existed in 723 AD. Many coins from the Augustus to Theodosius period were found there. Nearby are the municipalities of *Rifiano-Riffian* (<Lat. *Rufius)* and *Scena-Schenna (<Lat. Cinnius).* Nine names in the municipalities of the Burgraviato are also clearly of Latin origin and six of them are praedial: *Lagundo-Algund, Gargazzone-Gargazzon, Lana-Lana, Merano-Meran, Plaus-Plaus, Rifiano-Riffian, Scena-Schenna, Verano-Vöran* and *Ultimo-Ulten.*

With regard to Venosta, there are four names of municipalities of Latin origin: *Castelbello-Kastelbell, Curòn Venosta-Graun, Laces-Latsch* and *Prato allo Stelvio-Prad am Stilfser Joch.* Adding the ten pre-Roman toponyms, we note that no municipal name in Val Venosta is of German origin. The situation is not very different in the Burgraviato, where only one fifth of municipal names are not Latin or pre-Latin.

After the fall of the Roman empire, the area now coinciding with the Burgraviato came briefly under Franconian rule (about mid VI century) but unfortunately, as observed by Carlo Battisti, "Knowledge of the history of the Merano area in the palaeomedieval is incomplete: a basic problem is how to establish the beginning of Bavarian influence"[1]. The Longobardi founded the Duchy of Trento in 569 and also annexed the Burgraviato. In the meantime, the Baiuvari, who had already conquered the Isarco basin (590–592 AD) could have arrived in the Merano area from the Giovo Pass and the lower Val Passiria. However, according to Paulus Diaconus, this is unlikely to have happened before the death of Secondus of Trento, who recorded nothing about the Bavarian conquest of Merano.

In 830, the Tridentina county, constituted under the jurisdiction of the ex-Lombard duchy, extended along the Adige valley to Mortér di Venosta, thus including the present area of interest. The centre of gravity of this administrative area (i.e. the Burgraviato) was the Merano basin, which was under the feudal jurisdiction of the Episcopal Principality of Trento.

In 1027, Corrado II the Salico, a Roman-Germanic emperor, signed a diploma donating the *comitatus tridentino* (that also included the county of Venosta and Bolzano) to the church of Trento, investing the bishop with princely powers, irrespective of the jurisdiction of other rulers. As observed by Battisti, the area therefore "maintained its characteristics as Italian national land, despite being a direct feud of the Empire and living under Imperial German policy"[2]. Although the Ottoni favoured bishop princes over feudal forces that threatened Imperial authority, this policy was unsuccessful, due partly to the increasing influence of lords of the Ghibelline house of the Tirols in the Merano area. In 1140, Bertoldo and Alberto, sons of Alberto count of *Raetia Curiensis* of the *Vallis Venusta*, took the title of "Counts of Tirolo". Already owners of extensive lands in the Inn, Venosta and Engadine valleys, they built their castle in the South-Western part of the present Municipality of Tirolo (above Merano), on a hill that had belonged to a Benedictine convent, by then in ruins. This magnificent site dominated the strategic confluence of the Passirio with the Adige in the Merano basin. The influence of the Counts of Tirolo continued to grow at the expense of the episcopal principality.

2. The influence and prevalence of German

This was the period of Germanization of the area, since the Counts of Tirolo had a German orientation. In about 1230 the name Burggrafenamt appears for the first time as an administrative unit. It is derived from burgravius, a German term

1 C. Battisti & G. Giacomelli, *I nomi locali del Burgraviato di Merano*, Florence, 1968–70, vol. I, part I, p. 20.

2 C. Battisti & G. Giacomelli, *op. cit.,* vol. I, part I, p. 25.

with a Latin ending equivalent to praefectus urbis Tiroli, where the term urbs clearly indicates Merano. Indeed, this is where the judge known in 1200 as justiciarius in Merano resided [3].

In the XIII century, the jurisdiction of Merano included the municipalities of Naturno, Parcines, Lagundo, Plars, Rifiano, Maia, Avelengo and Merano, as well as the municipalities on the opposite bank of the Adige, that were previously a feud of the Counts of Ultimo, namely Ultimo, Marlengo, Lana and Tesimo. Understood in this sense, the Burgraviato is a set of heterogeneous centres consisting of three differentiated groups: the municipalities east of Venosta in the west, those constituting the more ancient nucleus in the centre (Tirolo, Caines, Rifiano, Val Passiria, Avelengo), and finally the lands of the *comitato* of Ultimo on the right bank of the Adige (Marlengo, Lana, Tesimo, Postàl and Gargazzone).

On 26th January 1363, Margarethe Maultasch ("wide mouth"), the last princess of Tirolo, gave up her feud to Rudolf IV of Habsburg. From that moment, Castel Tirolo and the surrounding land were no longer the heart and source of wealth of the Burgraviato, since transfer of property to the House of Austria amounted to handing over legal control to that dynasty (Castel Tirolo was abandoned and fell to ruin; only in 1985 was restoration completed and it now hosts a permanent exhibition of regional history).

After 1363, the County of Tirolo and practically the present Alto Adige followed the fate of the Habsburgs, except for the brief period of occupation by Napoleon. Germanization of place names became intense, but this was relatively recent, considering the long history described above. The area was also affected by circumstances that developed in the Middle Ages under neo-Latin administrative bodies on one hand Episcopal Principality of Trento) and German chancelleries (Counts of Tirolo and Ultimo) and trans-Alpine convents on the other.

For example, in Val Venosta the neo-Latin tradition continued for a long time, despite the foreign lords: about 1570, a local dialect, which in the upper valley continued until the Napoleonic period, was still spoken at Parcines[4]. These German or Germanized chancelleries clearly had the upper hand in the transcription of toponyms: indeed, they established the national custom of translating place names, whether true or presumed appellatives, only into their own language, or of adapting them to the language used in the chancelleries. As sustained by Battisti [5], "A Germanized or translated name cannot be considered

3 C. Battisti & G. Giacomelli, *op. cit.*, vol. I, part I, p. 29.

4 *Enciclopedia Treccani*, vol. XXXV, Rome, p. 122.

5 C. Battisti & G. Giacomelli, *op. cit.*, vol. I, part I, p. 30.

the name actually used in the place without further research, and is not sufficient proof of Germanization. Only the Registry that recorded the name is German". Giovanni Battista Pellegrini, who also studied the toponomastics of Alto Adige in detail, was of similar opinion: "One should not completely ignore the medieval situation of the region as far as the real linguistic aspect of toponymic terminology is concerned (...) Practically everywhere, landowner chancelleries gave local names forms in line with their own idioms, with adaptations and new creations. These names cannot be taken by historians as evidence that the population was already German-speaking"[6]. For example, when the high German phonetic shift is absent in a name of pre-Germanic origin, palaeo-German appropriation is impossible (see *Tirol-Tirolo* record below). The process of Germanization was completed later; pre-Latin or Latin place names were transformed or adapted after 1400. For example *Naifer Bach-Rio di Nova,* where *Naifer* is derived from "(terra)Nova", i.e. "land recently cultivated"; or *Ulfas Alpe-Alpe Ulvas,* where *Ulfas* is derived from the Latin *Ulva* = "sedge, swamp grass"; in 1230 there was still *Ancius Hano ouf Ulves*[7]. In the meantime, German toponomastics developed *ex-novo*.

The name *Alto Adige* was first introduced by Napoleon in fulfilment of the Treaty of Paris of 28th February 1810. It followed the example of the denomination of French departments, indicating all land south of the border, which stretched from Stelvio to Chiusa (a village north of Bressanone) and along the ridge of the Dolomites to Dobbiaco. The northern part of upper Adige as far as Merano and Chiusa was assigned to Bavaria and the southern part was divided into five districts (Trento, Rovereto, Riva, Cles, Bolzano), known as "*Dipartimento dell'Alto Adige*", and annexed to the Kingdom of Italy. *Südtirol* is a subsequent denomination. It first briefly indicated the ex-Dipartimento dell'Alto Adige (annexed to the Austrian Empire after the defeat of Napoleon), as well as the Bavarian branches of the Isarco, the canton of Dobbiaco, Ampezzo, Livinallongo and S. Candido. From 1824 to 1918 it indicated the present Trentino, while Alto Adige with Austrian Tirol and the Drava valley were called *Nordtirol.* The two parts constituted a single province *das Land Tirol.*

After the first world war and the defeat of Austria, the Treaty of Saint-Germain (1919) consigned Alto Adige to Italy, as agreed in 1915 with the Pact of London. *Südtirol* has now been the official name in German for more than

6 G. B. Pellegrini, *A proposito di bilinguismo nella toponomastica*, in Various Authors, *L'uso ufficiale del patrimonio dei nomi geografici,* Bolzano, 1986, pp. 115–121, p. 119.

7 J. Tarneller, *Die Hofnamen im Burggrafenamt und in den angrenzenden Gemeinden,* Wien, Archiv für Österreichische Geschichte, 1909, p. 213.

30 years, together with the name *Bozen*, for the province of "Bolzano-Alto Adige", which enjoys special autonomy; this name was included in the Constitution of the Republic of Italy in 2001.

3. A hundred years of Italian names

The question of official Italian-language toponomastics for Alto Adige has been considered important since the beginning of last century. Ettore Tolomei (Rovereto 1865 – Rome 1952), who was the main promoter of Italy's claim to Alto Adige from the end of the XIX century, was personally concerned with it. As a scholar and *irredentista,* he dedicated his whole life to these problems, especially toponomastics, founding the journal "*Archivio per l'Alto Adige*" in 1906, which is still published. He was nominated senator of the Kingdom of Italy in 1923.

The first edition of the *Prontuario dei nomi locali dell'Alto Adige* (vol. XV, part I, of the "*Memorie della Reale Società Geografica Italiana*", pp.140) was published in 1916 at the conclusion of the work of a commission of the Italian Royal Geographical Society of which Tolomei was president. It included all names (about 5000) of the Austrian Military Chart in scale 1:75000. It was the end point of a long series of studies that Tolomei had already partly done in 1906, the year in which he published his article ("*La toponomastica dell'Alto Adige*") in the first volume of the *Archivio.* The second edition of the *Prontuario dei nomi locali dell'Alto Adige* (published by the Istituto di Studi per l'Alto Adige, 218 pages) came out in 1929. The third edition was published in 1935, still in the "*Memorie della Reale Società Geografica Italiana*" (vol. XVI, part I, pp. 476).

Here I examine the later, which is the most up to date and complete. This edition still has official value, since it was confirmed by Ministerial Decree of 10th July 1940, emanated by Royal Decree no. 800 of 29th March 1923. It should also be recalled that bilingual toponomastics was confirmed by the De Gasperi-Gruber Agreement (1946), by the first Statute of Regional Autonomy (1948) and by the new Statute of Special Autonomy (1972).

The *Prontuario* is the list of place names of Alto Adige: a bilingual list in alphabetical order of about 8000 names that can be consulted in the form Italian – German or German – Italian. Under the letter "A", for example, we find *Algund-Lagundo* and under the letter "L", *Lagundo-Algund.* Toponyms have cartographic indications referring to a map in scale 1:25000 of the Istituto

Geografico Militare (IGM). The coordinates are based on the meridian of Rome (Monte Mario).

4. Eleven criteria for Italian place names

The criteria used by Tolomei and the commission over which he presided to determine the official Italian-language toponomastics of Alto Adige, with particular reference to the "Burgraviato di Merano" and the "Val Venosta", in are now identified, elaborated and indicated.

Today the "Burgraviato" is a district community in the Province of Bolzano composed of 26 municipalities (there are 116 in all of Alto Adige). Its territory centres on the Adige valley between Naturno and Nalles and all of the Val Passiria, and includes mainly mountain areas of the Alpi Venoste, the Ortles-Cevedale group and the Sarentino Massif.

List of municipalities (in Italian-German bilingual form):

Avelengo-Hafling, Caines-Kuens, Cermes-Tscherms, Gargazzone-Gargazon, Lagundo-Algund, Lana-Lana, Lauregno-Laurein, Marlengo-Marling, Merano-Meran, Moso in Passiria-Moos in Passeier, Nalles-Nals, Naturno-Naturns, Parcines-Partschins, Plaus-Plaus, Postàl-Burgstall, Provès-Proveis, Rifiano-Rifian, San Leonardo in Passiria-St. Leonhard in Passeier, San Martino in Passiria-St.Martin in Passeier, San Pancrazio-St. Pankraz, Scena-Schenna, Senale/San Felice-Unsere Liebe Frau im Walde/St. Felix, Tesimo-Thisens, Tirolo-Tirol, Ultimo-Ulten, Verano-Vöran.

The municipalities of *Lauregno-Laurein, Provès-Proveis* and *Senale/San Felice-Unsere Liebe Frau im Walde/St. Felix,* today in Alto Adige, are missing from the Prontuario because they were removed from the Province of Bolzano in 1927 and annexed to the Province of Trento.

Venosta is an area consisting of 13 municipalities. It is the name of the upper part of the Adige valley, from the river's sources near the Resia Pass, down to Tell, where the valley narrows and drops nearly 200 metres into the Merano basin.

List of municipalities (in Italian-German bilingual form):

Castelbello/Ciardes-Kastelbell/Tschars, Curòn Venosta-Graun, Glorenza-Glurns, Laces-Latsch, Lasa-Laas, Malles Venosta-Mals, Martello-Martell, Prato allo Stelvio-Prad am Stilfser Joch, Senales-Schnals, Silandro-Schlanders, Sluderno-Schluderns, Stelvio-Stilfs, Tubre-Taufers.

For every toponym in the Prontuario in German-Italian bilingual form (with respective cartographic indication), a record with progressive numbering was compiled. The record gives the following data:

a. municipality and any bilingual form of the toponym on the IGM map;
b. etymology with archival evidence of special interest for the phonetic and graphic evolution of the name;
c. the criterion used to determine the Italian name;
d. indications of a geographic nature or of general interest (see examples of records for Merano and Tirolo below).

Cartographic documentation of 46 IGM maps (scale 1:25000) was used. The maps are part of this study because only by systematic use of the maps was it possible to identify the sites of the toponyms and their municipalities. The number of records completed for the Burgraviato and Venosta was 1442 and 1401, respectively. After analyzing a total of 2843 records, one for each toponym studied, eleven categories underlying the toponomastic work of the Prontuario were identified. They were:

1. maintenance of toponym with phonetic adaptation;
2. maintenance of toponym with graphic adaptation;
3. maintenance of toponym without adaptation;
4. maintenance of a living Italian dialectal form;
5. restoration of a pre-Latin, Latin or medieval term with adaptation;
6. restoration of a pre-Latin, Latin or medieval term without adaptation;
7. translation into Italian;
8. translation into a dialect of the Triveneto area;
9. new creation by addition of determinative;
10. new creation by substitution;
11. omissions.

1. Maintenance of toponym with partial or total phonetic adaptation of the German term. This is sometimes used for names that have no meaning in modern German, e.g. *Andels-Andalo* (a word of obscure meaning in the municipality of Moso in Passiria valley); or *Agums-Agumes* (a place of uncertain etymon in the municipality of Prato allo Stelvio, Venosta). In this category we mostly have frequent phonetic adaptations of previous adaptations. See *Martschein-Marcena,* in the municipality of S. Pancrazio where the German toponym is a double diminutive <pre-L. MARRA "landslide" + ACEA + ONE. To make German names compatible with the Italian phonetic system, a final vowel is also added at the end; e.g. *Gargazon-Gargazzone*, *Marling-Marlengo* and *Naturns-Naturno* in the Burgraviato. In Venosta there are as many as eight

out of thirteen names of municipalities in this category and almost all are of pre-Latin origin: *Tschars* (word of uncertain etymon) becomes *Ciardes*; *Latsch-Laces (*Schneller[8] sustains that it could be an abbreviation of the Lat. DE PALATIIS, since Laces was an important place with a castle, but Pellegrini suggests a derivation from the neo-Lat. LAQUEUS "*Pinus mugo*"); *Laas-Lasa*; *Martell-Martello (*probably diminutive of the Alpine pre-Latin term MARRA "pile of stones")[9]; *Schnals* (from pre-L. CASEINA "alp") becomes *Senales*; *Schlanders-Silandro*; *Stilfs-Stelvio* and *Taufers-Tubre.*

2. Maintenance of toponym with graphic adaptation. This is a very narrow category in which we find for example names ending with the consonants -tz- that are reduced to -z- in the Italian form. For example *Allitz* becomes *Alliz*, *Parnetz-Parnez* (both in Lasa municipality in Val Venosta, words of uncertain etymon); *Kampei* with a "k" (in Ultimo municipality) becomes Campei with a "c" in the Italian form; *Getrums Spitze* becomes *Cima Ghetrum.* There are also names of German origin: *Soy (*from the appellative *SEEBER "at the lake")* becomes *Soi*; *Lohren (*<O.H.G. *LOH "wood")* becomes *Loren* (both toponyms in the municipality of Martello, in Val Venosta).

3. Maintenance of toponym without adaptation. In this case the toponym is transcribed without modification. Essentially names of pre-Latin or Latin origin, modified in the course of the centuries, were maintained. For example *Lazins-Lazins* (possibly from the neo-Latin LAQUEUS "*Pinus mugo*", in the municipality of Moso in Val Passiria); *Flim-Flim* (neo-Latin word < FLUMEN in the municipality of Ultimo; *Plars-Plars* (< pre-L. PALARIA < PALA "gently sloping meadows interrupting a steeper slope", in the municipality of Lagundo); *Verdins-Verdins* (pre-German toponym, possibly diminutive of VALLIS, in the municipality of Scena). It is also worth mentioning the famous *Lana-Lana* (municipality in the Burgraviato area), a praediality ending in -ANUM from Leonianum or Lucanius.

In Val Venosta, in this category we find almost exclusively names of pre-German origin, including two names of villages in the municipality of Stelvio: *Gomagoi* (< pre-L. CUMBA "valley") remains *Gomagoi* and *Trafoi* (from a pre-Indo-European root TER) remains *Trafoi.* As well, *Marzell (<pre-L.* MARRA "stony place"+ suff. ICEUS +ELLUS) remains *Marzell* (in the municipality of Senales); *Tabaretta* (< *pre-L.* TOB "gorge", or it could hide the pre-Latin denomination of "*pinaster*" TUBERES) remains *Tabaretta; Gadria* (could be a

8 C. Schneller, *Beiträge zur Ortsnamenkunde Tirols*, Innsbruck, 1893, p. 11.

9 C. Battisti, *I nomi locali del comune di Val Martello,* in *Archivio per l'Alto Adige*, Florence, 1974, p. 121.

development of <*Lat. QUADRIGA,* see the Engadinese *quadria, cudria "team of four oxen"*) remains *Gadria* (in the municipality of Silandro).

These toponyms are clearly already compatible with the Italian phonetic system. It is interesting that the percentage of this category is quite large, considering Venosta as a whole.

4. Maintenance of a living Italian dialectal form. Where possible, attempts were made to maintain a "living" Italian dialectal form. The most significant example is *Algund-Lagundo* (municipality in the Burgraviato). *Algund* is derived from the Lat. AD LACUNAM (1000 AD "*in loco qui dicitur Alagumna*"), though in 1894, Schneller wrote "Das Volk spricht Lagund" (p. 5 of his "*Beiträge zur Ortsnamenkunde Tirols*": thus the form *Lagundo* is clearly in this category. Also in the Burgraviato we have *Burgstall-Postàl* (name of municipality). *Burgstall* means "place where there was a castle or fort"[10]. *Postàl* also means "fort" and is a very old Trentino dialectal term, an adaptation of the German form, and was used by the community of Trentino origin that settled in the municipality. The -p- of the adaptation naturally indicates Bavarian pronunciation[11]. In the same area, in the municipality of Tesimo near the border with the municipality of Senale, we find *Gampen Joch – Le Palade. Gampen* is derived from the Latin CAMPUS; *Joch* means "mountain pass" and *Palade* is also a Trentino form meaning "defence with palisade", a fortification used from the XIII century; 1396 *Campenstein de Palladis,* 1518 *a Paladis*[12]. The reason for the choice of the Italian form is therefore clear and comes from the dialect of the nearby Val di Non.

In Venosta, two names of municipalities of pre-German origin are in this category. The first is *Graun-Curòn* (probably from CORONA "rock spur", see the Grisons term "*crun*" = terrace; the name is thought to come from the terrace of the chapel of St. Anna, 1147, *apud lacum Corum).* This word was already documented with the -o- variant, *Coròn,* in the maps of Cantelli (1686), Homann (1714) and Piccoli (1740)[13]. The second name of municipality is *Glurns* (probably from the pre-L. CALA with suffix -rn. The form *Glorenza* was already used on Italian maps in the first half of the XIX century (Civelli,1845, Perini, 1842)[14].

---

10 C. Battisti, *Glossario degli appellativi ricorrenti nella Toponomastica Atesina,* suppl. I, *Dizionario Toponomastico Atesino,* 2nd ed. with indices, Florence, 1940, p. 54.

11 C. Battisti & G. Giacomelli, *op. cit.*, 1968–70 (cf. municipality of *Postàl*).

12 C. Battisti & G. Giacomelli, *op. cit.*, 1968–70 (cf. municipality of *Tesimo*).

13 C. Battisti, *I nomi locali dell'Alta Venosta, parte I, Le Giurisdizioni di Castelnodrio e di Montemaria; Burgusio,* in *Dizionario Toponomastico Atesino*, vol. I, Florence, 1936, p. 197.

14 C. Battisti, *I nomi locali dell'Alta Venosta, parte II, Le Giurisdizioni di Malles, Glorenza e di Mazia,* in *Dizionario Toponomastico Atesino,* vol. I, Florence, 1937, pp. 775–776.

Two other examples are *Königspitze-Gran Zebrù* and *Zufall Ferner-Vedretta del Cevedale*, both toponyms of the Ortles-Cevedale massif on the border with Lombardy. The form *Zebrù* (of Bormian origin, perhaps from the pre-L. GIMBERU "cliff face" or from *cimbroi* "goat pasture" or from *cembrugi* "cliff face") is much older (1883) than *Königspitze,* which was introduced later by German mountaineers. With regard to the origin of *Königspitze*, Battisti[15] is sceptical about interpreting *König* as "king", which he considers an unlikely etymology for this name. Though poetic, the peak actually presents as a majestic wall and the name does not take into account the mentality of the valley dwellers. Its continuation WSW on one side of the Zebrù valley is the "Cima delle Miniere" that ends at the "Colle della Miniera", on the southern flank of which is an abandoned mine. *König* (dialectal form *Kunig*) could therefore be an adaptation of the earlier CUNICULUS "miniera", the area of which includes Alpine Lombardy and the Engadine. *Cevedale* is a "living" Solandro word on the Lombard side of the massif, and *Zufall* could even be a deformation of *Cevedale*. Another interesting example is *Langtaufers-Vallelunga*, where *Vallelunga* can be found on the Carta del Lombardo Veneto published by the Austrian Army Staff in 1837[16].

5. Adaptation of a pre-Latin, Latin or medieval term. Most toponyms in this category are neo-Latin names introduced into the region with the Roman occupation and Germanized over the centuries. In the Burgraviato (municipality of Lana) we find *Ackpfeif-Acquaviva*: at first sight it seems a German name but it is actually derived from the Latin AQUA VIVA and in 1272 it was still written *Achevive*. We also find *Gampen* (< Lat. CAMPUS), which returns to *Campo*, *Gfrill* (<Lat. CAPRILE) which returns to *Caprile*; *Kasatsch* (<Lat. CASA altered with the suffix -ACEA) returns to *Casaccia.*

In Venosta there are three municipal names in this category: *Kastelbell-Castelbello*, which until 1416 was written with a -c-[17]; *Prad-Prato in Venosta* (both clearly of Latin origin) and *Schluderns-Sluderno* (<pre-L. SALA "water channel", until 1259 documented as *Sludernes*, written with a -sch- since 1394[18]. Finally, the well known *Etsch* (<Lat. ATHESIS) returns to *Adige* and *Vintschgau* (<Lat. VENOSTES) returns to *Venosta*. In 717 AD we find *de Venostes*, in 831 *in Venustis,* and in 967 *vallis Venusta.* The name *Venusta* continues to be used by Italians and remains in constant use in the Latin chancelleries of the abbeys of Monte Santa Maria, Monastero and the Curia Coirese; it was also preferred by

15 C. Battisti, *op. cit.*, 1937, pp. 728–729.

16 C. Battisti, *op. cit.*, 1936, pp. 219–221

17 R. Staffler, *Die Hofnamen im Landesgericht Kastelbell*, in *Schlern-Schriften*, VIII, Innsbruck, 1925, pp. VIII–103.

18 C. Battisti, *op. cit.,* 1937, p. 600.

medieval Venostan notaries. The Germanized form *Vintschgau* is already used in German chancelleries in the second half of the XI century: 1077 AD *Finsgowe*, 1109 AD *Vinsgowe*. From 1374, the Austrian registry used the spelling *Vintschgau*. The initial substitution of “v” with “f” is typical of later modifications; substitution of “i” with “e” is a Bavarian trend[19].

6. Restoration of a pre-Latin, Latin or medieval term without adaptation. This category mainly concerns names of pre-German origin which were Germanized in time. For example, *Gand* (< pre-L. GANDA “moraine”) is restored to *Ganda*; *Graf* (pre-L. <GRAVA “sandy shore”) is restored to *Grava;* the toponym *Pfistrad Alpe-Alpe Viastrata* in the municipality of San Leonardo in Passiria is the XVIII century variant of *Vistrad* (still *Vistrad* in 1357) equivalent to VIA STRATA, recalling the Roman VIA STRATA of the Giovo pass. *Töll* (probably from a pre-L. TAL/TEL) is restored to *Tell.* The spelling *Töll* dates back to the XVI century and was handed down until the XIX century[20].

In Venosta, in this category we have the name of pre-German origin of the municipality of *Mals-Malles* (<pre-L. MAL “mountain”); indeed, *Malles* is a medieval form from 1094. The same is true of *Burgeis-Burgusio* (pre-German name of uncertain etymon), the Italian diction of which goes back to a medieval form of 1320[21]. The toponym *Ortler-Ortles* designates the summit of the Ortles-Cevedale range. The name of the mountain, probably neo-Latin from the diminutive of HORTUS “fenced area” was “Ortles” on Anich’s map of 1765, that is in a form with a neo-Latin ending, and remains thus in maps of the mid XIX century and the “*Bullettin Astronomique*” of 1887. For the official Italian form, the prior diction with the sigmatic plural was restored[22]. Another significant example is the name of the village *Eyrs-Oris* in the municipality of Lasa. The oldest documentation goes back to 1283 (*Aurs*) and according to Schneller (1894, p. 659) it is derived from *Ouris* <Lat. IN or SUB ORIS “riverside”). From *Aurs* it changed to *Aeures*, which improperly became *Eurs*, and finally according to Schneller “heute barbarisch Eyrs geschrieben” (= today barbarically written Eyrs). *Oris* is therefore the correct restoration of a name of Latin origin, subsequently Germanized.

7. Translation into Italian. This is the largest category. It contains words of German origin, most of which are common microtoponyms. We have a long series of *Alpe-Alpe*, or *Alpe-Malga*; *Wald-Bosco* or *Selva*, *Jöchl-Bocchetta*; *Scharte-Forcella*; *Hütte-Capanna* or *Rifugio*; *Schloss, Burg, Ruine* are translated

---

19 C. Battisti, *op. cit.*, 1936, pp. 67–68.

20 C. Battisti & G. Giacomelli, *op. cit.*, 1968–70 (cf. municipality of Parcines) and J. Tarneller, *op. cit.*, p. 103.

21 C. Battisti, *op. cit.*, 1936, p. 359.

22 C. Battisti, *op. cit.*, 1937, pp. 679, 726, 742, 743.

castello; *Spitze, Kopf, Kogl, Kofl* are translated *Cima* or *Punta*; *Bichl, Egg, Kopf* are rendered in Italian with *Colle* or *Dosso*. The very pertinent form "*novale*" (=land recently cultivated) is widely used to translate the German *Ried, Raut, Kreith*. In this group we also find all the hagionyms, including three municipalities in the Burgraviato, but no municipality name in Venosta.

8. Translation into dialect of the Triveneto area. The most significant example is the translation of HOF with *maso*, a term only used in Alto Adige. There is also a certain use of *lasta* to indicate the German *Platte*; *costòn* is equivalent to the German *Grat*. The dialectal noun *villa* is pertinently used for the German *Ort* and *Heim*, since "*villa*" may indicate a village or a part external to it.

9. New creation by addition of determinative. Generally in these cases the addition is a preposition or noun to complete the toponym, without modifying its original sense but highlighting the morphological or topographical aspect. For example *Berger-<u>Al</u> monte* is a common solution, as is *Pircher – Alle Betulle* (Pircher <M.H.G. BIRKE "birch") and *Pyla-Monte Pila* (in Val Venosta) or *Gribs-<u>Rio</u> Gris*.

10. New creation by substitution. This operation is sometimes motivated by the need to underline the municipality to which a place belongs, for example *Aschbach-Rio Lagundo*. In Venosta, words introduced by German mountaineering were eliminated: *Payerspitze-Punta Cristallo; Tuckett Spitze-Punta delle Baite*, where *Payer* and *Tuckett* were German mountaineers. In this category we also find some errors of interpretation. For example, in the Burgraviato (municipality of Moso) we have *Schönau-Belprato*, where *Schön* was interpreted as the German adjective for "beautiful". However, *Schönau* is a wrong transcription of *Schenau* from *Schenna* (name of the municipality) + *Au* "irrigated meadow near water". Thus the name is equivalent to "Meadows of Scena" (in *Schenner Awe*, 1288); this is a place north of Corvara in Passiria, the herds of which belonged to the municipality of Scena[23].

Controversial interpretations can also be found in Val Venosta: *Padöll* (<lat TABULATUM "wooden construction"+ ELLUS) was replaced by *Campitello*; *Konzen* (<pers. KUENZ) was paired with the noun *Cuna*. Substitution was also used for the difficult interpretation of the name *Bileben Wald* in Val Venosta: *Wald* means "wood, forest" and *Bileben*, an obscure term, is rendered with *di San Martino*. In other cases, the aim was simply to highlight topographic aspects: *Sauermoos-Palù di Mastaun* (*Sauer,* adj. "sour, acid" +*Moos* < O.H.G. MOS "marsh"). This solution was preferred because the place is near the peak of

23 C. Battisti & G. Giacomelli, *op. cit.*, 1968–70 (cf. municipality of Moso).

Mastaun in the municipality of Senales. Errors in etymology were only found in 2–3% of the 2843 place names examined.

11. Omissions. This category is in some ways the opposite to new creation by addition of determinative (category 9). Indeed, it sometimes involves elimination of terms that qualify a toponym; for example *Marlt Berg-Marlet* (in the municipality of Stelvio) or *Passeier Bach-Passirio* (municipality of Moso). On the other hand, when the toponym consisted of several words/names, we see that the one closest to the Italian tradition was left; in the Burgraviato, for example, *Hintere Eggen Spitze (Cima Sternai),* becomes *Cima Sternai* in Italian (Ultimo municipality). In Venosta we have (*Grazer Hütte) Tabaretta Hütte*, which becomes *Rifugio Tabaretta* (Stelvio municipality). Another interesting example regards a toponym in the municipality of Martello: *Gluder (Tair)-Pontara. Gluder* (dialectal form from glùdara "pile") has been cancelled. The word *Tair* is an apheretic form of *Pontair,* an adjectival derivative from the Lat. PUNCTUM (see also Trentino dialect "pontara"). In 1339 we find *Puntayr* and in 1624 the form *Pontair*[24]. With regard to the choice of the Italian form, we see that *Gluder* has been omitted because it was preferred to restore a name of Latin origin, still partly used in the XVII century, with Trentino dialectal adaptation.

However, the omissions are never "suppressions", otherwise the toponym would have disappeared completely. Why, then, do we sometimes find meticulous explanations with excessive simplifications? Are they inexplicable omissions or officializations of once-used oral forms? An answer may perhaps be found in the words of Tolomei, who sustained that the language spoken by the people is the "living source of toponomastics"[25].

A conclusion and two examples

Of the 2843 place names that I studied individually (out of a total of about 8000 in the Prontuario), 95% of the Italian forms, corresponding to 2700 place names, are correct and stylistically perfect. Two examples of records appear at the end of this paper. The Italian form of the bilingual toponomastics of Alto Adige has historically been the product of meticulous comparative research over many years, the scientific rigour and philological value of which are confirmed by scholars of the Italian and German schools. G. B. Pellegrini states that the Commission presided by Tolomei chose Italian dictions of German and Germanized names according criteria that were historically and toponomastically

24 C. Battisti, *op. cit.*, 1974, p. 139.

25 E. Tolomei, *Prontuario dei nomi locali dell'Alto Adige,* in *Memorie della Reale Società Geografica Italiana*, vol. XVI, part I, 3rd ed., 1935, Rome, introduction, p. 10.

valid[26]. According to Johannes Kramer, 90% were impeccable from the point of view of a Romance specialist[27].

5. Examples of records

Meran-Merano; 4 III SE (Merano) – 4019 – municipality

a – Merano; no German name

b – *Meran:* according to Schneller the name is related to the pre-Latin MARRA "landslide, moraine", but according to Battisti (1968), ignoring the suffix, the pretonic -e- can only have come from the mutation of -rj- into -ir-, as indicated by the older form: *Mairania,* 857 AD. According to Battisti, it is almost certainly a praedial name ending in *-anum* from *MARIUS,* an ancient noble Roman family name, also very common in northern Italy, documented as a surname in Veneto and the Transpadana, and characterized by the Osco-Latin root *marus.*
- 857 AD *Mairania;* 1237 *forum Mairani;* 1253 *de Merano;* 1266 *in burgo Merani;* 1292 *Merano,* whence the town has almost always been called *Meràn.* (Battisti, 1968–70).
- As indicated by the accent which conserves the Latin position, Germanization of the name is relatively recent (Pellegrini, 1985, p. 104).

c – Maintenance of a living Italian form without adaptation; in fact, an Italian-speaking community that used the name "Merano" has always lived in the town.

Tirol-Tirolo; 4 IV SE (Merano) – 4118 – municipality

a – Tirolo; no German name

b – *Tirol*: pre-Latin (Battisti, 1967, p. 67); 1142 *Tyral;* 1158 *Tiral;* 1163 *Tiralis, Tirallo.* This is Dante's *Tiralli*, but not *Teriolis* that appears in the "Notitia dignitatum utriusque Imperii" and indicates *Zirl* near Innsbruck (Battisti, 1968).

c – Maintenance with phonetic adaptation.

d – he consonant of the pre-Germanic name *Tirol* has not been modified and the accent is still on the last syllable: this demonstrates that the Germanization of the Merano area is about half a millennium behind, *cf.* its exact twin, the

---

26 G. B. Pellegrini, *Toponomastica italiana,* Milan, 1990, p. 416.

27 J. Kramer, *La toponomastica altoatesina di Ettore Tolomei – ieri e oggi,* in *Archivio per l'Alto Adige*, Florence, 1985, pp. 207–228, p. 221.

etymologically identical *Teriolis-Zirl* near Innsbruck. Palaeo-Germanic appropriation is therefore impossible (Battisti, 1967, p. 4).

Bibliography

Battisti C., *I nomi locali dell'Alta Venosta, parte I, le giurisdizioni di Castelnodrio e di Montemaria, Burgusio*, in *Dizionario Toponomastico Atesino*, vol. I, Florence, Rinascimento del Libro, 1936.

Battisti C., *I nomi locali dell'Alta Venosta, parte II, Le giurisdizioni di Malles, Glorenza e di Mazia,* in *Dizionario Toponomastico Atesino*, vol. I, Florence, 1937.

Battisti C., *Glossario degli appellativi ricorrenti nella toponomastica atesina, I, supplemento al Dizionario Toponomastico Atesino*, 2nd ed. with indices, Florence, 1940.

Battisti C., *Romanità e Germanesimo nel Burgraviato Meranese*, Florence, 1967, Istituto di Ricerche Onomastiche del CNR.

Battisti C. & Giacomelli G., *I nomi locali del Burgraviato di Merano, Florence,* Olschky, 1968–70, vol. I, parts I, II, III and vol. II, parts I, II, III series *Dizionario Toponomastico Atesino*.

Battisti C., *I nomi locali del Comune di Val Martello*, in *Archivio per l'Alto Adige*, Florence, 1974.

Kramer J., *Deutsch und Italienisch in Südtirol*, in *Reihe Siegen 23*, Heidelberg, K. Winter Univ. Verlag, 1981.

Kramer J., *La toponomastica altoatesina di Ettore Tolomei ieri e oggi*, in *Archivio per l'Alto* Adige, Florence, 1985.

Pellegrini G.B., *Problemi relativi alla toponomastica bilingue dell'Alto Adige*, in Massi E. (ed.), *Problemi della toponomastica italiana in Alto Adige, Atti della tavola rotonda svoltasi a Villa Celimontana il 25.10.1983*, Rome, 1985.

Pellegrini G.B., *A proposito di bilinguismo nella toponomastica*, in Various Authors, *L'uso ufficiale del patrimonio dei nomi geografici*, Bolzano, 1986.

Pellegrini G.B., *Toponomastica Italiana*, Milan, 1990.

Schatz J., *Wörterbuch der Tiroler Mundarten*, voll. 2, Innsbruck,1955, Universität Verlag Wagner.

Schneller C., *Beiträge zur Ortsnamenkunde Tirols*, Innsbruck, 1893–94–96.

Schöpf J.B., *Tirolisches Idiotikon*, Innsbruck, 1866, Druck und Verlag der Wagner'schen Universitäts-Buchhandlung.

Staffler R., *Die Hofnamen im Landesgericht Kastelbell*, in *Schlern-Schriften*, VIII, Innsbruck, 1925.

Tarneller J., *Die Hofnamen im Burggrafenamt und in den angrenzenden Gemeinden*, I Teil, Wien, 1909, aus dem Archiv für Österreichische Geschichte, 100. Band, I Hälfte, separat abgedruckt.

Tolomei E., *Prontuario dei nomi locali dell'Alto Adige*, in *Memorie della Reale Società Geografica Italiana*, vol. XVI, part I, 3rd ed., 1935, (1st ed. 1916), Rome.

Enciclopedia Italiana di Scienze, Lettere ed Arti, founded by Giovanni Treccani, vol. XXXV, Rome, 1949.

Along the streets of Trieste. Roads, culture and law between the Austro-Hungarian Empire and the Italian Republic

Davide Rossi

Summary

1. The "naming" State. The legislative ideology of toponymy

It seems that everything always starts from there.

It seems that everything always goes irresistibly back to that momentous decade which ended the XVIII century, with France and Paris taken by a *regenerative*[1] and furious storm, ready to wash away whatever might evoke the *Ancien Régime*[2].

However, if from a historical-legal point of view – much more in keeping with me – the French Revolution, between continuity and transformation, ideological plans and practical operations[3], clearly fulfilled the function of an interpretative watershed in terms of dogmatic and institutional categories, which were removed and replaced by a fundamentally new organizational system (making the historical distance between the "before" and the "after" seem emblematic), it is also very true – after careful deliberation – that the Revolution

---

1 The regenerative outcome of the French Revolution is clearly explained, in a pedagogical and educational way, in R. Isotton, *Brevi note sul "Plan d'éducation nationale di Michel Lepeletier de Saint-Fargeaux*, in A. Padoa-Schioppa, G.di Renzo Villata and G.P. Massetto (eds.), *Amicitiae Pignus. Studi in ricordo di Adriano Cavanna*, vol. II, Milan, 2003, pp. 1247–1287.

2 M. Fioravanti, *È possibile un profilo giuridico dello Stato Moderno?*, in *Scienza & Politica*, vol. XXXI, 2004, pp. 39–48.

3 This huge historiographic problem is simply touched in this essay. We remind, as general reference, the classics G. Tarello, *Storia della cultura giuridica moderna*, Bologna, 1976 and A. Cavanna, *Storia del diritto moderno in Europa. Le fonti e il pensiero giuridico,* vol. II, Milan, 2005, especially pp. 14–68.

influenced the urban structure, the rationalization of places and the decisions that reorganized their identity.

A truly *regenerative* finality that placed the citizen at the centre of the new century's society, reshaping not only customs and habits of mind, but also districts and departments, towns and villages, creating the development of residential housing areas without precedent[4]. A reorganization of the territory which, inevitably if not inexorably, aimed at optimizing resources, at making the system work through the *legal structure*, without which "no one could ever understand the historical significance of the modern State"[5]. Through the emergence of a new state entity, with its own original characteristics, bearer of the sovereignty principle, old peculiarities were subverted and the superiority of the general and abstract law over ancient privileges was affirmed. The modern State – fully legal and legalized – saw its tasks and functions widen; it emerged from the underworld of balances that it had guaranteed for centuries, and offered itself as a regulating – and functionalizing – element with its duties, expectations, power and purposes. A flow of systematizing actions in which the State consolidated its presence and authoritatively directed spaces and perceptions. The State itself rationalized the territory and its inhabitants, it organized the institutional structure into a pyramidal perspective in which the institutional bodies had to hierarchically answer to their superiors, and it required immanence towards the citizens[6], who had to be "rationalized" from birth to death. Official registering lost its religious connotation and became a prerogative of the State, and "the registration of birth is no longer a prerogative of the parson but, with priority, is now in the hands of the state registrar"[7]. In the same way, also toponymy – the naming of streets seen as the criterion of "the attribution of

---

4 We can consider the mid-1800 Paris and the Hausmannian politics as symbols of public areas' new exploitation and safeguarding, "that show a clear 'urban', economic and politic value", forerunning the Italian demographic increase of more than fifty years. On this subject, L. Lacché, *L'espropriazione per pubblica utilità. Amministratori e proprietari nella Francia dell'Ottocento*, Milan, 1995, pp. 543–638 (quotation at p. 547), and S. Maggi, *Le ferrovie*, Bologna, 2003.

5 M. Fioravanti, *È possibile un profilo giuridico dello Stato Moderno?*, *cit.*, p. 40.

6 The conquest of the separation of jurisdictional and administrative functions, during the XIX century, with "legal exceptions" in which the balancing role of the State continues, is described in L. Mannori, *Giustizia e amministrazione tra antico e nuovo regime,* in R. Romanelli (ed.), *Magistrati e potere nella storia europea*, Bologna, 1997, pp. 39–65.

7 S. Pivato, *Il nome e la storia. Onomastica e religioni politiche nell'Italia contemporanea,* Bologna, 1999, p. 20 (and at p. 51: "moreover, in 1815, the Restauration gave parsons back their exclusive competence on official registering and hence the control of names according to the Council of Trent").

names to places and public monuments, or of public use"[8] – becomes an affair of the State and of its institutions: the system which had, until then, been traditionally, "'spontaneous', namely a product of the feelings and words of the nation"[9], assumes an official character with the rational aim of identification. As there is a citizens' birth register, "so there also is a street register, both under the control of the administrative authorities"[10]. Throughout the XIX century, we almost see the dissipation of the mediating and balancing role of the State, which was concerned with achieving its aims with greater incisiveness by pursuing "a subjectivized public interest, considered as its own and that is authorized to prevail itself of any private interest, within the limits of the law"[11]. The principle of attributing street names is part of the revolutionary utopian result by which society's demand for radical changes in its structure underlines the need to transform places and their physicalness, due to a prevailing and characterizing political symbolism[12].

An uneven path, marked by uncertain legal categories and by a difficult approach of Jurists, who slowly "imagined" the State as a real interlocutor that was leaving doctrine behind and becoming more concrete[13]. In this perspective, the problem of the road network thus became an *administrative* problem

---

8 M. Pallottino, *Toponomastica*, in *Enciclopedia del Diritto*, vol. XLIV, Milan, 1992, p. 739.

9 And he continues: a toponymy "kept alive by an ordinary use without the interference of any authority, dependent on the change of its originating reasons and conditions", in M. Fanti, *Le vie di Bologna. Saggio di toponomastica storica e di storia della toponomastica italiana*, vol. I, Bologna, 2000, p. 12.

10 C.A. Mastrelli, L*'odonomastica nella legislazione italiana*, in *Rivista Italiana di Onomastica*, vol. IV, 1998, p. 424. The essay, a central point of departure, contains the history of regulations, in addition to the correct definition of terms. It is important to specify, without dilating on this subject, that if "in the ordinary use there is generally no difference between urban toponymy [of street or towns] and odonym, today it becomes fundamental". In fact, when "street naming creativity loses its spontaneity and is determined by administrative acts: in this new phase, it is not possible to talk about urban toponymy but we must talk about odonym", in C.A. Mastrelli, *Aspetti storico-linguistici della odonomastica*, in *Le città leggibili. La toponomastica urbana tra passato e presente. Atti del convegno di Foligno 11–13 dicembre 2003*, in *Bollettino della Deputazione di Storia Patria per l'Umbria*, vol. CI, 2004, pp. 61–62. A good key to the reading in G.B. Pellegrini, *Metodologia dell'indagine antroponimico-toponomastica*, in E. Vineis (ed.), *La toponomastica come fonte di conoscenza storica e linguistica. Atti del convegno della Società italiana di glottologia, Belluno 31 marzo–2 aprile 1980, Pisa*, 1981, pp. 11–28.

11 L. Mannari, B. Sordi, *Giustizia e amministrazione*, in M. Fioravanti (ed.), *Lo Stato moderno in Europa. Istituzioni e diritto*, Rome-Bari, 2002, p. 60.

12 Explanatory examples in M. Fanti, *Le vie di Bologna, cit.*, pp. 20–26.

13 On this play, between factuality and reality of the concept of State, P. Costa, *Lo Stato immaginario. Metafore e paradigmi nella cultura giuridica italiana tra Otto e Novecento*, Milan, 1986, p. 120 et seq.

requiring legal analysis[14], which was indicative of the social need that "directly embraces issues that care for the essential purposes of the State"[15]. Therefore, means of communication were seen as an important sphere of activity, with multidisciplinary theoretical principles and notions, for which the juridical side became essential, when "the direct activity of the State has to intervene and take the place of individual activities"[16]. Among the principal tasks of the State – or, more precisely, "in the content of the concept of the modern State, in which the public authority is the principal and essential actor in the progress of the community, which is the substratum of its characteristics"[17] – the organization of road communications is an integral part. They had to be made efficient and easily recognizable, suitable for favouring trade and the "movement and distribution of wealth"[18]. But street also has an *urban* meaning relating to the road system and to the rationalization of the internal areas of those *towns* that slowly become aseptic *municipalities*, with a strongly administrative and institutional character[19]. And municipal *urbanity* inseparably interwove itself with the language, whose function was no longer the old spontaneous medieval way of identifying places and territories, but instead became a way to ideologically put a mark on an everyday life coloured by names, dates and episodes that would encourage culture, favour a sense of belonging and identity and play a role in the conditioning of a united community.

The State understood the close link that binds "the structural and functional conception of language in considering that the meaning is no longer the conceptual content of linguistic signs, but a relation (or function) between the level of linguistic expression and the level of conceptual substance"[20], by

14 "The extension of the administrative power, and of its cases, was due to the development of civil societies, and the law gave poor protection to uncultivated times and places, even if they were mainly disposed … but, after nations' civilization, the law gave more protection to public things which were under the public administration power and not under the civil power… so, due to this law, the road organization was regulated by administrative bodies… and due to the aforesaid law the road direct administration was given to the administrative power", in G. Rocco, *Corso di diritto amministrativo*, vol. I, Napoli, 1850, p. 370.

15 C. Corradin and E. Peronac, *Le strade ferrate*, in V.E. Orlando (ed.), *Primo trattato completo di diritto amministrativo italiano*, vol. I, Napoli, 1850, p. 370.

16 *Ibidem*, p. 3.

17 *Ibidem*, p. 4.

18 *Ibidem*, p. 3.

19 F. Rugge, *Le nozioni di città e cittadino nel lungo Ottocento. Tra «patiforme sistema» e nuovo particolarismo*, in M. Meriggi and P. Schiera (eds.), *Dalle città alla nazione. Borghesie ottocentesche in Italia e in Germania*, Bologna, 1993, pp. 47–64.

20 L. Rosiello, *La semantica moderna e l'opera di Stephen Ullmann*, in S. Ullmann, *Semantica. Introduzione alla scienza del significato* (1962), Italian translation by A. Baccarat and L. Rosiello, Bologna, 1966, p. IX.

showing greater will and considering the relation between expression and the "names given".

"Word", "thing" and "sense" travel in parallel within society or, more generally, within a community identity: in the collective imagination, they inseparably link the idea or the perception of the *res* itself to an oral or written expression. A dependency between the expression and the content is established, as a general "reciprocal relation between the name and the sense, which enables them to mutually evoke each other"[21].

The difference between the "word" and the "thing" is a bumpy road that the historian well knows and he is well aware of the enormous mistake he risks making by using contemporary categories and images for past events[22]. However, "the attribution of names to species, to celestial bodies, to disease, always ends up snaring the denominated thing into a radical metaphor, and misappropriating the thing itself to the world"[23].

Names and concepts inexorably go arm in arm with history. They feed a cultural laboratory that portray changes and innovation, falsifications and metamorphoses, as "signals that, properly read, reveal currents of thought or feelings toward which the historian could not be indifferent"[24].

Therefore, the need to systematize the road network was driven by a practical demand to make road communication easier and to rationalize the territory[25]; but at the same time this requirement gave a sense of belonging to the community in the choice of place and street names. As well as the geometrical order, the numeration between right and left, the definition of places according to their importance and hierarchy, there was an administrative dynamism that wanted to express values and preferences, culture and civilization, through the formalization of street names whose choice suggested an ideological *imprinting*, an emotional value, a common feeling for the traditions of a nation – the Italian one – that was gradually being constructed. And the introduction of public street

---

21 S. Ullmann, *Semantica, cit.*, p. 96.

22 I have taken this simile – used in a different context – from the introduction of L. Mannari and B. Sordi, *Storia del diritto amministrativo,* Rome-Bari, 2001, pp. 6–15. For a close examination and good key to the reading, S. Ullmann, *Semantica, cit.,* pp. 90–106.

23 *Ibidem*.

24 M. Bloch, *Noms de personne et histoire sociale,* in *Annales d'Historie Économique et Sociale*, vol. IV, 1932, pp. 67–69, and S. Pivato, *Il nome e la storia*, *cit.*, p.13. From the methodological point of view, M. Bloch, *Réflexions d'un historien sur quelques travaux de toponymie*, in *Annales d'Historie Économique et Sociale*, vol. VI, 1934, p. 252.

25 A path that had begun during the French Revolution and reached Italy with the French Emperor's conquests, as above-mentioned; for further references, G. Simoncini, *La viabilità nelle città italiane del periodo napoleonico. Le fonti delle Archives Nationales di Parigi,* in *Storia Urbana*, vol. VI, 1982, p. 19.

lighting at the beginning of the nineteenth century marked "the accomplishment of this anything but metaphorical "brightening up" process of urban environment"[26]. As planned by the Unifiers in 1865, the constitutional outcome of the administrative system[27] certainly fits in with this perspective, by opening a new phase of urban space transformation and instilling a process that, in the years to come, would be momentous for institutional and *symbolic* organization.

The practical importance of the "communicative" value of street names was not supported by appropriate regulation on the reasons and systems for choosing them and therefore, the councils and peripheral administrations were given great freedom. There is no point in pausing over the fatally broad concept of "public road" as a space in which, regardless of legal ownership, the effective exercise of empiric power insists on the purpose of the promotion of the concept of a road, to be used indefinitely by users[28]. Liberal Italy is a patriotic and celebratory Italy, not supported by a central rational plan, nor by general pedagogic intentions, which gave local administrations plenty of room for movement[29]. In fact, there were no specific regulations planned and "there was no explicit reference to the Prefect's control on Councils relating to urban toponymy"[30]. Local administrations enjoyed a high degree of autonomy in the choice of names, often letting themselves go "to political factiousness or to delightfully country-

---

26 D. Marchesin, *Denominare e numerizzare la città: dall'antico regime alla Restaurazione*, in *Le città leggibili, cit.*, p. 137.

27 "There are enough signs to realize that this administrative unification was a constitutional event, in the sense that its construction and permanence became necessary to preserve the fabric of the State. All laws of 1865 are still in force, although in their guiding principles and ground rules, even if they were reproduced one or more times in subsequent laws", states G. Berti, *La responsabilità pubblica (Costituzione e amministrazione),* Padova, 1994, p. 197.

28 The confusion came from the vacuity of annex F of law no. 2248 of 1865, and was increased by terminological mistakes in reference to "country lanes" in the Italian legislative decree no. 1446 of 1st September 1918. Interesting key to the reading in E. Bonvicini, *La classificazione delle strade nei riflessi dell'articolo 29 cod. strad.*, in *Diritto Automobilistico*, vol. XX, 1955, pp. 71–80.

29 An accurate and precise reconstruction in G. Melis, *La legislazione sulla toponomastica dall'Unità ad oggi*, in *Le città leggibili, cit.,* pp. 89–97.
The fact that this subject did not attract the historians, legally speaking, is underlined by the almost total absence of monographs about the matter, the very few lines on rare articles or within the commentary of the *Testo Unico Comunale e Provinciale* (in addition to Astegno's work, mentioned by Melis. I quote, as an example, M. La Torre, *Commento al nuovo Testo Unico Comunale e Provinciale ed alle norme complementari*, Napoli, 1934, p. 165, where "street-naming" is not taken into account at all, neither in the index, and the only reference can be found under the paragraph "*L'oggetto dei regolamenti di polizia urbana – polizia stradale*"), and the absence of encyclopaedic entries about this subject, with the exception of the above-mentioned M. Pallottino, *Toponomastica, cit.* (see footnote 8).

30 G. Melis, *La legislazione sulla toponomastica, cit.,* p. 90.

flavoured conceitedness"[31]. At worst, the centralizing effort to remove, where possible, homonymy – and antinomy – of a Peninsula that had always been subdivided into local communities and tiny States, gave vent to an unrestrained toponymical revision, that binned millennial heritage in the name of celebratory intentions, patriotic Risorgimental evocations and moralistic efforts. The two-year period that follows Unification can be defined as a period characterized by "a sort of gutting of street names, which ... disfigured to a certain degree the topographic structure of built-up areas"[32], redrawing streets and squares, choosing heroes and models and consciously ignoring others.

An unprincipled and rarefied "cultural geography" ruled and it was this that, in the 1920s, urged the Parliament to regulate the choice of national street names choice with Italian legislative decree no. 1158 of 10th May 1923" (subsequently law no. 473 of 17th April 1925) which was later followed up by law no. 1188 of 23rd June 1927[33]. Conscious of the irrationality adopted in the sixty years after the Unification, the legislator authorities wanted to retrieve a systematic profile in the adoption of name choosing, with ministerial control through the intervention of the local Prefect, and more significantly, by the creation of cultural agencies that put a brake on local abuses and limited the unjustified – and often irrational – choices that sprang from exaggerated local pride. Thus, any change in old names had to be examined by the Ministry of Education through the Monuments and Fine Arts Bureau, and the choice of new names depended on the explicit opinion of the *Deputazioni* or the *Società di Storia Patria*, associations which promoted historical research within the local and regional area. In order to avoid emotional decisions or on-the-spur-of-the-moment choices, the discretionary power of the mayor – and shortly after of the *Podestà* entrusted with the task – was further limited by a time restriction that stated that the subject chosen for the street name had to have been dead for at least ten years[34]. However, parliamentary debate introduced the non-uninfluential derogation to this time restriction for "members of the Royal Family and those killed in battle or for the national cause" (as well as for the exceptional

31 G.R., *La disciplina giuridica della toponomastica stradale,* in *L'Amministrazione Italiana*, vol. XXIX, 1974, p. 217. The anonymous writer continues underlining that "it became more marked the tendency to replace illustrious names or historical dates and anniversaries with those of local personalities of small or no importance".

32 S. Raffaelli, *I nomi delle vie*, in M. Ornaghi (ed.), *I luoghi della memoria. Simboli e miti dell'Italia Unita*, Rome-Bari, 1996, pp. 215–242.

33 U. Maculan and F. Balmas, *Indicatore delle leggi e decreti del Regno d'Italia (dal 1861 al gennaio 1931)*, Rome, 1931, p. 1385. The complete chronology in C.A. Mastrelli, *L'odonomastica nella legislazione italiana, cit.* (see footnote 10).

34 This texts' forming procedure is optimally described in G. Melis, *La legislazione sulla toponomastica, cit.*, pp. 95–99.

hypothesis, directly under ministerial jurisdiction, for "people meritorious of the nation"). The "liberal" period for municipalities thus came to an end. They lost their discretionary power to a clear and rational legislative indication that reconciled peripheral and central lobbies and supported the cultural importance of toponymy through the intervention of such authorities as *Deputazioni* that guaranteed local historical traditions. Aware of the delicacy of the matter and of the multi-faceted expectations and aspirations involved – not only legal and institutional, but also urban, welfare, fiscal, moral, ethical and historical[35] – a fully participative system was introduced. A great deal of petitions with a variety of different aims were concerned, all equally interested in the regional organizational structure and in the cultural sensitivity that could be concretely expressed therein.

On the other hand, the solemnity and the symbolism that underlie modern toponymy cannot be identified – as we briefly tried to outline – in the administrative act which formalizes the name of a place. They do, in fact, mirror a historical outcome, a cultural revisionism and an intellectual decision that has more importance and meaning in the border areas[36] where the communities speak more languages and dialects, where folklore becomes more rarefied and the name of a road signifies a victory of one *faction* over another with considerable evocative value.

The city of Trieste and the northern part of the Adriatic Sea are the distinctive emblem of this process: the imperial past, powerful irredentism, annexation with Italy and the political crisis that coincided with the end of the Second World War – an open wound –, the loss of national sovereignty in some areas and the Italian re-conquest in others, that occurred with almost ten years delay.

2. Trieste, the *Sleeping Beauty*. A solution for all seasons

The XIX century, the age of the Risorgimento, had united the concept of nation and cultural identity, of ineluctable historical identity and incontrovertible

35 G. Casoni and E. Pigaiani, *Gli adempimenti istruttori concernenti l'intitolazione delle aree di circolazione*, in *Lo Stato Civile Italiano*, vol. C, 2004, pp. 128–130.

36 A problem referable not only to Julian March area, but to every border area, as described in G. de Vergottini, *Profili giuridici della toponomastica nella provincia di Bolzano*, in *Diritto e società*, 4/1986, pp. 651–659, an essay about the region of Alto Adige and in R. Barbagallo, *Caratteri e vicende della toponomastica in Valle d'Aosta*, ivi, 2/1989, pp. 361–364, an essay about the Savoia area.
Another testimony, although with "opposite effectiveness", in G.B. Pellegrini, *Toponimi slavi e "slavo-venetici" in Italia*, in *Rivista Italiana di Onomastica*, vol. II, 1996, pp. 70–79.

linguistic identity as the uniform aggregative outcome of a population in a modern political State that was schematically in the making. This rigid interpretation opened up cultural forms and models that were expressions of minorities with their principles and characteristics and cultural heritages to be protected, as the common link to folklore and traditions that only with the coming of democratic ordinance could enjoy indefeasible guaranties[37]. Border areas – and Trieste rightly falls into this category – are always inclined to precede these changes and become hybrid battlefields for fights and scraps between people and ethnic groups, each living their past as if the future should remain there, hidden somewhere behind the Isonzo river.

Trieste is, in fact, a border town[38] where toponymy is also an interpretative model and key reading.

It has an *internal* and an *external* toponymy. With the latter I refer to the irredentist myth that flooded the Italian peninsula with squares, roads and streets between the XIX and XX centuries. The irredentist dream and the desire for an anti-Austrian and united nation did not only dominate the political questions and newspapers of the time, but also bombarded the onomastic indexes[39] with references, with the aim of denying the historical, ethnic and cultural connections of these lands to the Austro-Hungarian Empire and claiming their *natural* and physiological link to Italy[40]. It was impossible to think of the process of national unification as complete without Trentino and Brenner, Trieste, the Istria

---

37 V. Piergigli, *Lingue minoritarie e identità culturali*, Milan, 2001, pp. 43–54.

38 The irredentist imagination and the value of Trieste is masterfully described in A. Ara and C. Magris, *Trieste. Un'identità di frontiera*, Turin, 2007.

39 Trieste, for its references and personalities, is second only to Rome, in S. Pivato, *Il nome e la storia*, *cit.*, p. 206. S. Raffaelli, *Il primo dopoguerra e il ventennio fascista*, in *Le città leggibili*, *cit.*, p. 157, reports a survey "of 1998 on the 200 most common odonyms of 8100 Italian Municipalities", from which we can infer that Trieste – with Trento, Nazario Sauro and Fabio Filzi, Fiume and Gorizia, Isonzo and Piave – is the most common and persistent.
And, in E. Caffarelli, *Odonomastica come impegno sociale e culturale*, in C.A. Mastrelli (ed.), *Odonomastica. Criteri e normative sulle denominazioni stradali. Atti del convegno di Trento, 25 settembre 2005*, Trento, 2005, p. 18: "Italy's most common city used in street-naming is Rome, followed by the reconquered towns of Trieste, Trento and Gorizia, and the most common river is Piave".

40 "At the outbreak of World War I, the Julian March, Istria and Dalmatia belonged to the Austro-Hungarian Empire, although they were inhabited by communities of Italian and Slavic culture. In fact, according to the census of 1910, based on the language in use, Trieste counted 171.522 native Italian speakers and 38.505 native Slavic speakers; while the entire Julian March counted 424.893 Italians, including the inhabitants of the Kingdom of Italy, and 446.691 Croatians-Slovenians", in P. Romano, *La questione del confine orientale e le due guerre mondiali*, in V. Piergigli (ed.), *L'autoctonia divisa. La tutela giuridica della minoranza italiana in Istria, Fiume e Dalmazia*, Padova, 2005, p. 223.

peninsula, Dalmatia and the Carnaro region. The national State, whose ethic edification as one single identified community, wanted road names to be a reminder of the turbulent Risorgimento period and ideologically aimed at arousing the population's conscience to complete – almost by popular acclaim – the annexation of the latter lands that were still to be conquered. A nomenclative frenzy resulted that went beyond the practical purposes of classification and started a distinctly cultural aim, a propulsive goal of civic consciences, a didactic and formative exegesis of collective perceptions, an ideological structure, as if streets were an open "political newspaper". The strong evocative power was reflected in the connotative use generated by the choice of names for the unredeemed lands, favouring an anti-Austrian climate and aspirations towards territorial revenge: terms were imposed – exogenous or applied street names with a Jacobin-style[41] – were used; terms that were completely out of the territorial context, chosen purely for political opportunism and to promote superior and national interests, as if to compensate for the linguistic gaps and extremely high illiteracy of the population, as well as to propose a coherent political plan.

Moreover, Trieste deserves a separate chapter, if only for its different institutional history and its multiethnic population. The interplay between political schemes and cultural inflections has made Trieste a town of many identities, more so than others, a bridge between the East and the West, a port of call for merchants and freight traffic, a place of encounter and confrontation between different schools of thought and aspirations. Trieste's toponymic history of the last century[42] shows this panorama accurately, as an instrument that confirms the dominance of one ethnic group over another, supremacy over minority. Trieste became a battlefield of either anti-Italian or anti-Austrian feelings depending on the moment, it made room for both the rhetoric of victory and hegemony. In a town that was undergoing continual and rapid changes, street names could become, depending on the moment, either indelible marks or fleeting memories of a changing territory.

The procedure of naming streets was never particularly complex resolved by simple government approval – generally from the imperial Lieutenant – after a proposal submitted by a specific organ of the City Council, namely the Municipal Delegation[43]. The *Costituzione della città immediata di Trieste* in 1850 had stated guidelines relating to administrative and institutional

41 E. Caffarelli, *Odonomastica come impegno sociale*, *cit.*, p. 17.

42 A really detailed key reading in E. Generini, *Trieste antica e moderna, ossia descrizione ed origine dei nomi delle sue vie, androne e piazze,* Trieste, 1884.

43 For further references, A. Tampus, *Vie e piazze di Trieste Moderna. Toponomastica stradale e topografia storica*, Trieste, pp. 21–26, and the above-mentioned bibliography.

subdivision[44]. The names chosen mainly referred to places, and were linked to geographical and popular reasons, to economic activities, to the public architecture or to the hydrographical situation[45]. The already precarious stability was broken by the Italian declaration of war against Austria – after the breaking of international obligations assumed within the Triple Alliance and Anglo-French negotiations[46] – on 24th May 1915, which was followed by an immediate compulsory administration of Trieste. Among the first measures adopted by the Imperial Commissioner, "maybe thinking that it would distort the Italian nature of the town"[47] was to "change part of the names of our lands, and substitute them with others"[48]. On 5th July – just two months after the Commissioner was installed – some of the streets to have their names changed were: *Via Vincenzo Bellini, Via Giuseppe Caprin, Via Giosuè Carducci, Via Felice Venezian, Via Nicolò Machiavelli,* as well as some squares: *Carlo Goldoni, Ruggero Manna, Gioacchino Rossini, Nicolò Tommaseo, Massimo d'Azeglio* and *piazza della Procureria*. Illustrious names with an evidently strong Italian parentage. Patriots of a rival nation with which they were at war and of whom it was more convenient to remove the memory. On the other hand, the town was filled with *artificial* streets and *unnatural* names: *via Laudon*, a general and famous Austrian warrant officer born in Livonia; *via Boroevic*, dedicated to the general who commanded an Austro-Hungarian army on the Italian front; *via Makart*, a painter from Salzburg; *riva Tegetthoff*, an admiral who distinguished himself in the famous Battle of Lissa; *via Hofer*, the leader of the Tyrolean insurrectionists,

---

44 The Municipality records confirmed the fact that this practice remained almost unaltered until the compulsory administration of Trieste, subject to the founding of *Commissioni per le nomenclature*. Further references in *Verbali della Delegazione Municipale di Trieste anche in sede di Consiglio*, year XLX – 1911, Trieste, 1911, p. 559: "No. IX–810/1–10: the proposals of *Commissione alla Nomenclatura delle vie*, concerning the denomination of some urban and suburban streets, are approved. During this meeting, the Honourable MP Puecher recommends to use abstract concepts in the street names choice in the future. The Honourable MP Mrach recommends to consider the local history in the choice of street names. The Honourable MP D'Osmo recommends to write under illustrious personalities' names, chosen to name a street, the date of birth and death and their title".

45 F. De Vecchi, *Il luogo e la storia. La toponomastica storica di Trieste alla scoperta del sito quale bene culturale*, vol. I, *Parte prima. Il borgo Teresiano*; vol. II, *Parte seconda. Il borgo Giuseppino*, Trieste, 1990–1992.

46 An interesting historiographic outline in G.E. Rusconi, *L'azzardo del 1915. come l'Italia decide la sua Guerra*, Bologna, 2005.

47 O. Ravasini, *Compendio di notizie su denominazioni delle località e strade di Trieste*, Trieste, 1918, to which followed a revised edition *Compendio di notizie sulla nomenclatura di località e strade di Trieste*, Trieste, 1929, from which – for the completeness and precision – I decided to extract the quotations, pp. 3–5.

48 *Ibidem.*

later shot by the French; *via Helgoland*, in memory of the battle in 1864 between the Austrians and the Danish; *piazza Maria Teresa*, the beloved Austrian empress of the XVIII century; *via Mozart*, the illustrious composer from Salzburg[49].

After having outlined this key, it was not surprising that on 11th November 1918 – when the first convocation of the Municipality after the reinstatement of the City Council by the Royal governor – subsequent to the Mayor's customary salutations, the names that had been changed just three years earlier by the imperial Commissioner, were re-established. Even before getting to the heart of the question about the value of the nominations and acts decided by the Commissioner or estimating the financial structure of the Municipality or establishing the relations to install in regard to the commitments previously taken by the Austrian Government, practical requirements imposed the restoration of *corso Vittorio Emanuele III, piazza dell'Unità, riva III ottobre, piazza Guglielmo Oberdan, riva Nazario Sauro, via Cesare Battisti*[50]. The use of categories connected to Italy and Italianism, to the memory of patriots or martyrs to freedom, to dates or events related to the Risorgimento, to the celebrations for the much-coveted unification, are all reflections and litmus papers for understanding that phenomenon that sees an inestimable instrument of cultural orientation and an identifying κοινή in the denomination of streets, squares and roads.

Trieste, in its uniqueness, as an expression of a seductive crossroads of culture and people, literature and history, faced the political problem of newly-achieved unification with a "national defence" approach, aligning itself with the ideals of the still immature new Italian middle class. The toponymic irredentism is a one-way choice geared to dismember the cultural versatility that marked the Austro-Hungarian Empire and to curb the cosmopolite atmosphere typical of places with a strong ethnic and trade interaction such as Trieste was in the mid-XIX century. The use of one name rather than another gave rise to feelings of frustration or to Slavic or Austrian rancour, nourishing conflicts and tensions among the various populations. The identity declaration of winning values – values to display on inscriptions, to be proud of because it is our hometown or because it promotes nationalism – was effectively expressed by the town's street names. Trieste lost the value of historical place names and inserted other names with a strong Italian and highly identificative character, sparking spiteful tension, the aftermath of which reverberated until the Second World War, and beyond.

49 *Ibidem*, pp. 211–214.

50 Archivio Generale del Comune di Trieste, *History Section*, folder G-8, 1915–1918 Council records, *Verbale della Giunta Municipale di Trieste – 11 novembre 1918*.

The hackneyed use of heroes and feats, local personalities or figures related to the at long last conquered Italianism, had a further aim with respect to plain opportunism, and attempted – through "toponymical cleansing – to organize the consensus or mould public opinion with a moralistic intent"[51]. The spreading of suffrage and trade union actions in the early XX century forced the State to make internal transformations as well as to increase the range of normative and institutional measures that would be necessary to regulate a cluster of private interests that were gradually to become public. The "administrative" or "mixed-class" State – as Massimo Severo Giannini[52] said – had made the areas governed by public power basically unlimited and these included – original as well as ineluctable – certainly the eccentric phenomenon of the ideological name. The system no longer took its inspiration from natural or historical origins, but became a *modus* of active participation and a cultural model itself for the spreading of "the Italian way of thinking".

The need for certainty, homogeneity, rationalization and good road traffic organization, as well as the need to clearly identify the areas of an urban centre, took a back seat in respect to prevailing nationalization, driven by the need to reduce minorities and to make the State's cultural structure almost monistic. Toponymy became a *cultural asset*, inevitably losing its function as a "historical turnaround, of scientific furnishings that might be compared, in the order of physical events, to the different deposits studied by geologists"[53].

Trieste's street-naming frenzy found a fertile breeding ground in the rise of Fascism, whose patriotic petitions and need for an ethically cultural doctrine coloured the ideological perspective through a "historical path that, without interruption, had begun in Imperial Rome, passed through the Risorgimento period achieved by the monarchy and, with the last war against the unredeemed lands, had at last been included into the Regime"[54].

The new fascist State – even if it was constantly coming up against the liberal doctrines that preceded it – tried to impose an "authoritarian twist in the principles of state law reversing the idea of a self-restraining State ... with the

---

51 E. Caffarelli, *Odonomastica come impegno sociale*, *cit.*, p. 24.

52 "The most common statement is that the State (identified as the sum of public powers of an internationally recognizable nation) is nowadays an "administrative State", namely an entity which provides potentially unlimited services to the community, controls and supervises the human nature condition"; on this subject, M.S. Giannini, *I pubblici poteri negli Stati pluriclasse*, in *Rivista Trimestrale di Diritto Pubblico*, 1979, pp. 390–395.

53 Biblioteca Universitaria di Bologna, *Lettera del Professor Ascoli, senatore del Regno, al Direttore generale della Statistica, circa la compilazione di una Toponomastica Italiana*, Milan, 1891, p. 1.

54 S. Raffaelli, *Il primo dopoguerra e il ventennio*, *cit.*, p. 155.

theory of a strong State whose nucleus lay in organicism … which had designed the State as an organic community whose life-force was superior to that of the people themselves"[55]. Cultural and institutional planning, which had been slowly spreading since the 1920s, included Italy's extension into the neighbouring territories – "those territories of Italian tradition of Julian March and Tridentine Venice and, for Dalmatia, Zara" – pursuant to peace treaties, the Kingdom's legislation and the issuing of "those legislative measures needed to create within them the rhythm of Italian life"[56]. These provisions also included the new, above-mentioned laws on toponymy of 1925–27, reference points in a procedure which tried to diffuse and centralize the choice of names by preserving the historical value and standardising the evaluation criteria[57]. In applying "laws no. 1322 of 26th September 1920 and no. 1778 of 19th April 1920, and on approval of the Commission, set up by the Royal Decree of 20th January 1921 with the aim to determine the general standards for choosing street names in the annexed lands and to propose the official reading of the names of Municipalities, hamlets and built-up areas of these lands, the Fascist government, with Royal Decree no. 800

55 F. Colao, *Due momenti della storia costituzionale italiana nella cultura giuridica tra Ottocento e Novecento: la «formazione del Regno d'Italia» e la «trasformazione dello Stato» dall'età liberale al fascismo*, in A.D. Benedictis, (ed.), *Costruire lo Stato, costruire la storia. Politica e moderno fra Ottocento e Novecento*, Bologna, 2003, pp. 236–238.

56 *La Legislazione fascista (1922–1928). Parte Prima. Ordinamento costituzionale dello Stato*, vol. I, Rome, p. 650.

57 In addition to the above-mentioned references, *La Legislazione fascista*, *cit.*, pp. 265–266. With regard to the aforesaid 1927 law, we remind the Home Office Document no. 16000.1 of 19th July 1927, which specified the law applications – "other cases of street names change, the choice of new streets and squares names, as well as the raising of monuments, memorial tablets and other mementos in public spaces, or in areas opened to the public" – its limits and dictations, the obligation imposed to "the Municipalities for revising street names and removing those monuments which contravene articles 2 and 3", the importance of "quickly execute the demanded fulfilments … [in order to avoid that] after the unsuccessful end of the agreed time-limit, measures without consultation must be implemented". The complete record in *Rivista Amministrativa del Regno*, vol. LXXVIII, 1927, p. 110 ("*Atti del Governo*" section). On 9th May 1928 the Home Office letter to the Prefects confirms the concern for those local authorities ignoring the new laws, and reminded that "article 5 of law no. 1188 of 23rd June 1927, gazetted on 18th July, establishing the change of street names in contrast with article 2, and removing monuments, memorial tablets and other mementos from public spaces which contravene article 3, if not explicitly authorized by the Monuments and Fine Arts Bureau, set to six months the time-limit from the coming into force of the aforesaid law, and disposed that the Prefects had to take the defaulting Municipalities' place, at the expense of the latter", in Archivio di stato di Trieste (from now onwards AST), Prefecture of Trieste, General Records, table 2100/1928 (*Affari Speciali dei Comuni*), folder no. 3047/19351, *Ministero dell'Interno – 9 maggio 1928.*

of 29 March 1923, thus determined the formalization of names of Municipalities and other areas in the annexed lands"[58].

However, this harmonization procedure was not as simple as imagined and local authorities were inclined to take liberties and practically decide autonomously on their own procedures, which were often on the limits of respect for the legislative provisions. The Royal Prefecture of Trieste was forced to intervene on several occasions, on urgent request of the Ministry, which was urging Municipalities not to ignore the law and to act correctly. On 19th November 1930, the Prefect – in relation to the ten years after the death of "people deserving of the nation" to whom a street name was to be dedicated – pointed out that authorization was not to be given before that time had elapsed and should then eventually be given "only to people who are truly deserving of the nation; and this rule, as with all exceptional regulations, is not to be broadly interpreted. It is therefore necessary that the existence of these extreme particulars is carefully verified before starting any kind of request"[59]. And on 30th June 1932 "the Head of Government stipulated that street names were to remain unchanged, except for very special cases for which the given regulations were to be applied"[60]. But evidently the local frenzy found no limits and, pedantically, after some years, on 23rd September 1936, the Royal Prefecture cautioned that "no *Podestà* could deliberate a street name" if the person had not been "dead for at least ten years, without the established authorization. Deliberations in contrast with those regulations would be overridden"[61].

Within this continually changing kaleidoscope, history and local traditions found their proper dimension in a difficult balance between nationals needs and the renewed Roman spirit.

In 1926 the Prefect's Commissioner, after having heard the opinion of the purposefully set up Commission, decided to change the name of *via Chiozza* to *via Crispi*, "because the patriotic Chiozza family would be remembered [in any case] by the old Trieste denomination of *Volti di Chiozza* under the *Assicurazioni Generali* building that had been built on the old arcade area"[62]. A twist that had neither rational common sense, nor was it linked to any logistical requirement or identity request, but was just a product of political decisions and ideological

58 *La legislazione fascista, cit.*, p. 674, in which a reference to the reinstatement of Italian surnames is made.

59 AST, Prefecture of Trieste, General Records, table 2100/1928 (*Affari Speciali dei Comuni*), folder no. 3047/19351, *Regia Prefettura di Trieste – 30 giugno 1932*.

60 *Ibidem, Regia Prefettura di Trieste – 30 giugno 1932.*

61 *Ibidem, Regia Prefettura di Trieste – 12 dicembre 1936.*

62 AST, Prefecture of Trieste, General Records, table 4128, "*toponomastica*" file, folder no. 3079, *Regia Prefettura di Trieste – 23 dicembre 1926*.

interpretations according to which a place changed its name on an opportunistic whim or due to pseudo-favouritism demands.

New official plans required that "all Municipality urban centres must have a main street named *Roma*, at the beginning X year"[63], and it was considered more than "a duty that a town commemorated the name of the Nation's sacred river, where the value of arms shone brightly"[64].

On 8th November 1929, on *Podestà* resolution, at the explicit request of the local population and after having heard the opinion of the Commission, it was decided that, in the area of *Villa Opicina*, *via Nazionale* and *Campo Romano* (in remembrance of the area thus called since "*terrazzani*" were found there as proof of Roman ruins)[65] would be introduced.

History, rituality, officialness and simple past interlinked in a nonsensical and disordered pattern: in relation to "new roads resulting from new construction", for the streets commonly known as "*Botta*" and vulgarly as "*Brigiacco*" the *Deputazione* "voted that the old names are to be preserved in subtitle since they do not contrast with the national spirit, however vulgar they might be, in terms of historical or juridical value"[66].

Political choice, expressed through non banal legal proceedings, used the law as a mere instrument to impose new languages linked to a clear and specific cultural *imprinting*; but at other times, this linguistic game re-launched normative transcendence from within the historical process, so that it could combine demands for keeping local traditions with local terminology or geographical spontaneity.

Public areas, where ideologies influenced toponymic decisions, could not in any case make a clean break with the past and with popular culture. One only has to remember what happened when – between 1934 and 1935 – the local section of ex *Don Bosco* students proposed that the appropriate authorities should name a street after their late institutor by modifying the *via del Bosco*, which, in their opinion, was of no historical or local relevance. However, the Ministry of Education itself intervened and actually opposed the suggestion, considering it as more correct to maintain the original name of *via del Bosco*. At that point, the Local Monument Commission intervened by proposing to name the then *via dei Lavoratori* after the generous priest, and thus everything was settled. Not without, however, a final intrusion by the Local Royal Monument Commission

---

63 Department of the Interior circular no. 15100/49840 of 3rd September 1931, in *Rivista Amministrativa del Regno*, Vol. LXXXII, 1931, p. 131 ("*Atti del Governo*" section).

64 AST, Prefecture of Trieste, General Records, table 4128, "*toponomastica*" file, folder no. 3079, *Regia Commissione Provinciale ai Monumenti per la provincia di Trieste – 14 settembre 1932.*

65 *Ibidem, Deliberazione del Podestà di Trieste – 8 novembre 1929.*

66 *Ibidem, Deliberazione del Podestà di Trieste – 3 dicembre 1927.*

for the Province of Trieste, that "after a long discussion, unanimously agreed not to change century-old streets (like *via del Bosco*) but that it would be better to change those streets that did not have a long local tradition. Reference is made to famous Italian personalities from the literary and arts field who cannot be classed among the greatest"[67].

However, it was celebratory enthusiasm that took the upper hand, in a frenzy of patriotic zeal: on 2nd September 1935 the *Reale Deputazione* declared "there are no objections to naming *largo Corsica* from a historical point of view; the name just has other contingent potential, and this judgment has been deferred to the Most Excellent Prefect's discretionary evaluation... since it is a reminder of when some Napoleonic followers stayed in Trieste, the place at issue could be named after one of them"[68]. The *Podestà*, however, maintained that, besides similarities in natural origins and language, between Trieste and the "generous land of Corsica, spiritual commitments were also established by the lengthy stay of some famous Corsicans (Caroline Bonaparte-Murat, Girolamo Bonaparte and his wife) … it was also found that some Adriatic land patriots, persecuted for their love of Italy, found free refuge in Corsica during hard times. It is therefore dutiful to honour this kind and heroic island, which is so passionately Italian in its history, language, folklore and traditions"[69] by giving its name to a street or a square in Trieste. In fact, we must not forget that "Trieste's Municipality, even before the Redemption, in interpreting the national feeling of its citizens, gave the town's streets and squares names that honoured Italy or symbolized Italianism. It is also noted that after the Redemption … other names were added as an expression of the principle of National unity and Italy now, led by the Duce and the Emperor-King, aims at liberating other Italian lands. The memory of *Nizza* as Garibaldi's home town and Corsica's long martyrdom, *via Nizza* and *via Corsica* should be entitled as such"[70].

It should also not be forgotten "that after 3 November 1918, the Municipality wanted to emphasize the principle of unity in urban toponymy in order to recreate the Italian family in one single national sector. The names recalled the historical, geographical and ethnic Italianism of Malta in remembrance of the fact that, in 1798, the Great Master of the Order of the Knights, Ferdinando Hompesch, appealed against the violation of the freedom of Malta. The Municipality was touched by the worthy battle that these Maltese brothers fought in order to defend the Italian language and way of thinking, for centuries the only

67 *Ibidem, Regia Commissione Provinciale ai Monumenti per la provincia di Trieste – 26 gennaio 1934.*

68 *Ibidem, Reale Deputazione di Trieste – 2 settembre 1935.*

69 *Ibidem, Deliberazione del Podestà di Trieste – 10 ottobre 1935.*

70 *Ibidem, Deliberazione del Podestà di Trieste – 3 dicembre 1940.*

light of civilization for those islands, and thus interpreted the feeling of the Trieste people and expressed national fraternity and solidarity to Malta citizen"[71]. Therefore, on 24th November 1934, the public authority decided to give its name to a new square.

In regard to those lands that had still not been redeemed and that therefore made the troubled course towards Italian unification incomplete – and how well this uneasiness was understood in Trieste – giving their name to an urban place or space might have been seen as a way to settle a small debt of gratitude .

But the historical moment was influenced by the immanent impact of the fascist culture, whose street name planning reflected the need to glorify the Regime and its different facets, characters and the celebrate State ethicalness as the only means by which society could completely merge and ensure itself of a sense of identity and statute. In fact, in 1938 it was pointed out that "due to its peripheral location and little importance, *piazza Caduti Fascisti* did not properly honour the memory of those who gave their lives for the Revolution"[72]; in October 1939, the *Regia Deputazione di Storia Patria per le Venezie* (associations which promoted historical research within the local and regional area) gave its authorisation – necessary for the naming of new or still unnamed streets – to name *via XXIII marzo*, the founding date of "the Italian Leagues of Combat, in honour of which the *Casa del Fascio*, which would become the new access to the aforesaid *piazza del Littorio*, was erected"[73].

On the occasion of the twenty-fifth anniversary of his death, the procedure began to commemorate Pio Riego Gambini, "killed at the battle of Podgora on 19th July 1915, founder of the Istrian Youth League and one of the more fierce leaders of Trieste and Istria's redemption youth movement as well as a brilliant speaker and writer. Considering that he has been commemorated with a public monument in *Capodistria* but that his memory has not yet been honoured in Trieste, where he carried out a large part of his mission, in consequence of the vote of the Venezia Giulia volunteers and interpreting the feelings and desires of the citizens, it is only dutiful to permanently commemorate this young fallen hero in our town. His name replaces *via Ferriera*, a denomination with no local historical interest"[74].

Although the process of naming still unnamed places was inevitably less complicated, changing a name, the legitimacy of which – based on popular use – was hard for public authority to touch, met with greater resistance and required

71 *Ibidem, Deliberazione del Podestà di Trieste – 24 novembre 1934.*

72 *Ibidem, Deliberazione del Podestà di Trieste – 13 marzo 1938.*

73 *Ibidem, Regia Deputazione di Storia Patria per le Venezie – 14 ottobre 1939.*

74 *Ibidem, Deliberazione del Podestà di Trieste – 14 luglio 1940.*

extremely good motives. The name change could not alter the town's history or memorials, nor could it create practical imbalance or confusion, but had to be vigorously justified. In 1940, the Italian Home Office "felt is their duty to pay everlasting homage to the memory of Trieste's gold medallist Arrigo Protti, who died heroically for the Empire and decided that naming a street with his glorious name was the most honourable way to commemorate him, especially since there were street names in Trieste's urban toponymy that could be changed with no offence to the town's history or memorials. Therefore, in view of laws no. 473 of 17th April 1925 and no. 1188 of 21st June 1927 on urban toponymy and in particular reference to art. 4, para. 2 of the aforesaid 1927 law, which gives the Italian Home Secretary the power to grant derogation to the regulation of article 2 of the same law, for people deserving of the nation, *galleria dei Mercanti* became *galleria Arrigo Protti*" and Trieste Municipality was authorised to continue and conclude the name change[75].

In a similar way, the introduction of racial laws imposed drastic controls and the purging of names which did not evoke Italianism[76], or even slightly hinted at a link with the Jewish race. The request in favour of "Vittorio Locchi, brilliant soldier and poet, who died in February 1917 as a consequence of the torpedoing of the ship which was transporting him to the Macedonian front, and who, in his wonderful poem "*Santa Gorizia*", immortalized the heroic deeds surrounding the liberation of this sister town"[77] was to replace the street named after the non-Aryan Giuseppe Revere. The street bearing the non-Aryan name of Leone Fortis[78] was to be dedicated to Lorenzo Lirenzetti, "Blackshirt of the National Security Volunteer Militia, Great War and Spanish Civil War soldier and gold medallist".

The same brief and highly rhetorical motives were applied to the "sanctification" of the Balbo road. With *Podestà* deliberation no. 863 of 6th July 1940 the then *via Moisè Luzzatto* was changed to *via Italo Balbo*, and also took the opportunity of including *via Belpoggio,* a continuation of *via Luzzatto*, into the new denomination. The Prefecture, on being called in on this matter, gave his favourable opinion on 23rd October, considering it "dutiful to immortalize the memory of the heroic quadrumvir Italo Balbo with a public act and giving one of the main streets of the town his glorious name was the most honourable way to

75 *Ibidem, Ministero dell'Interno – 3 marzo 1940.*

76 The reason of the Royal Decree no. 352 of 11th February 1923 was to thwart the use of foreign names, instead of Italian names, about the tax on memorial tablets written in a foreign language, in AST, Prefecture of Trieste, General Records, table 4128, "*toponomastica*" file, folder no. 3047/19349.

77 *Ibidem, Deliberazione del Podestà di Trieste – 6 luglio 1940.*

78 *Ibidem.*

commemorate him. Interpreting the unanimous feelings of the Trieste citizens, who demanded an everlasting homage to the memory of the air force hero killed in action in the sky over Africa, and in view of law no. 1188 of 6 June 1927 on urban toponymy, with particular reference to art. 4, para. 1, which does not authorize the application of the regulations of arts. 2 and 3, para. 1 of the aforesaid law, for people killed in battle, the Prefecture decided to give his name to a street denominated with a non-Aryan name". Within the short space of six months everything was settled, and on 7th December the superintendent Franco signed the resolution[79].

It was also interesting how the *Podestà*'s assurances to the Royal Prefecture, guaranteed that "this Administration had never thought of naming any of Servola's streets after a Dannecker". In fact, on 2nd March 1940, with a confidential note following a handwritten letter that was filed on 5th February, emphasis was placed on the fact that the Danneckers were "pure Austrians ... they did not feel the sacrosanct duty to Italianize their surname... and that few of them were among those glorious people killed on Spanish and African soil". It would therefore seem incongruous to name a street after a member of this family when there were so many young fascist martyrs killed in battle: "due to its hostile behaviour this family did not deserve ... political rehabilitation nor should the morality of the aforesaid village suffer the offence of slight matters which were not obvious to anyone"[80], in the hypothesis that favours should be asked or even in the case of corruption, should the Austrian nobles be selected.

Furthermore, there was no lack of artistic frenzy and sophisticated enthusiasm: on 13th July 1935 it was decided that, in consideration of "Verdi's stays in Trieste in 1850 and 1860, during which he frequented *Villa Severi* where he wrote a *berceuse* on a work by F.M. Piave, *Villa Severi*, demolished at the beginning of the XX century ... (and which stood adjacent to the named place), was to be replaced by *Villa dei Severi*, in memory of an unforgettable event during Verdi's stay in our town"[81]. Also Giovanni Pascoli was given an appropriate commemoration: the Municipality, which had always taken care to "commemorate the great names in the science, arts and Italian literary fields by naming urban roads after them, pointed out that Giovanni Pascoli, a lyrist of exquisite sensitivity, had so far been omitted. Following the citizens' vote, in view of law no. 1188 of 23rd June 1927 and noting that Giovanni Pascoli had lived from 1855 to 1912, thus exceeding the time period established by the

79 *Ibidem, Deliberazione del Podestà di Trieste n. 863 – 6 luglio 1940.*

80 All the quotations are taken from a confidential note of the *Podestà di Trieste alla Regia Prefettura – 2 marzo 1940, ibidem.*

81 *Ibidem, deliberazione del Podestà di Trieste – 13 luglio 1935.*

aforesaid law, the Municipality has decided to change the name of *via dell'Istituto*, a denomination with no historical or patriotic interest, to Pascoli"[82]. Additionally, in order to further clarify *via Caterina*, thus called "in remembrance of an old church dedicated to saint Catherine built at the beginning of the XVI century and demolished in 1770" and due to the large number of saints with the same name in the hagiography, it was decided to complete the name with "*da Siena*", thus identifying that *Caterina* as "Italy's most Italian saint"[83].

3. The Lord's ways are infinite

The institutional transition influenced by the fall of Fascism and the tortuous *road* in search of democracy, was characterised in Trieste by a sudden re-organizational phase which also included toponymy. The widespread removal of names linked to the twenty years of Fascism in Italy – which spontaneously characterized the initial months following the fall of Mussolini at that famous meeting of 25th July – as an ideological destruction of every emblem and "constitutive element of commemoration in public spaces"[84], was brusquely forced to slow down[85] due to the presence of the Nazi Germany army and the difficult political balancing act to which the northern part of the Adriatic Sea was subjected. On 17th November 1943 a missive reported how "the Vienna land office only made documents available with the German (or Slavic) names of villages and Municipalities. On the other hand, since German and Slavic street names were to be used to name villages and Municipalities again, and since it is difficult to choose Italian Municipalities and village names in a short time, please send a list of Municipalities and villages in your province specifying the German, Italian and Slavic name of those places ... in order to identify old names, it is possible to refer to ancient Austro-Hungarian Monarchy denominations"[86]. In this way, a stroke of the pen made urban history backslide

82 *Ibidem, Deliberazione del Podestà di Trieste – 6 luglio 1940.*

83 *Ibidem, Deliberazione del Podestà di Trieste – 30 ottobre 1940.*

84 For an overall view of the period between the fall of the Fascist Regime and the new institutional organization, R. Ridolfi, *La transizione democratica e la nascita della Repubblica*, in *Le città leggibili, cit.*, pp. 178–191. Quotation at page 176.

85 The different process which characterized "the other Italy", the Southern Kingdom, is described in S. Raffaelli, *Storia dell'odonomastica e stradari storici*, in C.A.Mastrelli (ed.), *Odonomastica, cit.*, p. 113.

86 AST, Prefecture of Trieste, General Records, table 4128, "*toponomastica*" file, folder no. 3079, *Regia Prefettura di Trieste – 17 novembre 1943.*

for more than twenty years, in search of a past organization that had been forgotten under the vibrant Italian irredentism.

A hybrid period marked the years of territorial division between areas A and B[87], encouraged by the imposed practicality of the moment and the need to return to normality, while freedom was being fervently welcomed in the rest of Italy.

Following "managerial resolution no. 356 of 14th June 1946, managerial resolution no. 407 of 6th July 1946 and managerial resolution no. 511 14th August 1946", on 3rd January 1947, the Municipality of Trieste decided to reinstate the old XIX century names, many of which had previously been modified. *Largo Roiano, via Belpoggio, via Felice Venezian, largo Risorgo, Via Raffaele Abro* – to name but a few since the list would be long and boring – all reappeared and *via Italo Balbo, piazza Caduti Fascisti, piazza Malta, corso del Littorio, via degli Squadristi, piazza dell'Impero*[88] all disappeared, like the rapid opening and closing of brackets. However, the operation was not quick enough in the eyes of the local press, in consideration of the fact that "after more than one year since the end of the war, fascist denominations or names in contrast with the then political situation had still not been removed from urban toponymy"[89].

However, if liberation from Fascism seemed, at first glimpse, almost natural, on the contrary there was more perplexity about those street names that reverberated people and events linked to the Great War or the Risorgimento, introduced by Fascism by way of commemoration and probably linked to it by a similar patriotic and national spirit, and which had become part of the collective identity heritage. On 15th April 1947, the Superintendence agreed with the Prefect about the idea of replacing *via Vittorio Emanuele*, *via Principe Umberto* and *via Nuova*, but suggested waiting to decide on the new names that had been suggested "whose message might evoke the Great War, which had had a strong impact on the Municipality of *Ronchi dei Legionari* ... it would therefore be opportune to postpone every name change due to their historical importance in the Italian Republic, of which the administration of this Municipality would soon be a part. Thus, it is hereby recommended to also wait before changing the

---

87 The special record enclosed to the *Memorandum of Understanding of London* permitted to recover the Italian sovereignty on Trieste only in 1954. "According to the peace treaty, Trieste could become a territory under the United Nation government; but, due to different problems, it was impossible to establish this regime and Trieste remained under a mixed military control: an area under the Yugoslav control, the other area under the English control", in G. de Vergottini, *Relazione*, in *Storia di terre italiane del nord-est. Istria, Venezia Giulia, Dalmazia dal 1800 ai giorni nostri. Atti del convegno. Sala Farnese, 1 febbraio 2003*, Bologna, 2006, p. 22.

88 AST, Prefecture of Trieste, General Records, table 4128, "*toponomastica*" file, folder no. 3079, *Comune di Trieste, Ufficio Lavori Pubblici – 3 gennaio 1947.*

89 *Ibidem, Comune di Trieste, Affari Generali al signor Presidente di Zona – 9 ottobre 1946.*

denominations *Duca d'Aosta* and *Gabriele D'Annunzio*, pending a new administrative position, in order to conform to Italian Republic guidelines"[90].

In 1946, the above-mentioned Arrigo Protti – already commemorated with a street name – together with other gold medal for military valour comrades Sergio Laghi and Odorico Panfili, was the subject of a complicated legal controversy. These three "holders" of streets names dedicated to them during the twenty years of Fascism in Italy, become the object of deliberation by the Town Council about the reinstatement of the old Trieste names. In fact, the President of the Municipality of Trieste thought it proper remove their position, since the measure to change urban toponymy was urgent but their situation still had to be carefully evaluated in the light of unknown reasons. In fact, it was still not certain whether the three soldier's had enlisted in the army of their own accord or whether they had been "called up and had therefore sacrificed their lives for military duties, from which they could not have shirked without being considered guilty of desertion". For his part, the President of the Region, even though he was aware of his role and *status* and was convinced that "purely as an advisory committee, there was no denying the right to express oneself about Municipality deliberations and decisions that would be taken in the future", "recognized his own juridical incompetence in the matter (and exonerated himself from expressing an opinion on Municipality deliberations, even if he was standing in for the *Giunta Provinciale Amministrativa – sede tutoria*)". Although he began from the assumption that the three soldiers could have been killed in the war in Africa while fulfilling their duties, he did not consider it appropriate to dishonour them by removing their names from urban toponymy. It was precisely this wordy dispute which prolonged the street name change procedure – which begun in November 1945 –, and the lengthiness of which, as already mentioned, was harshly criticized by the local press. The President of the Municipality of Trieste observed how "Local Council intervention could not be even justified by similar reference to the Regional Administrative Council deliberations because the change of old town street and square names did not come under its jurisdiction". The Local Council, whose powers were the same as that of the Prefect, should restrict its intervention only to legitimate questions – seeing that, whether in doctrine or in law, it is obvious that the judging authority never has the right to change the submitted document at issue, but only to give or deny its approval – because the Friuli-Venezia Giulia Monuments and Fine Arts Bureau was already dealing with the subject of Trieste's urban toponymy changes. If it should so excessively interpret its power given *ex-lege*, this would encourage

90 *Ibidem, Soprintendenza ai Monumenti, Gallerie e Antichità di Trieste – 15 aprile 1947.*

further restriction on the principle of a self-governing Municipality which had already been highly limited by "the centralizing Fascist laws"[91].

A doubt that also concerned the province: in fact, there was a profound fear about overdoing this *nominalistic purge*, in the knowledge of how hard it was to detect the dividing line between the old perspective of the State, which had characterized the Kingdom of Italy, and the new one, which characterized the road towards constitution that had just been taken, in a sort of metahistorical sublimation of the institutional profile. On 7th March 1950, the Monuments and Fine Arts Bureau asked the Prefecture of Trieste "to draw the Municipality of *San Dorligo della Valle*'s attention to law no. 1188 of 23rd June 1927, on the basis of which it was not permitted to change old street and square names which characterized the "local colour" of the village. In authorising the replacement of *piazza del Littorio* with *piazza Caduti della Liberazione*, it also advised the Municipality only to review those street names which were reminiscent of the old regime, and whose change would be examined as long as the new names related to local traditions"[92]. The previous November of 1949, the Municipality itself, considering that many streets and squares had been given Fascist denominations, decided to name each Municipality's main streets after a famous or historical national personality or national liberation hero: for this reason the main street become *via della Fratellanza*, *via Simon Gregorcic* and *piazza Vittime di Basovizza* made their appearance, and a commemoration to *Josip Srebrnic*[93] was suggested in place of *via Roma*.

Even more paradigmatic was the decision of the Municipality of Monfalcone, which did not found it at all hard to adapt itself to the "trend of the new times", and therefore considered it "necessary to remove, as soon as possible, all those names from streets or squares which did not suit with the present, giving these places back the old name or the one the citizens most wanted"[94]. But if we read the changes carefully, it is clear that only a little of the natural past was recovered, and preference was given to the – already mentioned – "trend of the new times": *via Romano Moise* became *via Giacomo Matteotti*, *via XXVIII ottobre* was named *via I maggio*, *via Macallè* became *via Tito Livio*, *piazza Albania* was changed to *piazza della Libertà*, *via D'Annunzio* was changed to *via San Giovanni Bosco*, *corso Vittorio Emanuele* was changed to *corso del Popolo*,

91 Almost every local administration, in addition to the headmaster of the Faculty of Arts and the Monuments and Fine Arts Bureau, played a leading role in this affair, due to the delicate choice to make and its consequences on the naming criteria. There are more than 30 documents on this subject in AST, Prefecture of Trieste, General Records, table 4128.

92 *Ibidem, Soprintendenza ai Monumenti, Gallerie e Antichità di Trieste – 7 marzo 1950.*

93 *Ibidem, Deliberazione del Comune di San Dorligo della Valle – 12 novembre 1949.*

94 *Ibidem, Deliberazione del Comune di Monfalcone – 7 settembre 1946.*

Piazza del Littorio became *piazza della Repubblica*, *viale Principe di Piemonte* became *viale Fratelli Rosselli*[95]. Terms that, non-coincidentally, were clearly evocative and allusive. The times had changed and the *streets* were humbly moving with them.

We have to wait for the Trieste completely return to Italian sovereignty to find some – poor – attempts to repress the tortuous choice of apologetic names, and to reconnect the link with traditions and the past. In the spring of 1956 a Commission for new urban street and square denominations was set up[96]. The fragmentary naming criteria adopted were stopped by the Monuments and Fine Arts Bureau which used its "cultural knowledge" with the clear intention to control the Town Council's hasty enthusiasm: thus, "the traditional name of "*Zudecche*", which appeared for centuries in the Municipality acts, could not be abolished without causing harm to the historical topographic studies of Trieste". Even the traditional name of "*Scoglio*" could not be abolished from urban toponymy, because "it referred to a big boulder that had forced the lower part of the old downhill slope of the peak *Vena di Trebiciano* and its little river, now hidden, to be built in an elbow shape. Several documents recalled the "*Scoglio* and the *Molino dello Scoglio*", of ecclesiastical property, located on the Rio (the Trieste's biggest river, that sprang from the suburban district of Cattinara) at the confluence of the little river "*Rio dello Scoglio*". Therefore, the name of "*Scoglio*" could not be moved elsewhere, because the boulder to which it refers is unmovable"[97]. The Monuments and Fine Arts Bureau also solicited for the restoration of the old name of "*Ponte dell'Aia*", "in homage to the historical topography of Trieste, and to let everybody know the meaning and origin of the evocative Friulian plural place-name "*Pon-d-àres*", where the *Rocciòlo* river, *Rozzòl* in local dialect, coming from *via della Tesa*, bent towards *via della Raffineria*. A bridge there once allowed wayfarers to travel from the town to the *Sette Fontane* valley"[98]. All these street-naming attempts were successful but they were only an exception – rather than the rule – of central administration influence.

95 *Ibidem*.

96 AST, Prefecture of Trieste, General Records, table 4128, "*toponomastica*" file, folder no. 3115, *Società Minerva di Trieste – 25 luglio 1956*.

97 All quotations in brackets are taken from *Ibidem, Soprintendenza ai Monumenti, Gallerie e Antichità di Trieste – 31 luglio 1956*.

98 *Ibidem*.

4. By way of conclusion. The view of the sea and the salty air

Streets, the State and border towns. There are many legal profiles linked to a subject such as toponymy, which captures the interests of historians, glottologists, sociologists, anthropologists, architects and linguists. Space assumes a hidden and unexpected ideological outcome[99], reflects daily experience and forms an indelibly confidential relationship with the people. Violating that link between urban denomination and reality, which comprises functional reasons, civic sensitivity and identity, the presence of markets, provisions, health centres or religious institutions, the State denies its past and makes the choice of street names and their classification one of its main goals. Even in a liberal and democratic system, political power becomes a "rational instrument for achieving well-defined and desirable purposes"[100]. The propagandistic and persuasive nature that the State has to ontologically incorporate in order to maintain a certain level of influence and balance among the government leaders, goes beyond economical, social, legal or bureaucratic relations to encroach upon unexpected areas. The choice of street names becomes *ideology*, a cultural effect which allows the ruling class to influence the citizens in terms of revered persons, eras, moments, battles. The State translates the ambitious project of moulding the citizens' culture with the simplest and most direct tool, i.e. the denomination of the places the citizens walk through and own, thus strengthening the educative role it has assigned itself. The particularistic decisions of peripheral administrations, perhaps more inclined to choose names linked to local reality, had to sift through legitimized cultural structures and models before giving their consent to what could legitimately be commemorated and what could not. Trieste is a clear example of a toponymical reality without historical *continuum*, but one marked by a cultural domestication of the different ethnic traditions where name choices were stratified according to ruling class of the time. It is therefore impossible to define a historical present, to recover the meaning of today in faraway roots, because the criteria for modifying street names became an instrument of cultural subjugation, the expression of historical phases that occurred very distant from one another, pictures of traditions which cannot be linked to the previous ones and which later generation would inevitably have found unfamiliar. Traces which appeared only to disappear quickly and then re-emerge on different perspectives, interpreting

99 It is interesting the historiographic perspective presented in B. Tobia, *Una patria per gli italiani. Spazi, itinerari, monumenti nell'Italia unita (1870–1900)*, Rome-Bari, 1991.

100 F. Neumann, *Premesse ad uno studio sul potere politico* (1950), in F. Neumann, *Lo Stato democratico e lo Stato autoritario*, Italian translation by G. Sivini, Bologna, 1973, p. 17.

political power in its most latent and unthinkable facets. The town appears "artificial", without the experience of life, deformed by political choices which overshadowed ideologies and by public commemorations branded into the citizens' memory and conscience. The naming campaign stopped at nothing, unheeding of the need for certainty, deaf to requests of simplicity and the usage of normally used street names: completely out of context[101].

The population, "a subject of needs and aspiration, but also an object in the government's hands, appears to be aware of what it wants from the government but unaware of how the government manipulates it"[102]. It is subject to administrative will, which is almost disrespectful to the past and, sometimes, even the cause of ethnic conflicts. Just take the example of the *corso Italia*: within the space of less than two hundred years this central arterial road of Trieste was named *contrada di Vienna*, *via del Corso*, *corso Vittorio Emanuele III* and *corso Tito;* the current name was given in 1955[103]. This road is a mirror of history, it englobes the town's cyclic nature, the ups and downs of the population and respect for the slow and gradual passing of time; a respect that was totally ignored at every political and regal change of hands, when the name of a road was not jealously guarded but altered because its links to the past did not concur with the time. Legal insights tried to do away with these spaces and cover up inconvenient evidence. Urban space became the symbol of depersonalization of relations and places, and the interplay between citizens and territory turned into a sort of theatrical play, where the latter imposed its conditioning and ideology on the former. However, the town "is the result of the sum of material signs that, in the course of history, have overlapped each other, been selected and frequently removed and which, in their entirety, express the culture, instinct and mentality of those who live there as well as the economical and political structures"[104]. Among these signs, the road towards modern day inexorably represents a clear political choice, and expresses the ideology of power. A bureaucratically rigid and legally formal option was preferred to the possibility to becoming culturally richer: Commissions created for this reason in local organisations were the proof; their evaluations were often – almost always – ignored in favour of political

---

101 G. Raimondi, *La toponomastica. Elementi di metodo*, Turin, 2003.

102 M. Foucault, *Sicurezza, territorio, popolazione. Corso al Collège de France 1977–1978*, Milan, 2005, pp. 85–86.

103 F. De Vecchi, *Il luogo e la storia*, vol. I, *cit.*, p. 32. The evolution of this important arterial road of Trieste can be found also in S. Raffaelli, *Il primo dopoguerra e il ventennio*, *cit.*, p. 156, footnote 2.

104 A. Grohmann, *Premessa*, *cit.*, p. 16.

decisions and partial assessment[105], which no hypothesis of legislative reform can remedy[106].

Maybe in a century it will no longer be possible to walk along *piazza Unità d'Italia*, passing all those wonderful palaces that seem to lead us down to the sea. To be sure, however, and it is more than wishful thinking, the view of the Gulf and the salty air will never be erased or forgotten.

Bibliography

Proceedings, journals, collected papers

Barbagallo R., *Caratteri e vicende della toponomastica in Valle d'Aosta*, in *Diritto e società*, 2/1989.

Bloch M., *Noms de personne et histoire sociale*, in *Annales d'Historie Économique et Sociale*, 1932.

Bloch M., *Réflexions d'un historien sur quelques travaux de toponymie*, in *Annales d'Historie Économique et Sociale*, 1934.

Bonvicini E., *La classificazione delle strade nei riflessi dell'articolo 29 cod. strad.*, in *Diritto Automobilistico*, 1955.

Caffarelli E., *Note ai margini, in Rivista Italiana di Onomastica*, 2000.

Casoni G., Pigaiani E., *Gli adempimenti istruttori concernenti l'intitolazione delle aree di circolazione*, in *Lo Stato Civile Italiano*, 2004.

Colao F., *Due momenti della storia costituzionale italiana nella cultura giuridica tra Ottocento e Novecento: la «formazione del Regno d'Italia» e la «trasformazione dello Stato» dall'età liberale al fascismo*, in De Benedictis A. (ed.), *Costruire lo Stato, costruire la storia. Politica e moderno fra Ottocento e Novecento,* Bologna, 2003.

Corradini C., Peronaci E., *Le strade ferrate*, in Orlando V.E. (ed.), *Primo Trattato completo di diritto amministrativo italiano*, vol. VII, First Part, Milan, 1914.

de Vergottini G., *Profili giuridici della toponomastica nella provincia di Bolzano*, in *Diritto e società*, 4/1986.

Fioravanti M., *È possibile un profilo giuridico dello Stato moderno?*, in *Scienza & Politica*, 2004.

105 C.A. Mastrelli, *Aspetti storico-linguistici*, *cit.*, pp. 69–73.

106 Detailed considerations in E. Caffarelli, *Note ai margini,* in *Rivista Italiana di Onomastica*, vol. VI, 2000, pp. 645–654.

Giannini M.S., *I pubblici poteri negli Stati pluriclasse*, in *Rivista Trimestrale di Diritto Pubblico*, 1979.

G.R., *La disciplina giuridica della toponomastica stradale*, in *L'Amministrazione Italiana. Rivista mensile delle Amministrazioni Statali, degli Enti Locali e delle Organizzazioni tributarie*, 1974.

Isotton R., *Brevi note sul "Plan d'education nationale" di Michel Lepeletier de Saint-Fargeaux*, in Padoa Schioppa A., di Renzo Villata G., Massetto G.P. (eds.), *Amicitiae Pignus. Studi in ricordo di Adriano Cavanna*, vol. II, Milan, 2003.

Le città leggibili. La toponomastica urbana tra passato e presente. Atti del convegno di Foligno 11–13 dicembre 2003, in *Bollettino della Deputazione di Storia Patria per l'Umbria*, 2004.

Mannori L., Sordi B., *Giustizia e amministrazione*, in Fioravanti M. (ed.), *Lo Stato moderno in Europa. Istituzioni e diritto*, Rome-Bari, 2002.

Mannari L., *Giustizia e amministrazione tra antico e nuovo regime*, in Romanelli R. (ed.), *Magistrati e potere nella storia europea*, Bologna, 1997.

Mastrelli C.A., *L'odonomastica nella legislazione italiana*, in *Rivista Italiana di Onomastica*, 1998.

Mastrelli C.A (ed.), *Odonomastica. Criteri e normative sulle denominazioni stradali. Atti del convegno di Trento, 25 settembre 2005*, Trento, 2005.

Pallottino M., *Toponomastica*, in *Enciclopedia del Diritto*, vol. XLIV, Milan, 1992.

Pellegrini G.B., *Toponimi slavi e "slavo-venetici" in Italia*, in *Rivista Italiana di Onomastica*, 1996.

Rugge F., *Le nozioni di città e cittadino nel lungo Ottocento. Tra «pariforme sistema» e nuovo particolarismo*, in Meriggi M., Schiera P. (eds.), *Dalle città alla nazione. Borghesie ottocentesche in Italia e in Germania*, Bologna, 1993.

Simoncini G., *La viabilità nelle città italiane del periodo napoleonico. Le fonti delle Archives Nationales di Parigi*, in *Storia Urbana*, 1982.

Storia di terre italiane del nord-est. Istria, Venezia Giulia, Dalmazia dal 1800 ai giorni nostri. Atti del convegno. Sala Farnese, 1 febbraio 2003, Bologna, 2006.

Vineis F. (ed.), *La toponomastica come fonte di conoscenza storica e linguistica. Atti del convegno della Società italiana di glottologia, Belluno 31 marzo–2 aprile 1980*, Pisa, 1981.

Archives and libraries

ARCHIVIO DI STATO DI TRIESTE
ARCHIVIO GENERALE DEL COMUNE DI TRIESTE, Sezione Storica
BIBLIOTECA UNIVERSITARIA DI BOLOGNA

Monographic studies

Ara A., Magris C., *Trieste. Un'identità di frontiera*, Turin, 2007.

Balmas F., Maculan U., *Indicatore delle leggi e decreti del Regno d'Italia (dal 1861 al gennaio 1931)*, Rome, 1931.

Berti G., *La responsabilità pubblica (Costituzione e amministrazione),* Padova, 1994.

Capanna A., *Storia del diritto moderno in Europa. Le fonti e il pensiero giuridico,* vol. II, Milan, 2005.

Costa P., *Lo Stato immaginario. Metafore e paradigmi nella cultura giuridica italiana tra Otto e Novecento*, Milan, 1986.

De Vecchi F., *Il luogo e la storia. La toponomastica storica di Trieste alla scoperta del sito quale bene culturale*, vol. I, *Parte prima. Il borgo Teresiano*; vol. II, *Parte seconda. Il borgo Giuseppino*, Trieste, Biblioteca Civica "A. Hortis", 1990–1992.

Di Simone M.R., *Istituzioni e fonti normative in Italia dall'Antico Regime al Fascismo*, Turin, 2007.

Fanti M., *Le vie di Bologna. Saggio di toponomastica storica e di storia della toponomastica italiana*, vol. I, Bologna, 2000.

Foucault M., *Sicurezza, territorio, popolazione. Corso al Collège de France 1977–1978*, Milan, 2005.

Generini E., *Trieste antica e moderna, ossia descrizione ed origine dei nomi delle sue vie, androne e piazze*, Trieste, 1884.

La Legislazione fascista (1922–1928). Parte Prima. Ordinamento costituzionale dello Stato, vol. I, Rome, Tipografia della Camera dei Deputati.

Lacché L., *L'espropriazione per pubblica utilità. Amministratori e proprietari nella Francia dell'Ottocento*, Milan, 1995.

La Torre M., *Commento al nuovo Testo Unico Comunale e Provinciale ed alle norme complementari*, Napoli, 1934.

Maggi S., *Le ferrovie*, Bologna, 2003.

Mannori L., *Sordi B., Storia del diritto amministrativo*, Rome-Bari, 2001.

Neumann F., *Lo Stato democratico e lo Stato autoritario*, Italian translation by G. Sivini, Bologna, 1973.

Ornaghi M. (ed.), *I luoghi della memoria. Simboli e miti dell'Italia Unita*, Rome-Bari, 1996.
Piergigli V. (ed.), *L'autoctonia divisa. La tutela giuridica della minoranza italiana in Istria, Fiume e Dalmazia*, Padova, 2005.
Piergigli V., *Lingue minoritarie e identità culturali*, Milan, 2001.
Pivato S., *Il nome e la storia. Onomastica e religioni politiche nell'Italia contemporanea*, Bologna, 1999.
Raimondi G., *La toponomastica. Elementi di metodo*, Turin, 2003.
Ravasini O., *Compendio di notizie su denominazioni delle località e strade di Trieste*, Trieste, 1918.
Ravasini O., *Compendio di notizie sulla nomenclatura di località e strade di Trieste*, Trieste, 1929.
Rocco G., *Corso di diritto amministrativo*, vol. I, Napoli, 1850.
Rusconi G.E., *L'azzardo del 1915. Come l'Italia decide la sua guerra*, Bologna, 2005.
Tampus A., *Vie e piazze di Trieste moderna. Toponomastica stradale e topografia storica*, Trieste, 1989.
Tarello G., *Storia della cultura giuridica moderna*, Bologna, 1976.
Tobia B., *Una patria per gli italiani. Spazi, itinerari, monumenti nell'Italia unita (1870–1900)*, Rome-Bari, 1991.
Ullmann S., *Semantica. Introduzione alla scienza del significato* (1962), Italian translation by A. Baccarani, L. Rosiello, Bologna, 1966.
Verbali della Delegazione Municipale di Trieste anche in sede di Consiglio, annata XLX – 1911, Trieste, Stabilimento Artistico Tipografico G. Caprin, 1911.

Second Part
Toponomastics as means of protection of linguistic minorities: legal issues in the comparative perspective

Topographic names and international law

Peter Hilpold

Summary

1. Introduction

At first sight, the naming of geographic sites is an inherently national issue. If it is true that sovereignty is on the retreat[1], it is also true that there are some core areas with regard to which States are eager to defend their prerogatives. Names and symbols are surely among them. At the same time, international issues and globalization in general are also encroaching upon naming in manifold ways.

1 See J.H. Jackson, *Sovereignty-Modern: A New Approach to an Outdated Concept*, in *American Journal of International Law,* 2003, pp. 782–802; O. Schachter, *Sovereignty – then and now*, in R.St.J. Macdonald, *Essays in Honour of Wang Tieya*, The Hague, 1993, pp. 671–688.

First of all, there is the question who "ownes" geographic names. While in an international society composed of widely unrelated subjects the right answer would not be difficult to find, in the "global village" where many local developments have international repercussions and viceversa a new sense of world citizenship, of a strong sense of responsibility towards developments in different regions of the world and of multiple identities arises. The ensuing commitment and the resulting sense of belonging engenders also the perception that there is a right to partake in the naming of the respective sites.

Then we have to keep in mind that peoples and cultures are moving and intermingling. As a consequence, and often also in anticipation of these changes, national borders are redrawn. Some peoples are outrightly seeking for territorial expansion, although both the instrument they employ to this end, war, as the ultimate goal they aspire at, the acquisition of territory by force, are clearly outlawed by international law[2]. All these changes are regularly associated with a renaming of topographic sites whereby it is often possible to take recourse to ancient names created by neighbouring peoples[3]. Often, however, new names are simply invented or created on the basis of shaky research[4]. Finally, there are many cases in which new names are created not by accident or "rediscovered" by incompetent research but they are rather the result of a willful attempt to justify territorial claims which should result in an annexation of territory or its secession.

Topographic names can also become an international issue when minority questions are involved. This is a very delicate issue and international law is moving very cautiously in this direction. In fact, as we will see later on, it cannot be denied that the recognition of minority rights of this kind might prelude farther-reaching demands. Nonetheless, there can be no doubt that at least some rights are granted also in this area and that the last years have witnessed an enormous strenghtening of the relevant provisions.

All the reasons mentioned so far indicating why international law has to deal with issues of geographic names in an ever more intensive way are of a rather

2 With regard to the outlawing of war it suffices to mention the Briand-Kellog-Pact and art. 2, para. 4 of the UN Charter. With regard to the prohibition of annexation of territory various norms can be mentioned, beginning with the Stimson doctrine of 1932 and including the prohibition of the use of force according to art. 2, para. 4 of the UN Charter, the right to self-determination and numerous soft-law instruments issued by institutions such as the CSCE/OSCE which are emphasizing the inviolability of national borders. It has also to be mentioned, however, that this clear prohibitions were often disregarded in the past and in particular in the immediate aftermath of World War II.

3 See, in this context, for example the "Macedonia question". Cfr. P. Hilpold, *Die Makedonienfrage*, in *Europa Ethnica*, 3/1993, pp. 113–120.

4 In this context also the term of "folk etymology" is used.

contentious nature. This may explain the reluctance with which this issue is taken up by the International Community. Thereby the point is often missed that the requirement to find international agreements for the naming of geographic sites is to a large extent a technical challenge required by the necessities of ever-increasing international exchanges. This is true both with regard to commercial exchanges and with tourism as with regard to other sporadic interaction as, for example, in the case of relief efforts when major disasters occur. According to the United Nations Group of Experts on Geographical Names "[c]onsistent use of accurate place names is an essential element of effective communication worldwide and supports socio-economic development, conservation and national infrastructure"[5]. Uncertainties with regard to the exact name of geographic locations are creating equivocies and additional costs. More and more the insight is growing that more relevance should be given to this aspect of topographic naming.

2. Activities by the United Nations in the field of topographic names – Standardization of Geographical Names

2.1 The institutional setting

Already when the great discoveries had come to an end and a common perception had come into life as to the extent and the geographic particularities of the globe the need was felt to standardize geographical names. In view of the rudimentary nature of international structures it was, however, no wonder that these attempts were not very effectual[6]. It was up to the United Nations to take up this challenge, at a time when the problem itself appeared to be even more pronounced than before.

The United Nations have been active in the field of Standardization of Geographical Names since the 1950's of the last century[7].

---

5 See the leaflet "*United Nations Group of Experts on Geographical Names – Consistent use of place names*", February 2001, http://www.un.org/depts/Cartographic/english/ungegn.pdf (5th April 2007).

6 On the history of international cooperation for the standardization of geographical names see N. Kadmon, *Toponymy – The Lore, Law and Language of Geographical Names*, New York, 1997, p. 219 et seq.

7 To be true, early preliminary activities in this field can be traced back to the year 1948. See for more details N. Kadmon, *Toponymy, cit.,* p. 233 et seq.

Already in 1959 the Economic and Social Council passed Resolution 715 A (XXVII) on the basis of which a Group of Experts on Geographical Names was set up[8]. Its terms of reference were the following:

(i) to consider the technical problems of domestic standardization of geographical names, including the preparation of a statement of the general and regional problems involved, and to prepare draft recommendations for the procedures, principally linguistic, that might be followed in the standardization of their own names by individual countries;
(ii) to report to the Council at an appropriate session on the desirability of holding an international conference on this subject and of sponsoring working groups based on linguistic systems;
(iii) to invite Governments of countries interested and experienced in the question to make available, at the request of the Secretary-General, and at their own expense, consultants to serve on the above group.

A first United Nations Conference on the Standardization of Geographical Names was held in Geneva in September 1967. These conferences take place every five years. They mark decisive steps in the ongoing process of harmonization of geographic names and at the same time they serve to redirect the relevant discussion towards new needs and requirements.

At the Geneva Conference of 1967 important recommendations were issued that influenced also the institutional underpinning of the relevant UN activities. On the basis of these recommendations, ECOSOC, in its resolution 1314 (XLVI) of 31st May 1968, approved the terms of reference for the United Nations Group of Experts on Geographical Names[9]. While the United Nations Conferences are responsible for setting the general framework and for the more basic, statutory work, the Group of Experts has an implementary function[10].

The main aims of this Group are the following[11]:

(a) To emphasize the importance of the standardization of geographical names at the national and international levels and to demonstrate the benefits to be derived from such standardization;

8 This group was first conceived as an Ad Hoc Group of Experts. By a ECOSOC decision of 4th May 1973 it was renamed in "United Nations Group of Experts on Geographical Names".

9 For the exact naming of this body see the previous footnote.

10 See N. Kadmon, *Toponymy, cit.*, p. 239.

11 See Subsidiary bodies of the Economic and Social Council and the General Assembly in the economic, social and related fields, E/2001/INF/3, 12th April 2001.

(b) To collect the results of the work of national and international bodies dealing with the standardization of geographical names and to facilitate the dissemination of these results to States members of the United Nations;
(c) To study and propose principles, policies and methods suitable for resolving problems of national and international standardization;
(d) To play an active role, by facilitating the supply of scientific and technical help, in particular to developing countries, in creating mechanisms for the national and international standardization of geographical names;
(e) To provide a vehicle for liason and coordination among member States, and between member States and international organizations, on work associated with the standardization of geographical names;
(f) To implement the tasks assigned as a result of the resolutions adopted at the United Nations Conferences on the Standardization of Geographical Names.

To further the aims stated above, the functions of the Group of Experts are[12]:

(a) To develop procedures and establish mechanisms for standardization in response to national requirements and particular requests;
(b) To undertake preparatory work for the periodic international conferences on the standardization of geographical names, to provide continuity for activities between conferences, and to provide leadership in the implementation of resolutions adopted at the conferences;
(c) To encourage the discussions and study of practical and theoretical steps directed towards standardization;
(d) To coordinate the activities of linguistic/geographical divisions formed to further the work at the national level, to encourage the active participation of countries and divisions, and to promote a degree of uniformity in the work undertaken;
(e) To create any necessary structure to supplement the work of divisions and to deal with issues beyond the scope of a division;
(f) To develop appropriate programmes to assist individual countries and group of countries, to achieve standardization where it is lacking;
(g) To make mapping organizations aware of the importance of using standardized geographical names;
(h) To maintain liason with international organizations dealing with related sujects and encourage group divisions to participate in the United Nations regional or other cartographic conferences;
(i) To work at the highest possible national, international and United Nations level to interrelate toponymy and cartography;

---

12 *Ibid.*

(j) To make standardization principles and standardized geographical names available as practical information for as wide a user community as possible, through all appropriate means.
Within this group, several working groups for specific tasks have been established. Inter alia they are setting up training courses in toponymy, the comparative study of the various systems of transliteration towards a single romanization system for each of the non-Roman writing systems and the production of international gazetteers.

The UNGEGN, which meets biennally, reports to the United Nations Conference on the Standardization of Geographical Names.

The UNGEGN is one of those UN bodies that are working quietly and efficiently far from the contentious, highly politicized areas that are standing at centre of public interest. The benefits of these harmonization activities are, on the other hand, very far-reaching and they concern:

"– trade and commerce;
- population censuses and national statistics;
- property rights and cadastre;
- urban and regional planning;
- environmental management – sustainable development and conservation;
- natural disaster relief, emergency preparedness and receipt of aid;
- security strategy and peacekeeping operations;
- search and rescue operations;
- map and atlas production;
- automatic navigation;
- tourism;
- communications, including postal and news services"[13].

2.2 General considerations on the way ahead

The work of UNGEGN reveals, however, at a closer look, also some problematic characters[14]. After the impetus of the first decades these activities seem partly to have last steam. There is still a consistent number of States that do not or not sufficiently participate at the relevant UN activities. The eight Conferences held

13 Cited according to UNGEGN, *Consistent Use of Place Names*, February 2001, http://www.un.org/depts/Cartographic/english/ungegn.pdf (5th April 2007).

14 See for more details the report prepared by H. Kerfoot, *The United Nations Conferences on the Standardization of Geographical Names ... Looking to the future*, United Nations Group of Experts on Geographical Names, Working Paper No. 55, Vienna, 28th March – 4th April 2006.

so far have produced 184 resolutions. This is a considerable number of documents and as a consequence oversight often gets lost. The great question is, how to make this situation more transparent and how to make norm creation more effectual. Doubts have been voiced whether the adoption of resolutions (which are in reality recommendations to ECOSOC) still constitute the most appropriate instrument to legislate in this field[15].

A better information policy would probably be helpful also in another area, namely with regard to the attempt to give guidance for topographic naming in minority areas or where indigenous populations are involved. To be sure, some noteworthy results have been achieved also in this area but it is also true, on the other hand, that progress has been slow and we are still far away from a clear, comprehensive set of rules that could be resorted to in this field. As we will see later on, several other international institutions are also active in this area. Probably all could profit from a better interconnection of these various activities.

Also the recommendation to create a national authority for geographical names has been heeded only in part. There is still quiet a large number of States that have no such authority. In this case, most often, military institutions have assumed the relevant tasks[16].

2.3 UN standardization of geographic names and the specific situation of minority areas and territories of indigenous peoples. The various resolutions

The relationship between nations and peoples at the one hand and the land on which they settle has been described the following way:

> "Nations and peoples are defined as much by their identifying characteristics as by the places in which they live. Groups of humans have established relationships between their identities and the land they occupy and have articulated those relationships in a geographical vocabulary of place names. Toponymy, therefore, is the eloquent reflection of the symbiotic relationship that exists between our planet and the societies that inhabit it"[17].

Of the 184 resolutions issued during the eight UN conferences on geographical names held so far, fifteen resolution have concerned national standardization. From the viewpoint of minorities, if not in general, the most important of these

15 *Ibid.*, p. 4.

16 This is also the case with Italy where the relevant institution is the "Istituto Geografico Militare".

17 See Commission de Toponymie du Quebec, *Promotion of Geographical Names Used by Minority Groups*, United Nations Group of Experts on Geographical Names, Working Paper No. 34a, Wien, 28t[h] March – 4th April 2006, p. 2, citing Henri Dorion, 1996.

resolutions is Resolution no. 4 issued on the first conference in Geneva in 1967[18]. This resolution is divided into five parts with the following headings:

- national names authority (recommendation A);
- collection of geographical names (recommendation B);
- principles of official treatment of geographical names (recommendation C);
- multilingual area (recommendation D) and
- national gazetteers (national gazetteers).

> Recommendation D – Multilingual areas
>
> "It is recommended that, in countries in which there exist more than one language, the national authority as appropriate:
>
> (a) Determine the geographical names in each of the official languages, and other languages as appropriate;
> (b) Give a clear indication of equality or precedence of officially acknowledged names;
> (c) Publish these officially acknowledged names in maps and gazetteers".

It is this a very far-reaching recommendation. If interpreted literally it requires any multilingual State to recognize the toponymy of all different groups. With the exception of the expression "as appropriate" this recommendation contains no safeguard clauses.

First of all, the State has an obligation to determine the geographical names in all the official languages. Therefore, it is to say, that this provision in this first part is very deferrent to national sovereignty. In fact it is the individual State which decides which languages are to be recognized the *status* of an official language. From this decision further international legal consequences ensue. On the other hand, it is known that in many cases multiethnic and multilingual States often do not give official *status* to the languages of the various groups they are composed of, even if they recognize them officially. Recommendation D goes, however, further, as it provides that also other languages should be considered in this context, "as appropriate". We find here, therefore, a double conditioning with regard to considerations of "appropriatedness". No minimum number of group members is required; there is no mentioning of a "minimum number". It is up to the respective State to judge whether the respective measure is appropriate. At the same time it is also clear that this judgement must not be abusive.

It is not necessary for the State to give equal *status* to the toponymy in the various languages. On the other hand, there is an obligation "to give a clear indication of equality or precedence of officially acknowledged names". It is up to the State to take the respective decision. The International Community has, on

18 *Ibid.*

the other hand, the right to know the results of this decision. The creation of transparency seems to be the paramount obligation. Under this perspective also the last obligation of Recommendation D is to be seen: the officially acknowledged names have to be published in maps and gazetteers.

With regard to these national gazetteers further information is given in Recommendation E of Resolution 4 of 1967:

> "It is recommended that each names authority produce, and continually revise, appropriate gazetteers of all its standardized geographical names.
>
> It is further recommended that, in addition to the standardized names, each gazetteers include, as a minimum, such information as is necessary for the proper location and identification of the named features.
>
> In particular, it is recommended that the following be included:
>
> (a) The kind of feature to which the name applies;
> (b) Precise description of the location and the extent, including a point position reference if possible, of each namend feature,
> (c) Provision for the parts of natural features to be additionally defined by reference to the whole and for the names of extended features to be defined as necessary by reference to their constituent parts;
> (d) Such information on administrative or regional areas as is considered necessary and, if possible, reference to a map or chart within which the features lie;
> (e) All officially standardized names for a feature, if there are more than one; and provisions for cross-reference to be made to names previously used for the same feature.
>
> When national authorities determine it possible, both technically and economically, they may include such information on geographical names as gender, number, definite and indefinite forms, position of stress, tone and pronunciation in the system of the International Phonetic Association and such other linguistic information as may lead to the better understanding and use of names both nationally and internationally".

Without doubt, the production of such gazetteers, though surely costly and work-intensive, constitutes an invaluable contribution on the way to a solution for the topographic problem that is both transparent and ponderated as well as suited for general acceptance.

The most important immediate addressees of these standardization activities are map and other editors. For these subjects specific recommendations have been spelled out[19]:

> "The Conference,
>
> [...]
>
> 1. Recommends that countries should be encouraged to publish and keep up-to-date toponymic guidelines for map and other editors which may enable cartographers of other countries to treat correctly all problems of cartographic toponymy of the countries that produced such guidelines, and which may be of help to all users in interpreting maps;

19 See IV/4.

2. Further recommends that those guidelines contain, inter alia and as appropriate, the following items:
   (a) Legal status of geographical names in the respective languages of multilingual countries;
   (b) Alphabets of the language or languages and furthermore, in the case of non-Roman alphabets and scripts, the officially introduced romanization keys;
   (c) Spelling rules for geographical names;
   (d) Aids to pronunciation of geographical names;
   (e) Linguistic substrata recognizable in the existing place names; but only as far as their knowledge may be of benefit to the cartographer;
   (f) Relationship between dialect(s) and standard language(s);
   (g) Peculiarities of dialect and area distribution of the main dialects;
   (h) Areal distribution of languages within multilingual countries;
   (i) Names authorities and measures taken in names standardization;
   (j) Source material;
   (k) Glossary of words necessary for the understanding of maps;
   (l) Abbreviations in official maps;
   (m) Administrative division

[...]"

On a whole, it can be said that these recommendations are expressing a clear preference for a general recognition of toponymy in all those languages that are spoken in a specific country. At the same time, the approaches chosen by the respective UN Conference are very prudent in the sense that they fully recognize the primary responsibility of the States for finding a solution that can find general acceptance.

The commitment to multilinguality cannot be said to be directly the expression of a favourable attitude towards linguistic and ethnic pluralism. The foremost goal is to make sure the "consistent use of accurate place names" and to this avail it is purported to give the broadest possible space to the toponymy effectively used in the various regions. If effective communication is to be achieved it is advisable to give preference to the so-called endonyms, i.e. to the place names used by the local population, in comparison to exonyms[20]. Often, for a place more than one endoynm exist and in this case the most extensive possible space has to be attributed to this plurality of names. Indirectly, of course, this attitude strenghtens also linguistic plurality as such[21].

---

20 Beside the need for standardization endonyms are also preferred because their use can cause political and cultural strains in international relations. See N. Kadmon, *Toponymy, cit.*, p. 84.

21 With regard to the use of exonyms it is to say, however, that the relevant UN bodies no longer take such a negative attitude. See, for example, Res. VIII/4:
"[...]
Noting that, notwithstanding the general goal of limiting the use of exonyms, in several countries there has been a tendency to increase their number,

At least in the first years this priority setting was very clear. This becomes evident from the resolutions II/36 and V/22 on "Problems of minority languages" and "Aboriginal/native geographical names" respectively.

"II/36 Problems of minority languages

The Conference

Noting that in some areas, e.g. the Lappish-speaking part of northern Europe, a minority language is spoken inside the territory of more than one country.

Noting further that geographical names in the minority language are sometimes spelt according to different principles in the different countries where the minority language is spoken,

Recognizing the desirability of a uniform treatment of the names in the minority language in such areas,

Recommends that, where possible, the countries in question, in consultation with native speakers of the minority language:

(a) Adopt a common orthography for all geographical names of the minority language;
(b) Use that orthography for the standardization of the place names in the minority language in their territory;
(c) Publish the standardized names in their official maps and national gazetters".

"V/22 Aboriginal/native geographical names

The Conference,

Aware that groups of aboriginal/native people exist in many countries throughout the world,

Also aware that these groups have their own languages, cultures and traditions,

Recognizing that the geographical names of these groups are a significant part of the toponymic tradition of every area or country in which they live,

Recognizing also that aboriginal/native people have an inherent interest in having their geographical nomenclature recognized as important,

1. Recommends that all countries having groups of aboriginal/native people make a special effort to collect their geographical names along with other appropriate information;
2. Recommends also that, whenever possible and appropriate, a written form of those names be adopted for official use on maps and other publications;
3. Recommends further that regional and international meetings be held to discuss the methodology for collecting and recording aboriginal/native geographical names".

In more recent times, the line between those activities within the UN that are directed at the mere name conservation for the purpose to make communication

---

Recognizing that measures such as the categorization of exonym use, the publication of pronunciation guides for endonyms, and the formulation of guidelines ensuring a politically sensitive use of exonyms would help in the reduction of the number of exonyms,
Recommends the establishment of a Working Group on Exonyms of the United Nations Group of Experts on Geographical Names, with the aim of preparing such measures as those mentioned above".

more effective and other activities that have as their goal the conservation of names which are important for the preservation of distinct group identities becomes more and more blurred. This fact received distinct expression in Res. VIII/1:

> "[...]
> Recalling the intent of the resolutions of earlier Conferences, namely, resolution 36 of the Second United Nations Conference on the Standardization of Geographical Names relating to multilingual geographical names and resolution 22 of the Fifth United Nations Conference on the Standardization of Geographical Names relating to the recording and use of aboriginal/native geographical names,
> Recognizing that there are many agencies throughout the world actively pursuing the retention/revitalization of minority and indigenous group culture through the recording, recognition and promotion of the toponyms representing such groups,
> Recognizing also that the promotion of this work will benefit the geographical names authorities and the United Nations, as well as provide valuable information for the community in general,
> [...]
> Recommends that geographical names authorities throughout the world be invited to present a summary of such activities for inclusion in a general report, scheduled to appear in 2007, on these activities to be prepared by the United Nations for subsequent dissemination to all interested parties".

In the same perspective Res. VIII/9 "Geographical names as cultural heritage" is to be read:

> "The Conference
> Recognizing the emphasis placed by delegates to the Eighth United Nations Conference on the Standardization of Geographical names on the importance of geographical names as part of a nation's historical and cultural heritage,
> Noting that the collection of geographical names in many countries of the world is made increasingly difficult as a result of the rapid pace of socio-economic change impacting on society and landscape,
> Recalling the recommendations made by the Second United Nations Conference on the Standardization of Geographical Names in its resolution 27, as well as the recommendations made by the Seventh Conference in its resolution VII/5, that measures be taken nationally to ensure that names that are yet to be collected are recorded through fieldwork according to local usage of name forms,
> Urges countries that have not already done so, to undertake both the systematic collection of geographical names and the promotion of a greater understanding among the wider public of the significance of inherited geographical names with respect to local, regional and national heritage and identity".

From the formulation of these recommendations a clear sympathy for the preservation of traditional geographical names transpires. The reason for this sympathy is to be found less in technical considerations directed at improving international communication as in a clear commitment towards the conservation of the cultural heritage which is here considered to be a value *per se.*

2.4 The protection of indigenous peoples by the UN, with a special perspective on the repercussions of these activities on topographic naming

As it is known, many intense and far-reaching activities have been undertaken within the UN in order to provide more efficient protection for indigenous peoples[22].

A great step forward in all the initiatives to strenghten the protection of indigenous peoples will be done once the Draft Declaration on the Rights of Indigenous Peoples will come into force. Much controversy has surrounded this declaration and in particular its provisions on self-determination. In 1996 this declaration has finally been approved by the Human Rights Council but it is still awaiting definite approval by the UN General Assembly. This declaration, in its art. 14, para. 1, addresses also the issues of place names:

> "Indigenous peoples have the right to revitalize, use, develop and transmit to future generations their histories, languages, oral traditions, philosophies, writing systems and literatures, and to designate and retain their own names for communities, places and persons".

On a whole, international law seems to be rather generous with respect to cultural rights of indigenous peoples. In many ways the rights of members belonging to such communities go beyond those of members of minorities.

An explanation for this different treatment is easy to find: Indigenous peoples usually pose no threat to the State they are living in. They are not aspiring at secession and they usually do not constitute a challenge to the respective governmental system. They mainly want to be left alone. On this basis States are usually prepared to make generous concessions to these groups. This context has to be kept in mind when the question is debated whether these special rules could be extended also to the area of minority protection in general. The state community has in the past clearly opposed such an extension. Although it is not always possible to determine exactly which peoples are to be considered as indigenous, most often this question poses no greater problems. State consensus does not go beyond this point and it is not up to the individual persons or groups to extend the purview of these provisions beyond the consensus found among the international legislators. Therefore, the very far-reaching way in which the

22 See, in particular, the Indigenous and Tribal Peoples Convention, adopted on 27th June 1989 by the General Conference of the International Labour Organization. This Convention No. 169 entered into force on 5th September 1991.

International Community seems to take care of the wishes of indigenous peoples in the field of geographic names should not lead to an easy generalization. Minority rights are granted under totally different circumstances. It is not rare that minorities are enjoying a rather strong position in a given State and that they are advancing demands for autonomy or even independent statehood. Under these conditions States will usually refrain from granting far-reaching concessions in the field of geographic names as these measures could further the process of self-determination.

In sum it has to be said that the provisions on demographic names for areas in which indigenous peoples are living have to be considered in isolation. No extension by analogy is possible.

3. European provisions

As it is known, there are two important European documents containing provisions on topographic names. Both documents have as their purpose the protection of national minorities (or, respectively, the protection of minority or regional languages): the European Framework Convention for the Protection of National Minorities and European Charter for Regional or Minority Languages. A few further documents which are also addressing the issue of topographic names but which are of minor importance will also be briefly commented upon within this chapter.

3.1 The European Framework Convention for the Protection of National Minorities (FCNM)

As it is known, the Framework Convention, which has entered into force on 1st February 1998 and has been ratified by thirty-nine States, is the first multilateral convention dedicated exclusively to issues of minority protection. At the time of its adoption by the Council of Europe's Committee of Ministers on 10th November 1994 this Convention was heavily criticised for being too vague and for offering too little to minorities or, respectively, to members of minorities. In the meantime, however, the overall judgment on this convention has changed profoundly. This change of perspective has mainly been brought about by the activity of the monitoring system which is composed, according to the articles 24 and 26 of the FCNM, by the Committee of Ministers and the Advisory Committee. In this system the Committee of Ministers is the political organ while the Advisory Committee has only an assisting, adjuvating function. In reality, however, it is the latter body the main contributions for the interpretation and for the practical application of the FCNM are coming from. This fact can be demonstrated very well also with regard to the interpretation and concrete application of art. 11, para. 11 containing the relevant provision on topographic names. This provision goes as follows:

> "In areas traditionally inhabited by substantial numbers of persons belonging to a national minority, the Parties shall endeavour, in the framework of their legal system, including, where appropriate, agreements with other States, and taking into account their specific conditions, to display traditional local names, street names and other topographical indications intended for the public also in the minority language when there is a sufficient demand for such indications".

Already a first reading of this provision reveals that this is the most cautiously worded norm of the whole convention. No other provision knows so many conditions and leaves, in its application, so much leeway to the States parties. At first sight this could be interpreted as a lack of consideration of minority interests in a very delicate field. In reality, however, this caution reflects the deep rift between the various negotiating parties on this issue. There was a strong opposition by several States towards the adoption of whatsoever provision on topographic names. Therefore, the fact that the actual art. 11, para. 3 of the FCNM has found entrance in the Convention is to be considered in itself an enormous achievement[23]. The far-reaching limitations and concessions mentioned above are to be considered the price for achieving agreement at all on a provision on this issue.

3.2 The single provisions of art. 11, para. 3 FCNM[24]

Notwithstanding all the limitations and exceptions mentioned above which shall be considered in greater detail below, first of all, due consideration shall be given to the positive achievements brought about by this provision.

Above all, it has to be kept in mind that this provision, whatever its meagre content, has been inserted into a multilateral provision which is, as already mentioned, dedicated exclusively to issues of minority protection and therefore to the protection of human rights. As a consequence, the provision of topographic names in the minority languages is no longer left to the discretion of individual States but in principle it constitutes a real international obligation for

23 See F. de Varennes, *Commentary to Art. 11 of FCNM*, in M. Weller (ed.), *The Rights of Minorities*, Oxford, 2005, pp. 329–363 (346 s.).

24 See P. Hilpold, *Ortsnamenregelungen aus völkerrechtlicher und aus europarechtlicher Sicht*, in *Juristische Blätter*, 129/2007, S. 228–236.

the whole, ever-increasing number of States which are parties to the FCNM. Of course, on a more restricted regional or even bilateral level, States can add to this obligation and provide for a more sophisticated protection even in this field[25]. On the other hand, it is made sure that concessions in this area cannot be made dependent from considerations of reciprocity or, once granted, be withdrawn at will.

It has furthermore to be noted that this provision refers not only to topographic names in the stricter sense (place names) but also to "street names and other topographical indications intended for the public" (also called the micro-topographic naming). While for "language signs, inscriptions and other information of a private nature visible to the public", according to art. 11, para. 2 FCNM persons belonging to a national minority have only the right to display them in his or her minority language and there is no corresponding duty for the respective State to take corresponding positive measures with regard to the micro-topographic naming in principle such an obligations exists.

This provision on micro-topographic names sheds also a different light on the ultimate purpose of topographic names in the minority language. It is wrong to contend that this purpose lies in the intent to demonstrate to the population as a whole that a minority group is living on a certain territory. Topographic names have rather the function to defend the identity of single minority groups. In fact, to provide for topographic names in the minority language means that the respective language gains acceptance and prominence. Equal treatment of the minority language signals that the State is taking care also for the minority groups and that no sense of inferiority should derive from the fact of belonging to such a group. An environment shall be created that reflects an overall positive attitude towards minorities[26].

With regard to the specific nature of this provision it can be stated that here the collective as such gains prominence. In fact, while modern minority rights law is clearly, in its essence, individualistic, there are also collective elements to be taken into consideration. There is probably no other field of minority law where this collective aspect is so pronounced as in this area. This fact has also implications for the implementation of this norms. Specific ways have to be found to give voice to the collective in order to determine whether such topographic names in the minority language should be introduced. What is more, it has to be assured that it is the minority as such that has to be asked for its

25 See also art. 18 para. 1 FCNM: "The Parties shall endeavour to conclude, where necessary, bilateral and multilateral agreements with other States, in particular neighbouring States, in order to ensure the protection of persons belonging to the national minorities concerned".

26 See extensively on this issue P. Hilpold, *Modernes Minderheitenrechts*, Wien/Baden-Baden/Zürich, 2001, p. 354 et seq.

opinion on this subject and not the population of a State as a whole as otherwise this provision would hardly ever be implemented.

It has also to be mentioned that art. 11, para. 3 is one of the few best-effort provisions of the FCNM. There is no immediate obligation to introduce topographic names in the minority language: parties shall only "endeavour" to this end. If we associate this fact with the circumstance that this provision as a whole is characterized by an unprecedented number of exceptions then the impression could arise that in the end in this area we are not confronted at all with a real legal obligation. This impression is, however, wrong.

In fact, it is not left to the discretion of the single State party whether to implement this provision or not. We are rather confronted here with a bona-fides-obligation and therefore art. 2 of FCNM applies:

> "The provisions of the framework Convention shall be applied in good faith, in a spirit of understanding and tolerance and in conformity with the principles of good neighbourliness, friendly relations and co-operation with States"[27].

There can be no doubt that in principle it is desirable that topographic names in the minority language are in place if the conditions mentioned in art. 11, para. 3 of the FCNM are fulfilled.

3.3 Limitations

First of all, this provision applies only to territories traditionally inhabited by minorities. This is remarkable, as otherwise the FCNM does not refer to limitations of this kind. As it is known, it is higly contested, both in literature as in practice, whether "new minorities", i.e. recent immigrants and persons who are not citizens of the respective country, can also benefit from minority rights provisions[28]. In the past, only those minorities were eligible for protection that had long-lasting ties with the territory they inhabited. In the meantime, however, this situation has changed. As minority rights are part of human rights it is the effective need for protection that has to be considered. New minorities can find themselves in a similar situation like traditional, long-established minorities and in this case they deserve similar protection. Of course, it is still legitimate to differentiale between these groups as to the extend, positive measures have to be

---

27 See with regard to this provision also P. Hilpold, *Commentary to Art. 2 of the FCNM,* in M. Weller (ed.), *The Rights of Minorities*, *cit.*, pp. 97–105.

28 See P. Hilpold, *Neue Minderheiten im Völkerrecht und im Europarecht*, in *Archiv des Völkerrechts*, 2004, S. 80–110.

granted. It is fully justifiable to grant more sophisticated rights to groups that have a stronger bond with a certain country.

As has become evident from the considerations undertaken so far, topographic names in the minority language are a very delicate issue. It seems, therefore, reasonable if such rights are granted only to traditional minorities. Furthermore, topographic names in the minority language usually give expression to a specific, long-standing relationship between a group and a certain region. This relationship is given only with traditional minorities and not with new minorities. Therefore, the condition mentioned seems to be deserve conditional approval.

Article 11, para. 3 requires furthermore that the respective area has to be inhabited by a "substantial number of persons". Again also this criterion has often, in the past, been resorted to for minority rights provisions to apply. On the other hand, it is also known that this criterion is not a generally recogized one. As has been evidenced by the Study undertaken by Francesco Capotorti, the number of group members necessary for the application of minority rights provisions cannot be determined in an abstract way. It is often said that the respective group has to be numerous enough in order to be able to maintain its specific identity and characteristics[29]. For different (positive) rights different minimum number requirements may be posed. Again, also in this case it seems to make sense to make the granting of rights in this area conditional upon the presence of a qualified number of minority members. As we will see later on, this provision has been interpreted, however, in a rather inconsistent way by the Advisory Committee.

This provision has to be applied by the State parties "in the framework of their legal system" and "taking into account their specific conditions". With regard to the first condition it has to be kept in mind that according to art. 27 of Vienna Convention on the Law of Treaties no party may invoke the provisions of its internal law as justification for its failure to perform a treaty.

In this context, however, no such leeway shall be granted to the individual States. The reference to the "framework of the legal system" shall rather provide some practical hints for the concrete application of this rather vague provision. By the reference to the "specific conditions" again a concession has been made to the States parties. Again, this provision reveals also the delicacy of the subject. The "specific conditions" this provision refers to, regard obviously elements outside the closer subject of geographic names. Therefore, it seems to be justified to take here into consideration even political elements. On the other

---

29 See E/CN.4/Sub.2/384/Rev. 1, 1979 and V. Grammatikas, *The Definition of Minorities in International Law: A Problem still Looking for a Solution*, in *Revue Hellenique de Droit International*, 52/1999, pp. 321–364.

hand, also this provision has always to be interpreted in good faith. It cannot constitute a facile excuse in order to circumvent the application of this provision.

Finally, art. 11, para. 3 requires "sufficient demand". This provision refers, of course, to the demand by the minority members. It does not seem to be justified to let the whole population of a certain country decide whether topographic names in the minority language shall find application. Usually the respective demand will be brought forward by the relevant minority organization. Also in this context, as with the exceptions mentioned above, the following ponderation has to be made: on the one hand, the restriction as such has to be taken as a fact as it was a precondition for the acceptance of this provision by the negotiating parties. On the other hand, it may not be applied abusively.

3.4 The practice of the Advisory Committee

As already mentioned, the Advisory Committee (AC) gives a decisive contribution for the practical application of the FCNM. In the few years of its activity it has given pivotal hints for the interpretation of this convention. This holds also true for art. 11, para. 3 even though the attitude taken by the AC in this field seems to be rather inconsistent and erratic.

Positively it has to be remarked that the AC has emphasized the need for transparence and the establishment of clear criteria[30]. Thereby, legal security is created. This was emphasized in the AC Report on Albania:

> "[T]he Advisory Committee is concerned by the lack of clear criteria concerning the display of traditional local names, street names and other topographical indications in minority languages intended for the public. The Advisory Committee therefore considers that the Government should examine the need for an adequate legal and administrative framework to govern the display of names and topographical indications in minority languages and adopt appropriate legislation in full conformity with Article 11 paragraph 3 of the Framework Convention. The Adisory Committee notes in this respect the comment of the Government in the State Report that 'a complete legal improvement of all the matters treated in this Article remains an issue to be dwelt upon in the future' [...]" [31].

Similar considerations can be found in the Report on Armenia:

> "The Advisory Committee finds that there is a lack of precision in Armenian legislation concerning the possibility of using minority languages in topographical indications. The Advisory Committee considers, despite the fact that there have been no complaints from the

30 See, in this context, the AC *Report on Estonia*, ACFC/INF/OP/I (2002) 005, 2001, para. 42.

31 Advisory Committee, *Opinion on Albania*, ACFC/INF/OP/I (2003) 004, 2002, para. 47.

persons concerned, that the authorities should supplement their legislation so as to ensure that the relevant provisions of the Framework Convention may be effectively implemented"[32].

It is interesting to note that the Advisory Committee requires the determination of clear criteria in this field even if there is no specific demand in respect. At first glance this requirement seems to conflict with the wording of art. 11, para. 3 of the FCNM which presupposes the existence of "a sufficient demand". This contrast is, however, only an apparent one. In fact, first of all, transparent legislation has to be set in place in order to make sure that the provisions on topographic names can be implemented if there is sufficient demand. This last condition has to be seen separately and will come into play subsequently. A significant demand for topographic names will most probably be brought forward only if there is a clear legal framework in place on which these demands can be based.

The most critical issue will always be, however, whether the relevant area is inhabited by a "substantial number of persons belonging to a minority". Although often the contrary is maintained, in this area there are no clear international criteria in place. Therefore, there was the hope that some clarification in this field would come from the Advisory Committee. This hope has been disappointed. The practice by the Advisory Committee has been described as "disconcerting from a legal point" and as expression of a "double standard"[33].

Thus, with regard to Austria, the AC greeted the judgment by the Austrian Constitutional Court according to which a minority constituting more than 10 percent of the population in a constitutionally protected minority area would suffice to make the right on topographic provisions, foreseen in the State Treaty of 1955, applicable[34].

In view of this statement it is baffling to read the relevant findings of the AC with regard to the Czech Republic:

"The Advisory Committee also notes that a provision of the new Act on municipalities (No. 128/2000) that entered into force in May 2000 authorises bilingual signs for topographical indications. Two conditions are laid down with regard to the bilingual signs: at least 20% of

---

32 Advisory Committee, *Opinion on Armenia*, ACFC/INF/OP/I (2003) 001, 2002, para. 103.

33 Cfr. the very poignant criticism of the AC's activity by F. de Varennes, *Commentary to Art. 11 FCNM*, in M. Weller (ed.), *The Right of Minorities*, *cit.*, p. 355.

34 See ACFC/INF/OP/I (2002) 009, 2002, para. 50: "The Advisory Committee particularly welcomes the Austrian Constitutional Court's interpretation of the second sentence of Article 7, paragraph 3 of the State Treaty as regards the threshold required for topographical indications to be displayed in minority languages. This interpretation, which is entirely in keeping with Article 11, paragraph 3 of the Framework Convention, represents a major improvement in the rights of persons belonging to national minorities [...]".

> the citizens residing in the municipality must consider themselves as persons belonging to the national minority concerned and, of these, at least 50% must request these signs. The Advisory Committee welcomes this development and expresses the hope that the new provisions will operate satisfactorily in practice"[35].

These thresholds for the application of bilingual topographic names are surely extremely high but they nonetheless found the approval by the AC[36].

Also in Romania high percentage requirements for the application of national legislation authorizing bilingual signs have found the approval by the AC[37].

On the other hand, the AC has been rather severe with Germany. This country was criticized in the context of topographic naming without reference to the actual size of the relevant minority:

> "The Advisory Committee finds that despite legal requirements to display topographical indications in the Sorbian language in areas traditionally inhabited by Sorbians, notably in the Land of Brandenburg, monolingual signs are only being replaced by bilingual ones at a very slow rate so that the whole operation could take several more years. The Advisory Committee considers that the German authorities should step up their efforts to speed up the full implementation of the legal provisions on bilingual signposting in areas traditionally inhabited by Sorbians"[38].

What seems, at first sight, so uneven and erratic, appears, however, at a closer consideration, far more considered. In fact, it is clear that the AC tried to obtain the utmost from the States parties subject to the monitoring process. The specific conditions were different in all cases. Some countries, such as Austria, have a long tradition in bilingual topographic naming. In other countries, such as the Czech Republic or Romania, there is no such tradition. From the former one can pretend more in absolute terms than from the latter. The approach taken by the Advisory Committee is to seek to convince the States parties to continously strenghten their minority protection standards, whereby, of course, the specific starting conditions have to be taken into consideration. On the other hand, these widely diverging findings reveal also that no general standards, at least of a numerical character, are in force in this field. Notwithstanding this fact, however, the States parties have to act in good faith and there can be no doubt that the best effort provision in art. 11, para. 3 FCNM has to be taken seriously. It can also be

---

35 See ACFC/INF/OP/I (2002) 002, 2002, para. 59.

36 In the meantime, in the Czech Republik the relevant provisions have been changed. Now a minority percentage of 10% is considered to be sufficient. Additionally, at least 40% of the resident adult minority population has to support this demand. Therefore, it can be said that the thresholds have been lowered but they are still high in an international perspective.

37 See ACFC/INF/OP/I (2002) 002, 2002, para. 59 approving a 20% criterion.

38 See ACFC/INF/OP/I (2002) 008, 2003, para. 86. See on all these findings also F. de Varennes, *Commentary to Art. 11 of FCNM*, *cit.*, p. 348 et seq.

said that the monitoring activity by the AC, the obligation by the States parties to emanate transparent legislation in this field and the continouing discussion between all the parties involved are all favouring the coming up of ever more precise standards and it cannot be excluded that in the future also general numeric standards will come into being.

3.5 The European Charter for Regional or Minority Languages

Less prominent than the FCNM is the European Charter for Regional or Minority Languages. One reason for this may lie with the fact that here languages stand at the middle of the interest and less people speaking them. Furthermore, the menu-approach, according to which each State party can choose among various obligations, enhances the lack of transparency surrounding this instrument as to the overall extent of the various obligations. Nonetheless, if the existing standards in the field of topographic naming in Europe have to be assessed due regard has to be paid also to this Charter. The relevant provision can be found in art. 10, para. 2g:

> "In respect of the local and regional authorities on whose territory the number of residents who are users of regional or minority languages is such as to justify the measures specified below, the Parties undertake to allow and/or encourage:
>
> [...]
>
> g) the use or adoption, if necessary in conjunction with the name in the official language(s), of traditional and correct forms of place-names in regional or minority languages".

The use of topographic names in the minority languages is seen here as an instrument to further strenghten the minority languages themselves. An overall environment positive to minority protection as such shall be created. There are no specific thresholds for the application of this provision. The only requirement is, that "the number of residents who are users of regional or minority languages is such as to justify" the respective measure.

By saying "use or adoption" this provision makes clear that it can also be necessary to reconstitute traditional topographic names[39]. If new topographic names are introduced it may be necessary to translate them into the minority language[40].

On a whole it can be said that the European Charter for Regional or Minority Languages pays little attention to the political connotation of topographic

39 See J.-M. Woehrling, *The European Charter for Regional or Minority Languages*, Strasbourg, 2006, p. 192 et seq.

40 *Ibid.*

naming. It evidences that topographic names in the minority or the regional language are an important, albeit subsidiary, instrument for the strenghtening of the position of these languages.

4. Further international law instruments

Several other international instruments make reference to topographic names for minorities. The relevance of these instruments has to assessed on a case by case basis. Generally it can be said that the more the relevant document assumes the character of a soft law instrument the more there is the preparation to make farer reaching concessions also in the field of topographic naming. It can further be noticed that the stronger the role played by States representatives in the elaboration of these documents the lesser seems to be the attention attributed to topographic names (and viceversa). Were minority representatives have been the leading forces for the elaboration of the respective instruments in some cases high relevance has been attributed to this issue. Thereby the importance of topographic names for the conservation of a minority identity has been rightly recognized. On the other hand, on this basis the respective documents risk becoming detached from reality.

Most prominent (and also most authoritative) in this field are surely the Oslo Recommendations regarding the Linguistic Rights of National Minorities of 1998.

This document contains the following recommendation:

> "In areas inhabited by significant numbers of persons belonging to a national minority and when there is sufficient demand, public authorities shall make provisions for the display, also in the minority language, of local names, street names and other topographical indications intended for the public".

In the Explanatory Note to this document we find the following clarification in respect to this provision:

> "Refusal to recognise the validity of historic denominations of the kind described can constitute an attempt to revise history and to assimilate minorities, thus constituting a serious threat to the identity of persons belonging to minorities".

Also Recommendation 1201 of the European Council Parliamentary Assembly of the year 1993, concerning an additional protocol to the EHRC, contains provisions on topographic naming in art. 7, para. 4:

> "In the regions in which substantial numbers of a national minority are settled, the persons belonging to that minority shall have the right to display in their language local names, signs, inscriptions and other similar information visible to the public".

This Recommendation has never been adopted, however, by the Council of Ministers.

This provision would have provided for very far-reaching concessions in the field of topographic naming. Only by the "substantial number" – requirement the scope of application of this provision would have been somewhat limited.

Other instruments, finally, seem to promise everything to everyone. In this context, the diverse proposals for the creation of a Group Rights Charta or for an additional protocol to the EHRC have to be mentioned. It seems that the guiding principle in the drafting process of these instruments was the intention to grant a maximum of rights to traditional, autochthonous groups. The question whether these demands were realistic and politically feasible was attributed minor relevance. As an example reference shall be made here to the Draft Convention on the Fundamental Rights of Ethnic Groups in Europe, prepared by the Federal Unit of European Nationalities of 1992.

This document contains the following provision:

> Art. 7: Right of Language
>
> "[...]
>
> In particular, groups and their members shall have the right to the use or equal status of their language in all legislative, public and administrative acts as well as in all fields of toponymy".

To this provision, the following interpretative comment was given:

> "Places shall be named and, where necessary, re-established to their original form in accordance with the relevant UN recommendations (UN Conference on the Standardization of Geographical Names, Geneva 1967, Resolution No. 4 and 20)"[41].

The right to topographic names in the minority language are guaranteed here without condition. There is no minimum threshold for this provision to apply. On a whole it can be said that this is a totally utopian and impractical approach. Approaches like these may have been engendered by a true will to help minorities but they can easily lead to the contrary as they can be seen as expression of an extreme, anatagonistic behaviour, pitting minorities against majorities without any sense for moderation.

---

41 See F. Ermacora, Ch. Pan, *Fundamental Rights of Ethnic Groups in Europe*, Wien, 1993, p. 79 et seq., referring also to the Stauffenberg Draft Charter for Ethnic Group Rights in the EC-12, 1988, art. 3j: "Ethnic groups collectively shall have the right to the installation of place name signs, directional signs and advertising signs in the language of the group" (unofficial translation, probably by Ermacora, Pan).

5. Conclusions

As evidenced at the beginning of this contribution, topographic naming is, first of all, a technical issue. A coherent, uniform usage of topographic names is a precondition for an effective international communication. Seen from this perspective it should be possible to solve all related questions in a calm atmosphere. At the same, however, the issue of topographic names is an enormously delicate one. Topographic names are seen as indicators of sovereign claims, they are evidence to the world of ancient settlement structures, they reflect the existence of minorities on a certain territory and they may be used – but also abused – as an argumentative tool in attempts to renegotiate state boundaries. Furthermore, however, topographic names are an important element for the strenghtening of a minority identity. The spectrum of rights which have to be respected in the field of minority protection is becoming ever larger. More and more the preparedness can be noticed to include among these rights also politically highly sensitive ones such as the right to topographic names in the minority language. It has been recognized that the feeling of belonging to a certain area constitutes an important element in the definition of a minority identity and this element becomes all the more important in a time of an ever accelerating globalization process. Of course, a difficult balancing between the various interests that are coming here into play has to be undertaken. A basic international consensus for the formulation of topographic names has to be found in any case as a matter of necessity: globalization requires security as to names and places. With regard to minority rights sovereign sensibilities are conflicting with a more self-conscious and a more assertive attitude taken by minority members. In general, the overall tendency is clear: topographic names expressed in the minority language are an important element of the minority culture. The growing *status* of international minority law leads to an ever-growing preparedness to tackle also this sensitive issue. The opposition against this tendency is a retreat fight: in a time when sovereignty becomes more and more relativized, when kin-States are more and more recognized as having a right and duty to act for "their" minorities abroad[42], when human rights are considered to be pivotal for the interpretation of international obligations, minority rights advocates and minorities themselves have the law on their side if they continue this struggle, with all due moderation, for the assertion of the right for

---

42 To be true, this right and duty does not go uncontested but, on the other hand, there are many elements evidencing that international minority law is attributing an important role to the kin-State. See on this issue P. Hilpold, Ch. Perathoner, *Die Schutzfunktion des Mutterstaates*, ("*The Kin State*"), Wien/Bozen/Berlin/Bern, 2006.

topographic names in the minority language. The situation is still evolving but it is fair to say that within the last ten years the rights of minorities have expanded enormously in this field. Whether this tendency will be set forth will depend very much from the question whether the overall positive attitude towards minority rights law will continue to last.

Bibliography

Monographs, articles, contributions in collective writings

de Varennes F., *Commentary to Art. 11 of FCNM*, in M. Weller (ed.), *The Rights of Minorities*, Oxford, 2005.

Ermacora F., Pan Ch., *Fundamental Rights of Ethnic Groups in Europe*, Wien, 1993

Grammatikas V., *The Definition of Minorities in International Law: A Problem still Looking for a Solution*, in *Revue Hellenique de Droit International*, 52/1999.

Hilpold P., *Die Makedonienfrage*, in *Europa Ethnica*, 3/1993.

Hilpold P., *Ortsnamenregelungen aus völkerrechtlicher und aus europarechtlicher Sicht*, in *Juristische Blätter*, 129/ 2007.

Hilpold P. *Modernes Minderheitenrecht,* Wien/Baden-Baden/Zürich, 2001.

Hilpold P., *Commentary to Art. 2 of the FCNM*, in M. Weller (ed.), *The Rights of Minorities*, Oxford, 2005.

Hilpold P., *Neue Minderheiten im Völkerrecht und im Europarech*t, in *Archiv des Völkerrechts*, 2004.

Hilpold P., Perathoner Ch., *Die Schutzfunktion des Mutterstaates* ("*The Kin State*"), Wien/Bozen/Berlin/Bern, 2006.

Jackson J.H., *Sovereignty-Modern: A New Approach to an Outdated Concept*, in *American Journal of International Law,* 2003.

Schachter O., *Sovereignty – Then and now*, in R.St.J. Macdonald, *Essays in Honour of Wang Tieya*, The Hague, 1993.

Kadmon N., *Toponymy – The Lore, Law and Language of Geographical Names*, New York, 1997.

Documents (on file with author)

Commission de Toponymie du Quebec, *Promotion of Geographical Names Used by Minority Groups*, United Nations Group of Experts on Geographical Names, Working Paper No. 34a, Wien, 28th March – 4th April 2006.

European Council, AC *Report on Estonia*, ACFC/INF/OP/I (2002) 005.

European Council, Advisory Committee, *Opinion on Albania*, ACFC/INF/OP/I (2003) 004.

European Council, Advisory Committee, *Opinion on Armenia*, ACFC/INF/OP/I (2003) 001.

European Council, Advisory Committee, *Opinion on Romania*, ACFC/INF/OP/I (2002) 001.

European Council, Advisory Committee, *Opinion on Austria*, ACFC/INF/OP/I (2002) 009.

Kerfoot H., *The United Nations Conferences on the Standardization of Geographical Names ... Looking to the future, United Nations Group of Experts on Geographical Names*, Working Paper No. 55, Wien, 28th March – 4th April 2006.

UNGEGN, *Consistent Use of Place Names*, February 2001, http://www.un.org/depts/Cartographic/english/ungegn.pdf (5th April 2007).

United Nations Organization, *United Nations Group of Experts on Geographical Names – Consistent use of place names*, February 2001, http://www.un.org/depts/Cartographic/english/ungegn.pdf (5th April 2007).

Woehrling J.-M., *The European Charter for Regional or Minority Languages*, Strasbourg, 2006.

The legal regulation of toponomastics in Italian law and the specific situation in Trentino-Alto Adige/Südtirol

Valeria Piergigli

Summary

1. Toponomastics and protection of linguistic minorities in Italian law: an overall view

Toponomastics, a science concerned with collecting and studying the origin, history and meaning of proper names of public places or places open to the public, fulfils many aims. Besides the practical function of knowledge and identification of places or geographical objects, toponyms also have communicative and cultural functions as well as a symbolic function in identifying geographic places and their communities or populations. Since they maintain the relationship of people to the land, they should be protected against erosion and facile attempts to change them from the outside. The requisite of clarity and the guarantee of immutability of public names are simultaneously the premise and corollary of formal operations of identifying place names usually expressed in the official language of the State[1].

1 The aims, content and partitions of toponomastics are studied by linguists and glottologists. See, beside the paper by C.A. Mastrelli in this volume, C.A. Mastrelli (ed.), *Odonomastica, Atti del Convegno, Trento, 25 settembre 2002,* Trento, 2005; E. Vineis (ed.), *La toponomastica come fonte di conoscenza storica e linguistica. Atti del convegno della Società italiana di glottologia*, Pisa, 1980; G. B. Pellegrini, *Teoria ed esperienza nella ricerca toponomastica*, in *Toponomastica trentina. Atti del convegno, Trento 28–29 maggio 1981*, Trento, 1982; Idem,

The attribution of names to places – whether to identify regional or single geographic entities – and their variations are of special importance when the places to be named evoke communities specifically characterised by differentiating factors – such as language and culture – with respect to the rest of the national population or the local majority population. In this case maintenance or recovery of place names by local authorities not only fulfils descriptive functions, but also protects the differential features of minority communities, usually aware of their specificity and wishing to conserve their cultural heritage. In this perspective, guarantee of the use of minority languages in toponomastics is a possible manifestation of the statute of protection of minorities and falls in the framework of determinations by public administrations on the subject of language policy.

The compactness and cohesion of minority communities, their concentration in defined geographic areas, autochthony, population density and the will of members to conserve community spirit and their heritage of historical, linguistic and cultural values are the requisites generally used in the legal regulation of minority languages and communities, especially when – as is usually the case – the criterion of territoriality rather than personality is favoured. The use of the minority language in toponomastics is closely linked to identification of geographical areas: more than in other sectors, the territoriality principle for the protection of minority identity is therefore expressed, for reasons intrinsic to toponomastics, in the determination of place names. For this purpose, it is first necessary to define the concept of "territory" in which the minority language is spoken, and to perform a census and periodic verification of the number of speakers of the minority language in that territory, and/or to define the borders of reference geographic contexts by appropriate formal provisions. On this subject, the European Charter for Regional or Minority Languages (1992), adopted by the Council of Europe, defines the "territory" as the geographic area in which the regional or minority language is spoken by a sufficient number of persons to justify adoption of measures of protection and promotion envisaged by the

Toponomastica italiana, Milan, 1990; C. Marcato, *Dizionario dei nomi geografici italiani*, Turin, 1992; A. Malossini, *Dizionario di toponomastica. I nomi geografici italiani*, Milan, 1997; E. Casti, *L'ordine del mondo e la sua rappresentazione. Seriosi cartografica e autoreferenza*, Milan, 1998; L. Cassi, P. Marcaccini, *Toponomastica, beni culturali e ambientali. Gli indicatori geografici per un loro censimento*, Rome, 1998. In the legal literature, see for a general framework: V. Italia, *La denominazione nel diritto pubblico*, Milan, 1966; G. de Vergottini, *Profili giuridici della toponomastica nella provincia di Bolzano,* in *Diritto e società,* 4/1986, pp. 651–652; M. Pallottino, *Toponomastica*, in *Enciclopedia del diritto,* XLIV, Milan, 1992, p. 739 et seq.

Charter (art. 1b), among which appears the use or adoption of traditional toponyms (art. 10, para. 2g).

In Italian law there is no general, exhaustive, legal regulation of toponomastics and the criteria for attributing names to places. The question therefore comes under somewhat deficient state laws, often dating back to the Fascist period[2], or sectorial laws that have stratified over the years, as well as rules passed by regional and local authorities. Similar fragmentation is found in laws about maintenance or restoration of traditional toponomastics as a measure for protecting minority linguistic identities, historically residing in the territories of many regions.

In the Italian Constitution, besides art. 6, which defines the fundamental principle of protecting linguistic minorities, there is also the text of art. 116 amended in 2001 (constitutional law no. 3/2001), which added the German and French translations of the Italian denominations of Trentino-Alto Adige/Südtirol and Valle d'Aosta/Vallée d'Aoste, formally approving the historical and linguistic features that earned those regions special autonomy when the Italian Republic was established[3]. Postponing analysis of the special statute of Trentino-Alto Adige/Südtirol[4], here it is worth recalling law no. 302/1997, among the state sources on protection of minorities (also) through toponomastics, which enacted the 1995 Framework Convention for the Protection of National Minorities[5]: art. 11, para. 3 encourages the Parties, in the ambit of their respective legal systems, and if appropriate in agreement with other States, to use the minority language in public local and topographic denominations under certain conditions (demographically substantial minority communities, established in a given geographic area, and sufficient demand). On the other hand, the Charter for Regional or

2 See Royal Decree 5th March 1911, instituting the "*Reale commissione per la revisione toponomastica della Carta d'Italia*" and law no. 68/1960 on the official cartography of the State, as well as Royal Decree no. 800/1923 about which see *infra* in this paper.

3 According to the Constitution, in Italy there are regions with ordinary statute and ordinary autonomy (art. 131) and regions with special statute and special autonomy (art. 116). The institution of the latter is mainly based on historical, linguistic, geographical peculiarities or economic reasons (Trentino-Alto Adige/Südtirol, Valle d'Aosta/Vallée d'Aoste, Sicily, Sardinia, Friuli-Venezia Giulia). Only within the special region Trentino-Alto Adige/Südtirol, besides the regional council, the provincial councils of Trento and Bolzano are granted legislative power (see *infra* § 3).

4 See § 2.

5 Like the European Charter for Regional or Minority Languages, the Framework Convention for the Protection of National Minorities, that came into force on 1st February 1998, is a multilateral convention drawn up by the Council of Europe. For the ratification *status* of both documents, see: http://conventions.coe.int.

Minority Languages[6] has not yet been ratified in Italy; as mentioned, among the many options of the contracting States, the Charter provides for use or adoption of traditional and correct forms of toponomastics in the regional or minority languages, together with the denomination in the official language of the State.

The state law for the protection of historical linguistic minorities (law no. 482/1999), which after a long and stormy procedure finally actuated art. 6 of the Constitution[7] in a general way, causing among other things erasure of the consolidated distinction between "recognized" and "non recognized" linguistic minorities, does not depend for operation of the protection measures envisaged – including restoration of local toponomastics – on periodic or other census of the percentage of speakers of the minority language and is based simply on the geographical fact. Municipal councils can decide to adopt toponyms in line with local traditions (art. 10 law no. 482/1999)[8] in addition to official toponyms, by defining the geographical areas of reference, as indicated by the law, which coincide with territorial and submunicipal areas. In a similar way, state law no. 38/2001 protecting Slovenian linguistic minorities in Friuli-Venezia Giulia envisages identification of municipalities or hamlets thereof, localities and bodies in which the Slovenian language is provided in addition to Italian for the purposes of toponomastic indications (art. 10)[9]. In addition, municipalities are

---

6 After signing the Charter on 27th June 2000, the bill of ratification and enactment was approved by Parliament and transmitted to the Senate in October 2003, where the procedure was interrupted (see *Atti Senato* no. 2545).

7 After stating that the official language of the Republic is Italian (art. 1), law no. 482/1999 stipulates in art. 2 that "... the Republic protects the languages and culture of the Albanian, Catalan, Germanic, Greek, Slovenian and Croatian populations and of those speaking French, French-Provencal, Friulan, Ladin, Occitan and Sard".

8 According to art. 3 of the law, delimitation of areas in which to apply the protection measures must be deliberated by interested provincial councils in response to request by a percentage of the local population (even not belonging to a minority language group) or a minority of the municipal council, or (in the absence of the above conditions) on the basis of the favourable outcome of consultation with the resident population (see also art. 1 decree of President of the Republic no. 345/2001 enacting law no. 482/1999). On the procedure and content of law no. 482/1999, see: S. Bartole, *Le norme per la tutela delle minoranze linguistiche storiche,* in *Le Regioni,* 6/1999, p. 1063 et seq.; E. Palici di Suni, *La legge italiana sulla tutela delle minoranze linguistiche storiche nel quadro* europeo, in *Diritto pubblico comparato ed europeo*, 1/2000, p. 101 et seq.; V. Piergigli, *La legge 15 dicembre 1999, n. 482 («Norme in materia di tutela delle minoranze linguistiche storiche») ovvero dall'agnosticismo al riconoscimento*, in *Rassegna parlamentare*, 3/2000, p. 623 et seq.; E. Malfatti, *La legge di tutela delle minoranze linguistiche: le prospettive e i problemi ancora aperti,* in *Rivista di diritto costituzionale*, 2001, p. 109 et seq.

9 Identification is performed by decree of the president of the regional government on the basis of a proposal of the joint institutional committee for problems of the Slovenian minority (art. 3) after hearing the bodies involved.

responsible for the denomination of towns and villages (art. 15, para. 4, legislative decree no. 267/2000, replacing art. 16, para. 2, decree of President of the Republic no. 616/1977).

Besides the state sources mentioned, various regional laws and local statutes reveal increasing attention towards protection and promotion of minority languages and their respective historical communities through regard for and recovery of traditional toponomastics, sometimes even instituting special bodies for technical and scientific support[10].

Once toponyms have been identified and reconstructed with the help of historians, geographers, linguists and oral and documentary sources, the most problematical profiles in the general provisions of laws protecting linguistic minorities, not only from the legal viewpoint, concern the choice of the most appropriate criterion to make the denominations thus acquired visible and the manner in which to transcribe them. Since a toponym cannot be divorced from the linguistic sign that represents it, transcription of place names assumes the existence of an idiom with alphabet and graphic rules, irrespective of whether we are dealing with the official language of the State or an unofficial regional or minority language. However, the language in which toponyms must be expressed may not be supported by writing, but handed down in dialect or only orally: in such situations it is not at all clear how toponyms should be codified. Besides, sometimes a minority idiom – especially if handed down orally or not supported by a kin-State beyond national borders – may occur in a plurality of linguistic variants within a given region or different regions of the same State. In such cases, before any public use of the idiom, an operation of linguistic normalization is necessary to identify, with the help of linguists and experts, a common or unified language[11].

---

10 Regarding regional legislative production, see articles 3 and 4 Piedmont law no. 11/2009; art. 1 Basilicata law no. 40/1998; art. 4e) Molise law no. 15/1997; art. 2 Friuli-Venezia Giulia law no. 15/1996 and art. 11 Friuli-Venezia Giulia law no. 29/2007 (the latter, which introduced the faculty of single-language toponomastics in Friulan, was declared not consistent with the Constitution by the Constitutional Court with judgment no. 159/2009, together with other provisions of the same regional law); art. 2 Veneto law no. 73/1994 and art. 9 Veneto law no. 8/2007; art. 1 Valle d'Aosta law no. 61/1976 and art. 3, para. 2a Valle d'Aosta law no. 47/1998; art. 24 Sardinia law no. 26/1997; art. 10 Trento Province law no. 18/1987, art. 2 Trento Province law no. 16/1987 and art. 19 et seq. Trento Province law no. 6/2008.

11 For example, in Italy, in order to develop the Friulan language "as a linguistic code suitable for all situations of modern life" (art. 10, para. 1b regional law 15/1996), the region Friuli-Venezia Giulia has the task of determining the official way to write Friulan and of promoting it (art. 13). Similarly, the Sardinian legislator makes the regional executive responsible for census of the linguistic repertoire of Sards, according to a project concerned with determining and making databases of the lexicons of the various communities and publishing the results of the

When the laws defining the determination of place names in areas with more than one language opt for combined use of the state and the minority languages, instead of a single language[12], there is the problem of deciding the typographic characters to use to express toponyms in the minority language. The writing of names in the state and the minority languages may be differentiated by using upper-and lower-case letters or large and small letters, with or without spaces; the importance of the denomination in the state language may be highlighted by placing it before the name in the minority language, or the toponym in the local idiom may be placed in brackets[13] or after a comma, followed by the name in the official language; the script or signs used may be different or of different colours[14] or it may be decided that the letters have to be of the same size for both denominations[15].

---

research, with the aim of producing general dictionaries of Sard and a linguistic atlas of Sardinia (art. 10, regional law 26/1997). For these laws see also footnote 10.

12 Especially in multilingual areas, toponyms may be expressed only in the official language of the State, or if preferred, only in the regional or minority language, as in Italy in the Ladin area of Fassa in Trento Province (art. 14 provincial law no. 16/1987, see § 3) and in Valle d'Aosta where application of so-called total or integral bilingualism accepted by the special statute, and reasons to do with the historical tradition of the area, have always enabled place names to be maintained in French alone without need for translation, except for the capital (*Aosta-Aoste*), despite attempts at Italianization during the Fascist period (see the legislative Decree Lieutenant of the Realm no. 545/1945 according to which the Valley council was to restore "place names suppressed or modified by the past regime" (art. 19) to their original form and law no. 61/1976 with which the region modified certain names of municipalities to bring them into line with more widely used historical names). The Valle d'Aosta region, where French is on an equal footing with Italian (art. 38 statute), has primary legislative power for "toponomastics" (art. 2v statute) and the power to legislate about the institution of new municipalities and modification of their borders and names, subject to consultation with the populations concerned (art. 42 statute), in line with the provisions of art. 133, para. 2 of the Constitution for ordinary regions. On the toponomastic rules in Valle d'Aosta, see: R. Barbagallo, *Caratteri e vicende della toponomastica in Valle d'Aosta,* in *Diritto e società*, 2/1989, p. 361 et seq.

13 On this subject, Royal Decree no. 800/1923 (*Determinazione della lezione ufficiale dei nomi dei comuni e di altre località dei territori annessi*) expressly kept in force by legislative decree no. 179/2009 (see footnote 49), establishes the possibility of authorizing the administrative authority to use a language different from the official language of the State for public signs, and stipulates that "the added name … must appear in second place, in brackets, and must not be written in characters more striking than those of the name in Italian" (art. 3).

14 See for example I. U. Libarona, *Apuntes juridicos sobre el paesaje linguìstico en euskal herrìa*, in *Revista de Llengua i Dret*, 1999, p. 149.

15 … as prescribed, for example in art. 1, para. 10 of Friuli-Venezia Giulia law no. 13/2000, in art. 9 of decree of President of the Republic no. 345/2001 (see footnote 8) and in art. 10 of the Croatian law of May 2000 on the use of the languages and writing of national minorities. If no official toponym exists, it is not excluded (in the case of bilingual indication) that the name in

The European Charter for Regional or Minority Languages and the Framework Convention for the Protection of National Minorities both envisage combined use of the state and minority languages for geographic names; more precisely, the intention of art. 11, para. 3 of the Framework Convention is not to introduce official recognition of local names in minority languages or to oblige national authorities to use the minority idiom only[16].

In Italian state and regional regulations, at least with regard to regions with ordinary statutes, the criterion of bilingualism is largely recognized in the interests of linguistic minorities in various public ambits[17] and the additional character of local toponyms are underlined with respect to those expressed in Italian. Thus, traditional names may be "added" or "placed beside" those expressed in Italian, or the place may be indicated "also" in the minority idiom, as envisaged by the municipal statutes and regulations as well as the road code[18], ensuring "graphic equality" of the name indicated in Italian and in the minority language[19].

---

the minority language precede instead of following that in the state language; see art. 2 of the order of the Spanish Ministry for Development of 28th December 1999 regarding proper names to be written on vertical motorway signs, according to which, in the absence of an official toponym, the name is written in the co-official languages of Spain, first in the language of the autonomous community and then in Castilian.

The UNGEGN (*United Nations Group of Experts on Geographical Names*), a specialized body of the United Nations to which Italy belongs, has long set out the criteria for the determination and writing of geographical names, also with regard to multilingual areas: on this subject, see Recommendation D on the standardization of geographical names in plurilingual regions (1967) and more recently the *Linee guida per la normalizzazione dei nomi geografici ad uso degli editori di cartografia ed altri editori* (2004), published by the Istituto Geografico Militare (www. igmi.org). To avoid arbitrary or imaginative determinations of toponyms and to preserve the historic and cultural value of the places to be named, these Guidelines suggest considering the historical background, local usage and, in the case of plurilingual toponyms, the respective manner of writing in the various languages. For more details, see P. Hilpold, *Topographic names and international law,* in this volume.

16 For these arguments, especially the content of art. 11, para. 3 of the Framework Convention, see Explanatory Report § 70 and the observations of F. de Varennes, *Commentary to Art. 11 of the FCNM*, in M. Weller (ed.), *The Rights of Minorities in Europe*, Oxford, 2005, p. 349.

17 On the bilingualism adopted by law no. 482/1999, according to the international guide-lines, see E. Palici di Suni, *Unitarietà della Repubblica e gruppi identitari: il caso delle minoranze linguistiche*, in S. Labriola (ed.), *Valori e principi del regime repubblicano, 1. Sovranità e democrazia*, tome II, Bari, 2006, pp. 662–663.

18 The current Italian road code gives local administrations the faculty of using "regional languages or local idioms of the area, in addition to the denomination in Italian, in signs indicating the border of a municipality" (art. 37, para. 2–*bis*, legislative decree no. 285/1992, added by art. 1 of conversion law no. 214/2003, amending law-decree no. 151/2003).

19 Art. 9 decree of President of the Republic no. 345/2001 (see footnote 8).

In practice, instead of promoting recovery of traditional place names and protection of minority communities, in certain regional contexts the scanty legislative indications contribute to interethnic tension. This is often due to omissions and failures of local legislators that enable disputable adaptations and translations, or even imaginative onomaturgy, in identifying and transcribing the place names.

2. Toponomastics and linguistic groups in Trentino-Alto Adige/Südtirol: from Italianization of the Fascist period to recognition of bi-tri-lingualism. Statutory principles and implementation

The legislation on toponomastics in Trentino-Alto Adige/Südtirol was influenced by historical events from the end of the World War I and laws passed during the Fascist regime. After Southern Tyrol – a traditionally German linguistic area – was annexed to Italy as Alto Adige, the advent of Fascism brought with it a programme aimed at eliminating German from schools and the municipal council of Bolzano and promoting Italianization of proper names, surnames, titles of nobility and translation of all local German and Ladin toponomastics into Italian. Royal Decree no. 800/1923[20], converted into law no. 473/1925, introduced Italian toponomastics, modifying the names of municipalities and places in the annexed territory and authorizing the Ministry for Internal Affairs to publish the definitive list of new names. With the ministerial decree of 10th July 1940, the official nature of the denominations contained in the third edition of the "*Prontuario dei nomi locali dell'Alto Adige*", published by the Royal Italian Geographical Society was recognized[21]. The subsequent German occupation (Sept. 1943–May 1945) led to effective reintroduction of German names, without eliminating the Italian toponomastics: indeed, ordinances dated 17th and 27th September 1943 gave councils the faculty to use bilingual names on signs indicating the edges of towns.

After the World War II, the Trentino-Alto Adige region was conceded special autonomy based on the Treaty of Paris (1946) (the so-called De Gasperi-Gruber

20 See footnote 13.

21 The cited legislation was based on work by Ettore Tolomei in the years 1906–1916 and on results of a commission nominated in 1921 by the Giolitti government. The Italianization of place names, including those of villages and non urban localities, had consisted in translation of existing names, including graphic and phonetic adaptations, and in the introduction of new names in Italian.

Agreement)[22], which enacted the principle of equal rights for Italian- and German-speaking citizens living in the Province of Bolzano and bilingual municipalities in the Province of Trento. In order to protect the ethnic character and the cultural and economic development of the German population, the Treaty stipulated among other things the use of "bilingual topographic nomenclature".

The first and second statutes of regional autonomy incorporated these provisions. In particular, the statute of 1948 made the Italian language official (art. 84), granted regional law the faculty of instituting new municipalities and modifying their borders and names (art. 7), gave the provinces primary legislative power on the subject of toponomastics[23], without modifying compulsory bilingualism in Bolzano Province (art. 11), stated that in said Province the public administration "had also to use German toponomastics for German-speaking citizens if the provincial law ascertained its existence and approved its diction" (art. 86), and finally imposed respect of the place names, culture and traditions of the Ladin population by provinces and municipalities (art. 87, para. 2).

The new statute of 1972 made the German and Italian languages equivalent in the region, subject to conditions and exceptions in articles 99 and 100, last paragraph, due to the fact that Italian is the official language of the State; it expressly included "protection of local linguistic minorities" among the national interests that the regional legislator is obliged to observe in exercising legislative power (art. 4); in line with the principle of linguistic separatism, it envisaged separate use of German and Italian in public sectors, except in cases specified by state rules for implementing the regional statute (so-called *norme di attuazione*)[24]

22 This agreement was Annex IV of the Peace Treaty between Italy and the allied and associated powers, signed in Paris on 10th February 1947. The Alto Adige question kept the Italian and Austrian Governments busy for nearly half a century and involved the De Gasperi-Gruber (1946) and Moro-Waldheim (1969) agreements, culminating in the drawing up of a special statute (constitutional law no. 5/1948) and its revision (the decree of President of the Republic no. 670/1972) that included commitments agreed by the two countries. Implementation of these measures by legislative and administrative acts officially sealed with the disclaimer by the Austrian authorities (1992), concluded the deal for the German-speaking community.

23 The so-called primary or exclusive legislative power, which is recognized only to regions with special statutes and to the Provinces of Trento and Bolzano, consists in the faculty of the regional/provincial bodies to pass laws without having to observe any state laws on the listed subjects but only respecting the Constitution and other limits established by the respective regional statutes.

24 With reference to regions having special statutes, the so-called *norme di attuazione* are state rules for implementing the regional statute; they consist in legislative decrees enacted by President of the Republic, which contain provisions aimed at implementing the regional statute and transferring administrative functions and personnel from the State to the region. The so-

(art. 100, para. 4), in order to favour the conservation of the minority cultural identity and avoid phenomena of assimilation. The said principle was explicitly derogated on the subject of toponomastics, where the provisions of the previous statute were confirmed: thus art. 8 no. 2 confirms provincial legislative competence and compulsory bilingualism in Bolzano Province, art. 7 maintains the competence of regional law for instituting new municipalities and modifying their borders and names, except those expressly listed in art. 3, which can only be modified by constitutional law[25], art. 101 is identical to the previous art. 86 and art. 102 confirms the right of Ladin populations (in both provinces) to uphold local toponomastics, among other things. The latter provision was subsequently modified to include Mocheno and Cimbrian populations as well as Ladins, in the municipalities expressly indicated in Trento Province as having the right to protection of local toponomastics and of their respective traditions[26].

In questions assigned to the competence of regions and provinces, including toponomastic determinations, state laws continue to apply until otherwise provided for by regional and provincial laws (art. 105)[27].

As far as statutory implementation through the so-called *norme di attuazione* is concerned, the decree of President of the Republic no. 574/1951 recognized the faculty to use local toponomastics in the Ladin valleys, in Ladin, Italian and German, thus permitting trilingual toponomastics there (art. 73); the decree of President of the Republic no. 526/1987, concerned with extending certain provisions contained in the decree of President of the Republic no. 616/1977 to autonomous regions and provinces, explicitly granted administrative functions proper to Italian municipalities in general to those in the Provinces of Trento and

called *norme di attuazione* are discussed below as far as they concern toponomastics in Trentino-Alto Adige/Südtirol.

25 The fact that art. 3 of the statute, like the previous statute, mentions certain municipalities and a village previously belonging to the Province of Trento that are incorporated into the Province of Bolzano, should be an impediment to any change in denomination by a source of law subordinate to the special statute, such as a regional law. On this subject, see G.. de Vergottini, *Profili giuridici*, *cit.*, pp. 655–656.

26 See art. 102 of the statute as modified by art. 4 of constitutional law no. 2/2001 (*Disposizioni concernenti l'elezione diretta dei presidenti delle Regioni a Statuto speciale e delle Province autonome di Trento e di Bolzano*).

27 As observed by E. Reggio D'Aci, *La regione Trentino-Alto Adige*, Milan, 1994, pp. 292–293, the expression "differently disposed" used in art. 105 should be understood as meaning "autonomously disposed", with the consequence that if the regional or provincial body exercises its legislative competence, in contrast or otherwise with state laws on the subject, promulgation of a regional or provincial law "acts as a resolutive condition for state laws in the sector". In the same sense, see also S. Bartole, *Regione Trentino-Alto Adige*, in *Enciclopedia giuridica*, XXVI, Rome, 1991, p. 3, that reports judgments no. 269/1974 and no. 28/1976 of the Constitutional Court.

Bolzano, provided those functions do not pertain to the responsibilities of the Region Trentino-Alto Adige or the autonomous provinces (art. 15); the decree of President of the Republic no. 574/1988 and subsequent amendments confirmed the equivalence of German and Italian in the region (art. 1) and combined use of both for acts concerning citizens in general, among other things (art. 4, para. 1)[28]. Names of places or buildings of public importance and road signs can be in this category[29].

Above-mentioned law no. 482/1999 confirmed the laws of protection in force in the Provinces of Trento and Bolzano in the various public sectors, deferring application of any more favourable measures envisaged by the law itself, with regard to Germanic populations and speakers of Ladin, to the so-called *norme di attuazione* (art. 18)[30].

3. Regional and provincial legislation: partial fulfilment and attempts to regulate between conflicting interpretations and conservation of the *status quo*

Before examining the realization of the statutory provisions locally, it is necessary to clarify the relation between regional and provincial laws in Trentino-Alto Adige/Südtirol, having the competence to institute new municipalities and modify their borders and names after consultation with the populations involved (art. 7 that defers to the regional law) and to regulate toponomastics subject to respect of bilingual denominations in Bolzano Province (art. 8, no. 2 that defers to the provincial law), respectively.

---

28 On compulsory joint use of Italian and German in acts regarding citizens in general, and especially in those indicating place names, the Constitutional Court – before adoption of the decree of President of the Republic no. 574/1988 – declared a law of the Province of Bolzano inconsistent with the Constitution. The provincial law had been challenged by the Government on the grounds that it did not have the Italian term "*maso avito*" before the German term "*Erbhof*" and because in requiring a public certificate for *masi aviti*, it admitted that it was provided on request in single-language form (Italian or German), violating compulsory joint use of both languages for legal acts and administrative certificates (judgment no. 188/1987). For a comment on the decision, critical with regard to the compulsory bilingual drafting of administrative certificates regarding *masi aviti*, mentioned by the Court, see P. Carrozza, *L'uso «disgiunto» della lingua tedesca al vaglio della Corte*, in *Le Regioni*, 6/1987, p. 1480 et seq.

29 See the decision of the Regional Court of administrative law, Province of Bolzano, no. 537/2002, *cit. infra* footnote 57.

30 In this sense, for example, art. 6 of legislative decree no. 261/2001 provides for application of the measures of law no. 482/1999 to the Province of Trento, as they are more favourable than the laws in force in that province.

It should first be clear that art. 7 of the statute is intended to refer to *all* municipalities. The literal interpretation of the provision is unacceptable: it would seem to limit regional competence to *newly instituted municipalities* and would subtract regulation of borders and names of *existing municipalities* from any other law. The paradoxical consequence would be that these ambits could not be modified because, according to this literal interpretation, regional law could not intervene as stipulated in art. 7 and there would be no other law competent to regulate borders and municipal names together.

Secondly, the apparent diversity of the matters governed by the two provisions in question should not give rise to doubts: indeed, the "denominations" of municipalities referred to in art. 7 fall in the broader sector of "toponomastics" mentioned in the subsequent art. 8, no. 2. Thus, a correct reading of the combined provisions should be in the sense of recognizing general competence of provincial law to govern local toponomastics, that is, *all place names in provincial territory*, except names of municipalities which would come under regional law[31]. In support of this reasoning, the Constitutional Court ruled that "toponomastics" include the "denomination of any type of place" and that "the determination of toponyms for villages must remain precluded to the Region Trentino-Alto Adige, because it has been incorporated in the general powers of the Provinces, which ... must extend to every type of place name, except that of municipalities"[32]. This judgment was made when the first statute of autonomy was in force, the relevant provisions of which were confirmed in the 1972 version.

This established, it remains to define whether regional law must be limited to the institution, denomination and variation of *single municipalities in specific cases*, or whether it can extend to regulation of *all* of municipal toponomastics. Under the first profile, numerous regional laws have been adopted in compliance

---

31 On the interpretation of arts. 7 and 8 of the regional statute, see the opinion of the District Attorney of the State of Trento of 21st April 2000, solicited by the council of the autonomous region regarding the bill of the council on "*Individuazione dei toponomi comunali nella Provincia autonoma di Bolzano – Proposta relativa alla toponomastica tesa a salvaguardare gli interessi di tutti e tre i gruppi linguistici del Sudtirolo*" (bill no. 5/1999). Under legal doctrine, see G. de Vergottini, *Profili giuridici*, *cit.*, p. 656; F. Bertoldi, *L'ordinamento costituzionale del Trentino-Alto Adige,* Milan, 1954, p. 187 et seq.; P. Cesareo, *L'autonomia della Regione Trentino-Alto Adige e delle province di Trento e Bolzano*, Milan, 1957, p. 193 and with different arguments, E. Reggio D'Aci, *La Regione Trentino-Alto Adige, cit.*, p. 108 et seq. and P. Hilpold, *La regolamentazione della toponomastica in Trentino-Alto Adige*, in J. Marko, S. Ortino, F. Palermo (eds.), *L'ordinamento speciale della provincia autonoma di Bolzano,* Padova, 2001, pp. 804–805.

32 Constitutional Court, judgment no. 28/1962, in *Giurisprudenza costituzionale*, 1964, p. 235 et seq.

with art. 7 of the statute, but there have been signs that extension of the subject to regional regulation could be problematical. On this point, two identical bills were presented by regional council in 1999 (no. 5/1999) and 2006 (no. 29/2006). On presentation of the first, the District Attorney of the State of Trento was consulted and expressed perplexity, but ruled in favour of regional initiative, considering admissible the faculty of the region to dictate general rules for municipal toponyms[33]. With regard to content, both bills, besides providing for abrogation of the state law (Royal Decree no. 800/1923) and the institution of a consultative commission for toponomastics in the Province of Bolzano, introduced the threshold of 20% for language groups (Italian, German, Ladin) in the municipality, according to the results of the last census, as a requisite for official denomination of municipalities in the respective languages. The percentage criterion of the language groups also determined the order in which the toponyms were to appear in road signs and indications of geographic localities.

Even admitting the competence of regional law to regulate all of municipal toponomastics, the bills in question contradict the fundamental principle that topographic indications in the Province of Bolzano must always be bilingual, irrespective of the demographic percentage of the language group[34]. Any departure from this would be failure to observe an international obligation and violation of an explicit statutory provision having the rank of constitutional law[35]. In fact, in these bills, not only is the stipulation of a minimum percentage of minority language speakers a condition for recognition of the right to use

33 In the opinion mentioned in footnote 31, the District Attorney of Trento held that since the bill in question "refers to the regulation of municipal names only, it does not *per se* appear outside regional competence, as defined by art. 7 of the statute". In the opposite sense, see P. Hilpold, *La regolamentazione della toponomastica, cit.*, p. 805, according to whom modification of the name of a single municipality in a specific situation remains of regional competence, whereas regulation of toponomastics is entirely of provincial competence; therefore, according to Hilpold, "modification of the name of a municipality, though occurring under regional law, must be compatible with the general order of toponomastics dictated by the Province".

34 This was the opinion of the District Attorney of Trento who among other things found that bill no. 5/1999 omitted the obligation, envisaged by the statute of autonomy, to hear the populations involved. He also found interference of the attributions of the toponomastics commission (in the process of being established) with the legal competence of the Province of Bolzano, lack of clarification of the legal value of the annex containing the list of municipal toponyms, and incompetence of a regional law to abrogate a state law such as Royal Decree no. 800/1923, according to the mechanism defined in art. 105 of the statute.

35 As a consequence of the provisions of the two regional bills, the use of German toponomastics would have been reintroduced in 108 municipalities of Südtirol in which the German language group constitutes more than 20% of the municipal population, while in 16 municipalities the Italian denomination would also have been maintained, since the Italian language group was above the indicated threshold.

bilingual toponyms, but consequently, failure to reach that percentage means official indication of the name of the municipality in one language only.

With regard to provincial initiatives, the activism of the Trentino legislator contrasts with the attempts at regulation of the Province of Bolzano, which has not yet adopted a law enacting the principle of bilingualism (art. 8, no. 2) or a law ascertaining the existence and approving the diction of the German names in order to legitimate their use by public administrations in provincial territory (art. 101).

The Province of Trento, where Ladin, Mocheno and Cimbrian communities live, has exploited the primary legislative competence assigned to it by art. 8, no. 2 of the statute since 1952 to dictate a general law on toponomastics[36] and then to compile the "*Dizionario toponomastico trentino*", which combines cultural aims with practical ones, offering municipalities in the province an instrument for correct denomination[37]. Besides official denominations attributed on the basis of provisions in force, the faculty of municipal administrations to add traditionally used local toponyms to the above denominations was subsequently envisaged[38]. Those provisions were abrogated and replaced by provincial law no. 16/1987 (*Disciplina della toponomastica*), which confirmed the aims and subject matter of the *Dizionario toponomastico trentino* and dedicated all of Item III to regulation of Ladin toponomastics in the Province of Trento, envisaging the possibility of expressing names of villages, roads, squares and public buildings in the Fassa area in Ladin alone. This rule was later modified to extend its application to the Mocheno and Cimbrian populations in the province, and in particular, joint use of names in Ladin, Mocheno or Cimbrian and Italian was provided for according to the identifications contained in the repertoire of toponyms, as well as use of solely Mocheno or Cimbrian denominations for localities in the municipalities of Fierozzo, Frassilongo, Palù del Fersina and Luserna (art. 17, prov. law no. 7/2004). Provincial law no. 6/2008 (*Norme di tutela e promozione delle minoranze linguistiche locali*) was passed more recently. With the intent of unifying and rendering organic the rules of the three linguistic communities, it again had articles on toponomastics. After hearing the respective toponomastic commission, the Province of Trento approves and updates the repertoire of toponyms for each linguistic minority "that includes locality names in the minority language and the corresponding name in another language, widely spoken at national or international level" (art. 19, para. 3); the repertoires are published in the official bulletin of the region and are part of the

36 Prov. law no. 2/1952.

37 Prov. law no. 2/1980.

38 Prov. law no. 43/1983.

Dizionario toponomastico trentino. Except for the names of municipalities (art. 3)[39] and road signs in minority areas, that must be written with graphic equality in the minority language and Italian, *preferential use of the minority language alone* is confirmed for indications and signs of localities and toponyms of the Ladin, Mocheno and Cimbrian communities (art. 19, paras. 6 and 7). Depending on the community, approval of village names and municipal deliberations on the names of roads, squares and public buildings pertains to the *Comun general de Fascia*[40] or the provincial executive, after hearing the respective toponomastic commissions.

As mentioned, the toponomastics situation in the Province of Bolzano is completely different. Apart from general laws on urban toponomastics[41], here, articles 8, no. 2, and 101 of the statute have not yet been actuated, although bills, programmes, coalition agreements and hearings of experts have not been lacking in the various terms of office and have kept the question alive within Government and among the local population. The question is only apparently exclusively cultural: it actually has considerable political and social impact. In the province, besides Ladins, Italians constitute a minority group in the larger German-speaking community. However, since its original drafting, the regional statute has preferred the expression "linguistic groups" to "linguistic minorities", recognizing limited legal *status* to the latter[42], except where explicit reference is made to "Ladin populations" or "German-speaking citizens". This choice of the statute framer, confirmed in bi-national countries such as Belgium and Canada (uninclined to use the term "linguistic minorities"), intended to underline an equality of the Italian- and German-speaking communities, and, in particular, to pursue the aim of ensuring special protection to the German component of the population of Alto Adige, by applying international rules, which arose from well-known historical events.

---

39 Art. 3 of prov. law no. 6/2008 gives the denomination in Italian and the respective minority languages of historical municipalities of the Ladin, Mocheno and Cimbrian communities, according to what had already been stipulated first by the legislative decree no. 321/1997, and later by the prov. law no. 4/1999.

40 The Province's administrative functions regarding, among other things, toponomastics in municipal territory where the Ladin community is established, are transferred to the *Comun general de Fascia* (art. 27 prov. law no. 6/2008 and art. 19 prov. law no. 3/2006).

41 See prov. law no. 5/1958, abrogated by prov. law no. 26/1975, in turn variously supplemented and modified.

42 See in this sense the provisions of arts. 56 and 92 of the statute and under legal doctrine, A. Pizzorusso, *Verso il riconoscimento della soggettività delle comunità etnico-linguistiche?*, in *Studi in memoria di C. Furno*, Milan, 1973, p. 739 et seq.

The provincial bills, variously promoted by majority and opposition parties[43] and presented uninterruptedly since the end of the 1980s, were particularly concerned with regulating confirmation of the existence and the diction of toponymns in German and Ladin, concentrating on: abrogation or maintenance of the state laws in force, except for any modifications to be deliberated through provincial law and as proposed by special commissions of experts; the institution of commissions or provincial consulting bodies for toponomastics to establish scientific and methodological criteria for toponomastic research and determination of toponyms or on use of the consulting body for ethnography and toponomastics as stated by provincial law no. 26/1975 referring to United Nations recommendations; and finally, repartition of attributions on the subject between the province and the municipalities. The *Südtiroler Volkspartei* (*SVP*) insists on the latter profile, proposing distinction between macro- and micro-toponomastics: the former including "the set of names of towns and all geographical names of water courses and mountains in the Province of Bolzano", the latter referring to "names of villages, sparse settlements and centres, land, brooks and the like ..." (art. 1, paras. 5 and 6, respectively, of prov. law no. 92/1991 and prov. bill no. 183/1992)[44]. Macrotoponomastics should be regulated by the province, unlike microtoponomastics. For the latter, delegated by the province, municipalities should decide autonomously whether to use mono-, bi- or tri-lingual denominations for geographical localities in their territory. This should overcome any possible controversial interpretation of the clause that stipulates bilingualism, since disagreement on the interpretation of that apparently clear clause has long impeded regulation of toponomastics in the Province of Bolzano. Indeed, according to most political representatives of the German population (especially the *SVP*) observation of the statutory obligation of bilingualism should not require double place names but only guarantee conservation of place names really existing in the Italian and German languages[45].

---

43 The most active political groups were the *Südtiroler Volkspartei* (*SVP*), *Union für Südtirol*, *Verdi* and *Alleanza Nazionale*.

44 Provincial bill no. 189/1992 (*Verdi*) refers to local microtoponomastics including the "official names of water courses and mountains in the Province of Bolzano, uninhabited places and land ..." (art. 4, para. 1). The so-called microtoponomastics actually ends up applying to most localities, the names of which are meant to be left to municipal councils, according to the bills mentioned.

45 The opposition parties and local press fear that delegation of microtoponomastics to municipal councils could lead to disappearance of the Italian names, since most of the municipalities in Bolzano Province are governed by the *SVP*.

To validate the proposal to officialise only toponyms expressed in German, an attempt was also made to recognize the German-speaking population of Alto Adige as "indigenous people" under the ILO Convention no. 169/1989 concerning indigenous and tribal peoples in independent countries and the then draft of the Declaration of Rights of Indigenous Peoples adopted in 1992. The latter guarantees, among other things, the right of such populations to protect "*... their own names of communities, places and persons*" (§10)[46].

Reference to the opportunity of considering the size of the different language groups appears in the bills, which reproposed a percentage criterion to choose the order in which scientifically confirmed bilingual or trilingual names should appear[47].

The council representatives of the former right-wing party *Alleanza Nazionale* always opposed any distinction between macro- and microtoponomastics: institution of two commissions of experts was suggested on the assumption that toponomastics must be considered a unitary category and that any attempt to

46 See the report accompanying provincial bill no. 75/1995 (*Union für Südtirol*). For a critical comment, see P. Hilpold, *La regolamentazione della toponomastica, cit.*, p. 806 et seq., which recalls that "indigenous peoples are ... those in a colonial context, who live in close contact with nature and intend to continue their existence in their original territory and according to their traditions and who do not seek more than partial integration in society through acquisition of the fruits of civilization" (p. 810), like the Sami in Scandinavia or the Indians of Canada. Moreover, the expression reported in the text was confirmed in the final version of the Declaration of rights of indigenous peoples, adopted by the General Assembly of the United Nations on 13th September 2007, according to which "*Indigenous peoples have the right to revitalize, use, develop and transmit to future generations their histories, languages, oral traditions, philosophies, writing systems and literatures, and to designate and retain their own names for communities, places and persons*" (art. 13, para. 1).

47 See art. 1, para. 8, prov. bill no. 183/1992 (*SVP*), art. 2, para. 2, prov. bill no. 57/2000 (*Verdi*), art. 2 prov. bill no. 143/2007 (proposed by the provincial council). Article 5 of prov. bill no. 43/2004 (*Union für Südtirol*) and art. 5 prov. bill no. 145/2007 (proposed by the provincial council), besides determining a minimum threshold of 20% for indications written in letters the same size for names of municipalities and minor places in Bolzano Province, listed the official plurilingual names of municipalities in the same Province (Appendix A), the official plurilingual names of villages and minor localities in the same Province (Appendix B) and the official plurilingual names of passes, valleys, mountains, water courses and lakes (Appendix C); the aim of the operation was to confirm the validity of the official names in use before the Royal Decrees of 1923–1940 came into force, for all localities not included in any of the three Appendices (arts. 2, 3 and 4 of both bills). See also provincial bills no. 159/2008 and no. 2/2008, both proposed by the provincial council. More recently, provincial bill no. 73/2010, presented by the provincial council, again proposed the percentage criterion for German, Italian and Ladin language groups in the respective municipal territories, according to the results of the last general census of the population, for the determination of the order to be followed in writing the toponyms, leaving unchanged the requirement that the names should have identical graphic importance (art. 2).

divide it amounted to violation of the statutory principles and criteria of the United Nations. The task of the commissions would be to ascertain toponyms in German and Ladin for approval under provincial law. The Province of Bolzano was also to have the faculty to impose penalties for violations of the law regarding application of Italian, German and Ladin place names (provincial bill no. 106/2006)[48].

Failure of the legislator of the Province of Bolzano to put pen to paper has maintained in force the law adopted in the Fascist period, that would cease to apply (art. 105 of the statute) when a provincial law on the subject is enacted[49].

4. Concluding remarks: the attitudes of States towards toponomastics, protection of linguistic minorities and the case of the Province of Bolzano

In general, comparative experience of minority protection does not reveal attitudes that could impede recovery of traditional place names, at least as far as laws are concerned. There is more diffidence when the positive measures invoked by members of minority communities include, for example, the guarantee of teaching of, or in, the minority language, or recognition of further and more onerous public uses of languages different from the official language of the State. The impression is that protection of minority languages through toponomastics is somehow underestimated and considered in a superficial manner by administrators, probably because it does not present any immediate risk for state homogeneity and territorial integrity. In other words, it seems that national authorities are not fully aware of the symbolic and highly identificative value of

48 Previously, the same council representatives suggested institution of a commission to ascertain the toponomastics of the Ladin populations and another commission for toponomastics of provincial competence. The second commission would propose (to the provincial council) modifications of the German toponyms ascertained and listed in the third edition of the above mentioned *Prontuario dei nomi locali dell'Alto Adige* published in 1935 by the Royal Italian Geographical Society (provincial bill no. 29/1999), maintenance of which was therefore provided for.

49 Against maintenance in force of the Royal Decree no. 800/1923 on the grounds of violation of provincial legislative competence, as defined in the special statute, and violation of art. 105 of the statute, the Province of Bolzano took the question of art. 1, paras. 1 and 2 of legislative decree no. 179/2009, to the Constitutional Court (case no. 23 of 22nd February 2010) that rejected the question because it was considered inadmissible (judgment no. 346/2010). As a consequence, the Constitutional Court simply confirmed the maintenance in force of the Royal Decree no. 800/1923, without entering upon the subject concerning the competences of the State and Province of Bolzano in the matter of toponomastics.

place names in minority languages for minority populations. This is confirmed by the generalized ratification of art. 10, para. 2g, on toponomastics of the Charter for Regional or Minority Languages by the signatory States; it is also confirmed by the reservations implied by non ratification of the various options, regarding the right to use the regional or minority language in administrative relations, in the text of the same provision. Such reservations demonstrate a cautious attitude, certainly not open to minority situations, at least in sectors in which state authority seems more directly involved[50].

Toponyms end up being included among generic expressions of minority cultural heritage to protect, often considered equivalent folklore and costumes. This means that the guarantee of use of a minority language for place names is low in a hypothetical ranking of public uses of minority languages. This attitude is reflected in the relative lack of attention towards technical aspects and in the practical problems that often emerge in naming places in minority languages.

In the Trentino-Alto Adige/Südtirol region, governance of toponomastics acquires an unusual profile because of the ethnic composition of the population protected by the regional statute and the so-called *norme di attuazione*. It has different connotations due to the primary legislative power attributed to the two autonomous provinces and that recognized to the regional council for municipal toponomastics. The Trentino legislator did not hesitate to exercise that power, taking care to legislate on the toponomastics of the Ladin, Mocheno and Cimbrian populations, whereas the legislator of the Province of Bolzano has not yet produced any exhaustive laws coherent with the provisions of the regional statute. The many fruitless attempts of the political forces so far show the difficulty of carrying out legislative reform, that in mixed-language areas requires tact due to the intimate connections it poses between linguistic groups, historical memory of places, and protection of the respective cultural heritage[51]. The different initiatives presented have only reignited discussion on aspects that should be indisputable, according to provisions of the regional statute enacting international obligations. As mentioned, the Treaty of Paris (1946) and the two

50 The Charter came into force on 1st March 1998 and determines that after accepting a minimum standard of protection (part II), signatory States can graduate their actions and choose, from among the alternatives proposed in part III and in the manner prescribed by arts. 2 and 3, those most appropriate for their specific environmental needs. More specifically, with reference to art. 10 that governs relationships with public administrations, art. 2, para. 2 stipulates that contracting States must ratify at least one option.

51 See periodic reports in the daily newspaper *Alto Adige* (http://altoadige.repubblica.it/). See also studies published by the *Centro Studi Atesini of Bolzano*, especially A. Mitolo, F. Bravi, *Aspetti politici e giuridici, storici e linguistici della toponomastica atesina,* 1984, and F. Bravi, *Toponomastica italiana nella provincia di Bolzano*, 1990.

versions of the regional statute approved compulsory bilingualism for place names in the Province of Bolzano, in derogation of the criterion of linguistic separatism passed in the region to protect linguistic groups. This obligation, explicitly approved for topographic indications, is also confirmed by art. 100 of the statute as enacted, and according to which public acts directed to an undifferentiated general population must be written both in Italian and German.

In the light of the above, the legal consequences should follow readily and be fairly linear. First of all, irrespective of reference to foreign experience often evoked by sustainers of German monolingualism for toponyms, there should be no doubt that the compulsory bilingualism approved by the statute cannot be modified by any internal source of law. Indeed, any derogation on the subject by state legislative decrees (the so-called *norme di attuazione*) or a provincial law would violate laws of constitutional rank, since the regional statute of autonomy was adopted by constitutional law.

Secondly, it is worth bearing in mind that the principle of equality of German and Italian in the region as well as the other protection measures, including bilingualism for toponomastics, were conceived by the Treaty of Paris and thus by the statutory legislator to protect the German language group, which is the majority in the Province of Bolzano but a minority in the region, not to protect the Italian language community[52]. Though a minority in the province, the Italian-speaking community is the major component of the population of the region and the State, where Italian is the official language, as now recognized expressly by art. 1 of law no. 482/1999[53]. This is confirmed by the fact that art. 1 of the Treaty attributes special protection to ethnic character and cultural and economic development – specifically and exclusively – of the German language group. Moreover, the text of art. 101 of the statute obliges public administrations in the Province of Bolzano to use also German toponomastics, after their existence has been ascertained as stipulated by provincial law. As a consequence, German toponyms are additional to, not substitutive of, Italian toponomastics, maintenance of which should not be in discussion, since intervention of the provincial legislator is required by the regional statute only to ascertain the existence and diction of the German toponyms. Thus, Italian toponyms cannot be removed according to the principle of bilingualism in art. 8, no. 2 of the statute, and their modification can be considered implicitly excluded, as contrary to art. 101.

---

52 For these observations, see G. de Vergottini, *Profili giuridici, cit.*, pp. 657–658.

53 In the course of the XVI legislature, for example, various constitutional bills have been presented, aimed at recognizing in the text of art. 9 or art. 12 of the Constitution the official character of the Italian language (see *Atti Camera* nos. 443, 730, 839, 2768 and 3148).

On the question of toponomastics in the Province of Bolzano, the state institutions have taken many positions and exerted pressures over the years: in 1997 the Parliament approved a decision that committed the Government, together with the Province of Bolzano, to promoting "any initiative useful to fully implement the provisions of the statute of autonomy on the subject of toponomastics", observing the statute "above all in its fundamental principle of bilingualism, expressed also in toponyms"[54] and the same year the Parliament asked the Government to clarify how it intended to proceed on the question of the request of the *SVP* to discuss regulation of toponomastics in the joint commission (the so-called *commission of six*) that provides consultation for the adoption of rules for implementing the statute[55]. With regard to the constitutional bills aimed at modifying the statute of autonomy of the regions, in the XV and XVI legislatures it was suggested, among other things, to review the provisions on toponomastics to ensure respect of bilingualism: in this sense, the bills proposed maintenance of existing Italian toponomastics, compulsory bilingualism for the new toponomastics (a function of the Province of Bolzano), bilingualism (and trilingualism in the Ladin valleys) for public signs giving precedence to the Italian names, and delegation to ordinary state law for penalties for non compliant administrations[56].

The lack of political agreement and the persistent non implementation of the statutory provisions by the provincial legislator are causing widespread discontent, especially among the Italian-speaking population that often witnesses the introduction of toponyms in German alone or imaginative translations into German of names originally expressed also in Italian, not only in out-of-the-way places, like forest roads and mountain tracks, but also in so-called hodonomastics (names of streets and public squares). So far, government warnings, issued to municipal councils not observing the principle of bilingualism, and complaints to the courts for violation of statutory obligations and laws have had little effect[57].

---

54 This was a resolution approved on 16th April 1997 by the First Permanent Commission of the Chamber of Deputies.

55 The interpellation was presented in session no. 208 of 10th June 1997.

56 Constitutional bill "*Modifiche allo statuto speciale per il Trentino-Alto Adige*" presented on 26th July 2006 (*Atti Camera* no. 1484) and similarly the constitutional bill presented on 14th May 2008 (*Atti Camera* no. 1043).

57 See the report on provincial bill no. 106/2006, at http://www2.landtag-bz.org/it/banche_dati/atti_politici/idap_elenco_trovati.asp.
With regard to the administrative cases, it is worth recalling the appeal to the Regional Court of Administrative Justice, Autonomous Section of Bolzano Province, presented in 2000 by several regional and provincial councillors against the Municipal council of Cortaccia and the Province of Bolzano, decided with decision no. 537/2002 (http:www//giustizia-

Bibliography

Barbagallo R., *Caratteri e vicende della toponomastica in Valle d'Aosta*, in *Diritto e società*, 2/1989.

Bartole S., Regione *Trentino-Alto Adige, in Enciclopedia giuridica Treccani*, XXVI, Rome, 1991.

Bartole S., *Le norme per la tutela delle minoranze linguistiche storiche*, in *Le Regioni*, 6/1999.

Bartole S., Olivetti Rason N., Pegoraro L. (eds.), *La tutela giuridica delle minoranze*, Padova, 1998.

Bertoldi F., *L'ordinamento costituzionale del Trentino-Alto Adige*, Milan, 1954.

Bravi F., *Toponomastica italiana nella provincia di Bolzano*, Bolzano, 1990.

Carrozza P., *L'uso «disgiunto» della lingua tedesca al vaglio della Corte*, in *Le Regioni*, 6/1987.

Cassi L., Marcaccini P., *Toponomastica, beni culturali e ambientali. Gli indicatori geografici per un loro censimento*, Rome, 1998.

---

amministrativa.it/). The applicants complained that the council had replaced bilingual road signs with signs in German alone. The judge agreed with the motives for the appeal and did not doubt that there was violation of the statute and decree of President of the Republic no. 574/1988, but dismissed the appeal for lack of active legitimacy, pointing out that the appeal should have been made by citizens resident in the municipality or by the majority of the Italian language group, according to art. 92 of the statute, or by the State that "is holder *ex lege* of qualified interest in legal challenge of administrative provisions considered to have been adopted in violation of art. 4 of decree of President of the Republic no. 574/1988 ...", which as is known, stipulates compulsory joint use of the Italian and German languages in acts addressed to citizens in general. Maintenance of the names written in German alone in the Municipality of Cortaccia was the effective result of the decision. A similar appeal was presented in 2001 by the hon. Gianfranco Fini (as vice president of the Council of Ministers and representing the State) and 500 other persons to the same court against the municipal council of Caldaro and the Province of Bolzano, because the council had deliberated a modification of the names of various streets and public squares, as well as villages, towns and localities in the municipality, introducing mostly names in German alone and consequently cancelling certain Italian names. The invitation of the government commissioner for the Province of Bolzano to the mayor of Caldaro to remove the illegal single-language signs and to replace them with bilingual ones had been in vain. In summer 2010, an inquiry was opened by the Prosecutor's Office to ascertain the subsistence of various offences in relation to the use of public finance to install signs in German alone on mountain paths. The defendant was the alpine association *Alpen Verein Südtirol*. A question was presented to Parliament (*Atti Camera* no. 5–02130, 18th November 2009) and was followed by signing of a memorandum of understanding between the state Government and the Province of Bolzano, to be advised by a joint commission of experts on the installation of bilingual or trilingual toponomastics on the mountain tracks (22nd September 2010).

Bronzetti G., *Le potestà legislative ed amministrative della regione Trentino-Alto Adige e delle province di Trento e Bolzano*, Trento, 1985.

Casti E., *L'ordine del mondo e la sua rappresentazione. Seriosi cartografica e autoreferenza*, Milan, 1998.

Cesareo P., *L'autonomia della Regione Trentino-Alto Adige e delle province di Trento e Bolzano*, Milan, 1957.

de Varennes F., *Commentary to Art. 11 of the FCNM*, in Weller M. (ed.), *The Rights of Minorities in Europe*, Oxford, 2005.

de Vergottini G., *Profili giuridici della toponomastica nella provincia di Bolzano*, in *Diritto e società*, 4/1986.

Di Michele A., Palermo F., Pallaver G., *1992: Fine di un conflitto. Dieci anni dalla chiusura della questione sudtirolese*, Bologna, 2003.

Hilpold P., *La regolamentazione della toponomastica in Trentino-Alto Adige*, in Marko J., Ortino S., Palermo F. (eds.*), L'ordinamento speciale della provincia autonoma di Bolzano*, Padova, 2001.

Italia V., La *denominazione nel diritto pubblico*, Milan, 1966.

Malfatti E., *La legge di tutela delle minoranze linguistiche: le prospettive e i problemi ancora aperti*, in *Rivista di diritto costituzionale*, 2001.

Malossini A., *Dizionario di toponomastica. I nomi geografici italiani*, Milan, 1997.

Mancini S., *Minoranze autoctone e Stato. Tra composizione dei conflitti e secessione*, Milan, 1996.

Mastrelli C. A. (ed.), *Odonomastica, Atti del Convegno, Trento, 25 settembre 2002*, Trento, 2005.

Mitolo A., Bravi F., *Aspetti politici e giuridici, storici e linguistici della toponomastica atesina*, Bolzano, 1984.

Palermo F., Woelk J., *Diritto costituzionale comparato dei gruppi e delle minoranze*, Padova, 2008.

Palici di Suni E., *La legge italiana sulla tutela delle minoranze linguistiche storiche nel quadro europeo*, in *Diritto pubblico comparato ed europeo*, 1/2000.

Palici di Suni E., *Intorno alle minoranze*, Turin, 2002.

Palici di Suni E., *Unitarietà della Repubblica e gruppi identitari: il caso delle minoranze linguistiche*, in Labriola S. (ed.), *Valori e principi del regime repubblicano, 1. Sovranità e democrazia*, tome II, Bari, 2006.

Pallottino M., *Toponomastica*, in *Enciclopedia del diritto*, XLIV, Milan, 1992.

Pellegrini G.B., *Teoria ed esperienza nella ricerca toponomastica*, in *Toponomastica trentina. Atti del convegno, Trento 28–29 maggio 1981*, Trento, 1982.

Pellegrini G.B., *Toponomastica italiana*, Milan, 1991.

Piergigli V., *La legge 15 dicembre 1999, n. 482 («Norme in materia di tutela delle minoranze linguistiche storiche») ovvero dall'agnosticismo al riconoscimento, in Rassegna parlamentare*, 3/2000.

Pizzorusso A., *Verso il riconoscimento della soggettività delle comunità etnico-linguistiche?*, in *Studi in memoria di C. Furno*, Milan, 1973.

Pizzorusso A., *Le minoranze nel diritto pubblico interno*, Milan, 1967.

Pizzorusso A., *Articolo 6*, in Branca G. (ed.), *Commentario della Costituzione*, Bologna-Rome, 1975.

Pizzorusso A., *Minoranze etnico-linguistiche*, in *Eniclopedia del diritto*, XXVI, Milan, 1976.

Pizzorusso A., *Libertà di lingua e diritti linguistici: una rassegna comparata*, in *Le Regioni*, 6/1987.

Pizzorusso A., *Minoranze e maggioranze*, Turin, 1993.

Poggeschi G., *Le nazioni linguistiche della Spagna* autonómica, Padova, 2002.

Reggio D'Aci E. *La regione Trentino-Alto Adige*, Milan, 1994.

Toniatti R., *Minoranze e minoranze protette: modelli costituzionali comparati*, in Bonazzi T., Dunne M. (eds.), *Cittadinanza e diritti nelle società multiculturali*, Bologna, 1994.

Vineis E. (ed.), *La toponomastica come fonte di conoscenza storica e linguistica. Atti del convegno della Società italiana di glottologia*, Pisa, 1980.

Protection of linguistic minorities and toponomastics in the Italian region Friuli-Venezia Giulia

Gugliemo Cevolin

Summary

1. Autonomous region Friuli Venezia-Giulia and linguistic minorities

The protection of minority languages in the legislation of the autonomous region Friuli-Venezia Giulia turns in the direction of the completeness of the discipline and toward a stable institutional framework. After the adoption of the state law no. 482/1999 (*Norme in materia di tutela delle minoranze linguistiche storiche*), its implementing regulation (decree of President of the Republic no. 345/2001) and the state law no. 38/2001 (*Norme a tutela della minoranza linguistica slovena della regione Friuli-Venezia Giulia*), a manifestation of this regional trend to protect different minorities is representend by the implementation of state laws on minorities with regional complete means of protection: for Slovenian minority the regional law no. 26/2007 (*Norme regionali per la tutela della minoranza linguistica slovena*); for the Friulan language the regional law no. 29/2007 (*Norme per la tutela, valorizzazione e promozione della lingua friulana*); for German minority the regional law no. 20/2009 (*Norme di tutela e promozione delle minoranze di lingua tedesca del Friuli-Venezia Giulia*). Furthermore, the autonomous region Friuli-Venezia Giulia has recently approved rules concerning the teaching of EU foreign languages (regional law no. 10/2009) and the preservation of Venetian dialect spoken in the region (regional law no. 5/2010).

2. Slovenian minority in the region

Before studying the level of protection achieved in the Italian system by the Slovenian minority[1] in the region it is necessary to direct the investigation toward a variety of measures such as international treaties, decisions of the Constitutional Court, arts. 3 and 65 of the regional statute, the state law no. 482/1999, the state law no. 38/2001 and the regional law no. 26/2007.

First of all, with regard to international treaties, it is worth recalling the Peace Treaty signed at the end of the Second World War and, secondly, the 1954 Memorandum of Understanding signed in London (so-called Memorandum of London) which provides rules for the inhabitants of the two areas, zone A and zone B, of the Free Territory of Trieste.

This Memorandum contains various provisions to protect members of the Yugoslav ethnic group in the area administered by Italy and the Italian ethnic group in the area administered by Yugoslavia: the Memorandum ensures to the two ethnic groups equal rights and treatment with others residents with regard to the political and civil rights, individual liberties, the attainment and exercise of public services and professions, in the matter of social assistance and pensions, in the use of language.

According to the rules laid down in the Memorandum, Yugoslav and Italian ethnic groups are free to use their language in official and personal relations with the administrative and judicial authorities of the two zones.

In Italian municipalities, in those electoral districts of the town of Trieste and in other municipalities in which members of the Yugoslav ethnic group are at least a quarter of the total population, inscriptions on public buildings and place names and road signs must be written in the language of Yugoslav ethnic group, as well as in the language of the Italian State.

The same protection is granted to the Italian ethnic group.

---

1 With regard to the Slovenian minority, see: S. Bartole, *Profili della condizione giuridica della minoranza linguistica slovena nell'ordinamento italiano*, in *Studi in onore di Manlio Udina*, Milan, 1975, II, pp. 1335–1375; R. Bin, *Regioni e minoranze etnico-linguistiche*, in *Le Regioni*, 4/1989; F. Rocco, *La disciplina di tutela della minoranza linguistica slovena e degli altri gruppi etnico-linguistici minoritari nel Friuli Venezia Giulia*, in *Miscellanea giuridica. Studi in onore di Ignazio Scotto*, Rome, 1992, p. 352 et seq.; L. Antonini, *Minoranza slovena ed uso della lingua nel processo: una tutela riconosciuta soltanto a Trieste?*, in *Le Regioni*, 4/1996, p. 716 et seq.

In the Yugoslav area, where Italian ethnic group is at least a quarter of the total population, inscriptions on public buildings and place names and road signs must be indicated in Italian, as well as in the language of the Yugoslav Government.

Even after the 1975 Treaty of Osimo (Ancona), the Italian Republic and the Socialist Federal Republic of Yugoslavia agree to maintain the domestic measures already taken under the special statute annexed to the above-mentioned Memorandum of London in order to maintain the level of protection for members of the two ethnic groups[2].

These principles need more specific agreements between Yugoslav and Italian States in order to be effective[3].

International treaties, legislative or administrative acts, the regional statute of Friuli-Venezia Giulia are the complex rules directed to the protection of the Slovene minority in the Provinces of Trieste and Gorizia. For a long time no form of protection is given to the Slovenian minority in the Province of Udine, less tied to the Yugoslavia. With the dissolution of the Socialist Federal Republic of Yugoslavia, the Republics of Slovenia and Croatia succeed the Socialist Federal Republic in the treaties system[4].

A very important step is the judgment no. 28/1982 of the Constitutional Court, which recognizes Slovene population in the territory of Trieste as “minority”, giving effect to art. 6 of the Italian Constitution and to art. 3 of the regional statute, at least for the region of Trieste[5]. The protection of the Slovenian

2 S. Bartole, *Profili della condizione della minoranza linguistica slovena nell'ordinamento italiano*, in *Studi in onore di Manlio Udina, cit.,* pp. 1335–1375; M. Udina, *Gli Accordi di Osimo. Elementi introduttivi e testi annotati,* Trieste, 1979; S. Bartole, *Tutela della minoranza linguistica slovena ed esecuzione del Trattato di Osimo*, in *Rivista di diritto internazionale*, 1977, p. 509 et seq.; E. Petrich, *Alcuni aspetti giuridico-internazionali delle disposizioni sulle minoranze nel Trattato di Osimo*, in *Bollettino d'informazione degli Sloveni in Italia*, 1–15 January 1979, p. 23 et seq.; G. de Vergottini, *Bilinguismo e ripristino della toponomastica italiana*, in G. de Vergottini (ed.), *Istria e Dalmazia. Un viaggio nella memoria, Atti del convegno di studi di Bologna, 10 marzo 1995*, Bologna, 1996, pp. 183–188.

3 A. F. Panzera, *La circolazione delle persone nei rapporti di vicinato italo-jugoslavi*, in A.M. Calamia, P. Mengozzi e N. Ronzitti (eds.), *I rapporti di vicinato tra Italia e Jugoslavia*, Milan, 1984, p. 215 et seq. and pp. 279–523.

4 About the possibility of renegotiation of the treaties see G. de Vergottini, *La rinegoziazione del Trattato di Osimo*, in *Rivista di studi politici internazionali*, 1/1993, pp. 77–91.

5 G. Mor, *L'uso ufficiale della lingua di una minoranza riconosciuta: il caso della minoranza slovena,*with regard to the Constitutional Court judgment no. 28/1982, in *Le Regioni*, 3/1982; Toniatti R., *La rappresentanza politica delle minoranze linguistiche: i ladini fra rappresentanza «assicurata» e «garantita»*, with regard to the Constitutional Court judgment 261/1995, in *Le Regioni*, 6/1995; M. Bertolissi, *La regione Friuli-Venezia Giulia dalla Costituente allo Statuto*, in *Le Regioni*, 4/1983, p. 817 et seq.; see Constitutional Court judgments no. 62/1992,

minority in the Province of Udine does not have immediately recognized protection. In relation to the level of protection the Slovenian minority is recognized as a "super-protected" minority[6] (along with the French-speaking minority in Valle d'Aosta and the German-speaking minority in Alto Adige) only after the approval of the state law no. 38/2001. In the matter of public signs and place names art. 10 of this law states the use of the Slovenian language alongside the use of the Italian one in signs of public offices, in official letters and, in general, in all public signs as well as in standards, as specified on the basis of the table included in art. 4.

The regional law no. 26/2007 provides the principles of cultural diversity and multiculturalism and fosters institutional relations with the Republic of Slovenia, the cooperation between the two minorities, Slovene minority in Italy, and the Italian one in Slovenia, with the possibility of establishing joint legal instruments[7]. The regional rules are written within the regional legal framework of the Euroregion[8] and the European Grouping for Territorial Cooperation (EGTC, Regulation EC no. 1982/2006 of the European Parliament and the Council of 5th July 2006)[9].

---

no. 271/1994, no. 16/1995, no. 15/1996 relating to the use of the German language in Trentino-Alto Adige/Südtirol in judicial cases; Council of State judgment no. 6817/2006 about bilingualism in administrative cases; with regard to the choice of language in the process see Constitutional Court judgment no. 377/2006; for the protection of linguistic minorities in the school see Constitutional Court judgment no. 430/2006.

6 See F. Palermo, *Le minoranze linguistiche in Italia dopo la legge generale di tutela*, in A. Lollini (ed.), *Pluralismo linguistico e costituzioni. Un'analisi comparata*, Meran, 2004, pp. 111–128.

7 For the first study about the regional legislation, see: *Slovit. Sloveni in Italia*, Anno IX, no. 11 (31st October 2007).

8 See G. de Vergottini, *Euroregione: quale giustificazione*, in *Coordinamento Adriatico*, 11–14/1994, pp. 11–12; Idem, *Regioni di confine comuni: dalla cooperazione alla istituzionalizzazione*, in *Rivista di studi politici internazionali*, 1/1995, pp. 61–79; G.. Cevolin, *Euroregioni, rapporti transfrontalieri e attività internazionale delle regioni nell'attuazione dell'art. 117 Cost. da parte della L. 5.06.2003, n. 131,* in L. Mezzetti (ed.), *La costituzione delle autonomie*, Napoli, 2004, pp. 309–350; Idem, *La cooperazione transfrontaliera come tecnica di tutela delle minoranze con particolare riguardo all'area dell'Italia orientale*, in V. Piergigli (ed.), *L'autoctonia divisa. La tutela giuridica della minoranza italiana in Istria, Fiume e Dalmazia,* Padova, 2005, pp. 437–465; L. Coen, *La realizzazione dell'Euroregione: un percorso complesso per un progetto necessario*, in Regione Autonoma Friuli Venezia Giulia (ed.), *Euroregione e cooperazione internazionale*, Udine, 2007, pp. 35–44; Idem, *La cooperazione territoriale come risorsa economica*, in R. Bin e L. Coen (eds.), *Poteri pubblici e sviluppo locale*, Padova, 2009, p. 77 et seq.

9 G. Cevolin, *Gli enti locali nel sistema europeo di cooperazione territoriale,* in *L'Amministratore locale*, 4/2007, pp. 38–41; A. Papisca (ed.), *Il Gruppo europeo di cooperazione territoriale. Nuove sfide allo spazio dell'Unione Europea*, Venice, 2009.

The regional law also promotes cooperation between the Slovenian, Friulan and German minorities (art. 4). In this law, it is important to mention the establishment of the Register of regional organizations of the Slovene linguistic minority (the registration in this book is a necessary prerequisite for the conclusion of agreements with the region and for access to the contributions required by law, art. 5) and the establishment of Organizations of the Slovenian linguistic minority, as institutions which represent the interests of this group (art. 6).

In conclusion, state and regional protection norms of the Slovene minority are complete and able to give the best protection to the Slovenian community as "super-protected minority" in the Italian law.

At this moment the Slovenian minority calls for increased funding from the region, even in relation to recent reductions in contributions due to the economic downturn. Language communities of Slavic origin settled in the valleys of Natisone, of Torre and Resia, in the province of Udine ask for protection of their traditional features and language which are different from those of the Slovenian national minority in the province of Trieste.

3. German language in the region

The German minority has gradually reached the goal of legislative recognition. Before 2009, in Friuli-Venezia Giulia the regional legislation adopted in order to protect the German minority was very limited. There were financial provisions contained in the regional law no. 4/1999 (art. 6, paras. 40, 41 and 41-*bis*), local provisions concerning funding for conservation projects of the German language and culture, provisions establishing associations and non-profit cultural organizations for specific research initiatives, teaching, publishing and audiovisual production and cultural shows. The regional legislation identifies the regional community of German culture as "the German-speaking community, including the variety *saurana* and *timavese* established in the municipalities of Sauris, of Paluzza (fraction of Timau[10]), Tarvisio, Malborghetto-Valbruna and Pontebba".

Finally, with the regional law no. 20/2009 for German-speaking minority in Valcanale (Kanaltal) in the village of Timau (Tischlbong) in the municipality of Paluzza and the municipality of Sauris (Zahre) all the German linguistic minorities of the region Friuli-Venezia Giulia recognized by the state law no. 482/1999 are ruled by specific provisions in all the different public sectors, included education, place names, media.

10 The hamlet of Timau belongs to the municipality of Paluzza.

The principles of respect for diversity and cultural integration guide the interpretation of the law.

The *saurana* and *timavese* variants, expressions of the ancient South Tyrolean-Bavarian type Carinthian, are also protected by the regional law.

The region can consult local associations for the protection of the German-speaking minorities; cultural and scientific institutions of minorities can be involved by the region for the promotion of linguistic and cultural heritage of German-speaking minority; the Province of Udine and the municipalities in the territory of linguistic protection co-operate with the region.

In order to ensure the reception of radio and television broadcasts in the German-speaking area, the region may support the implementation of the public service broadcasting and prepare appropriate agreements with RAI (Italian Radio Television) and commercial broadcasters in order to create local programs and services in German.

The law promotes regional cooperation through agreements and memoranda of understanding between the universities established in the region, other European universities, regions and local authorities which are present in the German-speaking minorities to improve the training and specialization of German minority language also for recognition of university diplomas and state exams that enable the exercise of professions.

The regional law provides forms of recognition of regional institutions and organizations which represent the German-speaking minorities in Friuli-Venezia Giulia and the regional commission for the German-speaking minority in the region, witch sets three-year plan up the general language policy for the German language, then approved by the regional council.

The feature of the German minority in the Southern Alps is its dispersion in "linguistic islands". For that reason the regional rules encourage cooperation between the German minority and the German-speaking European countries and between regional linguistic minorities.

In the matter of protection of cultural and linguistic diversities the municipalities, in their respective territories, may enter into agreements and arrangements with local authorities to carry out collaborative activities. This form of cooperation may become stable with the establishment of public and private offices.

4. Friulan language in the region

The patriarchal State of Aquileia, an original Christian tradition, an autonomous capacity to relate to the different peoples of Europe and anticipate an advanced form of democratic representation in the "Parliament of *Patrie dal Friûl*"[11], the recognition of the Friulan language as protected by the Italian Republic are elements that characterize Friuli[12].

In the years following the end of Fascism[13], the Association for Friulan autonomy (1945), the Committee for regional autonomy and the Popular Movement for the Friulan regional autonomy, through the writings of Gianfranco D'Aronco, Chino Ermacora, Pier Paolo Pasolini, Tiziano Tessitori and others, began to propose the establishment of the Friuli region. This proposal anticipates the legal recognition of the specificity of Friuli: the constitutional recognition of the principle of protection "by appropriate means" of linguistic minorities, the special autonomy (with Trieste)[14], the institution of the University of Friuli[15] and the legislative recognition of the Friulan language.

The regional law no. 15/1996 (*Norme per la tutela e promozione della lingua e della cultura friulane e istituzione del servizio per le lingue regionali e*

---

11 With regard to the "Parliament of *Patrie dal Friûl*" see: L. Casella (ed.) *Rappresentanze e territori. Parlamento friulano e istituzioni rappresentative territoriali nell'Europa moderna*, Udine, 2003; I. Cacciavillani, *Il parlamento della Patria del Friuli in epoca veneziana*, Venice, 2008.

12 About the Friulan history, see: P.S. Leicht, *Breve storia del Friuli*, Udine, 1976; G. C. Menis *Storia del Friuli. Dalle origini alla caduta dello Stato patriarcale (1420) con cenni fino al 20° secolo*, Udine, 2002; P. Paschini, *Storia del Friuli*, Udine, 2003.

13 For studies on the principle of autonomy in the Italian Constitution, see: M. Bertolissi, *La Regione Friuli-Venezia Giulia dalla Costituente allo Statuto*, in *Le Regioni*, 4/1983, p. 817 et seq.; S. Bartole (ed.), *Le Regioni alla ricerca della loro identità culturale e storica*, Milan, 1999; G. Cevolin, *Proposte e modelli di riferimento nel dibattito costituente sulle autonomie in Italia*, in *Storia contemporanea in Friuli*, n. 30, "*Costituzione e autonomie*", Proceedings of the Meeting of Udine, 4th–5th December 1998, Udine, 2000, pp. 77–107.

14 On the establishment of the autonomous region Friuli-Venezia Giulia, see: V. Buscema, R. Fusco, *La Regione Friuli-Venezia Giulia*, Milan, 1982, p. 1 et seq.; S. Bartole, *La Regione Friuli-Venezia Giulia di fronte al completamento dell'ordinamento regionale*, in *Le Regioni*, 5/1977; *Dibattito sulla regione. Quel trattino*, Udine, 1985; A. Agnelli, S. Bartole (eds.), *La Regione Friuli-Venezia Giulia. Profilo storico-giuridico tracciato in occasione del 20° anniversario dell'istituzione della Regione*, Bologna, 1987; G. Francescano, F. Salimbeni, *Storia, lingua e società in Friuli*, Rome, 2004; G. Ellero, *DAF Dizionario autonomistico friulano*, Codroipo, 2007.

15 F. Vicario, *Tarcisio Petracco (1919–2010). Il padre dell'università friulana*, in *Autonomie. Idee per il Friuli*, 23–24/2010, pp. 61–66; A. Persic, *La sfida di Tarcisio Petracco all'impossibile fino al traguardo contrastato di una Università friulana autonoma*, in *Autonomie. Idee per il Friuli, ivi*, pp. 67–83.

minoritarie) is the first law directed to the protection of the Friulan language. This law gives the region a legal instrument to pursue an active policy to conserve and develop the Friulan language and culture too.

The state law no. 482/1999 puts into practice the fundamental principle on the protection of minorities provided by art. 6 of the Constitution, which had been waiting to be carried out for over fifty years[16]. Friulans can be considered under all effects as members of a "recognized minority" (art. 2). This state law introduces a regulatory framework for the protection of language and culture of the population speaking Friulan, thus identifying the Friulan community among the minorities protected.

---

16 About the linguistic diversity in Italy, see: T. De Mauro, *Note sulle minoranze linguistiche e nazionali in Italia*, in *Il Mulino*, May–June 1979, p. 349–367. For important studies about minorities in the Italian legal system, see: A. Pizzorusso, *Le minoranze nel diritto pubblico interno*, Milan, 1967; Idem, *Commento all'articolo 6 della Costituzione,* in G. Branca (ed.), *Commentario della Costituzione*, Bologna, 1975, p. 303 et seq.; Idem, *Minoranze etnico-linguistiche*, in *Enciclopedia del diritto,* XXVI, Milan, 1976, p. 530 et seq.; F. Capotorti, *Study on the Rights of Persons Belonging to Ethnic, Religious and Linguistic Minorities*, New York, 1979; S. Bartole, *Minoranze nazionali*, in *Novissimo Digesto Italiano*, *Appendice*, V, Turin, 1984, p. 45 et seq.; R. Bin, *Regioni e minoranze etnico-linguistiche*, in *Le Regioni*, 4/1989, p. 1014 et seq.; M. Bertolissi, *Commento all'articolo 6 della Costituzione*, in V. Crisafulli, L. Paladin (eds.), *Commentario breve alla Costituzione*, Padova, 1990, p. 6 et seq.; M. Stipo, *Minoranze etnico-linguistiche*, in *Enciclopedia Giuridica Treccani*, XX, Rome, 1990, p. 3 et seq.; S. Bartole, *La tutela della minoranza slovena fra giurisprudenza costituzionale e legislazione ordinaria*, in *Giurisprudenza costituzionale*, 1992, p. 342 et seq.; G. de Vergottini, *Verso una nuova definizione del concetto di minoranza*, in *Regione e Governo locale*, 1995, p. 9 et seq.; V. Piergigli, *Diritti dell'uomo e diritti delle minoranze nel contesto internazionale ed europeo: riflessioni su alcuni sviluppi nella protezione dei diritti linguistici e culturali*, in *Rassegna parlamentare*, 1/1996, p. 33 et seq. After the state law no. 482/1999, see: S. Bartole, *Le norme per la tutela delle minoranze linguistiche storiche*, in *Le Regioni*, 6/1999, p. 1063 et seq.; V. Piergigli, *La legge 15 dicembre 1999, n. 482 ("Norme in materia di tutela delle minoranze linguistiche storiche") ovvero dall'agnosticismo al riconoscimento*, in *Rassegna Parlamentare*, 3/2000, p. 623 et seq.; Eadem, *Le minoranze linguistiche nell'ordinamento italiano: recenti sviluppi normativi*, in *Plurilinguismo. Contatti di lingue e culture*, 9/2002, p. 43 et seq.; Eadem, *Lingue minoritarie e identità culturali*, Milan, 2001; Eadem, *"Minoranze linguistiche"* and *"Diritti linguistici",* in M. Flores, T. Groppi, R. Pisillo Mazzeschi (eds.), *Dizionario: cultura dei diritti e dignità della persona nell'epoca della globalizzazione,* Turin, 2007, p. 930 et seq. and p. 385 et seq.; E. Malfatti, *La legge di tutela delle minoranze linguistiche: le prospettive ed i problemi ancora aperti*, in *Rivista di diritto costituzionale*, 2001, p. 109 et seq.; F. Palermo, *Le minoranze linguistiche in Italia dopo la legge generale di tutela*, in A. Lollini (ed.), *Pluralismo linguistico, cit.*, p. 111 et seq.; G. Cevolin, *L'istituzionalizzazione della tutela plurale delle lingue minoritarie dell'Alto Adriatico e il ruolo degli istituti culturali*, in A. Janežič (ed.), *Le comunità linguistiche di Alpe Adria. Ruolo e Prospettive per gli Enti e Istituti*, Udine, 2010, p. 33 et seq.

With the regional law no. 29/2007, the region implements the state law on the protection of minorities, in particular way with regard to the Friulan language within the region. This law provides one of the aims of the autonomous region in the protection, enhancement and promotion of the Friulan language as language of Friuli and even guarantees the various forms of local variants.

4.1 The area of settlement of the Friulan language

For the protection of linguistic minorities, the Italian Republic has chosen the model based on the identification of the territory where the system of minority protection has to be applied. The territorial area is defined according to the first regional law of protection (and even under the new legislation in 2007) by a decree of President of the regional government. The land area of protection should cover only the part of the region "where the Friulan language is traditionally and significantly spoken". The municipalities provide specific guidance. The area of settlement of the Friulan language is identified and defined under art. 5 of the law no. 15/1996 by presidential decree no. 412/1996 of the regional government. Approximately 80% of the municipalities in the region Friuli-Venezia Giulia are recognized within the territorial scope of the Friulan language.

4.2 The determination of the official spelling of the Friulan language and the toponymy

The issue of the official spelling is particularly sensitive from a linguistic point of view. From the literary point of view, Pier Paolo Pasolini expressed his poetry in several variations of the Friulan language. However, the process of standardization and normalization of the Friulan language is a necessary instrument for legal protection. With art. 13 of the law no. 15/1996, the region Friuli-Venezia Giulia has determined the official spelling of the Friulan language in accordance with the decision of the provincial council of Udine on 15th July 1986, in the text "The handwriting of Friulan normalized" written by prof. Lamuel Xavier (University of Girona) published in Udine in 1987, with an indication of some changes to the text, showing that the official spelling may be modified as a result of studies and comparisons. The benchmark was the spelling of the Friulan Philological Society and the law has taken measures to adopt changes in the marking of place-names and historical onomastics.

The Friulan language has many variations and it is not easy to find, from the linguistic point of view, a variant form which is more important than another one. A very difficult problem to be solved is the relationship between the official writing and its variants. The new regional no. law 29/2007 for the protection of the Friulan language, in different subjects provides for the protection of the different expressions of the Friulan language, with reference also to the field of toponymy: the region must respect the local variations of the name in the Friulan language of municipalities, villages and towns, in agreement with the municipalities (art. 11).

4.3 The protection of the Friulan language and the recent restrictive judgment of the Constitutional Court

The regional law no. 29/2007 extends linguistic rights in the public administration by establishing the duty for public institutions to provide "language policy plans", in the schools and in the matter of toponymy. In the new regional law it is very important the role of the *Agjenzie pe lenghe furlane*.

This law defines Friulan as "Friuli's own language"[17], specifies various guidelines (the respect of autonomies, citizens' free choice, flexibility of interventions) and recalls the fundamental international legal frameworks as the Universal Declaration of Human Rights, the European Convention on Human Rights and Fundamental Freedoms, the Central European Initiative Instrument for the Protection of Minority Rights, the OSCE documents signed by Italy, the European Charter for Regional or Minority Languages and the EU Treaty.

The legal meaning of "one's own language" has occurred in relation to the Catalan identity (*llengua pròpia*) in the statute approved by the Catalan Parliament in 1933 (art. 3) and is then reused in the 1979 statute of autonomy of Catalonia, which is reflected in the preamble of the law on the normalization of Catalan language adopted in 1983, retained in the 2006 statute of autonomy of Catalonia and developed in the sense of considering the use of Catalan language in public administration, media, schools and the recognition of Occitan as the language of Val d'Aran.

Article 10 of regional law no. 29/2007 introduces, within the delimited territory, the visual use of the Friulan language in street signs and, generally, in

17 For the concept of "one's own language", see: A. Milian Massana, *La exigencia de "al menos en catalán" como garantía de la presencia social de la lengua catalana*, in Various Authors, *Estudios jurídicos sobre la ley de política lingüística*, Madrid-Barcelona, 1999, p. 465 et seq.; G. Poggeschi, *Le nazioni linguistiche della Spagna* autonòmica, Padova, 2002, p. 79; I. Ruggiu, *Il nuovo Statuto catalano*, in *Le Regioni*, 2/2007, p. 281 et seq.; E. Aja, *La riforma dello Statuto catalano del 2006*, in *Diritto pubblico comparato ed europeo*, 3/2007, p. 1133 et seq.

any other sign visible to the public. About the place names in Friulan, the decision to establish the official Friulan name of towns and cities lies with ARLeF in agreement with the municipalities involved (in line with the provisions of the legislative decree no. 267/2000, local authorities can choose to make official the names in both Italian and Friulan or just in Friulan).

The Italian Government assumed the state law no. 482/99 as the parameter of constitutionality and contested the regional law on seven points. The judgment of the Constitutional Court no. 159/2009 declared the regional law on the protection of the Friulan language not consistent with the Constitution in several points[18].

An important point of conflict was the provision concerning the possibility to use "the Friulan language only" for place names; this provision, according to the Government, clashed with the law no. 482/99 and even with the constitutional principle of equality of all citizens.

In the matter of toponymy[19] the judgment of the Constitutional Court considered that the option, provided in the regional law for municipalities to adopt place names only in the Friulan language is also not consistent with the provision of the state law no. 482/1999 which authorizes the use of place names in the minority language but "in addition to the official place names".

Anyway the Constitutional Court's judgment no. 159/2009 is an important moment in the recognition and institutionalization of the discipline of the Friulan language.

The judgment confirms that the protection of the Friulan language is provided in the regulations for linguistic minorities in Europe. The nation-State of the XIX century must be considered outdated. The decision recognizes the Friulan language as "an element of individual and collective identity of vital importance" and points out the legal obligation to provide a legal framework, that removes the factual circumstances that might generate a discriminatory effect.

---

18 R. Toniatti, *Pluralismo sostenibile e interesse nazionale all'identità linguistica posti a fondamento di "un nuovo modello di riparto delle competenze" legislative fra Stato e Regioni*, in *Le Regioni*, 5/2009, pp. 1121–1149; E. Stradella, *La tutela delle minoranze linguistiche storiche tra Stato e Regioni davanti alla Corte costituzionale, ivi*, pp. 1150–1170; G. Cevolin, *Il giudice delle leggi interpreta restrittivamente il ruolo delle regioni nella tutela delle lingue minoritarie e indica la via per ottenere maggiori ambiti di tutela* (Sent. C. Cost. n. 159 del 2009), in G. Cevolin (ed.), *La tutela del friulano e del resiano davanti alla Corte Costituzionale e all'Unesco* (Proceedings of Udine 13th June 2009), in *Autonomie. Idee per il Friuli*, 20/2009, pp. 25–34; V. Piergigli, *La tutela delle minoranze linguistiche storiche nell'ordinamento italiano tra principi consolidati e nuove (restrittive) tendenze della giurisprudenza costituzionale*, at: www.associazionedeicostituzionalisti.it, 2010.

19 V. Piergigli, *La disciplina giuridica della toponomastica e la tutela minoritaria nell'ordinamento italiano. Spunti per una comparazione*, in P. Hilpold (ed.), *Minderheitenschutz in Italien*, Wien, 2009, pp. 159–193.

This interpretation is connected to the core principles of the Constitutional Court's judgments (no. 62/1992, no. 768/1988, no. 289/1987 and no. 312/1983). The Court said that the principal of substantial equality requires to ensure the effective participation of persons belonging to linguistic minorities in public life "through the right to use the language in institutional relations, including the right to education in minority languages, support for culture of the minority".

According to the interpretation of the judgment no. 159/2009 of the Constitutional Court, the protection of linguistic minorities (art. 6 of the Italian Constitution) can be effectively disciplined only by the State. In order to obtain a different and better protection of minority language than the one provided by the state law no. 482/1999, with regard to the Italian regions with a special statute (Friuli-Venezia Giulia, Valle d'Aosta/Vallée d'Aoste, Trentino-Alto Adige/Südtirol, Sicily and Sardinia) it is possible to approve legislative state decrees (so-called *norme di attuazione*)[20] with the contribute of joint committees composed of members of the State and the region involved (art. 18 state law no. 482/1999).

The implementing measures of the special statute of autonomy, taking an intermediate position between the constitutional and legislative ordinary norms, can contribute to the implementation of the regional autonomy (Constitutional Court judgment no. 213/1988). The Constitutional Court judgment no. 51/2006 found that the rules implementing the special statute can not be changed other than by acts adopted with the procedure laid down in the statutes, then prevailing on ordinary legislation.

In order to understand the possibilities offered by the legislative state decrees implementing the statute of the special regions it is sufficient to review the decrees implementing the statute of Trentino-Alto Adige for the protection of Ladin minority (recognized by the state law no. 482/1999), as well as of Mochena and Cimbrian populations (not expressly recognized by the above-mentioned state law) living in the Province of Trento (legislative state decrees no. 321/1997, no. 487/1998 about initiatives to receive radio and television programs in the Ladin language and other cultural areas in Europe, no. 344/1999 concerning amendments to the regulation of schools in Ladin, no. 262/2001, no. 177/2006).

In order to protect the Friulan language in a positive way it is necessary to achieve the levels approved by the State with regard to the regions Valle d'Aosta/Vallée d'Aoste and Trentino-Alto Adige/Südtirol, whose names are now

---

20 With regard to this kind of state provisions, see V. Piergigli, *The legal regulation of toponomastics in Italian law and the specific situation in Trentino-Alto Adige/Südtirol*, in this volume, footnote 24.

written in the Constitution in the respective minority language, besides the Italian one (art. 116 amended by the constitutional law no. 3/2001).

The recent judgment of the Constitutional Court no. 170/2010 recognizes a legislative action of even an ordinary region (Piedmont), especially in connection with the converging interests of preservation of cultural identity and heritage of their communities; however, it does not recognize the autonomous power to the region to "identify and protect … its own language", even beyond the languages recognized and established by the state legislature. What the Constitutional Court seeks to prevent is that the regional legislature set up its own community as a whole language minority to be protected under art. 6 of the Italian Constitution.

The decisions of the Constitutional Court no. 159/2009 and no. 170/2010 represent a recent restrictive tendency to not recognize the actual domains of regional legislation in the field of linguistic minorities.

After the constitutional reform of 2001 the Government has shown the availability of the State for a devolution of powers relating to education in the act added to the Memorandum of Understanding signed by the Office of the Prime Minister and the autonomous region Friuli-Venezia Giulia in December 2007. According to this Memorandum: "The Government and the region share the opportunity to start, in the manner provided for in the Constitution, the path to the region act to transfer the functions related to education in the context of the emerging lines nationwide. The transfer referred to in paragraph 1 will follow the principles of gradualism, in accordance with the interpretative and operational guidelines to be defined in the Joint Conference, without prejudice to the prerogatives of the State" (art. 8). At the meeting held in July 2010, the regional council of Friuli-Venezia Giulia has approved the motion no. 74 ("Guidelines to the political component of the regional joint committee for the current parliamentary term") recognizing the importance of the work of the joint committee to counter the "never slumbering tendency to flatten or "normalize" the levels of special autonomy" in the moment where art. 27 of the state law no. 42/2009, introducing into the Italian legal system the so-called fiscal federalism, defines for the special regions a different path from that of the ordinary regions. With this document, the regional council indicates to the joint committee the need to prepare a legislative text for the transfer to the region of the largest administrative functions relating to education and to provide for the transfer of financial resources and regulate the organization of the regional education offices (art. 2.1.1.1.).

The Friulan community does not require independence and has always pursued moderate versions of conceiving its own autonomy. The trends of devolution is one of the constants of the institutional setting as a factor of progress of European integration process. The assertion of a strong articulation of different levels of government is an expression of participatory democracy at the institutional and functional levels[21].

Bibliography

Azzena A., *Prospettive di cooperazione interregionale mediante trattati internazionali e superamento della riserva del 'potere estero' dello stato centrale*, in *Le Regioni*, 1/1985.

Barbera A., *Gli accordi internazionali tra Governo, Parlamento e corpo elettorale*, in *Quaderni costituzionali*, 3/1984.

Bartole S., *Lo statuto di autonomia della provincia di Bolzano e la riforma della costituzione italiana – prospettive per l'autonomia*, at: www.eurac.edu/Press/Academia/10/Artikel1.asp.

Bartole S., Olivetti Rason N., Pegoraro L., *La tutela giuridica delle minoranze*, Padova, 1998.

Bertolissi M. *Identità e crisi dello stato costituzionale in Italia*, Padova, 2002.

Calliari F., *La minoranza ladino-dolomitica. Costituzione, statuto d'autonomia, leggi regionali e provinciali,* Rimini, 1991.

Capotorti F., *Study on the Rights of Persons Belonging to Ethnic, Religious and Linguistic Minorities*, New York, 1979.

Capotorti F., *Il regime delle minoranze nel sistema delle Nazioni Unite e secondo l'art. 27 del patto sui diritti civili e politici*, in *Rivista internazionale dei diritti dell'uomo*, 1992.

Capotorti F., *La disciplina internazionale per la tutela delle minoranze: traguardi recenti*, in *I diritti dell'uomo*, 1/1993.

Caravita B., *La Costituzione dopo la riforma del titolo V. Stato, Regioni e autonomie fra Repubblica e Unione europea*, Turin, 2002.

Ceccanti S., *Tra tutela delle minoranze e rischi etnicistici*, in *Giurisprudenza costituzionale*, 1998.

Cerri A., *Libertà, eguaglianza, pluralismo nella problematica della garanzia delle minoranze*, in *Rivista trimestrale di diritto pubblico*, 1993.

Cevolin G., *Lingue di confine*, in *LiMes. Rivista italiana di geopolitica, Quaderno speciale Lingua è potere,* December, 2010.

---

21 F. Tönnies, *Comunità e società* (Berlin 1920), Milan, 1963; J. Habermas, *L'inclusione dell'altro. Studi di teoria politica*, Milan, 1998; W. Hanriette, *L'avventura delle lingue in Occidente*, Bari-Rome, 1999; F. Viola, *Identità e comunità. Il senso morale della politica*, Milan, 1999; A. de Benoist, *Identità e comunità*, Napoli, 2005; G. Nevola, *Democrazia, Costituzione, Identità. Prospettive e limiti dell'integrazione europea*, Turin, 2007; V. Cuccia, *Libertà di espressione e identità collettive*, Turin, 2007.

Cevolin G., *Le radici e le lingue: l'Europa pluriverso linguistico*, in Various Authors, *Questione di radici. La modernità e il suo attraversamento nell'Europa del XXI secolo*, Rimini, 2010.

Cisilino W., *La tutela delle minoranze linguistiche. Analisi della normativa statale e regionale, con particolare riguardo alla lingua friulana*, Udine, 2004.

Dentesano E., *Compendio di bibliografia per la toponomastica friulana*, Udine, 2006.

G. de Vergottini, *Multiculturalismo, minoranze linguistiche ed immigrazione*, in Bonazzi T., Dunne M. (eds.), *Cittadinanza e diritti nelle società multiculturali*, Bologna, 1994.

de Vergottini G., *La protection constitutionelle des nouvelles minorités*, in *Revue belge de droit constitutionnel*, 4/1995.

de Vergottini G., *Verso una nuova definizione del concetto di minoranza*, in *Regione e governo locale*, 1/2 1995.

de Vergottini G., *La protection des minorités entre garantie des droits linguistiques et bilinguisme,* in *Annuaire Européen,* Vol. XLIV, 1998.

Flick G.M., *Minoranze ed eguaglianza: il diritto alla diversità e al territorio come espressione dell'identità nel tempo della globalizzazione*, in *Politica del diritto*, 1/2004.

Fois P., *La protezione internazionale delle minoranze: il caso dell'Europa*, in M. Pinna (ed.), *L'Europa delle diversità. Identità e culture alle soglie dei terzo millennio*, Milan, 1994.

Lazzaro F. M., *La cooperazione fra regioni comunitarie alla luce della riforma costituzionale italiana*, in *Le istituzioni del federalismo*, 2/2003.

Mazzarolli L., *La tutela delle minoranze linguistiche nella Costituzione del nuovo Titolo V*, in *Le Regioni*, 5/2003.

Mezzetti L., *Le democrazie incerte. Transizioni costituzionali e consolidamento della democrazia in Europa orientale, Africa, America Latina, Asia,* Turin, 2000.

Montanari L., *I diritti dell'uomo nell'area europea tra fonti internazionali e fonti interne*, Turin, 2002.

Palermo F., *Diritto costituzionale comparato dei gruppi e delle minoranze*, Padova, 2008.

Palici di Suni Prat E., *Intorno alle minoranze*, Turin, 1999.

Piergigli V., *Lo statuto Istriano e il bilinguismo al vaglio delle autorità croate*, in *Quaderni costituzionali*, 3/2001.

V. Piergigli, *Lingue minoritarie e identità culturali*, Milan, 2001.

V. Piergigli (ed.), *L'autoctonia divisa. La tutela giuridica della minoranza italiana in Istria, Fiume e Dalmazia*, Padova, 2005.

Pizzorusso A., *Le minoranze nel diritto pubblico interno*, Milan, 1967.
Pizzorusso A., *Minoranze e maggioranze*, Turin, 1993.
Ruggeri A., *Sovranità dello Stato e sovranità sovranazionale, attraverso i diritti umani, e le prospettive di un diritto europeo "intercostituzionale"*, in *Diritto pubblico comparato ed europeo*, 2/2001.
Toniatti R., *La tutela delle minoranze linguistiche: il paradigma pluralista della nuova democrazia europea*, in Various Authors, *Le role des langues minoritaires dans la vie publique. Proceedings of the meeting: "Le role des langues minoritaires dans la vie publique", Saint-Vincent 23–24 June 2000*, Aosta, 2001.
Zanghì C., *Le minoranze: storia semantica di un'idea*, in *Rivista internazionale dei diritti dell'uomo*, 5/1992.

The languages of France and toponomastics

Antonella Benazzo

«Les noms de lieux sont donc comparables aux monnaies, aux médailles et aux inscriptions. Ce sont des fossiles dialectaux. Ils doivent être regardés et respectés comme des reliques de la religion du sentiment national ; ils comptent au nombre de nos titres de propriété ou même de nos titre de noblesse... Les noms sont les meilleurs témoins d'anciens dialectes en voie de recul ou complètement disparus. La toponymie générale de la France porte l'empreinte des couches superposées des langues qui se sont succédé sur telles ou telles parties de notre sol : ibère, ligure, celte, romaine, franque, germaine, normande, arabe, anglaise, etc. Les noms de lieux ont donc une histoire, ou plutôt sont le reflet de l'histoire du pays. Ils sont des survivances et comme des épaves, laissées sur place par de civilisation éteintes».

Jean Brunhes, *Géographie humaine de la France. Introduction générale, Tome I de l'Histoire de la nation française*, Gabriel Hanotaux (ed.), Paris, Société de l'Histoire Nationale et Plon-Nourrit, 1920, p. 296.

«Le retour à la tradition est un mythe. Aucun peuple ne l'a jamais vécu. La recherche d'identité, le modèle, pour moi, il est devant soi, jamais en arrière. Et je dirai que notre lutte actuelle, c'est de pouvoir mettre le plus possible d'éléments appartenant à notre passé, à notre culture dans la construction du modèle d'homme et de société que nous voulons pour l'édification de la *polis*. Notre identité, elle est devant nous».

Jean-Marie Tjibaou, *La présence kanak*, Alban Bensa, Eric Wittersheim (eds.), Paris, Odile Jacob, 1996, p. 185.

Summary

1. Toponomastic policy from preservation of cultural heritage to aspirations of linguistic conquest

The majority of contemporary States are linguistically heterogeneous, both from the perspective of individual linguistic practices and toponomastics. Despite this, the processes of edification of nation-States have been characterized by the imposition (often progressive rather than sudden) of a dominant language that becomes official at the expense of others. This generally also affects the dimension linking single communities with their territory through place names that symbolically delimit space, evoking sentiments of belonging to a specific cultural and linguistic identity. Since toponomastics concerns the attribution of names to places and public monuments, it does not solely serve the practical purpose of geographical identification, but also an essential communicative and cultural function. In this sense, the various policies on toponomastics can be an important instrument for valorisation and protection of linguistic minorities in the territory of a State, or conversely, a means for slowly or suddenly assimilating them into the culture of a dominant majority[1].

Though imposition of an official language may be a reason for changing place names, this usually does not overcome centuries of toponomastic practices, unless there exists a policy in this sense. There are currently many factors (changes in international balance and the crisis of nation-States, resurgence of ethnic conflicts, permeability of national borders to major international migrations, advance of processes of supranational integration in Europe, globalisation and international terrorism) favouring perception of a threat to linguistic, religious and cultural identify of nation-States and, in parallel, the realisation of progressive erosion of the linguistic heritage constituted by minority languages, at least within States and territories where no specific instruments of valorisation and protection are provided by the law. Within this scenario, the will to preserve linguistic wealth as part of the national and European heritage is testified by approval of the European Charter for Regional or Minority Languages of 1992 and the Framework Convention for the Protection of National Minorities of 1995. Both treaties, which have to be ratified by new States wishing to join the

1 A well-known example is that of the German population of Trentino-Alto Adige/Südtirol, see: G. de Vergottini, *Profili giuridici della toponomastica nella provincia di Bolzano*, in *Diritto e società*, 4/1986, p. 651 et seq.; P. Hilpold, *La regolamentazione della toponomastica in Trentino-Alto Adige*, in J. Marko, S. Ortino, F. Palermo, *L'ordinamento speciale della provincia autonoma di Bolzano*, Padova, 2001, p. 801. See also V. Piergigli, *The legal regulation of toponomastics in Italian law and the specific situation in Trentino-Alto Adige/Südtirol*, in this volume.

European Union, expressly consider toponomastics among the tools for protecting linguistic minorities[2].

This trend is also confirmed by the resurgence of autonomist and nationalist movements that use the defence of languages and dialects as a vehicle for polemical claims related to identity. For example, in post-Franco Spain, the Autonomous Communities were recognised to have sovereignty on the subject of linguistic policy and some chose monolingualism, restoring original Catalan, Basque and Galician place names at the expense of Castilian, the official language of Spain[3]. In the case of Baltic States that regained full sovereignty after collapse of the Soviet Union, rejection of the ex-occupying power also manifested through complete revisitation of toponomastics maps, from which all possible references to the Russian language were fastidiously removed, despite the fact that many Russians had chosen to continue to live in these States or had lived there since birth.

The case of Latvia is emblematic: the country is traditionally populated by various ethnic minorities, the largest of which is the Russian community. Before Soviet occupation in 1940, the Latvian Constitution did not contain any reference to language, which was only introduced in 1998, when Latvian was constitutionalised as official language[4]. The country has undoubtedly undergone a process of Russianisation, which did not occur through linguistic assimilation but rather through economic planning common to the area of Soviet countries and through internal immigration that increased the Russian presence from 18% to 42% of the resident population. One of the first measures adopted by the national Government after the achievement of independence in 1991 was to

2 Specifically, the European Charter for Regional or Minority Languages states: "Within the administrative districts of the State in which the number of residents who are users of regional or minority languages justifies the measures specified below and according to the situation of each language, the Parties undertake, as far as this is reasonably possible: ... the use or adoption, if necessary in conjunction with the name in the official language(s), of traditional and correct forms of place-names in regional or minority languages" (art. 10, para. 2g). The Framework Convention for the Protection of National Minorities states: "In areas traditionally inhabited by substantial numbers of persons belonging to a national minority, the Parties shall endeavour, in the framework of their legal system, including, where appropriate, agreements with other States, and taking into account their specific conditions, to display traditional local names, street names and other topographical indications intended for the public also in the minority language when there is a sufficient demand for such indications" (art. 11, para. 3). See also P. Hilpold, *Topographic names and international law,* in this volume.

3 Regarding the Catalan experience, see G. Poggeschi, *Le nazioni linguistiche della Spagna* autonómica, Padova, 2002, p. 185 et seq.; Idem, *I diritti linguistici. Un'analisi comparata,* Rome, 2010, p. 157 et seq., and Idem, *Place names in Spain: the prominence of the linguistic pluralism of the* Estado autonómico, in this volume.

4 Constitution (*Satversme*) of the Latvian Republic (Constitution 1922, am. 2002), art. 4.

replace all signs of public places and roads, previously bilingual in Latvian and Russian, with exclusively Latvian inscriptions. The Law on Languages of 1992, formally aimed at restoration and valorisation of Latvian, was evidently animated by linguistic nationalism particularly hostile to the Russian-speaking population. This is demonstrated by the reduction of Russian schools and compulsory transcription of names on personal official certificates and documents into Latvian using the Latin alphabet. In addition, the Citizenship Law of 1994 imposed the naturalization of persons born in Latvia after 1940, with the effect of excluding about 22% of the population from voting. The perplexity and objections raised by European institutions during the phase of negotiations for entry into the EU, which occurred in 2004, induced a change in the electoral legislation[5] and a certain opening towards Russian schools, but the Government did not change its policy of promoting monolingualism. With regard to toponomastics, the Council of Ministers adopted various dispositions in 2000. These establish strict rules for observation of Latvian language and spelling in place names, placing them under supervision of the Minister for Justice[6]. However, the result of this linguistic policy seems to have been almost exclusively to create tensions between the Latvian and Russian communities, missing the opportunity of creating a bilingual State in which the two languages could coexist and be equally transmitted to new generations[7].

The case of States implementing valorisation of the autochthonous linguistic heritage is different. An example is the African State of Upper Volta, an ex-colony of France, whose name originates from its major river. Independent since 1960, the State took the name of Burkina Faso in 1984. This name is a synthesis of two terms from the principal autochthonous idioms, meaning "land of men of integrity or whole men". Something similar may be happening in the archipelago of New Caledonia, named by its discoverer James Cook, inspired by the ancient Latin name for Scotland. Since 1946, it has been a French overseas territory (today a territorial grouping *sui generis*), undertaking the difficult and uncertain road to independence[8]. *La Nouvelle Calédonie*, also known to the French as *Le*

---

5 See C. Taube, *Latvia: Political participation of linguistic minorities*, in *International Journal of Constitutional Law*, 2003, p. 511

6 See H. Guillorel, *Territoire de la langue et toponymie officielle*, in *Droit et Cultures*, 2002, p. 42.

7 In this sense, see S. Panov, *Discours nationaliste et politique linguistique en Lettonie indépendante*, in *Mots, Langue(s) et nationalisme(s)*, n. 74/2004, p. 125 et seq.

8 The decision was postponed to a referendum scheduled for 2014, but the outcome is anything but certain, since Kanaks are only 45% of the population. On the institutional and legislative details of Caledonian autonomy, see J.-Y. Faberon, *Nouvelle-Calédonie et Polynésie française: des autonomies différentes*, in *Revue française de droit constitutionnel*, 68/2006, p. 691; D. Custos, *New Caledonia, a Case of Shared Sovereignty within the French Republic:*

Caillou (the pebble), is *Kanaky* (from the term *kanak*, man) for the autochthonous population.

The only explicit reference to recognition of names in local language in the whole body of legislation governing the languages of France is found in the Noumea Accord of 1998 (recognised in Title XIII of the French Constitution) reached after gory battles between the autochthonous independence movement and French descendents that brought the archipelago to the brink of civil war. Between 1984 and 1988, the violent claims of the robust Kanak independence movement were, among other things, for recognition of land titles of customary law, cancelled by French domination and progressive expropriation of native land. In art. 1.5 of the Agreement, possible adoption of signs of New Caledonian identity, such as a new name, an anthem and a flag expressing "Kanak identity and the shared future of all inhabitants" is contemplated. This hypothesis, that calls for a *loi du pays* voted by a 3/5 majority of members of the Caledonian assembly, has not yet been discussed, although a compromise on the name *Kanaky Nouvelle Calédonie* seems to be emerging[9]. Article 1.3.1 of the Agreement also establishes that: "Kanak place names will be identified and legally protected, according to the rules applicable to historical monuments". The provision, enshrined in a paragraph dedicated to cultural heritage, is intended to consider the special link between the collective identity of the Kanak people and the earth, a fundamental element that enables family genealogies to be traced and the plan of clans, tribes, districts and *customary areas* to be determined. *Coutumières* (customary areas) are special subdivisions, like French administrative subdivisions, each having its own institutions and coinciding in practice with the traditional land of each tribal community[10].

Thus, toponomastics has become one of the manifestations of Kanak cultural rehabilitation after 150 years of colonial domination that cancelled, deformed

---

Appearance or Reality?, in *European Public Law*, 2007, p. 97. The last and controversial constitutional revision that implemented the Noumea Accord in relation to the right to vote was adopted with Constitutional Law no. 2007–237 of 23rd February 2007 modifying art. 77 of the Constitution, by which electors were limited to persons present in New Caledonian territory in 1999 and their descendents. For a criticism, see O. Gohin, *Quand la République marche sur la tête. Le gel de l'électorat restreint en Nouvelle-Calédonie*, in *Actualités juridique.-Droit administratif*, 2007, p. 800.

9 See D. Custos, *New Caledonia, a Case of Shared Sovereignty within the French Republic: Appearance or Reality?*, *cit.*, p. 120.

10 On the value of place names in Kanak social and political structure, see A. Bensa, *La mémoire des lieux chez les Kanak Nouvelle Calédonie (Grande Terre)*, in *Ateliers*, 1997, p. 83 et seq.; for the political, historical and geographic implications of the name of this French overseas territory, see M. Darot, *Calédonie, Kanaky ou Caillou? Implicites identitaires dans la désignation de la Nouvelle-Calédonie*, in *Mots*, 53/1997, pp. 8–25.

and replaced traditional place names. Recovery of the original names is the subject of a special agreement between the State, the New Caledonia territorial community and the three provinces into which the archipelago is divided. The project spans seven years, beginning in 2002[11]. The agreement regulates the research required to reconstruct the history of place names, envisaging collaboration between provinces, municipalities and the autochthonous customary authorities (Area Councils, Council of Grand Chiefs and Tribal Councils). Once identified, the place names must be approved by all the authorities involved; municipal councils will have the task of preparing the signs with the help of local artists, and the provinces will provide finance. French toponyms will continue to appear in bilingual signs where the Kanak names will have priority position with respect to the language of colonisation, out of respect for the cultural diversity of a population currently consisting of 30% French immigrants and their descendents, 45% Kanak and the rest recent Asian immigrants. The indications in autochthonous language, however, only have memorial value and as a tourist attraction: despite the wishes of the customary authorities, France does not yet recognise its official character, except as far as application of the special land regime is concerned[12].

Hence, there is reason to doubt the authentic will to favour Kanak cultural emancipation, especially considering the French legislator's recent proclivity for so-called memorial law[13], or solemn declarations, often without any legal effect, adopted in relation to dramatic historical events, with the presumed intention of reducing or neutralising their importance in the building of collective memory. In particular, the law of 23rd February 2005, *portant reconnaissance de la Nation et contribution nationale en faveur des Français rapatriés*, aroused lively debate. It stipulated that "school curricula recognise the positive role of French presence overseas" (art. 4, para. 2). The sentence seemed a justification of colonisation and a disavowal of French responsibility for difficult relations with the populations of her colonies; it was abrogated the following year, but its meaning echoed the much broader details on the role of the French coloniser contained in the Preamble of the Noumea Accord.

Toponomastic choices are therefore hardly ever neutral, even when they are generically justified as defence of linguistic heritage. Current trends in Western

11 *Accord particulier entre l'Etat et la Nouvelle Calédonie*, concluded on 22nd January 2002 according to art. 215 law no. 99–209 of 19th March1999 regarding New Caledonia.

12 Notes on the idiosyncrasies of this regime in J.-Y. Faberon, *Nouvelle-Calédonie et Polynésie française*, *cit.*, p. 704.

13 See P. Fraisseix, *Le Droit mémoriel*, in *Revue française de droit constitutionnel*, 2006, p. 483 and E. Cartier, *Histoire et droit: rivalité ou complémentarité?*, in *Revue française de droit constitutionnel*, 2006, p. 519 et seq.

countries seem to oscillate between two opposite ideological positions. On one hand, there is the recovery-of-cultural-heritage perspective, generally taken by classic national States, that seeks to go back to the historical origin of place names. However, a static image tends to hide the hegemonic processes that occurred in the course of time. A different approach is usually found at the level of regional or local policy, that claims linguistic reconquest through new mapping that observes the current dynamics of living languages and stimulates their use[14]. A conciliation of the two aspirations, mirrored in the various options of monolingualism or bi-plurilingualism, may be fraught with problems of geographical standardization but remains largely practicable in other sectors of toponomastics, for example local signposting.

2. Toponomastics in France: the general framework

France has not escaped these tensions, despite strong attachment to revolutionary ideas of the unity of the French people and *République* and the equality of all citizens, on the basis of which exclusive use of French is imposed in the public sphere, fuelling entrenched diffidence towards recognition of collective linguistic rights or peripheral centres of public power, considered dangerous symptoms of national disintegration. This is why France has not signed the Council of Europe's Framework Convention for the Protection of National Minorities, has not ratified the European Charter for Regional or Minority Languages, has expressed reserves that prevent application of art. 27 of the International Covenant on Civil and Political Rights, and on the whole has schizophrenically defended multilingualism and promoted French internationally, while failing to recognise linguistic minorities at home[15].

Indeed, France, together with Italy, is the European State with the greatest linguistic diversity[16]. According to linguist Bernard Cerquiglini's report to the French Government in 1999, in anticipation of ratification of the European Charter for Regional or Minority Languages, as many as 75 languages or dialects, different from official French, 35 in continental France alone and the others in overseas territories and departments, are traditionally spoken by French

14 In this perspective see H. Guillorel, *Territoire de la langue et toponymie officielle*, *cit.*, p. 33.

15 See among others T. Gründler, *La République française, une et indivisible?* in *Revue de droit public*, 2007, p. 476.

16 See A. Nanchi, *Vers un statut des minorités en droit constitutionnel français*, Clermont-Ferrand, 2006, p. 3.

citizens in the territory of the Republic[17]. The same heterogeneity is also testified by place names, which in continental France often carry more or less evident traces of Catalan, Basque, Breton, German or Occitan origins.

The case of France can also be demonstrative of the complexity of choices that public powers are called to make with a view to protection of regional languages in the matter of toponomastics. A grid with variables to consider for an assessment of the political nodes implicit in toponomastic practices should at least consider the different categories of place names, the level on the geographic scale of places, the processes of transformation of names and the position of toponomastic authorities[18].

Conflicts between national and local languages affect the various categories of toponyms differently: for example, in Alsace and the neighbouring Moselle, only the names of large cities are francised (*Straßburg* has become *Strasbourg*; *Obernai* is the French contraction of the German *Oberehnheim*), while the Germanic character of the name of small towns has been conserved almost everywhere (e.g. *Mittelhausbergen* in Bas-Rhin) and names in the land register are the original German-Alsatian ones. Examples of the same dynamics elsewhere are the francisation of the Occitan Tolosa that becomes *Toulouse*, or the Catalan *Perpinyà* that has become *Perpignan*; the conservation of place names in Basque (*Ainhoa* in the Atlantic Pyrenees), Breton (*Kermoroc'h* in Côtes-d'Armor), Catalan (*Banyuls-dels-Aspres* in the Eastern Pyrenees), Corsican (*San-Gavino-di-Carbini* in the Southern Department of Corsica), and

17 See B. Cerquiglini, *Les langues de la France, Rapport au Ministre de l'Education Nationale, de la Recherche et de la Technologie, et à la Ministre de la Culture et de la Communication*, April 1999 (www.culture.gouv.fr/culture/dglf/lang-reg/rapport_cerquiglini/langues-france.html). Note that the languages and dialects censured in the Report have very differentiated sociolinguistic statutes: living languages spoken by millions of citizens are grouped with essentially written languages close to extinction for virtual absence of maternal or oral transmission. The current statute of the languages of France recognises a territorial link, and hence the character of regional language, in the case of Alsatian, Basque, Breton, Catalan, Corsican, Western Flemish, Moselle francique, Franco-Provençal, several variants of *Langue d'Oïl* (Franc-Comtois, Walloon, Champenois, Picard, Norman, Gallo, Poitevin, Saintongeais, Lorrain, Bourguignon-Morvandiau) and *Langue d'òc* or *Occitan* (Gascon, Languedocian, Provençal, Auvergnat, Limousin, Vivaro-Alpine). Non-territorial languages, namely those spoken by a significant number of French citizens without being the official language of a State and thus at risk of extinction are: dialectal Arabic, Western Armenian, Berber, Spanish Hebrew, Romany and Yiddish. Overseas, there are 15 variants of Creole having a French (Martinique, Guadalupe, Reunion, Guyana) or Anglo-Portuguese lexical basis (Guyana), 28 Kanak languages in New Caledonia, seven different local dialects in French Polynesia, Maori and Malagasy on the island of Mayotte, and Wallisian and Futunan in the Wallis and Futuna islands.

18 See H. Guillorel, *Territoire de la langue et toponymie officielle*, *cit.*, p. 35.

so forth. In general, microtoponomastics in France is a rather stable category that testifies very ancient languages, as in the case of the names of rivers or mountains, and the relative lack of interest in redefinition during construction of the nation-State.

Processes of linguistic hegemony must also grapple with the time dimension. The national or official character of a language generally depends on affirmation of the written form via cartography or the creation of standard geographical nomenclature by reference to ancient legal texts or land registers instituted in France in the early XIX century. Current valorisation of the notion of cultural and linguistic heritage urges the translation into writing of thousands of places that risk disappearing with the people still able to name them orally. If historical recovery is contemplated, it is also necessary to decide how far back to go, which is not easy in a country like France in which processes of transformation of toponyms have occurred over a long historical period and to different degrees in the various historical provinces. Denomination processes themselves are a factor of considerable complexity, since Francisation of a toponym may occur by literal or phonetic transcription, following an adaptation or a translation or even a simple accident due to poor copying. For example, the simple inversion of a letter changed the town of *Saint-Onen-la-Chapelle* in Brittany, which takes its name from a Breton saint, into *Saint-Ouen-la-Chapelle*, which refers to a Catholic saint much more common in French hagiotoponyms. This error persisted for a long time on French geographic maps.

The position of toponomastic authorities obviously has implications for linguistic policy. In the case of France, strictly political authorities have not always been necessary and they currently occupy an eminent position in administrative and relatively independent para-administrative bodies at national and local levels[19].

The French situation is quite diversified in the degree of self-inclusion of ethnic and linguistic identity of the various local communities and their claims. The highest political tensions manifested in New Caledonia, French Polynesia and Corsica, but there are other communities that aspire to recognition of their linguistic identity in Brittany, Alsace and the Basque and Occitan parts of the country.

19 See *infra*, § 4.

3. The origins of the linguistic hegemony of French and slow assimilation of minority languages

The idea that France unified the State through an active policy of promotion of French at the expense of provincial languages is a stereotype that is not confirmed by historical studies but rather is derived from a modern view of the problems and potential of state linguistic policy. The link between language, territory and national identity did not manifest clearly before the XIX century[20] and an active policy of promotion of French is only found among the policies of governments of the Fifth Republic in the last fifty years[21]. Nevertheless, the act of making French the official language of the nation generally continues to be ascribed to the ordinance: "*pour la réformation et abbréviation des procès*" signed by Francis I in the Castle of Villers-Cotterêts on 15th August 1539[22]. Article 111 of the text imposed the use of the "French mother tongue" for acts of notaries and court judgments instead of an often rudimentary and incomprehensible Latin.

In actual fact, the *Ancien Régime* only pursued the Francisation of legal language, without any ideology aimed at imposing national linguistic uniformity or the cancellation of provincial languages, indeed considered to have historical and cultural value equal if not superior to that of the French of Paris[23]. Besides, in the expression of the ordinance, the various provincial vernaculars were

20 See E. J. Hobsbawm, *Nations and Nationalism since 1780: Programme, Myth, Reality,* Cambridge, 1990, p. 19 et seq.

21 See J. Ziller, *Le droit français de la langue, entre le mythes d'une tradition interventionniste et la réalité de nouvelles angoisses*, EUI Working Paper LAW 10/2006, p. 2 (http://www.iue.it).

22 The ordinance of 1539 is still law today for decisions of the Appeal Court regarding whether a defence memoire presented at a penal hearing must be in French (*Cour cass., ch. crim.*, 4th March 1986, *Turkson*) or whether a sentence containing an untranslated clause in American can be rejected (*Cour cass., 2ème ch. civ.*, 11th January1989, *Soc. Composants et Produits Electroniques C. Soc. TRW Inc*). For a documented historical reconstruction, see : S. Soleil, *L'ordonnance de Villers-Cotterêts, cadre juridique de la politique linguistique des rois de France?*, in A.-M. Le Pourhiet (ed.), *Langue(s) et Constitution(s),* (*Colloque de l'Association française de droit constitutionnel, Rennes, December 2000*), Aix-Marseille, 2003, p. 19 et seq.; see also F. Melin-Soucramanien, *Le statut des langues régionales ou minoritaires: la «tolerance constitutionnelle» française*, *ibidem*, p. 7, who plausibly interprets the ordinance of 1539 as the first instance of a rule on the compulsory use of French in the public sphere.

23 The so-called *Langue d'Oïl* spoken in the Northern part of the Loire was not a homogeneous language outside the narrow limits of individual historic provinces or large cities and the more educated classes. In other words, a person from Lorraine and another from Normandy had little possibility of understanding each other at the time. See G. Zink, *L'ancien français*, Paris, 1987, p. 25.

generally understood to be included, as shown by subsequent royal edicts that expressly offered the alternative of French or vernacular language. In any case, this was the prevalent interpretation as testified by court practice at least until approval of the *Code Napoleon*[24]. Indeed, after 1620 the requirements of political, administrative and judicial unification of the Realm led to the enactment of rules that imposed French in the drafting of legal acts in certain non-French-speaking provinces (Catalonia, Flanders, Loraine, Alsace, the Béarnaise area in the Atlantic Pyrenees where Basque was spoken, but not in Brittany), but it was the aim of political unity that in many cases led to these measures being accompanied by observation of cultural and linguistic diversity "of ways, customs, laws and language"[25]. This was noted by the revolutionaries in observing that knowledge of French was, if anything, a prerogative of the *élite*, but far from common in most of the population: "*Le despotisme maintenait la varietés des idiomes*"[26].

The Revolution's first approach to the problem of provincial languages actually had a liberal fingerprint: the directives of the general assembly were translated into all the idioms of the nation and a system of public education was contemplated. With the Jacobin radicalisation, generalised prohibition of languages different from French was imposed by a short-lived law of 1794. Repression of local languages was therefore a limited episode, and the revolutionary intention of the spread of French as a national language was only achieved progressively and much later.

In the course of the Restoration and the Second Empire (1814–1870), little progress was made in this direction: in 1832, written French was required for access to public office and in 1859, more than three centuries after the edict of Villers-Cotterêts, the Appeal Court recognised the legal obligation of French in the drafting of public acts. It was not until the Third Republic (1870–1940) and approval of the Ferry law of 1882 that the revolutionary ambition of creating a

24 See P. Cipolla, *L'Ordonnance criminelle di Luigi XIV e la lunga marcia verso la codificazione*, in *Politica del diritto*, 2005, p. 497.

25 For example, in Alsace, annexed in 1648. Despite the auspices of an exponent of state centralism of the stature of Louis XIV and his minister Colbert, Catholic priests in the region were invited to celebrate mass in German to counter the Lutheran influence, central government directives were broadcast in French and German and the administrative officials of the Realm usually relied on Alsatian in oral communications. The same logic was applied in Corsica, annexed to the Realm in 1768: at least half of the sovereign Council consisted of Corsican citizens, bilingual schools were envisaged and Italian was widely tolerated in legal acts. See S. Soleil, *L'ordonnance de Villers-Cotterêts, cit.*, pp. 26–27.

26 From Bertrand Barère de Vieuzac's report on languages to the Committee of Public Health (27th January 1794), in M. de Certeau, D. Julia, J. Revel (eds.), *Une politique de la langue. La Révolution française et les patois*, Paris, 1975, p. 296.

compulsory system of public education and the effective spread of French was achieved. The law contained nothing about local dialects, which were certainly advanced more by the zeal and hostility to *patois* of teachers animated by the Jacobin revolutionary spirit than by any assimilationist will of the legislator[27].

From the early XVIII century, French was widespread as the language of culture and social class prestige in all the European courts, without that being the consequence of any particular linguistic policy. Similarly, in France, the erosion of provincial vernaculars occurred as a result of the enormous gravitational force exercised by the political and cultural centre of Paris, which was already a megalopolis in the XIII century. Things changed in the course of the XX century, when the language of international communication shifted towards the Anglo-American axis, relegating French to the position of minority language on the world scene.

These are the dynamics that led the Fifth Republic to inaugurate an authentic policy in active defence of French: two centuries after Cardinal Richelieu conceived the *Académie française*, the task of normalising French was taken up directly by state institutions such as the High Committee for the Defence and Expansion of French, created in 1966 (and dissolved in the '80s), the task of which was to preserve the purity of the language against foreign influence and dialectal forms. In 1972, ministerial commissions were instituted to replace foreign words that had come into use with appropriate French terms, which were to be binding for the administration. In the same view, the Bas-Lauriol law of 1975 on the use of French was approved, introducing specific sanctions. However, the law remained largely unimplemented and does not seem to have significantly influenced the behaviour of French citizens. Almost in parallel, a prudent linguistic policy of promotion of regional languages was inaugurated with the Deixonne law of 1951, which concerned the teaching of local languages and dialects, and with the Haby law of 1975, which envisaged the possibility of teaching regional languages and culture throughout the school period.

Intensification of initiatives towards European political integration and fears of loss of national identity again fuelled French language protectionism, leading to a revision of the Constitution in 1992, which in coincidence with approval of the Treaty of Maastricht, included a first paragraph in art. 2 of the Constitution: "The language of the Republic is French". Though partially corrected by the Constitutional Council, the regulations for implementation, approved with the Toubon law in 1994, tended to reproduce the logic of the previous Bas-Lauriol law in regulating the right of citizens to use French in five particular sectors (teaching, public competitions, research, worker protection and consumer

27 See J. Ziller, *Le droit français de la langue*, *cit.*, p. 4.

protection)[28]. In 1999, the Constitutional Council used the new inclusion of art. 2 of the Constitution as grounds to declare the constitutional inconsistency of the European Charter for Regional or Minority Languages.

4. Constitutional recognition of French and regulation of other languages of France

The new draft of art. 2 of the French Constitution has not really changed French legislation[29]. According to the Constitutional Council, the provision should be interpreted to mean that French is the official language of the public service and legal persons who exercise a public function, as already established by the Bas-Lauriol law of 1975. In examining the text of the Toubon law, the Constitutional Council reduced its scope, observing, among other things, that "*la langue française évolue, comme toute langue vivante, en intégrant dans le vocabulaire usuel des termes de diverses sources, qu'il s'agisse d'expressions issues de langues régionales, de vocables dits populaires, ou de mots étrangers*"[30]. The Council concluded that compulsory use of official terminology can only be imposed in the public service but not on public or private bodies and radio and television. In particular, art. 3 of the law, which imposed the use of French for all inscriptions and announcements having the purpose of informing the public, whether displayed or made in public streets, places open to the public or on common means of transport, was declared unconstitutional. Basically, the interpretation of the legislator, the Constitutional Council and the supreme magistrature was what counted for understanding not so much *whether* use of regional languages was permitted, as much as *in what cases* their use was prohibited.

28 For an analysis of this legislation see A. Somma, *La politica linguistica del legislatore nelle esperienze italiana e francese*, in *Politica del diritto*, 1997, p. 58 et seq.

29 On the anomaly of a constitutional linguistic provision protecting the majority or national language, see G. Carcassonne, *Droit constitutionnel*, Paris, 2000, p. 44. In the Italian literature, also in relation to the coeval adoption in Italy of the law on historical linguistic minorities no. 482/1999 that opens with a similar provision ("The official language of the Republic is Italian"), see S. Ceccanti, *Francia e Italia di fronte alle differenze di sesso e di lingua: crisi comune delle certezze consolidate ed esiti diversi*, in *Diritto pubblico comparato ed europeo*, 1/2000, p. 91.

30 Law no. 94–345 DC of 29th July 1994, *Loi relative à l'emploi de la langue française*, *cons.* 6.

Article 2 of the Constitution has been analysed more than once by the Constitutional Council, which progressively defined its limits[31], especially in relation to other languages of France. The best-known and most controversial decision was undoubtedly the one regarding the ratification of the European Charter for Regional or Minority Languages, in which the Council considered whether ratification would be contrary to the new paragraph of art. 2 of Constitution and also to the principles of indivisibility of the Republic, equality of citizens and unity of the French people, proclaimed by arts. 2 and 3, as these are "fundamental principles that oppose recognition of collective rights to any group, whether defined by a community of origin, culture, language or belief"[32].

Thus, the Constitution does not impose an absolute obligation to use French, but undoubtedly the constitutional reform of 1992 and the Constitutional Council's interpretation of it in 1999 impeded the policy of progressive opening to regional languages that began in 1951 with the Deixonne law on teaching of local languages and dialects.

However, there are very clear limits to the use of regional languages, derived from the conflict caused by their use in the public service, prevalently in relation to the space to be given to their teaching. For example, jurisprudence has established that in public or publicly financed schools, French must take priority, but today bilingual schools in which equal time is dedicated to two languages are also substantially allowed[33]. The State has made some significant steps in the training of qualified teachers of Breton, Basque, Corsican, Creole and Catalan; the first public competition for teachers of Alsatian, Moselle *francique* and Occitan was held in 2002. Again, New Caledonia, where Melanesian languages have priority over French, is an exception. Other exceptions for French overseas

---

31 In the most recent decision, handed down on 28th September 2006, concerning the Agreement for application of the Convention of 2006 on European patents, the Constitutional Council examined art. 2 for the first time in the framework of control of international commitments, following a parliamentary petition alleging that France's renunciation of complete transcription of European patents into French, according to the Agreement, violated the constitutional right to use French. The Council rejected the petition on the grounds of absurd linguistic nationalism, with motivations that could lead to future greater openness of the constitutional judge. See M. Verpeaux, *La défense désespérée de la langue française*, in *Recueil Dalloz*, 2/2007, p. 120 et seq.

32 Law no. 99–412 DC of 15th June 1999, *Charte européenne des langues régionales ou minoritaires, cons.* 6.

33 With regard to Breton schools practising "immersion" teaching, the Council of State established that the possibility of exemption from compulsory use of French in teaching to enable learning of a regional language in public schools financed by the State was only allowed if a dominant position was ensured for the language of the Republic. See *Conseil d'Etat, Conseil National des Groupes Académiques de l'enseignement Public, UNSA et autres*, no. 248192–248204, decision of 29th November 2002.

communities include the possibility of making tests in local language facultative in competitions for access to public functions.

Various provisions of legislative or regulatory rank widening the range of measures directed at protecting regional languages have been added to definetions of the limits of their usage in the public sphere in France, without yet leading to their complete recognition for public uses. Among legislative provisions, law no. 99–533 of 25th June 1999 (*Loi d'orientation pour l'aménagement et le développement durable du territoire*) introduced the policy of support for regional languages among the measures aimed at regional management and sustainable development, specifying that collective cultural services aimed at ensuring "the promotion and diffusion of French together with protection and transmission of regional or minority cultures and languages" (art. 14).

Regarding overseas departments, the *Loi d'orientation* no. 2000–1207 of 13th December 2000 recognises all languages used in these territories as part of the national linguistic heritage that can benefit from active state policy to favour their use (art. 34). Special provisions concern the promotion of Kanak culture in New Caledonia: for this purpose law no. 89–524 of 27th July 1989 institutes an agency to valorise the Kanak linguistic heritage and encourage forms of cultural expression in craft, audiovisual and artistic sectors. As already mentioned, toponomastics has received special attention prescribing restoration of place names in Kanak. With law no. 84–747 of 2nd August 1984 and law no. 96–142 of 21st February 1996 (now art. L 4433–27 of the *Code général des collectivités territoriales*), the French Parliament transferred competence in cultural matters, with special reference to initiatives in the sector of regional languages, promoted by or at least after consultation with the relevant territorial communities, to the regions of Guadalupe, Guyana, Martinique and Reunion. A similar provision defines the competence of the region Corsica (art. L 4422–37 of the code).

The Government also adopted regulations in line with this new dash towards minority languages, especially in the cultural sector[34]. With law no. 85–1006 of 23rd September 1985, a National Council of Regional Languages and Cultures was instituted at the prime minister's office; its task was to study questions regarding linguistic and cultural support and promotion, and to offer consultation for the definition of ministerial policy.

A symbolic turning point was the subsequent law no. 2001–950 of 16th October 2001, which transformed the General Delegation for the French Language into the "*Délégation générale à la langue française et aux langues de France*" (DGLFLF); its task was to "contribute to the conservation and

---

34 A review is provided by V. Eysseric, *Le corpus juridique des langues de France,* Paris, 2005.

valorisation of the languages of France, or the languages different from French spoken on national territory and which are part of national cultural heritage" (art. 2) and to coordinate state policy in sectors governed by the Ministry for Culture and Communication. In 2002, another law (no. 2002–898 of 15th May 2002) for the first time expressly included protection and valorisation of the languages of France among the tasks of an administrative authority, namely the Minister for Culture and Communication. The subsequent regulations of 11th September 2003 regarding organisation of the DGLFLF amplified the tasks of the Delegation with regard to the languages of France, specifying coordination functions in contributing to the development and valorisation of the languages of France and in ensuring observation and evaluation of linguistic practices, through appeal to the administrations and research organisations competent in this sector (art. 5).

On 4th October 2003, the first *Assises nationales des langues de France* were held in Paris; this was an unusual national meeting organised by the State at the initiative of the Minister for Culture. It was attended by various members of Parliament and representatives of local communities, associations, media and universities. The need to provide French regional and minority languages with organic governance, showed by the Government in its 2004 report to Parliament on application of the Toubon law, was strongly expressed[35]. However, political will to act has been slow to manifest. The last proposal for constitutional recognition of regional languages was presented in 2006 by the Breton deputy Marc Le Fur on an impromptu occasion (debate of a bill concerning New Caledonia) when he requested approval of an amendment to art. 2, para. 1 of the Constitution adding the words "in observation of the regional languages that are part of our heritage"[36]. The proposal was voted 44 *for* and 57 *against*, a better result than that of Le Fur's previous attempt in 2005, presented together with the 2007 presidential candidate, François Bayrou, and that of prime minister Jospin's attempt in 1999 that aimed to introduce a new provision consenting ratification of the European Charter for Regional or Minority Languages, against opposition by the Constitutional Council[37]. Repeated failure of these proposals show that the question of linguistic differences in France is a delicate subject that divides the political parties transversely but that has not prevented concrete steps in the direction of their protection.

---

35 Available at: http://www.culture.gouv.fr/culture/dglf/rapport/2004/Rapport_au_parlement_2004.pdf.

36 *Assemblée Nationale, Session ordinaire 2006–2007, 93e séance*, 13th December 2006.

37 In this case it regarded approval of a new art. 53, para. 3 stating that "The Republic may ratify the European Charter for Regional and Minority Languages signed on 7th May 1999".

Finally, the constitutional reform (so-called Constitutional Law of Modernisation of Institutions of the Republic, no. 2008–724 of 23rd July 2008) introduced a new provision in art. 75–1, according to which "*Les langues regionales appartiennent au patrimoine de la France*". However, the effect of the provision is largely symbolic and without immediate consequences in legal terms. The "cultural" connotation of regional languages, besides not questioning the primacy of French as public language, does not alter the principle by which use of a language different from French is a freedom, not a right[38].

5. Legislation and practice in toponomastics: names of municipalities, departments, regions and road signs

Now the historical, political and legislative context can be completed with the rules and practices of toponomastics. As we have seen, the transition from oral to written forms proves determinant in the officialisation of place names and thus of the prevalence of a national language over varieties of pre-existing languages and also of the possibility of reconstructing the philology and linguistic transformations of individual toponyms. As far as France is concerned, toponomastics acquired a scientific character roughly in the second half of the XIX century, when topographic dictionaries were produced for all departments, according to a project dating back to 1870, only partially completed. The evolution of each toponym was described in great detail, generally going back to the Middle Ages. A systematic study of toponomastics only began with the work of Auguste Longnon (*Noms de lieux de France*) published in 1920, subsequently expanded with many other studies that generally classify place names according to linguistic layers in time and the type of place (river, mountain, cultivated and uncultivated land, human settlement, places of worship, place of production, and so forth)[39].

On the basis of laws, some of which date back to 1884, attribution of official character to place names in the French system is only the task of the Government or national legislator for names of administrative bodies[40], periodically subject to

38 See summary in C. Le Bris, *Les Langues régionales dans la Constitution*, in *Revue de droit public*, 2009, p. 787 et seq.

39 Among general studies, see for example C. Rostaing, *Les noms de lieux*, Paris, 1997 and S. Gendron, *L'origine des noms de lieux en France: essai de toponymie*, Paris, 2003. Recently many up-to-date studies on regional and local toponomastics have also become available.

40 The denomination or change of name of municipalities and departments requires a government decree (arts. L 2111–1 and L 3111–1 *Code général des collectivités territoriales,* respectively) whereas the change of name of a region requires a law of Parliament (art. L 4121–1).

census by the Home Ministry and communicated to the National Institute of Statistics and Economic Studies (INSEE), which has the task of managing the databank and providing data. Naturally, this is not a small task from the viewpoint of linguistic uniformisation of national territory, considering the extreme administrative subdivision of the country since the French Revolution, when *arrondissements,* cantons and municipalities were created in order to rationalise many of the present departments[41]. The revolutionary aim of creating immediate identification of the various ambits with the State was pursued not only by dividing land but also by naming departments after rivers and mountains in order to transmit a new memorisation of the physical territory that could cancel the historical and political references of the preceding provinces.

In the same technocratic spirit, the regions, which are functional entities rather than identity spaces, were created starting from 1956. Reference to regional languages in France therefore does not necessarily refer to administrative regions. Indeed, certain areas that united historically or linguistically homogeneous provincial communities were divided between two regions, as in the case of Brittany, Normandy, Savoy and Vendee. Most regions except Alsace and Corsica, where the situation is more homogeneous, do not correspond to the territory of any historical community; examples are the regions Centre, Rhône-Alpes and Pays-de-la-Loire. The consequence is that French citizens do not feel any historical, cultural or linguistic identification with their region, but rather with their municipality or directly with the State[42]. This does not prevent citizens

41 The subdivision of French territory can be regarded as an example of the motto *divide and rule.* In 1789 the present 329 *arrondissements*, 3879 cantons and 36771 municipalities were created; in 1790, 83 departments were instituted (today there are more than 100). In 1956, 22 regions were formed. The last administrative partition introduced by the national legislator was the *pays*, created in 1995 by law no. 95–115 (*Loi d'orientation pour l'aménagement et le développement du territoire*) effectively inspired by the will to unite territories having geographic, economic, cultural or social cohesion, but the bodies actually only have consultative functions. The resulting institutional overlap was not accompanied by clearly defined partition of roles. Even after the reform on decentralised organisation of the Republic in 2003, partition of roles continues to depend largely on the legislator and not the Constitution, except in part for overseas territories. See among others M.-C. Pontorehau, *Recenti sviluppi della centralizzazione alla francese*, in *Le Regioni*, 6/2005, p. 1083; A. Fais, *La décéntralisation e la sperimentazione normativa in Francia*, in *Autonomie*, 2006, p. 465; M. Calamo Specchia, *Le asimmetrie funzionali e istituzionali del decentramento alla francese e l'orbita europea: una forza gravitazionale ancora troppo debole?*, in *Federalismi.it*, 3/2007 (on line).

42 See J.B. Auby, *Il ruolo e l'identità delle istituzioni regionali in Francia: recenti sviluppi*, in *Le Regioni*, 2/2001, p. 249 et seq.

from re-identifying with their territorial community[43], provided any changes in borders aimed at reflecting homogeneous groupings of population are introduced by sufficiently participative procedures, as shown for example in Corsica (paradoxically), which opposed reunification of its two departments in 2003[44].

On the other hand, no specific rules regard the denominations of places different from administrative entities. Insomuch as such places are of local interest, they are legitimately in the ambit of the bodies representing the respective territorial communities. In particular, the need for prior authorisation by the prefect for the names of streets and public places was abolished by the law of 31st December 1970, and the *loi de décentralisation* of 1982 eliminated all power of the prefect to approve or annul deliberations of the municipal councils. Only administrative judges can examine the decisions of municipal councils. Since 1988, the State Council (Dubois case) is only authorised to verify the absence of manifest errors of evaluation and to determine whether decisions of the municipal council respond to municipal interest and are in line with laws and general legal principles. Cases of annulment are in fact very rare[45].

Ultimately, the officiality of place names different from those of administrative entities depends on the functions performed by major institutions operating at the central level but relatively independent from the Government, namely the National Geographic Institute (IGN) and more recently the National

---

43 In this sense see for example A. Nanchi, *Vers un statut des minorités en droit constitutionnel français*, *cit.*, p. 82, that underlines how the rules in force give the national legislator the opportunity to valorise the link of people with their territory. According to art. L 4122–1 of the current *Code général des collectivités territoriales*, changes in regional borders are the responsibility of the legislator, after consultation with the regional councils involved, whereas changes in municipal borders are the responsibility of the Government according art. L 2112–1 et seq. of the same code.

44 The referendum of approval on 6th July 2003 narrowly rejected the proposal to reform the institutional setting of Corsica and create a single territorial community with greater powers, replacing the two departments and the region. This outcome was probably the result of political opposition rejecting this initiative of the central Government due to insufficient local participation. See G. Allegri, *Quali prospettive dopo il no al referendum in Corsica?* in *Federalismi.it*, 5/2003 (on line).

45 See for example *Tribunal administratif de Nice*, dec. of 24th March 2006, in *Actualités juridique-Droit administratif*, 22nd May 2006, p. 1038, annulling the decision of the municipal council of Nice to name a public space after Jacques Medecin. Through manifest error of judgment, the prefect of Alpes-Marittimes appealed on the grounds that the merit of Medecin (former mayor of the city, repeatedly condemned for corruption and abuse of office) was not unanimously recognised in the municipality. There are two criteria for legal assessment of public celebration: maintenance of public order and evaluation of local interest in celebrating a certain person. The two criteria are related in the sense that disorder or protests could arise if a public space were named after a controversial figure.

Toponomastics Commission (CNT), which among other things drafts and proposes bills for laws and regulations on the subject. The written and oral forms of French toponyms are derived from local use, which this Commission is specifically charged with enforcing. Thus, particularities of the various local vernaculars are generally maintained in official French toponyms.

The IGN is mainly concerned with normalisation of geographic names in the field of French and international cartography. Since the 1950s, it has carefully recovered and preserved names often derived from local use that may have been altered by wrong transcription, phonetic adaptation and inappropriate Francisation. A survey of toponyms in use, concluded in 1997, listed about two million names that are now the basis of the toponomastic data for 1:25,000 maps and enabled important normalisation of dialectal toponymy. It is interesting that even in the latest edition of the glossary, regional languages are not yet mentioned but rather "dialectal terms"[46].

The National Toponomastics Commission was instituted at the National Council of Geographic Information (an interministerial body of government consultation) with an act of 26th July 1985, modified by an act of 28th September 1999, to "contribute to the conservation and coherent development of the toponomastic heritage of France". A regulation of 2000 specified its organisation and functions which are currently shared between three subcommissions with distinct tasks (creation of a database of national toponomastics; documentation and international relations; normalisation of toponyms), in which the main national authorities on the subject are represented, for example the General Delegation of French and the Languages of France, INSEE, the land registry, IGN and public and university bodies such as the *Ecole des hautes études en sciences sociales,* the Direction of the Archives of France and the National Library of France.

Specific local offices, instituted by active bilingual territorial communities, have recently been added to this plethora of central public authorities. Their task is to integrate toponomastic data in local languages through documentary research and field interviews. They play the role of privileged local referents for Government on cultural and linguistic policy. For example, the Office of the Breton Language, created in 1999 and financed by the region of Brittany and Loire Atlantique with the task of studying sociolinguistic aspects of spoken Breton, provides consultancy for toponyms and microtoponyms of the land register to the territorial communities. Similar bodies are the Institute of Occitan Studies and the Inter-Regional Centre of Occitan Development (CIRDOC), the

---

46 S. Lejeune, E. Calvarin (eds.), *André Pégorier. Les noms de lieux en France. Glossaire de termes dialectaux*, 3rd ed., Paris, 2006.

Public Office of the Basque Language and the Institute of Catalan Studies. These bodies play an essential role in finding homogeneous, rational formulas for bilingual signs, a field completely without regulation at national level.

Indeed, regardless of the official or unofficial character of place names, an element indicative of the level of protection and of effective linguistic pluralism of an area is the use of bilingual or multilingual signposting. The presence of bilingual signs may sometimes only indicate the evolutionary stage of any claims in this sense, but in any case it is an important incentive for orthographic normalisation of place names and local linguistic variants, as well as reinforcing the perception of identity and specificity of a place, which can immediately be linked to one of its most representative traits. It is also useful in border regions, determining communicative continuity that favours integration of populations of neighbouring countries. This is a relatively recent but fast-growing phenomenon, especially in Western countries, linked to increased international mobility of persons and awareness of the frequent lack of correspondence between the administrative borders of States and ethnic-linguistic divisions. The introduction of bilingual panels is costly and requires organisation and coordination between local and national authorities, calling both for research into methods enabling efficacious perception of information for the purposes of road safety, and for time and resources to identify and normalise local toponyms according to a national standard.

A minimum form of protection is the simple indication of certain toponyms in place signs (at the beginning and end of towns, street names, signs indicating places of cultural interest) without the minority language being official and often using minor characters with respect to those of the national language. Greater protection is indicated by widespread adoption of bilingual town signs and road signs; normally the national idiom precedes the one in local language, in letters of the same size but typographically different, in order to maintain the sense of prevalence of the national language. The effective application of bilingualism in signposting occurs when the local and national versions are given equal *status* in all types of indications, according to a priority usually linked to the linguistic prevalence of the population. In this case the local language may take priority position if the number of speakers constitutes a majority, as occurs for example in Alto Adige/Südtirol. A stronger form of protection of the minority language occurs in the transition to monolingualism, with indications offered only in the local language, generally assisted by co-officiality with respect to the national language (for example in Catalonia) or according to more flexible modes as in Finland, where signposting is also in the second national language if residents speaking that language reach a certain numerical threshold.

When uniform regulation is lacking at national level and the initiative is left to the various road authorities, there are usually more advanced forms of bilingualism in the local and urban networks but often not uniform or standardized. France is such a case[47], where widely different behaviours are recorded in the territories of the main ethnic and linguistic minorities, which despite the prohibition of languages different from French in public life, have developed bilingual road signs. The general rule continues to be French monolingualism on national routes, but a campaign of vandalism against road signs, especially in Corsica, induced the Government to formulate legislative changes that allow local representatives to use road signs providing "local information". National Government tolerance of bilingual signs has been a fact for many years (at least since 1980), but continues to lack explicit legislative references. In any case, the State refuses to subsidise this type of initiative.

Bilingual signs are nevertheless used widely in the departments of Western Brittany (French/Breton, departments of Finistère, Côtes-d'Armor and Morbihan), Alace (French/German), certain municipalities of Occitania (French/local variant of Occitan), department of Western Pyrenees (French/Catalan) and Atlantic Pyrenees (French/Basque). Signs are (sometimes) given in different typographic characters so as to emphasise the officiality and priority of French, and should be brought up to date: the local language is written in italic letters of the same size, despite the recommendations of local toponomastic offices that the same characters should be used. In various cases, at least in minor municipalities of Brittany, the French place name copies the Breton name; in Alsace and the nearby Moselle region, the German names of small towns have been conserved almost everywhere and the land registries conserve the original German or Alsatian names; at Strasbourg bilingual signs are limited to certain streets in the historic centre. However, in recent years Alsace too has increased its *démarche identitaire* by recovering Alsatian street names that have undergone multiple translations in the course of time, to the point of becoming incomprehensible.

The uniformity and widespread nature of bilingual signs for towns and directions in Corsica (in French/Corsican throughout the island), as well as for municipal, department and national roads, constitutes an exception in *France metropolitaine*. Some municipalities of the interior also display direction signs solely in Corsican.

---

47 According to law no. 2004–809 of 13th August 2004 (*Loi relative aux libertés et responsabilités locales*), road management (excluding major arteries) is transferred to departments that apply for it, together with ownership of the relevant land (transferred by the State) and the respective liens, rights and duties. The transfer becomes active by decree of the Council of State (art. 18).

6. Unanswered questions on toponomastic policy in France

If it is currently the task of French local communities to decide whether to use local bilingual signs, the State has not offered incentives or formulated uniform reference criteria but has merely manifested a certain tolerance. Constitutional recognition of regional languages in 2008, with the rewriting of art. 75–1 of the Constitution, should at least permit normalisation of urban bilingual signs by the State[48]. However, the provision does not have any automatic effect regarding ratification of the European Charter for Regional Languages.

Among the 39 commitments made by France on signing the European Charter for Regional or Minority Languages (it was necessary to ratify at least 35), there was also art. 10, para. 2g that states: "In respect of the local and regional authorities on whose territory the number of residents who are users of regional or minority languages is such as to justify the measures specified below, the Parties undertake to allow and/or encourage (…) the use or adoption, if necessary in conjunction with the name in the official language(s), of traditional and correct forms of place-names in regional or minority languages".

It is noteworthy that in establishing the inconsistency of the Charter with the French Constitution, the Constitutional Council recognized that none of the commitments made were contrary to the Constitution in principle (last *considérant* of the decision of 1999) and that they were also measures already largely applied in France in favour of regional languages.

The 1998 report of the constitutionalist Guy Carcassonne, solicited by the prime minister Lionel Jospin, listed at least 52 commitments among the 94 envisaged by the treaty, ratification of which would not have involved problems of constitutionality, since questions on the use of regional languages in the public service and commitments involving obligations for the State, particularly financial ones, were essentially excluded. The choices finally made by the French Government were therefore even more cautious than the already prudent proposals of the report.

Regarding the cited provision of art. 10, Carcassonne observed its relatively non-bindng nature, according to reasoning that was later shared by the Constitutional Council: "*Le g du paragraphe 2 concerne lui aussi une faculté déjà couramment, et officiellement, pratiquée: celle de donner aux toponymes leur forme traditionnelle, conjointement avec celle de la langue officielle. Il n'est, pour s'en convaincre, que de circuler, par exemple, sur des routes bretonnes, basques ou alsaciennes pour découvrir que de très nombreux noms de lieux (et pas toujours eux seulement), apparaissent en version bilingue sur des*

48 See C. Le Bris, *Les Langues régionales dans la Constitution*, *cit.*, p. 813.

panneaux indicateurs. Étant entendu que, d'une part, il ne s'agit pas d'instaurer une obligation et que, d'autre part, cet usage ne peut être autorisé que conjointement avec l'utilisation du français et non en se substituant à elle, cette disposition est compatible avec la Constitution"[49].

The opinion of the Council of State in 1996 was of the opposite sign. The Council accepted the substantial content of the provision in considering art. 10 of the Charter as one of the insuperable obstacles to constitutional compatibility: the administrative judge was concerned with the fact that ratification by France was not a purely formal operation but that it involved policies of effective promotion of regional languages. In fact, this could be said to be the aim of the treaty, despite the flexibility of choices conceded to ratifying States[50]. This objection prompted the Government to accompany signing of the European Charter of Languages with an interpretive declaration having the purpose, among other things, of reducing the effect of art. 10[51].

Indeed, viewed as a positive state action in favour of regional and minority languages, art. 10 of the Charter raised very complex problems that presupposed precise and delicate political choices, at the time absent from French legislation, except for the special case of New Caledonia: first of all, the definition of the relationship between the numerical importance of minority subjects in a certain territory and incitement to observe traditional place names. The denomination or re-denomination of places involves social and spatial questions that do not necessarily coincide with the linguistic practices of citizens, whose direct involvement is always advisable by consultations in sensitive areas. In the

49 G. Carcassonne, *Etude sur la compatibilité entre la Charte européenne des langues régionales ou minoritaires et la Constitution, Rapport remis au Premier Ministre, La Documentation Française*, 1998, § 134, p. 91.

50 *Charte des langues régionales ou minoritaires, Avis du Conseil d'Etat*, 24th September 1996, § IV: "*D'autre part, l'État ne sautait raisonnablement esquiver la difficulté créée par les prescriptions de l'article 10 relatif à l'usage des langues régionales ou minoritaires par les autorités administratives et les services publics, en retenant dans cet article quelques mesures marginales, apparemment compatibles avec l'obligation d'utiliser le français à condition que ce ne soit pas à titre exclusif. Cette option ne permettrait pas de donner consistance à la politique qu'il ne serait engagé à mettre en œuvre à la partie II, et qui consiste bien à promouvoir l'usage de ces langues dans la vie publique au même titre que dans la vie privée*".

51 The declaration attached to ratification of the treaty emphasised that the intention of France did not in any way correspond to recognition of minorities but rather to promotion of the European linguistic heritage, in line with the Preamble to the Constitution which ensures equality of all citizens and unity of the French population. The Government of the Republic also interpreted art. 7–1, lett. d) and arts. 9 and 10 of the Charter as aimed at establishing a general principle in line with art. 2 of the Constitution (basically: only French is the official language of the State) and the facultative character of the teaching of regional and minority languages on French territory.

absence of specific legislative and constitutional guarantees and in a context of fragmentation of the territorial communities, as in France, it is easy for bad dynamics to set in rather than virtuous practices.

An example: in 2005, the Council of the Department of Morbihan in Southern Brittany decided unanimously to extend bilingual signs in French/Breton also to departmental roads of Gallo territory in the Eastern part of the region, irritating the Breton population and above all the local minority which considered itself prevalently French-speaking and quite insensitive to the presumed effect of attracting tourism. According to an association of citizens formed to fight this innovation (and its costs, to be borne completely by the department)[52], local politicians considered Gallo identity unremunerative as an image, being a language with Roman roots, which unlike Breton (of Celtic origin), is not so easy to distinguish from French; thus Gallo identity was violated, first with French and then with Breton.

It is also necessary to evaluate the meaning of the expression in art. 10 of the Charter: "traditional and correct forms of toponomastics in regional and minority languages". What may these forms be, in a case such as France in which the processes of transformation of toponyms have occurred over a very long period and to different degrees in the various parts of the country? The approach to recovering the linguistic heritage used by the French State does not coincide with local policies of recognition of the Breton, Basque and Occitan toponomastic heritage that claims a minimum of linguistic reconquest in a panorama that has clearly undergone direct and indirect Francisation. Indeed, these communities are generally not satisfied by the rehabilitation and diffusion of place names in regional language based on philological or documentary reconstruction. They also seek, where possible, to introduce new toponyms derived from oral traditions that are probably the only ones that can symbolically reanimate their areas, restoring the dignity and value of minority languages, helping to avoid the risk of a museographic-type operation, or worse a merely folkloristic one, which would not be understood by the population.

Bibliography

Aime M., *Eccessi di culture*, Turin, 2004.

Allegri G., *Quali prospettive dopo il no al referendum in Corsica?*, in *Federalismi.it*, 5/2003 (on line).

52 *Association d'opposition à la signalisation bilingue en pays gallo* (http://aosb.free.fr/).

Auby J.B., *Il ruolo e l'identità delle istituzioni regionali in Francia*, in *Le Regioni*, 2/2001.
Bensa A., *La mémoire des lieux chez les Kanak Nouvelle Calédonie (Grande Terre)*, in *Ateliers*, 1997.
Calamo Specchia M., *Le asimmetrie funzionali e istituzionali del decentramento alla francese e l'orbita europea: una forza gravitazionale ancora troppo debole?*, in *Federalismi.it*, 3/2007 (on line).
Carcassonne G., *Droit constitutionnel*, Paris, 2000.
Carcassonne G., *Etude sur la compatibilité entre la Charte européenne des langues régionales ou minoritaires et la Constitution, Rapport remis au Premier Ministre,* Paris, 1998.
Cartier E., *Histoire et droit: rivalité ou complémentarité ?*, in *Revue française de droit constitutionnel*, 2006.
Cassia P., *Le droit de la rue*, in *Pouvoirs*, 2006.
Ceccanti S., *Francia e Italia di fronte alle differenze di sesso e di lingua: crisi comune delle certezze consolidate ed esiti diversi*, in *Diritto pubblico comparato ed europeo*, 1/2000.
Cerquiglini B., *Les langues de la France, Rapport au Ministre de l'Education Nationale, de la Recherche et de la Technologie, et à la Ministre de la Culture et de la Communication*, Paris, 1999.
Cipolla P., *L'Ordonnance criminelle di Luigi XIV e la lunga marcia verso la codificazione*, in *Politica del diritto*, 2005.
Custos D., New *Caledonia, a Case of Shared Sovereignty within the French Republic : Appearance or Reality ?*, in *European Public Law*, 2007.
Darot M., Calédonie, *Kanaky ou Caillou? Implicites identitaires dans la désignation de la Nouvelle-Calédonie*, in *Mots*, 1997.
de Certeau M., D. Julia, J. Revel (eds.), *Une politique de la langue. La Révolution française et les patois*, Paris, 1975.
de Vergottini G., *Profili giuridici della toponomastica nella provincia di Bolzano*, in *Diritto e società*, 4/1986.
Eysseric V., *Le corpus juridique des langues de France, Délégation Générale à la langue française et aux langues de France*, Paris, 2005.
Faberon J.-Y., *Nouvelle-Calédonie et Polynésie française: des autonomies différentes*, in *Revue française de droit constitutionnel*, 2006.
Fais A., *La décéntralisation e la sperimentazione normativa in Francia*, in *Autonomie*, 2006.
Fraisseix P., *Le Droit mémoriel*, in *Revue française de droit Constitutionnel*, 2006.
Gendron S., *L'origine des noms de lieux en France: essai de toponymie*, Paris, 2003.

Gohin O., *Quand la République marche sur la tête. Le gel de l'électorat restreint en Nouvelle-Calédonie*, in *Actualités juidique-Droit administratif*, 2007.
Gründler T., *La République française, une et indivisible?*, in *Revue de droit public*, 2007.
Guillorel H., *Territoire de la langue et toponymie officielle*, in *Droit et Cultures*, 2002.
Hilpold P., *La regolamentazione della toponomastica in Trentino-Alto Adige*, in Marko J., Ortino S., Palermo F., *L'ordinamento speciale della provincia autonoma di Bolzano*, Padova, 2001.
Hobsbawm E. J., *Nations and Nationalism since 1780: Programme, Myth, Reality*, Cambridge, 1990.
Knaebel G., *La rue mémoire: écriture du politique*, in *Pouvoirs*, 2006.
C. Le Bris, *Les Langues régionales dans la Constitution*, in *Revue de droit public*, 2009.
Lejeune S., E. Calvarin (eds.), *André Pégorier. Les noms de lieux en France. Glossaire de termes dialectaux*, Paris, 2006.
Melin-Soucramanien F., *Le statut des langues régionales ou minoritaires : la «tolérance constitutionnelle» française*, in A.-M. Le Pourhiet (ed.), *Langue(s) et Constitution(s)*, Aix-Marseille, 2003.
Nanchi A., *Vers un statut des minorités en droit constitutionnel français*, Clermont-Ferrand, 2006.
Panov S., *Discours nationaliste et politique linguistique en Lettonie indépendante*, in *Mots*, 2004.
Piergigli V., *Minoranze linguistiche (Diritto costituzionale comparato)*, in *Enciclopedia giuridica Treccani*, vol. XX, Rome, 2005.
Poggeschi G., *Le nazioni linguistiche della Spagna* autonómica, Padova, 2002.
Poggeschi G., *I diritti linguistici. Un'analisi comparata,* Rome, 2010.
Pontorehau M.-C., *Recenti sviluppi della centralizzazione "alla francese": aspettando l'atto terzo*, in *Le Regioni*, 6/2005.
Rostaing B., *Les noms de lieux*, Paris, 1997.
S. Soleil, *L'ordonnance de Villers-Cotterêts, cadre juridique de la politique linguistique des rois de France?*, in A.-M. Le Pourhiet (ed.), *Langue(s) et Constitution(s),* Aix-Marseille, 2003.
Somma A., *La politica linguistica del legislatore nelle esperienze italiana e francese*, in *Politica del diritto*, 1997.
Taube C., *Latvia: Political participation of linguistic minorities*, in *International Journal of Constitutional Law*, 2003.
Various Authors, *Langues régionales: langues de France, langues d'Europe*, Paris, 1999.

Verpeaux M., *La défense désespérée de la langue française*, in *Recueil Dalloz*, 2007.

Ziller J., *Le droit français de la langue, entre le mythes d'une tradition interventionniste et la réalité de nouvelles angoisses, EUI Working Paper Law*, 10/2006.

Zink G., *L'ancien français*, Paris, 1987.

Belgium: only by name?
Vanishing federalism and invisible minorities

Susanna Mancini

Summary

1. Introduction

The Belgian system is to a much larger extent than that of any other deeply divided State, the result of political tensions and contradictory projects. It is a system that does not resemble any other federal model. In fact, its whole constitutional odyssey was carried on with no reference to other federal experiences, or to any previously identified theoretical models[1]. All comparative and definitional efforts at capturing it are therefore of little use.

The State reform that transformed a unitary State into a fully-fledged federation was carried out in order to respond to ongoing crises and political deadlocks; as a result, it is characterized by a logic of compromise. In many cases, compromise meant the adoption of structurally contradictory constitutional norms, which reflect the often irreconcilable views of the two linguistic groups, the Flemish and the Francophone, on how to shape the structure of the State.

---

1 M. Uyttendaele, *Précis de droit constitutionnel belge. Regards sur un système institutionnel paradoxal*, Bruxelles, 2005, p. 823.

Moreover, Flemish and Francophone Belgians do not differ only on the ground of language. They are also separated by deeply different cultural, ideological and religious traditions that date back to the pre-unitary State time. Such differences are reflected in the federal structure. Belgium is, in fact, the State of two peoples, with different identities[2], that agreed on a constitutional compromise on the basis of parity. Place names in Belgium faithfully reflect the language-related conflict that shapes the country's constitutional setting. Therefore, before analyzing the regulation of "place names", it is necessary to provide an overview of the Belgian federating process and of the Belgian federal system.

2. From the unitary State to the federation: 1830–1993

2.1 From the hegemony of French to linguistic territoriality (1830–1963)

Belgium constitutes a paradigmatic example of "centrifugal" federalism. Born as a unitary State, it adopted the federal formula after a constitutional odyssey towards territorial decentralization, in the hope of solving the tensions between its two main linguistic communities: the Francophone and the Flemish. The process of separation between these two linguistic groups is "just as old as the very formation of the national State"[3]. The Flemish speakers are approximately 5.9 million, that is 57,6% of the State population. They are mainly concentrated in the Northern region, usually referred to as Flanders. The Francophones are 3,3 million (32,4%) and live in the Southern region, or Wallonia, while in the country's capital region, Brussels, (960.000 inhabitants, that is 9,3% of Belgium's population) about 85–90% speak French. Finally, after the first world war, a small German speaking community of about 70.000 people was added to the country through annexation and constitutes the majority in a number of Eastern municipalities.

Belgium seceded from the United Kingdom of the Netherlands after the "August Revolution" of 1830, which was a product of the alliance between the Francophone bourgeoisie and the Catholic Church. The new State was shaped as a parliamentary monarchy with an electoral system based on a property

2 W. Dewachter, *De dualistisce identiteit van de Belgische maatschappij*, Amsterdam, 1992, p. 28, quoted by A. Alen, *Nationalism-Federalism-Democracy. The Example of Belgium*, in *Revue Européenne de Droit Public*, 5, 1, 1993, p. 71.

3 S. Noiret, *Le revisioni costituzionali in Belgio: un cammino difficile verso il federalismo o l'agonia dello stato nazionale?*, in Z. Ciuffoletti, S. Noiret (eds.), *I modelli di democrazia in Europa e il caso italiano*, Florence, 1992, p. 175.

assessment franchise, that favored the French-speaking *élite*. The latter put an end to the multilingual system that the Flemish had experienced under King Willem I of the Netherlands, where both Dutch and French were *de jure* and *de facto* the official languages. It is true that art. 23 of the 1830 Belgian Constitution protected linguistic freedom: this provision, however, played into the hands the Francophone *élite*, which controlled every aspect of public and cultural life, to speak "*où et quand elle le désirait, la langue qui avait ses preferences*"[4]. A government decree of 16th November 1831 declared French the sole official language with respect to legislation, administration, the courts, the church, schools, universities and the army. The fact that the majority of the population[5] spoke a "barbarian and imperfect dialect of Dutch"[6] was simply not taken into account.

The reasons for this are manifold. In part they have to do with the "*politique hégemonique du francais*" in this part of Europe and with the choice of the Constitution framers to build up a francophone public space. It should not be forgotten, however, that at that time, Flemish was not yet a unitary or codified language. A number of *thiois* dialects were spoken by the rural population of Flanders, while the upper class commonly spoke French[7]. Language and class were strictly entangled: therefore, it would be simplistic to say that, in spite of their numeric superiority, the "Flemish" as a whole were banished to the role of a dominated minority. Most (lower class) Flemish were certainly conscious of their linguistic distinctness and discriminated against on the ground of language, but the domination and discrimination were to be put down to other (bourgeois) members of their own linguistic group, that choose to speak French (the so-not too politely-called *Fransquillons*). This proves the relativity of the concept of "minority" and demonstrated that numerical inferiority may not necessarily be the determinative attribute.

A first wave of reaction against this unjust linguistic *status* was sparked by a convergence between the social and economic changes provoked by industrialization, and some striking judicial proceedings such as the trials of the Flemish Coucke and Goethals, held before the *Court of Assize* of Hainaut where they were sentenced to death without having understood a single word throughout the entire criminal proceedings brought against them.

---

4 M. Ruys, *Les Flamands, un peuple, un mouvement, une nation en devenir*, Tielt, 1973.

5 In 1864 the Flemish were 2.4 millions and the Francophones were 1.8 millions.

6 J. De Meyer, *Beschouwingen over het federalisme in Belgie*, in *De Gids o Maatschappelijk Gebied*, 1962, p. 473, quoted by A. Alen, *Nationalism-Federalism-Democracy, cit.*, p. 45.

7 A. Von Busekist, *La Belgique. Politique des langues et constrution de l'Etat de 1780 à nos jours*, Paris-Bruxelles, 1998, XII ("Introduction").

After that the Parliament enacted a series of acts introducing bilingualism, albeit only within Flanders (the situation was therefore asymmetrical, as the Flemish region became in principle bilingual, while the rest of the country remained monolingual), making it possible to use Flemish in criminal proceedings (1873) and in the state administration (1878). Much of this legislation, nevertheless, remained dead letter.

The adoption of a block-vote system (1893) and, later, of male universal suffrage (1911), strengthened the Flemish presence in the political sphere: as a consequence the Equalization Act of 1898 repealed the decree of 1831 and made Flemish an official language on an equal footing with French. A subsequent law of 1921 introduced the principle according to which the administration was compelled to use the language of the region.

Such improvements provoked a strong reaction among the French speakers. Walloons and French speaking residents of Brussels started to fear that bilingualism in the whole country would make Flemish more competitive in the workplace and take jobs away from French-speakers in Wallonia. In 1912 the Congress of Liege introduced the principle of "administrative separation," in order not to oblige French-speaking civil servants to learn Flemish. The Walloon socialist leader J. Destrée, published his "Letter to the King on the separation of Wallonia and Flanders"[8], in which he proposed to transform Belgium into a Union of two free and independent peoples. Paradoxically, by fighting the introduction of a bilingual system at the beginning of the XX century, francophone Belgians set the basis for the adoption of the principle of territoriality based on linguistically uniform regions, that would prove later critical to the defense and promotion of the Flemish language. On the other hand, monolingualism was also convenient for the Flemish, who anticipated that its imposition "would accelerate the assimilation of the small, but strategic French-speaking bourgeois minority in the Flemish urban centers"[9].

The second wave of language laws, adopted in the 1930s, moved towards territorial monolingualism in Flanders and Wallonia and bilingual institutions in Brussels as well as in areas with linguistic minorities. The core law of 1932 regulated the use of languages in the administration and in its dealings with the public. These laws were more comprehensive than their XIX century predecessors, and more evenly implemented, except in Brussels.

---

8 J. Destree, *Lettre au Roi sur la séparation de la Walloonie et de la Flandre*, Paris-Gembloux, 1968.

9 L. Hooghe, *Belgium: Hollowing the Center*, in N. Bermeo, U.M. Amoretti (eds.), *Federalism, Unitarism and Territorial. Cleavages*, Johns Hopkins University Press, 2003, chapter 3.

At this stage of the process, linguistic territoriality was not rigidly applied. The boundaries of the three linguistic territories were adjusted every ten years on the basis of the results of a population census. As a result of the first two censuses many more "Flemish" municipalities had become "francophone" or "bilingual" than the other way around. Flemish territory was lost around Brussels, partly to Wallonia and partly to Brussels. In this phase, therefore, the application of territoriality was widely mitigated by the acceptance of "natural" linguistic changes in social reality. But precisely for this reason, it failed as a means of protection of Flemish. Indeed, each census pushed Flemish further North, thus formalizing the natural francophonization of Flanders[10]. The frustration which followed on the Flemish side had a crucial consequence, as it transformed prior linguistic concerns into territorial claims: the aim of the Flemish movement became the definitive demarcation of linguistic borders.

The census-based system came to an end in 1961, after the boycott by 300 Flemish burgomasters of the language questions in the census, which resulted in blocking the adjustment of the linguistic borders and practically forced the national Government to drop questions on language usage from subsequent population censuses.

The political resources of the Flemish political class had by then considerably strengthened, mainly thanks to two factors. In the first place, there had emerged "a class of Flemish politicians who had been educated entirely in Dutch-speaking schools and/or universities and who were thus more vocal in demanding a strict observance of the language laws. Secondly, while Wallonia had been the industrial heart of Belgium, the decay of its post-war coal and steel industries shifted the bulk of socio-economic policy-making to Flanders. Unlike Wallonia, Flanders did not have to go through a painful restructuring of its heavy industries. It was more successful in attracting foreign direct investment and developing medium-sized enterprises and service industries"[11].

A series of reforms in the field of language rights took place between 1962 and 1966 and gave birth to three monolingual regions (Flemish, Francophone and German-speaking), and a bilingual one (the 19 Brussels municipalities). With the exception of latter, the degree of linguistic homogeneity within the new regional boundaries was very high. It was not, however, absolute, as in both the

---

10 X. Delgrange, *Le fédéralisme belge: la protection des minorités linguistiques et idéologiques*, in *Revue de droit public et de la science politique en France et à l'étranger*, 1994, p. 1164 et seq.

11 W. Swenden, *Belgian Federalism, Basic Institutional Features and Potential as a Model for the European Union*, Paper presented at the RIIA Conference – Governing Together in the New Europe, Robinson College, Cambridge UK, 12th–13th April 2003 and published by the London Institute of International Affairs, 2003.

Flemish and the Francophone regions there were, respectively, Francophone and Flemish enclaves. Among the latter, the more problematic case was that of the Fourons, six French-speaking municipalities that used to be part of the French-speaking district of Liege and were included in that of Limburg, within the Flemish region. The protest, organized by the *Rétour à Liège* ("Return to Liège") party grew until it became a national issue when the burgomaster refused to officially speak Flemish. The district of Liege called a referendum: 93% of the *fouronnais* voted against the inclusion of their municipalities in the Limburg district; however, the Flemish majority in the national Parliament refused to change the linguistic borders. This conflict was actually solved only in 1988, without modifying the regional boundaries, but by freezing the application of territoriality, that is, by granting the francophone *fouronnais* the right to vote in the French speaking constituency of Verviers[12].

As a consequence of these reforms, the Walloon "psychological" minority, became a linguistic minority[13], conscious of its disadvantaged position within what it began to call *un état belgo-flamand.* It tried to advocate for a non territorial protection of language rights, specifically in the field of education, in order to protect all French speakers irrespective of their location, but first the European Court of Human Rights [14] and then, in a widely changed institutional

12 The Fourons case represents an exception in the Belgian system. Another exception is that of the municipality of Commines that was moved from Flanders to Wallonia in 1962 and where there was a Flemish speaking minority. The Flemish claimed and obtained a regime of reciprocity with the Fourons municipalities. See E. Witte, *Language and Territoriality: A Summary of Developments in Belgium,* in *International Journal of Group Rights*, 1993, p. 219.

13 X. Delgrange, *Le fédéralisme belge, cit.*, p. 1165.

14 European Court of Human Rights, *Belgian Linguistic Case* of 23rd July 1968, (Application Nos. 1474/62, 1677/62, 1691/62, 1769/63, 1994/63 and 2126/64 Ser. a, vol. 6). Certain measures of the Belgian Government that denied French-speaking students living in Dutch-speaking unilingual regions from state subsidized education in French in those regions were challenged for violation of the right to education, the right to respect for private and family life, and the right against discrimination under the European Union's Convention for the Protection of Human Rights and Fundamental Freedoms (paragraph 2 of the facts at 3 of the Court's judgment: "The Applicants, who are parents of families of Belgian nationality, applied to the Commission both on their own behalf and on behalf of their children under age, of whom there are more than 800. Pointing out that they are French-speaking or that they express themselves most frequently in French, they want their children to be educated in that language"). The Court did not find the Belgian Government's measures discriminatory or arbitrary. The pursuit of linguistic unity within the unilingual regions was based on the objective fact that a large majority of the population in the regions spoke only one of the two national languages. Furthermore the measures were based on a public interest, namely, to ensure that all schools dependent on the State and existing in a unilingual region conducted their teaching in the language which was essentially that of the region, hence promoting among pupils a knowledge in depth of the usual language of the region.

context, the Belgian *Cour d'Arbitrage*[15], frustrated such attempts, declaring the principle of territoriality compatible with, respectively, the European Convention of Human Rights and the Belgian Constitution.

2.2 The first steps towards federalism: the state reforms of 1970–1971

At the end of the 1960's, despite the growing tension between the two linguistic communities, both agreed on the necessity to overcome the unitary formula through a process of decentralization. The Francophones felt that the Walloon interests were hurt by the Flemish majority at the national level and that a more regionalized system was necessary to adopt the measures that Wallonia needed to face its economic crisis. The Flemish, on their side, were conscious of the importance of the decentralization process in guaranteeing their cultural and linguistic autonomy.

The creation in 1963 of the linguistic regions (which are not political structures with their own bodies, but rather simply a way to divide the federal territory) was a milestone in the history of Belgian federalization, as it set the basis of the future federal system. First of all, the existence of linguistic regions is the condition for rendering linguistic legislation operational (which, as we will see, is a critical feature of Belgian federalism); in the second place, the regions offered a territorial basis for the exercise of the future Community competences; finally, they anticipated the division of the State in four territorial areas: the Flemish Region, the Walloon Region, the Region of Brussels-Capital and the German Community [16].

The first crucial step in the process of dismemberment of the unitary State took place in 1970–1971, with the creation of three cultural Communities[17]: the Flemish and the French ones were granted (limited) legislative competences in the fields of education, cultural matters and the use of languages, while the German community could enact only administrative (secondary) acts. The 1970–1971 reforms gave birth, albeit only in principle, also to three (political) Regions (Flemish, Walloon and Brussels-Capital), thanks to the adoption of art. 107*quater* of the Constitution. The Regions have powers with regard to economic and employment policy, environmental and energy policy, local authorities, roads, transportation, etc. Obviously, the reform aimed at satisfying the claims

15 See A. Alen, P. Peeters, *The Competences of the Communities in the Belgian Federal State: The Principle of Exclusivity Revisited*, in *European Public Law*, 2/1997, p. 165 et seq.

16 M. Uyttendaele, *Précis de droit constitutionnel belge, cit.*, p. 823.

17 This took place through a constitutional amendment that led to the adoption of arts. 3*bis*, 3*ter* and 59*bis* and 59*ter*.

and needs of both linguistic groups. The Flemish obtained a certain degree of cultural and linguistic autonomy, through the creation of the cultural Communities, while the Regions were supposed to respond to the need of a separate economic development for Wallonia. The Regions, however, did not become effective before 1980–1988, because the implementation of art. 107*quater* required an over-qualified (*cumulative*) parliamentary majority, which proved impossible to reach, mainly because of the divergences regarding the *status* of Brussels. The Francophones favored the creation of an autonomous Region, while the Flemish wanted the capital either to be jointly governed by the two cultural Communities, or transformed in a federal district[18].

The constitutional reform of 1970 was not confined to the territorial decentralization of state powers. It also deeply modified the criteria of representation of the linguistic groups in the central legislative and the executive organs, a particularly troubling issue for the French-speaking minority, which had already experienced in the Fourons affair the frustration of being outnumbered by the Flemish majority. The solution was a compromise which basically transformed Belgium in a bilateral and parity based State.

The federal Government must have an equal number of Flemish and French speaking ministers, apart from the so called "asexual" prime minister, who can be indifferently French or Dutch speaking. The governmental decision-making process is governed by negotiations: all decisions must be adopted with a formula which is in between absolute majority and unanimity: dissenting ministers, in fact, may only aquiesce or resign[19]. The seats in the two chambers are assigned according to a proportional system based on the number of voters, which in principle favors the Flemish majority. In order to maintain a balance between the two groups, however, the reform introduced a number of correctives. To understand how they work, one must take into account that according to art. 43 of the Constitution "the elected members of each chamber are divided into a French linguistic group and a Dutch linguistic group". The first mechanism, which protects the French-speaking minority, is the so called alarm-bell procedure ("*sonnette d'alarme*")[20], according to which each linguistic group may block the legislative procedure in all "sensitive" matters. If at least three quarters of the members of one of the linguistic groups sign a motion, declaring "that the provisions of a draft bill or of a motion are of a nature to gravely damage relations between the communities. the parliamentary procedure is

18 In the difficulties of reaching an agreement see: M. Uyttendaele, *Le fédéralisme inachevé*, Bruxelles, 1991, p. 287.

19 X. Delgrange, *Le fédéralisme belge, cit.*, p. 1174, note 77.

20 If at least three quarters of the members of one group sign a motion the procedure is suspended and the motion is referred to the Government which plays an arbitration role.

suspended … and the motion referred to the Council of Ministers which, within thirty days, gives its justified recommendations on the motion and invites the implicated Chamber to express its opinion on these recommendations" (art. 53 of the Constitution of 1993).

Another corrective measure aims at avoiding that fundamental (quasi-constitutional) legislation – e.g, laws regulating linguistic and institutional subject matters –, be adopted against the will of one linguistic group, thus protecting both the Flemish and the Francophones is the rule according to which to adopt such laws, a double or "cumulative" majority is required, that is an overall two thirds majority in each chamber and a majority in each linguistic group. This mechanism grants a *de facto* veto power to both linguistic groups, but it relies on a difficult requirement, the two-thirds majority, which can be reached only on the basis of an agreement among six parties, "with the risks in terms of incoherence and heterogeneity that this implies"[21].

Moreover, as it presupposes the division of MPs in linguistic groups, this corrective measure does not protect German speakers, as there is no German linguistic group in Parliament[22].

Finally each linguistic group can in practice veto constitutional reforms, given that a majority within the two communities – and the two linguistic groups which represent them in Parliament – is not only necessary from a political standpoint, but also a numerical necessity for the amending procedure, which culminates in a two-thirds majority of the total votes cast in both houses of the federal Parliament (art. 131 of the Constitution).

2.3 The reforms of the 1980's: the compromise over the "Brussels question"

The constitutional amendments and the legislative reforms of the 1980's strengthened the *status* of the Communities, which ceased to be qualified as "cultural" and were granted new competences. One notable responsibility that was (almost) completely transferred to the Communities is education[23]. The expansion of Community powers was carried on much to the detriment of regional competences, especially in Flanders, where it was decided in 1980 to merge the institutions of the Community and those of the Region.

The reforms also gave birth to a new judicial organ, the *Cour d'Arbitrage*, which initially had basically the role of solving responsibility conflicts between

21 X. Delgrange, *Le fédéralisme belge, cit.*, p. 1177, note 98.

22 *Ibid.*, p. 1175 et seq.

23 See on this point J. Bourtenbourg, *L'enseignement et la communautarisation*, in *Administration Publique Trimestrielle,* 1988, p 183 et seq.

the central State and its sub-units (Communities and Regions), but was later transformed into a full-fledged Constitutional Court. The Court's composition reflects the bipolar and parity-based nature of the Belgian State, as it must have an equal number of Flemish and Francophone members (a rule which also applies to the *Conseil d'Etat* and to the Court of Cassation).

In 1988 it was finally possible to reach a compromise on the thorny "Brussels question". The capital was organized as an autonomous and fully bilingual Region, although with a lesser degree of autonomy in as compared to the other Regions. Within the regional system, the Flemish minority enjoys a very high degree of protection. The alarm bell procedure, in fact, applies to the Regional Councils, and so does the principle of parity of the regional executive organ. Moreover, the latter's decision-making process are governed by the consensus procedure that also applies to also applies to the federal Government. In other words, the Flemish population in Brussels (less than15%) is protected to the same extent and through the same mechanisms that apply at the federal level to the French speaking population (33%).

2.4 The 1993–2001 reforms: the (con)federal Constitution

The state reform of 1993 turned Belgium into a fully-fledged federal State. The 1993 Constitution declares at art. 1: "Belgium is a federal State made up of communities and regions".

The responsibilities of the Communities and the Regions were further expanded, through the adoption of art. 35 of the Constitution, according to which "The federal authority only has power in the matters that are formally attributed to it by the Constitution" and "The Communities and the Regions, each in its own field of concern, have power for the other matters." Article 35 is thus shaped as a typically federal clause; however, in the Belgian case its application is made difficult by the unclear line between the competences of the Communities and those of the Regions; and the vague terms in which the powers of the central State are expressed.

The revised Constitution of 1993 introduced several changes concerning the relationship between the legislative and the executive organs, including constructive non confidence-vote; moreover, it drastically changed the composition of the senate and adjusted it to the new federal reality. However, the new senate, unlike in other federal States, does not completely represent the federate entities. The former provincial senators have been replaced by a new group of senators, who are appointed by and from the community councils. The Flemish and French communities are equally represented in this group with ten community senators each, while the German community appoints one community senator. More than half of all senators are directly elected at the federal level. Consequently, the protection of minorities is really only a matter for the linguistic groups that may rely on the "alarm procedure" and on the system of the special majority vote described above. Beside that, at least one Flemish speaking senator and at least six French speaking senators must, on the day of their election, reside in the bilingual region of Brussels-Capital.

Finally, a new state reform took place in 2001. More powers were transferred to the Communities and the Regions, with regard to agriculture, fisheries, foreign trade, development cooperation, auditing of electoral expenses and the supplementary financing of the political parties. The Regions became responsible for twelve regional taxes, and local and provincial government became a matter for the Regions, including supervision on municipal elections. The functioning of the Brussels institutions was also amended during this last state reform, which resulted among other things in a guaranteed representation of the Flemish inhabitants of Brussels in the legislative Council of the Brussels-Capital Region.

3. Belgian federalism today: a logic of compromise and contradiction

3.1 An asymmetrical dual-layered structure: the overlapping of powers

Belgium is made up of two different types of state sub-units, the Communities and the Regions. The latter (the Walloon region, the Flemish region and the Brussels region) should not be confused with the linguistic regions to which the Constitution refers at art. 4 ("Belgium has four linguistic regions: the French-speaking region, the Dutch-speaking region, the bilingual region of Brussels-Capital and the German-speaking region"), which are not politically autonomous sub-entities and simply constitute the territorial foundations for the three "political" Regions. Nevertheless, there is no total overlap: the Flemish Region overlaps with the Dutch linguistic region, and the Brussels Region overlaps with the Brussels-Capital linguistic region, but the Walloon Region overlaps with both the French and the German linguistic regions. The three "political" Regions have a directly elected council and an executive organ and can enact decrees with the same force of federal laws in various fields: economic and employment policy, environment, local authorities, transport etc. The three Communities are: the Flemish Community, which comprises the Flemish-speakers in Wallonia and in Brussels; the French Community which comprises Francophones in Wallonia and in Brussels and the German Community, which comprises the Germans that constitute the majority of the population in the eastern municipalities of the country. In principle, just like each Region, also each of the three Communities has its own parliamentary Council and executive organ, and is entrusted with constitutionally assigned powers in the fields of education, culture, health and social policy.

Thus, at least in theory, Regions and Communities are separated sub-entities, with their own political organs that exercise competences in different fields. In practice, however, there is a significant overlap between both the organs and competences of a Region and a Community. Both the Flemish and the French Communities, in fact, ended up by being also territorially structured. Initially, at the time when they were created, they were thought in "corporative" terms, as a response to the hopes of the Francophones to unify all French-speaking Belgians, though preserving the linguistic rights of those living in Flanders. The linguistic dimension was therefore a crucial issue in their creation: while there is a Region of Brussels-Capital, there is no Brussels Community, just as there is no homogeneous linguistic culture in Brussels. The initial project, however, was not successful. According to the Court of Arbitration, the competences of both Communities and Regions can be exercised only within their territory[24]. So, today, the principle of "personality" only applies as far as Brussels goes, since the French Community has no authority over Francophones who live in the Flemish Region and the Flemish Community has no authority over the Flemish speakers who live in the Walloon Region.

The Flemish Community and Region even merged their institutions. Today, there are only one Flemish government and one Flemish parliamentary Council, catering for Regional competences (for citizens located in the Flemish region) and Community competences (addressing all inhabitants of the Flemish region and the Flemish-speakers in Brussels).

On the opposite, the French Community and Walloon Region have not been merged. Separate Regional and Community parliaments and governments continue to exist, although the French Community parliament is entirely composed of MPs who have been directly elected to the Brussels and Walloon regional parliaments respectively.

The reason for this difference is threefold. First of all, while there is a concurrence between the Flemish Community and the Flemish Region, the Walloon Region covers two linguistic Regions: French and German. This means that certain regional powers in Wallonia are exercised by the German Community. In the second place, while Flemish inhabitants of Brussels represent a very

24 A. Alen, P. Peeters, *The Competences of the Communities, cit.*, p. 165 et seq.

small share of the total group of Flemish Belgians, *les Bruxellois Francophones* are a much larger share of Francophone Belgians with a strong tradition of "sociological and political independence with regards to Wallonia"[25].

Moreover, to understand this deep asymmetry, one must bear in mind that the two types of subunits respond to different cultural (and, actually, philosophical) identities: that of the Walloons, which is inspired by the French theory of the nation-State, and that of the Flemish, which is more sensitive to the Germanic tradition of the *Volk.* These two different identities have shaped the actual functioning of the federal system, and produced a deep institutional asymmetry between North and South. In Flanders, the Community exercises both the competences of the Community and those of the Region; in Wallonia, after a first period of effective coexistence of the two sub-entities, the Region has clearly surpassed the Community, which has for all practical purposes been dismantled[26]. Powers of the French Community are therefore exercised by the Region and also by the French Community Commission in Brussels. The German Community exercises all community powers as well as some regional competences and the Brussels Region disposes of all regional competences. Finally, in the Brussels regional territory, both the French and the Flemish Communities exercise competences in fields such as education and culture.

3.2 The problem of minority rights

As it emerges from the description of its actual functioning, Belgian federalism is not based on the equality among its territorial sub-units, but rather on that of its two main linguistic groups. Language rights are therefore a key element in the Belgian federal structure, but also a particularly problematic one. Linguistic territoriality has been applied in Flanders in very strict terms. Flemish has been imposed at all levels: in legislation, the administration, the schools and universities, the courts, private enterprises, with no possible exception, apart from the "*régime de facilité*" which is applied in six municipalities in the periphery of Brussels and consists in a quasi-bilingual system in the fields of education and public administration. It would not be accurate to define the "*régime de facilité*" as a means of minority protection. In the Flemish view, the system is just a temporary solution that serves as a prelude to the linguistic assimilation of the French-speaking population[27].

---

25 *Ibid.,* p. 165.

26 X. Delgrange, *Le fédéralisme belge, cit.*, p. 1167.

27 In this logic, the Province of Brabant, which is located on the border of the two regions and includes Brussels, has been divided in Flemish Brabant and Walloon Brabant, so to reduce the

The truth is that the Belgian system structurally excludes the possibility of protecting linguistic minorities. In the first place, minorities are not legally defined as such. Linguistic groups enjoy an equal *status* and are therefore protected through the territorial and institutional state organization itself, as well as through ordinary legislation, applicable to all groups, and not through special constitutional clauses and/or special autonomy.

In practice, however, the system shows a certain degree of similarity to the French "neutral" State model, in the sense that it results in a sum of strictly homogeneous sub-units, in which the elevation of collective linguistic goals over individual linguistic rights results in the weakening of the latter.

The region of Brussels-Capital represents an exception, in that both the French and the Flemish Communities exercise competences in fields such as education and culture. It has been pointed out that this overlapping of regional and community levels constitutes a good solution, because "the region gives protection to the French-speaking Brussels population with a built-in protection for the Dutch-speaking population", while the "presence of the Communities … guarantees the cultural and social rights of each group" and that the positive aspect of the system is that it offers "choice to the population"[28].

This choice, however, is denied to the rest of the population by the strictly monolingual systems applied within the other two regions. In the latter, the situation is in fact similar to that of a typically monolingual State: there is only one official language and linguistic freedom of those who do not belong to the majority group is highly limited. This results in a high degree of protection of the linguistic rights of the individuals belonging to each majority group within the two main regions, but also in the discrimination of "regional" minorities, which are not recognized as such, that are subject to a duty of linguistic assimilation. The definition of linguistic minorities in Belgium is a particularly thorny issue. The difficulties do not concern the federal level, where only German speakers can be viewed as a linguistic minority, but rather the *status* of trapped minorities within the two monolingual regions. According to Resolution 1301 (2002) of the Parliamentary Assembly of the Council of Europe on "The Protection of Minorities in Belgium", such groups (Francophones in Flanders and in the German-language Region, as well as Flemish and German speakers in the

---

number of municipalities that requires the application of the "*régime de facilité*" (as well as, according to X. Delgrange's malicious interpretation – *Le fédéralisme belge, cit.*, p. 1181 – in order to weaken the ties between Walloons and Francophones bruxellois).

28 W. Pas, *A Dynamic Federalism Built on Static Principles: The Case of Belgium*, in G. A. Tarr, R. F. Williams, J. Marko (eds.), *Federalism, Subnational Constitutions and Minority Rights*, Praeger, 2004, p. 164.

French-language Region) could actually be regarded as linguistic minorities[29]. Such recognition, however, is likely to challenge the principle of territoriality, which "remains the fragile and therefore static basis on which the actual Belgian state rests"[30]. It is not by chance that Belgium signed the Framework Convention for the Protection of National Minorities in 2001[31] but made the reservation that "the notion of national minority will be defined by the Belgian inter-ministerial conference on foreign policy".

3.3 The impact of linguistic federalism on the regulation of place names

The regulation of place names faithfully reflects the Belgian federal structure. Moreover, the Belgian system in this field is not in accordance with international standards concerning place names, which are contrary to the translation of place names, and in favour of the preservation of the original linguistic form.

In Wallonia and Flanders, place names and road signs are strictly subject to the rule of linguistic territoriality. This means that in Flanders, French place names are translated into Flemish, while Flemish names appear translated into French in Wallonia. So, the Walloon city of *Liège*, is indicated only in the form "*Luik*" in Flanders, as well as *Mons*, which in French means "mountain" is

---

29 This Resolution represents an important step forward with respect to the traditional view, expressed in the Human Rights Committee decision in the Ballantyne case according to which "the minorities referred to in article 27 (of the 1966 Covenant) are minorities within … a State, and not minorities within any province" (11.2) See Human Rights Committee, 47th session, Communications Nos. 359/1989 and 385/1989, *John Ballantyne and Elizabeth Davidson, and Gordon McIntyre v. Canada*, views adopted on 31st March 1993.

30 W. Pas, *A Dynamic Federalism, cit.*, p. 173.

31 In the framework of the Council of Europe, the European Charter for Regional or Minority Languages (1992) and the Framework Convention for the Protection of National Minorities (1994) form an important site for the gradual development of a minimum standard with regard to the legal position of regional and minority languages. The Framework Convention is self-executing, but only regarding the loose commitments that the States have undertaken towards the minorities. Beyond this point, the execution of this convention requires special regulations in order to be effective at domestic level. Both the Framework Convention and the Charter on Languages have entered into force in 1998. Neither of the two is as yet so universally accepted as the European Convention of Human Rights, but the number of States parties is rising. The Framework Convention is much closer to become a genuine pan-European standard. It has now been ratified by 39 States and the only ones missing, apart from some mini-States, are Turkey and four EU States: Belgium, France, Greece and Luxembourg. See S. Mancini, B. De Witte, *Language Rights as Cultural Rights: A European Perspective,* in F. Francioni, M. Scheinin (eds.), *Cultural Human Rights*, Leiden-Boston, 2008.

translated in Flemish road signs as "*Bergen*". The same logic applies, of course, in Wallonia, where the Flemish town of *Brugge* becomes "*Bruges*".

The regulation of place names, therefore, is symptomatic of the failure on the original idea behind the creation of the Communities. These were initially thought as "corporate" entities, as a response to the demands of the French speakers to unify their entire linguistic group (that is, the French speaking Belgians living in Wallonia, Brussels and Flanders). The linguistic dimension was therefore a crucial feature of the Communities. The Court of Arbitration made clear that both the regions as well as the Communities could exercise their powers only within their territorial boundaries, thus emphasizing once again the importance of linguistic territoriality.

Again, the region of Brussels, represents an exception, because bilingualism is mandatory for all public signs except those relating to the French or the Flemish community. In the capital, the use of both languages is systematic, not only for place and street names, but also in the public transportation system. All street signs begin with the French words "*rue*," "*avenue*," "*boulevard*," and end with the Flemish version words "*straat*," "*laan*," "*dresses*." In the region of Brussels-Capital the signs indicating names of cities are also both in French and in Flemish. The French and the Flemish versions usually appear juxtaposed from left to right (e.g., *Liège/Luik*, *Antwerpen/Anvers*).

In the German-speaking community – the only one where there is no language conflict – the official inscriptions are usually bilingual with a predominance of German. In the municipalities, signs tend to be in German, according to the Belgian system of monolingualism, but some municipalities use both German and French, although not for street names, which are almost always in German, as well as road signs. The regulation is, thus, similar to the one in Flanders and Wallonia, with one important difference: the signs of French and Flemish cities and place names are (almost never) translated and keep their name in the original language. Occasionally, however, the German translation appears next to the name in the original language (e.g.: *Lüttich-Liège*), while in rare cases only the German translation appears (*Löwen* instead of *Leuven*).

4. Conclusions: towards separation?

As the regulation of place names demonstrates, the core of the Belgian State and the basis of its functioning at all levels are the two largest linguistic communities. As described above, the federal Government must always decide by consensus. In the federal Parliament, the agreement between the two linguistic groups is also always necessary, as each of them may block the legislative procedure in all "sensitive" matters, and veto constitutional reforms.

Also "at the European Union level, regional and community governments can shape the position of the Belgian state or even speak on its behalf when it comes to their constitutionally-specified jurisdiction. Basically, when a Council of Ministers discusses policy-making in an area where either the Community or the Region is competent in Belgium, then it is up to the relevant units to flesh out a position. This involves a fair degree of compromise between Regions or Communities since they need to agree for a Belgian position to take shape"[32].

At all levels and for all purposes, the federal system is based on a necessary consensus between Flemish and Francophone Belgians. Here, however, lies the paradoxical character of the system: federalization was made necessary because of the presence of two deeply divided groups with a high degree of reciprocal mistrust, but the condition for the federation to function is the agreement between the two.

The bipolar character of Belgium is not confined to its state organization, but it extends to virtually every aspect of public life. for a long time there has not been a "Belgian" cultural life, a "Belgian" university, a "Belgian" public opinion, "Belgian" media or a "Belgian" party system. "The three major political parties – each electorally threatened by a nationalist movement – were torn apart" between the 1960's and 1970's. "In 1967, the Christian Democrats split into a Flemish and Francophone party in the wake of an acrimonious linguistic confrontation around the catholic university of Louvain"[33], a century-old (mainly) francophone university located in the Flemish Brabant, which was split in two (Leuven and Louvain-la-Neuve), because it challenged the Flemish claim of a linguistically homogeneous region[34]. Finally, "The unitary Socialist Party held out until 1978, though the two wings gained de facto autonomy in the early 1970s"[35]. So, unlike in other multiethnic federations (India, Switzerland and to a certain extent Canada), the party system on Belgium is not an element of

32 J. Van Ginderachten, *The Belgian Federal Model,* at http://www.ecsanet.org/conferences/ecsaworld2/Ginderachter.htm.

33 W. Swenden, *Belgian Federalism, cit.*

34 *L'Université de Louvain et la question linguistique*, in *Courrier Hebdomadaire*, Centre de Recherches et d'Information politiques, 1968, p. 394 et seq.

35 W. Swenden, *Belgian Federalism, cit.* For a comprehensive overview of historical development of the Belgian party system see S. Noiret, *Political Parties and the Political System in Belgium before Federalism*, 1830–1980, in *European History Quarterly* (SAGE, London Oaks and New Dehli), vol. 24 (1994), pp. 85–122.

cohesion among the different state components[36], but, quite to the contrary, a propeller of centrifugal tendencies.

At the time of this writing, Belgium has been unable of forming a Government since almost a year, breaking the record for the world's longest wait for a government. A similar crises occurred in 2007, when a last-minute stopgap coalition put an end to a 192 days of political deadlock[37].

---

36 R. Paddison, *Il federalismo: diversità regionale nell'unione nazionale*, in G. Brosio (ed.), *Governo decentralizzato e federalismo*, Bologna, 1995, p. 39 et seq., providing an illuminating discussion of the role of national political parties in multiethnic federations.

37 On 19th December 2007, the former prime minister Guy Verhofstadt, a Flemish liberal, assembled a stopgap coalition after 192 days of embarrassing political deadlock. Even forming a temporary Government proved difficult because of the deep and bitter division between north and south. The crisis had started after the June elections. In Belgium, the national Governments are formed after complex negotiations among the parties, divided as these are by ideology and by language. In this case, the process required the appointment by the King of an "*informateur*" and also of a "*démineur*" (mine sweeper), as the formation of a new Government was expected to be exceptionally complicated. Both came to the conclusion that the only coalition possible was the so-called "Orange-Blue" formula consisting of the CD&V-NVA (Flemish Christian Democrats), MR (French speaking Liberals), Open VLD (Flemish Liberals) and the CDH (French speaking Christian Democrats). However, Yves Leterme (Flemish Christian Democrat – CD&V) the "*formateur*", appointed by the King as, failed for the impossibility of reaching an agreement on the state reform and the division of the electoral district BHV (see below). In order to unblock the situation, the King appointed an "*explorateur*" (explorer), who recommended to re-appoint Leterme as "*formateur*" to resume the negotiation process. Despite his decision not to open discussions on the State Reform or the electoral district BHV, Leterme failed again.

Due to this time-consuming working method, for the first time in Belgian history the Federal Parliament started its activities while government negotiations were still going on. On 7th November 2007, the parliamentary Commission on Interior affairs voted in favor of the division of the electoral district "Brussels-Halle-Vilvoorde" ("BHV"). The issue of the electoral district BHV is a symbolic and tense issue. BHV is the electoral district that brings together Brussels and a number of Flemish communities (Halle-Vilvoorde). This means that the District covers the territory of Brussels, which is bilingual, but also part of the monolingual Flemish Region. The fact that "Brussels-Halle-Vilvoorde" is one electoral district, means that the 150,000 French speaking Belgians who live in the Flemish municipalities of this district, have the opportunity to vote for French speaking candidates of Brussels for the European and Federal elections. The division of this district is a long-standing demand of Flemish politicians, and has been revived following a recent judgment of the *Cour d'Arbitrage* that ruled the unconstitutionality of the district structure.

For the first time in Belgian history, the Flemish MPs took advantage of their numerical superiority and voted without the agreement, and actually radically against the French speaking MPs for the separation of BHV. Their vote had mainly a symbolic meaning: apart from the activation by the Francophone MP's of the "conflict of interest" resolution and of the "alarm bell" procedure, the law was not voted in a plenary session and this means that it will not be possible within the upcoming year to formally enact it.

These crises provide unequivocal signs that the Belgian tradition of compromise may no longer ensure the functioning of the federal system.

The crises also demonstrate very clearly that the Belgian structure is confederal rather than federal. The country survives and its political institutions work, only as long as its two founding peoples want, and are able to, make it survive and function.

The Belgian Constitution did not enshrine a secession clause; this right, however, is implicitly embedded in the very logic of the Belgian system. Liberal federations are reluctant to enshrine a secession clause in the Constitution precisely because it suggests the coexistence of more than one people within a State, that possesses a form of "quiescent" sovereignty, while, as the American Supreme Court put it, in most federal contexts the Constitution "in all its provisions, looks to an indestructible union"[38].

Moreover, in a federal context, the constitutional right to secede may be used strategically by the state sub-units, taking advantage of the right to secede in order to seek gains having little to do with secession. The democracy and transparency of decision-making processes may be threatened when the right of secession is exploited by the most populous or richest subunits, taking advantage of their greater bargaining power to put forward non-negotiable demands in search of immediate gains instead of compromise solutions, to the detriment of the national interest. In such cases cooperation between the State's components is replaced by forms of autonomous development, reducing the level of interdependence among the subunits.

The Belgian people seem actually to be aware of the *de facto* existence of a withdrawal clause. In December 2006, the (public) Wallonian national broadcast outlet, RTBF, broadcast a grotesque joke throughout the country. In the middle of a popular TV-program, a special news edition was broadcast. "Good evening, tonight in a special reunion of the Flemish parliament, Flanders has declared itself unilaterally independent. The King has fled the country, citizens cannot cross the borders anymore". There followed a number of interviews with "real" Ministers and MPs, that took a part in the performance. The reactions were of many kinds; the (Southern part of the) country did panic and practically no one thought that secession would be impossible.

Moreover, the risk that the Belgian system embodies, which is clearly manifest in view of the absence of a supremacy clause for federal sources of law in the constitution, results in a de-legitimization of the latter, which becomes

38 U.S. Supreme Court, *Texas v. White,* 74 U.S. 700, 726 (1869).

more of a "compact" between States rather than a "Constitution over them"[39]. In other words, the federal formula in its Belgian application does not attain its main objective, which is to conciliate unity with diversity. Instead, this federal formula has a disintegrating role that is likely to bring about a deeper separation between the linguistic communities.

Bibliography

Alen A., *Nationalism-Federalism-Democracy. The Example of Belgium*, in *Revue Européenne de Droit Public*, 5, 1, 1993.

Alen A., Peeters P., *The Competences of the Communities in the Belgian Federal State: The Principle of Exclusivity Revisited*, in *European Public Law*, 2/1997.

Bermeo N., Amoretti U.M. (eds.), *Federalism, Unitarism and Territorial. Cleavages*, Johns Hopkins University Press, 2003.

Bourtenbourg J., *L'enseignement et la communautarisation*, in *Administration Publique Trimestrielle*, 1988.

Calhoun J.C., *A Discourse on the Constitution and Government of the United States*, reprinted in Calhoun J.C., *The Papers of John C. Calhoun* 69, Clyde N. Wilson & Shirley B. Cook (eds.), University of South Carolina 2003.

Z. Ciuffoletti, S. Noiret (eds.), *I modelli di democrazia in Europa e il caso italiano*, Florence, 1992.

Delgrange X., *Le fédéralisme belge: la protection des minorités linguistiques et idéologiques*, in *Revue de droit public et de la science politique en France et à l'étranger*, 1994.

De Meyer J., *Beschouwingen over het federalisme in Belgie*, in *De Gids o Maatschappelijk Gebied*, 1962.

Destree J., *Lettre au Roi sur la séparation de la Walloonie et de la Flandre*, Paris-Gembloux, 1968.

Dewachter W., *De dualistisce identiteit van de Belgische maatschappij*, Amsterdam, 1992.

Francioni F., Scheinin M. (eds.), *Cultural Human Rights*, Leiden-Boston, 2008.

Hooghe L., Belgium: *Hollowing the Center*, in N. Bermeo, U. M. Amoretti (eds.), *Federalism, Unitarism and Territorial. Cleavages*, Johns Hopkins University Press, 2003.

---

39 See J. C. Calhoun, *A Discourse on the Constitution and Government of the United States*, reprinted in J. C. Calhoun, *The Papers of John C. Calhoun* 69, p. 82, Clyde N. Wilson & Shirley B. Cook (eds.), University of South Carolina 2003.

L'Université de Louvain et la question linguistique, in *Courrier Hebdomadaire, Centre de Recherches et d'Information politiques*, 1968.

Mancini S., De Witte B., *Language Rights as Cultural Rights: A European Perspective*, in Francioni F., Scheinin M. (eds.), *Cultural Human Rights, cit.*

Noiret S., *Le revisioni costituzionali in Belgio: un cammino difficile verso il federalismo o l'agonia dello stato nazionale?*, in Ciuffoletti Z., Noiret S. (eds.), *I modelli di democrazia in Europa e il caso italiano, cit.*

Noiret S., *Political Parties and the Political System in Belgium before Federalism, 1830–1980*, in *European History Quarterly* (SAGE, London Oaks and New Dehli), vol. 24 (1994).

Paddison R., *Il federalismo: diversità regionale nell'unione nazionale*, in Brosio G. (ed.), *Governo decentralizzato e federalismo*, Bologna, 1995.

Pas W., A *Dynamic Federalism Built on Static Principles: The Case of Belgium*, in Tarr G.A., Williams R.F., Marko J. (eds.), *Federalism, Subnational Constitutions and Minority Rights*, Praeger, 2004.

Ruys M., *Les Flamands, un peuple, un mouvement, une nation en devenir*, Tielt, 1973.

Swenden W., *Belgian Federalism, Basic Institutional Features and Potential as a Model for the European Union*, Paper presented at the RIIA Conference – Governing Together in the New Europe, Robinson College, Cambridge UK, 12th–13th April 2003 and published by the London Institute of International Affairs, 2003.

Tarr G.A., Williams R.F., Marko J. (eds.), *Federalism, Subnational Constitutions and Minority Rights, cit.*

Uyttendaele M., *Précis de droit constitutionnel belge. Regards sut un système institutionnel paradoxal*, Bruxelles, 2005.

Van Ginderachten J., *The Belgian Federal Model*, at http://www.ecsanet.org/conferences/ecsaworld2/Ginderachter.htm

Von Busekist A., *La Belgique. Politique des langues et constrution de l'Etat de 1780 à nos jours, Paris-Bruxelles*, 1998.

Witte E., *Language and Territoriality: A Summary of Developments in Belgium*, in *International Journal of Group Rights*, 1993.

Topographic naming in Austria

Peter Hilpold

Summary

1. Introduction

In Austria, the question of topographic naming enjoys high-standing importance in the political discussion. The official attitude towards this issue has not only become one of the most important benchmarks for the openess towards minority issues in general but it is also a mirror for broader trends in the dialogue between the main political parties. Legally speaking, the issue of topographic naming is of concern for several minority regions in Austria. In fact, however, it has become a contentious question only in the Federal Land of Carinthia. There, on the other hand, the subject of topographic naming transcends by far what usually is to be seen a technical question in the field of minority protection. The emotionality by which this dispute is characterized hints at deeper lying conflicts dating back to territorial struggles leading to the drawing of much-contested border lines. In an ethnically and linguistically mixed region, a situation so typical for the old Austrian-Hungarian empire, the drawing of border lines was *per se* a difficult issue. As long as these borders remained contested or, to put it more modestly, as long as the fear should persist that the other side could one day openly put in question these borders, topographic naming remains an issue of high political importance. In fact, in this context the names used in sign posts could easily be misread as justifications for territorial claims.

As a consequence of the extremely emotional value attributed to the issue of topographical naming it was difficult for the Austrian Government or, respectively, for the Austrian Parliament, to find a solution that would not stir further rancour. Thus, the Austrian Constitutional Court had to step in to fill the most evident gaps. This jurisprudence met with criticism for two reasons: first of all, the Constitutional Court was ill-suited to assume the role of a legislator. Some decisions set new material law which could not easily be desumed from constitutional provisions. Secondly, this jurisprudence was to be seen as problematic from the viewpoint of the constitutional division of powers. On the other hand it is true that by this intervention by the Constitutional Court it was possible to overcome a long-standing impasse.

2. The relationship between topographic naming and minority protection

There can be no doubt that the provisions on bilingual topographic names are, first of all, expression of a minority protection intent. At the same time it has to be taken into consideration that the provisions on topographic naming are usually qualified, from a human rights perspective, as collective rights, even though this qualification is not unproblematic. If we are putting these two elements together it would appear that the extent to which bilingualism in topographic naming is granted will generally depend from the strength of the various minority groups. On a practical level, however, the situation is more complicated. In fact, the international and constitutional obligations in the field of topographic naming have remained, for a long time, largely unimplemented. For some, a vicious circle was thereby established: the failure to implement minority protection provision has contributed to the weakening of the minority groups and as a consequence, the reduced strenght of the group could be used by the Government as a pretext to further lower the protective measures. Therefore, the question arose, whether the historic strenght of the group (say, in 1955) should be taken as a reference. Though the adoption of such an approach may be required by considerations of political justice, in practice some sort of compromise will be necessary, as will be stated below.

Topographic naming makes part of the general language provisions in favour of minorities and therefore the relevant norms have to be interpreted according to similar criteria. Viewed more closely there is, however, a great difference between provisions relating to the use of minority languages before public institutions and provisions on topographic naming. According to the Austrian Constitutional Court[1] the inherent function of the provisions on topographic naming is to give evidence to the public that a larger group of minority members

1 See VfSlg. 12.836/1991, 16.404/2001 and V 131/03 of 14.12.2004.

is living – in an "eye-catching" manner – [2] on a certain territory. It is evident that the Constitutional Court has oversimplified the problem with this statement. In fact, as will be shown with this contribution, scope and function of topographic naming goes far beyond. Bilingual topographic names have not been introduced in the interest of the majority but in the immediate interest of the minority and their members. As a corollary of these considerations it has to be remembered that the strength of the various minorities is of pivotal importance for the implementation of these provisions.

The most recent census is of 2001. The figures exposed below have to be read, however, with caution. The counting of a minority is always a problematic issue as minorities often fear that this process is detrimental to their interests[3]. In view of past experiences[4] members of minorities often refuse to be officially counted. Accordingly, there is no official counting of a minority affiliation in Austria. In the past, in Austria the "mother tongue" was counted. This was considered to be discriminatory by the minorities as there could be an inclination for an affiliation to the German language group. The requirement to indicate the "language of everyday life" (*Umgangssprache*) is surely more minority-friendly. For some, however, this requirement is too minority-friendly. On the other hand, there can be no doubt that a census, in what ever form formulated, tends rather to under-estimate the strength of a minority than to overstate it. As a consequence, minority representation organization indicate far higher numbers.

3. The relevant constitutional provision

Article 7, para. 3 of the Austrian State Treaty concerning the rights of the Slovenian and Croatian minorities goes as follows:

> "In administrative and judicial areas of Carinthia, Burgenland, and Styria with Slovenian, Croatian and mixed populations, the Slovenian and Croatian languages shall be permitted as official languages in addition to German. Signposts and signs in these areas shall be in the Slovenian and Croatian as well as German languages".

---

2 The Constitutional Court used the term "*ins Auge springend*".

3 See generally and with relation to South Tyrol P. Hilpold, *Minority Census and Declaration of Membership to a Minority – A Pillar of the South Tyrolean Autonomy under International Scrutiny*, in *Italian Yearbook of International Law*, XV, 2005, pp. 81–109.

4 See P. Hilpold, *Modernes Minderheitenrecht*, Wien/Baden-Baden/Zürich, 2001, p. 392 et seq. Thus, for example, in 1938 the Roma population in Austria was first registred and afterwards murdered by the National Socialists.

On a whole, this provision can be considered to be very minority-friendly. As atates are generally very reluctant to grant to their minorities specific rights in this field – and this has been true even more so in the past – these provisions of 1955 constitute a very modern and advanced regulation. The practical implementation of this provision has constituted, however, a very irksome process. The reason for this difficulties cannot only be found, in the fact, already mentioned that the issue of topographic naming in minority areas is very controversial. In fact, the implementation process of art. 7, para. 3 of the State Treaty revealed that the wording of the relevant provision in the State Treaty is rather ambigous.

The Constitutional Court ruled that art. 7, para. 3, first sentence of the State Treaty is self-executing[5]. Due to the close relationship between the first and the second sentence in art. 7, para. 3 ("in such districts [...]") this qualification has been extended to the second sentence and on this basis the Constitutional Court was able to rule also on the application of this provision.

4. What are "administrative and judicial areas"?

First of all, it was unclear what was meant with "administrative and judicial areas". In the meantime there is a general consensus that these expressions are not of a technical character in the sense that they had to correspond squarely to political units with the same naming in Austria. Special care has to be taken to find units with which minority groups truly can identify themselves. On a practical level these are usually municipalities ("*Gemeinden*"). Therefore, reference has to be made to municipalities – or territorial subdivision of municipalities ("*Ortschaften*") – when it has to be determined whether we are in the presence of a "mixed" population[6]. Furthermore, according to the Constitutional Court, the obligation set by the State Treaty applies also for municipalities ("*Gemeinden*") or single localities ("*Ortschaften*") qualified as

---

5 See VfSlg. 9744/1983.

6 See extensively, P. Hilpold, *Modernes Minderheitenrecht, cit.*, p. 277 et seq. as well as D. Kolonovits, *Sprachenrecht in Österreich*, Wien, 1999, p. 138 et seq. See also VfGH 13.12.2001 G 213/01, V 62,63/01:
"*Von all dem ausgehend ist dem Begriff 'Verwaltungsbezirk' gemäß Art. 7 Z 3 zweiter Satz des Staatsvertrages von Wien, insoweit es um das Verfassen von 'Bezeichnungen und Aufschriften ... topographischer Natur' in Form der in Rede stehenden straßenverkehrsrechtlichen Hinweiszeichen geht, aber ein Verständnis beizulegen, das sich an den tatsächlichen, d.h. – gegebenenfalls – ortschaftsbezogenen, Siedlungsschwerpunkten der betreffenden Volksgruppe orientiert. Demgemäß sind unter dem Begriff 'Verwaltungsbezirk' in diesem normativen Zusammenhang auch 'Ortschaften' im mehrfach erwähnten gemeinderechtlichen Sinn zu verstehen*".

such by the Road Traffic Act (*Straßenverkehrsordnung*)[7]. Curiously, this Act became an important vehicle for the implementation of the international and constitutional obligations to install bilingual sign posts. It was also this Act which allowed individuals to act for the implementation for this right before the Constitutional Court. In fact, speed limitations according to the Road Traffic Act apply to municipalities or single localities if apposite signs indicate their beginning and end. These indications have to be made in a correct language – if legally required also in a bilingual way[8]. In view of this situation, members of the Slovene minorities who were passed a fine for exceeding speed limitations in municipalities or single localities with a Slovene minority but with no bilingual signposts made their way to the Constitutional Court. They contested the traffic mandate before the Courts and at the end, the relevant question laid before the Constitutional Court. By this way it was possible for individuals to contest the non-implementation of group rights, although some lawyers expressed doubts whether this process was legally correct.

5. What are municipalities with "mixed population"?

The next question that was to be addressed regarded the definition of "Slovenian, Croatian and mixed population". It was obvious from the beginning that there are no municipalities in Austria with a majority of Slovenian and Croatian population. This formulation has, therefore, not to be understood literally but rather contextually. It is clear that municipalities with a mixed population of German and Slovenian or German and Croatian residents are meant.

Said this, it was to clarify what was meant with the term "mixed population" according to the State Treaty. With other words: it was clear that the presence of very small minority groups could not justify the demand for bilingual signposts. The question was, then, what was the percentage of minority members requested for a village to be considered as of "mixed population". As the State Treaty of 1955 contains no indications in this regard it has to be looked out for other documents which could be taken as an interpretative guide.

---

7 See VfSlg 16.404/2001.

8 As Rudi Vouk, the lawyer who brought this case before the Constitutional Court, has pointed out place-name signs (such as "St. Kanzian" in the respective case) "declare the boundaries of of the locality and at the same time prescribe a speed limit [...]. In the legal sense these place-name signs are in effect an ordinance". Cited according to *Österreiches Volksgruppenzentrum*, 2nd Report on the implementation of the European Framework Convention for the Protection of National Minorities, Wien, 2007, p. 88.

As already mentioned above, it was the Constitutional Court which had to bring important clarifications about. The compromise, formulated by the Constitutional Court, took the following form:

- the relevant data should be gained through a more generic process[9];
- the relevant percentage should refer to a longer period.

This said, it was still to be determined what actually the percentage was, starting from which a "mixed population" can be considered to be given. Those few authors who expressed an opinion in this regard did not manage to bring much clarity to this subject. As a good example in kind one can refer to Theodor Veiter, in the past one of the most prolific authors on Austrian minority law. On various occasions he expressed different ideas in this regard. One time he wrote that a percentage of 10% was sufficient[10] and on another occasion he was of the opinion that the threshold should not, in any case, exceed 20%[11]. It was also said that every percentage between a range of 5–25% would be in conformity with international law[12]. For at least two reasons these proposals seems to be of little help: first of all, the fact that they diverge widely demonstrates that there is no consensus in this area. Secondly, even if it would be possible to narrow these differences the considerable extent of these ranges makes them widely useless.

It could, therefore, be tried to seek clarification via an historic interpretation approach[13].

As it is known, already after the First World War Austria had to assume minority protection obligations through the Treaty of Saint Germain of 1919. According to art. 68 of this Treaty protective measures have to be granted only if minority members represented a "considerable proportion" of the respective population. During the negotiations for the State Treaty a similar clause was also discussed but in the end it did not find its way in the final text of the treaty. This

---

9 See VfGH 12.836/1991.

10 See Th. Veiter, *Das Recht der Volksgruppen und Sprachminderheiten in Österreich*, Wien, 1970, p. 539.

11 See Th. Veiter, *Das Österreichische Volksgruppenrecht seit dem Volksgruppengesetz von 1976*, Wien, 1979, p. 112.

12 See F. Matscher, *Die Stellung der Minderheitensprachen in Österreich*, in F. Koja, G. Stourzh (eds.), *Schweiz – Österreich, Ähnlichkeiten und Kontraste*, Wien 1986, pp. 103–122 (111). For F. Sturm, *Der Minderheiten- und Volksgruppenschutz*, in R. Machacek et al. (eds.), *Grund- und Menschenrechte in Österreich*, vol. II, N.P. Engel: Kehl am Rhein, 1992, pp. 77–111, this range should go from 10–20% (ibid., p. 106).

13 See art. 32 VCLT.

fact has been interpreted as an expression of the intent to require a rather low threshold for the minority protection provisions to apply[14].

After the uncertainties as to the exact minority size needed had lasted for decades in 2000 the Austrian Constitutional Court finally made important clarifications: a minority percentage of 10,4% was in any case sufficient for the protection provisions to apply[15]. As a consequence, it can be said that the relevant percentage is not a strictly fixed number but rather of an indicative nature. In 2001 the Constitutional Court transposed this figure to the area of topographic naming[16].

For the following figures see European Council, Second Report Submitted by Austria Pursuant to art. 25, para. 1 of the Framework Convention for the Protection of National Minorities of 1st December 2006[17].

Population according to everyday language and nationality – 2001 Census

Everyday language	Total numbers for nationality		Place of birth			
	absolute	in %*	in Austria	in %*	abroad	in %*
Burgenland-Croat	19,374	5.9	18,943	11.3	431	0.3
Romany	4,348	1.3	1,732	1.0	2,616	1.6
Slovak	3,343	1.0	1,172	0.7	2,171	1.3
Slovene	17,953	5.4	13,225	7.9	4,728	2.9
Czech	11,035	3.3	4,137	2.5	6,698	4.2
Hungarian	25,884	7.8	9,565	5.7	16,319	10.0
Windisch**	567	0.2	547	0.9	20	0.0

* *Percentages refer to the total number of indications of a non-German everyday language*

** *A variety of the Slovene language, interspersed with German vocabulary*

14 See G. Stourzh, *Um Einheit und Freiheit. Staatsvertrag, Neutralität und das Ende der Ost-West-Besetzung Österreichs 1945–1955*, Wien, 1988, p. 159.

15 See the decision of 4th October 2000, V 91/99–11. This decision regarded the municipality of Ebensdorf and concerned the Slovene Language Decree. On the basis of this decision Slovene had to be accepted as an official language before municipal authorities also in Ebensdorf. Due to the strict connection between the provisions on the use of minority languages before public authorities and the use of these languages for signposts it was only a matter of time before also the provisions on bilingual topographic naming should find a more extensive application.

16 See the decision of 13th December 2001, G 213/01, V 62, 63/01.

17 ACFC/SR/II(2006)008.

6. The implementation of the relevant provisions

6.1 Implementation as a controversial process

An important step for the implementation of the topographic provisions contained in the State Treaty was set in 1972 when the "Signposts Act" ("*Ortstafelgesetz*") was adopted[18]. According to this Act, 205 municipalities in Carinthia should obtain bilingual signposts. This act which was adopted only with the votes of the socialist members of the Parliament was opposed by the main actors in this area: for many members of the Slovene minority it was too restrictive, for German nationalist groups in Carinthia, like the "*Kärntner Abwehrkämpferbund*" it was much too generous. All bilingual signs were removed by force within a short period of time. The Austrian Government did not insist on the implementation of this Act and tried rather to find a consensual solution. Intense negotations set in and the result was the "Austrian Group Rights Act" ("*Volksgruppengesetz*") which contained *inter alia* a regulation for the question of topographic naming. The Signposts Act of 1972 was formally repealed[19]. For two reasons minority representatives were sceptical towards the new situation that had come about:

- first of all, they were not satisfied with the modalities a special census, designed to implement the new rules that were to be enacted, had been carried out;
- secondly, the obligation to instal bilingual signposts applied only to municipalities with a minority presence of at least 25% while for the Signposts Act of 1972 a percentage of 20% had sufficed[20]. The justification delivered by the Government for this restrictive approach was shaky. In fact, according to the Government this requirement corresponded to general international law criteria[21]. In reality, however, no such rule could be desumed from international law[22].

---

18 See BGBl. 270/1972 of 6th July 1972.

19 See § 24 para. 3 of the Austrian Group Rights Act.

20 See § 2 para. 1 no. 2 of the Group Rights Act 1976.

21 In particular, the Government had referred to minority provisions attached to the London Memorandum for Trieste of 1954. According to these provisions it was planned, amongst others, to install bilingual topographic signpost in areas with a minority presence of at least 25%. These provisions were, however, never put in effect and in 1976, when the Group Rights Act was issued, they were no more in force.

22 See, more extensively, P. Hilpold, *Modernes Minderheitenrecht*, *cit.* and Idem, *Der Ortsnamenstreit in Kärnten und in Südtirol aus rechtsvergleichender und völkerrechtlicher Sicht*, in 125 *Juristische Blätter,* 2/2003, pp. 92–105 (93).

At the end, even this very demanding Act was implemented only in part.

Only in 2001 the 25%-criterion was set aside by the Constitutional Court as described above[23].

6.2 The present situation

Over the years the situation consolidated somewhat and in the last years considerable progress has been made in the attempt to find a solution that would satisfy, to a certain extent, the aspirations of all the parties involved.

At present, in Austria bilingual signposts apply for the Slovene minority in Carinthia and for the Croatian and the Hungarian minority in Burgenland.

While the implementation of the relevant provisions has been (and, to a certain extension, continous to be) very contentious with regard to Carinthia, in Burgenland the relevant measures – which came very late – were adopted in a calm political climate.

The relevant Topographical Ordinance for Burgenland[24] went into effect on 22nd June 2000. It refers to 28 municipalities and to 47 places for which also Croat names apply. With regard to the Hungarian minority living in Burgenland there are four municipalities and/or places for which the respective designation has official *status* also in the Hungarian language.

Topographic naming in Carinthia is now regulated by a Topographical Ordinance of 2006[25]. On the basis of this Ordinance the number of municipalities with bilingual signpost has been considerably enlarged. Nonetheless, in the aftermath further municipalities were added to this list by the Constitutional Court. The Constitutional Court has also taken a clear stance against any attempt to circumvent the relevant obligation. Thus in 2006[26] this Court ruled, for example, that the obligation to instal bilingual signposts was not fulfilled by the installation of an additional (smaller) sign with Slovene names.

On a whole, this subject is still in fermentation. The Constitutional Court has given important guidelines for the implementation of art. 7, para. 3, second sentence of the Austrian State Treaty. Nonetheless, it is also clear that the Constitutional Court cannot fully take the place of the legislator. Notwithstanding the fact that the Constitutional Court has repeatedly returned to this issue many elements still remain uncertain. There are two reasons why this will be the case also in the future:

---

23 Decision of 13th December 2001, G 213/01, V 62, 63/01.

24 See BGBl. II 170/2000.

25 Published in BGBl. 245/2006.

26 See V 81/2006.

– first of all, Court rulings, which are passed in view of a specific controversy, can never do fully justice to a reality which is enormously complex and variegated;
– secondly, even if the legislator acts these rules can again be set aside by the Constitutional Court which bases its findings on a higher-ranking constitutional norm.

This controversy could be closed only if a general consensus was found on the issue of topographic names and if this consensus could be transformed in an act of constitutional rank. Of course, such an approach would also have drawbacks as this would practically paralyze the further development of these rules while the public discussion is still under way. On a whole, however, the stability brought about by such a consolidation of the rules would be surely beneficial and would by far outweigh the drawbacks associated with the loss of dynamics in the whole legislative development. The main problem lies, of course, in finding such a consensus that would mirror a general compromise. In a political landscape in Austria that has been characterized in the last years by major shifts it is not easily forseeable when and how a compromise on this eminently political issue can be found.

At the same time it has also to be remembered that the need to find a satisfactory solution in the field of topographic naming is not only commanded by constitutional obligations but to the same extent also by international law obligations. In this context not only the Austrian State Treaty has to be mentioned but also the European Framework Convention on National Minorities (FCNM) of 1995[27]. Although the relevant provision in art. 11, para. 3 appears, at first sight, rather vague[28], the process of implementation for this provision has given further clarity to this norm. The Advisory Committee on the Framework Convention for the Protection of National Minorities has repeatedly admonished invidual parties to this convention to give effective implentation to this

27 See on this subject P. Hilpold, *Ortsnamenregelungen aus völkerrechtlicher und aus europarechtlicher Sicht – unter besonderer Berücksichtigung der Kärntner Ortstafelfrage*, in *Juristische Blätter*, 129/2007, pp. 228–236.

28 "In areas traditionally inhabited by substantial numbers of persons belonging to a national minority, the Parties shall endeavour, in the framework of their legal system, including, where appropriate, agreements with other States, and taking into account their specific conditions, to display traditional local names, street names and other topographical indications intended for the public also in the minority language when there is a sufficient demand for such indications".

provision[29] and it has also expressed its approval for the judgment of the Austrian Constitutional Court of 13th December 2001[30].

It is to be expected that the further development of the situation in Austria with regard to topographic naming will be closely followed by the treaty organs of the Framework Convention.

Bibliography

Hilpold P., *Modernes Minderheitenrecht*, Wien/Baden-Baden/Zürich, 2001.

Hilpold P., *Der Ortsnamenstreit in Kärnten und in Südtirol aus rechtsvergleichender und völkerrechtlicher Sicht,* in *Juristische Blätter*, 125, 2/2003.

Hilpold P., *Minority Census and Declaration of Membership to a Minority – A Pillar of the South Tyrolean Autonomy under International Scrutiny*, in *Italian Yearbook of International Law*, XV, 2005.

Hilpold P., *Ortsnamenregelungen aus völkerrechtlicher und aus europarechtlicher Sicht – unter besonderer Berücksichtigung der Kärntner Ortstafelfrage*, in *Juristische Blätter*, 129/2007.

Kolonovits D., *Sprachenrecht in Österreich*, Wien, 1999.

Kolonovits D., *Ortstafelerkenntnis (VfGH 13.12.2001, G 213/01, V 62 63/01) – Umsetzung möglich?*, *Juristische Ausbildung und Praxisvorbereitung (JAP*), 2001/2002.

Kolonovits D., *Commentary to Art. 7 Z 2–4 Staatsvertrag von Wien*, in Korinek K., Holoubek M., *Österreichisches Bundesverfassungsrecht*, *Kommentar*, 7. Lfg., Wien, 2005.

Kolonovits D., *Aktuelles Erkenntnis des VfGH (12.12.2005, V 64/05) zur Aufstellung von zweisprachigen Ortstafeln in Kärnten*, *migralex,* 1/2006.

---

29 See, for example, Advisory Committee, *Opinion on Albania*, ACFC/INF/OP/I (2003) 004, 2002, para. 47 and Advisory Committee, *Opinion on Armenia*, ACFC, INF/OP/I (2003) 001, 2002, para. 103.

30 See the *Opinion on Austria* of 16 May 2002, ACFC/INF/OP/I(2002)009, para. 50: "The Advisory Committee particularly welcomes the Austrian Constitutional Court's interpretation of the second sentence of Article 7, paragraph 3 of the State Treaty as regards the threshold required for topographical indications to be displayed in minority languages. This interpretation, which is entirely in keeping with Article 11, paragraph 3 of the Framework Convention, represents a major improvement in the rights of persons belonging to national minorities. The Advisory Committee considers it important that this ruling, which comes from the highest Court of the State which deals with constitutional issues, be respected and implemented by the various authorities concerned at all levels. In this context, the extremely negative reaction of the Governor of Carinthia gives rise to deep concern [...]".

Matscher F., *Die Stellung der Minderheitensprachen in Österreich*, in Koja F., Stourzh G. (eds.), *Schweiz – Österreich, Ähnlichkeiten und Kontraste*, Wien, 1986.

Stourzh G., *Um Einheit und Freiheit. Staatsvertrag, Neutralität und das Ende der Ost-West-Besetzung Österreichs 1945–1955*, Wien, 1988.

Sturm F., *Der Minderheiten- und Volksgruppenschutz*, in Machacek R. et al. (eds.), *Grund- und Menschenrechte in Österreich*, vol. II, N.P. Engel, Kehl am Rhein, 1992.

Veiter Th., *Das Recht der Volksgruppen und Sprachminderheiten in Österreich*, Wien, 1970.

Veiter Th., *Das Österreichische Volksgruppenrecht seit dem Volksgruppengesetz von 1976*, Wien, 1979.

Winkler G., *Zweisprachige Ortstafeln und Volksgruppenrechte*, in *Zeitschrift für Öffentliches Recht*, 57/2002.

Topographical names and minority rights: the case of Switzerland

Lidija R. Basta Fleiner and Thomas Fleiner

Summary

1. Topographical names and linguistic rights: particularities of the Swiss case

Swiss policy of topographical names as a means of protecting and promoting minority rights is indeed specific; it displays many dimensions, providing for a variety of approaches and solutions. This is mainly due to the following two reasons: 1) particular minority rights concept; 2) close linkage between topographical indications' policy and collective nature of linguistic minority rights that base on territoriality principle.

Furthermore, today, it is the language which persisted as the key element of communal identity in a multilingual Switzerland.

1.1 Swiss minority rights concept

Swiss understanding of minority rights builds on three pillars: a) Swiss concept of nation; b) federalism and power-sharing, including specific relationship between federalism and democracy; c) group rights approach and territoriality in minority policy. Major religious and linguistic diversities are cross-cutting. No linguistic or religious group in Switzerland has a "mother canton"; Swiss citizens belonging to traditional religious and linguistic communities can at the same time be a majority or a minority in a political process.

a) *Swiss nation concept.* Swiss multicultural, composed nation ("*Willensnation*" – nation by will) consists of democratically integrated traditional linguistic and religious groups, sharing a common will to preserve and promote these traditional diversities. Inter-communal piece is one of major legitimating values of the Swiss State. A permanent search for consensus instead of overruling is notorious for the Swiss democratic political culture. The notions of "majority" and "minority" actually have little meaning, and there is no specific provision protecting minorities as such in the federal Constitution[1].
b) *Federalism and power sharing.* Since the first federal Constitution adopted in 1874, democratic pluralism has been primarily conceived as a co-existential *modus vivendi* for religious and linguistic groups. Swiss federalism guarantees strong cantonal autonomy but also gives great importance to the municipal autonomy (self-rule and communal civism). On the other hand, thanks to a major role of direct democracy instruments – popular initiative and referendum – Switzerland could embrace an integrative power-sharing model among different linguistic and religious groups. Popular initiatives and referendum are about concrete political issue, which could in one case build alliance along linguistic, in other case, along religious lines. Here, it is important to point out the following: whereas religious diversity – as a rule – plays no major role today, the cleavages between urban and rural areas have been increasingly affecting results of public voting[2].

---

1 In this sense the Swiss Constitution transcends modern constitutionalism, which considers cultural homogeneity of the nation as a condition *sine qua non* for democracy. A nation-State concept builds instead on the nation composed of democratically integrated traditional linguistic and religious communities. Cf. Th. Fleiner, L.R. Basta Fleiner, *Constitutional Democracy in a Multicultural and Globalised World*, Berlin-Heidelberg, 2009, p. 511.

2 In the last constitutional referendum (13th February 2011) the majority of the cantons and of the peoples rejected a proposal to prohibit soldiers keeping their arms at home. In this vote the rural areas were in favour of the actual tradition while the urban areas preferred the prohibition of arms at home (http://www.admin.ch/ch/d/pore/va/20110213/det554.html, accessed 28th February 2011).

c) *Group rights approach and territoriality in minority policy: a general overview.* This element of Swiss minority rights approach is critical for understanding the specificities and many varieties in the Swiss policy of topographical names as a means to protect and promote minorities. The federal Ordinance on Geographical Names[3] gives the cantons and municipalities the competences to formulate their policies in this respect. Together with the latest federal Guidelines on Geographical Names[4], it provides for a legal framework delegating the cantons and even municipalities to substantiate their policies on topographical names. Given that out of 26 Cantons three are bilingual (Bern, Fribourg and Valais) and one is trilingual (Graubünden/ Grisson) cantonal and municipalities policies on geographical names are part and parcel of the overall territoriality-based linguistic policies, containing both sides of the coin.

Historically, the territoriality principle connected specific sets of rights and duties to a certain territory (as opposed to the principle of personality which links rights to respective groups of individuals), and guaranteed full religious sovereignty to single cantons. Once again: religious identities initially played a major role in maintaining peaceful coexistence between Protestants and Catholics. Today, however, linguistic diversities create more tensions. Swiss Constitution, as revised in 1999[5], calls for the respect and maintenance of the traditional language territories: the language traditionally spoken by the population of a territory shall have the *status* of an official language. Each canton autonomously designates its official language. Sometimes this causes problems in bilingual and one trilingual canton since the cantons also decide which languages shall be official languages in their territory for the communication with cantonal and municipal authorities. The cantons are thus requested to protect indigenous linguistic minorities also on smaller territories. Such constitutional solutions aim at preserving peaceful relations among different linguistic groups. On the other hand, they inevitably restrict individual linguistic rights. For instance, every Swiss citizen, irrespectively of his/her mother tongue, is educated in the official language of the territory where he/she lives, and has to use respective official language in communication with public authorities[6].

3 Verordnung No. RS 510.625 über die geographischen Namen from 1st January1971, last revision entered into force on 1st July 2008.

4 Toponymische Richtlinien der Schweiz, 1. Ausgabe 2010, Bundesamt für Landestopographie, Wabern (CH).

5 The Constitution has been in force since 1st January 2000, after a referendum had taken place.

6 More: see *infra* footnote 9, further *infra* § 1.3.

1.2 Multilingualism in Switzerland

The identity of Switzerland as a nation-State primarily builds on its four different national languages: German, French, Italian and Romansh. Three of these languages are at the same time the main languages of the neighbour-countries of Switzerland[7] (Germany, Austria, Liechtenstein, France and Italy). For more than 200 years multilingualism has been a key element of the Swiss identity[8]. As a consequence, the freedom of language cannot be treated only as an individual right. In case of Switzerland, the fundamental in this right covers not only individual human dignity but also the dignity of linguistic community. On the other side, multilingualism did not lead to a linguistic homogenisation of the country. The only exception was foundation of the new canton of Jura by inner secession from the canton of Bern, including only French-speaking part of the Jura region. Actually, the borderlines of the cantons do not overlap with linguistic borderlines. More notably, the cantons have preserved their own traditional multilingualism[9].

1.3 Federal constitutional framework for multilingualism

According to the Preamble of the Constitution, Switzerland's identity as a country is defined by its unity in diversity. It is a nation composed of different cantons, religions, languages and cultures[10]. Swiss State not only respects but also promotes its diversities as one of its main duties (art. 2 of the Constitution). Each traditional cultural community must be supported in order to be able to

7 See: L.R. Basta, Th. Fleiner, *Federalism and Multiethnic States: the Case of Switzerland*, 2nd ed., Fribourg 2000. According to the statistics from the year 2000, out of seven million inhabitants 63% are German, 20.4% French, 6.5% Italian, 0.5% Romansh and 9% have other original languages than the communities speaking one of the four national languages of Switzerland. While German and French have always been considered as main languages, Italian and Romansh are considered as languages under threat. They have diminished in the last ten years as original languages. Increased has however the diversity of the languages. Already 16.6% of the population indicate that they speak at home a different language than one of the national languages. This is an increase of 3% within only 10 years. In: G. Lüdi, I. Werlen, *Sprachenlandschaft in der Schweiz*, Swiss Federal Statistical Office, Bern, 2000, p. 7 et seq.

8 It was during the French occupation that Napoleon changed Switzerland into a trilingual country. Since then cantonal borderlines and linguistic borderlines have not coincided.

9 Cf. A. Auer, *D'une liberté non écrite qui n'aurait pas dû l'être : la "liberté de la langue"*, in *Zeitschrift für Aktuelle Juristische Praxis (AJP)*, 1992, p. 955 et seq.

10 Article 1 of the federal Constitution before the 1999 revision read as follows: "Together, the peoples of the 23 sovereign cantons of Switzerland united by the present alliance, to wit: Zurich, Berne, Lucerne, Uri and Jura, form the Swiss Confederation".

develop its own identity within the unity of the composed nation. Article 70 of the Constitution further clarifies this basic constitutional principle: according to para. 3, the Confederation and the cantons have a duty to foster mutual exchange of different language communities; in addition, according to para. 4, the Confederation has to grant subsidies for the specific tasks of multilingual cantons. Moreover, para. 5 of this article provides that the Confederation has also to care for the sustainability of the Italian and Romansh languages, which are spoken by the smallest cultural communities of Switzerland[11].

Multilingualism not only influences handling of different languages, it determines even the structure of the country and its cantons, districts and, in particular, its municipalities. In several multilingual cantons the municipalities are the bearer of the right to determine the official language right (historically even of the official religion). Also the actually worldwide unique directorial governmental system of the seven federal councils, influenced by the French directory of the revolutionary French Constitution of 1795, is as an institutional design aimed at accommodating the diversity of the country. The Federal Council is composed of seven pair members individually elected by the Federal Assembly, and represents different linguistic regions and communities (art. 175). Each of the three linguistic communities (the French and Italian community is considered as belonging to the Latin speaking community) is thus represented in the Government.

1.4 Different understanding of language rights

1.4.1 Freedom to use any language

Until the 1999 constitutional revision, the right to use freely one's language was guaranteed in Switzerland by the Federal Tribunal, as an "unwritten fundamental right"[12]. The Tribunal linked the freedom of speech to the official language of a

11 The federal Constitution now in force mentions the word "language" thirteen times (art. 4, art. 8, para. 2, art. 18, art. 31, art. 69, para. 3, art. 70, paras. 1 to 5, arts. 71 and 175 para. 4, as well as art. 188, para. 4). This is an indication that the Constitution considers language as a potential for conflicts on one side, and on the other, as an asset. As a matter of comparison: the word "*lingua*" in the Italian Constitution is mentioned twice, the word "*langue*" in the French Constitution and "*Sprache*" in the German Fundamental Law is mentioned only once. The Constitution of the multilingual Spain contains five, the Constitution of Belgium seven references to language. Even the treaty of Lisbon of the European Union refers to language only five times.

12 Since the famous decision of 31st March 1965, BGE 91 I 480, the right to use freely own language has been considered by the Federal Tribunal as an unwritten constitutional right

canton, saying that each canton or municipality had according to the principal of territoriality the competence to determine its official language to be used by the administration, the courts and in public schools[13]. Moreover, the cantons could oblige parents to provide for their children to have some education in the official language of the canton of their domicile.

The Constitution in force since January 2000 provides explicitly in its art. 18 for "the individual freedom to use any language". This right includes all languages and dialects. Even languages which are not any more used or which are secret are protected.

1.4.2 Balancing between individual and collective language rights. A particular challenge for multilingual Switzerland

Multilingual Switzerland faces a special challenge as regards balancing of linguistic diversity between individual and collective level. Article 18 of the Constitution provides a constitutional basis for such balancing in a combination of the right to use freely own language as provided in art. 18 of the Constitution, and the principle of territoriality implied in art. 70, para. 2, namely: "The cantons shall decide on their official languages. In order to preserve harmony between the linguistic communities the cantons shall respect the traditional territorial distribution of languages and take account of indigenous linguistic minorities".

According to this provision, the principle of territoriality apparently limits the right to a free use of language[14]. The main reason why the Federal Tribunal gave priority to the principle of territoriality already before the 1999 constitutional revision over the individual freedom of language was its concern about freedom and harmony among different indigenous linguistic communities. Accordingly, the Federal Tribunal explicitly decided: "If the Federal Tribunal would not

---

linked to art. 116 of the former Constitution: "According to scholarship, the freedom of language belongs to the unwritten constitutional rights of the Constitution. To this concept we agree" (translation by Th. Fleiner). See also the non published decision of 3rd June 1932 Zähringer and consorts against the Council of the State of the Canton of Tessin, quoted in: C. Marti-Rolli, *La liberté de la langue en droit suisse,* Zurich, 1978, p. 16. More on the development of the liberty of language: D. Richter, *Sprachenordnung und Minderheitenschutz im schweizerischen Bundesstaat; Realivität des Sprachenrechts und Sicherung des Sprachenfriedens,* Berlin-Heidelberg, 2005, p. 219 et seq.

13 BGE 91 I 480, Consideration II.2, 31st March 1965.

14 More in depth on the freedom of language: D. Richter, *Sprachenordnung und Minderheitenschutz im Schweizerischen Bundesstaat, cit.*, p. 145 et seq.

respect this limitation, a contradiction between the legal order and the reality may occur and thus endanger language peace"[15].

In a nutshell, the understanding of the-rule-of-law equality principle, which underlies the Swiss Constitution, can be formulated as follows: in order to remain legitimate, multinational federal States have to balance individual equality and freedom with those of constitutive communities, giving legal guarantees for the citizens to enjoy in the first instance equal opportunities within their own cultural community. The "public interest" of a language community has to be balanced with the public interest of the entire federation. The consequence is a privileged *status* for traditional languages as national languages.

1.4.3 A privileged status *for traditional languages as national languages*

According to art. 4 of the federal Constitution, Switzerland recognizes four different languages as national languages. With this provision the Constitution guarantees first of all to all persons belonging to German, French, Italian and Romansh speaking communities the freedom of language and the equality in rights of all citizens speaking either of these languages. This provision guarantees first of all these languages originally spoken in Switzerland a special protection in terms of freedom of language. Whoever speaks one of the national languages has the right to address himself or herself to federal authorities in his native language, based on the fundamental right to use freely own language. However, this protection is limited by the principle of territoriality. Based on their constitutional autonomy, the cantons determine their official language valid for the entire territory of the canton[16]. According to art. 70, para. 1 of the federal Constitution, official languages are German, French and Italian, and for communication with Romansh speaking persons also Romansh[17].

The fact that Switzerland recognizes all four national languages on equal footing has far-reaching impact for the policy on geographical names. Each

15 BGE 122 I 236, E. 4, 15th July 1996.

16 Those, who for this reason would claim the right to address their cantonal authorities in a national language which is not recognized by the canton as its official language, cannot claim insist on their freedom of language because of the principle of territoriality (Decision of the Federal Tribunal 10th June 2003 (1P.327/2003), Consideration, at 4).

17 The Swiss currency is named Frank. This label has been borrowed from the French currency in the XIX century. On the Swiss banknotes Frank translated into all four different Swiss national languages. If Switzerland for practical reasons can only use one language, one uses the old Latin language. Thus the abbreviation of Switzerland is CH which counts for "*Confoederatio Helvetica*". The latter wording is e.g. used on the coin of five Swiss franks.

canton has its own tradition with regard to topographical indications. Moreover many names and labels have a strong historical background, going back to the language of the middle-ages. Swiss federal authorities had to take this into account when legally laying down common principles for geographic-names policies in the country[18].

Because the languages traditionally spoken in Switzerland are on equal footing irrespective of how big are linguistic communities, the Constitution does not declassify any of the languages to a minority language. In addition, collective linguistic rights have to be balanced with the need for mutual understanding among the different communities speaking national languages. Finally, one has also to provide measures in order to guarantee particularly the sustainability of language communities which are under the threat to disappear.

Further important effect of such a constitutional politics of multilingualism in Switzerland is that national languages should not be exposed to the free market system of unlimited competition. If small communities are in danger to disappear because of the rule of free market, measures need to be implemented to support those endangered communities.

Last but not least, measures sustaining traditional language communities may often also lead to delimit the liberty of language of minorities living in this specific area[19]. The freedom of language of the persons speaking national languages is – within the frame of the principle of territoriality – only guaranteed provided it does not endanger the traditional homogeneity of the indigenous language of the territory. The individual right has to withdraw before the collective right of the language community. Collective rights and individual rights have to be balanced. The more the sustainability of the language community is in danger, the more the individual right to use freely own language may be limited.

Taken altogether, the above discussed particularities of Switzerland as traditionally multilingual State and society have had a decisive impact on the many facets of decentralized policy on geographic names as a means of protecting and promoting minority rights. These have been reflected already at federal level. Here some examples: the Lake of Geneva, in German "*Genfer*

18 Decree on Geographical Names from 21st May 2008, SR 510.625.

19 During the First Monitoring Cycle under the Framework Convention for the Protection of National Minorities, the Swiss Government defended territoriality principle for compulsory schooling as aimed at essentially preventing the Germanisation of the traditionally French-speaking part of Bern canton through the creation of German-language private schools. In this case, traditional linguistic identity as a condition for inter-communal peace has for Swiss multicultural society a higher value than individual freedom (Cf. GVT/COM/INF/OP/I(2003)007 at 17–18).

See", is translated into French as "*Lac Léman*", the "Lake of Constance" in French is called "*Bodensee*" in German. Even for Switzerland, *Suisse*, in German is often used the word "*Eidgenossenschaft*", which could hardly be translated either in French, Italian, Romansh or English.

2. Decentralized and diversified policy of topographical names in Switzerland

2.1 Overall approach assessed with a view to minority protection

The State Report of Switzerland under the First Cycle of Monitoring the implementation of the Framework Convention for the Protection of National Minorities (FCNM) of the Council of Europe mapped out an overall approach of Switzerland to geographical names regarding art. 11, para. 3 of the Convention as follows: "The determination of place names comes fundamentally within the competence of the cantons, or even the municipalities. As far as the Confederation is concerned, it has adopted an ordinance concerning the names of places, municipalities and stations. It includes provisions on collecting, spelling and changing the names of places, municipalities and stations. The main criterion used in collecting and changing names is accuracy. In the (trilingual)[20] canton of Graubünden, many place names and names of districts and municipalities in the Romansh region were formerly indicated in German. [...] Today most districts, municipalities and places have their authentic name"[21].

The First Opinion on Switzerland issued by the Advisory Committee under the FCNM (ACFC) welcomed the fact that art. 11, para. 3 of the Framework Convention is very widely achieved in practice, also as regards topographical indications in Romansh in Graubünden[22] (First Opinion). Nonetheless, this indeed positive assessment of the ACFC in view of the geographical-names policy as an instrument of minority protection needs to be context-related, in order to understand that the situation is till far from being optimal. Traditionally, Romansh has several different idioms. In order to treat this minority language on equal footing it had to agree to a common but artificial standard language ("*Rumanch Grischun*"). Still many people in this area consider that this artificial language has been imposed by the German speaking majority. Most recently an association for traditional Romansh languages has been founded in Graubünden,

20 Official languages are Romansh, German and Italian.

21 ACFC/SR(2001)002, at 65.

22 ACFC/INF/OP/I(2003)007.

with an aim to get popular approval for coming back to traditional idioms as official languages. Given the role that initiative and referendum play in Swiss political life already at a communal level, this initiative coming from the civil society may have considerable impact, not least by putting this issue high on political agenda in a number of municipalities.

2.2 Ordinance on Geographical Names from May 21, 2008[23]

Based on the above discussed constitutional principles affecting policy on geographical names, the Ordinance in fact brings into effect constitutionally guaranteed sovereignty of the cantons as regards official languages, including their autonomy to delegate to their municipalities the decision on official language for topographical indication. The only purpose explicitly laid down in the Ordinance is to guarantee that "for official use, geographical names have to be used by all authorities consistently" (art. 1).

Under this regulation fall the "names of municipalities, localities, streets, stations and of topographical objects such as farmland and names of fields, waters, lakes, waterfalls, water-sources, ponds, alps, valleys, mountains, hills, cultural objects as castles, monasteries, churches, chapels, official buildings such as schools, hospitals, mountain huts, bridges, tunnels, airports and mountain passes" (art. 3). Geographical names must be simple to write and read, and they are generally accepted if possible and reasonable, they are used according to the standard language of the region in question. The cantons provide by their rules and regulations as to who is competent to decide on geographical names on their territory. They also set up Cantonal Commissions for the Glossary and each canton has also a commission for the nomenclature (arts. 8 and 9).

Geographical names and their spellings can only be changed *in the public interest* (art. 4, italics by authors)[24]. According to the rules for the names of

---

23 SR (Systematic Collection of Federal Legislation) 510.625.

24 In its already mentioned State Report for the FCNM monitoring, the Swiss Government flagged the principles of proportionality and public interest when commenting art. 11, para. 1, related to wording of signs, *inscriptions and other information of a private nature visible to the public* (italics by authors). The matter concerned a building regulation in a mainly Romansh-speaking municipality where luminous signs are permitted in Romansh only. Reacting in its Comments on the Committee's remark in the First Opinion that "Romansh could be protected just as well by an obligation to put up bilingual private signs, and encourages the competent authorities to look into this possibility" (note 21 *supra*, p. 64), the Government even in this case justifies its giving preference to public interest over individual freedom as follows: "[...] the Federal Tribunal considered that, given the perilous situation of Romansh, the measures concerned, which were designed to safeguard both the extent and the homogeneity of the

official measurements, issued by the Federal Office of Topography, the language of regions must be respected. The Office issues recommendations for the names of municipalities, localities, streets and addresses of buildings. The Federal Office of Transportation has the competence of issuing guidelines for the spelling of the names of railway stations (art. 6)

As regards the competence of municipalities to decide on geographical names, the Ordinance again provides a legal framework within which the Swiss municipalities, in compliance with cantonal law, can exercise their autonomy: the name of a municipality has to be accurate and clear for the entire Switzerland; it should not lead to any mistake of mixing up with the name of another municipality; in the following cases the name of the municipality needs an addendum: a) the same name is used for several municipalities; b) the name of several municipalities is spelled differently but orally used in the same way (art. 10).

In practice, particularly the multilingual cantons have very different solutions for their bilingual municipalities. In the canton of Grison there is a municipality "*Bivio*" with even three traditional languages: Romansh, Italian and German. In the bilingual canton of Berne a special statute has entered into force, giving the municipalities of the bilingual town of *Bienne* a special collective right, i.e., power to decide within their own competence on the topographical indications in their territory. In the city of Fribourg the conflict over the names of the streets has been still going on. The names of the streets have different meaning in German and French respectively. For instance, for one street the French name is "*Grand Rue*" and the Swiss German name is "*Riichegasse*" (the street of the rich)! The German village *Düdingen* is called "*Guin*" in French. In the bilingual canton of Valais, the French name for the river Rhone is "*Rhône*" in French, but "*Rotte*" in the Swiss German dialect of the canton Valais.

2.3 General Guidelines on Writing Geographical Names, issued in 2010[25]

As provided by art. 5 of the above-mentioned Ordinance 510.625, the Swiss Office for Topography issues every year guidelines for the use of geographical

---

mainly Romansh areas, could be said to involve a major public interest and that in the case concerned a painstaking assessment of the various interests at stake had led to the conclusion that there was an overwhelming case for prohibiting signs in a language other than Romansh" (GVT/COM/INF/OP/(2003)007, p. 16).

25 Accessed 28th February 2011: http://www.cadastre.ch/internet/cadastre/de/home/docu/kva/vd-express.parsys.74574.downloadList.49972.DownloadFile.tmp/avexpress201010beilagede.pdf.

names[26]. These guidelines have been written taking into account specificities of all four national languages in Switzerland. Accordingly and in compliance with the Ordinance, cantonal nomenclature commissions throughout Switzerland decide on the homogeneous spelling of geographical names.

2.3.1 German

Geographical names are usually spelled orally by the peoples speaking Swiss-German dialect in dialect. However, writing depends on the type of name. Names of municipalities, localities, stations and streets are written in a language close to standard German (e.g. *Zürich* instead of *Züri*, *Huttwil* instead of *Huttu*). The same applies for generally known names of topographical objects, such as mountains and rivers (e.g. *Matterhorn* instead of *Horu*, *Rhein* instead of *Rii*). On the other side, the fieldnames, as well as the names of topographical objects not generally known, are written according to the dialect version of the name as it is used in the locality, loyal to the oral version.

2.3.2 French

Until the XIX century a provincial French language was mainly spoken in Western Switzerland (Romandie). Exceptions of this practice were the areas of today's canton Jura, the Jura region in the canton of Bern, and the close board area of northern Neuchâtel. In this area the French dialect of the Burgundy was spoken. Finally in all three language areas the *Langue d'Oïl* was embraced, which was mainly spoken in Paris.

Written standardization of this language started already in middle-ages. Today, one can hear the *patois* (local dialect) in every day life only in Evolène (Val d'Hérens, canton Valais). In the canton of Fribourg there are only small groups in the area of Gruyère who still insist keeping the *patois*. The French speaking cantons have passed their own rules and regulations on geographical names. However there are almost no differences in spelling topographical indications, since in all cases the modern French language applies.

---

26 The Guidelines build on the reports of the UN Group of Experts on Geographical Names (UNGEGN) founded in 1982 at the IV United Nations Conference on the Standardization of Geographical Names.

2.3.3 Italian

The Italian speaking area includes the territory of the Italian speaking canton of Tessin/Ticino and Italian speaking territories of the canton of Grison, such as Misox, Bergell and Puschlav. Because a great majority of indigenous people still speak many traditional dialects, the latter are sustained also by policy on geographical names. This especially applies for geographical names of the official measurements. The reports and official documents of the canton of Tessin/Ticino also use such names according to the municipalities' rules, including spelling. This cantonal assignment is effectuated in the *Repertorio toponomastico ticinese*, to be found in the *Archivio di Stato del Cantone Ticino*. More notably, the Report includes also the Italian speaking areas of the canton of Grison.

In the official measurement of the canton of Tessin all names which can be italianised are registered in modern Italian. The rest of those names which etymologically cannot any more be reconstructed are edited in the local dialect.

Initially, including the federal Guidelines on Geographical Names from 1948, there were established no spelling rules for Italian names. However, the canton of Tessin/Ticino edited such rules already in 1940. As in all other cantons, the *Commissione Cantonale di Nomenclatura* decides on spelling of geographical names.

2.3.4 Romansh

This language is spoken only in the areas of canton of Grison. There are five different idioms: *Sursilvan* (the upper part of the canton), *Sutsilvan* (the middle part, Domleschg, Schams), *Surmiran* (middle Grison, Oberhalbstein), *Putèr* (upper Engadin) and *Vallader* (lower Engadin andValley of Münster). Since 1982 the *Rumantsch Grischun* is used as standard language for Romansh.

Today the Surselva and the lower Engadin and the valley of Münster are considered as Romansh speaking. Other municipalities are settled by peoples who up to 90% speak German.

Geographical names are collected in two volumes of the Romansh book of names. The book updated and edited in 1939 and 1964. These volumes contain all names which are used in traditional areas of with Romansh language, but they also contain German and Italian geographical names. A municipality is considered as traditionally Romansh when the majority of the inhabitants spoke Romansh in the year 1880.

In these traditionally Romansh areas in 1880, more than 30 official names of municipalities are today in German and in Italian language because of the change of the composition of the population. In this case the former Romansh names are not any more used officially but they are added and typographically clearly distinguished. This rule applies only to the municipalities with actually clear German predominance, such as the areas in middle Grison (Sutselva, Surmeir) and in the upper Engadin (Putèr).

The waters are written only according to the language of the local environment. An exception has been made only for the lake traditionally called "*Lej da Segl*". Because of the navigation needs the name "*Silsersee*" has been introduced. For a reader of maps this should help him identify the location.

Mountains on the language border-line have almost always two names. Generally known notions which are not Romansh – coming from the literature of the Alps – are always additionally translated into Romansh, for instance "*Biancograt*" into "*Cras Alva*".

3. Conclusion

Notwithstanding its specificities and a strongly decentralized and diversified policy on geographical names, Switzerland apparently fulfils commendably the international standards for displaying and using topographical indications to sustain linguistic identities of its traditional communities. In doing so by a consistent, constitutionally based policy of special protection for smaller linguistic communities (positive measures), Romansh in particular, Switzerland demonstrates a forceful example of providing "full and effective equality" in its minority policies, as laid down in art. 4 (paras. 2 and 3) of the FCNM[27], without even pursuing a concept of "majority" and "minority". More importantly, the cross-cutting of cleavage patterns along both religious and linguistic lines apparently play in hand for such a policy. It is the combination and proportional balancing in public interest of individual and collective linguistic rights which results in a special mix of multilingualism in Swiss linguistic policy at the federal level and a kind of "inter-lingualism" at cantonal and municipal level. Until now it proved to be the only viable strategy, conducive to a minority-

27 "The Parties undertake to adopt, where necessary, adequate measures in order to promote, in all areas of economic, social, political and cultural life, full and effective equality between persons belonging to a national minority and those belonging to the majority. In this respect, they shall take due account of the specific conditions of the persons belonging to national minorities.
The measures adopted in accordance with paragraph 2 shall not be considered to be an act of discrimination".

friendly linguistic policy in general, and those on geographical names in particular.

Bibliography

Auer A., *D'une liberté non écrite qui n'aurait pas dû l'être: la "liberté de la langue"*, in *Zeitschrift für Aktuelle Juristische Praxis (AJP)*, 1992.

Basta L.R., Fleiner Th., *Federalism and Multiethnic States: the Case of Switzerland*, 2nd ed., Fribourg, 2000.

Fleiner Th., Basta Fleiner L.R., *Constitutional Democracy in a Multicultural and Globalised World*, Berlin-Heidelberg, 2009.

Lüdi G., Werlen I., *Sprachenlandschaft in der Schweiz*, Swiss Federal Statistical Office, Bern, 2000.

Marti-Rolli C., *La liberté de la langue en droit suisse*, Zurich, 1978.

Richter D., *Sprachenordnung und Minderheitenschutz im schweizerischen Bundesstaat. Realivität des Sprachenrechts und Sicherung des Sprachenfriedens*, Berlin-Heidelberg, 2005.

Place names and minority language protection in the United Kingdom

Dewi Llŷr Jones

Summary

1. Introduction

The United Kingdom of Great Britain and Northern Ireland is a monarchical, unitary State composed of the countries of England, Scotland, Wales and Northern Ireland. As is to be expected, such an amalgamation of individual countries and of culturally and historically distinct peoples initially gave rise to significant linguistic divergences through the whole of the Union. To a large extent, these differences have remained in existence until today, despite the contrasting ways in which the constituent countries of the Union were united with the dominant military and political force of England. Indeed, as will be discussed later in the chapter, alongside English, the language of the majority, there are six minority native languages spoken in the United Kingdom today: Irish; Scots; Ulster-Scots; Scottish Gaelic; Cornish; and Welsh[1]. A seventh

1 As recognised for the purposes of: Council of Europe, European Charter for Regional or Minority Languages, 5th November 1992, CETS No. 148 (Charter for Regional or Minority Languages).

language, Manx Gaelic, is also recognised as a minority language on the Isle of Man, a Crown dependency[2].

This chapter aims to provide an evaluative account of the United Kingdom's legislative and policy framework on the protection of three of these languages, with particular consideration given to place names in the minority languages in question[3]. This will include consideration of the reception, implementation and impact in the United Kingdom of the Council of Europe's Framework Convention for the Protection of National Minorities[4] and its Charter for Regional or Minority Languages[5]. Finally, the chapter will also analyse the legislation of the United Kingdom Parliament and the National Assembly for Wales on the Welsh language[6] and of the Scottish Parliament's legislation on Scottish Gaelic[7]. Conclusions will then be drawn as to the strengths and weaknesses of the various governmental policies on the minority languages in question and on whether further legislation is needed to protect the various languages of the United Kingdom. In this context, consideration will also be given to place names in the minority native languages.

2. Historical development and governmental structure

Wales

In order to appreciate the social, political and legal context of the United Kingdom's minority languages, one must have also an understanding of its historical formation and governmental structures. Since this chapter will concentrate on the native languages of Wales and Scotland, it is important not only to consider the historical origins of the Union of those countries with

---

2 Manx Gaelic falls outside the scope of this chapter since the Isle of Man is not part of the United Kingdom.

3 The chapter will concentrate mainly on the minority languages of Scotland and Wales: Scots, Scottish Gaelic and Welsh. However, some attention will also be given to the other three languages, especially in the context of the Charter for Regional or Minority Languages.

4 Council of Europe, Framework Convention for the Protection of National Minorities, 1st February 1995, CETS No. 157 (Convention for the Protection of National Minorities).

5 Charter for Regional or Minority Languages.

6 Primarily the Laws in Wales Act 1535 (27th Henry VIII chapter 26) (Laws in Wales Act 1535) (initially entitled the Act for Law and Justice to be Ministered in Wales in like Form as it is in the Realm (27th Henry VIII chapter 26)), the Welsh Courts Act 1942 (Welsh Courts Act), the Welsh Language Act 1967, the Welsh Language Act 1993 and the Welsh Language (Wales) Measure 2011 (Welsh Language Measure).

7 Gaelic Language Act 2005 (Acts of the Scottish Parliament 7) (Gaelic Language Act).

England in the sixteenth and eighteenth centuries respectively[8], but also to understand the process of devolving some legislative powers back to those countries at the end of the XX century[9]. The devolution process and its consequences are of particular relevance here since, by today, the devolved governments of Wales and Scotland are responsible for formulating policy and for legislating on their own domestic linguistic affairs.

Whilst a significant proportion of today's Wales was brought under the direct control of the English Crown in 1282 and 1283[10], the whole of the country was not united with England until the enactment of the Laws in Wales Acts of 1535 and 1542/3. From that time onwards, the Parliament at Westminster, London, was the sole legislator for Wales and its language[11]. This was to remain the case for over four and a half centuries, until the incoming Labour government of 1997 established the National Assembly for Wales in May 1999 as a democratically elected body, accountable to the Welsh electorate[12]. Whilst the initial powers of the Assembly were limited to secondary legislative powers in eighteen fields of competence[13], including the Welsh language, its significance was increased greatly by the enactment of the Government of Wales Act 2006. Under the provisions of this statute, the Assembly gained the power to pass so-called "Measures" on devolved matters[14], provided that the central Parliament had conferred the competence upon the Assembly to do so in the specific field in

8 Wales was united with England by the Laws in Wales Act 1535 and the Laws in Wales Act 1542/3 (34th/35th Henry VIII chapter 26) (initially entitled the Act for Law and Justice to be Ministered in Wales in like Form as it is in the Realm and the Act for Certain Ordinances in the King's Dominion and Principality of Wales (34th/35th Henry VIII chapter 26)). Scotland and England were united by means of the Scottish Parliament's Union with England Act 1707 (Union with England Act 1707) and the English Parliament's Union with Scotland Act 1706 (6th Ann chapter 11) (Union with Scotland Act 1706). Together, the Acts are popularly known as the Acts of Union of 1707.

9 By virtue of the Government of Wales Act 1998 (GoWA 1998) and the Scotland Act 1998 (Scotland Act).

10 Edward I had conquered the last of the Welsh princes, Llywelyn ap Gruffudd and Dafydd ap Gruffudd in 1282 and 1283. Edward I then imposed elements of the English common law into the former Principalities of Wales by enacting the Statute of Rhuddlan 1284. For a general overview, see T. G. Watkin, *The Legal History of Wales*, Cardiff, 2007, pp. 99–106.

11 Wales had returned 24 Members of Parliament following the enactment of 1535 Act. As will be shown later, the 1535 Act itself had included a much-despised clause regarding the *status* and use of the Welsh language.

12 The Assembly was established through the enactment of the Government of Wales Act 1998. The Government's proposals had been approved by the Welsh electorate in a popular referendum held in September 1997.

13 GoWA 1998, sch. 2.

14 Government of Wales Act 2006, s. 93 (GoWA 2006).

question[15]. Given that Assembly Measures are the same in effect as Acts of Parliament[16], since May 2007, the Assembly has been able to ask Parliament for permission to pass primary legislation in various fields, including the Welsh language[17]. As will be seen later in the chapter, this was to be one of the first priorities of the Welsh Assembly Government that entered office in May 2007.

Scotland

In many ways, the historical development of Scottish governance is notable by its differences to the development of Welsh governance. Whereas the whole of Wales had been conquered and assimilated into the English Crown by 1536[18], Scotland kept its independence until 1707[19], despite sharing a Monarch with England from 1603 onwards[20]. Moreover, in stark contrast to the way in which Union had been imposed on Wales, the Treaty of Union that was to finally unite Scotland and England had to be approved expressly by the Scottish Parliament[21]. Importantly, the Acts of Union also provided specifically for the continued existence of the Presbyterian Church in Scotland and the Scottish legal system[22].

---

15 Schedule 5 of the Government of Wales Act 2006 contains a list of 20 fields in which the National Assembly for Wales may ask the United Kingdom Parliament for the competence to pass a Measure.

16 GoWA 2006, s. 94(1). See also National Assembly for Wales, *Measures. What is a Measure/ Proposed Measure?*, available at <http://www.assemblywales.org/bus-home/bus-legislation/ bus-legislation-guidance/bus-legislation-guidance-measures.htm> accessed 12th November 2010.

17 At the time of writing in January 2011, it had been agreed by the Assembly and by the United Kingdom Parliament that a referendum would be held in Wales on 3rd March 2011 on the issue of granting further powers to the Assembly. A 'Yes' vote in the referendum would see the Assembly gain the power to pass Acts of the National Assembly, whereby the Assembly would receive legislative competence in all the subjects listed in Schedule 7 to the Act, without firstly having to ask the central Parliament for such competence. A "No" vote would see the *status quo* being preserved.

18 Laws in Wales Act 1535.

19 Scotland and England were united to form Great Britain by the passing of the Union with Scotland Act 1706 and the Union with England Act 1707.

20 Upon the death of Elizabeth I of England in 1603, James VI of Scotland also became James I of England. From then until the union of 1707, except for the Interregnum years of 1649–1660, the Monarch of England was also the Monarch of Scotland, despite the two Crowns remaining independent.

21 The Scottish Parliament approved the Treaty on 16th January 1707. The English Parliament did likewise on 6 March 1707.

22 The *status* of the Presbyterian Church had been secured initially by the Scottish Parliament's Protestant Religion and Presbyterian Church Act 1707. The Act was then safeguarded by the

As a result, even after the Union of the Parliaments of the two countries had been completed on 1st May 1707, Scotland had retained two key institutions which were to become a focus for Scottish identity and unity.

The fact that the Scottish Parliament had chosen voluntarily to end its own existence and had succeeded in imposing some key terms into the Union agreement made the situation in Scotland quite different to the one in Wales. Partly as a result, Scotland was granted dedicated representation within the United Kingdom central Government decades in advance of Wales[23]. It was also more prominent in its calls for establishing a form of self-government towards the end of the XX century[24]. As a result of numerous factors, including perceived greater public support and a more developed national debate about self-governance, the 1997 Labour Government's proposals for devolution in Scotland were much more advanced than the ones for Wales. Eventually put into force by the provisions of the Scotland Act 1998, the recommendations of its 1997 White Paper were for an elected parliamentary body with full law-making powers for Scotland[25].

In comparison with the original powers of the National Assembly for Wales, the Scottish Parliament was regarded from the outset as a strong legislative body with primary law-making powers in wide-ranging fields of competence. Even today, whereas the strengthened Government of Wales Act 2006 only lists the matters in which the National Assembly *has* competence to pass Measures, the Scotland Act grants the Scottish Parliament the power to pass Acts in *all* fields, except the ones that are listed as reserved for the United Kingdom Parliament[26]. Given that only a handful of these reserved matters are related specifically to culture[27], it is evident that the Scottish Parliament is granted the competence to legislate on practically all Scottish cultural affairs, including languages. Since the Scottish Government has been granted wide-ranging executive powers to

---

Union with Scotland Act 1706 and the Union with England Act 1707. The Scottish legal system had been preserved by art.19 of the Treaty of Union.

23 By way of example, the office of Secretary for Scotland was established in 1885. The corresponding office of Minister for Welsh Affairs was not established until 1951. Scotland's representation gained full Secretary of State *status* in 1926, whilst Wales had to wait until 1964.

24 The Scottish Constitutional Convention had been established in 1988 as a multi-party, multi-civic group, organisation to call for devolution to Scotland. Its 1995 paper provided the basis for much of the Government's 1998 White Paper. The 1995 paper is available at Scottish Constitutional Convention, *Scotland's Parliament, Scotland's Right*, available at <http://www.almac.co.uk/business_park/scc/scc-rep.htm> accessed 12th November 2010.

25 The Scottish Office, *Scotland's Parliament,* White Paper, Cm 3658, 2007.

26 Scotland Act, s. 28, sch. 5.

27 Scotland Act, sch. 5, head K – Media and Culture.

correspond to the legislative powers conferred upon the Parliament[28], there is little doubt that the 1998 devolution settlement permits the devolved Scottish administration to develop and execute progressive policies on its national languages[29]. The extent to which it has done so will be examined in the latter part of the chapter.

3. Demographics and territorial subdivisions

In order to be able to appreciate trends related to the United Kingdom's minority languages, one must also have a background understanding of the State's demographics. It is very difficult, for example, to understand the level of protection that should be afforded to any minority language without understanding the position of the majority and their language. In this instance, it is vital to understand the dominance of England and English. In the case of Scotland and Wales, as will be shown later in the chapter, it is also important to comprehend the structure of local government since it is these regional authorities that are responsible for implementing numerous linguistic policies, especially with regards to place names.

According to the latest available statistics at the time of writing, the population of Wales in mid-2009 was 2.999 million and the population of Scotland was 5.194 million. This is in comparison with Northern Ireland's 1.789 million and England's 51.810 million[30]. Put another way, 84% of the United Kingdom's population live in England, 8% live in Scotland and 5% live in Wales. As would be expected, England's dominant population is also mirrored by its representation at the United Kingdom Parliament, where 533 of 650 MPs (82%) are returned from English constituencies, 59 (9%) are from Scottish constituencies, 40 (6%) are from Welsh constituencies and 18 (3%) are from Northern Irish constituencies.

In terms of local government structure, Scotland is subdivided into 32 council areas by the Local Government etc. (Scotland) Act 1994, which came into effect

28 Scotland Act, s. 54.

29 A new Scotland Bill was introduced to the United Kingdom Parliament on 30th November 2010. Once enacted, it will increase the Scottish Parliament's taxation powers and legislative competencies in some respects. However, it will not affect the Scottish Parliament's ability to legislate on culture, including the languages of Scotland.

30 Office of National Statistics, *Population Estimates,* June 2010, available at <http://www.statistics.gov.uk/pdfdir/pop0610.pdf> accessed 13th November 2010.

on 1st April 1996[31]. On the same date, Wales was divided into 22 unitary authorities by the Local Government etc. (Wales) Act 1994. Despite the different nomenclature, the Scottish councils and the Welsh unitary authorities operate in very similar ways as they are all single-tier authorities, responsible for all local government matters within the boundaries of their geographical areas. Importantly for these purposes, they are also responsible for the formation and implementation of their own language schemes under the Welsh Language Act 1993 and the Gaelic Language (Scotland) Act 2005.

4. Linguistic background and trends

Although this chapter concentrates mostly on the minority languages of Scotland and Wales, it is also worth noting some key statistics about the United Kingdom's other minority languages and who has de facto policy control over them.

Northern Ireland – Irish and Ulster Scots

Of the six minority languages spoken in the United Kingdom today, two are spoken in Northern Ireland. The first, Irish, has had a question asked about it in the decennial census since 1991. In that year, the census recorded that 131,974 of those over three years old and resident in Northern Ireland could speak Irish (8.8% of the over three year old population)[32]. By the 2001 census, 106,844 of those over three years old and resident in Northern Ireland could speak Irish (6.6% of the over three year old population)[33].

The number of Ulster Scots speakers on the other hand is notoriously difficult to assess. This is primarily due to the fact that competence in the language has

31 Interestingly for these purposes, under the Local Government (Gaelic Names) (Scotland) Act 1997, a Scottish council area which opts to have a Scottish Gaelic name may be known as the Gaelic *comhairle,* rather than a council.

32 Northern Ireland Statistics and Research Agency, *1991 Census data Irish Language Report*, available upon request from the Northern Ireland Statistics and Research Agency. Details available at <http://www.nisra.gov.uk/Census/Previous%20Census%20Statistics/1991Census Statistics.html> accessed 13th November 2010.

33 Northern Ireland Statistics and Research Agency, *Table KS24 Knowledge of Irish*, available at <http://www.nisranew.nisra.gov.uk/Census/Census2001Output/KeyStatistics/keystats.html#dsi trict council level> accessed 13th November 2010. The figure of 6.6% does include those who can "speak and write Irish" due to a change in the classifications. This may account partly for the percentage decrease from 1991 to 2001.

never been the subject of a census question. As a result, estimates can vary dramatically. A report prepared for the Council of Europe on the implementation of the Charter for Regional or Minority Languages with regards to Ulster Scots noted that one estimate placed the number of speakers at 100,000 between Northern Ireland and the Republic of Ireland. A second survey indicated that there were in the region of 35,000 Ulster Scots speakers in Northern Ireland alone[34]. However, it is suggested that neither of these figures should be regarded as completely accurate. The Northern Ireland Statistics and Research Agency has committed itself to include a question on competence in Ulster Scots in the next census, due to be held in March 2011[35]. It is only after the results of this survey are published will it be possible to have a true indication of the numbers involved and thus understand properly the distinct needs of the language.

As was suggested in the section on governance in the United Kingdom, when a devolved administration has been established in one of the constituent countries of the Union, executive and legislative competence on the minority languages of the country in question has been conferred upon the devolved body. This is the case in Northern Ireland, where legislative competence over both Irish and Ulster Scots has been conferred upon the Northern Ireland Assembly[36], and the Northern Ireland Executive is under a statutory duty to adopt strategies for both languages[37]. However, at the time of writing in January 2011, the power-sharing Executive in Northern Ireland had yet to adopt its language strategy and had emphasised that it saw no need for the Assembly to legislate on any of the country's minority languages[38]. As a result, it could be argued that very little

34 Public Foundation for European Comparative Minority Research 2006–2007, *Ulster-Scots in the United Kingdom through the lenses of the European Charter for Regional or Minority Languages*, available at <http://languagecharter.eokik.hu/docs/byLanguage/Ulster-Scots_in_the_UK.doc> accessed 13th November 2010.

35 Northern Ireland Statistics and Research Agency, *The 2011 Census of population in Northern Ireland proposals*, available at <http://www.nisranew.nisra.gov.uk/census/pdf/proposals.pdf> accessed 13th November 2010.

36 The Northern Ireland Assembly was established by the Northern Ireland Act 1998 (Northern Ireland Act). It has primary legislative power in all matters, apart from those specifically excepted by Schedule 2 or reserved to the United Kingdom Parliament by Schedule 3.

37 Northern Ireland Act, s. 28(d), as amended by the Northern Ireland (St. Andrews Agreement) Act 2006 and the Northern Ireland (St. Andrews Agreement) Act 2007.

38 The failure to adopt a language strategy can be attributed to political disagreements within the power-sharing Executive. Contrary to the advice of the Council of Europe's Committee of Experts, the Executive has proposed to create a single strategy for both languages, *A Strategy for Indigenous or Regional Minority Languages*. Discussions are ongoing. See Northern Ireland Assembly Committee for Culture, Arts and Leisure Official Report, *Language Strategy: Ministerial Briefing 1st July 2010*, available at <http://www.niassembly.gov.uk/record/committees2009/CAL/100701_LanguageStrategyMinisterialBriefing.htm> accessed

progress is being made currently as far as the formal protection of Northern Ireland's minority languages is concerned.

County of Cornwall – Cornish

Unlike all the other minority languages spoken in the United Kingdom, Cornish is spoken in a region that is not represented by a devolved administration. As a result, the promotion and protection of the Cornish language is left primarily to the Cornwall Council unitary authority. The reports compiled on behalf of the Council of Europe reveal that the Committee of Experts are satisfied with the work of the Council in this respect and that it has worked well in partnership with the Cornish Language Partnership in establishing various initiatives to promote the language[39].

It should also be noted that no questions on Cornish language skills have ever been asked in the United Kingdom census and that, therefore, accurate statistics are difficult to obtain. However, the Council of Europe's reports note that there are in the region of 300 effective speakers of Cornish in the County[40]. The 2011 United Kingdom census will allow residents to name their main language if it is a language other than English (or Welsh in Wales), but it seems unlikely that this change will lead to more accurate statistics on the number of Cornish speakers since most will probably denote English as their main language.

Wales – Welsh

The Welsh language has gone through somewhat of a revival during the last few decades. After nearly a century of decline in the percentage of Welsh speakers in Wales[41], census statistics show that the situation stabilised between 1981

1st December 2010; Northern Ireland Assembly, *Minute of proceedings Monday 8 November 2010*, available at <http://www.niassembly.gov.uk/minutes/2007mandate/minutes/2010/101108.htm> accessed 1st December 2010.

39 Public Foundation for European Comparative Minority Research 2006–2007, *Cornish in the United Kingdom through the lenses of the European Charter for Regional or Minority Languages*, available at <http://languagecharter.eokik.hu/docs/byLanguage/Cornish_in_the_UK.doc> accessed 20th November 2010; Council of Europe, *Application of the Charter in the United Kingdom 3rd Monitoring Cycle*, available at <http://www.coe.int/t/dg4/education/minlang/report/EvaluationReports/UKECRML3_en.pdf> accessed 20th November 2010.

40 *Cornish in the United Kingdom* (see footnote 39).

41 From 54% in 1891 to 19% in 1981 (percentages of the over 3 year old population). Office for National Statistics, *Proportion of People Able to Speak Welsh*, available at

(503,532 speakers, 19.0% of the over three year old population) and 1991 (508,098 speakers, 18.7% of the over three year old population). The number of speakers has since gone on to show signs of growth. The 2001 census recorded 582,368 Welsh speakers in Wales (20.8% of the over three year old population)[42] and indications suggest that similar results are expected at the 2011 census[43].

Since the remainder of the chapter will focus mostly on policy and legislation on the Welsh language in Wales, it suffices to say for now that by today, the National Assembly for Wales and its Government are the principal policy makers and legislators on the Welsh language. Their recent actions will be evaluated in the latter part of the chapter.

Scotland – Scots and Scottish Gaelic

Similarly to the situation of Ulster Scots in Northern Ireland, statistically accurate information relating to the number of Scots speakers in Scotland is difficult to find. Again, this is due to the fact that Scots has never been the subject of a census question, primarily due to its linguistic similarity to the English language. Nevertheless, various estimates have been ventured regarding the number of speakers, including one by the General Register Office for Scotland in 1996 which put the number at a substantial 1,500,000[44]. If accurate, this would clearly put Scots in a relatively healthy position. However, in the absence of more dependable statistics, it may be unwise to form such firm and positive conclusions at this stage.

Following pressure from Scots language campaigners and the Council of Europe's Committee of Experts[45], the General Register Office for Scotland has committed itself to survey the number of Scottish residents with Scots language

---

<http://www.statistics.gov.uk/downloads/theme_compendia/fow/Wales.zip> accessed 20th November 2010.

42 Welsh Language Board, *Census 2001: Main Statistics About Welsh*, available at <http://www.byig-wlb.org.uk/English/publications/Publications/332.doc> accessed 20th November 2010.

43 Welsh Language Board, *Welsh Language Use Surveys of 2004–06*, available at <http://www.byig-wlb.org.uk/english/publications/publications/welsh%20language%20use%20surveys%202004-06.pdf> accessed 20th November 2010.

44 I. Máté, *A Report on the Scots Language Research carried out by the General Register Office for Scotland in 1996*, Edinburgh, 1996.

45 See Public Foundation for European Comparative Minority Research 2006–2007, *Scots in the United Kingdom through the lenses of the European Charter for Regional or Minority Languages*, available at <http://languagecharter.eokik.hu/docs/byLanguage/Scots_in_the_UK.doc> accessed 2nd December 2010.

competence in the 2011 census[46]. It could be argued that only after the results of this survey are made public will the devolved Scottish administration be able to form effective policies to protect and promote the language.

In contrast to the position regarding Scots, the number of Scottish Gaelic speakers is easily ascertainable. Census questions have been asked about Scottish Gaelic competence since 1881. The analysis of the census responses show that the number of Scottish Gaelic speakers has reduced dramatically since that time, and that the downwards trend is continuing[47]. There were 79,307 Scottish Gaelic speakers in 1981 (1.6% of the over three year old population)[48], 65,978 speakers in 1991 (1.4% of the over three year old population) and 58,652 speakers in 2001 (1.2% of the over three year old population)[49]. Although the rate of regression has reduced in recent times, the overall picture is still one of decline. It is also acknowledged that, due to the average age of the current speakers, numbers will continue to drop in the immediate future[50]. As will be seen in the last part of the chapter, in order to attempt to stem the reduction in the number of speakers, the last few years have seen a concerted attempt by the Scottish Government and Parliament to increase the protection given to Scottish Gaelic by means of fresh policies and new legislation. The same is true to a lesser extent of their actions with regards to the Scots language.

Isle of Man – Manx Gaelic

Although a Crown Dependency and not part of the United Kingdom, the current statistics related to Manx Gaelic are useful as background information. The 2001 census noted that 1,689 of the Isle of Man's residents can speak, read or write

---

46 Scots linguistic competence will be measured in Scotland alone. General Register Office for Scotland, *Scotland's Census 2011 Specimen Questionnaire*, available at <http://www.gro-scotland.gov.uk/files2/the-census/scotlands-census-2011-specimen-questionnaire.pdf> accessed 2nd December 2010.

47 Despite a 9.2% increase from 1961 to 1971 (increase from 80,978 to 88,415 speakers).

48 General Register Office for Scotland, *Census 1981 Gaelic Report,* Edinburgh, 1983.

49 General Register Office for Scotland, *Scotland's census 2001 Gaelic Report,* available at <http://www.gro-scotland.gov.uk/files1/stats/gaelic-rep-english-commentary.pdf> accessed 2nd December 2010.

50 Bòrd na Gàidhlig, *The National Plan for Gaelic 2007–2012*, available at <http://www.bord-na-gaidhlig.org.uk/National-Plan/National%20Plan%20for%20gaelic.pdf> accessed 1st December 2010.

Manx Gaelic (2.2% of the island's population)[51]. As would be expected, policy making responsibility for the language lies with the Government of the Isle of Man.

5. Language legislation in the United Kingdom

The United Kingdom Parliament has no tradition of legislating on minority languages in general. It has enacted numerous pieces of primary legislation that refer specifically to individual minority languages, but it has never sought to pass a piece of legislation with blanket protection for all the United Kingdom's indigenous minority languages. It has never attempted to legislate specifically for the protection or promotion of place names in the minority languages either. Instead, it has opted to protect minority language speakers by numerous different means, including securing their rights not to be unjustifiably discriminated against as part of a racial group in general anti-discrimination legislation. This was done initially by means of the Race Relations Act 1976[52], and more recently by the Equality Act 2010[53]. However, as will be seen below, this has proved quite problematic in some respects.

The 1976 Act prohibited two types of racial discrimination in the fields of: employment; the provision of goods and services; education; and the provision of public functions. Firstly, it made direct discrimination illegal, i.e. it prohibited anyone from treating another person less favourably on racial grounds[54]. Significantly, it also prohibited indirect discrimination. Such indirect discrimination would occur where a person, A, imposed an unjustifiable detrimental condition or requirement on another person, B, but also applied the same condition or requirement to *all* racial groups. B would then have to prove that the proportion of people from his or her racial group capable of satisfying the requirement was considerably smaller than the proportion of persons from other racial groups[55]. Put another way, to be illegal, the detrimental condition had to be of general application, but affect a considerably greater proportion of B's racial

---

51 Economic Affairs Division, Isle of Man Government, *Isle of Man Census Report 2001 Volume 2*, available at <http://www.gov.im/lib/docs/treasury/economic/census/reportvolume2.pdf> accessed 10th December 2010.

52 As amended by the Race Relations (Amendment) Act 2000.

53 The Equality Act 2010 (Equality Act) came into force on 1st October 2010 and repealed the Race Relations Act 1976 (RRA) in its entirety. However, since all the relevant case law refers to the RRA, it will also be discussed.

54 RRA, s. 1(1)(a).

55 RRA, s. 1(1)(b).

group than of other racial groups. In the context of the United Kingdom's minority language speakers, this latter provision potentially prohibited, for instance, an employer in Wales from imposing an unjustifiable detrimental condition which had a greater negative effect on the Welsh-speaking racial group within his employment. However, this statement presupposes that Welsh-speaking Welsh people, for example, would classify as a separate racial group to non-Welsh speaking Welsh people. If this were not the case and there only existed one generic "Welsh" racial group, it would be practically impossible for Welsh speakers in Wales to prove that a particular condition indirectly discriminated against them.

The case of *Gwynedd County Council v. Jones and Another*[56] established conclusively that there could be no such thing as a Welsh-speaking racial group, only a general Welsh racial group. The Tribunal noted that section 3 of the 1976 Act had deemed that a racial group should be defined by reference to colour, race, nationality or national origins and that there was no mention of language. It also referred to past cases that listed the factors which should be considered in determining the existence of a racial group, of which a shared language was just one consideration[57]. As a result of these factors, the two applicants in the instant case were held to be part of a wider Welsh racial group and, therefore, could not prove indirect discrimination.

Although the *Jones*[58] case only referred to the Welsh language and the Welsh racial group, it can be assumed that the same principles would be applied to all the United Kingdom's minority languages. Despite arguments that speakers of other languages, such as Scottish Gaelic[59], would be in a better position to prove the existence of a separate racial group, the situation was regarded as generally unsatisfactory. As is noted by Bamforth et al., "The present approach in *Jones* ignores the way in which linguistic differences can lead to differences within groups such as Welsh and Scottish; and also the way in which language can be

---

56 *Gwynedd County Council v. Jones and Another* [1986] ICR 833 (EAT). The case itself concerned two non-Welsh speaking Welsh people who claimed that they had been indirectly discriminated against as part of a non-Welsh speaking Welsh racial group as they had been rejected in their job applications for which knowledge of Welsh was deemed essential. The Employment Appeal Tribunal held that linguistic background alone was insufficient to define a racial group. As a result, the condition was not contrary to the 1976 Act since the two applicants were part of the racial group that *could* satisfy the requirement.

57 *Mandla (Sewa Singh) v. Dowell Lee* [1983] ICR 385 (HL). The other factors included: a long shared history; cultural tradition; common descent or origin; a common literature; and a common religion.

58 *Jones* (see footnote 56).

59 W. McLeod, *Autochthonous Language Communities and the Race Relations Act*, [1998] 1 WJCLI <http://webjcli.ncl.ac.uk/1998/issue1/mcleod1.html> accessed 19th December 2010.

the source of discrimination and disadvantage"[60]. Following the case, it appeared that the only way in which a Welsh speaker in Wales could rely on the provisions of the Race Relations Act 1976 to prove discrimination on linguistic grounds would be under the direct discrimination route of section 1(1)(a). Although such an action did prove successful in the case of *Cowell v. Williams*[61], it appears that the threshold for success was a high one. In order to make a successful claim, the applicant had to prove that they were personally treated less favourably on racial grounds. In some circumstances, as was the case in *Cowell,* such racial grounds could involve requirements or conditions relating to a minority language.

Due to the difficulties of proving indirect racial discrimination on linguistic grounds under the 1976 Act, language campaigners welcomed the United Kingdom central government's announcement in February 2005 that it would review and reform the country's discrimination laws. However, the government's June 2007 consultation paper[62] was received with apprehension by bodies such as the Welsh Language Board. In their consultation response, the Board urged the central Government to include Welsh speakers as a named group in a list of those who were to receive protection from indirect discrimination[63]. They also expressed surprise that the consultation paper had failed to mention the Welsh language, or any other minority language, at any stage. Nevertheless, it appears that the Board's representations were ignored since the same criticisms can also be made of the subsequent White Paper[64] and of the eventual Equality Act 2010, as neither includes any specific reference to minority languages. Instead, the Act seeks to consolidate and clarify all the United Kingdom's pre-

60 N. Banforth, M. Malik and C. O'Cinneide, *Discrimination Law: Theory and Context,* London, 2008, p. 820.

61 *Cowell (t/a The Stables) v. Williams* (EAT, 28 February 2001). In this case, Mr Williams had been instructed by his employer, Mrs. Cowell, not to speak Welsh with his Welsh-speaking colleagues. His refusal to comply led to a deterioration in their relationship and to Mr Williams' eventual dismissal. The Employment Tribunal held that he had been discriminated against on racial grounds since his ethnic origins meant that the employer's request had put Mr Williams under a disadvantage. As a result, he was treated less favourably, contrary to s. 1(1)(a) of the RRA. The employer's subsequent appeal failed on all grounds.

62 Department for Communities and Local Government, *Discrimination Law Review: A Framework for Fairness: Proposals for a Single Equality bill for Great Britain*, available at <http://www.communities.gov.uk/documents/corporate/pdf/325332.pdf> accessed 19th December 2010.

63 Welsh Language Board, *The Welsh Language Board's Response to the Discrimination Law review Consultation Paper,* available at <http://equalities.gov.uk/nosearch/pdf/Welsh%20 Language%20Board%20(Rees).pdf> accessed 17th December 2010.

64 Government Equalities Office, *Framework for a Fairer Future – The Equality Bill,* White Paper, Cm 7431, 2008.

existing anti-discrimination legislation on the basis of sex, race, age, disability, sexual orientation and religion or belief.

In reality, the Equality Act 2010 only makes slight changes to the position of minority language speakers who seek a ruling that they have been discriminated against on linguistic grounds. They can still claim that they have been directly discriminated against, provided that the court or tribunal is satisfied that they received less favourable treatment on grounds of race[65]. In this respect, it is worth noting that the Equality Act also reverses the burden of proof on applicants. Once some evidence of less favourable treatment has been submitted, the onus is then on the respondent to provide a satisfactory explanation[66]. The 2010 Act also still prohibits disproportionate indirect discrimination on grounds of race, but with one slight change. Rather than demanding evidence that the proportion of persons from the applicant's racial group that can comply with a requirement is considerably smaller than the proportion of persons that can comply from other racial groups, the 2010 Act asks for evidence that the condition places people from the victim's racial group at a particular disadvantage in relation to other racial groups[67]. In one way, this seems to lower the threshold somewhat. However, in reality, it will remain practically impossible for a minority language speaker to bring an action for indirect discrimination on linguistic grounds in their home country, since no real additional guidance is given on the meaning of a racial group[68]. As a result, it is very likely that the pre-2010 case law on indivisible racial groups will still apply – i.e. to refer to the previous example, the Welsh speaking Welsh still cannot compare their position as a distinct racial group to non-Welsh speaking Welsh people.

6. The Council of Europe's protection mechanisms

Since there are no general Acts of Parliament on the United Kingdom's minority languages, and due to the inherent difficulties in pursuing the indirect

65 Equality Act, s. 13(1).

66 Equality Act, s. 136. In reality, this change will only have a minimal practical effect since the majority of courts and tribunals had already adopted such a practice informally, before the enactment of the 2010 Act. It should also be noted that courts and tribunals are permitted to infer unlawful discrimination where the respondent's explanation is not satisfactory. See *King v. Great Britain – China Centre* [1991] EWCA Civ. 16. In the case of minority language speakers wishing to prove direct discrimination, the court could consider recurring patterns of behaviour that seemingly place the applicant under a disadvantage.

67 Equality Act, s. 19, para. 2 (b).

68 Equality Act, s. 9 defines race.

discrimination route, attention will also be given to the Council of Europe's mechanisms for protecting minorities and their languages. In the United Kingdom context, these are the Framework Convention for the Protection of National Minorities and the European Charter for Regional or Minority Languages.

The Convention for the Protection of National Minorities was signed by the majority of the Council of Europe's Member States, including the United Kingdom, in February 1995. It subsequently came into force in the United Kingdom in May 1998. As is well documented, the overall aim of the Convention is to protect the rights of national minorities generally, including some of their linguistic freedoms. These include the right of the minorities: to receive education in their own language[69]; to use their language in cultural affairs[70]; to freedom of expression in the minority language[71]; and to free use of their language generally, including with the authorities where possible[72]. Interestingly for these purposes, the Convention also specifies that minorities are to be able to "display traditional local names, street names and other topographical indications" in their own minority languages[73]. Therefore, by ratifying the Convention, the United Kingdom Government has committed itself to ensuring that the above linguistic rights are protected for all its designated minorities. In this context, the United Kingdom's national minorities are the Welsh, Scottish and Irish. The people of Cornwall have been excluded from the Convention's scope on the grounds that the central Government does not believe that they satisfy the definition of a "racial group" under the Race Relations Act 1976 and Equality Act 2010. As a result, the provisions of the Convention cannot apply to the Cornish language.

It has been commented that the Convention for the Protection of National Minorities is aimed primarily at the European States that still oppress the most basic human rights of their national minorities, and as such, is marginal in more democratically-developed countries. The Convention has also been criticised for its vague language, its lack of genuine enforcement mechanisms, and its nondescript sanctions for breaches[74]. Whilst there may be an element of truth in some of the above, it could be argued that the Convention still has an important role to play in the United Kingdom nowadays. In submitting progress reports to the Advisory Committee every five years, the central Government must provide

---

69 Convention for the Protection of National Minorities, art. 14.

70 Convention for the Protection of National Minorities, art. 5.

71 Convention for the Protection of National Minorities, art. 9.

72 Convention for the Protection of National Minorities, art. 10.

73 Convention for the Protection of National Minorities, art. 11, para. 3.

74 G. Lewis, *Hawl i'r Gymraeg*, Talybont, 2008, p. 60.

an accurate account of the ways in which the Convention's aims are being achieved. Where necessary, the Committee will then ask the State for further clarification on ambiguous points[75] and make recommendations where it is felt that more could be done to protect the minorities in question. In this manner, the Convention has been effective in bringing areas of weakness to the public's attention and in putting political pressure on the central Government to resolve various situations[76]. In terms of linguistic issues, the reports of the Advisory Committee have also been successful in bringing deficiencies to light regarding the rights of Irish, Scots and Ulster-Scots speakers. In particular, the Committee's second report highlighted the need for the Scots language to be given more respect within administrative and governmental institutions and for a language act to be passed on Northern Ireland's minority languages[77]. In turn, the central Government then has had to respond to the points raised and commit itself to improvements.

Nevertheless, it must be acknowledged that the Council of Europe's main instrument for the protection of minority languages is its Charter for Regional or Minority Languages, initially opened for signature in 1992. The United Kingdom subsequently signed the document in March 2000 and brought it into force in July 2001. In doing so, it gave the so-called level 3 higher protection *status* to Irish, Scottish Gaelic and Welsh. Eventually, it also gave the lower, level 2, *status* to Cornish, Scots, Ulster Scots (and Manx Gaelic on behalf of the government of the Isle of Man).

Similarly to the Convention on National Minorities in some respects, the Charter for Regional or Minority Languages can be criticised for allowing member States excessive leeway in deciding on the level of protection to be

---

75 For example, the Committee asked for further clarification on the way in which minorities could use minority languages in their place names. See the government's response in their second State report. Department for Communities and Local Government, *The United Kingdom's Second Report to the Council of Europe under the Framework Convention for the Protection of National Minorities*, available at <http://www.coe.int/t/dghl/monitoring/minorities/3_FCNMdocs/PDF_2nd_SR_UK_en.pdf> accessed 21st December 2010.

76 By way of example, the Advisory Committee's first report noted concerns about, inter alia, the general rights of gypsies and travellers. The central Government responded by including provision about their rights in the Housing Act 2004. All State Reports and Advisory Committee Reports are available at: Council of Europe, *State Reports*, available at <http://www.coe.int/t/dghl/monitoring/minorities/3_FCNMdocs/Table_en.asp#United_Kingdom> accessed 21st December 2010.

77 Advisory Committee on the Framework Convention for the Protection of National Minorities, *Second Opinion on the United Kingdom Adopted on 6 June 2007,* available at <http://www.coe.int/t/dghl/monitoring/minorities/3_FCNMdocs/PDF_2nd_OP_UK_en.pdf> accessed 21st December 2010.

given to a language. In effect, the level 2 protection given to three of the United Kingdom's languages only denotes that the Government has committed itself to a few key symbolic principles on the languages in question, and only if the position of the languages require or permit the adoption of such objectives in the first place[78]. Even where the State has opted to give a language level 3 protection within part of its territory, it retains significant scope for discretion. Of the 68 undertakings or pledges a State can make with respect to any single language, it only has to adopt 35 in order for the language to qualify for the higher level of protection. In the United Kingdom context, the central Government has committed itself to 36 undertakings with regards to Irish, 39 with regards to Scottish Gaelic, and to 52 with regards to Welsh[79]. The State has yet further scope for discretion, even within the undertaking to which it has committed itself, since it then chooses one of up to four specific commitments under that broad heading. By way of example, in the field of primary education, a State can choose to accept to undertake:

> "(...) [W]ithin the territory in which such languages are used, according to the situation of each of these languages, and without prejudice to the teaching of the official language(s) of the State:
> to make available primary education in the relevant regional or minority languages; or
> to make available a substantial part of primary education in the relevant regional or minority languages; or
> to provide, within primary education, for the teaching of the relevant regional or minority languages as an integral part of the curriculum; or
> to apply one of the measures provided for under i to iii above at least to those pupils whose families so request and whose number is considered sufficient; (...)"[80].

It will be seen from the above Charter extract that, assuming that the State decides to make an undertaking in the field of primary education in the first place, it can then opt for the minimal commitment of merely making available some primary education in the language concerned. Nonetheless, on the other hand, it could also choose the most far-reaching option of committing itself to providing primary education in the minority language concerned whenever requested to do so by a child's family.

There is little doubt that the way in which the Charter was drafted allows the most ambitious member States to set themselves progressive and comprehensive goals for their minority languages. However, conversely, the scope for state

78 Charter for Regional or Minority Languages, art. 7.

79 Public Foundation for European Comparative Minority Research, *Number of Undertakings*, available at <http://languagecharter.eokik.hu/docs/BasicData/number_of_undertakings_abc.pdf> accessed 21st December 2010.

80 Charter for Regional or Minority Languages, art. 8, para. 1b.

discretion could also mean that the more cautious or conservative States could give effect to the Charter without committing itself to any significant or new undertakings. To some extent, this is true of the United Kingdom's approach to the Charter. Rather than set progressive, forward thinking goals for its level 3 languages, it seems that the central Government sought to commit itself to a minimal amount of meaningful targets. Indeed, in many instances, it seems that the Government's approach was to merely note what the situation was at the time of ratification, without having regard to the way in which language provision could be developed in future. In fact, it could be claimed that the Government set itself numerous targets that were much lower than what had already been achieved. One such example concerns Welsh-medium primary education. As is noted above, in this context the State had the choice of committing itself to an undertaking ranging from (i) ensuring at least some Welsh-medium primary education to (iv) providing such education to families upon request. Eventually, the United Kingdom Government opted for the minimal choice (i). However, if one considers the successes that had already been achieved in the field of Welsh-medium education at that time, it is difficult to understand why the Government failed to set itself more worthwhile targets. By 2000/2001, the year in which the Charter came into force, 49,422 primary school pupils (out of a total of 285,786 – 17.2%) were in designated Welsh-medium schools and 281,275 had some Welsh language classes (out of a total of 285,786 – 98.4%)[81]. It should also be noted that the Education Reform Act 1988 had made the study of Welsh compulsory in all state primary schools in Wales from 1990 onwards, as is indicated in the 98.4% statistic above. Therefore, without having to pledge itself to any unrealistic goals, it appears that the United Kingdom Government could have committed itself to option (iii) easily – making Welsh an integral part of the curriculum (as it had been since 1990). There are many other instances of such extremely unambitious targets[82].

Another popular complaint regarding the Charter for Regional or Minority Languages concerns its monitoring procedure. In this respect, the procedure for the Charter is similar to the one for the Convention for the Protection of National Minorities in that there is a duty on national Governments to submit progress reports at set dates. In this instance, the reports are submitted at three year intervals. They are inspected by the Committee of Experts, who are then responsible for on-the-spot visits to the States and for forming the Council's

81 Statistics for Wales, *Schools in Wales: General Statistics 2009*, available at <http://wales.gov.uk/docs/statistics/2009/091029schoolsgen09ency.pdf> accessed 21st December 2010.

82 G. Lewis, *Hawl i'r Gymraeg, cit.*, p. 57.

monitoring cycle reports. Generally, the reports draw attention to the deficiencies in a State's implementation of Charter undertakings. However, there is no formal mechanism for individuals to bring specific complaints to the attention of the Committee, only through hearsay and evidence sessions during the on-the-spot visits. This is one of the most common criticisms of the current regime. Nevertheless, it is clear from examining the monitoring reports that the opinions of the minority language speakers are noted and can be included in the reports themselves[83]. More generally, the main criticism that can be made of the monitoring reports is that, by definition, they can only comment and make recommendations on the State's own chosen undertakings. As explained above, where the State has opted to follow a conservative route, as is the case in the United Kingdom, there is relatively little scope for criticism. Nonetheless, despite a lack of formal sanctions against a non-compliant State, the reports are a valuable tool in bringing any serious and persistent failures to the attention of the public and the wider international community. In the United Kingdom's case, the majority of issues are raised in relation to the general *status* of the Scots and Ulster Scots languages, and on the lack of a language strategy in Northern Ireland generally. Comparatively few issues are raised regarding the Welsh language, and, since the enactment of the Gaelic Language (Scotland) Act 2005, the concerns regarding Scottish Gaelic have reduced[84].

7. Language legislation and policy in Wales

As explained above, for various reasons, relatively little protection is given to the Welsh language and its speakers by means of anti-discrimination legislation and by the Council of Europe's agreements alone. This is especially true with regards to Welsh language place names. As a result, it is also necessary to examine domestic legislation and policies, most of which emanate from the United Kingdom Parliament and central Government.

83 In the United Kingdom context, abundant references are made to complaints being made to the Committee on issues such as: lack of funding for the Scots language (Monitoring Report no. 2); the fact that the Northern Ireland executive aims to introduce a language strategy which makes Ulster Scots and Irish equal in *status*, contrary to the advice of the Committee of Experts; and the fact that the Ulster Scots academy had never materialised (both in Monitoring Report no. 3).

84 All State Reports and monitoring reports are available at, Council of Europe, *Reports and Recommendations*, available at <http://www.coe.int/t/dg4/education/minlang/Report/default_en.asp#United> accessed 21st December 2010.

In comparison to the other minority languages in the United Kingdom, the Parliament at Westminster has legislated relatively frequently on the Welsh language, although not always to its benefit. The first time it did so was in the Laws in Wales Act 1535, when, *inter alia*, it sought to make the English language the official language of public life in Wales and to prohibit monoglot Welsh speakers from holding public office:

> "Also be it enacted by the Authority aforesaid that all Justices, Commissioners, Sheriffs, Coroners, Escheators, Stewards, and their Lieutenants, and all other Officers and Ministers of the Law, shall proclaim and keep the Sessions Courts, Hundreds, Leets, Sheriffs Courts, and all other Courts in the English Tongue; (...) and also that from henceforth no Person or Persons that use the Welsh Speech or Language, shall have or enjoy any manner Office or Fees within this Realm of England, Wales, or other the King's Dominion, upon Pain of forfeiting the same Offices or Fees, unless he or they use and exercise the English Speech or Language"[85].

Legally, this remained the case for over four centuries. However, despite the negative impact of the so-called language clause, the Welsh language survived[86]. Indeed, by the time of the 1891 census, 910,289 of those resident in Wales could speak Welsh, including 508,036 monoglot Welsh speakers[87]. Nevertheless, despite its apparent good health at the turn of the century, by the 1930s and 1940s it was clear that the language was in decline: the percentage of Welsh speakers in Wales had reduced from 54% in 1891 to 37% in 1931 and an estimated 33% in 1941[88]. Therefore, partly in response to popular protests in Wales regarding the falling number of speakers and the subservient *status* of the language, particularly in the legal world, the wartime Parliament enacted the Welsh Courts Act 1942[89].

The 1942 Act provided that, "the Welsh language may be used in any court in Wales by any party or witness who considers that he would otherwise be at any disadvantage by reason of his natural language of communication being Welsh"[90]. The same section of the Act also expressly repealed the infamous language clause of the Laws in Wales Act 1535/6[91]. However, it can be argued

85 Laws in Wales Act 1535, s. 17.

86 On the impact of religion and nonconformism on the language, see: G. H. Jenkins, *The Welsh Language Before the Industrial Revolution,* University of Wales Press, 1997; J. Davies, *The Welsh Language*, University of Wales Press, 1999, p. 23.

87 *1891 Census of England and Wales, Vol IV General Report,* Cm 7222, 1893–4.

88 *Proportion of People Able to Speak Welsh* (see footnote 41).

89 D.H. Davies, *The Welsh Nationalist Party 1925–1945,* Cardiff, 1983; J.G. Jones, *The National Petition on the Legal Status of the Welsh Language 1938–1942*, in *Welsh History Review*, 18/1996, p. 92.

90 Welsh Courts Act, s. 1.

91 Laws in Wales Act 1535, s. 17.

that in all other respects, the general impact of the Act was very limited and that it could only be felt from within the four walls of the courtroom. Other than granting a conditional right to use the language in court, the Act failed to address any issues regarding the *status* of the language and the rights of its speakers. In fact, as was subsequently shown in the case of *R v. Merthyr Tydfil Justices, ex p. Jenkins*[92], the Act's impact was very limited even within the court structure. The judges in this 1966 case emphasised that parties would not be permitted to use the Welsh language in any proceedings unless (i) the court believed them to be under a disadvantage, or (ii) the parties themselves considered themselves to be under a genuine disadvantage from not being permitted to do so. Ultimately, either way, it was a matter for the court's discretion. Since the defendant in the case in question was an English-speaking schoolteacher, the court had no difficulty in deciding that he had no right to address the court in Welsh.

As can be deduced from the above analysis of the 1942 Act, it proved to be of no assistance in any attempt to reduce the rate of decline in the percentage of Welsh speakers. By 1961, the percentage of Welsh speakers in Wales had reduced to 26% of the population[93]. This fact, and the continued deficiencies in the *status* of the Welsh language, led to mass direct action protests by organisations such as the newly-formed Welsh Language Society from the early 1960s onwards. As will be discussed later in the chapter, a significant proportion of the Society's protests were aimed at the English-only road signs in Wales at the time. Such protests led directly to the central government commissioning the Hughes-Parry report in 1963[94] and to the eventual enactment of the Welsh Language Act 1967. However, as was the case with the Welsh Courts Act 1942, the 1967 Act did very little to protect or promote the Welsh language and the rights of its speakers. Nonetheless, it did succeed in providing Welsh speakers with an unqualified right to use their language in the Welsh courts, thus removing the need to show a disadvantage from not being permitted to do so as provided for by the 1942 Act[95]. The 1967 Act also permitted an appropriate government minister to prescribe Welsh versions of statutory forms and documents for the first time, subject to the proviso that if there were ever a conflict between the English and Welsh version of a text, the English version would prevail automatically[96].

Whilst the Welsh Language Act 1967 was of some symbolic significance, Welsh language speakers had to wait until the enactment of the Welsh Language

92 [1967] 1 AER 636 (HC).

93 *Proportion of People Able to Speak Welsh* (see footnote 41).

94 Welsh Office, *Legal status of the Welsh language,* Cm 2785, 1965.

95 Welsh Language Act 1967, s. 1(1).

96 Welsh Language Act 1967, s. 2.

Act 1993 for any real increase in the *status* of the language. At the time of writing in January 2011, this Act remained the most recent enactment currently in force exclusively on the Welsh language. As such, the 1993 Act is worthy of attention. In contrast to its predecessors, the Act sought to give the Welsh language official recognition in fields other than the administration of justice. It did so by providing that in the course of public business generally, "the English and Welsh languages should be treated on a basis of equality"[97]. It also re-enacted without practical change the provisions of the 1967 Act on the right to use the Welsh language in legal proceedings[98].

The most notable innovation brought about by the 1993 Act was the establishment of the Welsh Language Board as a statutory body[99], charged with the somewhat vague duty of, "promoting and facilitating the use of the Welsh language"[100]. Amongst other things, the Board was to be responsible for the implementation of the language scheme system, also introduced by the 1993 Act[101]. In this context, section 5 of the Act notes that certain public bodies are expected to publish[102], with the prior approval of the Welsh Language Board[103], a scheme outlining the public services that they pledge to provide through the medium of Welsh. Since the Board plays an integral part in the drafting of a body's language scheme in the first place, it can also reduce the potential for an organisation to set itself under-ambitious targets. Therefore, whilst the Act does not give Welsh speakers enforceable rights to receive Welsh medium services, it does place public authorities under a duty to designate their Welsh language obligations. It should also be noted that although the Act mainly applies to public sector organisations, it can also apply to private sector companies that exercise functions of a public nature[104]. Private companies such as water and electricity

97 Welsh Language Act 1993, s. 5(2).

98 Welsh Language Act 1993, s. 22. On the *status* of the Welsh language in the courts, see: R Léwis, *Cyfiawnder Dwyieithog? Bilingual Justice?*, Llandysul, 1998; G. P. Davies, *The Legal Status of the Welsh Language in the Twentieth Century*, in G. H. Jenkins and M. A. Williams (eds.), *Let's Do Our Best for the Ancient Tongue,* Cardiff, 2000; J. Williams, *Welsh language in law and governance*, in *Welsh Journal of Law and Policy*, 4/2005, p. 143; C. Huws, *The Language of Heaven and the Language of the Courts*, in *Cambrian Law Review*, 2007, p. 118.

99 Welsh Language Act 1993, s. 1.

100 Welsh Language Act 1993, s. 3(1).

101 Welsh Language Act 1993, s. 5.

102 The public bodies that are given notice to do so by virtue of section 7 of the Welsh Language Act 1993.

103 Welsh Language Act 1993, s. 14.

104 Welsh Language Act 1993, s. 6(1)(o).

service providers have been obliged to produce Welsh language schemes under this section[105].

Whereas the above provisions extended the scope of the Welsh Language Act 1993 into the private sector to a minimal extent, there is no doubt that the Act was aimed primarily at public sector organisations. This is one of the major criticisms that have been made of the Act; that it neglected to consider the possibility that statutory provision was also needed on the Welsh language in the private sector. The Act has also been condemned for failing to create sufficiently rigorous monitoring and enforcement regimes. Whilst the Welsh Language Board can conduct statutory investigations into suspected breaches of language schemes under section 17 of the Act, there are no formal sanctions that can be brought against an offending body, other than the publication of a report and[106], ultimately, referral to the relevant Welsh Assembly Government Minister[107]. There is, for instance, no recourse to civil or criminal penalties. Nevertheless, despite these criticisms, and even though the Act prolonged the pre-existing ambiguity regarding the *status* of the Welsh language in Wales[108], the Act should be regarded as an important stepping stone on the road to securing increased protection for the language. Indeed, as will be seen below, the 1993 Act became somewhat of a blueprint for the Gaelic Language (Scotland) Act that the Scottish Parliament enacted in 2005.

As noted above, the Welsh Language Act 1993 is the last piece of legislation to come into force on the Welsh language. However, any discussion on minority language protection in Wales would be incomplete without consideration of the devolved administration and its enabling Acts. The first of these Acts, the Government of Wales Act 1998, not only established the National Assembly for Wales as a parliamentary body, but also ensured that the Welsh language was integral in all that it did: section 32 of the 1998 Act gave the Assembly the power to do anything it considered appropriate to support the Welsh language;

---

105 See, for example, Welsh Water, *Welsh Language Scheme*, available at <http://www.byig-wlb.org.uk/english/publications/publications/welsh%20language%20scheme%20-%20welsh%20water.pdf> accessed 21st December 2010; Scottish Power, *Welsh Language Scheme*, available at <http://www.byig-wlb.org.uk/english/publications/publications/welsh%20language%20scheme%20-%20scottishpower.doc> accessed 21st December 2010.

106 Welsh Language Act 1993, s. 19.

107 Welsh Language Act 1993, s. 20.

108 The Act fails to note that the Welsh language is an official language in Wales. However, in Parliamentary debates on the Welsh Language Bill, the Prime Minister, the Right Honourable John Major MP, noted that in the government's opinion, the Welsh language was already an official language in Wales: "We believe that Welsh already enjoys official *status* in Wales. A general declaration in the Bill would have no practical effect and would probably only increase legal uncertainty", House of Commons Debate 13th July 1993, vol. 228, col. 827.

section 47 ensured that the Assembly treated the English and Welsh languages equally in the conduct of its business; and sections 66 and 122 provided that all the Assembly's secondary legislation was to be made bilingually. The same provisions were substantially re-enacted by the subsequent Government of Wales Act 2006[109].

However, despite the importance of both Government of Wales Acts in this context, the main focus of this section should be on the policies and legislation proposed by the Welsh Assembly Government. In early 2003, the Government published its *Iaith Pawb* policy document, outlining the way in which it aimed to create a truly bilingual Wales[110]. As a first step, it set itself the extremely ambitious targets of achieving the following by 2011: increasing the percentage of Welsh speakers in Wales by 5% from the 2001 figures; arrest the decline in the number of communities where Welsh is spoken by over 70% of the population; increase the percentage of children receiving Welsh medium pre-school education; and increase the range of services that can be delivered through the medium of Welsh. Whilst the policy was rightly criticised for failing to explain in sufficient detail how the Government intended to reach its goals, and for failing to provide sufficient financial support, there is no doubting its overall ambition[111]. By today, it seems clear that the Government will fail in some of its targets, including its flagship goal of increasing the percentage of Welsh speakers by 5%.[112] Nevertheless, this has not deterred the current coalition government from committing itself to further Welsh language policies. In its One Wales agreement document, the Labour and Plaid Cymru Government pledged to seek competence to legislate on the Welsh language by means of Assembly Measure[113]. This became one of the new government's first priorities when it entered into office in July 2007.

---

109 GoWA 2006, ss. 78, 98(5), 156. On the process of legislating through the medium of Welsh, see: K. Bush, *Legislating in Welsh: Resuming an Old Conversation*, in *Cambrian Law Review*, 2007, p. 84; G. Griffiths, *The Challenge of Legislating Bilingually*, in *Cambrian Law Review*, 2007, p. 104.

110 Welsh Assembly Government, *Iaith Pawb: A National Action Plan for a Bilingual Wales*, available at <http://wales.gov.uk/depc/publications/welshlanguage/iaithpawb/iaithpawbe.pdf;jsessionid=2cDLNqcTpzW23vXhnYLTqV88XF9cZKh8PCLQrCHn0k1KtKPLG4V9!1876000129?lang=en> accessed 21st December 2010.

111 H. Gruffudd, *Bylchau yn Iaith Pawb,* in *Barn*, December/January, 2002–2003, p. 20; N. Thomas and H. Gruffudd, *An Action Plan for Welsh*, in *Planet,* 157/2003, p. 77.

112 *Welsh language use surveys of 2004–06* (see footnote 43).

113 The Labour and Plaid Cymru Groups in the National Assembly, *One Wales: A Progressive Agenda for the Government of Wales*, available at <http://wales.gov.uk/strategy/strategies/onewales/onewalese.pdf?lang=en> accessed 21st December 2010.

As provided for by section 95 of the Government of Wales Act 2006, any request by the Assembly for further legislative competence must be approved by both Houses of Parliament at Westminster. Consequently, in summer 2007, the new Welsh government immediately entered into negotiations behind closed doors with the central Government regarding the form and content of the proposed competence conferral order. Whilst the content of the governmental discussions may still be confidential, it is no secret that it proved difficult to find consensus between both governments; the Assembly's request for legislative competence was not finally approved until February 2010. As a result, the subsequent legislation, the Welsh Language (Wales) Measure, was not passed by the Assembly until December 2010 and is not scheduled to receive Her Majesty's approval until 9th February 2011. Whilst it may be difficult to forecast the exact consequences of the Measure at this stage, the wording of the legislation itself makes it clear that the Measure, once implemented, will bring about a highly significant change in the *status* of the Welsh language.

Firstly, the 2011 Measure will finally resolve the unanswered questions regarding the *status* of the Welsh language in Wales. Section 1(1) of the Measure States unequivocally that "The Welsh language has official *status* in Wales". However, it is unlikely that this section will be the main focus of the Measure once it is brought into force. Section 2 of the Measure will establish the office of the Welsh language commissioner, who will be entrusted with the task of promoting and facilitating the use of the language. The commissioner's office will eventually replace the Welsh Language Board, which is to be abolished by virtue of section 143. Primarily, the role of the commissioner will be to regulate the standards system which is to be imposed by the Measure[114]. The successor to the current language scheme system, the so-called standards will be imposed on certain bodies by the commissioner[115], after being initially drawn up by the Welsh Ministers[116]. Whilst it is difficult to forecast the content of the imposed standards with any certainty, mainly due to the fact that no examples of such standards have been included in the Measure itself, they appear likely to be a more developed form of language scheme obligations. Importantly, the Measure also extends the range of bodies that may be required to comply with the requested standards. Whereas the Welsh Language Act 1993 was concerned mainly with the language schemes of public authorities and a few private companies, under the 2011 Measure, the Welsh language commissioner will be able to impose specific standards on a much wider range of private sector bodies.

114 Welsh Language Measure, s.26.

115 Welsh Language Measure, s. 44.

116 Welsh Language Measure, s. 25.

Eventually, these may include companies such as bus and railway operators, post offices and telecommunication companies[117]. Once standards are imposed on such a body, the commissioner will have responsibility for monitoring compliance[118]. The commissioner's office will be able to investigate complaints either on its own initiative or on behalf of citizens, and will then be able to publish its findings in a report. Where necessary, the commissioner will also be able to impose a civil penalty of up to £5,000 on any body or persons deemed to be in breach of its obligations[119], subject to an appeal to the newly-formed Welsh Language Tribunal on the grounds that the commissioner erred in finding a breach in the first place[120]. Interestingly, the commissioner will also have the power to investigate any alleged instances of interference with a person's freedom to use the Welsh language in any context within Wales[121]. Although it will not be possible to impose any significant punitive sanctions where such interference is found, the commissioner will be able to publish a report of its findings and refer it to the relevant Welsh Minister[122].

8. Place names and road signs in Wales

As indicated above, the issue of bilingual place names and road signs has been an extremely contentious one in Wales since the mid 1960s. At that time, practically all road signs in Wales were in English only, and as such, were regarded by the Welsh Language Society as an obvious and symbolic target for their direct action campaigns. Whilst the newly-established Welsh Office could authorise Welsh or bilingual road signs on a one-off basis upon requests by local authorities, they were clearly reticent in doing so and completely rejected the idea that councils could be given blanket permission to erect all road signs within their areas bilingually[123]. They were, however, more forthcoming in allowing local authorities control over place name signs on the boundaries of towns and villages, deeming that signs of this nature were to be regarded as advertisements

117 Welsh Language Measure, schs. 7–8.
118 Welsh Language Measure, s. 71.
119 Welsh Language Measure, s. 83.
120 Welsh Language Measure, s. 95.
121 Welsh Language Measure, s. 111.
122 Welsh Language Measure, s. 118.
123 P. Merriman and Rh. Jones, *"Symbols of Justice": the Welsh Language Society's campaign for bilingual road signs in Wales, 1967–1980,* in *Journal of Historical Geography*, 35(2), 2009, pp. 350–357.

rather than road signs[124]. As a result, it was road signs that bore the brunt of the Welsh Language Society's campaign from 1967 onwards[125]. In the period between October of that year and December 1972, the Society's civil disobedience campaign included the illegal painting over of monolingual English signs and their ultimate removal and destruction. The campaign led to over two hundred campaigners being arrested and to a significant number of the Society's members being imprisoned[126]. Nevertheless, in August 1969 the central Government reiterated its objection to the approval of bilingual road warning signs, regulatory signs or direction signs[127].

The seeds of the government's change of policy on bilingual road signs were eventually sown in February 1971 when the Secretary of State for Wales commissioned an independent committee of inquiry into the possibility of permitting bilingual road signs in Wales. The Bowen Committee's final report, published in August 1972, recommended that bilingual road signs be approved throughout Wales, and that the Welsh language text should be placed first on such signs, before the English language text[128]. However, whilst the Government agreed to the principle of bilingual road signs a few months later in November 1972, it disagreed with the recommendation that the Welsh language should be placed first[129]. As a result of this difference of opinion, and due to the inherent

124 P. Merriman and Rh. Jones, *"Symbols of Justice"*, *cit.*, p. 357. In this context, it should be noted that a significant proportion of the place name signs in Wales at the time would have been anglicised versions of the original Welsh names (e.g. the anglicised spelling Caernarvon was used instead of the Welsh language spelling, Caernarfon). The Welsh Office thus confirmed in 1968 that local authorities had permission to change the name to the Welsh version or to a bilingual one. In many instances, where the common English and Welsh names were significantly different (i.e. had different etymological roots, e.g. Swansea/Abertawe, or where the English translation of the Welsh name was significantly different, e.g. Ammanford/Rhydaman) the local authority would wish to keep both names on its signs. The Welsh Office confirmed that this was also acceptable. As a result, place name signs in Wales today can be: in Welsh only; in English only; bilingual (either from the same etymological roots, or from different ones).

125 On the general history of the Welsh Language Society in this period, see: C. Davies, *Cymdeithas yr Iaith Gymraeg*, in M. Stephens (ed.), *The Welsh Language Today,* Llandysul, 1973; C. Williams, *Non-violence and the development of the Welsh Language Society, 1962–c.1974,* in *Welsh History Review*, 8/1977, p. 426; D. Phillips, *The History of the Welsh Language Society*, in G.H. Jenkins and M.A. Williams (eds.), *cit.*

126 P. Merriman and Rh. Jones, *"Symbols of Justice"*, *cit.*, p. 358.

127 Committee of Inquiry into Bilingual Traffic Signs, *Bilingual Traffic Signs: Report of the Committee of Inquiry Under the Chairmanship of Roderic Bowen 1971–1972,* Cm 5110, 1972, pp. 112–116.

128 Committee of Inquiry into Bilingual Traffic Signs, *Bilingual traffic signs, cit.*, p. 78.

129 T. Fishlock, *Government Agrees in Principle to Welsh Road Signs in Two Languages*, *The Times,* London, 30th November 1972, p. 4.

costs of replacing all the country's monolingual road signs, the process of erecting bilingual road signs dragged on through the 1970s. Indeed, many local authorities chose not to replace their English-only signs at all until the late 1970s[130]. In order to attempt to resolve the situation, and thus placate the Welsh Language Society, the central Government announced its current policy of allowing local councils the choice of which language should come first on its road signs in April 1980[131].

The current situation regarding bilingual place names and road signs in Wales is inextricably linked to the protests of the 1970s and the central Government's response to the various campaigns. As is indicated above, Welsh local authorities retain full control over place names, i.e. the names of cities, towns and villages[132], whilst government still has a role to play where road signs are concerned[133]. Additionally, within the cities, towns and villages in question, section 64 of the Town Improvements Clauses Act 1847 and section 18(1) of the Public Health Act 1925 permit local councils to "alter the name of any street, or part of a street, or (…) assign a name to any street, or part of a street, to which a name has not been given"[134]. As a result, legally, Wales's unitary authorities are given free reign as far as place names and street names are concerned[135]. However, in the context of street names, it is also important to consider the potential impact of Welsh language schemes. As is noted above, all public bodies in Wales, including the 22 unitary authorities, are under a duty to form and adhere to their own Welsh language schemes. Whilst concerns have been noted regarding the monitoring structures of the language schemes, there is evidence to suggest that the very existence of the schemes has had a positive effect on Welsh language names for streets and certain geographical features. Regardless of the percentage of Welsh speakers resident in their areas, all

130 P. Merriman and Rh. Jones, *"Symbols of Justice", cit.*, p. 371.

131 T. Jones, *Government to Spend £1m in support of Welsh Language*, *The Times,* London, 16th April 1980, p. 5.

132 Section 76 of the Local Government Act 1972 permits a local authority to change the name of a "community" within its area. Section 27(4) of the same Act, as amended by section 8 of the Local Government (Wales) Act 1994, also enabled councils to prescribe bilingual names for communities by 1st October 1997.

133 In many instances, the issue of place names and road signs are intertwined, since the majority of road signs also contain place names. As many of the road signs in question are the responsibility of the Welsh Assembly Government (see below), it is vital that the local authorities and Assembly Government are in agreement about the acceptable form of the place name. The Welsh Language Board's Place-Names Standardisation Team and Advisory Service have an important role to play in this respect.

134 Public Health Act 1925, s. 18(1).

135 Subject to the content of footnote 133.

22 unitary authority language schemes refer to such names in some way. As expected, the commitments vary from one authority to the next. For example, Anglesey County Council (with 60.1% of its population able to speak Welsh)[136] pledges that it:

> "[W]ill employ only the Welsh version of place-names, names of rivers, mountains, etc. (...) Where a new street or estate is being named, the new name will be based on indigenous, historical Welsh names of the area. When a new name has to be coined, this will be done in Welsh only"[137].

Newport City Council on the other hand (with 10.0% of its population able to speak Welsh)[138] also makes firm and far-reaching commitments:

> "Since the Council has the right to decide on the names of new streets, it recognises the importance of giving appropriate consideration to local opinion. The policy in relation to new names will be to adopt a bilingual name that is consistent with the heritage and history of the area. (...) All road signs and pedestrian and other street furniture signage within the City centre will be fully bilingual (...) All other public information signs, notably highway signs and markings that are the responsibility of the City Council will be replaced with bilingual signs (...)"[139].

It must also be noted that, where necessary, Wales's unitary authorities and Assembly Government can consult the Welsh Language Board's Place-Names Advisory Service for expert advice when seeking a standardised Welsh place name. In turn, the Advisory Service will consult the well established principles of its Standardisation of Place-Names Team when advising such a body[140]. Although the Board does not presently offer advice on Welsh versions of street names and the like, it is does have a guidance document for local authorities that need to coin Welsh names for streets or new developments[141]. It is assumed that

---

136 *Census 2001: Main Statistics About Welsh* (see footnote 42).

137 Isle of Anglesey County Council, *Welsh Language Scheme*, available at <http://www.anglesey.gov.uk/upload/public/attachments/78/languagescheme.pdf> accessed 4th January 2011.

138 *Census 2001: Main Statistics About Welsh* (see footnote 136).

139 Newport City Council, *Welsh Language Scheme*, available at <http://www.newport.gov.uk/stellent/groups/public/documents/plans_and_strategies/cont499493.pdf> accessed 4th January 2011.

140 The Welsh Language Board has had responsibility for the Standardisation of Place-Names Team since 2001. Prior to that time, it was under the control of the Welsh Assembly Government. Although it does not have a statutory duty in this regard, the Welsh Language Board's Standardisation Team has an important role to play, especially in the discussions between the Ordinance Survey, local authorities and the Welsh Assembly Government.

141 Welsh Language Board, *Guidelines for Language Officers for the Standardisation of Place-Names and Street Names*, available at <http://www.byig-wlb.org.uk/English/publications/Publications/4437.pdf> accessed 4th January 2011.

responsibility for the Advisory Service and the Standardisation Team will be transferred to the Welsh language commissioner's office once established.

As noted, the situation regarding road signs in Wales is somewhat different to the legal position of Welsh place names or of the names of streets and geographical features. Generally, the road signs that are permitted in England, Scotland and Wales today are all listed and pictured in the Traffic Signs Regulations and General Directions 2002[142]. However, the included signs are all monolingually English. Bilingual or Welsh versions of the approved signs are authorised by virtue of Regulation 4(1) of the Traffic Signs (Welsh and English Language Provisions) Regulations 1985[143], which provides that "A sign shown in a diagram in Schedule 1 with the prefix 'W' followed by a diagram number may be used in Wales in place of a sign bearing the same diagram number without the prefix 'W' in Parts I or II of Schedule 1 to the Main Regulations". Therefore, local authorities in Wales *may* use any road signs that have been prescribed by the 1985 order (or have been added subsequently). It should also be noted that further, non-prescribed, signs, including bilingual ones, can be approved by a Welsh Assembly Government Minister on a one off basis[144].

As is seen above, there is no obligation on Welsh unitary authorities to use the prescribed bilingual signs on the roads within their control; the regulation only States that they can do so if they desire. However, again, the effect of the Welsh language schemes must be considered at this point. The majority of Wales's unitary authority language schemes contain reference to road signs, as is seen in the above extract from Newport City Council. A further example can be seen in Gwynedd Council's language scheme, where it is stated that, "All signs, including road and directional information signs, erected by the Council or on its behalf (...) shall be in Welsh or in bilingual form"[145]. Again, there is no doubt that the language scheme system has been successful in this respect; it should be regarded as one of the plethora of reasons why practically all road signs in Wales

---

142 SI 2002/3113 (Traffic Signs Regulations 2002).

143 SI 1985/713 (Bilingual Traffic Signs Regulations 1985).

144 Section 8 of the Traffic Signs Regulations 2002 notes the National Assembly for Wales has unlimited power to authorise a sign that has not been prescribed by the 2002 Regulations. The powers were initially provided for by section 64(2) of the Road Traffic Regulation Act 1984 (Road Traffic Act 1984), which noted that a Secretary of State may approve such a sign on a one off basis. The National Assembly for Wales (Transfer of Functions) Order 1999, sch. 1, SI 1999/672, transferred the relevant functions of section 64(2) to the National Assembly for Wales. By virtue of sch. 11 (paras. 30–37) of the Government of Wales Act 2006, they are now exercisable by the Welsh Ministers.

145 Gwynedd Council, *Welsh Language Scheme*, available at <http://www.gwynedd.gov.uk/upload/public/attachments/1040/Cynllun_Iaith_2010_S.pdf> accessed 4th January 2011.

today are bilingual, despite the lack of legislation making such signs compulsory throughout the country.

In the context of road signs, it must also be understood that the Welsh Assembly Government retains responsibility for all major roads (i.e. trunk roads and motorways) in Wales. As a result, legally, the Welsh Government also has the choice of only using monolingual English signs on its roads. However, once again, Welsh language schemes have a bearing, since the Welsh Assembly Government has its own scheme, approved in December 2006:

> "The signs for which we are responsible (mostly motorway and trunk road signs) will be bilingual. Signs which are in English only at the moment will be made bilingual when they are replaced (…) We will produce bilingual versions of prescribed traffic signs for use by Local Authorities in Wales. We propose to complete prescribed bilingual sign design drawings, which we expect Local Authorities to use, by spring 2007"[146].

9. Language legislation and policy in Scotland

In contrast to the position of the Welsh language, the Parliament at Westminster has never enacted general legislation on Scottish Gaelic or Scots. As a result, no provisions have been made at the United Kingdom level on the *status* of the languages, nor has the central Government sought to protect the languages in any comprehensive way. Nevertheless, Scottish Gaelic has been mentioned in various Acts of Parliament from the late nineteenth century onwards, but only in very limited contexts. For example, the Crofters Holdings (Scotland) Act 1886 noted that one of the three members of the Crofters Commission had to be a Scottish Gaelic speaker[147]. The language has also been mentioned in Scottish education acts since 1918, whereby local education authorities are under a duty to secure adequate provision of Scottish Gaelic teaching in the Gaelic-speaking areas[148]. However, other than in these two narrowly defined areas, and in the field of public broadcasting[149], no provisions have been made regarding the

---

146 Welsh Assembly Government, *Welsh Language Scheme*, available at <http://wales.gov.uk/depc/publications/welshlanguage/languagescheme/scheme06.pdf?lang=en> accessed 4th January 2011.

147 Crofters Holdings (Scotland) Act 1886, s. 17. The Commission is a land court to resolve disputes between crofters and their landlords. Similar or identical requirements have been enacted by the Small Landholders (Scotland) Act 1911, s. 3; Crofters (Scotland) Act 1993, s. 1(5).

148 Education (Scotland) Act 1918; Education (Scotland) Act 1945, s. 1(1); Education (Scotland) Act 1980, s. 1(5).

149 Broadcasting Act 1990, s. 183; Broadcasting Act 1996, ss. 32, 95.

general protection or *status* of Scottish Gaelic[150]. On the other hand, no enactments at all have been made about the *status* of the Scots language in any field[151].

As was the case for Welsh speakers until the latter half of the twentieth century, the lack of protection and official *status* for the Scottish languages has caused significant difficulties for their speakers. In the case of the Scots language, as identified by the Council of Europe's Committee of Experts, the lack of protectionist domestic legal provisions makes it very difficult to "provide a stable foundation for the language in public life" and to create any comprehensive national policy framework for the language[152]. Critically, it is also felt that the lack of official *status* has contributed to the fact that there is, debatably, no standardised form of written Scots to this day. In turn, this makes it very difficult for the language to be used in any formal context, including in education. It could also lead to Scots speakers themselves questioning the *status* of the language. By way of example, a recent survey showed that 64% of those questioned did not "really think of Scots as a language – it's more just a way of speaking" and 67% noted that they "probably use Scots, but am not really aware of it"[153]. The same types of problems apply to a lesser extent with regard to Scottish Gaelic. There is, for instance, no right to use the language in the Scottish courts[154]. The case of *Taylor v. Haughney*[155] in 1982 is still authority for the fact that the language of the Scottish courts is English, and that Scottish Gaelic speakers have no right to use the language unless they can show that they do not understand English. The only apparent exception to this rule, according to the United Kingdom's submission to the Council of Europe's Committee of Experts, is that provision has been made for the use of Scottish Gaelic in the civil courts of Lochmaddy, Portree and Stornoway[156].

---

150 Section 6(1) of the British Nationality Act 1981 also deems that in order to become a naturalised British citizen, a person must have sufficient knowledge of English, Welsh or Scottish Gaelic.

151 Section 23 of the National Heritage (Scotland) Act 1985 permitted the Secretary of State to make grant payments to any body that promotes the development or understanding of cultural affairs. This could include organizations involved with Scottish Gaelic or the Scots language.

152 *Scots in the United Kingdom* (see footnote 45).

153 Scottish Government Social Research, *Public Attitudes Towards the Scots Language*, available at <http://www.scotland.gov.uk/Resource/Doc/298037/0092859.pdf> accessed 7th January 2011.

154 See W. McLeod, *Official Status for Gaelic: Prospects and Problems*, in *Scottish Affairs*, 21/1997, p. 95.

155 (1982) SCCR 360 (HCJT).

156 Public Foundation for European Comparative Minority Research 2006–2007, *Scottish-Gaelic in the United Kingdom through the lenses of the European Charter for Regional or Minority*

Since there are very little relevant pieces of United Kingdom legislation to consider in this context, attention must be given to devolution and its effects on Scotland's languages. As noted above, the Scotland Act 1998 established a Scottish Parliament with primary law making powers. It was also responsible for conferring wide-ranging competencies on the Scottish executive, including powers over Scottish Gaelic and Scots. However, in contrast to the Government of Wales Acts of 1998 and 2006, the Scotland Act 1998 made no explicit provision about languages. Whereas the Welsh enabling Act had ensured that the Welsh language played a prominent role from the outset[157], its Scottish counterpart remained silent on the corresponding issue. Instead, language matters were provided for by the Scottish Parliament's Standing Orders; rule 7.1 of the current edition states that, "Parliament shall normally conduct its business in English but members may speak in Scots Gaelic or in any other language with the agreement of the Presiding Officer". Rule 7.2 further provides that "Any person addressing the Parliament on the invitation of the Parliament in accordance with Rule 15.3.5, may do so in any language other than English with the agreement of the Presiding Officer"[158].

Debatably, Scottish Gaelic has gained most out of the establishment of the Scottish Parliament and Government thus far. However, that is not to say that the Scots language has not benefited also. By way of example, the second Scottish executive, in office from 2003 to 2007, included reference to the language in Scotland's curriculum, "A Curriculum for Excellence", for the first time[159]. The same executive also attempted to introduce a general policy framework on both Scotland's minority languages in February 2007[160]. However, a new government entered office in May 2007, thus ending the implementation process prematurely. Nonetheless, no real momentum was lost in this respect as the newly elected SNP government also brought with it a manifesto pledge to promote "an increased awareness of Scots and its literature. This will include introducing a question on Scots in the census and ensuring that European

---

Languages, available at <http://languagecharter.eokik.hu/docs/byLanguage/Scottish-Gaelic_in_the_UK.doc> accessed 7th January 2011.

157 GoWA 1998, ss. 32, 47, 66, 122.

158 The Scottish Parliament, *Standing Orders of the Scottish Parliament*, available at <http://www.scottish.parliament.uk/business/so/sto-c.htm> accessed 7th January 2011.

159 The Executive included reference to the 'diversity of languages in Scotland, including Scots' in its subsequent 2006 guidance document. Scottish Executive, *A Curriculum for Excellence: Building the Curriculum 1*, available at <http://www.ltscotland.org.uk/Images/building_curriculum1_tcm4-383389.pdf> accessed 7th January 2011.

160 Scottish Executive, *A Strategy for Scotland's Languages: Draft Version for Consultation*, available at <http://www.scotland.gov.uk/Resource/Doc/163888/0044602.pdf> accessed 7th January 2011.

obligations to develop the language are honoured. We will actively encourage the use of Scots in education, broadcasting and the arts"[161].

In attempting to honour the above manifesto pledges, the SNP government gave priority to conducting various audits and surveys of the Scots language. As was indicated in the first two monitoring reports of the Council of Europe's Committee of Experts, traditionally, there has been significant shortage of reliable information concerning Scots language provision[162]. Consequently, it has been extremely difficult for any government to form effective policies for the protection of the language. However, as a result of the Scottish government's initial audit[163], which was published in January 2009, and its subsequent survey[164], published in January 2010, it may be possible for future Scottish governments to pursue more effective policies to increase the *status* of the language. In the meantime, the evidence of the Council of Europe shows that there has already been a promising increase in the practical *status* and respect given to the language[165].

Despite the recent improvements in the *status* of the Scots language, its position is still not as advanced as the situation of Scottish Gaelic. The Gaelic Language (Scotland) Act 2005 is highly significant in this regard since it is the first piece of legislation to be enacted solely to increase the *status* of Scottish Gaelic. Similarly to the Welsh Language Act 1993, the 2005 Act established the Bòrd na Gàidhlig, the Gaelic Language Board, as a statutory body with responsibility for the general promotion of Scottish Gaelic. The Bòrd is further charged with ensuring that Scottish Gaelic becomes an official language in Scotland through: increasing the number of speakers; increasing the use and understanding of the language; and facilitating access to Scottish Gaelic and Gaelic culture[166]. Under section 2 of the Act, the Bòrd was expected to outline its strategy for achieving the above goals by publishing a national Gaelic language plan, which it eventually did in March 2007[167]. Although the Welsh Language Board is not under a corresponding statutory duty in Wales, the similarity in the roles of the two bodies continues under section 3 of the 2005 Act, where

---

161 SNP, *Manifesto 2007*, available at <http://www.snp.org/system/files/manifesto+programme.pdf> accessed 7th January 2011. The manifesto also made corresponding pledges regarding Scottish Gaelic.

162 *Scots in the United Kingdom* (see footnote 45).

163 Scottish Government Social Research, *Audit of Current Scots Language Provision in Scotland*, available at <http://www.scotland.gov.uk/Resource/Doc/258124/0076555.pdf> accessed 7th January 2011.

164 *Public Attitudes Towards the Scots Language* (see footnote 153).

165 *Application of the Charter in the United Kingdom 3rd monitoring cycle* (see footnote 39).

166 Gaelic Language Act, s. 1.

167 *The National Plan for Gaelic 2007–2012* (see footnote 50).

provision is made for the Bòrd to issue notices on relevant public authorities to create and publish Gaelic language plans. Subject to an appeal against the imposition of such a notice in the first place[168], the public authorities in question must outline the services which they pledge to provide in Scottish Gaelic. As was the case in Wales, the Bòrd then has a role to play in both the approval of the scheme and in monitoring a body's compliance with it[169]. The fact that the plans have to be eventually approved by the Bòrd means that it has significant indirect input into their content. In terms of its ultimate sanctions, the Bòrd can compile a report on any breach and direct it to the Scottish Ministers, who in turn can lay it before the Scottish Parliament. However, as was the case in Wales under the 1993 Act, no further or punitive sanctions can be brought against a body which is in breach of its obligations. To date, 13 organisations have had their language plans approved, and a further 29 plans are in the pipeline[170]. The approved plans include four from Scottish local authorities – the Highland Council, Argyll and Bute Council, Comhairle nan Eilean Siar and Glasgow City Council.

The similarities between the Welsh language schemes in Wales and the Gaelic language plans in Scotland make it inevitable that at least some of the same weaknesses appear in both regimes. For instance, it could be argued that, as was the case in Wales, the compliance monitoring procedure established by the 2005 Act is weak, primarily due to the lack of effective sanctions. It could also be said that both the Welsh and Scottish Acts give insufficient attention to the use of the languages in the private sector. Indeed, whilst the Welsh Language Act 1993 permits the Board to place demands on a limited number of private companies, the 2005 Scottish equivalent fails to mention private sector organisations at all. As a result, the Bòrd's interactions with private companies are based wholly on the goodwill of the organisations in question; the Bòrd has no statutory duties in this respect, other than the general responsibility for promoting the language. Finally, in contrast to the situation in Wales since 1967, the 2005 Scottish Act fails to provide a right for Scottish Gaelic speakers to use their language in a court of law. Whilst the Scottish Courts service may eventually have a language plan approved to address this deficiency in some way, the current situation in Scotland remains as unsatisfactory now as it was following the *Taylor* case in 1982[171].

168 Gaelic Language Act, s. 4.

169 Gaelic Language Act, ss. 5–6.

170 Bòrd na Gàidhlig, *Gaelic Language Plans*, available at <http://www.gaidhlig.org.uk/en/work/gaelic-language-plans.html> accessed 7th January 2011.

171 *Taylor v. Haughney* (see footnote 155).

10. Place names and road signs in Scotland

In the context of place names and road signs in Scotland, the focus of this section will be on Scottish Gaelic. This is primarily due to reasons outlined elsewhere in the chapter regarding the close linguistic proximity of the Scots and English languages and the perceived lack of a standardised written form of Scots. However, where there is a desire for the use of a standardised Scots place name or sign, most of the principles that are discussed below with regards to Scottish Gaelic are equally applicable to Scots.

The legal position of bilingual place names and road signs in Scotland is very similar to the Welsh situation. Briefly, it can be said that de facto responsibility for choosing the place names displayed on boundary signs, i.e. the names of villages, towns and cities, lies with local authorities. In doing so, they can opt to have an English-only name, a Scottish Gaelic-only (or Scots-only) name, or a bilingual name. However, since practically all place names will also be used on road signs in Scotland, it is vital that the local authorities in question also gain the approval of the Scottish Government when choosing to name or re-name a community. As a result, the work of the Gaelic place-name advisory partnership, the Gaelic Place-Names of Scotland, is of great significance. Established in 2006, the partnership, in which Bòrd na Gàidhlig is a member, is responsible for providing guidance to Scottish local authorities, to the Scottish Government, and to the Ordinance Survey on authoritative Scottish Gaelic place names. In doing so, it consults the National Place-Names Gazetteer[172] and its own well-established orthographic principles[173]. As was the case with respect to the Welsh Language Board's Standardisation of Place-Names Team, there is no statutory force to the partnership's recommendations. However, it seems unlikely that any local authority would choose to disregard its opinions without very good reason. As will be seen below, the language plans of the relevant local authorities may also have an impact in its choice of place names.

Similarly to Welsh local authorities, Scottish councils have a free choice when choosing names for streets or new developments. In Scotland's case, this is by virtue of section 97 of the Civic Government (Scotland) Act 1982: "A local authority may, in relation to any road in their area – (a) give such name to it as they think fit (…)". However, even in this respect, the considered opinions of the

172 Gaelic Place-Names of Scotland, *National Place-Names gazetteer*, available at <http://www.ainmean-aite.org/Database.asp> accessed 10th January 2011.

173 Gaelic Names Liaison Committee, *Orthographic Principles*, available at <http://www.ainmean-aite.org/UserFiles/File/GNLC%20Orthographic%20Principles%202006.pdf> accessed 10th January 2011.

Gaelic Place-Names of Scotland partnership can be considered[174]. Additionally, it must be remembered that under the authority of section 3 of the Gaelic Language (Scotland) Act 2005, the Scottish councils in question may be placed under an obligation to create a Scottish Gaelic language plan. It is clear from the four local authority plans to be approved thus far that they can have a genuine impact on Scottish Gaelic street names, place names, and on road signs. By way of example, the Highland Council's language plan provides:

> "Town, city and village welcome signs and Council road signs will be bilingual (...) When existing signs require to be replaced due to age or damage, bilingual signs will be erected (...) The adoption of Gaelic names will be encouraged on new streets and developments, using local historic and cultural connections wherever this information is available (...) When existing street name signs require to be replaced due to age or damage, the new signs will be bilingual"[175].

A further example comes from Comhairle nan Eilean Siar's language plan:

> "All street names in the Western Isles will be bilingual, with the Gaelic name first, and in a bolder type, to give it prominence (...) Placenames in the Western Isles should appear in Gaelic only. However, it may be necessary to have some exceptions to this policy, in cases where Gaelic and English vary significantly e.g. 'An t-Ob' and 'Leverburgh'"[176].

In the context of road signs, it has been explained elsewhere in the chapter that there is an exhaustive pictorial list of approved signs in the Traffic Signs Regulations and General Directions 2002[177]. Consequently, any council in England, Scotland and Wales can erect such signs on its roads without further authorisation. However, as noted, the signs contained in the 2002 Regulations are all in English-only. Whilst Welsh local authorities have the choice of choosing a sign that is approved in the Traffic Signs (Welsh and English Language Provisions) Regulations[178], there is no corresponding instrument for Scottish Gaelic signs. As a result, legally, a Scottish local authority that wishes to erect a bilingual road sign of a particular nature must approach the Scottish Government for permission to do so. In practice, the local authority in question will be encouraged to consult the Gaelic Place-Names of Scotland partnership

---

174 Gaelic Place-Names of Scotland, *Gaelic Street Name Guidance*, available at <http://www.ainmean-aite.org/UserFiles/File/Gaelic%20Street%20Names%20-%20Sraidean.pdf> accessed 10th January 2011.

175 Highland Council, *Gaelic Language Plan*, available at <http://www.highland.gov.uk/NR/rdonlyres/D97AF968-4CF7-4DAA-BEE4-F458B0C7A2CD/0/HCGLPE280508.pdf> accessed 10th January 2011.

176 Comhairle nan Eilean Siar, *Gaelic Language Plan*, available at <http://www.cne-siar.gov.uk/sgioba/documents/languageplan/plan_e.pdf> accessed 10th January 2011.

177 Traffic Signs Regulations 2002.

178 Bilingual Traffic Signs Regulations 1985.

for research to establish the correct and appropriate Gaelic forms. As is the case in Wales, the Scottish Government has the power to grant authorisations of non-prescribed signs by virtue of section 64(2) of the Road Traffic Regulation Act 1984[179].

Therefore, bilingual road signs are permitted in Scotland. However, in contrast to the situation in Wales, certain signs have to be approved by the Scottish Government. Whilst bilingual road signs are widespread in Scotland today, especially in the Western Isles, on roads in the Scottish Highlands[180], and on roads leading to the ferry ports to the Western Isles, the fact that they have to be approved by the Scottish Government is a significant hindrance.

11. Concluding remarks

The United Kingdom's minority languages live in the shadow of one of the world's most dominant languages, English. Despite the traditional lack of statutory protection, and in spite the ever-increasing influence of English-language culture, six indigenous languages have survived to this day. Nevertheless, the position of all six is precarious. As was shown in the section on recent trends in the number of speakers, all the languages have suffered significant decline in the last century. It is also apparent that the number of speakers continues to drop at an alarming rate in respect of some of the languages, including Scottish Gaelic. However, the introduction of devolution to the United Kingdom at the end of the twentieth century has, debatably, brought a new dawn for its indigenous languages. By today, the languages of Scotland and Wales, for instance, do not have to compete for precious parliamentary time at Westminster in order to have new policies and legislation debated and approved. In this context, both Scottish Gaelic and Welsh have already benefited from the increased attention that can now be given to their plight. Scots has also benefited to a lesser extent.

Although the position of Scots, Scottish Gaelic and Welsh is far from uniform, it is clear that the devolution process has brought considerable

---

179 Section 64(2) of the Road Traffic Act 1984 provided that a Secretary of State may approve such a sign on a one off basis. The Scotland Act 1998 (Transfer of Functions to the Scottish Ministers etc.) Order 1999, sch. 1, SI 1999/1750, transferred the relevant functions of section 64(2) to the Scottish Ministers.

180 See, for instance, the Scottish Executive, *Bilingual Road Signs Get Green Light*, available at <http://www.scotland.gov.uk/News/Releases/1999/10/84807339-9b7d-4fee-b2ed-b2c0c4a71b5d> accessed 10th January 2011.

improvements in their *status* and profile[181]. It is very doubtful, for instance, whether the Scots language would have been the subject of detailed surveys and audits if the Scottish Parliament had not been established in 1999. It is even more dubious whether any legislation would have been enacted on Scottish Gaelic if a democratically elected Scottish body had not been created. In this context, the Gaelic Language Act 2005 should be regarded as an important and symbolic first step on the road to establishing official standing for the language. The Welsh experience has shown that, in time, the language plan model can be built upon to achieve such a *status*. This has been confirmed in Wales through the enactment of the Welsh Language Measure 2011. Although it may not be possible to predict the long term effects of the Measure with any certainty, it is highly likely that its provisions on language standards will lead to an increase in the number of public and private sector services provided through the medium of Welsh.

However, despite the above improvements to the *status* of the languages, there are still several grounds for concern. A notable example relates to the views of the Committee of Experts that there is no standardised form of written Scots[182]. This is one area that will need to be addressed as a matter of urgency by the incoming Scottish Government after the May 2011 elections. There are also significant deficiencies that need to be tackled with regards to road signs and place names in Scots, Welsh and Scottish Gaelic. In regards to road signs, the fact that there is no Scottish Gaelic equivalent to the Bilingual Traffic Signs Regulations 1985 in Wales is a cause of concern in itself, since it potentially places an excessive amount of discretionary power in the hands of the Scottish Government. Whilst the attitude of successive Scottish Governments has been favourable towards both Scots and Scottish Gaelic, placing Scottish bilingual road signs on a legislative footing would remove the potential for the issue to become politicised. In the Welsh context, it could also be argued that there is a need for central Government to update the 1985 Regulations, since many more signs have been approved on a one off basis by the Secretary of State, the National Assembly and the Welsh Ministers since that time. Further, in terms of place-names, it could be argued that the roles of the Welsh Language Board's Place-Name Advisory Service and the Gaelic Place-Names of Scotland partnership should be placed on a more formal footing. Legislation could give statutory force to the recommendations made by both organisations, thus ensuring consistency in Scottish Gaelic and Welsh language place names. Whilst there is very little evidence to suggest that their opinions are disregarded by local authorities at present, the potential for inconsistency still exists.

---

181 *Application of the Charter in the United Kingdom 3rd Monitoring Cycle* (see footnote 39).

182 *Scots in the United Kingdom* (see footnote 45).

Nevertheless, despite the above concerns, the three minority languages of Scotland and Wales appear to be in positions of growth in many respects. Even if the number of Scottish Gaelic speakers continues to fall in the 2011 census, as expected, there are several causes for optimism. New regimes have recently been established for all three languages, and as such, the coming months and years will prove crucial for their future prosperity.

Bibliography

– – 1891 Census of England and Wales, Vol. IV General Report, Cm 7222, 1893–4.

Advisory Committee on the Framework Convention for the Protection of National Minorities, *Second Opinion on the United Kingdom Adopted on 6 June 2007*, available at <http://www.coe.int/t/dghl/monitoring/minorities/3_FCNMdocs/PDF_2nd_OP_UK_en.pdf> accessed 21st December 2010.

Banforth N., Malik M. and O'Cinneide O., *Discrimination Law: Theory and Context*, London, 2008.

Bòrd na Gàidhlig, *The National Plan for Gaelic 2007–2012*, available at <http://www.bord-na-gaidhlig.org.uk/National-Plan/National%20Plan%20for%20gaelic.pdf> accessed 1st December 2010.

Bush K., *Legislating in Welsh: Resuming an Old Conversation*, in *Cambrian Law Review*, 2007.

Comhairle nan Eilean Siar, *Gaelic Language Plan*, available at <http://www.cne-siar.gov.uk/sgioba/documents/languageplan/plan_e.pdf> accessed 10th January 2011.

Committee of Inquiry into Bilingual Traffic Signs, *Bilingual Traffic Signs: Report of the Committee of Inquiry Under the Chairmanship of Roderic Bowen 1971–1972*, Cm 5110, 1972.

Council of Europe, *Application of the Charter in the United Kingdom 3rd Monitoring Cycle*, available at <http://www.coe.int/t/dg4/education/minlang/report/EvaluationReports/UKECRML3_en.pdf> accessed 20th November 2010.

Davies C., *Cymdeithas yr Iaith Gymraeg*, in Stephens M. (ed.), *The Welsh Language Today*, Llandysul, 1973.

Davies D. H., *The Welsh Nationalist Party1925–1945*, Cardiff, 1983.

Davies G. P., *The Legal Status of the Welsh Language in the Twentieth Century*, in Jenkins G. H. and Williams M. A. (eds.), *Let's Do Our Best for the Ancient Tongue,* Cardiff, 2000.

Davies J., *The Welsh Language*, University of Wales Press, 1999.

Department for Communities and Local Government, *Discrimination Law Review: A Framework for Fairness: Proposals for a Single Equality Bill for Great Britain*, available at <http://www.communities.gov.uk/documents/corporate/pdf/325332.pdf> accessed 19th December 2010.

– – *The United Kingdom's Second Report to the Council of Europe under the Framework Convention for the Protection of National Minorities*, available at <http://www.coe.int/t/dghl/monitoring/minorities/3_FCNMdocs/PDF_2nd_SR_UK_en.pdf> accessed 21st December 2010.

Economic Affairs Division, Isle of Man Government, *Isle of Man Census Report 2001 Volume 2*, available at <http://www.gov.im/lib/docs/treasury/economic/census/reportvolume2.pdf> accessed 10th December 2010.

Fishlock T., *Government Agrees in Principle to Welsh Road Signs in Two Languages, The Times*, London, 30th November 1972.

Gaelic Names Liaison Committee, *Orthographic Principles*, available at <http://www.ainmean-aite.org/UserFiles/File/GNLC%20Orthographic%20Principles%202006.pdf> accessed 10th January 2011.

Gaelic Place-Names of Scotland, *Gaelic Street Name Guidance*, available at <http://www.ainmean-aite.org/UserFiles/File/Gaelic%20Street%20Names%20-%20Sraidean.pdf> accessed 10th January 2011.

General Register Office for Scotland, *Census 1981 Gaelic Report,* Edinburgh, 1983.

– – *Scotland's census 2001 Gaelic Report*, available at <http://www.gro-scotland.gov.uk/files1/stats/gaelic-rep-english-commentary.pdf> accessed 2nd December 2010

– – *Scotland's Census 2011 Specimen qQuestionnaire*, available at <http://www.gro-scotland.gov.uk/files2/the-census/scotlands-census-2011-specimen-questionnaire.pdf> accessed 2nd December 2010.

Government Equalities Office, *Framework for a Fairer Future – The Equality Bill*, White Paper, Cm 7431, 2008.

Griffiths G., *The Challenge of Legislating Bilingually*, in *Cambrian Law Review*, 2007.

Gruffudd H., *Bylchau yn Iaith Pawb*, in *Barn,* December/January, 2002–2003.

Gwynedd Council, *Welsh Language Scheme*, available at <http://www.gwynedd.gov.uk/upload/public/attachments/1040/Cynllun_Iaith_2010_S.pdf> accessed 4th January 2011.

Highland Council, *Gaelic Language Plan*, available at <http://www.highland.gov.uk/NR/rdonlyres/D97AF968-4CF7-4DAA-BEE4-F458B0C7A2CD/0/HCGLPE280508.pdf> accessed 10th January 2011.

Huws C., *The Language of Heaven and the Language of the Courts*, in *Cambrian Law Review*, 2007.

Isle of Anglesey County Council, *Welsh Language Scheme*, available at <http://www.anglesey.gov.uk/upload/public/attachments/78/languagescheme.pdf> accessed 4th January 2011.

Jenkins G. H., *The Welsh Language Before the Industrial Revolution*, University of Wales Press, 1997.

Jones J. G., *The National Petition on the Legal Status of the Welsh Language*, 1938–1942, in *Welsh History Review*, 18/1996.

Jones T., *Government to Spend £1m in support of Welsh Language*, *The Times*, London, 16th April 1980.

Labour and Plaid Cymru Groups in the National Assembly, *One Wales: A Progressive Agenda for the Government of Wales*, available at <http://wales.gov.uk/strategy/strategies/onewales/onewalese.pdf?lang=en> accessed 21st December 2010.

Lewis G., *Hawl i'r Gymraeg*, Talybont, 2008.

Lėwis R., *Cyfiawnder Dwyieithog? Bilingual Justice?,* Llandysul, 1998.

Máté I., *A Report on the Scots Language Research carried out by the General Register Office for Scotland in 1996,* Edinburgh, 1996.

McLeod W., *Official Status for Gaelic: Prospects and Problems,* in *Scottish Affairs*, 21/1997.

– – *Autochthonous Language Communities and the Race Relations Act*, [1998] 1 WJCLI <http://webjcli.ncl.ac.uk/1998/issue1/mcleod1.html> accessed 19th December 2010.

Merriman P. and Jones Rh., *'Symbols of Justice': the Welsh Language Society's campaign for bilingual road signs in Wales, 1967–1980,* in *Journal of Historical Geography*, 35(2) 2009.

National Assembly for Wales, *Measures. What is a Measure/Proposed Measure?,* available at <http://www.assemblywales.org/bus-home/bus-legislation/bus-legislation-guidance/bus-legislation-guidance-measures.htm> accessed 12th November 2010.

Newport City Council, *Welsh Language Scheme*, available at <http://www.newport.gov.uk/stellent/groups/public/documents/plans_and_strategies/cont499493.pdf> accessed 4th January 2011.

Northern Ireland Assembly Committee for Culture, Arts and Leisure Official Report, *Language Strategy: Ministerial Briefing 1 July 2010,* available at <http://www.niassembly.gov.uk/record/committees2009/CAL/100701_LanguageStrategyMinisterialBriefing.htm> accessed 1st December 2010.

Northern Ireland Assembly, *Minute of Proceedings Monday 8 November 2010*, available at <http://www.niassembly.gov.uk/minutes/2007mandate/minutes/2010/101108.htm> accessed 1st December 2010.

Northern Ireland Statistics and Research Agency, *1991 Census Data Irish Language Report*, available upon request from the Northern Ireland Statistics and Research Agency. Details available at <http://www.nisra.gov.uk/Census/Previous%20Census%20Statistics/1991CensusStatistics.html> accessed 13th November 2010.

– – *Table KS24 Knowledge of Irish*, available at <http://www.nisranew.nisra.gov.uk/Census/Census2001Output/KeyStatistics/keystats.html#dsitrict council level> accessed 13th November 2010.

– – *The 2011 Census of Population in Northern Ireland Proposals*, available at <http://www.nisranew.nisra.gov.uk/census/pdf/proposals.pdf> accessed 13th November 2010.

Office for National Statistics, 'Proportion of people able to speak Welsh' available at <http://www.statistics.gov.uk/downloads/theme_compendia/fow/Wales.zip> accessed 20th November 2010.

– – *Population Estimates, June 2010*, available at <http://www.statistics.gov.uk/pdfdir/pop0610.pdf> accessed 13th November 2010.

Phillips D., *The History of the Welsh Language Society*, in Jenkins G. H. and Williams M. A. (eds.), *Let's Do Our Best for the Ancient Tongue*, Cardiff, 2000.

Public Foundation for European Comparative Minority Research 2006–2007, *Cornish in the United Kingdom through the lenses of the European Charter for Regional or Minority Languages*, available at <http://languagecharter.eokik.hu/docs/byLanguage/Cornish_in_the_UK.doc> accessed 20th November 2010.

– – *Number of Undertakings*, available at <http://languagecharter.eokik.hu/docs/BasicData/number_of_undertakings_abc.pdf> accessed 21st December 2010.

– – *Scots in the United Kingdom through the lenses of the European Charter for Regional or Minority Languages*, available at <http://languagecharter.eokik.hu/docs/byLanguage/Scots_in_the_UK.doc> accessed 2nd December 2010.

– – *Scottish-Gaelic in the United Kingdom through the lenses of the European Charter for Regional or Minority Languages*, available at <http://languagecharter.eokik.hu/docs/byLanguage/Scottish-Gaelic_in_the_UK.doc> accessed 7th January 2011.

– – *Ulster-Scots in the United Kingdom through the lenses of the European Charter for Regional or Minority Languages*, available at <http://language

charter.eokik.hu/docs/byLanguage/Ulster-Scots_in_the_UK.doc> accessed 13th November 2010.

Scottish Constitutional Convention, *Scotland's Parliament, Scotland's Right*, available at <http://www.almac.co.uk/business_park/scc/scc-rep.htm> accessed 12th November 2010.

Scottish Executive, *Bilingual road signs get green light*, available at <http://www.scotland.gov.uk/News/Releases/1999/10/84807339-9b7d-4fee-b2ed-b2c0c4a71b5d> accessed 10th January 2011.

– – *A Curriculum for Excellence: Building the Curriculum 1*, available at <http://www.ltscotland.org.uk/Images/building_curriculum1_tcm4-383389.pdf> accessed 7th January 2011.

– – *A Strategy for Scotland's Languages: Draft Version for Consultation*, available at <http://www.scotland.gov.uk/Resource/Doc/163888/0044602.pdf> accessed 7th January 2011.

Scottish Government Social Research, 'Audit of Current Scots Language Provision in Scotland' available at <http://www.scotland.gov.uk/Resource/Doc/258124/0076555.pdf> accessed 7th January 2011.

– – *Public Attitudes Towards the Scots Language*, available at <http://www.scotland.gov.uk/Resource/Doc/298037/0092859.pdf> accessed 7th January 2011.

Scottish Power, *Welsh Language Scheme*, available at <http://www.byig-wlb.org.uk/english/publications/publications/welsh%20language%20scheme%20-%20scottishpower.doc> accessed 21st December 2010.

SNP, *Manifesto 2007*, available at <http://www.snp.org/system/files/manifesto+programme.pdf> accessed 7th January 2011.

Statistics for Wales, *Schools in Wales: General Statistics 2009*, available at <http://wales.gov.uk/docs/statistics/2009/091029schoolsgen09ency.pdf> accessed 21st December 2010.

The Scottish Office, *Scotland's Parliament*, White Paper, Cm 3658, 2007.

The Scottish Parliament, *Standing Orders of the Scottish Parliament*, available at <http://www.scottish.parliament.uk/business/so/sto-c.htm> accessed 7th January 2011.

Thomas N. and Gruffudd H., *An Action Plan for Welsh*, in *Planet*, 157/2003.

Watkin T. G., *The Legal History of Wales*, Cardiff, 2007.

Welsh Assembly Government, *Iaith Pawb: A National Action Plan for a Bilingual Wales*, available at <http://wales.gov.uk/depc/publications/welshlanguage/iaithpawb/iaithpawbe.pdf;jsessionid=2cDLNqcTpzW23vXhnYLTqV88XF9cZKh8PCLQrCHn0k1KtKPLG4V9!1876000129?lang=en> accessed 21st December 2010.

– – *Welsh Language Scheme*, available at <http://wales.gov.uk/depc/publications/welshlanguage/languagescheme/scheme06.pdf?lang=en> accessed 4th January 2011.

Welsh Language Board, *Census 2001: Main Statistics About Welsh*, available at <http://www.byig-wlb.org.uk/English/publications/Publications/332.doc> accessed 20th November 2010.

– – *Guidelines for Language Officers for the Standardisation of Place-Names and Street Names*, available at <http://www.byig-wlb.org.uk/English/publications/Publications/4437.pdf> accessed 4th January 2011.

– – *The Welsh Language Board's Response to the Discrimination Law Review Consultation Paper*, available at <http://equalities.gov.uk/nosearch/pdf/Welsh%20Language%20Board%20(Rees).pdf> accessed 17th December 2010.

– – *Welsh Language Use Surveys of 2004–06,* available at <http://www.byig-wlb.org.uk/english/publications/publications/welsh%20language%20use%20surveys%202004-06.pdf> accessed 20th November 2010.

Welsh Office, *Legal Status of the Welsh Language*, Cm 2785, 1965.

Welsh Water, *Welsh Language Scheme*, available at <http://www.byig-wlb.org.uk/english/publications/publications/welsh%20language%20scheme%20-%20welsh%20water.pdf> accessed 21st December 2010.

Williams C., *Non-violence and the development of the Welsh Language Society, 1962–c.1974*, in *Welsh History Review*, 8/1977.

Williams J., *Welsh Language in Law and Governance*, in *Welsh Journal of Law and Policy*, 4/2005.

Place names in Spain: the prominence of the linguistic pluralism of the *Estado autonómico*

Giovanni Poggeschi

Summary

1. Introduction. Place names as the yardstick against which to measure various language policies

Place names accompany us through our lives. The science of toponomy relates to the history of places, as the immediate reflection of ideological choices or of national history. Saint Petersburg has no longer been Leningrad since Russia chose a liberal-democratic and capitalist model; Istanbul is no longer Constantinople in republican Turkey, even though the Greeks still give it this name. The choice of a geographical name is therefore not neutral, even when it appears that there are no evident linguistic conflicts. It has not crossed anyone's mind to put up a sign saying "*Crasplàn*" rather than Crespellano (province of Bologna), or "*Napule*" instead of Naples, but many Italian municipalities run by the Northern League Party have made choices of this kind ("*Nuàra*" for Novara, "*Seriat*" per Seriate, and many others), though they have been withdrawn once the majority has changed political hue, as occurred in Bergamo.

In the Spanish State comprised of autonomous communities[1],where there are six autonomous communities which grant official *status* to the regional language

1 The expression "State comprised of autonomous communities" may be synonymous with a "regionalised State" but, given the importance of the Spanish model, I prefer to use the former expression. However, in using this expression, I refer exclusively to the specific model designed under the 1978 Constitution which has then developed down to today, and do not use

alongside Castilian, and three providing more mundane forms of protection for local dialect[2], the issue of place names provides a direct illustration of the efficacy, intensity and nature of the various regional and local language policies. This paper deals with toponomy as the science of place names, including both renowned and important places (macro-toponomy) as well as less known places of strictly local importance (micro-toponomy). However, for the sake of completeness, reference will also be made to the use of language in road signs and shop names (in Castilian "*rotulación*") that come together to make up what is defined as the "linguistic environment" of a given area, city, region or State, as well as the related question of the names of local authorities.

In order to clarify the terminology used, "place name" will in this paper be taken to refer to the general body of place names, road signs ("*rotulación*"), the action of placing road signs ("*rótulos*"), consisting in the signs placed in a clearly visible place at the entrance to a factory, office, street etc. in order to make them known to the public; similarly, "name" will refer to the "given name" which, in the case of local authorities, "is conferred according to an administrative procedure with the purpose and result that the local authorities adopt or change the authority's own name to one that is different from that of other local authorities, in such a way that the former may be distinguished form the latter"[3]. There is no doubt that the three concepts are inter-related, given that road signs include place names and the names of local authorities[4].

Minority protection is a dimension, or a cross-cutting issue[5], on which the legislative and regulatory powers of the different levels of local government intersect[6]. Place names and also road signs are also areas characterised by the

---

it in a prognostic manner for the future (other than in relation to an accentuation of certain problem issues).

2 Most recently, art. 15 of the statute of Castille-León, approved in December 2007, provides for the protection of the language model for Leónese and for Galician, limited to the areas where they are spoken.

3 F.M. Díaz-Guerra, J. Vernet Llobet, *El régim jurídic de la llengua en la retolació pública, la toponímia i la denominació dels ens locals a Catalunya*, in *Revista de Llengua i Dret*, 16/1991, p. 87. The "*rotulación*" may therefore be public or private depending on the party concerned.

4 *Ibidem*, p. 87.

5 The objective is therefore the "establishment of the language regime within which the activities constituting these powers are exercised, regardless of whether these are vested in the State or the autonomous community": J.M. Pérez Fernández, *Principios del régimen juridico-lingüístico: en especial, el estatuto de oficialidad*, in J.M. Pérez Fernández (ed.), *Estudios sobre el estatuto jurídico de las lenguas en España*, Barcelona, 2006, p. 56.

6 On minority protection as a specific area of law, see F. Palermo, *Titolo V, minoranze e norme d'attuazione degli Statuti speciali*, in *Forum on line Quaderni costituzionali:* http://www.forumcostituzionale.it/site/index.php?option=com_content&task=view&id=8&Itemid=0. Another view, endorsed by a technical opinion of an uncited expert from the Italian Province of

fact of their "instrumental" nature with regard to the powers of the body vested with furthering the public good or of whoever administers it, or regulates it in the case of private activities[7].

Place names and road signs therefore make a significant contribution to the "linguistic environment" of a place[8], defining at the same time its history and relative political choices. Both public and private choices contribute to shaping the linguistic environment of a given place, for example in the name chosen for a restaurant or a shop which may, where linguistic regulation is not particularly restrictive, also be in a language other than the official one for that place, whether it be foreign ("*Hard Rock Cafe*") and/or a dialectical variant of the official language ("*la budghéina*", small shop in Bolognese dialect)[9].

Bolzano (on which, see V. Bocci, *La salvaguardia delle minoranze linguistiche dopo la riforma del Titolo V della Costituzione: ancora sulla permanenza dell'interesse nazionale*, also available at the website cited above) would have as its immediate consequence under Italian law the conclusion that minority protection is an area reserved to the legislative and regulatory jurisdiction of the regions and (with particular force) of the autonomous provinces of Bolzano and Trento, given its absence from the list of matters reserved to the State under art. 117 of the Italian Constitution as amended in October 2001. On the protection of minorities as a "cross-cutting issue", in which both the regions and the state may intervene but regarding which the latter retains the duty and must guarantee the maintenance of a certain degree of unity in the definition of minority policies, see L.A. Mazzarolli, *La tutela delle minoranze linguistiche nella Costituzione del nuovo Titolo V*, in *Le Regioni*, 5/2003, pp. 727–736. A detailed analysis of the concept of minority is provided in V. Piergigli, *Lingue minoritarie e identità culturali*, Milan, 2001, p. 53 et seq.

7 I. Urrutia Libarona, *Apuntes jurídicos sobre el paisaje lingüístico en Euskal Herria*, in *Revista de Llengua i Dret*, 31/1999, p. 130.

8 The concept of "linguistic environment" or "linguistic aspect" ("*visage linguistique*") has been particularly developed within the Canadian literature, and in particular that of Québec, which is one of the most studied (and closely followed) under comparative law. On language rights in Québec, see J. Woehrling, *La cohabitation linguistique au Canada: les politiques linguistiques du Québec, de l'État fédéral canadien et des provinces anglophones*, in *Revista Vasca de Administración Pública*, no. 69 (II), 2004, pp. 315–345.

9 There are cases within comparative law of obligations also for private individuals to use (at least) one official language: for example the "*Charte de la langue française*" in Québec, also referred to as "Law 101", was the object of censure by the Canadian Supreme Court, in particular in two judgments from 1988, due to the "excessive" nature of some of its provisions on the exclusive use of French that infringed freedom of expression, which certainly protects the right to express oneself in one's own language, but does not guarantee the right to express oneself exclusively in one's own language: see D. Loprieno, *La politica linguistica del Québec tra diritti individuali e diritti collettivi*, in S. Gambino, C. Amirante (eds.), *Il Canada. Un laboratorio costituzionale. Federalismo, Diritti, Corti*, Padova, 2000, pp. 321–323. Another case of "severe" language legislation, due to the fact that the official language is weak within the international and regional context (i.e. the Baltic region) is Latvia, regarding which I refer to G. Poggeschi, *Language policy in Latvia*, in *Noves SL. Revista de sociolingüística*,

It has been the task of dictatorships, carried out with tenacity and diligence, to cancel the public use of place names in minority languages[10]. More simply, and less traumatically, linguistic policies, including those of democratic States, have chosen to privilege a standard form compared to dialects.

However, democracies have usually made an effort to respect the local place names of minorities in different ways depending on their different ideological choices. France, which as is known is regarded as a country providing a low level of protection for minorities[11], has in certain cases safeguarded traditional place names in areas where there is a regional or minority language[12], and at times has chosen to "frenchify" names which were originally the official place names in other languages, creating hybrids which are difficult to justify from a historical or linguistic point of view, but thereby avoiding the hypothetical requirement for names in two languages[13].

It may already be noted from these initial reflections how the issue of place names may become a sensitive issue when it involves linguistic or national minorities[14]. It is a flag, an immediately tangible sign of the identity of a place. At the level of science based on history and on philology, it may not necessarily be a harbinger of conflicts, but simply of diachronic events that have now been digested without trauma: an inhabitant of Paris does not yearn for the name

---

Barcelona, 2004 (available also in Catalan), published also on the website http://www6.gencat.net/llengcat/noves/hm04tardor/poggeschi1_3.htm. Regarding the "at least in Catalan" clause contained in various provisions of the 1998 Catalan Law on language policy, under which the use of another language is not excluded, though the use of Catalan must be guaranteed, see A. Milian Massana, *La exigencia de "al menos en catalán" como garantía de la presencia social de la lengua catalana*, in Various Authors, *Estudios jurídicos sobre la ley de política lingüística*, Madrid – Barcelona, 1999, pp. 465–510.

10 A striking example was the course of action followed in the South Tyrol by Senator Tolomei, who Italianised many place names, at times relying on the existing Latin root, and at others in an arbitrary fashion, with sometimes grotesque results.

11 On the protection of minorities in France as protection of linguistic diversity, see F. Benoît-Rohmer, *Les langues officieuses de la France*, in *Revue française de droit constitutionnel*, 45/2001, pp. 3–29.

12 There are many local choices underlying this. For example, place names are very prominent in the local Celtic language in Brittany, whilst in many cities in the *Pays d'Oc*, even where this language is little spoken, there are signs in the *Langue d'Oc* ("*carrièra*" alongside "*rue*").

13 There are numerous examples of this in Alsace: the name *Sélestat*, a city in the middle of Alsace, would be *Schlettstadt* in German. Rather than a literal translation, which often occurred in the Italian South Tyrol, a choice was made for a vaguer assonance with the original name which at the same time frenchifies it. See A. Richert, *Noms de lieux en Alsace*, Paris, 1986.

14 The term "national minorities", initially circumscribed to the situation in Central and Eastern Europe, entered into common usage also throughout the rest of Europe following the adoption by the majority of European States of the "Framework Convention for the Protection of National Minorities", adopted by the Council of Europe in 1994.

Lutezia, nor a Bolognese that of *Felsina* (unless he or she belongs to a group of Etruscan enthusiasts).

Spain is a very interesting and topical "*case study*" both for ideological/ political as well as national reasons, which are moreover interrelated with one another. Although the term "minorities" is banned, with the concepts of nationality and linguistic rights applying in its stead, we find the typical dynamics of relations between majority and minority, often marked by conflict (in which moreover the minority on state level may become the majority on regional or local level). Spain is a pluri-lingual and regional State, in a nutshell pluri-national, in which these two characteristics are recognised under constitutional law, and are visible also in the provisions governing place names which will be discussed in sections three and four, after a necessary recognition of the general legislation on multilingualism which draws its legitimation from the text of the Constitution.

2. Official pluri-lingualism as provided for under the 1978 Constitution and its legislative and regulatory development by the autonomous communities

Before addressing the question of place names, it is necessary to sketch out a brief constitutional history of language legislation in Spain, starting from 1978[15], the year in which the new Constitution restored democracy and designed the successful State comprised of autonomous communities.

The foundation for the complex and detailed regulation of linguistic rights is art. 3, which provides as follows:

> "1. Castilian is the official language of the State. All Spaniards have the duty to know it and the right to use it.
> 2. The other Spanish languages shall also be official within the ambit of the respective autonomous communities in accordance with their own statutes.
> 3. The wealth of linguistic pluralism in Spain is a cultural patrimony which shall be the object of special respect and protection".

The legislative structure of the Spanish Constitution, including in particular Title VIII which provides for the existence of autonomous communities and the overall system of competences resulting from it, also informs art. 3 of the

15 For a more detailed study, see G. Poggeschi, *Le nazioni linguistiche della Spagna* autonómica, Padova, 2002.

Constitution[16]. There is no statement as to what the "other Spanish languages" are which may be granted official *status* under the terms of the statutes of the autonomous communities concerned, but it is known that they are Catalan[17], Basque and Galician, and it is the task of the regional legislature to specify the extent of joint official *status*.

In any case, the Constitution already enshrines the principle of the joint official *status* of Castilian alongside the relevant regional language, and in drafting the self-government statutes nobody was in fact able to object to the conferral of official *status* on Spain's other languages[18], alongside obviously the principle of the official *status* of Castilian throughout Spain, "irrespective of the State (*stricto sensu*), regional or local nature of the various public powers" (Constitutional Court, judgment no. 82/1986).

The more circumspect literature on linguistic rights in Spain hence felt that in order for the official *status* of the other Spanish languages to be truly effective in the respective autonomous communities, it was necessary for the initiative involving the regionalisation process to be successful[19]. It was indeed fully successful, in various States, which included periods of rapid expansion as well as indecision, caught between the opposing forces of asymmetry and the tendency towards uniformity in the autonomous communities. However, it can be said today that the model of the State comprised of autonomous communities has been successfully implemented[20], so much so that it has been considered as one of the examples of a decentralised State most admired within comparative law[21], in spite of the fact that it has emitted some crisis signals over recent years,

---

16 A. Milian Massana, *La regulación constitucional del multilinguismo*, in *Revista española de derecho constitucional*, 10/1984.

17 Here Catalan is considered to include its variant officially called Valencian. Although under different names, there is nevertheless a "Catalan language environment" defined by the Catalan "*Law on language policy*", no. 1 of 1998. On the legal implications of this issue, see P. Pérez Tremps, *El ámbito lingüístico catalán*, in Various Authors, *Estudios jurídicos sobre la ley de política lingüística*, *cit.*, pp. 547–576.

18 G. Poggeschi, *Le nazioni linguistiche della Spagna* autonómica, *cit.*, p. 79.

19 A. Milian Massana, *Ordenament linguistic (EAC 3)*, in *Comentaris sobre l'Estatut d'Autonomia de Catalunya*, vol. 1, Barcelona, 1988, p. 172.

20 On the assessment of the State comprised of autonomous communities, see the detailed and excellent account of E. Aja, C. Viver Pi-Sunyer, *Valoración de 25 años de autonomía*, in *Revista española de derecho constitucional*, 69/2003, pp. 69–113.

21 The literature on the Spanish State comprised of autonomous communities is now extensive. I note only the following, in addition to the work cited in the previous footnote: J.J. Solozábal Evchevarría, *Las bases constitucionales del Estado autonómico*, Madrid, 1998; in Italian, F. López Aguilar, *Lo Stato* autonómico *spagnolo*, Padova, 1999; for a critical account, above all with regard to peripheral nationalisms (including in particular Catalan and Basque nationalism), see R. Blanco Valdés, *Nacionalidades históricas y regiones sin historia*, Madrid, 2005.

specifically in relation to the possibility of it evolving towards an asymmetrical confederation, or a symmetrical federation, or ultimately return to a tendency towards a latter-day centralism.

As far as the modulation of the official *status* of regional languages is concerned[22], the autonomous legislative basis of which is provided by the statutes, the literature is practically unanimous is considering them identical to Castilian[23]. As is the case for Castilian, *status* as an official language translates first and foremost into the duty to learn it at school; another central aspect is the use of the co-official language at all levels of the public administration. Another area in which the co-official *status* is apparent is that of place names.

The individual autonomous communities have developed a very detailed *corpus* (which is of considerable size in the case of Catalonia and the Basque Country) of language rights, with a series of laws ad regulations based on the respective local government statutes. The so-called normalisation laws in the 1980s constituted the general basis for subsequent legislation and regulation of detailed self-government provisions and, in the case of Catalonia, were followed by the 1998 law on language policy, the most complete example of general legislation regulating language rights and duties anywhere in Europe[24].

As regards the question at issue in this study, there is a partial instance of joint official languages in cases involving place names of national interest (*Donostia/ San Sebastián*), but the general rule is that the place name has official *status* according to the legislation of the autonomous community, which means that the place name will generally be expressed in the official regional language, which is historically the traditional language. Nonetheless, there remains scope for decision by the central State although, as will be seen in the next section, state legislation has been used also to endorse the validity of place names in the co-official regional languages of the autonomous communities.

3. The regulation of place names by the central State

The central legislative has taken responsibility for the possible confusion caused by the sharing of competence over place names between the State and the autonomous communities under Royal Decree no. 334 of 12th February 1982,

22 On which most recently, see J. Vernet, *El pluralismo lingüístico*, in J. Vernet, R. Punset, *Lenguas y Constitución*, Madrid, 2007, p. 36 et seq.

23 E. Argullol Murgadas, *Estudio*, in Various Authors, *La lengua de enseñanza en la legislación de Cataluña*, Barcelona, 1994, p. 387 et seq.

24 An initial commentary is contained in G. Poggeschi, *La nuova legge linguistica catalana nel quadro dell'evoluzione dello Stato regionale spagnolo*, in *Le Regioni*, 5/1998, pp. 1107–1144.

prior the laws on the linguistic normalisation of the autonomous communities but after the statutes confirming competence over language already specified under art. 3 of the Constitution.

The preamble to the Decree immediately admits that "since certain doubts have arise in the application of current legislation on road signs and transport and communication signage, as well as in the distribution of powers over such matters, it appears appropriate to establish, within the framework of the Constitution, the joint official *status* of Castilian alongside the languages of certain autonomous communities"[25].

Article 1 provides that "within the territory of the autonomous communities established with a different official language from Castilian, road signs or indications written on roads and motorways, or at railway stations, bus stations and ports, ports of general interest, airports open to commercial traffic, border posts and other installations, or in the provision of services of general public interest under the competence of the autonomous communities or the State administration, and if appropriate operated the concessionaires of the latter, shall be expressed in Castilian and in the other official language of the autonomous community which is recognised under the respective self-government statute".

The second article adds that "the implementation of prior legislation shall be a matter for the public administration, and for the bodies or concessionaires responsible for roads, stations, airports, installations and services. This implementation shall be conditional upon the fact that each of the autonomous communities to which these provisions refer shall enact, within the ambit of it own sphere of powers, a provision regulating the use of Castilian identical to that enacted in this royal decree".

The general rule is, as will be seen in the next paragraph, that of automatic competence with regard to the names of all localities and settlements; however, in order to amend the names of the autonomous communities and the provinces it is necessary to enact a state law. This was the case for the Catalan *Girona* and *Lleida* (Law no. 2 of 28th February 1992) and for the Galician *A Coruña* and *Ourense* (Law no. 2 of 3rd March 1998)[26].

As regards a change in name to the autonomous communities, it is sufficient here to cite Law no. 13 of 25th April 1997 in order to illustrate the procedure by which the province of the Balearic Islands, the *Baleares* in Castilian, officially became *Illes Balears* in Catalan.

---

25 This text, along with the others relating to place names and legal provisions of the central State and Catalonia, may be consulted at http://www6.gencat.net/llengcat/legis/nor-topo.htm.

26 In the previous official version, in Castilian, respectively Gerona, Lérida, La Coruña and Orense.

Powers over traffic and rail transport, the regulation of land transport which passes through the territory of more than one autonomous community and over state-owned infrastructure remains under the exclusive competence of the central State[27].The expansion of the concept of joint official *status* in the six autonomous communities concerned has meant that signs are usually bilingual even if they refer to matters under state competence.

4. Place names as governed by the autonomous communities. The powers of the municipalities and of other sub-state bodies

It clearly follows from the above that the territorial body that has played the greatest part in the legislation on place names in Spain is the autonomous community[28], without however disregarding the role of the smaller local authorities. Naturally the question arises only when there are two or more official languages within the autonomous community even if, in theory, also some monolingual autonomous communities could in future exercise powers over place names by reference to a past in which other languages were spoken within their territory (for example, in Andalusia, Arabic or Judeo Spanish).

A central point relates to the competence over the local authorities: the State is generally reserved the right to define the "*bases*" of the legal arrangements governing the public administrations, whilst competence over the "local arrangements" is generally a matter for the autonomous communities (which are for example governed by art. 160 of the new Catalan statute). In any way, the procedure for changing a name is an executive decision reserved to the autonomous community, but the right to initiate the procedure is normally vested in the local authority[29]. On the other hand, it does not appear that the districts have any significant powers in this area, as the intermediary level of government between the municipalities and the provinces and other smaller local authorities.

As is the case in other areas in which the language factor has an impact, the legal instruments on which the policies and language regulations of the autonomous communities are based are regional laws on normalisation or language and the relative implementing decrees. The analysis of the legislation

---

27 I. Urrutia Libarona, *Apuntes jurídicos sobre el paisaje lingüístico en Euskal Herria, cit.*, p. 150.

28 In many legal systems, regional legislation appears to be the most appropriate instrument for regulating the question of language: see G. Poggeschi, *Le nazioni linguistiche della Spagna* autonómica, *cit.*, p. 390 et seq.

29 F.M. Díaz-Guerra, J. Vernet Llobet, *El régim jurídic de la llengua en la retolació pública, la toponímia i la denominació dels ens locals a Catalunya, cit.*, p. 92.

on place names may therefore easily be conducted on a case by case basis, that is for each autonomous community in which the language factor is legally regulated.

Euskadi

The question of place names in the Basque country, or *Euskadi* in *Euskera*[30], differs from Catalonia, the other autonomous community which vigorously claims broader self-government powers[31], due to the non-legal fact of the nature of the local language *Euskera* which differs significantly from Castilian, not having any Latin or even Indo-European root[32]. The situation of linguistic decline, above all during the Franco period, resulted in many places in the abandonment of traditional place names, which the institutions of the autonomous community have been attempting to reverse since the re-establishment of democracy and regional autonomy[33].

Euskera is a minority language even inside the Basque Country, and has been the object of a powerful, and partially successful, campaign of protection and reinforcement[34], above all through the education system[35] and a widespread

30 The now widespread use of the terms Basque, *Euskadi* and *Euskera* are testament to the strong impact of regional policies reinforcing and providing greater visibility to Spanish languages other than Castilian.

31 In reality, the draft reform of the statute of *Euskadi* is much more radical than that for Catalonia (it proposes a kind of association on equal footing between the Basque Country and Spain), so much so that it has not gone beyond the stage of a draft within the autonomous community. See G. Poggeschi, *Prove tecniche di "soberanismo" basco all'esame (rinviato) del "Tribunal Constitucional" spagnolo*, in *Diritto pubblico comparato ed europeo*, 3/2004, pp. 1119–1126.

32 http://www.euskara.euskadi.net/r59-738/es/contenidos/informacion/6669/es_2427/es_12442.html.

33 I. Urrutia Libarona, *Apuntes jurídicos sobre el paisaje lingüístico en Euskal Herria*, in *Revista de Llengua i Dret*, 31/1999, pp. 125–180.

34 From the vast bibliography, see E. Cobreros Mendazona, *El régimen jurídico de la oficialidad del euskera*, Oñate, 1989; I. Agirreazkuenaga Zigorra, *Diversidad y convivencia lingüística. Dimensión europea, nacional y claves jurídicas para la normalización del euskera*, Donostia, 2003.

35 Within the autonomous community of *Euskadi*, it differs from that of Catalonia: whereas for the latter the choice has been that (controversial, but considered lawful from the constitutional point of view by judgment no. 337/1994 of the Constitutional Court) of a single education network, made possible also by the common features shared by Castilian and Catalan, both derived form Latin, in Euskadi there are three types of schools: Castilian monolingual schools, Basque monolingual schools and bilingual schools: see G. Poggeschi, *Le nazioni linguistiche della Spagna* autonómica, *cit.*, pp. 231–236. On *Euskera* in the Basque education system, see

language policy involving all institutional levels of government (although a central role is played by those directly dependent upon the autonomous community of *Euskadi*)[36]. A fundamental role in the recovery of the language is played by the *Euskaltzaindia*, the Royal Academy of the Basque Language, which is, pursuant to art. 6, para. 4 of the statute, the "official consultative institution on *Euskera*"[37].

The self-government statute, the so-called statute of Gernika of 1979[38], is the legal basis defining the official *status* of *Euskera* (art. 6, obviously alongside Castilian, which is official throughout Spain), subsequently specified under the *Euskera* normalisation Law no. 10 of 24th November 1982, which was the first of this category of legislation to be enacted in Spain.

The provision that is of interest here is art. 10 of the *Euskera* normalisation Law, which provides as follows:

> "1. The official name of the territories, municipalities, settlements, geographical places, streets and, in general, of the place names of the autonomous Basque community shall be determined by the government, the local government bodies of the historical territories and the local corporations within the ambit of their respective competences respecting, in all cases, the Basque, Romance or Castilian original with the academic spelling in each language".

The above article is a compendium of public law and a precise statement of the principle of subsidiarity. It must at this stage be recalled that the institutional structure of the autonomous community of *Euskadi* presents itself as a kind of Federation of historical[39] or self-governing territories, that is Álava, Guipúzcoa

---

most recently I. Urrutia Libarona, *Derechos lingüísticos y euskera en el sistema educativo*, Pamplona-Iruña, 2005.

36 *Ibidem*, pp. 273–281.

37 On the controversy relating to the monopoly of the *Euskaltzaindia* on consultancy concerning the Basque language, see G. Poggeschi, *Le nazioni linguistiche della Spagna* autonómica, *cit.*, pp. 125–128, in particular in note 15.

38 The choice of place name made there was Basque, but the most important and significant artwork of the last century remains the *Guernica* by Pablo Picasso, in Castilian.

39 From the vast bibliography on historical rights, a concept obviously related to that of "historical territories", see M. Herrero de Miñón, *Derechos Históricos y Constitución*, Madrid, 1998; M. Herrero de Miñon, E. Lluch (eds.), *Derechos históricos y constitucionalismo útil*, Madrid, 2001 During the drafting of the new statute for Catalonia, the issue of historical rights extended to Catalonia, and therefore now recognised only to *Euskadi* and Navarra, was much debated. Article 5 of the draft statute specified that "The self-government of Catalonia is based on the historical rights of the Catalan people, which this statute incorporates and reaffirms". Following an negative opinion of the *Consell Consultiu*, the regional body that also has the function of issuing a prior judgment on the constitutionality of Catalan self-government norms, the reference to historical rights is found in the preamble to the definitive version of the statute of Catalonia, as well as in art. 5, which reiterates it and specifies its legal scope. "The self-government of Catalonia is also based on the historical rights of the Catalan people, its age-old

and Vizcaya. Pursuant to art. 2 of the statute, these, along with Navarra, "have the right to form part of the autonomous community of the Basque Country".

There are two specific organs that are competent to promote *Euskera* and exercise important powers over place names. These are the *Consejo Asesor del Euskera* and the *Dirección de Promoción del Euskera de la Viceconsejería de Política Lingüística*. The former body is regulated by Basque Government Decree no. 3076 of 13th July 2000 on the "Culture Department": according to art. 1 of this Decree, the Department "is organised as the organ for exchange provided for under art. 29 of Law no. 10/1982 of 21st November (normalisation of *Euskera*, note added), for the study, channelling and coordination of the efforts and activities of the various institutions, both public and private, involved in the task of linguistic normalisation".

A permanent body within the *Consejo Asesor* is the *Comisión Especial de Toponimia*, established specifically "due to the nature and special characteristics of the task of normalisation of place names and the diverse nature of the administrations implied by the officialisation of place names ... to provide consultancy and make proposals relating to the determination, amendment and recovery of the place names of the autonomous community of the Basque Country ..." (art. 13 of Decree no. 3076 of 2000 of the Basque Government).

Article 16 of Decree no. 3076 of 2000 lists the functions of the "Special Commission on Place Names" which consists, *inter alia*, of consultancy (which in the author's view is mandatory according to a reading of paragraph one) for the autonomous administration "on the needs and priorities relating to the collection, recovery, inventory and conservation of the places names of the autonomous community of the Basque Country", consultancy on the same

institutions and the Catalan legal tradition, which this statute incorporates and updates pursuant to art. 2, the second transitional provision and other Constitutional principles, resulting in the recognition of a special position of the Generalitat vis-à-vis civil law, language culture, their protection within education and the institutional system into which the Generalitat is organised". That "also" and the incorporation of historical rights into the statute ensure that the arrangements are constitutional (or rather, should ensure this, since in order to be certain about this assertion it will be necessary to await the judgment of the Constitutional Court on the Catalan statute). The Constitutional Court had denied any constitutional relevance to historical rights, ruling that "The Constitution is not the result of a pact between historical territorial entities which preserve certain rights prior to the Constitution and which have higher *status* to it, but is on the contrary a rule of the founding authority which imposes itself with general binding force over the matters within its scope, and there are no prior 'historical' rights that remain external to it" (judgment no. 76/1988, paragraph 2 of the conclusions on points of law). The issue is not simply one of theoretical interest, but would have very practical consequences: the original thinking of the framers of the new Catalan statute sought to associate the assumption of new powers with the existence of historical rights, an operation which, as seen above, is not possible according to the letter and spirit of the current Spanish Constitution.

questions for local authorities where the latter request it (paragraph two) and the drawing up of an annual report on its activities (paragraph three).

A more recent provision, Basque Government Decree no. 1068 of 14th February 2006 which (re)defines the organisational structure of the Culture Department, specifies under art. 16, para. 2c the tasks of the *Dirección de Promoción del Euskera de la Viceconsejería de Política Lingüística* cited above including, *inter alia*, the "normalisation of place names in road signs and in the linguistic environment in general, when this is not a matter for the special Commission on Place Names of the *Consejo Asesor del Euskera*".

The organ cited above took steps to subject the place names of three historic provinces to review: in Álava alone, 30,000 place names were subject to review[40]. This effort is framed against the more general policy of promoting the Basque language which has involved[41] – albeit subject to the difficulties associated with the actual socio-linguistic situation and the contact with two languages with significant international standing, namely Castilian and French[42] – copious legal regulation[43]. In recent years, the Constitutional Court has twice been called upon to rule on the constitutionality of provisions of the autonomous community of *Euskadi* on language competences and the administration of justice, by judgments no. 253 of 11th October 2005 and no. 270 of 13th September 2006, both of which ruled unconstitutional the powers of the autonomous community of *Euskadi* on the language skills necessary in order to occupy specific jobs within the justice system (which as such should have fallen under state competence)[44] located within the territory of the autonomous community.

---

40 The data may be consulted at: http://www.euskara.euskadi.net/r59-15853x/es/euskara_eaetoponimia/bases/consultaBD_sel.asp?ilocal=c.

41 Proposals for a more incisive language policy are contained in I. Agirreazkuenaga Zigorra, *El euskera en el marco del autogobierno. Propuestas de futuro*, in *Revista Vasca de Administración Pública*, 75/2005.

42 I. Urrutia Libarona, *Estatuto jurídico del euskera en el Paía Vasco*, in J.M. Pérez Fernández (ed.), *Estudios sobre el estatuto jurídico de las lenguas en España*, *cit.*, p. 417.

43 For the years immediately prior to the drafting of this article, see E. Cobreros Mendazona, , *La normativa sobre el euskera publicada en 2005*, in *Revista Vasca de Administración Pública*, 74/2006, pp. 289–296; Idem, *La normativa sobre el euskera publicada en 2006*, in *Revista Vasca de Administración Pública*, 77/2007, pp. 99–106.

44 For the most recent considerations on the question of languages and justice, see R. Punset, *Algunas cuestiones controvertidas en materia de cooficialidad lingüística*, in J. Vernet, R. Punset, *Lenguas y Constitución*, *cit.*, pp. 73–77.

The 1982 statute of the *Comunidad Foral* of Navarra ("*Ley Orgánica de Reintegración y Amejoraminto del Régimen Foral de Navarra*") dedicates art. 9 to the question of language.

The law on language for Navarra, the "*Ley del vascuence*" or no. 18 of 15th December 1986, supplements the provisions of the statute, and has the characteristic of dividing the territory of the "*Comunidad Foral*" into three areas, depending on the historical and socio-linguistic situation[45]. There is a mono-lingual Castilian area, one Basque and one mixed. In the first area Basque and Castilian each enjoy official *status*, whilst in the mixed area, which is a "*tertium genus*", although there are not two official languages, there is "some official use of *Euskera*, both in teaching as well as the possibility for the law to provide that citizens use Basque – with full validity and efficacy – in their conduct or relations with the public administrations in the mixed area"[46].

The "*Ley del vascuence*" dedicates art. 8 to place names:

> "1. The place names of the self-governing community shall be officially denominated in Castilian and Basque, in accordance with the following provisions:
>   a. In the Basque speaking area, the official name shall be in Basque, unless there is a distinct name in Castilian: in this case both shall be used.
>   b. In the mixed and non-Basque speaking area the official name shall be the current name unless, for those expressed in Castilian, there is a distinct name in Basque: in this case both shall be used.
> 2. The Government of Navarra shall determine in accordance with paragraph 1 of this Article, having obtained the opinion of the Royal Academy of the Basque Language, the place names of the self-governing community as well as the official names of the territories, settlements and inter-urban roads, and shall report on this to Parliament. The names of inter-urban roads shall be determined by the relevant municipality.
> 3. The names adopted by the Government, according to the provisions of the above paragraphs, shall be the legal names for all purposes within the territory of Navarra, and signs must comply with them. The Government of Navarra shall regulate the normalisation of public signage, respecting in all cases the international rules that the State has adopted".

The political reality of Navarra is very different from that of neighbouring *Euskadi*, to which it is obviously tied by a very strong bond. This desire for differentiation has resulted in choices by the government of Navarra over recent years watering down the recovery policy for Basque. This process – which is

45 See X. Arzoz Santisteban, *La convivencia lingüística en Navarra*, in *Revista Vasca de Administración Pública*, no. 69 (II), 2004, pp. 35–100.

46 I. Agirreazkuenaga Zigorra, *Diversidad y convivencia lingüística. Dimensión europea, nacional y claves jurídicas para la normalización del euskera*, *cit.*, p. 214.

considered to run contrary to Spain's ratification of the 1992 European Charter for Regional or Minority Languages of the Council of Europe in an opinion issued by experts from the Council[47] – mirrors the self-government decree no. 29 of 10th February 2003, the purpose of art. 16 of which appears to be the conversion of Castilian into the only language within the cultural environment of the mixed area, in contrast to what has occurred in previous years[48].

The linguistic policy of Navarra therefore runs fundamentally contrary to that of most other autonomous communities, which tend to strengthen their own regional languages, as a demonstration of the profound differentiation of the Spanish State comprised of autonomous communities also in regional language policies[49].

Catalonia

The 1979 self-government statute, which already enshrined the dual official *status* of Catalan alongside Castilian, was replaced by the new statute in 2006[50], and the law on language normalisation of 1983 was replaced by the 1998 law on language policy[51]. The 2006 statute has been the object of certain challenges, two

---

47 X. Arzoz Santisteban, *Estatuto jurídico del euskera en Navarra*, in J. M. Pérez Fernández (ed.), *Estudios sobre el estatuto jurídico de las lenguas en España, cit.*, p. 397. Doubts on the practice of Navarra relating to the media with reference to the European Charter, as in a judgment of the Navarra Court of Justice of 1994, have been expressed by I. Agirreazkuenaga Zigorra, *La Carta Europea de las Lenguas Regionales o Minoritarias*, in J.M. Pérez Fernández (ed.), *Estudios sobre el estatuto jurídico de las lenguas en España, cit.*, pp. 133–138.

48 X. Arzoz Santisteban, *Estatuto jurídico del euskera en Navarra, cit.*, p. 404.

49 Within this context that is little inclined towards the reinforcement of the Basque language, the publication by the Basque Government (not by chance in 2000, under a government different from that which was less favourable to the promotion of the Basque language) of the book *Toponimia de Navarra. Criterios de Normalización Lingüística y Nomenclátor de Localidades*, edited by the Royal Academy for the Basque Language along with the Council of Navarra and *Euskera* must be emphasised.

50 On which I refer, as regards the Italian literature, to M. Iacometti, *La laboriosa approvazione di un nuovo Statuto per la Catalogna*, in *Diritto pubblico comparato ed europeo*, 2/2006, pp. 614–639; G. Poggeschi, *La definitiva approvazione del nuovo Statuto di autonomia della Catalogna. Un passo in avanti verso una maggiore asimmetria dell'Estado autonómico?,* in *Diritto pubblico comparato ed europeo*, 3/2006, pp. 1340–1352; I. Ruggiu, *Il nuovo Statuto catalano*, in *Le Regioni*, 2/2007, pp. 281–313 and E. Aja, *La riforma dello Statuto catalano del 2006*, in *Diritto pubblico comparato ed europeo*, 3/2007, pp. 1133–1155. The articles cited all contain references to the already copious Spanish literature on this matter.

51 This law has been defined as "second generation" compared to the previous one: E. Pons Parera, *Estatuto jurídico de las lenguas en Cataluña*, in J.M. Pérez Fernández (ed.), *Estudios sobre el estatuto jurídico de las lenguas en España, cit.*, p. 294; on the Catalan language law,

of which were of considerable size[52]. After a wait of four years due to internal problems[53], the Constitutional Court issued the important judgment no. 31 of 28th June 2010, which essentially safeguards the central core of the State, negating however its scope for innovation and moderating the use of exclusive competences[54]. The statute's articles governing place names were upheld; on the other hand, the Court ruled unconstitutional the expression "*preferential use*" which art. 6 imposed for the public administration and public means of communication in Catalonia[55].

Already Decree no. 106 of 16th April 1982, which restates the definition laid down by Royal Decree no. 334 of 12th February 1982, provided for the compulsory use of Catalan, without however excluding the use of the other official language.

The issue of place names receives specific attention under art. 18 of the law on language policy:

"1. The sole official form of the place names of Catalonia shall be that in Catalan, in agreement with the linguistic standards of the Institute of Catalan Studies, except those from the Val d'Aran, the official form of which shall be in Aranese.
2. The determination of the names of the municipalities and districts shall be governed by the legislation on local authorities.
3. The determination of the names of urban streets and of settlements of any type shall be a matter for the municipalities, whilst the determination of other place names in Catalonia shall be a matter for the Government of the *Generalitat*, including inter-urban roads, irrespective of the body responsible for them.
4. The names referred to in paragraphs 2 and 3 shall be the legal names for all purposes and signs must comply with them. It shall be a matter for the Government of the *Generalitat* to regulate the normalisation of public signage, respecting in all cases the international rules that have been transposed into domestic law".

---

see in Italian G. Poggeschi, *La nuova legge linguistica catalana nel quadro dell'evoluzione dello Stato regionale spagnolo*, in *Le Regioni*, 5/1998, pp. 1107–1144.

52 These were the challenges by the *Partido Popular* and by the *Defensor del Pueblo* concerning, *inter alia*, various aspects related to symbolic issues (the classification of Catalonia as a nation) and substantive (the powers "locked in" by Catalonia).

53 For greater detail, see M. Iacometti, *Ricusazioni "a raffica" per il* Tribunal Constitucional, in *Diritto pubblico comparato ed europeo*, 2/2007, pp. 1031–1051.

54 For a commentary on the Constitutional Court judgment no. 31/2010, see the special online issue of the *Revista catalana de Dret Públic*: http://www10.gencat.net/eapc_revistadret/recursos_interes/especial%20estatut/documents%20especial%20estatut/document.2010-07-15.7236299341/ca.

55 See in this regard the comments included in the special online issue of the *Revista catalana de Dret Públic* cited in the previous note, by A. Milian Massana, X. Muro Bas, A.M. Pla Boix and E. Pons Parera.

The article cited above was implemented specifically by Decree no. 78 of 8th February 1991 on the use of place names, as amended by Decrees no. 59 of 23rd February 2001 establishing the Commission on Place Names and no. 6 of 23rd January 2001 regulating the procedure for changes to the names of population centres and decentralised municipal bodies[56]. The regulation of the names of local authorities in Catalonia has also been the object of the recent Decree no. 139 of 26th June 2007, issued accordingly following the enactment of the self-government statute of 2006.

According to art. 1 of this legislation, "the names of the municipalities of Catalonia shall be those included in the Register of local authorities of Catalonia". Articles 2 and 6 govern the change and rectification of place names. Changes in place names are governed by art. 2: they are ordered by the municipality concerned by majority vote approved by those entitled on the municipal council, which may also request an opinion from the Institute of Catalan Studies (IEC). According to art. 3, if the latter does not state its opinion before the time limit specified, the change of name is considered to have been accepted. If the opinion of the Institute of Catalan Studies is not favourable to the change, the municipality must make a decision within a time limit of three months. It may restate its choice by absolute majority, whilst if on the other hand it does not make a decision, it will be considered to have discontinued the procedure. This thus amounts to a good combination between political will and the respect for the linguistic and historical criteria safeguarded by a prestigious institution such as the Institute of Catalan Studies.

It can already be understood from the example provided that Catalan legislation on language rights and duties is the body of law that is most developed from the entire Spanish State, and this broad reach also relates to place names. The degree of detail in language regulation in Catalonia is moreover unrivalled throughout Europe, with the partial exception of *Euskadi* and the South Tyrol.

The new self-government statute for Catalonia, which confirms the tendency towards hyper-regulation also over language issues, dedicates two provisions to place names, namely art. 151 and art. 155. Both form part of a very long list of the competences of the *Generalitat*: according to the first (point b), it is responsible for "… the name and choice of the capital city and the symbols of the municipals and other local authorities, place names and the determination of special arrangements". The second, governing "intellectual and industrial property", provides under paragraph 2b that the competences of the *Generalitat*

56 This provision, along with the others in this area adopted by the central State and the autonomous community of Catalonia, may be consulted at http://www6.gencat.net/llengcat/informe/catala/dictamen.pdf

include "the legal and procedural defence of the place names of Catalonia applied to the industrial sector".

This means that private initiative is also subject to linguistic duties, according to principles laid down by the 1998 law on language policy[57]. It is clear that where the regional legislature has also taken steps to regulate language use in the industrial sector, which is normally governed by principles of private law, the public *status* of this language is already fairly strong, being guaranteed both under applicable legislation as well as policy choices and their social force. The "threat" for Catalan comes not only from Castilian, but also from English, the language of the multinationals that are present in large numbers of the most economically developed of the autonomous communities throughout Spain, but which are not happy at the imposition of a local language such as Catalan, as important as it may be[58]. This is therefore the reason for the provisions such as those cited from art. 155, which cannot even be remotely conceivable in other linguistic realities.

The decided prevalence of the use of Catalan in certain contexts (such as place names and education)[59] is thrown into doubt today by the ruling in judgment no. 31/2010 of the Constitutional Court that the expression "*uso preferente del catalán*" is unconstitutional.

The Balearic Islands

The joint official *status* of Catalan, in the variant used in the Balearic Islands, and of Castilian was already enshrined under art. 3 of the self-government statute (basic law of 25th February 1983)[60]. The subsequent law on linguistic normalisation, no. 3 of 29th April 1986, dedicates art. 14 to the issue of place names:

57 On the issue of usage in public and private, see A. Milian Massana, *Público y privado en la normalización lingüística*, Barcelona, 2000.

58 The technique sought by the Catalan authorities with the multinationals is the use of agreements which "advise" the latter also to use Catalan, which would however in practice prove to be compulsory under Catalan legislation. The use of agreements in any case avoids the imposition of penalties, which is disliked by both parties.

59 The predominance of the use of Catalan in public education was also placed in doubt by the case law of the Supreme Court following judgment no. 31/2010 of the Constitutional Court, in judgments of 9th, 13th and 16th December 2010.

60 For a detailed analysis of the *status* of Catalan in the Balearic Islands, see B. Colom Pastor, *Estatuto jurídico del catalán en las Illes Balears*, in J. M. Pérez Fernández (ed.), *Estudios sobre el estatuto jurídico de las lenguas en España, cit.*, pp. 325–347.

“1. The sole official form of place names of the Balearic Islands shall be that in Catalan.
2. The determination of the official names of the municipalities, territories, settlements, inter-urban roads in general and the place names of the autonomous community shall be matter for the Government of the autonomous community, in agreement with the opinion of the University of the Balearic Islands. The names of urban streets must be determined by the relevant municipalities, also subject to the requirement of consultancy mentioned above, giving preference to the traditional popular place name and to elements of autochthonous cultures.
3. These names shall be the legal names for all purposes and signs must comply with them”.

Decree no. 36 of 23rd April 1989 on place names contains a list of the official versions of place names in the autonomous community. The weight of tourism, the primary industry of the Balearic Islands, also impinges upon the reality of place names: whilst it may be so that Catalan names are the official ones, to give an example of a renowned locality, the Castilian name *Ibiza* is much more widespread throughout the world than the Catalan name *Eivissa*, also thanks to a car model which uses the Castilian version. This shows that at times the official version, which correctly mirrors the local reality, is not mirrored by an equal international diffusion of the terms for certain localities that are famous throughout the world. It is important to add to this the fact that the mass presence of tourists, including in particular many Germans, has developed a micro-toponomy and commercial signage in German, which obviously does not have any impact on the traditional names of localities, though it certainly does on the linguistic environment[61].

Valencia

The question of place names in Valencia cannot be analysed without reference to the linguistic and terminological conflict which sees the supporters of the unity of the Catalan language pitched against the so-called “secessionists”, that is those who consider Valencian to be a distinct language from Catalan[62]. The official name is the Valencian language, but linguists (except a small minority, who are certainly not the most accredited) are agreed in considering Valencian to be a variant of Catalan or at the very least as forming part of the same linguistic family. Some judgments have endorsed this position[63], but the term Valencian

61 The same applies to the English “colonies” in the autonomous communities of Valencia and Murcia and in Andalusia, which are no longer comprised of tourists, but permanent residents.

62 G. Poggeschi, *Le nazioni linguistiche della Spagna* autonómica, *cit.*, pp. 356–376.

63 A very detailed recent account is contained in J. Ochoa Monzó, *Estatuto jurídico del valenciano*, in J.M. Pérez Fernández (ed.), *Estudios sobre el estatuto jurídico de las lenguas en España*, *cit.*, pp. 352–362.

remains the official one. Moreover, not all those who speak Valencian deny the unity with Catalan; historical reasons explain this terminology which, for legal reasons, is also used here[64].

In fact, art. 7 of the first self-government statute for Valencia from 1982 states that Castilian and Valencian both have official *status*, though limited the official *status* of the latter to the areas where it is traditionally spoken, and hence to the exclusion of the internal area that is entirely Castilian speaking. The new statute from 2006, this time in art. 6, essentially confirms the provisions contained in the latter on linguistic matters, with the significant novelty of the definition of Valencian as the "own language" of the autonomous community.

The Valencian law on language, which is called the "*Law on the use and teaching of Valencian*", or Law no. 4 of 23rd November 1983, dedicates art. 15 to place names:

> "1. The determination of the official names of the municipalities, territories, settlements, geographical places, inter-urban roads and place names of the Valencian community shall be matter for the Council of the Valencian Generalitat, in accordance with the legal procedures provided for. The names of urban streets shall be determined by the relevant municipalities.
> 2. The decisions adopted by the Council, in accordance with the provisions of the previous paragraph, shall be the legal names for all purposes, and public signs are to be displayed in accordance with them according to procedures to be determined by regulation, and without prejudice to the respect due to international rules signed by the State in this area.
> 3. Any municipalities that have names in the two languages of the community shall display their name in both.
> 4. The names adopted by the Council in accordance with the provisions of paragraph one shall be displayed in signs in the two official languages, insofar as the official name permits".

The regulations implementing this Law are contained in Decree no. 58 of 13th April 1992 governing the procedures for changing the names of municipalities. The Ordinance of 1st December 1993 of the regional department of education and science, implementing Decree no. 145 of 24th November 1986, provides for the use of the official languages in place names, road signs and public services located within the territory of the autonomous community.

Galicia

Galician (*gallego*, or *galego* in the local language), a language closely related to the neighbouring Portuguese, receives protection under the 1981 self-govern-

64 See, for an analysis of language rights in the Valencian community, M. Alcaraz Ramos, *El régimen jurídico de las lenguas en la Comunidad Valenciana*, Alacant, 1999.

ment statute for Galicia, the only which dared to provide, under art. 5, for the obligation to know Galician, a requirement ruled unconstitutional by judgment no. 84/1986, which recalled that the only duty in terms of language knowledge, according to art. 3 of the Constitution, applies in respect of Castilian[65].

Galician, which statistics indicate as the healthiest regional language in terms of the percentage of people who regularly speak it, is in actual fact in a less advanced situation of normalisation compared to Catalan[66], the public presence of which is certainly broader and qualitatively more significant within the cultural industry and in various contexts, including universities[67]. Contrary to what has occurred in Catalonia and the Basque Country, there has not been a regular development in Galicia of the language legislation contained in the statute and the normalisation law[68]. The change in the governing majority in the autonomous province in 2005, now supported by a coalition of socialists and nationalists from the *Bloque Nacional Galego*, and no longer the Popular Party and its charismatic former President Fraga, appears to have given a certain impetus to language policy in Galicia. A bill for a new language law is currently before the autonomous Parliament.

The law on language normalisation, no. 3 of 15th June 1983, provides as follows:

---

65 It is worth citing the clarification contained in the judgment under examination in the second paragraph of the conclusions on points of law: "... this duty (to know Galician, note added) is not imposed by the Constitution and does not relate to the joint official *status* of Galician. Article 3, para. 1 of the Constitution imposes a general duty to know Castilian as the official language of the State; this duty is consistent with other provisions of the Constitution which recognise the existence of a common language for all Spaniards, the knowledge of which may at all times be presumed, irrespective of questions such as residence or current address. On the other hand, the same does not apply to the other Spanish languages with joint official *status* in the respective autonomous communities, because the article cited does not impose that duty for them. Nonetheless, this cannot be considered discriminatory, since the prerequisites noted above that underlie the requirement to know Castilian do not apply to the other joint official languages. The absence of any constitutional duty to know Galician has nothing to do with the provisions of the self-government statute of Galicia concerning the right of Galicians to know and use the language of their Community (art. 27, para. 20), aimed at guaranteeing its 'normal and official use' (art. 5, para. 3); since the requirement to know *Gallego* is not a simple instrument for carrying out the corresponding duties and exercising the powers mentioned above, as the representative for the *Xunta* (the regional executive, note added) of Galicia avers, without prejudice to the fact that the goal of the public action carried out to this effect may be to ensure that Galician citizens have knowledge of this language".

66 Data which on the other hand encourage moderate optimism have been published in A. Nogueira López, *Estatuto jurídico de la lengua gallega*, in J. M. Pérez Fernández (ed.), *Estudios sobre el estatuto jurídico de las lenguas en España*, *cit.*, p. 449 et seq.

67 It is sufficient to count the legal textbooks in Catalan compared to those in Galician.

68 A. Nogueira López, *Estatuto jurídico de la lengua gallega*, *cit.*, pp. 452–453.

"1. The only form of place names shall be that in Galician.
2. The determination of the official names of the municipalities, territories, settlements, inter-urban roads and place names of Galicia shall be a matter for the Xunta of Galicia. The names of urban streets shall be determined by the relevant municipality.
3. These names shall be the legal names for all purposes and signs must comply with them. The Xunta of Galicia shall regulate the normalisation of public signage, respecting in all cases the international rules signed by the State".

The decrees implementing the provisions of the normalisation law are no. 43 of 23rd March and no. 132 of 6th September 1984, which respectively provide for the functions and composition of the Commission on place names and the procedure for the recovery of Galician place names. Four decrees adopted between 1996 and 2003, establish the official place names for the four provinces, A Coruña, Lugo, Ourense and Pontevedra.

Aragon

The autonomous community of Aragon, tied by historical bonds of a federal nature with Catalonia, is considered to be Castilian territory. However within its borders, especially in the more remote Pyrenean areas, Aragonese continues to be spoken, a dialect similar to Castilian but endowed in any case with its own peculiar characteristics. In certain areas bordering with Catalonia, the so-called *franja*, Catalan is spoken.

Under the self-government statute, which recently entered into force on 23rd April 2007, art. 1 classifies Aragon as a "historic nation", whilst art. 7 is dedicated to the Aragonese "languages and dialects". According to art. 7, para.1, "the languages and dialects of Aragon constitute one of the most significant expressions of the historical and cultural patrimony of Aragon and a social value of respect, cohabitation and comprehension". Article 7, para. 2 provides that such matters may only be regulated under primary legislation. The future law on languages in Aragon, which has remained in draft form for years, "will determine the areas where the use of languages and dialects of Aragon predominates (and will) regulate their legal *status* ...".

Article 7 of the statute on place names is not cited, though it figures indirectly in Regional Decree no. 206 of 22nd July 2003 approving the General Regulation under Law no. 8 of 17th December 1998 on the "Roads of Aragon", art. 108 of which provides that road signs are to be bilingual, respecting the languages and dialects of Aragon[69]. Law no. 7 of 9th April 1999 on the local administration in Aragon provides in art. 23 that:

> "The names of the municipalities shall be in Castilian or in the traditional language of the place name. Notwithstanding the foregoing, in those areas of the Aragonese territory in which the use of another language or dialect is common, the government of Aragon may also authorise, pursuant to a well-founded request, the joint use of the name in this language".

Decree no. 346 of 19th November 2002 confirms the previous provision, adding however the legislation contained in art. 68 on the procedure for changing the name of a municipality.

The law on the Aragonese cultural heritage, no. 3 of 10th March 1999, is another legal instrument implementing the provisions of the statute[70], art. 4 of which regulates the *status* of "minority languages" (Aragonese and Catalan).

The protection of the languages and dialects of Aragon within a less conflictual socio-linguistic context than the neighbouring Catalonia (the same applies for Asturias, as will be seen in the next section) shows how the identity factor is valorised in order to reinforce cultural and political claims, perhaps in a manner which may appear unnatural and forced, but which occurs within the dynamic of Spanish regionalism, which privileges "differential facts"[71].

Asturias

Article 1 of the statute of the Principality of Asturias of 1981 provides that "The *bable* shall receive protection. Its use, dissemination through means of communication and teaching shall be promoted, respecting in all cases the local variants and the voluntary nature of its learning". A specific regional law on the "dialect", on the *bable* or Asturian, implements the general provision laid down by the statute, namely the "*Ley de uso y promoción del bable/asturiano*", approved by the regional parliament on 23rd March 1998. Asturian has a "semi-official" *status*[72], in a similar manner to Aragonese (Aranese is on the other hand official

69 On the legal *status* of the languages and the dialects of Aragon, see J.I. López Susín, *Estatuto jurídico de las lenguas en la Comunidad Autónoma de Aragón*, in J.M. Pérez Fernández (ed.), *Estudios sobre el estatuto jurídico de las lenguas en España*, *cit*., pp. 215–248.

70 Also the previous self-government statutes contained an article dedicated to the language question of Aragon, but the current version is much more detailed.

71 For further considerations on this point, see G. Poggeschi, *Le nazioni linguistiche della Spagna* autonómica, *cit*., p. 389 et seq.

72 See for more detail, J. M. Pérez Fernández, *El marco legal del asturiano: vías hacia el reconocimiento efectivo de los derechos lingüísticos*, Oviedo, 2005; G. Poggeschi, *Le nazioni linguistiche della Spagna* autonómica, *cit*., pp. 376–385.

for a reduced territory within Catalonia). This "semi-official *status*" applies to the entire territory of the autonomous community.

Article 15 of the above law is entirely dedicated to place names (*Topónimos*):

> "1. The official denomination of the place names of the autonomous community of the Principality of Asturias shall be in their traditional form. When a place name is in general use in its traditional form and in Castilian, the denomination may be bilingual.
>
> 2. In accordance with the procedures to be determined by regulation, it shall be a matter for the government Council, having obtained an opinion from the Committee on Place Names of the Principality of Asturias, and without prejudice to the municipal and state competences, to determine the place names of the autonomous community".

The above provision therefore stresses the fact that the traditional denomination, i.e. that in Asturian, is the official one, and relates to the names of the municipalities, parishes and all settlements, as is naturally the case, given the competence of the Principality over local government (art. 11, para. 10 of the self-government statute).

The self-government decree no. 38 of 4th April 2002, which regulates the *Junta Asesora de Toponimia del Principado de Asturias*, is particularly important. The functions which art. 3 of that decree specifies consist in the issue of opinions relating to place names, according to different procedures. The procedure for determining place names initiates with a request from the regional department of culture, acting *ex officio* or following an application by a municipality or a rural fraction [*concejo* (*conceyu* in asturiano) and *parroquia rural*]. The *Junta Asesora* then issues an opinion, having heard also the local authorities, and the regional council then determines the official place names by decree.

The *Junta Asesora de Toponimia del Principado de Asturias* meets at least three times per year, and also whenever it is convened by its Chairman. Its task is significant in a land where place names have undergone changes over the course of the centuries and, at least according to the purists, deformations. Various decrees on the recovery of traditional Asturian place names have been issued over recent years[73], and it appears that something has therefore changed within the autonomous community of Asturias through an awareness of the problem, and the use of the legal instruments of self-government in order to resolve the problems of place names, "one of the most painful aspects of the Asturian linguistic reality"[74].

---

73 For a list, see J.M. Pérez Fernández, *Estatuto jurídico de la lengua asturiana*, in J.M. Pérez Fernández (ed.), *Estudios sobre el estatuto jurídico de las lenguas en España*, *cit.*, p. 277.

74 *Ibidem*, p. 275. In an attempt at greater elegance, I have translated at "painful" the much stronger adjective "*sangrantes*" ("bloody").

5. Conclusions

The legislation on place names in Spain reflects the great linguistic, historical and legal variety of the country. The "linguistic environment" is therefore highly variegated. The recent phenomenon of mass immigration into this country, with the emergence of commercial signs relating to shops aimed at an Arab, central African or other public (the numerous Latin American migrants are already integrated through their knowledge of the common Castilian language), has accentuated this change.

The current reform process for the autonomous statutes is today a matter of attention for political and legal observers[75]. The evolution of Spanish self-government also has consequences in the area of place names: the policy of dual official *status* or of the promotion of dialects tends to lead towards the placing of an emphasis on "differential facts", including in place names. Besides, as is confirmed not only by the Spanish experience relating to "mere dialects", but also that of France and Italy, "there is no need for a language to have joint official *status* in order to be a feature of the linguistic environment"[76].

In a Spain that is increasingly autonomous and increasingly multi-ethnic, if therefore place names are to follow the logics of natural evolution (the manner and intensity of which is albeit unpredictable) of a greater autonomy for the autonomous communities, then signage ("*rotulación*") will reflect the diversity of languages and cultures that also UNESCO has shown it holds to heart in the "Convention on the Protection and Promotion of Diversity of Cultural Expressions"[77]. It is important moreover not to underestimate the separatist tendencies of *Euskadi* and Catalonia: especially in the latter autonomous community, the delusion brought about by judgment no. 31/2010 appears to have reinvigorated that sentiment, which in any case had never abated. A decisive transformation into a pluri-national and asymmetrical federal State would be an extreme solution but useful in order to guarantee the survival of the Spanish State.

---

75 From the copious literature, see R. Tur Ausina, *Stato delle autonomie e riforme statutarie*, in *Diritto pubblico comparato ed europeo*, 2/2007, pp. 630–633.

76 I. Urrutia Libarona, *Apuntes jurídicos sobre el paisaje lingüístico en Euskal Herria*, *cit.*, p. 137.

77 On this point I refer to G. Poggeschi, *La "Convenzione sulla protezione e la promozione della diversità delle espressioni culturali" dell'UNESCO entra a far parte del corpus legislativo italiano. Una novità nel panorama degli strumenti giuridici internazionali?*, in *Aedon*, 2/2007 at: http://www.aedon.mulino.it/archivio/2007/2/poggeschi.htm.

Bibliography

Agirreazkuenaga Zigorra I., *Diversidad y convivencia lingüística. Dimensión europea, nacional y claves jurídicas para la normalización del euskera*, Donostia, 2003.

Agirreazkuenaga Zigorra I., *El euskera en el marco del autogobierno. Propuestas de futuro*, in *Revista Vasca de Administración Pública*, 75/2005.

Agirreazkuenaga Zigorra I., *La Carta Europea de las Lenguas Regionales o Minoritarias*, in Pérez Fernández J. M. (ed.), *Estudios sobre el estatuto jurídico de las lenguas en España*, Barcelona, 2006.

Aja E., Viver Pi-Sunyer C., *Valoración de 25 años de autonomía*, in *Revista española de derecho constitucional*, 69/2003.

Aja E., *La riforma dello Statuto catalano del 2006*, in *Diritto pubblico comparato ed europeo*, 3/2007.

Alcaraz Ramos M., *El régimen jurídico de las lenguas en la Comunidad Valenciana*, Alacant, 1999.

Arzoz Santisteban Xabier, *La convivencia lingüística en Navarra*, in *Revista Vasca de Administración Pública*, no. 69 (II), 2004.

Arzoz Santisteban X., *Estatuto jurídico del euskera en Navarra*, in Pérez Fernández J.M. (ed.*), Estudios sobre el estatuto jurídico de las lenguas en España*, Barcelona, 2006.

Argullol Murgadas E., *Estudio, in Various Authors, La lengua de enseñanza en la legislación de Cataluña*, Barcelona, 1994.

Benoît-Rohmer F., *Les langues officieuses de la France*, in *Revue française de droit constitutionnel*, 45/2001.

Blanco Valdés R., *Nacionalidades históricas y regiones sin historia*, Madrid, 2005.

Bocci V., *La salvaguardia delle minoranze linguistiche dopo la riforma del Titolo V della Costituzione: ancora sulla permanenza dell'interesse nazionale*, at: http://www.forumcostituzionale.it/site/index.php?option=com_content&task=view&id=8&Itemid=0

Cobreros Mendazona E., *El régimen jurídico de la oficialidad del euskera*, Oñate, 1989.

Cobreros Mendazona E., *La normativa sobre el euskera publicada en 2005*, in *Revista Vasca de Administración Pública*, 74/2006.

Cobreros Mendazona E., *La normativa sobre el euskera publicada en 2006*, in *Revista Vasca de Administración Pública*, 77/2007.

Colom Pastor B., *Estatuto jurídico del catalán en las Illes Balears*, in Pérez Fernández J.M. (ed.), *Estudios sobre el estatuto jurídico de las lenguas en España*, Barcelona, 2006.
Díaz-Guerra Ferran M., Vernet Llobet J., *El régim jurídic de la llengua en la retolació pública, la toponímia i la denominació dels ens locals a Catalunya*, in *Revista de Llengua i Dret*, 16/1991.
Gambino S., Amirante C. (eds.), *Il Canada. Un laboratorio costituzionale. Federalismo, Diritti, Corti*, Padova, 2000.
Herrero de Miñón M., *Derechos Históricos y Constitución*, Madrid, 1998.
Herrero de Miñon M., Lluch E. (eds), *Derechos históricos y constitucionalismo útil*, Madrid, 2001.
Iacometti M., *La laboriosa approvazione di un nuovo Statuto per la Catalogna*, in *Diritto pubblico comparato ed europeo*, 2/2006.
Iacometti M., *Ricusazioni "a raffica" per il Tribunal Constitucional*, in *Diritto pubblico comparato ed europeo*, 2/2007.
López Aguilar F., *Lo Stato autonomico spagnolo*, Padova, 1999.
López Susín J.I., *Estatuto jurídico de las lenguas en la Comunidad Autónoma de Aragón*, in Pérez Fernández J.M. (ed.), *Estudios sobre el estatuto jurídico de las lenguas en España*, Barcelona, 2006.
Loprieno D., *La politica linguistica del Québec tra diritti individual e diritti collettivi*, in Gambino S., Amirante C. (eds.), *Il Canada. Un laboratorio costituzionale. Federalismo, Diritti, Corti*, Padova, 2000.
Mazzarolli L.A., *La tutela delle minoranze linguistiche nella Costituzione del nuovo Titolo V*, in *Le Regioni*, 5/2003.
Milian Massana A., *La regulación constitucional del multilinguismo*, in *Revista española de derecho constitucional*, 10/1984.
Milian Massana A., *Ordenament linguistic (EAC 3)*, in *Comentaris sobre l'Estatut d'Autonomia de Catalunya*, vol. I, Barcelona, 1988.
Milian Massana A., *La exigencia de "al menos en catalán" como garantía de la presencia social de la lengua catalana*, in Various Authors, *Estudios jurídicos sobre la ley de política lingüística*, Madrid – Barcelona, 1999.
Milian Massana A., *Público y privado en la normalización lingüística*, Barcelona, 2000.
Nogueira López A., *Estatuto jurídico de la lengua gallega*, in Pérez Fernández J.M.(ed.), *Estudios sobre el estatuto jurídico de las lenguas en España*, Barcelona, 2006.
Ochoa Monzó J., *Estatuto jurídico del valenciano*, in Pérez Fernández J.M. (ed.), *Estudios sobre el estatuto jurídico de las lenguas en España*, Barcelona, 2006.

Palermo F., *Titolo V, minoranze e norme d'attuazione degli Statuti speciali*, in *Forum on line Quaderni costituzionali* at: http://www.forumcostituzionale.it/site/index.php?option=com_content&task=view&id=8&Itemid=0

Pérez Fernández J.M., *El marco legal del asturiano: vías hacia el reconocimiento efectivo de los derechos lingüísticos*, Oviedo, 2005.

Pérez Fernández J.M. (ed.), *Estudios sobre el estatuto jurídico de las lenguas en España*, Barcelona, 2006.

Pérez Fernández J.M., *Principios del régimen juridicolingüístico: en especial, el estatuto de oficialidad*, in Pérez Fernández J.M. (ed.), *Estudios sobre el estatuto jurídico de las lenguas en España*, Barcelona, 2006.

Pérez Tremps P., *El ámbito lingüístico catalán*, in Various Authors, *Estudios jurídicos sobre la ley de política lingüística*, Madrid – Barcelona, 1999.

Piergigli V., *Lingue minoritarie e identità culturali*, Milan, 2001.

Poggeschi G., *La nuova legge linguistica catalana nel quadro dell'evoluzione dello Stato regionale spagnolo*, in *Le Regioni*, 57/1998.

Poggeschi G., *Le nazioni linguistiche della Spagna autonómica*, Padova, 2002.

Poggeschi G., *Language policy in Latvia*, in *Noves SL. Revista de sociolingüística*, Barcelona, 2004 (available also in Catalan at the website: http://www6.gencat.net/llengcat/noves/hm04tardor/poggeschi1_3.htm).

Poggeschi G., *Prove tecniche di "soberanismo" basco all'esame (rinviato) del "Tribunal Constitucional" spagnolo*, in *Diritto pubblico comparato ed europeo*, 3/2004.

Poggeschi G., *La definitiva approvazione del nuovo Statuto di autonomia della Catalogna. Un passo in avanti verso una maggiore asimmetria dell'Estado autonómico?,* in *Diritto pubblico comparato ed europeo*, 3/2006.

Poggeschi G., *La "Convenzione sulla protezione e la promozione della diversità delle espressioni culturali" dell'UNESCO entra a far parte del corpus legislativo italiano. Una novità nel panorama degli strumenti giuridici internazionali?*, in *Aedon*, 2/2007: http://www.aedon.mulino.it/archivio/2007/2/poggeschi.htm.

Pons Parera E., *Estatuto jurídico de las lenguas en Cataluña*, in Pérez Fernández J. M. (ed.), *Estudios sobre el estatuto jurídico de las lenguas en España*, Barcelona, 2006.

Reposo A., *Profili dello Stato* autonomico. *Federalismo e regionalismo*, Turin, 2000.

Richert A., *Noms de lieux en Alsace*, Paris, 1986.

Ruggiu I., *Il nuovo Statuto catalano*, in *Le Regioni*, 2/2007.

Solozábal Evchevarría J.J., *Las bases constitucionales del Estado autonómico*, Madrid, 1998.

Tur Ausina R., *Stato delle autonomie e riforme statutarie*, in *Diritto pubblico comparato ed europeo*, 2/2007.

Urrutia Libarona I., *Apuntes jurídicos sobre el paisaje lingüístico en Euskal Herria*, in *Revista de Llengua i Dret,* 31/1999.

Urrutia Libarona I., *Derechos lingüísticos y euskera en el sistema educativo*, Pamplona-Iruña, 2005.

Urrutia Libarona I., *Estatuto jurídico del euskera en el Paía Vasco*, in Pérez Fernández J.M. (ed.), *Estudios sobre el estatuto jurídico de las lenguas en España*, Barcelona, 2006.

Various Authors, *La lengua de enseñanza en la legislación de Cataluña*, Barcelona, 1994.

Various Authors, *Estudios jurídicos sobre la ley de política lingüística*, Madrid – Barcelona, 1999.

Vernet J., *El pluralismo lingüístico*, in Vernet J., Punset R., *Lenguas y Constitución*, Madrid, 2007.

Woehrling J., *La cohabitation linguistique au Canada: les politiques linguistiques du Québec, de l'État fédéral canadien et des provinces anglophones*, in *Revista Vasca de Administración Pública*, no. 69 (II), 2004.

Minority protection and regulation of place names in Croatia

Francesco Palermo

Summary

1. Introduction. Toponomastics as basic minority rights and its difficult implementation in Croatia

Toponomastics is a multifaceted subject involving various disciplines in which linguistic, historical, ethnographic, cultural and of course legal profiles intertwine. In a legal key, the study of toponomastics regards the regulation of names of public places[1] or more broadly, the "denomination of any kind of place"[2]. The most delicate and complex sector of the legal dimension of toponomastics regards regions in which different autochthonous groups live[3], due to the high

1 See M. Pallottino, *Toponomastica*, in *Enciclopedia del diritto*, vol. XLIV, Milan, 1992, p. 739 et seq. and G. de Vergottini, *Profili giuridici della toponomastica nella provincia di Bolzano*, in *Diritto e società*, 4/1986, p. 651 et seq. See also V. Piergigli, *The legal regulation of toponomastics in Italian law and the specific situation in Trentino-Alto Adige/Südtiro*l, in this volume.

2 Italian Constitutional Court, judgment no. 28/1964 (in *Foro italiano*, 1964, I, p. 875).

3 Hence those generated "after processes of formation of States or due to territorial changes and not as a result of immigration" (J. Woelk, *La tutela giuridica delle minoranze: modelli, strumenti e prospettive*, in E. Pföstl (ed.), *Valorizzare le diversità: tutela delle minoranze ed*

political-symbolic potential related to the use of minority languages for official place names, which evidently express "ownership" (or "co-ownership") of a region by a group. Like the right of individuals to have names, the right of places to have names is an essential and primary factor for a group, legitimizing its presence in a region, and therefore its survival as a group. This is a minority right that could be defined "existential", since it is functional for the recognition and existence of the minority group, at least those with national or ethnic-linguistic character[4].

In this context, the situation of the Republic of Croatia is particularly significant, due to the complexity of the questions implied (historically and legally) and the recent rapid evolution of minority rights in general, and toponomastic rights in particular, in its regulations.

The present analysis illustrates the legal regulation of toponomastics in minority languages in Croatia, with particular reference to the use of Italian, in the general context of protection of national minorities as it has been evolving in the brief history of post-Yugoslavian Croatia. The temporal dynamics will be the thread and background of the study, being an essential factor for the understanding of the current legal situation and its origins (paras. 1.1 and 1.2). Moreover, the right to toponymy in minority languages (particularly Italian) needs to be examined in the context of minority linguistic rights envisaged by the Croatian regulations and defence of those rights (para. 2). In this perspective, it is also necessary to consider the contribution of constitutional law in defining the entity, protection and limits of national minority toponomastic rights in a given language, as well as the fundamental role of "international conditionality" for the development of the "minority constitution"[5] in Croatian law (para. 3), finally drawing conclusions from the data examined (para. 4).

1.1 Development of Croatian laws on protection of minorities: the two phases

Since its adoption in 1990, the Croatian Constitution has dedicated much attention to the treatment of national minorities. Two phases in the constitutional

---

Europa multiculturale, Rome, 2003, p. 59), which excludes other types of communities, even residing in the same place, such as immigrant and nomad communities, whose linguistic toponomastic rights are not in fact recognized.

4 See also F. Palermo, J. Woelk, *Diritto costituzionale comparato dei gruppi e delle minoranze*, Padova, 2008, p. 172 et seq.

5 The term "minority constitution" is used by R. Toniatti, *La rappresentanza politica delle minoranze linguistiche: i ladini fra rappresentanza «assicurata» e «garantita»*, note to Constitutional Court no. 261/1995, in *Le Regioni*, 6/1995, p. 1271 et seq.

evolution of independent Croatia can be distinguished. The first coincides with the era of the first president Franjo Tudjman (1990–1999) who governed Croatia with an iron fist and impatience of ethnic-linguistic pluralism, advancing a repressive, nationalistic policy in which minorities were regarded as disturbing the identification of state and nation proclaimed in the preamble to the Constitution, which in its original version defined Croatia as "the nation State of the Croatian people and the state of members of other nations and minorities who are its citizens: Serbs, Muslims, Slovenes, Czechs, Slovaks, Italians, Hungarians, Jews and others"[6]. Although the Constitution envisaged broad rights for national minorities and adoption of constitutional legislation on the subject already in 1991, the provisions remained substantially unimplemented in this phase, seeming more a concession to international pressure than a true commitment[7].

The second phase began with the death of Tudjman and democratization of the country (1999–2000) and is still underway. With the development of democracy and the slow but visible affirmation of the rule of law[8], national minority rights were also promoted and gradually made effective by a change of overall political attitude towards constitutional provisions regarding minorities and above all by approval of the new constitutional law on rights of national minorities in 2002[9]. As further explained below, effective protection of minority rights – including toponomastic rights in one's own language – has developed[10] since then, though shadow zones, regarding among other things the full effectiveness of toponomastic rights in national minority languages, remain. In

6 See I. Di Carlo, *La questione delle minoranze nelle procedure di aggiornamento degli accordi di Osimo*, in *La comunità internazionale*, V. LI, 2/1996, p. 317 et seq.

7 See J. Marko, J. Kregar, *Il sistema politico croato. Alcuni problemi di consolidamento della democrazia*, in S. Bartole, P. Grilli di Cortona (eds.), *Transizione e consolidamento democratico nell'Europa centro-orientale. Elites, istituzioni e partiti,* Turin, 1998, p. 145 et seq.

8 For more details, see the assessment of the European Commission, Final report "*Reinforcement of the rule of law. Division of competencies and interrelations between courts, prosecutors, the police, the executive and legislative powers in Western Balkan countries (strategic studies in CARDS 2003)*", published in full at: http://www.kfunigraz.ac.at/suedosteuropa/media/Finalreport.pdf.

9 See A. Petričušić, *Constitutional Law on the Rights of National Minorities in the Republic of Croatia*, in *European Yearbook of Minority Issues*, vol. 2, 2002/2003, Leiden/Boston, 2004, p. 607 et seq. In Italian, with special reference to regulation of political representation contained in the law, see also C. Casonato, *La rappresentanza politica della comunità italiana in Slovenia e Croazia*, in V. Piergigli (ed.), *L'autoctonia divisa. La tutela giuridica della minoranza italiana in Istria, Fiume e Dalmazia*, Padova, 2005, p. 313 et seq.

10 As recognized also by the international community. For all, see the Second Opinion of Croatia adopted on 1st October 2004 by the Advisory Committee for the protection of national minorities instituted by the Framework Convention of the Council of Europe, ACFC/INF/OP/II(2004)002.

more recent times, the previous openness towards minority rights has become significantly less convincing, and this trend has a negative impact on the practical enjoyment of minority rights, including the use of minority languages for topographical indications.

The Constitution, amended in significant parts regarding minority rights in 1997 and 2001, now contains various provisions on the subject. The preamble still contains the nationalistic definition of Croatia as the "nation State of the Croatian people", but besides the increase in the number of national minorities expressly recognized (Germans, Austrians, Ukrainians and Ruthenians were added in 1997), its political interpretations has profoundly changed. Among the provisions relevant to the present study, it is worth mentioning art. 3, which includes "national" equality among the values of the Republic, in the sense of equality of national groups living in Croatia; art. 12 establishes Croatian as official language and Latin as the alphabet throughout national territory (para. 1), ensuring by law that in certain places "other languages and Cyrillic script or other alphabets may become co-official" (para. 2); the fundamental art. 15 ensures equality of rights to all national minorities (para. 1) and gives them preferential and guaranteed political representation (para. 3), as well as linguistic rights and cultural autonomy (para. 4), all, however, subject to constitutional law (para. 2); art. 82 stipulates that laws governing the rights of national minorities require a qualified majority of 2/3 of parliamentary representatives for their adoption and amendment[11].

In this constitutional framework, it is evident that the main source of national minority rights in Croatia is the constitutional law on the rights of national minorities stipulated by art. 15, para. 2 of the Constitution. Current constitutional law on the point dates back to 13th December 2002[12]. This is a very modern[13] law that widely protects and guarantees recognized national minorities, although, as we shall see, its implementation is not yet complete due to political, social and economic obstacles. Adoption of the constitutional law of 2002 springs from Croatia's commitment, on admission to the Council of Europe (1996), to modify

11 The Constitution also envisages that all civil, political, social and cultural rights be guaranteed irrespective of ethnic origin and that all can freely associate to protect or promote their social, economic, political, national and cultural aims (art. 44). All have access to public offices and services (art. 12) and religious freedom is guaranteed (art. 41). See J. Marko, *Die rechtliche Stellung der Minderheiten in Kroatien*, in J.Abr. Frowein, R. Hofmann, S. Oeter (eds.), *Das Minderheitenrecht europäischer Staaten*, vol. 2, Berlin et al., 1994, p. 88 et seq.

12 Ustavni zakon o pravima nacionalnih manjina, in *Official Gazette* (Narodne Novine) 155/2002. See footnote 8.

13 Written with the fundamental contribution of the Commission for Democracy through Law of the Council of Europe (Venice Commission).

the previous controversial legislation adopted in 1992, immediately after independence. This legislation was modified and suspended several times and was a tool of Tudjman's nationalist regime.

The true problem upstream of the first legislation on minorities was the numerical strength of the Serbian population[14], which among other things had a majority in the South-Eastern region of Krajina. When Croatia achieved independence during the Balkan wars, the Serbs proclaimed the Serbian Republic of Krajina, occupying about 1/3 of the country with military forces until 1995, when the Croatian army finally conquered the contested territory, expelling a large proportion of the Serbian population[15]. In this context, the general law protecting national minorities[16], and the specific law dedicated to the Serbian minority[17], remained unapplied, especially due to the *de facto* independence of the Krajina region. In 1995, when Krajiina was reannexed and suitable conditions for applying the minority laws were restored, the Parliament decided to suspend application of the laws for reasons related to the hostilities just concluded.

As a result of strong pressure by the Council of Europe to reintroduce and improve the suspended legislation[18], in May 2000 (a few months after the death of Tudjman) the Croatian Parliament partly reintroduced the suspended legislation and amended it to enable proportional political representation of the Serbian population, but did not reintroduce the part regarding self-government of minorities[19]. This timid step forward was not enough to ensure full implementation of the Constitution as far as national minority rights were concerned, and under further pressure from the international community, bills to further modify the previous legislation were presented. These bills still proved too timid and met

14 About 12%, against 0.5% Italians, for example. No other minority reached 1% of the population.

15 Comparing the censuses of 1991 and 2001, we see that at national level the Croatian group was 72% in 1991 and 90% ten years later, whereas the Serbian minority dropped from 12% in the census of 1991 to 7.4% in 2001. Current estimates indicate that Serbs account for no more than 4.5% of the total population of Croatia. Between the two censuses, Serbs decreased by 65%, but all other minorities also decreased (Montenegrins –49%, Slovenes –41%, Macedonians – 32%, Ruthenians –28%, Hungarians –25%, Ukrainians –20%, Slovaks –15%, Italians –7%, Bosnians/Muslims –7%), except for Roma, Albanians and Germans. See Croatian Office of Statistics: www.dzs.hr/.

16 Constitutional law on human rights and freedoms and on the rights of ethnic and national minorities or communities in the Republic of Croatia, *Official Gazette* 65/1991 and subsequent modifications (and suspensions).

17 Charter of Rights of Serbs and other nationalities in the Republic of Croatia, *Official Gazette* 31/1991.

18 See resolution of the Parliamentary Assembly of the Council of Europe no. 1185/1999.

19 C. Casonato, *La rappresentanza politica*, *cit.* (see footnote 9).

harsh criticism by international organizations[20]. Progressive opening of the political climate enabled completely new legislation that replaced the previous laws to be presented and approved in December 2002.

1.2 Toponomastics rights in minority languages in Croatia: general characteristics and respective endogenous and exogenous factors

The constitutional law of 2002 had a broad scope, with particularly significant innovative aspects, in line with the latest legislation on the subject. It aims to be a true "constitution" for minorities in Croatia, almost like a single law covering the whole subject of minority rights (from education to language usage, political representation, self-government, mass media and consultation procedures), without completely succeeding due to certain necessary cross-references to related laws[21] – cross-references that as we shall see break up the legal framework of toponomastics. It is modern because to endeavours to define a national minority[22], envisages "latest generation" minority rights such as cross-border cooperation, dedicates much space to sectors such as the media and is generally deeply influenced by the latest international ideas on the subject,

20 For example, in its Opinion of 2000, the Venice Commission stated that the proposed amendments to the constitutional law of 1991 "do not seem to adequately meet the political needs of minorities in Croatia". Venice Commission, *Opinion on the Croatian Constitutional Law Amending the Constitutional Law of 1991*, 16–6–2000, CDL-INF (2000) 10.

21 For example, the legislation on free association, telecommunications, elections, etc. Among the main laws protecting minorities in Croatia, we recall the law on proper names of 1992, the law on radiotelevision of 1992 (and subsequent amendments in 1998, 2001 and 2003) and above all the law on education in national minority languages of 2000 (*zakon o odgoju i obrazovanju na jeziku i pismu nacionalnih manjina*, in *Official Gazette* 51/2000), which will be discussed further on.

22 The definition in art. 5 is however based on the classic elaboration of Capotorti dating back to the 1970s, and establishes that a national minority is "a group of Croatian citizens whose members settled traditionally in the territory of the Republic of Croatia, who have ethnic, linguistic, cultural and/or religious characteristics different from those of other citizens and who wish to preserve those characteristics". However, introduction of this definition creates a contradiction with the preamble of the Constitution, at least formally: indeed, the preamble contains a list of recognized ethnic minorities (extended after the reforms of 1997 and 2001, but still potentially "closed"), whereas the constitutional law of 2000 contains a procedural criterion and therefore introduces the principle of the "open" catalogue of national minorities recognized or recognizable by Croatian law. On this point, see A. Petričušić, *op. cit.*, p. 612.

especially the Council of Europe's Framework Convention for the Protection of National Minorities of 1995[23], which largely inspired it[24].

In the context of the constitutional law of 2002 and related regulations, the two main profiles for the purpose of this paper emerge. On one hand, protection of minorities unfolds on two levels in Croatia, the local (linguistic rights, educational rights, etc.) and the national one (political representation, self-government of groups and their representative and consulting bodies); on the other hand, the right to toponomastics in minority languages comes under the exclusively local dimension of protection of minorities, being recognized only in areas where minorities exist and above all being delegated for implementation to regional or municipal rule. As we shall see, delegation of the practical aspects of toponomastics in minority languages to local regulations causes various persisting problems of effective guarantee. Finally, as a general rule, and as occurs almost everywhere, also in Croatia the heavy and penetrating laws protecting minorities relegates toponomastics to a secondary plane, helping to make it an "underestimated" right with respect to its true structural importance[25].

Before presenting a detailed analysis of the laws on toponomastics, a further basic consideration is necessary. As we have just seen, the development of constitutional and legislative control of minority rights in Croatia is largely due to the influence of the international community[26]. However, the low consideration accorded to toponomastics in the (hypothetical) hierarchy of minority rights is also a factor in international law, which does not yet seem to have fully realized the importance of the right to toponymy in minority languages, to judge from the few documents dedicating attention to the problem, and the fact that those that do are often limited to generic statements[27]. Thus the right to minority

---

23 In force since 1998 (ETS 157).

24 Croatia ratified the Framework Convention in 1997. See M. Mancini, *La tutela della minoranza italiana in Slovenia e Croazia: lo stato dei rapporti internazionali*, in V. Piergigli (ed.), *L'autoctonia divisa, cit.*, p. 263 et seq.

25 For these considerations in general see V. Piergigli, *The legal regulation of toponomastics in Italian law, cit.* and *Concluding remarks,* in this volume.

26 See M. Dicosola, *Stati, nazioni e minoranze. La ex Jugoslavia tra revival etnico e condizionalità europea*, Milan, 2010.

27 The most emblematic example is art. 11, para. 3 of the Framework Convention for the Protection of National Minorities of the Council of Europe, 1995, that states: "In areas traditionally inhabited by *substantial numbers* of persons belonging to a national minority, the Parties shall *endeavour, in the framework of their legal systems*, including, where appropriate, agreements with other States, and taking into account their *specific conditions*, to display traditional local names, street names and other topographical indications intended for the public also in the minority language *when there is a sufficient demand* for such indications" (our italics). The "official" explanatory report of the Convention stresses that "this provision does not imply any official recognition of local names in the minority languages" (see Council

language toponomastics in Croatia has enjoyed an "entrainment effect" from international laws on the protection of minorities, but as such is mainly anchored in internal control from constitutional, legislative and regulatory sources.

2. Linguistic rights of minorities and toponomastics in minority languages. From closure to openess

Reconstruction of the normative framework ensuring general linguistic rights, especially the right to toponymy in minority languages, calls for analysis of different laws, sometimes in contradiction with each other. The overall picture is complex but it is worth considering a diachronic view to comprehend the transition from a closed system to one of linguistic openness towards national minorities, as well as the recent re-emergence of nationalistic trends.

2.1 Linguistic rights ...

As to linguistic rights of the Italian minority, the first reference is the Constitution, followed by the bilateral Treaty between Italy and Croatia of 1996[28]. The preamble of the Constitution recognizes the Italian community as a national minority. As already mentioned, art. 12, para. 2 states the principle of territorial delimitation of minority linguistic rights (including toponomastic rights), in a framework of co-officiality with Croatian, "in individual local units", or theoretically at municipal level[29].

Besides territorial limitation, there is also numerical limitation. According to the old constitutional law of 1992 on human rights and freedoms and rights of ethnic and national communities or minorities (amended in 2000 and then

---

of Europe, *Framework Convention for the Protection of National Minorities. Collected Texts*, Council of Europe Publishing, Strasbourg, 3rd ed., 2005, p. 29). Point 3 of the Oslo Recommendations of the OSCE High Commissioner on National Minorities on the latter's linguistic rights (1998): "In areas inhabited by significant numbers of persons belonging to a national minority and *when there is sufficient demand*, public authorities shall make provision for the display, also in the minority language, of local names, street names and other topographical indications intended for the public". All these documents are available at: OSCE/Council of Europe, *National Minority Standards. A compilation of OSCE and Council of Europe texts*, Council of Europe Publishing, Strasbourg, 2007.

28 For further references see M. Mancini, *La tutela della minoranza italiana in Slovenia e Croazia, cit.*, p. 268.

29 According to art. 3 of the law on local and regional self-government of 2001, "local units" are municipalities and towns or cities.

incorporated in the constitutional law of 2002), the introduction of co-official use of minority languages (and thus bilingual place names) is affected by the numerical size of the national minority, which has to be a majority in municipal territory in order to become co-official. Co-officiality is not automatic where a minority group holds a majority, but under such conditions may be decided by municipal authorities[30].

These rigid limits weakened when Croatia entered what we have called the second phase of its policy towards minorities. In 2000, the law on the use of national minority languages and alphabets in the Croatian Republic excluded certain ambits from co-officiality (art. 3)[31] but conserved rights recognized by international treaties (for the case of the Italian minority, cross-reference was made to the bilateral Treaty of 1996, which contains more favourable provisions, and to the Memorandum of 1954 and the Treaty of Osimo of 1975)[32]. This tangle of norms has a basic corollary: for minorities whose rights are guaranteed by international treaties, linguistic co-officiality may be independent of (the very strict) general provisions (the need for minorities to represent the majority in municipal councils), if co-officiality of the minority language is in any case envisaged by the statute of the municipality or region. Thus the power to introduce co-officiality ceases to be a solely municipal prerogative, because it can be exercised by the region; the ambit of application however remains municipal[33] or even sub-municipal[34].

---

30 I. Di Carlo, *op. cit.*, recalls that on this point there was disagreement due to recognition of co-officiality of Italian in several municipalities in which the Italian group was not the majority.

31 Minority language and alphabet cannot be used for example towards central bodies of state administration, commercial courts, the administrative court, the Supreme Court and the Constitutional Court.

32 The same holds for other international treaties ratified by Croatia. More generally on this point, see M. De Ciuceis, *L'uso della lingua nei rapporti con la pubblica amministrazione e nell'amministrazione della giustizia*, in V. Piergigli (ed.), *L'autoctonia divisa*, *cit.*, especially p. 342.

33 With regard to the regional dimension, in fact, co-officiality of a minority language, established by regional statute, only regards regional bodies "that carry on activity in the interests of self-government" (art. 8). More specifically, the law of 2000 establishes that in municipalities, cities and regions where the language and script of a national minority is in official joint use, the activity of municipal and town councils, municipal cabinets and regional assemblies and cabinets is conducted in Croatian language and Latin characters as well as in the language and script of members of the national minority. Article 9 states that municipalities, towns and regions, in which there is official joint use of the language and script of the national minority, must guarantee citizens the right to bilingual or plurilingual public documents and bilingual or plurilingual printing of forms for official use. Article 13 states that in municipalities, towns and regions where there is official joint use of the language and script of the national minority, the first written act of an administrative procedure is sent to the party in Croatian and Latin letters

The change could not have been more radical. As far as linguistic rights (including toponomastics) were concerned, the change went from a numerical criterion, extremely difficult to meet, to a political criterion. Now regional or municipal statutes decide the introduction of co-officiality of a minority language and therefore minority language toponomastics. From a legal point of view, this new provision remains an exception (this is so for the law of 2000 and the subsequent general constitutional law of 2002, which confirms the general scope of application at municipal level)[35], although its practical effect is actually revolutionary, marking a transition from widespread official monolingualism to application of linguistic rights (including toponomastics) for certain minorities. The constitutional law of 2002 later endeavoured to "close the circle", maintaining the numerical criterion generally for the introduction of linguistic co-officiality at municipal level by regional or municipal statutes, but lowering it considerably: no longer a majority, as previously required, but a third of the population of the local administrative area involved must belong to the national minority, the language of which it is intended to officialise.

Summing up, the complex fabric of laws and their temporal succession indicates a difficult transition from a formally promotional linguistic regime[36], which was actually extremely limiting for national minority linguistic rights (municipal ambit, municipal competence and majority of the population requirement), to much more open control that while maintaining only a municipal scope of application, enables its activation by municipal and regional statutes, makes generalized reference to international law (bilateral and multilateral) and lowers to one third the minimum threshold of minorities in a municipality contemplating introduction of linguistic equality.

---

as well as in the language and script in official joint use of the national minority. Article 24 states that if the municipality, town or region does not pass use of the language and script of the national minority with the statute, or if they decide contrary to that law, the director of the central body of the State administration suspends implementation of the statute, or any of its provisions, orders direct application of the law and presents the government with a proposal to open a procedure to assess the constitutionality and legality of the statute or another general act of the municipality, town or region.

34 According to art. 6 of the law of 2000, the municipal statute can only stipulate equality of the minority language and Croatian in certain areas, so that not all the sub-municipal administration may be bilingual, but toponomastics and hodonomastics are certainly bilingual.

35 The link between the general constitutional law of 2002 and the law on minority language and alphabet of 2000 is art. 7 of the former, which preserves the rights defined by special laws. The law of 2000 is therefore defined as special (*lex specialis*) with respect to the constitutional law of 2002.

36 For this category, see R. Toniatti, *Minoranze e minoranze protette: modelli costituzionali comparati*, in T. Bonazzi, M. Dunne (eds.), *Cittadinanza e diritti nelle società multiculturali*, Bologna, 1994, p. 273 et seq.

2.2 ... and toponomastic rights in minority languages

With specific reference to toponomastics, art. 10 of the law on minority languages and alphabets of 2000 establishes that "in municipalities and cities in which a minority language and alphabet are in co-official use, the following can be written in bilingual or multilingual form of the same size: road signs and other traffic signs, names of streets and squares, names of places and geographic sites". Moreover, "members of national minorities have the right to freely use their language and alphabet in private and in public, including the right to use symbols, inscriptions and other information in their language and alphabet, in accordance with the law". The right to toponymy in minority languages is not expressly mentioned: the law envisages the right to indicate "inscriptions" or "information" in the minority language, which is functionally the same, though undoubtedly the legal definition implies a restrictive and bureaucratic conception of toponomastics[37].

Still on the subject of the relationship between the laws of 2000 and 2002, the latter makes express mention of linguistic minority toponomastic rights. Article 13 reads: "the law that regulates use of minority language and alphabet and/or the statutes of local self-governing units must determine measures to conserve traditional names and signs, attribute traditional denominations to places, streets and squares and assign names of persons and events significant in the history and culture of national minorities in Croatia, in areas traditionally and most abundantly inhabited by members of the national minorities".

The competence thus defined is generally bestowed on the state by specific laws on minority questions, in particular, as far as we are concerned, the law on languages of 2000 and the "general" law of 2002. However, these laws delegate application to municipalities by provisions of municipal or regional statutes. In practice, municipalities can adopt "measures to protect traditional names and signs", "attribute traditional names to places, streets and squares" and if the original names are unavailable or do not exist, attribute names of figures and historical events that contributed to the history and culture of the national minority (art. 12, para. 1, constitutional law 2002).

The actual implementation of these measures, as mentioned, is delegated to municipal statutes. With regard to the Italian minority, the statute of the region where it is settled, Croatian Istria[38], is of fundamental importance.

37 C. Pan, *Die Minderheitenrechte in Kroatien*, in C. Pan, B.S. Pfeil (eds.), *Minderheitenrechte in Europa. Handbuch der europäischen Volksgruppen*, vol. 2, Wien et al., 2006, p. 217.

38 According to the census of 2001, the number of Italians in Croatia was 19,636. The region with the greatest Italian minority is Istria, with 14,284. It is followed by Primorje-Gorski Kotar with

2.3 Italian toponomastics in the Istrian statute and municipal statutes

The history of the Istrian statute is long and complex[39]. The first statute of the region was approved on 30th March 1994. On 14th April of the same year the central Government proposed taking as many as 35 articles of the statute to the Constitutional Court. These articles were alleged to violate the Constitution and the 1992 constitutional law on human rights and freedom of ethnic communities and minorities in force at the time. The Court admitted most of the Government's observations, cancelling 18 provisions of the Istrian statute, nine of which regarded protection of the Italian community[40].

The political change towards minorities after the death of Tudjman was soon felt even in Istria[41]. In April 2001, urged by the new legislative framework, the regional assembly approved the new statute, which was not only more attentive to the minority question in general, but above all finally authorized (hitherto absent) regional competence on the subject of linguistic co-officiality.

The Istrian statute of 2001 endeavoured to give full equality to the Croatian and Italian languages. Article 6 in its original form established equality of the two languages throughout the region. The Government again contested the provisions in May 2001[42], especially those regarding protection of the Italian minority, but while the judgment was pending, decided to withdraw the case after a political agreement between the regional assembly and the Minister for Justice, which led to certain changes in the statute, finally approved in November 2001[43].

3539 and Požega-Slavonia with 788. The majority of Italians live in the municipalities of Buie (5528), *Pula/Pola* (5375), *Rovinj/Rovigno* (2169), *Rjeka/Fiume* (3330) and Pakrac (869). The expression "Croatian Istria" refers not only to the geographical region of Istria belonging to the Republic of Croatia ("Istria" in the present paper). It is well known that geographical Istria is divided among three States: Croatia, Slovenia (municipalities of *Piran/Pirano*, *Izola/Isola* and *Koper/Capodistria*) and Italy (only the municipality of Muggia).

39 For detailed reconstructions and further references see M. De Ciuceis, *op. cit.*, especially p. 344 et seq. and G. Poggeschi, *Le minoranze nazionali nei Paesi dell'Europa centrale ed orientale*, in E. Pföstl (ed.), *Valorizzare le diversità, cit.*, in particular p. 232 et seq.

40 See judgment U–II–433/1994. On the question see also V. Piergigli, *Lo statuto istriano e il bilinguismo al vaglio delle autorità croate*, in Quaderni costituzionali, 3/2001, p. 630. See also below at § 3.

41 See M. De Ciuceis, *op. cit.*, p. 346.

42 M. Seppi, *op. cit.*, p. 400.

43 V. Piergigli, *Lo statuto istriano, cit.*, p. 631.

The present art. 6 of the statute recognizes co-officiality of Italian, placing it under local self-governmental control[44], and waiving the initial ambition to extend bilingualism to all public bodies and offices in the region[45].

The regulation of toponomastics provides both protection and promotion. The former emerges in art. 14, which assigns competence to the regional government, including "protection of the historical, cultural and national heritage, typical products of Istria and place names" (point 3), according to the concept that place names are cultural goods. The promotional dimension emerges in art. 21 of the statute, according to which "the Istrian region promotes the social, regional, natural, ethnic, cultural and other features of Istria" (para. 1) and "promotes popular Istrian customs, celebration of popular holidays, protection of original place names and local language" (para 2), especially through education ("teaching of the social environment") and training. Finally, art. 25, para. 1, point 2 guarantees typographic equality of toponomastic indications[46], and art. 26 emphasises the provisions of national law with regard to the municipal or sub-municipal dimension of application of linguistic rights[47].

However, as stated above, Croatian governance of minority language toponomastics (and more generally minority linguistic rights) is a stratified system that transfers the whole weight of practical protection to municipalities, thus entrusting the guarantee of a constitutional right to an administrative body. Croatian law on the point is like a many-layered cake: international law (directly applicable by virtue of the supremacy of international law stated in the Constitution), the Constitution, the constitutional law of 2002 and the various special laws (especially the law of 2000 on minority languages and alphabets) and where relevant, as in the case of Istria, the regional statute. However, the only edible layer of the cake is the lowest one: the municipal statute. This merely administrative declination of a constitutional right clearly causes systemic

44 In fact art. 6 as modified in November 2001 states: "In the Region of Istria, the Croatian and Italian languages are equivalent for official use as concerns the work of regional bodies for local self-government".

45 M. De Ciuceis, *op. cit.*, p. 348.

46 The provision envisages bilingualism "in writing, with letters of the same size, the tables of the representative, executive and administrative bodies of the Region, and of legal persons with public authorizations".

47 According to art. 26, "in part or all of the territory of the municipalities and towns of the Region Istria, in which members of the Italian national community live, subject to their statutes, the Croatian and Italian languages are equivalent in official use". This provision reiterates the national law, notably the criterion stated in art. 6 of the law of 2000 on the use of minority languages and alphabets.

problems and problems with guarantees, being entrusted to merely local dynamics[48].

However, with regard to the Italian minority, from an operational point of view, municipal protection of toponomastic rights is nowadays rather widespread and accepted. Many municipal statutes implement the principle of bilingual toponomastics when the numerical conditions defined by the constitutional law of 2002 are met[49].

Among them, an example of the content and techniques of guarantee of this right is the statute of the town of *Pula/Pola* (1994), which stipulates that the town must "fulfil tasks regarding promotion of its historical, artistic, cultural, linguistic, ethnic and environmental identity, in particular observing original toponomastics" (art. 14) and guarantees "members of ethnic and national communities or minorities" "freedom of expression of their national group, free use of their language and script, cultural autonomy, protection of equal participation in public affairs in line with the Constitution, the law, the present Statute and the general and individual acts of the town bodies" (art. 97, para. 1). According to a particularly significant provision, "members of the autochthonous Italian national community are ensured full affirmation of their individual and collective identity, irrespective of their share in the population" (art. 97, para. 2): this provision is now in line with repeal of the numerical criterion as required by the constitutional law of 2002 and international treaties, but which before this law could at most be interpreted as being of a planning nature, because they could not be applied independently of the numerical clause. In other words, this is a courageous provision for the period in which it was approved and has clear symbolic meaning in the determination of the plurilingual and pluricultural identity of Istria and the town of *Pula/Pola* in particular[50]. In line with the above rules, and with special regard to toponomastics, it is stipulated that "road signs bearing place names, street names and names of squares should be in Croatian and Italian" (art. 109).

---

48 It is therefore sometimes criticized by independent observers, e.g. the report of the Croatian Helsinki Committee, Report on the implementation of the Framework Convention of Council of Europe on the Protection of Minorities in Republic of Croatia (*sic!*, so the English version ...) of 1999, available at http://www.minelres.lv/reports/croatia/NGO/croatia_NGO.htm.

49 For the texts of the statutes see: http://dev.eurac.edu:8085/mugs2/do/browse.

50 The preamble to the Istrian statute opens invoking "Istria, a pluriethnic, pluricultural and plurilingual community", see G. Poggeschi, *op. cit.*, p. 233. The fact that this provision was introduced in 1994, in a legal and political context that did not favour it, shows the "positive" side of the coin of fragmentation of language rights entrusted to municipalities alone, because this fragmentation ended up loosening the grip of what was then repressive legislation.

The statute of the town of *Rovinj/Rovigno* (1993) also establishes co-officiality of the Italian language (art. 7), with special reference to "the right to cultural initiative and activity, printing rights, respect of toponyms and popular customs and traditions" (art. 17, para. 1) in order to create "the conditions necessary to ensure that the complete public and official life of the town is conducted with full equality of both languages" (art. 17, para. 2). The provisions of the statute of the municipality of *Novigrad/Cittanova* (1993) are even more detailed, not only recognizing co-officiality (art. 8) but also ensuring members of the Italian community "the right to free and equal use of their language and script, to develop their culture, to fly their flag and exercise other rights defined by the Constitution, the law, the present Statute and other provisions" (art. 15). Regarding toponomastics in the broad sense, it is established that "on municipal territory, all provisions, public signs, notices posted on notice boards of state bodies, the magistrature, independent bodies, local administration, firms, institutions and shops must be in Croatian and Italian using the same letters", a particularly pervasive provision also extending to the private sector. A similar and equally broad provision is found in other statutes, such as that of the municipality of *Umag/Umago* (1993) that in declining the principle according to which "the whole public and social life is conducted with total equality of rights of both languages and forms of script" (art. 13), stipulates that "on municipal territory all provisions, public signs, notices, and printed material of physical and legal persons and all written and oral communications in general are conducted in Croatian and Italian" (art. 14).

3. Constitutional jurisprudence and international monitoring

The legislation on minority linguistic (and specifically toponomastic) rights in Croatia and its practical application by local government shows an overall asymmetrical linguistic policy. The regional and numerical limits contained in the national legislation and complete transfer of implementation of these rights to municipal level lead to diversified treatment of the different national minorities and different degrees of protection of minority communities depending on the municipality involved. Despite this regional asymmetry, the Italian minority proves on the whole to be much better guaranteed and protected than others, being covered by the bilateral Treaty and by virtue of the generally promotional approach of the Istrian statute and the various municipal statutes.

The attitude of internal jurisprudence and the soft jurisprudence of international control bodies[51] with regard to this situation shows that on this subject, national judges are on the whole deferent to the laws and substantially accompany their evolution[52], while the international bodies played a prime role in urging the change in favour of minority rights, which Croatia enacted after the Tudjman era.

With regard to internal jurisprudence, three significant cases demonstrate this evolution. The first is the briefly mentioned judgment of the Constitutional Court to the Government's contestation of the first Istrian statute of 1994[53]. In this judgment, the strong argument enabling the Court to declare various provisions of the statute to be unconstitutional was the excessive fragmentation and "localization" of competences. In upholding the Government's observations, the Court confirmed that only the Constitution and the law can recognize or limit individual freedoms and rights in observation of the principle of equality between all citizens of the Republic, irrespective of the region in which they live. According to the Court, the power to intervene on the principle of equality belonged exclusively to the State. It followed that only the State could regulate special minority rights, as exceptions to the principle of equality. However, this argument contains a basic contradiction, because if the State governs minority rights, transferring their implementation to local level, the responsibility for defective implementation cannot fall solely on the shoulders of local administrations. It is true that the court ruled that the content of the first Istrian statute exceeded its competence on this point (*ultra vires*), but a basic contradiction emerges clearly from the argument: the system transfers the implementation of rights completely to local levels, leaving large margins of discretion to broaden or restrict the range of interpretation left to local

---

51 In particular, the reports of the Advisory Committee set up by the Framework Convention of the Council of Europe were defined as "soft jurisprudence" by J. Packer, *Situating the Framework Convention in a wider context: achievements and challenges*, in Council of Europe (ed.), *Filling the Frame. Five years of monitoring the Framework Convention for the Protection of National Minorities*, Council of Europe Publishing, Strasbourg, 2004, p. 45.

52 For more details see F. Palermo, *Domestic enforcement and direct effect of the FCNM*, in A. Alen, B. de Witte, P. Lemmens, A. Verstichel (eds.), *The Framework Convention for the Protection of National Minorities: a useful pan-European instrument?,* Antwerp et al., 2008, pp. 187–214.

53 Judgment U–II–433/1994, on which see also point 2.3 above and footnote 37. For detailed analyses in Italian, see V. Piergigli, *Lo Statuto istriano e il bilinguismo al vaglio delle autorità croate*, *cit.*, p. 631, G. Poggeschi, *op. cit.*, p. 232, M. De Ciuceis, *op. cit.*, p. 348, M. Seppi, *Lo Statuto istriano. Vecchie e nuove problematiche*, in V. Piergigli (ed.), *L'autoctonia divisa*, *cit.,* p. 383 et seq. and Osservatorio sui Balcani, *Istria: tra Croazia ed Europa*, http://www.osservatoriobalcani.org/article/articleview/140 (2001).

governments. As demonstrated, the judgment of the Constitutional Court and the whole affair of the first Istrian statute show that at least in the first phase after independence, the linguistic policy applied was not at all coherent with the policy declared[54].

The second case arose from an administrative appeal of the Istrian regional government against an order imposed by the Ministry of Public Administration to remove bilingual signs displayed in the regional headquarters and offices of the town of *Pazin/Pisino*[55]. The case was complex and essentially administrative. What counts for our purposes was that at the end of a long line of reasoning, the Court rejected the case of the Istrian administration, but basically on the grounds of the principle *tempus regit actum*: indeed, the Court ruled that the legislative situation in 1998 enabled central authorities to remove the bilingual signs, whereas subsequent evolution of the laws at least partly changed the picture. This judgment is emblematic of the transition from the restrictive regime for minorities before the changes of the year 2000, and the subsequent promotional regime.

The third decision of the Constitutional Court does not directly concern a toponomastic problem, but more generally the basic question of how to interpret minority rights with reference to the principle of equality. In its judgment on the first Istrian statute, adopted in the Tudjman era, the Court considered that the principle of equality could only be declined by the national legislator and that minority rights were strict exceptions to the formal principle of equality. In a subsequent judgment, typical of the "second phase", the Court read minority rights as implementation and no longer as exception to the principle of equality, on the basis of international developments on the subject. In the contestation of the constitutionality of the constitutional law on the representation of minorities in political bodies (which contained positive actions for political representation of national minorities), the Court gave direct application to art. 4, para. 3 of the Framework Convention for the Protection of National Minorities, which establishes that "full and effective equality between persons belonging to a national minority and those belonging to the majority in all areas of economic, social, political and cultural life" "shall not be considered to be an act of discrimination". For the Court[56], attribution of special electoral rights to national

54 V. Piergigli, *L'Europa centro-orientale e la tutela minoritaria*, in Eadem (ed.), *L'autoctonia divisa, cit.*, p. 487.

55 Constitutional Court, judgment U–III–322/1999 (handed down in 2001).

56 Constitutional Court, judgment U–I–732/1998 (12th April 2001, Official Journal 36/2001).

minorities was not an exception to the principle of equality, but a direct implementation of international standards on the point[57].

From these examples it can be seen that the interpretation of the Constitutional Court on minority rights in general and toponomastic rights in particular ran parallel to evolution of the legislation and the overall political climate towards minorities. The "progress" made by Croatia has also been widely recognized by international control bodies. In this sense, comparison of the first two *State Reports* presented to the Council of Europe by Croatia under the Framework Convention for the Protection of National Minorities is enlightening. The first (1999)[58] is still coloured by sharply nationalistic tones, only partly tempered by the diplomatic language[59]. The second, presented after the constitutional law of 2002[60], has a radically different legal framework and the language reflects the change in perspective between the two constitutional laws and the transformation of Croatia from a defensive nationalistic State to a model of legislation promoting minority rights[61].

Likewise, the assessments of the Advisory Committee set up by art. 25 of the Framework Convention and the Committee of Ministers of the Council of Europe between the first and second control cycles on implementation of the convention are also extremely different. The First Opinion and even the First Recommendation of the Committee of Ministers found excessive delay in

57 Cf. the even more decisive judgment of the Constitutional Court of 17th Sept. 2003, U–I/1681/2003. This case was lodged by the Italian union and the Serbian national council against the electoral law.

58 http://www.coe.int/t/e/human_rights/minorities/2._framework_convention_(monitoring)/2._monitoring_mechanism/3._state_reports_and_unmik_kosovo_report/1._first_cycle/1PDF_1st_SR_Croatia.pdf (ACFC/SR(1999)005 of 16th March 1999).

59 For example, in the report it states that the statistical data on minorities (then going back to 1991) are on the whole relatively non indicative of the real situation, because in the meantime there occurred "the aggression on Croatia in 1991, the occupation of one quarter of its territory, genocide, ethnic cleansing of all the non-Serbian population, Croats as well as members of national minorities such as Hungarians, Slovaks, Czechs, Ruthenians, Ukrainians, Roma, Germans, Austrians and others. Non-Serbian inhabitants were either killed or forcibly driven out from their centuries old habitat" (p. 1). This language colours the whole report and tends to justify non application of rights then envisaged, on the basis of the dual premise of Serbian aggression and the ensuing emergency situation for Croatian unity.

60 http://www.coe.int/t/e/human_rights/minorities/2._framework_convention_(monitoring)/2._monitoring_ mechanism/3._state_reports_and_unmik_kosovo_report/2._second_cycle/1PDF_2nd_SR_Croatia.pdf (ACFC/SR/II (2004)002 of 13th April 2005).

61 The second State Report under the Framework Convention appears in explicit denial of the first one. In fact, it expressly affirms that: "Since the First Report on the implementation of the Framework Convention, national minority rights have been greatly improved, especially in the legislative sphere and in the exercise of rights to minority culture and language" (p. 1).

implementing laws protecting minorities (the constitutional law of 1992), especially locally[62], namely, the level at which the guarantee of bilingual toponomastics is implemented.

The most recent developments, however, show a much more conservative attitude by the Croatian authorities with regard to the implementation of minority rights, including the use of minority languages in place names. The step back does not go as far as to modify the current legislation, but affects implementation of the relevant laws, notably the Constitutional Law on the Rights of National Minorities. The shortcomings in the implementation of several key provisions of the law, such as the right to proportional representation of minority communities in the civil service, are sharply outlined in the Advisory Committee's Third Opinion on Croatia, adopted in 2010[63]. With particular regard to the right to display place names in minority languages, the Committee "notes with regret that the situation concerning use of minority languages for topographical indications has not changed significantly in Croatia since the last monitoring cycle. Although the Law on Use of Language and Script of National Minorities and the Constitutional Law on the Rights of National Minorities came into force in 2000 and 2002, respectively, application of the law, which rests primarily with local authorities, is seriously lacking, especially in areas inhabited by many members of the Serb minority"[64]. The Committee "recalls its recommendation in the second opinion and strongly urges the Croatian authorities to take more proactive measures to ensure that the provisions of the Constitutional Law pertaining to the implementation of art. 11 of the Framework Convention be implemented, including at regional and local level"[65]. Such stalling in the implementation of key minority rights is systematic and pervasive and is seen as a step back towards intolerance, as if "the exam" had already been passed. It is noteworthy that this regressive attitude was also remarked with regret by the European Commission in its latest progress reports on Croatia[66].

---

62 In its first resolution on Croatia of 6th February 2002, the Committee of Ministers wrote: "Especially at local level, some authorities appear reluctant to implement measures to remedy the negative consequences of discriminatory practices and other minority-related problems that occurred in the past, to ensure that such problems do not occur in today's Croatia" (ResCMN(2002)1, sub 1).

63 Adopted on 28th May 2010.

64 Third Opinion on Croatia, at § 141.

65 Third Opinion on Croatia, at § 143.

66 See in particular Progress Reports 2009 and 2010, available at: http://www.delhrv.ec.europa.eu/?lang=en&content=2781.

4. Conclusions

Two main coordinates of protection of minorities in Croatian law, with particular regard to the right to toponymy in minority languages, can be drawn from the above. On one hand, minority linguistic rights (especially the right to place names in minority languages) are extremely asymmetrical; on the other, Croatia was rapid in changing nationalistic legislation, repressive of minority identities, into an extremely advanced system with regard to legal instruments protecting the rights of national minorities. However in the last few years, this positive trend seems to have waned significantly, if not ceased all together.

With regard to the first profile, the salient points of the current legislation on the right to toponymy in minority languages (especially in Italian) form an intricate and not always linear complex of laws of different rank and impact, from international sources to the statutes of municipalities, and can be summarized as follows. The Italian community is regarded as an autochthonous national minority[67], a prerequisite for the implementation of rights connected to this *status*, in particular the use of the language in private and public life and at official level[68]. The Italian minority also enjoys the right to free use of its language in private and public, including the resulting right to display inscriptions and information in Italian[69]. A prerequisite for the use of the minority language for place names is recognition of co-officiality of the minority language[70], which is possible at municipal level when at least one third of the citizens of the municipality belongs to the national minority or when this is in any case envisaged by international agreements binding Croatia (as in the case of the Italian minority)[71], irrespective of numbers. Co-officiality of the minority language can also be declared by regional administrations, not with reference to its territory but only its bodies operating in municipalities and cities for the purposes of self-government[72]. In this framework, the rights attributed to toponomastics regard the names of places, geographical sites, streets, squares, road signs and in some cases, when contemplated by municipal statute, also the

67 As stated by the preamble of the Constitution in its 1997 version and art. 5 of the constitutional law of 2002.

68 Art. 7 of the constitutional law of 2002.

69 Art. 10 of the constitutional law of 2002.

70 According to the principle defined in art. 12 of the Constitution as specified by art. 10 of the law on languages and alphabets of minorities of 2000.

71 In particular, for the Italian minority, the bilateral Treaty of 1996 and as far as they apply, the provisions of the Treaty of Osimo of 1975 and the Memorandum of 1954.

72 Art. 12 of the constitutional law of 2002.

signs of commercial activities and shops. Names in minority languages must have the same typographic relief as those in Croatian[73].

Thus there are cities and municipalities that declare or otherwise the co-officiality of a minority language in their area or part thereof[74], through their statutes, determining the place and street names to use, adopting measures to preserve traditional names and signs and attributing traditional names or names of persons or events significant for the history and culture of the minority to places, streets and squares[75]. Although the region of Istria was able to obtain a limited margin to act on this subject[76], the terminal of minority linguistic rights and especially Italian toponomastics remains the municipality. This leads to fragmented protection, varying in intensity and degree of guarantee from place to place. In such a fragmented situation, the role of constitutional jurisprudence, which has gradually modified its initial position that minority rights were exceptions to the principle of equality of citizens, and therefore subject to close scrutiny, in favour of general inclusion of same in the principle of equality, in line with the legislative and political evolution of Croatian laws on the subject, is clearly noteworthy.

The second profile, regarding the rapid development of the "minority constitution" in Croatia, emerges from prior elements and is more general in character. In legally and politically configuring its relationships with minorities, Croatia took a common course for Central-Eastern European countries[77]: the attainment of independence as a nation-State was accompanied by legislation (and practice) aimed at affirming the mono-national character of the constituted State, under the guidance of a charismatic ultra-nationalist leader. However, the nationalistic attitude immediately encountered strong international pressure to temper the more extreme aspects of the legislation[78], increasing the contrast between internal political-constitutional lines aimed at strengthening pre-dominance of the majority, and the conditions imposed by the international community for full acceptance of the new State, which needed to be included in the new international context. The first change of political generation (the death

73 Art. 10, para. 1 of the law of 2000.

74 Art. 10, para. 2 of the law of 2000.

75 Art. 13 of the constitutional law of 2002.

76 Apart from the power to indicate co-officiality in its statute, to be anyway implemented at municipal level, the current statute allows the Istria Region to promote protection of original place names through knowledge of the social environment where the minority was settled (art. 21, para. 2), to regulate protection of place names (art. 14, point 3) and to require bilingualism in the tables of representative, executive and administrative bodies of the region and of legal persons with public authorizations (art. 25, para. 1).

77 See V. Piergigli, *L'Europa centro-orientale*, *cit.*, p. 469 et seq. and G. Poggeschi, *op. cit.*

78 See M. Dicosola, *op. cit.*

of President Tudjman) had to occur for this conflict to resolve in favour of the framework of protection of minorities imposed by the international community. If this path was common to many other Central-Eastern European countries (from Estonia to Slovakia, Latvia and Serbia), the Croatian experience was nevertheless faster and more accentuated. In a very short period, Croatia accepted radical change.

The constitutional law of 2002, in particular, was very advanced from this point of view in the comparative and incredibly rich panorama of minority rights, if compared not only with the previous situation in Croatia, but also with that of many other countries, including Western ones. However, it is clear that a hierarchy of rights like the one contemplated by the intricate Croatian legislation on minorities cannot be completed, as it were, in a single day. Thus certain key provisions for effective and efficacious protection of minorities are still unimplemented[79].

This is also true for toponomastics. Faced with rather generous regulation, practical implementation still has some gaps, due also to asymmetry. However, if the present situation still shows some shadow areas from a synchronic perspective, a diachronic view of the rapid and extremely incisive evolution of minority rights in Croatia since the death of Tudjman and the attainment of democracy, shows a radically different picture. Croatia has certainly made protection of minorities one of its main strengths for accreditation with the international community, and has largely succeeded. Of course the process may have begun by external induction through the well-known phenomenon of conditionality (that enabled Croatia to enter the Council of Europe relatively quickly, but not yet the European Union)[80], and in any case, whatever the cause, it seems undeniable that the country moved at record speed to construct a pluralistic system, also from the ethnic-linguistic viewpoint, building legislation that promotes its national minorities after years of extreme nationalism. In common with several other recent democracies in Central, Eastern and South-

---

79 Among these, the definitive establishment of a system that fully promotes political representation. For example, the positive acts stipulated on the subject of elections, especially by art. 15 of the constitutional law of 2002, are still at odds with the old practice of imposing alternative votes for general elections and election of minority representatives. In this way, political participation of minorities, though defined extremely generously in the constitutional law, is much restricted with the system of quotas and reserved seats, because those who vote for minority candidates are still excluded from the general vote. See on this point the second report of the Advisory Committee of the Council of Europe (ACFC/SR/II (2004)002 of 13th April 2005), *cit.*, p. 33.

80 In general and with many references: L. Appicciafuoco, *Integrazione dei Balcani occidentali nell'Unione europea e principio di condizionalità,* in *Diritto pubblico comparato ed europeo*, 2/2007, p. 537 et seq.

Eastern Europe, however, consolidation of minority rights is still not fully achieved. The pendulum continues to swing between convinced recognition of the multiethnic character of Croatian society and nationalistic temptations, aimed at reducing as much as possible the practical scope of minority rights. While the path towards a multiethnic democracy seems irreversible, its practical implementation is still conditioned by political pressures and sometimes even boycotted by nationalistic forces.

Bibliography

Appicciafuoco L., *Integrazione dei Balcani occidentali nell'Unione europea e principio di condizionalità*, in *Diritto pubblico comparato ed europeo*, 2/2007.

Bartole S., *La Convenzione-quadro del Consiglio d'Europa per la protezione delle minoranze nazionali*, in *Rivista italiana di diritto e di procedura penale*, 2/1997.

Casonato C., *La rappresentanza politica della comunità italiana in Slovenia e Croazia*, in Piergigli V. (ed.), *L'autoctonia divisa. La tutela giuridica della minoranza italiana in Istria, Fiume e Dalmazia*, Padova, 2005.

Council of Europe, *Framework Convention for the Protection of National Minorities. Collected Texts*, Council of Europe Publishing, Strasbourg, 3rd ed., 2005.

Croatian Helsinki Committee, *Report on the implementation of the Framework Convention of Council of Europe on the Protection of Minorities in Republic of Croatia*, 1999, in: http://www.minelres.lv/reports/croatia/NGO/croatia_NGO.htm.

De Ciuceis M., *L'uso della lingua nei rapporti con la pubblica amministrazione e nell'amministrazione della giustizia*, in Piergigli V. (ed.), *L'autoctonia divisa, cit.*

de Vergottini G., *Profili giuridici della toponomastica nella provincia di Bolzano*, in *Diritto e società*, 4/1986.

Di Carlo I., *La questione delle minoranze nelle procedure di aggiornamento degli accordi di Osimo*, in *La comunità internazionale*, V. LI, 2/1996.

Dicosola, M., *Stati, nazioni, minoranze. La ex Jugoslavia tra revival etnico e condizionalità europea*, Milan, 2010.

European Commission for Democracy through Law, *Opinion on the Croatian Constitutional Law Amending the Constitutional Law of 1991*, 16th June 2000, CDL-INF (2000).

European Commission, *Final report "Reinforcement of the Rule of Law. Division of competencies and interrelations between courts, prosecutors, the police, the executive and legislative powers in the western Balkan countries (strategic studies in CARDS 2003)"*, at: http://www.kfunigraz.ac.at/suedost europa/media/Finalreport.pdf.

Mancini M., *La tutela della minoranza italiana in Slovenia e Croazia: lo stato dei rapporti internazionali*, in Piergigli V. (ed.), *L'autoctonia divisa, cit.*

Marko J., *Die rechtliche Stellung der Minderheiten in Kroatien*, in Frowein J. Abr., Hofmann R., Oeter S. (eds.), *Das Minderheitenrecht europäischer Staaten*, vol. 2, Berlin et al., 1994.

Marko J., Kregar J., *Il sistema politico croato. Alcuni problemi di consolidamento della democrazia*, in Bartole S., Grilli di Cortona P. (eds.), *Transizione e consolidamento democratico nell'Europa centro-orientale. Elites, istituzioni e partiti*, Turin, 1998.

OSCE/Council of Europe, *National Minority Standards. A compilation of OSCE and Council of Europe texts*, Council of Europe Publishing, Strasbourg, 2007.

Osservatorio sui Balcani, *Istria: tra Croazia ed Europa*, http://www.osservatorio balcani.org/article/articleview/140 (2001).

Packer J., *Situating the Framework Convention in a wider context: achievements and challenges*, in Council of Europe (ed.), *Filling the frame. Five years of monitoring the Framework Convention for the Protection of National Minorities*, Council of Europe Publishing, Strasbourg, 2004.

Palermo F., Woelk J., *Diritto costituzionale comparato dei gruppi e delle minoranze*, Padova, 2008.

Pallottino M., *Toponomastica*, in *Enciclopedia del diritto*, vol. XLIV, Milan, 1992.

Pan C., *Die Minderheitenrechte in Kroatien*, in Pan C., Pfeil B.S. (eds.), *Minderheitenrechte in Europa. Handbuch der europäischen Volksgruppen*, vol. 2, Wien et al., 2006.

Petričušić A., *Constitutional Law on the Rights of National Minorities in the Republic of Croatia*, in *European Yearbook of Minority Issues*, vol. 2, 2002/2003, Leiden/Boston, 2004.

Pföstl E. (ed.), *Valorizzare le diversità: tutela delle minoranze ed Europa multiculturale*, Rome, 2003.

Piergigli V. (ed.), *L'autoctonia divisa. La tutela giuridica della minoranza italiana in Istria, Fiume e Dalmazia*, Padova, 2005.

Piergigli V., *Lo statuto istriano e il bilinguismo al vaglio delle autorità croate*, in *Quaderni costituzionali*, 3/2001.

Poggeschi G., *Le minoranze nazionali nei Paesi dell'Europa centrale ed orientale*, in Pföstl E. (ed.), *Valorizzare le diversità, cit.*

Toniatti R., *La rappresentanza politica delle minoranze linguistiche: i ladini fra rappresentanza «assicurata» e «garantita»*, in *Le Regioni*, 6/1995.

Toniatti R., *Minoranze e minoranze protette: modelli costituzionali comparati*, in Bonazzi T., Dunne M. (eds.), *Cittadinanza e diritti nelle società multiculturali*, Bologna, 1994.

Verstichel A., Alen A., de Witte B., Lemmens P. (eds.), *The Framework Convention for the Protection of National Minorities: a useful pan-European instrument?*, Antwerp, 2008.

Verstichel A., *Representation and identity. The right of persons belonging to national minorities to effective participation in public affairs. Content, justification and limits*, PhD, EUI, Florence 2007.

Woelk J., *La tutela giuridica delle minoranze: modelli, strumenti e prospettive*, in E. Pföstl (ed.), *Valorizzare le diversità, cit.*

Toponomastics as an instrument of protection and valorisation of the Italian community in Slovenia

Carlo Casonato

Summary

1. Some categories of the study: toponomastics as an instrument of oppression or valorisation of the identity of minority populations

Toponomastics, i.e. the identification and attribution of public place names or the "denomination of any type of place"[1], is not a neutral subject that can always and

---

1 For legal defining aspects, see C.A. Mastrelli, *Toponomastics and its partitions,* in this volume, G. de Vergottini, *Profili giuridici della toponomastica nella provincia di Bolzano,* in *Diritto e società*, 4/1986, p. 651 et seq. and M. Pallottino, *Toponomastica*, in *Enciclopedia del diritto,* vol. XLIV, Milan, 1992, p. 739 et seq. The broad definition cited is from Italian Constitutional Court judgment no. 28 of 2nd April 1964 in which among other things the range to give to the term toponomastics is debated.

exclusively be based on impartial options of a scientific nature; rather, it is an activity that also largely depends on discretional choice of an ideological or broadly political character, aimed at achieving at least partly predetermined results. This profile manifests in areas where more than one language is spoken, where the following approaches can be used, according to the overall policy adopted for minority rights: a) a "repressive nationalist" model imposing monolingual place names; b) a "multinational egalitarian" model that considers the various languages as equal; c) a "multinational promotional" system of imperfect plurilingualism in which other variously protected languages are used alongside an official language[2].

The potentially instrumental character of toponomastics, used for oppression of minorities rather than to protect and valorise them, also emerges in relation to some of its functions. Since it can be used not only for knowledge, identification and communication of places, but also with the cultural and symbolic function of hiding or revealing the link between a geographical area and the people living there[3], it can also be used to negate or assimilate the identity and linguistic specificities of the respective populations, or to promote their respect and valorisation.

From these viewpoints, toponomastics can lend itself equally to attempts to strike the resident population, denying its identity and uprooting its linguistic and symbolic relationship with the area (e.g. the practice of forcible replacement of place names and proper names)[4], or to the recovery, protection and promotion of identities through restoration and valorisation of traditional place names. Under certain conditions (numbers, political and social homogeneity, majority or minority will, autochthonous character), toponomastics can be a powerful instrument of minority protection and promotion, favouring respect and strengthening the identity of the populations in question[5].

---

2 See R. Toniatti, *Minoranze e minoranze protette: modelli costituzionali comparati*, in T. Bonazzi, M. Dunne (eds.), *Cittadinanza e diritti nelle società multiculturali*, Bologna, 1994, p. 292 et seq.

3 See V. Piergigli, *The legal regulation of toponomastics in Italian law and the specific situation in Trentino-Alto Adige/Südtirol,* in this volume.

4 For example, the "Italianization" conducted by senator Tolomei in Alto Adige in the first half of the XX century.

5 Some conditions necessary for minority protection in terms of toponomastics are common to other instruments of minority protection (including minority numbers, homogeneity, political and social cohesion, minority and majority will) and some other conditions are peculiar to toponomastics (the presence and knowledge of a language or idiom among members of the minority population, concentration in a particular area, stability of the link with the area, autochthony). Among others, see V. Piergigli, *The legal regulation of toponomastics in Italian law, cit.,* in this volume. In more general terms, J. Woelk, *La tutela giuridica delle minoranze:*

On this point, the procedure used to identify place names could profit from involving subjects who express minority culture. In deciding place names to assign, the technical-scientific part of the commission could be supplemented with persons representing the sensibility and will of the group to be protected and valorised, in order to make the choice of place names fully respectful of traditional linguistic names in use[6].

Toponomastics lends itself to minority protection and valorisation prevalently in terms of regional rather than personal protection, and with reference to autochthonous populations, in whom the link between the linguistic dimension and residence in a region is relatively stable and historical.

Assuming that toponomastics respects the real linguistic situation and is aimed at protection and valorisation of minority populations living in a region, this paper considers the forms, sources and content that toponomastics has taken in Slovenia as far as the Italian community is concerned.

2. The link between protection of toponomastics and the autochthonous character of the Italian population in Slovenia: historical notes

If the autochthonous character of a population living in a region is one of the conditions for recognition of toponomastics respectful of that population's language, it is worthwhile briefly outlining aspects of the history of the Italian community living in what is today the Republic of Slovenia.

Since the foundation of Aquileia in the II century BC and for about seven centuries of dominion, the Roman Empire partly Romanized the autochthonous populations and partly transferred Italic people to the Istrian area[7]. After subsequent periods of domination of the area by Byzantines, Longobards, Franks, the Republic of Venice and the Hapsburgs of Austria, the demographics of the Istrian area were variegated and complex, nevertheless maintaining a large

---

modelli, strumenti e prospettive, in E. Pföstl (ed.), *Valorizzare le diversità: tutela delle minoranze ed Europa multiculturale*, Rome, 2003, p. 59.

6 On this aspect, we shall see the importance of the municipal level in exercising competence on toponomastics. For example, the statute of the city of Capodistria states that the Council of the self-governing National community, via councillors representing the Italian National Community, must decide the toponomastics of towns, streets and squares in mixed areas of the municipality. See below.

7 Beyond my extreme summary, see among others B. Benussi, *L'Istria nei suoi due millenni di storia*, Trieste, 1924 and V. D'Alessio, *Il cuore conteso. Il nazionalismo in una comunità multienica. L'Istria asburgica*, Napoli, 2003.

Italian-speaking population. In the early XX century, Istria counted a slight relative Serbo-Croatian majority (41%) and more than 36% of Italian-speaking citizens[8]. At the end of the first world war, Istria was part of Italy and Fiume became a free State (1920–1924). Since Gentile's scholastic reforms of 1923 in the subsequent Fascist period, the area underwent forcible linguistic "de-Slavisation" and imposition of exclusively Italian place names and surnames[9].

At the outbreak of the second world war, Italy expanded into the Balkans[10], overcoming the resistance of local forces by particularly brutal methods, which after the war and after liberation of the border by the forces of Tito and the Soviet Union, were turned against any Italian suspected of having collaborated with the Fascist government or the German occupying forces. In the ambit of the Peace Treaty of Paris in 1947, the Free Territory of Trieste was proclaimed. Like zone A, it was assigned to Allied control, whereas zone B came under Yugoslavian control[11]. The violence perpetrated against Italians, extreme poverty, anticipated discrimination and certain provisions of the Treaty of Paris led to a gradual forced "de-Italianization" of those areas, inducing most of the Italian population to leave zone B and seek refuge within the new borders of Italy. Those who opted to remain were consigned to an extreme minority condition[12].

A later step determinant for the purposes of the present research was the Memorandum of Understanding of London, 1954, in which besides not confirming the existence of the Free Territory of Trieste[13], it was decided to end military government of the two zones and to annex zone A to Italy and zone B to the Yugoslavian Federation. Besides providing certain principles of protection for the Italian and Slav minorities in the areas assigned to Yugoslavia and Italy,

8 See G. Perselli, *I censimenti della popolazione dell'Istria, con Fiume e Trieste, e di alcune città della Dalmazia tra il 1850 e il 1936*, Trieste, 1993.

9 See P. Romano, *La questione del confine orientale e le due guerre mondiali*, in V. Piergigli (ed.), *L'autoctonia divisa. La tutela giuridica della minoranza italiana in Istria, Fiume e Dalmazia*, Padova, 2005, p. 230 et seq., who recalls the order of the Prefect of Pola: "To remove the deformations of surnames perpetrated by Slav politician in recent decades, I order that the surnames of the citizens of this municipality be written as listed below".

10 The Pacts of Rome signed with the Kingdom of Croatia in 1941 established that Lubiana, Ragusa, Cattaro, Spalato and Sebenico became part of Italy and that Dalmazia come under Italian governorship. Like the considerations that follow, see among others P. Romano, *La questione del confine orientale e le due guerre mondiali, cit.*, p. 233.

11 Without prejudice for the sovereignty of the Italian State. For our purposes, zone B is home to what is now an Italian-speaking minority.

12 About 300,000 Italians left, with cases such as the city of Pola, where 28,000 out of a total of 30,000 citizens left in the space of a few months. Istria lost about half of its population.

13 The Free Territory of Trieste never consolidated as such, due to lack of agreement on nomination of its governor at the United Nations Security Council.

respectively, the special statute attached to the Memorandum provided for protection of cultural development and freedom to use one's own language with administrative and legal authorities. As well, the right of minority ethnic groups living in the Free Territory of Trieste and in what had been zones A and B, but only in these, to place names in their own languages, was recognized in municipalities in which the groups constituted at least a quarter of the local population[14].

The importance of this transition was that the Memorandum fixed a principle that would become a constant in the history of the Italian minority in Slovenia, according to which the forms and strength of protection of the Italian community depended largely on where they lived: in particular, persons living in what had been zone B enjoyed a much more effective statute of protection, that cannot be compared with that of residents in "the rest of Slovenia". Despite rhetorical exaltation of pluriethnicity by the new Socialist Federal Republic of Yugoslavia, Italians living outside ex-zone B, and therefore not covered by the specific provisions of the special statute, were particularly penalized, because they could only invoke a generic and difficult-to-enforce principle of non discrimination regarding human rights and basic freedoms, such as that contained in the Universal Declaration of Human Rights of 1948, mentioned in the Peace Treaty[15].

To continue this very brief reconstruction of the major historical passages concerning Italian toponomastics in Slovenia, the Treaty of Osimo of 1975 should be recalled. Besides tracing the final border between Italy and Yugoslavia, the two States formally abrogated the Memorandum and related documents (including the special statute), promising to maintain all internal

---

14 "In the area under Italian administration inscriptions on public institutions and the names of localities and streets shall be in the language of the Yugoslav ethnic group as well as in the language of the administering authority in those electoral districts of the Commune of Trieste and in those other communes where the members of that ethnic group constitute a significant element (at least one quarter) of the population; in those communes in the area under Yugoslav administration where the members of the Italian ethnic group are a significant element (at least one quarter) of the population such inscriptions and names shall be in Italian as well as in the language of the administering authority". See the special statute annexed to the Memorandum of Understanding between the governments of Italy, United Kingdom, United States of America and Yugoslavia concerning the Free Territory of Trieste, signed in London on 5th October 1954, reported in Italian in L. Paladin, *Commento allo Statuto della Regione Friuli-Venezia Giulia*, Udine, 1969, p. 265 et seq., available also at http://www.trattatodiosimo.it/memorandum.htm.

15 See M. Mancini, *La tutela della minoranza italiana in Slovenia e Croazia: lo stato dei rapporti internazionali*, *cit.*, p. 265; G. Conetti, *Aspetti giuridici delle relazioni dell'Italia con la Slovenia e la Croazia*, in T. Favaretto, E. Greco (eds.), *Il confine riscoperto*, Milan, 1997, p. 51 et seq.

measures, adopted in favour of Italian and Yugoslav minority linguistic groups, in force.

In the early 1990s, Slovenia achieved independence together with Croatia and was recognized as a sovereign State that could ratify international treaties. However, Slovenia (unlike Croatia)[16] did not exploit the dimension of international pacts in order to protect (among other things) the toponomastics of the Italian-speaking population.

3. Regulation of Italian toponomastics in Slovenia in international law: weak protection among missing agreements, soft law and self-commitment

Having briefly outlined events surrounding the autochthony of the Italian population (mainly living on the coast) in what is today the Republic of Slovenia, and having identified the original traditional character of the link between area of residence and forms of protection of toponomastics, it is now worth looking at the sources and contents of specific forms of protection. In this section, continuing the historical approach, the fabric of regulation of Italian place names in Slovenia is analyzed starting from international sources.

With a view to recognition of Slovenia (and Croatia) by the international community, Italy wrote an agreement aimed at homogeneous protection of the Italian minority which would be divided by a national border once the two States were created. However, just before the meeting to sign the Memorandum of Understanding (15th January 1992), Slovenia declined to sign the agreement on the grounds of the absence of a provision establishing a principle of reciprocity for the Slovenian minority in Italy[17]. Despite this opposition, which persists and has prevented signing of the agreement, a few months later Slovenia declared that it was "taking over from ex-Yugoslavia" and felt bound by the provisions, among others, of the Treaty of Osimo, which in turn referred to the substance of the special statute annexed to the Memorandum of Understanding, art. 6 of which was designed to protect place names of the Italian minority in Slovenian

16 On protection of Italian toponomastics in Croatia, see F. Palermo, *Minority protection and regulation of place names in Croatia*, in this volume.

17 See historical annotations in M. Mancini, *La tutela della minoranza italiana in Slovenia e Croazia: lo stato dei rapporti internazionali*, *cit.*, p. 266.

municipalities in ex-zone B where the group constituted at least a quarter of the population[18].

Other documents of international character can be considered in this analysis, recalling that since 1992 Slovenia has officially been a member of the United Nations. Although the Universal Declaration of Human Rights is substantially irrelevant on this subject, the International Covenant on Civil and Political Rights of 1966 contains a general principle of equality and non discrimination, also on a linguistic basis (art. 26) and admonishes States against depriving minorities of "the right to enjoy their own culture [...] or to use their own language" (art. 27)[19].

To specify these principles, but merely as an instrument of soft law, it is also worth recalling the Universal Declaration of Linguistic Rights, adopted with UNESCO support at Barcelona in 1996, in which the public powers of ratifying States are invited to adopt all appropriate measures to apply the principles of protection of minority languages. With regard to toponomastics, art. 32 of the Declaration recognizes the right of linguistic communities "to use place names in the language proper to the territory, both orally and in writing, in the private, public and official spheres" and "the right to establish, preserve and revise autochthonous place names. Such place names cannot be arbitrarily abolished, distorted or adapted, nor can they be replaced if changes in the political situation, or changes of any other type, occur".

In the framework of the Organization for Security and Co-operation in Europe (OSCE), let us recall the *Oslo Recommendations Regarding the Linguistic Rights of National Minorities* of 1998 that invite States where substantial minorities reside and request toponomastic protection to provide same for public places[20].

---

18 In general, see I. Di Carlo, *La questione delle minoranze nelle procedure di aggiornamento degli accordi di Osimo*, in *La comunità internazionale*, 1996, p. 317 et seq.

19 In 1993, Slovenia also ratified the Covenant's first facultative protocol, which enables citizens of member States to consult the Committee of Human Rights about questions regarding violations of rights mentioned in the Covenant: see M. Mancini, *La tutela della minoranza italiana in Slovenia e Croazia: lo stato dei rapporti internazionali*, *cit.*, p. 278. Here it is also worth mentioning the Declaration of Rights of Persons Belonging to National, Ethnic, Religious and Linguistic Minorities, approved by the Commission of Human Rights in December 1992, and considered a document implementing and completing art. 27 of the Covenant, as well as the first major change of course in attitudes towards minorities in terms of "dynamic element indispensable for the overall development of the society in which they live", from a viewpoint that is no longer "mere pacification of conflicts and preventive limitation of latent hotbeds of insurrection": E. Pföstl, *Introduzione. Il ritorno al multiculturalismo*, in E. Pföstl (ed.), *Valorizzare le diversità: tutela delle minoranze ed Europa multiculturale*, *cit.*, p. 20.

20 We refer to art. 3: "In areas inhabited by significant numbers of persons belonging to a national minority and when there is sufficient demand, public authorities shall make provision for the

Similarly, the *Instrument for the Protection of Minority Rights*[21], adopted under the Central European Initiative, of which the commitment towards minorities is still only politically binding, is also briefly resumed in the more recent *Plan of Action 2007–2009* adopted in Tirana in November 2006[22].

In general terms, as just shown, the protection of Italian toponomastics in Slovenia is linked to a declaration of substantial respect of the Treaty of Osimo, as far as international law is concerned, and to the principles of generic linguistic protection contained in the Covenant on Civil and Political Rights. This does not mean that the other documents cited cannot orientate (in terms of mere persuasion) Slovenia to protect and valorise place names in minority language. Still in the framework of international law, a slightly different discourse regards the documents adopted by the Council of Europe.

3.1 Protection under the Council of Europe

Slovenia became a member of the Council of Europe in May 1993 and ratified the European Convention on Human Rights in 1994. For our purposes, the Convention only contains a generic principle of non-discrimination, which it may not be possible to interpret as a source of independent autonomous rights, but rather as a general clause to be interpreted only in relation to positions already expressed envisaged in the Convention[23].

The European Charter for Regional or Minority Languages of 1992, ratified by Slovenia in October 2000, is at least theoretically more interesting. In considering use of minority languages in private and public as "an inalienable

---

display, also in the minority language, of local names, street names and other topographical indications intended for the public". The whole document can be found at http://www.osce.org/documents/hcnm/1998/02/2699_en.pdf.

21 Article 13 of the document states: "In conformity with their national legislation, States may allow, where necessary through bilateral agreements with other interested States, in particular with neighbouring States, the display of bilingual or plurilingual local names, street names and other topographical indications in areas where the number of persons belonging to a national minority reaches, according to the latest census or other methods of ascertaining its consistency, a significant level. The display of signs, inscriptions or other similar information of private nature also in the minority language should not be subject to specific restrictions, other than those generally applied in this field".

22 See http://www.ceinet.org/download/CEI_PoA_2007-2009.pdf.

23 With specific reference to minority topics, see among others: E. Pföstl, *Introduzione. Il ritorno al multiculturalismo, cit.*, p. 21. In general: M. de Salvia, *Compendium della CEDU – Le linee guida della giurisprudenza relativa alla Convenzione europea dei diritti dell'uomo*, Napoli, 2000, and C. Defilippi, D. Bosi, R. Harvey (eds.), *La Convenzione Europea dei diritti dell'uomo e delle libertà fondamentali commentata ed annotata*, Napoli, 2006.

right conforming to the principles embodied in the United Nations International Covenant on Civil and Political Rights, and according to the spirit of the Council of Europe Convention for the Protection of Human Rights and Fundamental Freedoms", this document offers a specific and detailed series of measures for protecting and valorising languages used by minority populations. In this perspective, art. 10 (para. 2g) of the Charter stipulates that the parties pledge to permit and promote "the use or adoption, if necessary in conjunction with the name in the official language(s), of traditional and correct forms of place-names in regional or minority languages". In this connection, it is pacifically considered that Italian meets all the conditions to be considered a "minority language" in Slovenia[24].

Despite these measures, the Charter also aims to protect and promote regional or minority languages, *not* linguistic minorities (preamble) and therefore even if it aims to improve the situation of persons speaking those languages, with the objective of developing pluralism and European cultural wealth, it cannot be considered an instrument of direct protection of minorities[25].

In general terms, the Charter has also had little effect, not leading to identification of generally agreed and implemented standards of minority protection, despite the fact that it sets out mechanisms for monitoring application of its principles by a committee of experts having the task of evaluating the relations of single States (see below)[26]. In order to provide stronger guidelines for European States, without exactly defining legal constraints, the Council of Europe therefore drafted the Framework Convention for the Protection of National Minorities. This specific instrument for the protection of minority groups was adopted in 1995 and ratified by Slovenia in March 1998 and contains specific measures on toponomastics. It commits ratifying States to adopt

---

24 Article 1 of the Charter defines regional or minority languages as those traditionally used in the territory of a State by citizens of that State who form a group, numerically inferior to the rest of the population of the State; and that are different from the official language/s of the State; this expression "does not include either dialects of the official language(s) of the State or the languages of migrants". For the sake of clarity, it should be recalled that Slovenia declared Italian to be a regional or minority language, according to the Charter: M. Mancini, *La tutela della minoranza italiana in Slovenia e Croazia: lo stato dei rapporti internazionali*, in V. Piergigli (ed.), *L'autoctonia divisa, cit.*, p. 279.

25 Point 11 of the Explanatory Report of the Charter continues: "For this reason emphasis is placed on the cultural dimension and the use of a regional or minority language in all the aspects of the life of its speakers. The Charter does not establish any individual or collective rights for the speakers of regional or minority languages". On this subject, see J. Woelk, *La tutela giuridica delle minoranze: modelli, strumenti e prospettive*, in E. Pföstl (ed.), *Valorizzare le diversità: tutela delle minoranze ed Europa multiculturale, cit.*, p. 85.

26 E. Pföstl, *Introduzione. Il ritorno al multiculturalismo, cit.*, p. 28.

"adequate measures in order to promote, in all areas of economic, social, political and cultural life, full and effective equality between persons belonging to a national minority and those belonging to the majority" (art. 4, para. 2), and aims to "promote the conditions necessary for persons belonging to national minorities to maintain and develop their culture, and to preserve the essential elements of their identity, namely their religion, language, traditions and cultural heritage" (art. 5, para. 1). In the furrow of these principles, the document calls the parties to endeavour to "recognise that every person belonging to a national minority has the right to use freely and without interference his or her minority language, in private and in public, orally and in writing" (art. 10, para. 1). As mentioned above, besides observation of names and surnames in the minority language, with specific reference to toponomastics, the Framework Convention reads: "The Parties undertake to recognise that every person belonging to a national minority has the right to display in his or her minority language signs, inscriptions and other information of a private nature visible to the public. In areas traditionally inhabited by substantial numbers of persons belonging to a national minority, the Parties shall endeavour, in the framework of their legal system, including, where appropriate, agreements with other States, and taking into account their specific conditions, to display traditional local names, street names and other topographical indications intended for the public also in the minority language when there is a sufficient demand for such indications" (art. 11, paras. 2 and 3).

Although the law specifically mentions toponomastics in minority languages and expresses duty (with frequent use of the formula "shall"), its content reflects extreme caution, resuming two objective and subjective requisites (number and will or demand, respectively) already seen in the OSCE Recommendations of Oslo, thus leaving wide discretion to States as regards the *an* and the *quomodo* of protection[27].

In resuming and re-elaborating values and principles already contained in other international documents, the Framework Convention – also by virtue of its

27 See R. Toniatti, *La tutela delle minoranze linguistiche: il paradigma pluralista della nuova democrazia europea*, in Various Authors, *Le rôle des languages minoritaires dans la vie publique*, *Actes du Séminaire di Saint-Vincent*, 2000, p. 42, who after illustrating the provisions on toponomastics contained in the Framework Convention, the European Charter for Minority Languages and OSCE framework, concludes: "The different formulations of these texts confirms that the paradigm of cultural pluralism gives way to the much more consolidated majority decisional mechanism in legislation, at the price of providing much weaker legal guarantees".

framework character – contains prevalently programmatic provisions that are not directly applicative or legally binding[28].

Despite these weaknesses, the Charter and the Framework Convention define a mechanism of monitoring that obliges the parties, periodically and when requested by the Committee of Ministers of the Council of Europe, to send the General Secretariat of the Council of Europe a report on the State of application of the principles defined in the laws. With the help of an Advisory Committee, the Committee of Ministers evaluates the state of implementation and the effective degree of minority protection, sending the States its opinions, which have attained primary political and diplomatic importance. For expositional reasons, this will be discussed after considering the relative lack of European sources and the wealth of national sources, which in Slovenia deal with toponomastics in the Italian language.

4. "We all are ... majorities": notes on the lack of provisions protecting minority toponomastics and minorities in the European Union

Slovenia has been a member of the European Union since May 2004; thus EU law could be another point of reference for the protection of Italian place names. Since 1993, respect of minorities is one of the political criteria of Copenhagen necessarily to be respected for joining the European Union; after the entry into force of the Lisbon Treaty, the same principle can now be found in primary law (art. 2 of the Treaty on European Union: TEU). However, beyond this general declaration and anti-discrimination measures (art. 19 of the Treaty on the Functioning of the European Union, TFEU, however does not specifically mention language among the grounds of forbidden discrimination), EU law does not offer any express measures for the protection and valorisation of linguistic minorities, not to mention toponomastics in minority language. The paradox is that since the European Union adopted the Copenhagen criteria, double standards are applied *vis-a-vis* "old" members and candidate States who are thoroughly screened regarding their compliance with the criterion of respecting minority rights[29]. The EU's only concern seems to be the respect of cultural diversity and

28 See J. Woelk, *La tutela giuridica delle minoranze: modelli, strumenti e prospettive*, *cit.*, p. 87 et seq.

29 B. De Witte, *Politics vs Law in the EU Approach to Ethnic Minorities*, in J. Zielonka (ed.), *Europe Unbound. Enlarging and Reshaping the Boundaries of the European Union*, Routledge, 2002, p. 137 et seq., writes about protection of minorities as an "article for export

the principle of non-discrimination. Thus, in 1993, the Treaty of Maastricht introduced a general obligation for member States to "respect national and regional diversity", a clause that does not directly indicate at minority protection. Nor does the Treaty of Amsterdam (1999) go beyond the above mentioned clauses of combating discrimination on the basis of nationality, race or ethnic origin[30].

Besides the recognition of the rights of members belonging to minority-groups in art. 2 TEU, as part of the protection of Human Rights, neither the Charter of Fundamental Rights of the European Union nor the two Treaties contain anything more than a prohibition of discrimination on the basis of membership of a national minority (art. 21 of the Charter) and respect for cultural and linguistic diversity (arts. 22 of the Charter, and 165 of the TFEU)[31].

In a nutshell, *de jure condito,* it can be said that the principle of protection and promotion of minorities, not to mention their linguistic expression in terms of traditional place names, is not included in the legislation of the European Union. Inverting the saying that in Europe we are all minorities, from the legal point of view it seems that we all are rather ... majorities (and thus do not need protection)[32].

Nevertheless, as already mentioned and as we shall see below, the will of Slovenia to join the European Union and thus the need to respect the criteria of

---

but not for domestic use". See also the prohibition of discrimination on grounds of nationality and racial or ethnic origin in the TFEU (among others, see arts. 10, 18 and 19).

30 On the relation between the EU and minorities, besides the already cited J. Woelk, *La tutela giuridica delle minoranze: modelli, strumenti e prospettive,* cit., p. 93 et seq. and B. De Witte, *Politics* vs. *Law in the Eu Approach to Ethnic Minorities,* p. 137 et seq., see also P. Hilpold, *Minderheiten in Unionsrecht*, in *Archiv des Völkerrechts,* 2001, p. 432 et seq.; G. von Toggenburg, *A Rough Orientation through a Delicate Relationship: The European Union's Endeavours for its Minorities,* in S. Trifunovska (ed.), *European Minorities and Languages,* The Hague, 2001, p. 205 et seq.; Idem (ed.), *Minority Protection and the Enlarged European Union: The Way Forward,* Budapest, 2004; N. Nic Shuibhne, *EC Law and Minority Language Policy. Culture, Citizenship and Fundamental Rights,* The Hague-London-New York, 2002; R. Toniatti, *Il multiculturalismo nell'ordinamento giuridico dell'Unione europea,* presented at the conference *Società multiculturale e Stato democratico,* Paestum, 18th–19th May 2007.

31 Among others, see C. Piciocchi, *L'identità culturale e la Carta dei diritti fondamentali dell'Unione Europea*, in R. Toniatti (ed.), *Diritto, diritti, giurisdizione. La Carta dei diritti fondamentali dell'Unione Europea*, Padova, p. 119 et seq.

32 We also refer to the paper by R. Toniatti, *Il multiculturalismo nell'ordinamento giuridico dell'Unione europea, cit.* In a different perspective, see E. Pföstl, *Introduzione. Il ritorno al multiculturalismo, cit.,* p. 37, according to which "recent developments in the jurisprudence of the Court of Justice on the question of fundamental rights demonstrates that the teleological interpretation of community constitutional principles and those of member States can provide a satisfactory level of protection of rights, also in the case of minorities".

Copenhagen, including the respect for minorities, were fundamental pressures towards adoption of laws protecting minorities and above all towards their implementation with effective measures, which have bestowed importance and concrete significance on provisions that in other parts of the Balkans have often remained empty phrases.

5. The stronger internal minority protection: constitutional law

In the absence of a bilateral agreement with Italy, international and supranational law seem very weak protection for the Italian minority in Slovenia and its toponomastics, at least legally speaking. However, more important elements can be found in internal law, starting from constitutional rank, albeit not yet explicitly. The Constitution of the Republic of Slovenia of 1992 tackles the theme of the Italian (and Hungarian) minority, framing it in a setting of general protection and valorisation of its characteristics[33]. Article 5 proclaims that the Republic "shall protect and guarantee the rights of the autochthonous Italian and Hungarian national communities", whereas on the subject of language, it is stated that while the "official language in Slovenia is Slovene" in "those municipalities where Italian or Hungarian national communities reside, Italian or Hungarian shall also be official languages" (art. 11)[34]. Though other constitutional provisions go into more detail about the instruments of minority protection[35], there is no specific clause dedicated to the right to express traditional toponomastics in Italian. However, along the lines of part of the Slovenian legislation, it seems correct to apply an interpretation permitting the principle of co-officiality specified by art. 11 to be separated from the rule according to which also the Italian toponomastic dimension is directly

33 In general, among others, see P. Nikolic, *I sistemi costituzionali dei nuovi Stati dell'ex-Jugoslavia*, Turin, 2002, p. 131 et seq.

34 In general, see P. Roter, *Language Issues in the context of Slovenian Smallness*, in F. Daftary, F. Grin, *Nation-Builiding, Ethnicity and Language Politics in Transition Countries*, European Center for Minority Issues, Open Society Institute, Budapest, 2003, p. 211 et seq., also available at: http://lgi.osi.hu/publications/2003/248/ECMI-Vol-II.pdf.

35 See in particular art. 64 on special rights of the Italian and Hungarian autochthonous communities in Slovenia that begins: "The autochthonous Italian and Hungarian national communities and their members shall be guaranteed the right to use their national symbols freely and, in order to preserve their national identity, the right to establish organisations and develop economic, cultural, scientific, and research activities, as well as activities in the field of public media and publishing".

recognized, though not explicitly, at constitutional level[36]. The right of the Italian community to express its identity also through place names therefore seems to be a principle implied not only by the spirit of the Slovenian Constitution. However, as such, acts are needed to specify content, entity and limits.

A first finding on this subject regards the relationship between art. 5 of the Constitution and art. 5 of the special statute annexed to the Memorandum of Understanding of 1954, in which, as already mentioned, it is expressly recognized that inscriptions of public bodies and place as well as street names in ex-zone B, where members of the Italian ethnic group constituted at least a quarter of the population, are also in Italian. This provision, though not expressly ratified in any subsequent bilateral treaty, was the subject of a declaration linked to the Treaty of Osimo, in which Slovenia pledged to maintain in force measures already adopted in favour of the Italian linguistic group. From a substantial viewpoint, it can therefore be interpreted to mean that Italian toponomastics in that area could be among the rights of the autochthonous community that the Republic of Slovenia "protects and guarantees" and has perhaps constitutionalised according to art. 5 of its Constitution.

Regarding determination of the territory within which these rights can be exercised, it is useful to refer to the law on the formation of municipalities and the determination of their territories, adopted in 1994. This act determines the criteria for identifying "mixed-ethnic areas", which, as far as the Italian group is concerned, include the areas thus defined in the statutes of the municipalities of Capodistria, Isola and Pirano[37].

To implement protection of Italian for toponomastics, there are sources of primary rank that act both at substantial and procedural level.

---

36 I refer, among others, to Z. Antonič, A. Zorman, *Linguistic and Sociocultural Transition in Slovenia: The Italian Ethnic Group, Past and Present*, in *Transition Studies Review*, 2004, p. 171 et seq. Also: M. De Ciuceis, *L'uso della lingua minoritaria nei rapporti con la pubblica amministrazione e nell'amministrazione della giustizia*, in V. Piergigli (ed.), *L'autoctonia divisa, cit.*, p. 352 et seq.

37 The statute of the municipality of Capodistria (art. 7) defines the following localities as mixed-nationality areas: Ankaran-Ancarano, Barizoni-Barisoni, Bertoki-Bertocchi, Bošamarin-Bossamarino, Cerej-Cerej, Hrvatini-Crevatini, Kampel-Campel, Kolomban-Colombano, Koper-Capodistria, Prade, Premacan-Premanzano, part of the town of Spodnje Škofije (Valmarin), Šalara-Sallara and Škocjan-San Canziano. The statute of Isola identifies Dorava pri Isoli, Jagodje, Livada, Polje pri Izoli as mixed-ethnic areas (art. 4). The statute of Pirano (art. 3) names the following mixed-nationality areas: Pirano, Portorose, Lucia, Strugnano, Sezza, Sicciole, Parezzago and Dragogna.

6. Primary and statutory laws on "substantial protection" of Italian toponomastics

The starting point to examine the legislation that defines, from a substantial viewpoint, the protection of Italian toponomastics consists in the Act on public usage of Slovenian language, approved in July 2004. This law confirms the principle, first only implied through interpretation as we have seen, that Slovenian is the official language and "the language of oral and written communication in all spheres of public life in the Republic of Slovenia, except when Italian and Hungarian are official languages in accordance with the Constitution of Slovenia, and when the provisions of international treaties that are binding for the Republic of Slovenia specifically allow also the usage of other languages" (art. 1). With reference to the enduring substantial validity of the special statute of the Memorandum of Understanding, it can therefore be said that this law stresses the rule of co-officiality, according to which the use of Italian and Italian toponomastics follows the same rules as the use of Slovenian, but limited to ethnically mixed areas, thus exempting protection from the objective requisite that the numerical size of the minority group be at least a quarter of the total population, as defined by the special statute. This principle is also expressed in art. 3, according to which "in the territory of municipalities where the Italian or the Hungarian national community lives, the public usage of Italian or Hungarian as official languages shall be guaranteed in the manner as regulated by this Act for the public usage of Slovenian and in accordance with the provisions of individual sector-specific acts".

Article 20, para. 1 also provides that "public warnings, written and oral instructions, information and proclamations in the Republic of Slovenia shall be in Slovenian, and, if necessary or customarily practiced, also in other languages". Including toponomastics in the subject of this provision (public notices, signs and proclamations) and broadly interpreting the requisite of necessity, also in view of the "custom" of speaking Italian in mixed-language areas, it can be concluded, confirming the principle implied by the Slovenian Constitution and repeated by primary sources, that place names must also be expressed in the Italian language and according to Italian denominations in mixed-ethnic areas identified in the statutes of the municipalities of Capodistria, Isola and Pirano. Within this general framework and proceeding from general to specific, it now becomes clearer how Italian toponomastics is regulated by the statutes of municipalities containing mixed-ethnic areas[38].

38 The texts of the statutes and part of the legislation cited are available from the site of the Accademia Europea di Bolzano: http://www.eurac.edu/Org/Minorities/IMR/index.htm or

First of all, account must be made of municipal competence on minority and ordinary toponomastics. This competence was defined in 1980 by the Act regulating Naming and Registration of Settlements, Streets and Buildings in which "denominations, redenominations (...) of towns and streets and definitions of settled areas" are generally attributed to the municipal assembly; this competence is confirmed by the law on local self-government bodies approved in 1993, which provides that "in areas inhabited by members of the Italian and Hungarian ethnic communities, councils implement the special rights of ethnic communities" (art. 5).

On the basis of this, the statute of Capodistria (2000) provided the municipality with a bilingual denomination: *Mesta Obcina Koper – Comune Città di Capodistria*. The act also designates a general framework of protection and valorisation of the Italian component, stipulating that: "in harmony with the Constitution, the principles of state legislation and the present statute, the Municipality ensures citizens belonging to the autochthonous Italian national community a position permitting conservation and affirmation of their national identity" (art. 6). With regard to linguistic questions, art. 92 states that "members of the Italian national community are guaranteed the right to freely manifest their nationality, to express and develop their culture and to use their language"; finally, on toponomastics, the statute specifies that "public signs in nationally mixed territory are bilingual" (art. 117). The so-called municipal decree on visual bilingualism of 1998 (decree on public implementation of bilingualism in mixed-ethnic areas) adds that "all writing on signs and road maps, road signs, street signs and signs displayed in stations and stops of public transport (...) and in town public transport vehicles, except place names not in mixed-nationality areas" (art. 6) must be bilingual (art. 5), where bilingual writing is "in Slovenian and Italian with letters of the same form and dimensions" and "graphical representation may be different in the two languages but must occupy the same space and one of the two languages must not appear to be in a subordinate position with respect to the other" (art. 2)[39].

Besides these provisions, art. 118 of the statute of Capodistria imposes widespread recognition and use of Italian toponomastics by public bodies: "In exercising their activities, municipal administrations and other municipal offices,

---

http://xoomer.alice.it/histria/links.htm. See also the research contained in the graduate thesis of A. Lucianer, *La toponomastica italiana in Croazia e Slovenia*, Trento, 2006.

39 In the municipality of Capodistria, this decree confirms Ankaran-Ancarano, Barizoni-Barisoni, Bertoki-Bertocchi, Bošamarin-Bossamarino, Cerej-Cerei, Hrvatini-Crevatini, Kampel-Campel, Kolomban-Colombano, Prade, Premančan-Premanzano, Šalara-Sallara, Škocjan-San Canziano and area no. 243 (part of the town of Spodnje Škofije – area of Valmarin) as mixed-nationality areas.

as well as those of other local autonomous communities, firms and public bodies having public functions, must use names of streets and towns in mixed-nationality areas in their Slovenian and Italian versions".

The statute of the town of Isola (1995) also defines a bilingual municipal name: *Obcina Izola – Comune di Isola*. Citing the above constitutional principles and those of national laws, broad protection of the autochthonous Italian national community is envisaged, with the specification that "in mixed-nationality (bilingual) territory, including the town of Isola and the villages of Dorava and Jagodje, Slovenian and Italian are languages of equal *status* in public and social life". Although there are no express provisions for minority toponomastics, the principle of co-officiality certainly covers that linguistic dimension as well.

The statute of the municipality of Pirano (1995) dedicates a whole part to the Italian national community and its members. For our purposes, special rights in general and the right to express and develop one's national identity and to freely use one's language (art. 65) are guaranteed. This type of cross-reference certainly also protects the Italian toponomastic dimension.

7. Primary and statutory laws on "procedural protection" of Italian toponomastics

Besides defining provisions for the substantial protection, expressed or implied, of toponomastics in Italian language and according to Italian denominations, the various legislative levels in Slovenia also define a *procedure* for concretely identifying traditional names to attribute to public places. The procedure aims to ascertain denominations and to take into due account minority sensibilities, as well as envisaging direct participation of members of the Italian national community. Thus the mechanisms of political representation of the Italian population in municipal assemblies competent on the subject of toponomastics offer participative procedures that ensure fuller democracy before the decision and more fairly shared and more effective results after the decision[40].

The first (general) provision to consider is art. 9 of the above Act on local self-governing bodies, which among other things links determination of the name of the municipality to historical aspects which have to be ascertained by persons who have authentic living memory of the traditional (minority) dimension. Article 8 of the Act regulating Naming and Registration of Settlements, Streets and Buildings of 1980 already specifies that in mixed areas, the minority

40 On the potential of political representation for minority protection, see C. Casonato, *Minoranze etniche e rappresentanza politica: i modelli statunitense e canadese*, Trento, 1998, p. 68 et seq.

community takes part in the decision-making process regarding the names of towns and streets. Since municipal councils have competence in minority toponomastics, it is also worth mentioning the Act on administrative elections and local autonomy, which stipulates that 10% of councillors' seats on local councils in which autochthonous national communities live, are reserved for their direct representatives.

Another related dimension of local Italian representation in Slovenia, from the viewpoint of protection of representative toponomastics and under the procedural perspective chosen here, are the self-governing communities of local nationalities. These self-governing bodies are organs of public law based and legitimized by art. 64 of the Constitution, as implemented by the Act on self-governing communities of nationalities. Constituted at municipal level, these organs aim to protect the interests of Italians in the municipalities of Capodistria, Isola and Pirano[41].

In concrete terms, in Capodistria, the self-governing communities of local nationality must express an opinion, which is obligatory and binding, on town toponomastics in mixed-nationality areas as well as generally on the regulation of visual bilingualism (art. 97 of the statute)[42]. While the statute of the city of Isola stipulates that the self-governing community of Italian nationality must generally be concerned with the particular rights of Italian-speaking citizens, as well as promoting their interests (art. 43), Pirano Council envisages that the same community must express an obligatory binding opinion on decisions regarding toponomastics and the use of local names in mixed-nationality territory (art. 66).

---

41 The councils of these communities consist of components elected on the basis of the law on administrative elections. Only members of the community have the right to active and passive vote, which is exercised on the basis of electoral lists managed by the community and controlled by agents of the Home Ministry. See C. Casonato, *La rappresentanza politica della comunità italiana in Slovenia e Croazia*, in V. Piergigli (ed.), *L'autoctonia divisa, cit.*, p. 332 et seq.

42 On the other hand, a non binding opinion is obtained on the symbols of the municipality: C. Casonato, *La rappresentanza politica della comunità italiana in Slovenia e Croazia*, *cit.*, p. 333.

8. Conclusions: toponomastics and protection of the Italian community in Slovenia

The Italian ethnic group in Slovenia consists of about 2200 persons and is 0.11% of the population[43]. Considering the small size of the group and its coexistence with many other ethnic minorities, the community is sustained by apparently complete and exemplary legal protection[44].

A series of favourable conditions prompted the framers of the Slovenian Constitution and the national and municipal legislator to adopt legislation and constitutional measures ensuring significant protection to the Italian community. Among the positive factors was international political and diplomatic influence, principally the need to observed the Copenhagen criteria in order to join the European Union, the economic and political importance of Italy (homeland of the minority beyond the Slovenian border) and the presence of a Slovenian ethnic group on Italian soil. These and other forces led Slovenia to formulate Italian and Hungarian minority laws, the content and sources of which are summarized below.

First of all, the Slovenian Constitution attributes a series of special and additional rights to the Italian and Hungarian populations with respect to the weak rights envisaged for other minority groups (arts. 5 and 64), in prime position, for our purposes, co-officiality of the Italian language in mixed-ethnic areas (Koper-Capodistria, Izola-Isola, Piran-Pirano). As developed by primary legislation and the statutes of the three municipalities involved, this has led to equal *status* of Slovenians and Italians in mixed-ethnic areas, irrespective of minority numbers, creating an almost perfect bilingual toponomastic model in which the only difference, limited to certain areas, consists in the precedence of the Slovenian name (Act on public usage of Slovenian language 2004). Along with this principle of substantial protection, a procedure of co-decision ensures

---

43 See the results of the census of 2002 and the indications offered by M. De Ciuceis, *L'uso della lingua minoritaria nei rapporti con la pubblica amministrazione e nell'amministrazione della giustizia*, *cit.*, p. 353. In the First Report of the *Advisory Committee* of the Framework Convention of the Council of Europe of June 2004, 3762 native speakers of Italian and 2258 members of the Italian minority were counted. However, since 1991, the population that declares itself to be ethnically Italian has fallen by 700: see *Rapid Reports*, no. 93/2003, *Statistical Office of the Republic of Slovenia* in the Second Report of Slovenia to the Council of Europe, 6th July 2004 (available from the site of the Council of Europe: http://www.coe.int.).

44 See P. Blair, *The Protection of Regional and Minority Languages in Europe*, in *Euroregions*, V, 1993, p. 38; M. Klemenčič, J. Zupančič, *The effects of the dissolution of Yugoslavia on the minority rights of Hungarian and Italian minorities in the post-Yugoslav States*, in *Nationalities Papers*, IV, 2004, p. 853 et seq.

participation of representatives of the Italian national self-governing communities in the identification of local names through obligatory binding opinions.

Good protection and valorisation of the Italian population, including Italian toponomastics, is ensured by this legislation, in contrast to the poor guarantees still afforded to other minority groups, such as Bosnians, Croatians, Serbs and Romany. With regard to monitoring of implementation of the Framework Convention (14th June 2006), a recent resolution of the Committee of Ministers of the Council of Europe concluded that: "[Hungarians and] Italians continue to enjoy a high level of protection, and a climate of mutual understanding characterises the relations between these minorities and the majority"[45].

Bibliography

Antonič Z., Zorman A., *Linguistic and Sociocultural Transition in Slovenia: The Italian Ethnic Group, Past and Present*, in *Transition Studies Review*, 2004.

Benussi B., *L'Istria nei suoi due millenni di storia*, Trieste, 1924.

Blair P., *The Protection of Regional and Minority Languages in Europe*, in *Euroregions*, V, 1993.

Bonazzi T., Dunne M. (eds.), *Cittadinanza e diritti nelle società multiculturali*, Bologna, 1994.

Casonato C., *La rappresentanza politica della comunità italiana in Slovenia e Croazia*, in Piergigli V. (ed.), *L'autoctonia divisa. La tutela giuridica della minoranza italiana in Istria, Fiume e Dalmazia*, Padova, 2005.

Casonato C., *Minoranze etniche e rappresentanza politica: i modelli statunitense e canadese*, Università degli Studi di Trento, 1998.

Conetti G., *Aspetti giuridici delle relazioni dell'Italia con la Slovenia e la Croazia*, in Favaretto T., Greco E. (eds.), *Il confine riscoperto*, Milan, 1997.

D'Alessio V., *Il cuore conteso. Il nazionalismo in una comunità multienica. L'Istria asburgica*, Napoli, 2003.

Daftary F., Grin F., *Nation-Builiding, Ethnicity and Language Politics in Transition Countries*, European Center for Minority Issues, Open Society Institute, Budapest, 2003.

De Ciuceis M., *L'uso della lingua minoritaria nei rapporti con la pubblica amministrazione e nell'amministrazione della giustizia*, in Piergigli V. (ed.), *L'autoctonia divisa, cit.*

45 The resolution is available from the site of the Council of Europe: http://www.coe.int.

de Salvia M., *Compendium della CEDU – Le linee guida della giurisprudenza relativa alla Convenzione europea dei diritti dell'uomo*, Napoli, 2000.

de Vergottini G., *Profili giuridici della toponomastica nella provincia di Bolzano*, in *Diritto e società*, 4/1986.

De Witte B., *Politics vs. Law in the Eu Approach to Ethnic Minorities*, in Zielonka J. (ed.), *Europe Unbound. Enlarging and Reshaping the Boundaries of the European Union*, Routledge, 2002.

Defilippi C., Bosi D., Harvey R. (eds.), *La Convenzione Europea dei diritti dell'uomo e delle libertà fondamentali commentata ed annotata*, Napoli, 2006.

Di Carlo I., *La questione delle minoranze nelle procedure di aggiornamento degli accordi di Osimo*, in *La comunità internazionale*, 1996.

Hilpold P., *Minderheiten in Unionsrecht*, in *Archiv des Völkerrechts*, 2001.

Klemenčič M., Zupančič J., *The effects of the dissolution of Yugoslavia on the minority rights of Hungarian and Italian minorities in the post-Yugoslav States*, in *Nationalities Papers*, IV, 2004.

Mancini M., *La tutela della minoranza italiana in Slovenia e Croazia: lo stato dei rapporti internazionali*, in Piergigli V. (ed.), *L'autoctonia divisa, cit.*

Nic Shuibhne N., EC *Law and Minority Language Policy. Culture, Citizenship and Fundamental Rights*, The Hague-London-New York, 2002.

Nikolic P., *I sistemi costituzionali dei nuovi Stati dell'ex-Jugoslavia*, Turin, 2002.

Paladin L., *Commento allo Statuto della Regione Friuli-Venezia Giulia*, Udine, 1969.

Palermo F., Woelk J., *Diritto costituzionale comparato dei gruppi e delle minoranze*, Padova, 2008.

Pallottino M., *Toponomastica*, in *Enciclopedia del diritto*, vol. XLIV, Milan, 1992.

Perselli G., *I censimenti della popolazione dell'Istria, con Fiume e Trieste, e di alcune città della Dalmazia tra il 1850 e il 1936*, Trieste, Centro Ricerche Storiche di Rovigno, 1993.

Pföstl E. (ed.), *Valorizzare le diversità: tutela delle minoranze ed Europa multiculturale*, Rome, 2003.

Piciocchi C., *L'identità culturale e la Carta dei diritti fondamentali dell'Unione Europea*, in Toniatti R. (ed.), *Diritto, diritti, giurisdizione. La Carta dei diritti fondamentali dell'Unione Europea*, Padova, 2002.

Piergigli V. (ed.), *L'autoctonia divisa. La tutela giuridica della minoranza italiana in Istria, Fiume e Dalmazia*, Padova, 2005.

Romano P., *La questione del confine orientale e le due guerre mondiali*, in Piergigli V. (ed.), *L'autoctonia divisa, cit.*

Roter P., *Language Issues in the context of Slovenian Smallness*, in Daftary F., Grin F., *Nation-Builiding, Ethnicity and Language Politics in Transition Countries*, European Center for Minority Issues, Open Society Institute, Budapest, 2003.

Toniatti R. (ed.), *Diritto, diritti, giurisdizione. La Carta dei diritti fondamentali dell'Unione Europea*, Padova, 2002.

Toniatti R., *Il multiculturalismo nell'ordinamento giuridico dell'Unione europea*, presented at the conference *Società multiculturale e Stato democratico*, Paestum, 18th–19th May 2007.

Toniatti R., *La tutela delle minoranze linguistiche: il paradigma pluralista della nuova democrazia europea*, in Various Authors, *Le rôle des languages minoritaires dans la vie publique, Actes du Séminaire di Saint-Vincent*, 2000.

Toniatti R., *Minoranze e minoranze protette: modelli costituzionali comparati*, in Bonazzi T., Dunne M. (eds.), *Cittadinanza e diritti nelle società multiculturali*, Bologna, 1994.

Various Authors, *Le rôle des languages minoritaires dans la vie publique, cit.*

von Toggenburg G. (ed.), *Minority Protection and the Enlarged European Union: The Way Forward*, Budapest, 2004.

von Toggenburg G., *A Rough Orientation through a Delicate Relationship: The European Union's Endeavours fot its Minorities*, in S. Trifunovska (ed.), *European Minorities and Languages,* The Hague, 2001.

Woelk J., *La tutela giuridica delle minoranze: modelli, strumenti e prospettive*, in Pföstl E. (ed.), *Valorizzare le diversità*, Rome, 2003.

Toponomastics and protection of ethnic (national) minorities: legislation and practice of the Republic of Serbia

Boris Krivokapić

Summary

1. Introduction

The toponomastic issues in Serbia are inseparable from the issue of official use of languages, especially the national minority ones, the official use of the Serbian language being, for obvious reasons, indisputable[1]. Therefore, for better

---

1 For the official use of language in general, and particularly in comparative law (in legislation and practice of a number of the European States), see: B. Krivokapić, *Službena upotreba jezika u međunarodnom pravu i novijem zakonodavstvu nekih evropskih država* (*Official Use of*

understanding of the problem a beforehand basic knowledge of essential facts about ethnic structure and legal order of Serbia is needed. Only upon such a basis an adequate understanding of concrete solutions is possible, as well as the evaluation of relevant practices.

1.1 Republic of Serbia: basic facts

The Republic of Serbia is among the States that emerged on the foundations of the former *Socialist Federal Republic of Yugoslavia* (SFRY), once well-known and appreciated for its liberal policy towards national minorities. It appeares that the roots of such a long time positive practice have been deep. Despite certain excesses, especially during the armed conflicts in some parts of the former SFR of Yugoslavia, all ex-Yu republics – now sovereign States – have generally preserved a relatively fair attitude toward position and special rights of national minorities, Serbia included.

Following the SFR of Yugoslavia's disintegration for a time (since 1992) existed the Union of Serbia and Montenegro – the *Federal Republic of Yugoslavia* (FR of Yugoslavia)[2], to be transformed in 2003 into a short-lived unusual and very loose form of association named the *State Union of Serbia and Montenegro (SCG)*. Finally in 2006 Montenegro declared its sovereignty thus making the Republic of Serbia an independent State too. Consequently, the position of national minorities, as well as other related issues, were no more subject to a double (federal and republic) legislation (as used to be the case), but only the Serbian one. Namely, with independence Serbia became a unitary State. Accordingly, instead of one or another form of federal order, once legal and political reality in former Yugoslavia, a more simple legal order came into being.

As the use of national minority languages in toponomastics is our central topic here, the relevant Republic of Serbia legislation will be surveyed, i.e. the relevant provisions of the 2006 Constitution, laws and other legal acts directly dealing with the discussed issues. In the same context, a survey of the international legal obligations of Serbia related to this particular field of social relations will be

---

Language in International Law and Recent Legislation of a Number of the European States), Belgrade, 2004; B. Krivokapić, *O nekim problemima službene upotrebe jezika u unutrašnjim porecima država* (*Some Issues of the Official Use of Languages in the Interior State Order*), in *Anali Pravnog fakulteta u Beogradu,* 2/2005, pp. 92–129.

2 More on position of national minorities in the FR of Yugoslavia, official use of languages included, see, among others: B. Krivokapić, *Ethnic Minorities in the Federal Republic of Yugoslavia and their rights*, in *Yugoslav Law,* 2–3/1994, pp. 63–71; 1/1995, pp. 3–21.

given. And finally, a more objective insight into the current practices is indispensable. However, before all the mentioned considerations, a brief discussion of the ethnic structure of Serbia is necessary because, at least in this country, the ethnic (national) minorities practically coincide with the linguistic ones.

In any case, it should be observed that all further considerations relate only to that part of the state territory of Serbia which is actually under its jurisdiction. It is well-known that under provisions of the UN Security Council Resolution 1244 (as of 1999) the Southern autonomous province of Serbia – Kosovo and Metohija (hereinafter: Kosovo) – has been subject to the international rule[3].

Meanwhile (17th February 2008) this territory declared independence, and a number of States recognized it as a sovereign State[4]. Despite the fact, Serbia still considers Kosovo and Metohija its territory, insisting that its independence was an illegal act, contrary to the related norms and principles of both the international public and internal Serbian law. The majority of the UN members (directly or indirectly) share the Serbian stand[5].

The legal *status* of Kosovo is by no means subject of this paper. All briefly mentioned in here should only indicate the actual state of affairs, especially that the legislation of the Republic of Serbia is *de facto* not in effect in Kosovo territory. Therefore, the issues of official use of language in general, and that of national minority languages in particular, in Kosovo will be left aside, and our discussion focused on the so called Central Serbia (Serbia proper) and its Northern autonomous province – Vojvodina, well-known for many ethnic minorities living there.

1.2 Ethnic structure

The wars, international sanctions, general insecurity, poor standard of living and the like, have considerably influenced the ethnical structure of Serbia. A part of population emigrated – either to the neighbouring or the developed Western

3 I.e. the United Nations Interim Administration Mission in Kosovo – UNMIK, since 2008 operating in cooperation with the European Union.

4 Up to 3rd September 2010, 70 UN members and the Republic of China (Taiwan) have recognized Kosovo independence.

5 Only 36.5% of the UN members (of 192) have recognized Kosovo independence.

countries[6] – while, in the same time, huge numbers of refugees from other regions of the former SFRY came to Serbia[7].

In any case, Serbia is still a multinational State, with high percentage of members of national minorities. It is especially so in Vojvodina.

According to the latest census (as of 31st March 2002), the ethnic structure of Serbia (without Kosovo) is as follows[8]:

National affiliation	**Republic of Serbia**	**Central Serbia**	**Vojvodina**
Serbs	6,212.838	4,891.031	1,321.807
Hungarians	293.299	3.092	290.207
Bosniacs	136.087	135.670	417
Roma	108.193	79.136	29.057
Yugoslavs	80.721	30.840	49.881
Croats	70.602	14.056	56.546
Montenegrins	69.049	33.536	35.513
Albanians	61.647	59.952	1.695
Slovaks	59.021	2.384	56.637

6 A relatively high number of Serbs emigrated, as well as of the other nations (national minorities). In search of a better life many left for the West (mostly to the EU, USA, Canada, Australia, etc.); a considerable number of national minority members went to the respective former Yugoslav republics, i.e. their respective national States.

7 During the armed conflicts in the region (1991–1995), Serbia received a great number of refugees from other republics of former Yugoslavia. Despite a certain percentage of other nations, quite understandably Serbs by then living in other former Yugoslav republics prevailed. According to the census the Commission for Refugees of the Republic of Serbia organized in cooperation with the UNHCR, there were 537,937 refugees in Serbia in 1996 (233,000 from Bosnia-Herzegovina, and 291,000 from Croatia). As the situation normalized in the following years, number of refugees constantly decreased mostly due to their admission to the Serbian citizenship, and less to their return to the countries of origin (177,000), leaving to third countries (some 30,000), or death (about 36,000). According to the UNHCR data, 98,739 refugees were evidenced in Serbia in 2009, majority from Croatia and Bosnia-Herzegovina. The most relevant statistical and other data on refugees in Serbia are to be found at the High Commissioner for Refugees site: http://www.unhcr.org and the Commissariat for Refugees of the Republic of Serbia: http://www.kirs.gov.rs.

8 *Etnički mozaik Srbije prema podacima popisa stanovništva 2002* (*Ethnic mosaic of Serbia according to the 2002 census*), Belgrade, 2004, Ministarstvo za ljudska i manjinska prava Srbije i Crne Gore.

National affiliation	Republic of Serbia	Central Serbia	Vojvodina
Vlachs	40.054	39.953	101
Romanians	34.576	4.157	30.419
Macedonians	25.847	14.062	11.785
Bulgarians	20.491	18.839	1.658
Bunyevtsi	20.021	246	19.766
Muslims	19.503	15.869	3.634
Ruthenians	15.905	279	15.626
Others[9]			
Total	7,498.001	5,466.009	2,031.992

According to the census, beside Serbs some thirty other ethnic communities live in the Republic of Serbia.

Generally speaking, in the Republic of Serbia (without Kosovo) live 1,285.163 members of other nations, that is national minorities, presenting 17,14% of its total population. In Central Serbia live 574.978 (10,52%) of them, and in Vojvodina 710.185 (amounting to 35% of its total population).

In that respect, the Republic of Serbia is a multinational State in which, beside its majority population, live members of other nations (ethnic minorities) who, in certain local units, are a majority population.

1.3 Official use of language

The Republic of Serbia recognizes full freedom of use of minority languages, meaning a national minority members may use their language: 1) in private (exg. at home, with friends), 2) in public (in the streets, media, in communication with state organs, etc.), and 3) officially.

The official use of minority languages signifies their use in court and other state organ procedures (that is, possibility that these procedures as such might, under certain conditions, be conducted in minority languages), in Parliament and

9 In Serbia as a whole (without Kosovo): Slovenes – 5,104; Gorans – 4,581; Germans – 3,901; Russians – 2,588; Czeks – 2,211; Jews – 1,158; Egyptians – 814; Šokci – 717; Hashkali – 584; Greeks – 572; Turks – 522; Tsintsars – 293, etc.

other state bodies, in documents and certificates, etc[10]. However, this article is mostly limited to the use of national minority languages and script in writing of local toponyms, names of settlements, streets, squares, and other toponyms. The legal order of Serbia explicitly treats such a writing as an instance of the official use of national minority language.

2. Legal scope

The legal framework of the field is defined by internal (domestic) regulations on one hand, and by international law, i.e. mostly by relevant multilateral and bilateral treaties binding for the Republic of Serbia, on the other hand.

The internal regulations include republic regulations in effect on national level (the Constitution of the Republic of Serbia, laws and regulations), but also the provincial ones (bylaws of the autonomous province, decisions and general acts), regulations of units of local self-government (municipal and city by-laws, and the like).

2.1 Constitution of the Republic of Serbia (2006)

1) Fundamental constitutional solutions

The new Constitution of Serbia (as of 8th November 2006)[11] in its art. 1 declares that Serbia is a State of the Serbian nation and all its citizens, founded on the rule of law and social justice, principles of civil democracy, human and minority rights and freedoms, and committment to the European principles and values.

A special chapter is devoted to the rights of national minority members, while a number of other Constitution provisions also deals with issues important for the position of that category of citizens[12]. In the art. 75, para. 1 the Constitution stipulates – beside rights granted to all other citizens – that the members of national minorities are guaranteed additional individual or collective rights. The

10 See for more details: B. Krivokapić, *Official use of language in international law and recent legislation of some European countries*, *cit.*, pp. 51–80.

11 Službeni glasnik Republike Srbije (*Official Gazette of the Republic of Serbia*), 83/2006. The text of the Constitution and other most important regulations could be found, among others, (also in English) at the site of the National Assembly of the Republic of Serbia, http://www.parlament.sr.gov.yu/content/cir/index.asp.

12 Among others, arts. 3; 8; 12; 34, para. 6; 38; 50, para. 3; 176–193; 194, paras. 4–5; 200, paras. 4, 6–7, 9; 201, para. 4; etc.

former are exercised individually, and the latter in community with others, in accordance with the Constitution, law and international treaties.

Consuming their collective rights, either directly or via their representatives, national minorities participate in decision-making or themselves decide on various issues related to their culture, education, information as well as the *official use of language and script* (our italics), in compliance with the law. To consume their right to self-government in the fields of culture, education, information and official use of language and script, the members of national minorities could elect their national councils, in compliance with the law (art. 75, paras. 2–3 of the Constitution)[13].

In that relation it should be noted that though art. 10, para. 1 of the Constitution stipulates that in the Republic of Serbia the Serbian language and Cyrillic script are in official use, the very next paragraph of the same article (art. 10, para. 2) allows for the official use of other languages and scripts, specifying that such a practice will be regulated by law in compliance with the Constitution.

As for the subject herein of direct interest, the provisions of the art. 79 of the Constitution are of particular importance since, in listing of the most substantial special rights of national minorities, it explicitly underlines that, apart from other rights, national minorities will have the right that:

> "traditional local names, names of streets, settlements and topographic names are also written in their languages, in areas where they make a significant majority of population"[14].

Thus the Constitution unequivocally recognizes the right of national minorities in communities where they are present in considerable percentage to the official use of their language and script, that is in writing of local names, names of settlements and topographic signs. And all that in conjuction with the Serbian language and Cyrillic script, not instead of it ("*and* in their language").

---

13 The 2002 Law on Protection of Rights and Freedoms of National Minorities has already introduced national councils as cultural autonomy institutions, endowed with some legal-public authority. The Law will be subject to further discussion in this article.

14 The whole provision is as follows: "Members of national minorities will have the right to: express, preserve, foster, develop and publicly express their national, ethnic, cultural, and religious specificity; use their symbols in public places; use their language and script; have proceedings also conducted in their language before state bodies, organizations with delegated public authority, bodies of autonomous provinces and local self-government units, in areas where they make a significant majority of population; to education in their language in state and provincial institutions alike; to establish educational institutions of their own; use of their name and family name in their language wherever they make a significant majority of population; to complete, timely and objective information in their own language, including right to expression, receiving, sending and exchange of information and ideas; establishment of their own mass media in accordance with the law".

Recognizing this right to national minorities, the Constitution creates a necessary legal framework leaving more specific conditions and modalities of its exercise to other relevant laws. The latter should neither annul nor restrictively interpret this right. It follows from the art. 18 which stipulates that:

> "Human and minority rights guaranteed by the Constitution shall be implemented directly.
>
> The Constitution shall guarantee, and as such, directly implement human and minority rights guaranteed by the generally accepted rules of international law, ratified international treaties and laws. The law may prescribe manner of exercising these rights only if explicitly stipulated in the Constitution or necessary to exercise a specific right owing to its nature, whereby the law may not under any circumstances influence the substance of the relevant guaranteed right.
>
> Provisions on human and minority rights shall be interpreted to the benefit of promoting values of democratic society, pursuant to valid international standards in human and minority rights, as well as the practice of international institutions which supervise their implementation".

Having in mind that the international treaties binding for Serbia also partly regulate these matters, it is interesting to see how the Constitution treats the international legal obligations of the country.

The treatment is, in general, positive and meets standards of a modern European State. Thus art. 16, para. 2 provides that:

> "Generally accepted rules of international law and ratified international treaties shall be an integral part of the legal system in the Republic of Serbia and applied directly. Ratified international treaties must be in accordance with the Constitution".

Even this brief survey supports conclusion that the Constitution of Serbia creates a pretty good legal framework for generally favourable position of national minorities and, particularly, explicitly provides not only for freedom of use of minority languages, but also for certain types of their official use, among others in toponomastics.

2) Opinion of the Venice Commission

Though judged by the solutions it offers in the field of minority rights (and, consequently, regarding official use of their languages and scripts), Constitution of the Republic of Serbia udoubtedly belongs to the best European documents of the kind, evaluation of the respective issues of the European Commission for Democracy Through Law (Venice Commission) raised an intriguing problem.

Namely, in its Opinion of 17th–18th March 2007[15] the Commission notes that[16], according to the art. 10 of the Constitution of Serbia, Serbian language and Cyrillic script are in official use in Serbia. In this connection, the Commission remarks that, compared to the 1990 Constitution, the level of protection of linguistic minorities has been reduced since art. 8 of the former Constitution explicitly stipulated official use of the Latin script under conditions provided by law. On the other hand, on the grounds of arts. 14, 18, para. 2 and 75 of the current Constitution the Commission underlines that the intention of constitution-makers to guarantee protection of minorities is indisputable. In this respect, the Commission concludes that it finds unclear the reasons why the Constitution omits legal protection of the Latin script, which majority of national minority members prefer to use. And the more so, because under provisions of the art. 20, para. 2 of the Constitution, the achieved level of human and minority rights is not to be reduced.

With no intention to deal in further detail with the Commission's Opinion, it is necessary to remark that this is an interesting case clearly pointing to all the traps an analysis of legal system of a foreign State inevitably poses[17]. Namely, good will and competence of the Commission members beyond any question, it could be easily seen that what we are facing here is a misunderstanding, very likely as an outcome of the insufficient knowledge of Serbian realities and the ways respective social relations are regulated.

It will suffice to highlight few moments that, conditionally speaking, the Venice Commission missed:

– the former Constitution of 1990 was also giving preference to the Serbian (Serbo-Croat, as then called) language in official use. Article 8 of the 1990 Constitution says:

> "In the Republic of Serbia the Serbo-Croat language and Cyrillic script are in official use, while the Latin script is in official use as provided by law.

---

15 European Commission for Democracy Through Law (Venice Commission), *Opinion on the Constitution of Serbia*, adopted by the Commission at its 70th plenary session (Venice, 17th–18th March, 2007), CDL-AD(2007)004, www.venice.coe.int/docs/2007/CDL-Ad(2007) 004-e.pdf.

16 European Commission for Democracy Through Law (Venice Commission), *Opinion on the Constitution of Serbia, op.cit.*, "*Article 10 – Language and Script*", p. 5.

17 It maybe of interest to remark that the Commission adopted its Opinion on the grounds of comments submitted by experts from Austria (*Mr. C. Grabenwarter*), United Kingdom (*Mr. J. Jowell*), Poland (*Ms. H. Suchocka*), Finland (*Mr. K. Tuori*), and Belgium (*Mr. J. Velaers*), i.e. countries that have nothing in common with legal system of Serbia, or former Yugoslavia.

In the regions of the Republic of Serbia where nationalities[18] live, in official use are also their languages and scripts, as provided by law"[19].

- The 2006 Constitution changes regulation of the matter only in that it: 1) instead of Serbo-Croat speaks of Serbian language (respecting the fact that after Croatia and Serbia became independent States, their once unique language also separated); 2) puts together in the same sentence the provision on legal regulation of official use of the Latin script, and the provision on official use of other languages and scripts (where it belongs); 3) omits from the respective provision the explicit mentioning of minorities speaking instead of official use "of other languages and scripts", making clear it is regulated by law in accordance with the Constitution. Namely, art. 10 of the 2006 Constitution verbatim says:

  "In the Republic of Serbia in official use is the Serbian language and script. Official use of other languages and scripts is regulated by law, grounded on Constitution".

In this connection it should be mentioned that the right of minorities to official use of their languages and scripts, as well as concrete forms of its expression is regulated by the Constitution itself. When it comes to toponomastics it suffices to mention again the already quoted provision of the art. 79, para. 1 of the Constitution.

That provision *does not specify official use of any other language, except Serbian*. The provision only regulates how the Serbian language will be officially used, as the official language and the language of the majority population (such a solution is usual in almost all contemporary States). And, the original script of the Serbian language is Cyrillic. This provision in no way reduces national minority rights – the official use of their languages and scripts is realized in compliance with the adopted solutions, after the rules of their languages and orthography. In other words, the provision actually specifies how the Serbs will use their language. The use of Latin script of other nations is by no means jeopardized – whenever the official use of any of the languages using Latin script (Albanian, Croat, Hungarian, Slovakian, etc.) is stipulated, its member has the right to use that script (Latin), to receive correspondence from state organs thus written, to have names of settlements, streets, and the like thus written, and so on. Moreover, the Latin script is not the script of all national minorities. A number of national minorities in Serbia use Cyrillic or some other

18 Then an official term for ethnic minorities.

19 Constitution of the Republic of Serbia, Službeni glasnik Republike Srbije (*Official Gazette of the Republic of Serbia*), 1/1990.

script as their national script – to mention just Bulgarians, Montenegrins, Macedonians or Ruthenians, whose script is Cyrillic[20].

In other words, we do not see anything disputable in the provisions of the art. 10 of the current Constitution of the Republic of Serbia. The fact is that it, in conjuction with other constitutional solutions and relevant laws, in no way limits or reduces the official use of national minority languages[21]. It does not regulate the script of *minority languages* when in official use, but the script of the *Serbian*, that is, the official, majority language.

2.2 Substantial legal solutions

The series of laws and regulations regulate the issues we are dealing with in this paper. For our purposes we will briefly discuss only the most important ones.

1) Law on Official Use of Languages and Scripts (1991)[22]

2.2.1 Introduction

The Law was enacted in July 1991, that is while the Socialist Federal Republic Yugoslavia still existed. Clearly, this is the act of Serbia as a member to the former ("old") Yugoslav federation. It regulates the official use of majority (Serbian) language and Cyrillic script, but also provides for conditions and ways of the official use of national minority languages.

---

20 With certain specific features pertinent to a given language (some specific letters).

21 For a bit more critical review of the Venice Commission Opinion, see: S. Antonić, *Venecijanska komisija i ćirilica* (*Venice Commission and the Cyrillic Script*), in *Nova srpska politička misao* (*New Serbian Political Thought*), special edition 2/2008, pp. 133–138; www.nspm.rs/srbija-medju-ustavima/venecijanska-komisija-i-ćirilica.html. The author (a well-known Serbian political analyst), among other, writes that "The Venice Commission knows [this is said ironically] that national minorities in Serbia prefer to write and read Serbian in Latin than in Cyrillic script. Therefore it criticizes Constitution writers for depriving them of their right and pleasure. Paradox is that the provision in mind regulates official use of the Serbian language. Article 10 does not say that now on the Hungarian language in Serbia will be written in Cyrillic or that Bulgarian language in its official use in Serbia will be written in Latin script. No, the article only regulates how *Serbian* language will be written in its official use. The simpliest question arises: What national minorities have to do with the decision which script Serbs will officially use in the Serbian State? And how does it at all interferes with any previous right? And what is that new, the most recent and only in Serbian case declared minority right "to prefer use of Latin script" in writing or reading Serbian language?".

22 Službeni glasnik Republike Srbije (*Official Gazette of the Republic of Serbia*), 45/1991.

With minor changes mainly regarding punishments stipulated for its violation, that law was in effect for 19 years. By the beginning of 2010 it was subject to certain more crucial changes to be later discussed, but is still in effect[23].

2.2.2 Basic solutions

The Law in its text before the changes of 2010, in the first place in its art. 1, para. 1 stipulates that the Serbo-Croatian language is in official use in the Republic of Serbia. When representing the Serbian linguistic expression the language is also called Serbian, and as such is called Serbian in further text[24]. However, the first article explicitly stipulates that in parts of Serbia inhabited by members of national minorities, the languages and scripts of national minorities are also in official use beside Serbian (art. 1, para. 3).

It is worth mentioning that among other forms of official use of languages and scripts the Law explicitly notes their use in writing of names of places and other geographical toponyms, names of streets, squares, names of state bodies, organisations and firms, publishing of public calls, information and warnings, as well as in writing of other public inscriptions (art. 3, para. 2).

The Law generally stipulates that roadsigns and traffic directions on international and magistral roads, as well as names of places and other geographic toponyms are to be written in Serbian language, both in the Cyrillic and Latin script. The roadsigns and traffic directions on other roads (in other words: roads of lower importance), names of streets, squares and other public inscriptions could also be written in both Cyrillic and Latin scripts (art. 5, paras. 1 and 2).

However, according to the provisions of art. 19, in regions where also national minority languages are in the official use, names of places and other geographical toponyms, names of streets and squares, names of state bodies and organisations, roadsigns, information and public warnings, as well as other public inscriptions will be written also in national minority languages (that is, in conjuction with Serbian).

In connection with this kind of official use of national minority languages, the provisions of the art. 11, paras. 1 and 2, are of special interest since they stipulate that municipalities[25] in which members of national minotiries live determine

---

23 More on the 1991 Law (before changes of 2010) and desirable ways of its amendments see: B. Krivokapić, *A Contribution to the initiative for New Legislation of the Republic of Serbia Relating to Official Use of Language,* in *Yugoslav Law,* 3/2003, pp. 5–26.

24 Though formally unchanged until 2010 provisions on Serbo-Croatian language became obsolete, due to practical separation of Serbian, Croatian and Bosnian language.

25 Basic units of local self-government.

when national minority languages are also in official use, regulating these matters in municipal bylaws.

The provisions of art. 7 stipulate that in the official use the text in languages and script of national minorities is written after the text in Serbian, below or on its right side, in letters of the same size and type. If more than one national minority language is in official use, texts in these languages are written after the text in Serbian in scriptic order (art. 7, para. 2).

The Law stipulates (art. 7, para. 3) that geographic names and proper nouns in public inscriptions will not be replaced by other names or nouns, and will be written in national minority languages in accordance with the spelling rules of those languages.

The Law, among others, defines financing of its implementation by bodies and organizations in which rights and obligations by this Law are realized (art. 21); explicitly stipulates that monitoring of implementation of its provisions will be within the domain of the respective activities of the ministries in the spheres of administration, transport, urbanism and housing-communal affairs, culture and health (art. 22); and, finally, stipulates penalties for violations of its provisions, including those in the sphere of official use of national minority languages in writing of names of places and other geographical toponyms, names of streets and squares, etc. (arts. 23, 26).

2.2.3 Evaluation of adopted solutions

Generally speaking, the solutions this Law provides (even before changes and amendments of 2010) deserve positive evaluation. It explicitly recognizes various forms of official use of languages and scripts of national minorities, including those in the domain of writing of names of settlements, streets and squares, geographic toponyms, etc. Still, some weaknesses were noted, mostly regarding two controversial questions[26].

First, under provisions of this Law local self-government bodies are responsible for introduction of the official use of national minority languages but, since the Law does not provide for objective criteria of such a practice, it is left to municipalities to freely decide if such a need really exists on their territory. As a consequence, in practice arised different interpretations and different solutions in different municipalities.

26 We have already discussed these problems in our paper: B. Krivokapić, *Protection of linguistic minorities and toponomastics in Serbia*, in G. de Vergottini, V. Piergigli (eds.), *La toponomastica in Istria, Fiume e Dalmazia. Profili giuridici,* vol. I, Florence, 2009, p. 224.

The second objection relates to the already mentioned art. 7, para. 3 which stipulates that geographic toponyms and proper names are unchangable. In other words, the Law offers a contradictory solution: namely, writing of these names in minority languages and scripts is allowed, but with preservation of respective names in Serbian. This actually means that the name of a place (as usual in Serbian language) is simply re-written in accordance with grammar and orthography of a national minority language (script). So, for example, the name of the city *Subotica* is to be written after Hungarian orthography (as "*Szubotica*"), but could not be replaced by a *Hungarian name* of the place ("*Szabatka*").

2.2.4 The recent changes

By the beginning of 2010 (5th May 2010) was adopted the Law on Changes and Amendments of the Law on Official Use of Languages and Scripts[27], which in the Law as whole settled certain solutions in a different way, erased some disputable provisions, changed certain articles or replaced them with a new text, with one completely new article added. The Law on Changes and Amendments has total of 8 articles, the last one specifing the Law will come into effect the eighth day from its publishing in "Official Gazette".

Though the matter is regulated by the art. 6, it should be immediately mentioned that the first innovation is that in the Law on Official Use of Languages and Scripts as a whole the word "nationality" was replaced by the words "national minority". It is a terminological solution expressing changes in the naming of ethnic minorities, and is in compliance with international standards[28], but also with the 2006 Constitution and its solutions[29].

The provisions of the art. 1 of the Law on Changes and Amendments change the Law on Official Use of Languages and Scripts in yet another way adjusting it to new reality: by a brief and clear formulation the article specifies that in Serbia the Serbian language (thus former mentioning Serbo-Croatian is omitted) is in official use.

---

27 Službeni glasnik Republike Srbije (*Official Gazette of the Republic of Serbia*), 30/2010. Also to be found at: www.parlament.gov.rs/content/lat/akta detalji.asp?Id=836&t=Z#.

28 With the Framework Convention for the Protection of National Minorities (1995) adopted in the Council of Europe, but also in series of other international documents (of UN, OECD, etc.).

29 More on different naming, see: B. Krivokapić, *Problem naziva manjina – nacionalne, etničke ili...? (Problem of naming minorities – national, ethnic, or...?*), in *Prava čoveka* (*Human rights*), 5–6/2003, pp.19–41.

Article 2 erases a vague paragraph 3 of the art. 7, which contained already mentioned disputable solutions.

Article 3 erases arts. 8 and 9 which regulated certain issues of official use of Latin script. These solutions are in compliance with art. 10 of the 2006 Constitution as already mentioned. However, doing so it does not jeopardize the use of Latin script when it comes to the official use of language and script of a national minority. Anyway, art. 10 of the original Law of 1991 remained unchanged, and says:

> "When in compliance with provisions of this Law a text is also written in Latin script, text in Latin script will be written after the text in Cyrillic script, below or on the right side of it".

By the art. 4 the Law on Changes and Amendments of the Law on Official Use of Languages and Scripts former art. 11 is replaced by a completely new art. 11. The new article instead of the earlier solution by which municipalities (units of local self-government) in which national minorities live were free to decide themselves when on their territory also national minority languages were in official use. Since, as already mentioned, no further objective criteria were given, it was possible that municipalities with absolutely no good reason did not introduce a national minority language into the official use. New art. 11 clearly regulates the matter:

> "At the territory of a local self-government unit where a national minority members traditionally live, their language and script might be in equal official use.
>
> A self-government unit will be obliged to introduce into an equal official use the language and script of a national minority if the percentage of that national minority in total population at its territory is 15% according to the latest census.
>
> The official use of national minority languages from the paragraph 1 of this article particularly entails: use of national minority languages in administrative and court procedures and conducting of the administrative procedure and court procedure in the national minority language; use of the national minority language in communication with citizens of organs with public authority; issue and keeping of official records and collections of personal data in national minority languages and acceptance of these documents in these languages as valid; use of national minority languages in ballot-papers and voting material; use of national minority languages in functioning of representation bodies.
>
> *At territories from paragraph 2 of this article, names of organs with public authority, names of self-government units, settlements, squares and streets and other toponyms will be written also in the language of a national minority in question, according to its tradition and orthography* (our italics).
>
> National minority languages that are in official use of the organs of an autonomous province are specified by its statute.
>
> Laws and regulations are also published in national minority languages, in compliance with particular law.

Members of national minorities whose number in total population of the Republic of Serbia is at least 2% according to the latest census might address republican organs in their own language and have the right to receive answer in the same language.

Members of national minorities whose number in total population of the Republic of Serbia is under 2% according to the latest census, might address republican organs in their own language and have the right to receive answer in the same language via a self-government unit in which the language of that national minority is in official use, in which case that self-government unit provides for translation and covers costs of translation of the document sent to the republican organ and of the answer of that organ".

We deliberately quoted new art. 11 *in extenso*, though most of its provisions do not directly deal with the issues of the official use of languages in toponomastics. We did so for a number of reasons: first, it is the only article of this Law that is completely replaced. Then, insight into the total text of new art. 11 provides for understanding of the place and role this Law devotes to the official use of national minority languages and scripts in toponomastics. It obviously treats the issue as an important part of the corpus of minority rights, i.e. protection of national minorities.

As for concrete solutions, particular attention should be paid to the following:

- in contrast to the old solutions, new art. 11 speaks not only about use, but of *the equal* use of national minority languages and scripts;
- an innovation is also the solution by which a local self-government unit is obliged to introduce the language and script of a national minority into the equal use, if the percentage of a respective minority members is 15%. In this way a local self-government unit is prevented from not introducing in equal official use the language and script of a national minority with significant share in the population of that unit. Not only a very precise criteria (15% percent of a national minority members according to the latest census) is defined, but it is also specified that the equal introduction of the language and script is done by the highest sel-government unit's act – its statute;
- the mentioned solutions are in full compliance with the respective solutions of the Law on Protection of Rights and Freedoms of National Minorities (2002), which will be discussed later. In other words, new art. 11 introduces not only more precise and democratic solutions, but also eliminates disbalance between the two most important legal regulations in the field.

Article 5 of the Law on Changes of the Law on Official Use of Languages and Scripts introduces a new art. 18a. However important in itself, it is irrelevant here for it deals with guarantees of the right of national minority members to free choice and use of personal name and names of his/her children, as well as to enrollment of these personal names in all public documents.

And, finally, art. 7 of the Law on Changes and Amendments of the Law on Official Use of Languages and Scripts does not change any particular article of the original law of 1991, but amends it, making more precise that:

> "That national minority language that is in official use in a local self-government unit on the day this law comes into effect, will remain in the official use there".

It is a very important solution, specifying in this matter the general principle that the achieved level of minority protection is not to be reduced[30].

2.2.5 Evaluation of changes and amendments made

By the cited changes and amendments the 1991 Law was finally adjusted in its solutions both to the needs of everyday life, and to the 2006 Constitution and solutions of other regulations, above all the Law on Protection of Rights and Freedoms of National Minorities (2002), which comprehensively grants rights of national minorities and their members.

Generally speaking, in the Republic of Serbia Serbian language is still in the official use (it is a constitutional solution, but also understandable as such), but also is guaranteed and in a better way regulated the equal official use of other languages, or more precisely, national minority languages. It is true that a question could be asked why it took so long, i.e. why these changes and amendments were made four years after the new Constitution came into effect. Though excuses could be found in referring to the turbulent developments on the Serbian political scene, as well as in the overloaded Parliament engaged in adoption of huge number of new regulations, still an impression remains that changes and amendments of such an important regulation had to be done much earlier.

2) Law on Protection of Rights and Freedoms of National Minorities (2002)[31]

This Law was enacted as the law of the FR of Yugoslavia made of two associated Republics – Serbia and Montenegro. Despite that since 2003 it has

30 The provision of other two articles of the Law on Changes and Amendments of the Law on Official Use of Languages and Scripts (meaning arts. 6 and 8) were earlier discussed at the beginning of this survey.

31 Službeni list Savezne Republike Jugoslavije (*Official Gazette of the Federal Republic of Yugoslavia*), 11/2002.

been implemented as a Serbian regulation[32]. When Montenegro parted in 2006, and Serbia turned to a sovereign State, the Law was formally in effect as law of the Republic of Serbia.

Though relatively highly evaluated both in the country and abroad, some of its solutions, generally speaking, could have been somewhat better[33]. In a comprehensive, modern and generally high quality way it regulates rights and legal *status* of national minority members. In its 25 articles the Law actually regulates all substantional issues relevant for safeguarding undisturbed living, full equality and development of national minorities in Serbia. Among others, the Law explicitly stipulates that "persons belonging to national minorities can freely use their language and script in private and in public" (art. 10).

As for the official use of national minority languages particularly in writing of names of places, streets, topographic names and the like, especially important are provisions of its art. 11, paras. 1 and 3, entitled "*Official use of language and script*":

> "On the territory of a local self-government unit, where national minority members traditionally live, their language and script might be in equal official use.
>
> A local self-government unit is obliged to introduce the language and script of a national minority in official use always if the percentage of that national minority in the total population on its territory reaches 15% according to the latest census.
>
> In the unit of local self-government where the language of a national minority is in official use at the moment of the enactment of this Law, it shall remain in official use".

Further paragraphs of the same article more precisely define various issues relevant for the official use of national minority languages[34], paragraph 5 being of particular importance:

---

32 Under art. 64, para. 2 of the Constitutional Charter (2003) of then existing State Union of Serbia and Montenegro provisions, the laws of the FR of Yugoslavia elsewhere from the affairs of Serbia and Montenegro were to be applied as laws of member States until the member States enact new laws, except laws the parliament of member States decide not to be implemented. The text of the Constitutional Charter could be found (also in English) on the site of the Ministry of Foreign Affairs of Serbia: http://www.mfa.gov.yu/Srpski/Facts/ustavna_povelja_s.html.

33 More on this: B. Krivokapić, *Serbia and Montenegro: the New Legal Framework for the Protection of Ethnic Minorities,* in *Revue québécoise de droit international*, vol. 16.1, 1/2003, pp. 61–100.

34 Use of national minority languages in administrative and court procedures, and procedings of administrative and court procedures in national minority languages, use of national minority languages in communication of authorities with public powers with citizens; issuing of public documents and keeping of official records, collections of personal data in national minority languages, and acceptance of such documents in those languages as equally valid; use of minority languages on ballot-papers and election materials, use of minority languages in procedings of representative bodies, etc.

> "On the territories from paragraph 2[35], names of organs with public authority, names of local self-government units, settlements, squares and streets and other toponyms are also to be written in the language of the respective national minority according to its tradition, grammar and ortography".

Hence, this Law too explicitly allows for official use of languages and scripts of national minorities, including in the writing of names of local self-government units, settlements, squares, streets and other toponyms. The use of these languages and scripts is *equal,* i.e. *in conjuction with* the Serbian language and script, not instead of it.

Obviously, both the 1991 Law and the Law on Protection of Rights and Freedoms of National Minorities allow that units of local self-government when find it necessary may introduce a national minority language into the official usse. However, the new Law on Protection of Rights and Freedoms of National Minorities introduces certain important positive innovations, into the legal order, such as:

- introduction of a national minority language into the official use (including writing of mentioned names and toponyms) is *mandatory* in those local self-government units where the share of a given national minority is 15% or more of the total population of that unit. This is an important improvement. Besides, as already mentioned, national minority languages *could* be introduced to official use even if percentage of a given minority is lower than 15%;
- in local self-government units where the language of a national minority is in the official use (including writing of the herein mentioned names) at the moment of enactment of this Law, it shall remain in official use (regardless of possible later changes in ethnic structure of population – even if it in the meantime considerably decreases the percentage in the overall population)[36];
- all names (of local self-government units, settlements, squares and streets, and other toponyms) are also written in the language of respective minority *in line with its tradition* and orthography. Hence, contrary to solutions of the 1991 Law (before the changes and amendments of 2010), the new Law provides that names in question are to be written in line with tradition of a given ethnic group, and not by sheer transcription of the Serbian name to the minority language, that is, by writing Serbian name in script and in line with orthography of the minority language.

---

35 That is, territories of local self-government where the percentage of members of national minority in total population reaches 15% according to the latest census.

36 This solution is not derived only from the quoted provisions of art. 11, para. 3 of the Law, but also from its provision in the art. 8, which generally guarantees protection of acquired rights to the members of national minorities.

Since their solutions were partly different (in collision), for some time the question was which of two laws (the one of 1991 or that of 2002) was of superior legal power. In that connection, a lot more was in favour of new Law – the one on the protection of minority rights. First, for reasons of hierarchy of legal acts (it was enacted on federal level as an act of the FR of Yugoslavia); second, because it was harmonized with the ratified international treaties; and, third, due to the fact that it was later enacted (*lex posterior derogat legi priori*). In the meantime, these dilemmas faded away and if any inconsistency arose, the Law on Protection of Rights and Freedoms of National Minorities (2002) was senior in practice, with its more modern and liberal solutions.

Finally, the Law on Changes and Amendments of the Law on Official Use of Languages and Scripts (2010), which took over more liberal and modern solutions of the Law on Protection of Rights and Freedoms of National Minorities (2002) as already said, that inconsistency was formally eliminated.

2.3 Other regulations of the Republic of Serbia

Of course, many practically important issues connected to names of settlements, streets, squares and toponyms in national minority languages are, by their very nature, regulated by other laws and sub-laws. However, such regulations do not introduce any substantionally new solutions; their scope is to define more precisely ways the relevant solutions of the Constitution and basic laws (The Law on Official Use of Languages and Scripts and The Law on Protection of Rights and Freedoms of National Minorities) are enacted.

1. So, for example, *The Law on Local Self-Government (2007)*[37] specifies that local self-government exists in municipalities, cities and the city of Beograd (art. 1, para. 2). Article 20, para. 32, and art. 34 specify that municipality, via its organs, in compliance with the Constitution and law, among other things, "takes care of consumation, protection and promotion of human rights and individual and collective rights of national minority members and ethnic groups"; "decides on official use of languages and scripts of national minorities on the territory of municipality in question"; and "takes care of public information of local importance, and provides for conditions of public information in Serbian language and national minority languages used at the municipal territory", and the like.

Article 91 specifies that local self-government symbols might be displayed only in conjuction with the state symbols. It specifies that in the official premises

37 Službeni glasnik Republike Srbije (*Official Gazette of the Republic of Serbia*), 129/2007.

of the local self-government unit are displayed only the state symbols, symbols of national minority whose language is in official use at the territory of that local self-government unit, as well as the symbols of that local self-government unit itself; the display of the autonomous province's symbols is to be regulated by regulations of its own[38].

Article 93 directly deals with toponomastics and therefore is of special interest here:

> "A local self-government unit's assembly sets up holidays and decides on street, square, city district, hamlet and other parts of settlement names at its territory, with a beforehand approval of the ministry in charge of local self-government affairs.
>
> If in a local self-government unit a national minority language is in official use, in the procedure of re-naming streets, squares, city districts, hamlets and other parts of settlements the opinion of the respective national council will be acquired".

Thus the Law takes into account the fact that in Serbia the official use of national minority languages is allowed and regulated, among other domains, also in naming and writing names of streets, squares, city districts and other settlements, and underlines that any change of these names occurs, approval of the respective national minority, or more precisely, its national council, is necessary.

And finally, important is art. 98 which specifies that in nationally mixed local self-government units councils for interethnic relations will be established, as independent working bodies comprised of representatives of the Serbian nation and national minorities. Further art. 98, para. 2 specifies that, in compliance with this Law, local self-government units having more than 5% of a national minority in total population, or over 10% of all national minorities in total population, according to the latest census in the Republic of Serbia, will be considered as mixed. Members of the Serbian nation and national minorities with over 1% share in total population of a self-government unit will have their representatives in the council. The council is in charge of realization, protection and promotion of national equality, in compliance with law and statute, while its concrete scope of activity, structure, selection of members and modes of activity are subject to decision of local self-government unit's assembly. Of its stands and proposals the council informs local self-government assembly which is obliged to give opinion about it at its first next session, but not later than within 30 days. The assembly and executive bodies of a local self-government unit are obliged to submit proposals of all their decisions relevant for national equality to the council asking for its opinion. And finally, by the art. 99, para. 11, council for interethnic relations is granted the right to initiate before the Constitutional

---

38 We mention here local self-government unit symbols for these may have text in minority languages.

Court a procedure of evaluation of constitutionality and legality of a given decision or other act of the local self-government unit if the council considered it a direct violation of rights of members of the Serbian nation and national minorities represented in the council for interethnic relations. The same conditions met, the council is granted the right to initiate procedure of evaluation of compatibility of a decision or other act of a self-government unit with the statute before the Supreme Court.

The above mentioned solutions should be a serious guarantee that the official use of languages and scripts, national minorities included, will be in compliance with law, in the domain of toponomastics as well.

2. From a practical point of view, some other regulations are also interesting, especially the *Law on Territorial Organization of the Republic of Serbia* (2007)[39] which specifies that the territorial organization of the Republic of Serbia consists of municipalities, towns and the city of Beograd, as its territorial units, and autonomous provinces, as forms of territorial autonomy (art. 2). The Law further stipulates that the territory of municipalities, towns and the city of Beograd is made of settlements, or more precisely of areas covered by land registers of respective territorial units (art. 3, para. 1), etc.

Of particular interest here is that this Law fixes names of municipalities and towns, settlements and land registers, as well as modes of their change (art. 4, para. 2). It further specifies that settlements might be named after geographic, ethnographic, historical or other terms, or a late prominent personality (art. 7); that a local self-government unit's assembly, citizens, local neighbourhood community, or other interested community organs might initiate change of settlement's name previously given by this Law, initiate naming of a newly established settlement, or a procedure to pronounce a settlement ceased to exist (art. 8, para. 1). Beforehand opinions of respective organs of territorial autonomy and local self-government unit's assembly (art. 8, para. 2) are needed for change of name of the existing settlement, naming of a newly established one, or pronoucement that a settlement ceased to exist. The Law also specifies that the Government will regulate how settlements, streets, squares, buildings and house numbers will be signified (art. 10).

In its arts. 16 and 20–21, the Law gives a list of all municipalities (150) and towns (23 and the city of Beograd) in the Republic of Serbia, with their exact names, headquarters and other relevant data.

3. Directly relying on art. 10 of the Law on Territorial Organization of the Republic of Serbia, identical to the one in the old Law on Territorial

39 Službeni glasnik Republike Srbije (*Official Gazette of the Republic of Serbia*), 129/2007.

Organization of the Republic of Serbia[40], the Government adopted its *Decree on Setting up of House Numbers, Numeral Signification of Houses, Streets and Squares*[41]. In its art. 3, para. 1 the Decree specifies that names of settlements, streets and squares are written in compliance with the law regulating official use of languages and scripts within the framework of protection of national minority rights and freedoms, in its sections regulating official use of languages and scripts.

In its arts. 20 and 22[42] the Decree also specifies the mode of signification of settlement, street and square names, further precising (art. 20, paras. 2–3) that the name of a settlement is displayed on an enabelled board (65x40 cm in size) and, if a display is multilingual, on a bigger board (65x60 cm). Bigger enabelled boards are also mandatory in cases of multilingual writing of street and square names (art. 23)[43]. And quite understandably so, because if smaller multilingual boards would be simply illegible.

Worth mentioning are the solutions specifying that the Service[44] is obliged to display the name of a settllement within 15 days from the date when the decision on naming or re-naming settlement is published in the *Official Gazette of the Republic of Serbia* (art. 21), or, in case of the name of a street or square, within 30 days from the date of receival of the decision of municipal or city organ in charge of naming or re-naming streets and squares (art. 24), along with decision that the costs of displaying names of streets and squares covers the city, or municipality on territory of which a street or square is located[45].

Very important are the provisions prohibiting unauthorized display or removal of boards with names of settlements, streets and squares (art. 4), and stipulating fees for persons who disallow putting boards with street and square names on their houses, or objects, as well as for unauthorized persons who display, dismount, destroy, damage or mar appearance of the board with a settlement, street or square name (art. 29). In such cases, the fees are stipulated also for a legal entity and a responsible person of a legal entity.

---

40 Službeni glasnik Republike Srbije (*Official Gazette of the Republic of Serbia*), 47/1991, 79/1992, 82/1999, 47/1994.

41 Službeni glasnik Republike Srbije (*Official Gazette of the Republic of Serbia*), 110/2003, 137/2004, 58/2006, also at: www.podaci.net/ zl/2109676/U-ukbozb0BO-0658.html.

42 These general solutions specify that at the entrance to a settlement display of its name is mandatory; the board shall be put on roads at the entrance to a settlement, on the right side of the road; on pillars 2.5 m. high a 65x40 cm enamelled sheet metal board hangs, with a written name of the place, written in white letters on dark blue background, etc.

43 Instead of regular 50 x 30 cm, multilingual boards are 50 x 55 cm.

44 An authorized organization unit of the Republican Geodesy Office in a given municipality or city – Land Register Office (art. 2 of the Act).

45 Art. 23, para. 3 of the Act.

4. *The Law on Establishment of Certain Autonomous Province Competencies*[46] also dealt with issues related to naming of settlements. That act, sometimes called the Omnibus Law, regulated transfer of some of republican competencies to provincial level, among other things, in the domain of regulation of the right to official use of languages. Its art. 18 ("Official Use of Languages and Scripts") specified that the autonomous province via its bodies, and in compliance with the law regulating the official use of language and script: 1) more precisely regulated the official use of languages and scripts of national minorities and monitored implementation of regulations settling these matters; and 2) monitored implementation of the law. The Law defined the position of autonomous province, without stating which province it was about (hence, both provinces – i.e. AP of Vojvodina and, once conditions met, AP of Kosovo and Metohija).

A new *Law on Establishment of Autonomous Province of Vojvodina Competences* was adopted in 2009[47], clearly related only to the Northern Serbian province (Vojvodina). The Law contains basically the same solutions, as its art. 76 ("Official Use of Languages and Scripts") stipulates that the Autonomous Province of Vojvodina, via its organs, more precisely regulates official use of languages and scripts at its territory, in compliance with law. Through its organs, and in compliance with law regulating official use of languages and scripts, the Province also exercizes supervision, but only as a delegated job. As stipulated by its art. 90, by the date this Law comes to effect previous Law on Establishment of Certain Autonomous Province Competencies ceased to be valid.

5. Other laws, in any possible way related to protection of national minority rights, especially those adopted over the last five-six years, are also more or less relevant for regulation and realization of official use of national minority languages in the domain of writing names of cities, other settlements, streets and the like in these languages and scripts.

In this respect, the *Law on National Minority National Councils* (2009)[48] adopted on 31st August 2009 is of special interest here. It regulates competencies of national councils in the fields of culture, education, information and official use o languages and scripts, procedure of their election, their funding and other questions relevant for national councils functioning.

In its art. 2, para. 2 the Law specifies that national council represents national minority in spheres of education, culture, information in national minority language and official use of language and script, participates in decision-making

46 Službeni glasnik Republike Srbije (*Official Gazette of the Republic of Serbia*), 6/2002.

47 Službeni glasnik Republike Srbije (*Official Gazette of the Republic of Serbia*), 99/2009.

48 Službeni glasnik Republike Srbije (*Official Gazette of the Republic of Serbia*), 72/2009. Also at: www.puma.vojvodina.gov.rs/dokumenti/zakoni/Zakon ns.pdf.

or decides upon issues pertinent to these fields, and founds relevant institutions, commercial societies and other organizations. Besides, in compliance with law and its statute, national council, through its organs, independently: initiates adoption of laws and monitors their implementation as well as that of other regulations in spheres of culture, education, information and official use of language and script (art. 101, paras. 1–9); participates in drafting of regulations and proposes changes and amendments of regulations settling constitutionally granted national minority rights in spheres of culture, education, information and official use of languages and scripts (art. 10, paras. 1–10); proposes special regulations and temporary measures in spheres pertinent to realization of right to self-government with the view to full equality of national minority members and citizens of majority population (art. 10, paras. 1–11); initiates procedure before the Constitutional Court, Ombudsman, provincial and local ombudsman and other relevant bodies whenever finds a violation of constitutional and legally granted national minority rights and freedoms occured (art. 10, paras. 1–12); takes stands and undertakes measures in connection with issues directly influencing position, identity and rights of national minority (art. 10, paras. 1–14), etc.

The provisions of the art. 22 which regulate national council's competencies in the domain of official use of languages and scripts are of special importance here, and therefore worth to be *verbatim* quoted:

"National council:

1) Fixes traditional names of self-government units, settlements and other geographic names in the national minority language if national minority language is in official use at the territory of a given self-government unit; names thus fixed by national council become names in official use in conjuction with names in Serbian language, and are published in the "Official Gazette of the Republic of Serbia", or when national council's headquaters are in the Autonomous Province of Vojvodina – in the "Official Gazette of the Autonomous Province of Vojvodina";
2) Proposes display of local self-government unit, settlements and other geographic names in the national minority language;
3) Proposes official use of a national minority language and script in a given self-government unit;
4) Proposes re-naming of streets, squares, city districts, hamlets, other settlements and institutions proved to be of onsiderable importance for a given national minority;
5) Gives opinion in the procedure of naming streets, squares, city districts, hamlets and other settlements, if at the territory of a self-government unit or inhabited place a national minority language is in official use;
6) Proposes organ in charge to monitor official use of a national minority language and script;
7) Proposes measures and activities organs in charge are to take in translation of regulations to national minority languages being in official use;

8) Undertakes measures and activities in promotion of official use of national minority language and script;
9) Decides on other issues in the field to which is entitled by law, autonomous province or local self-government unit act".

The provisions of the art. 23, para. 1 are important as they stipulate that particular acts – among others, those mentioned above in art. 22 of this Law – adopted without appropriate proposal or opinion of national council are illegal and invalid.

6. Many other laws are also of interest here. Thus, for example, the *Anti-Discrimination Law* (2009)[49] in its definition of prohibition of discrimination mentiones prohibition of discrimination based upon national affiliation or ethnic origin and language (art. 2, para. 1), and among serious forms of discrimination classifies instigation and forging of inequality, hate and intolerance based upon national racial or religious affiliation and language (art. 13, para. 1). The Law also explicitly forbids discrimination of national minorities and their members based upon their national affiliation, ethnic origin, religious beliefs and language, and stipulates that modes of realization and protection of national minority rights are regulated by special law (art. 24).

Even laws that do not explicitly mention toponomastics, official use of languages or protection of minority rights, are of considerable importance. So, for instance, the *Law on Responsibility for Violation of Human Rights* (2003)[50] defines: forms and particulars of violation of human rights that are grounds for investigation of responsibility; persons subject to procedure of investigation of responsibility for violation of human rights; principles and rules of investigation of responsibility for violation of human rights, and other relevant issues.

2.4 Vojvodina Regulations

As an autonomous province of the Republic of Serbia Vojvodina, due to its multiethnic composition[51], regulates these issues by some of its own acts. The latter shall be in compliance with the Constitution and laws of the Republic of

49 Službeni glasnik Republike Srbije (*Official Gazette of the Republic of Serbia*), 22/2009.

50 Službeni glasnik Republike Srbije (*Official Gazette of the Republic of Serbia*), 58/2003.

51 According to the latest census, out of total Vojvodina population 1,321.807 (65%) declared themselves as Serbs, Hungarians 290,207 (14.4%), Slovaks 56,637 (2.8%), Croats 56,546 (2.8%), Yugoslavs 49,881 (2.6%), Montenegrins 35,513 (1.7%), Rumanians 30,419 (1.5%), Roma 29,057 (1.4%), Bunyetsi 19,766 (1%), Ruthenians 15,626 (0.8%), Macedonians 11,785 (0.6%), Mulsmims 3,634 (0.2%), Albanians 1,695 (0.1%), etc.

Serbia, actually being only a further elaboration of already established solutions[52].

1. First, the old *Statute of the AP of Vojvodina* (1991)[53], as the supreme legal act of the Province, had some provisions granting official use of national minority languages. Its art. 6 stipulated the official use of minority languages in the work of provincial organs, in conjuction with the Serbo-Croatian language and Cyrillic script. Even more interesting is the provision of art.10, paras. 1–4 which specifies that the AP of Vojvodina granted official use of languages and scripts of national minorities in conjuction with official use of the Serbo-Croatian, in compliance with law.

A new *Statute of the Autonomous Province of Vojvodina*[54] was adopted in 2009. Already in its first article (art. 1, para. 2) the Statute underlines that Vojvodina is the region where multiculturality, multiconfessionality and other European principles and values have been traditionally nourished. Consequently art. 7, para. 1 of the Statute specifies that multilingualism, multiculturalism and multiconfessionalism as universal values are of special importance for Vojvodina. In that connection, art. 7, para. 2 stipulates that the duty of all provincial organs and organizations is that, within their rights and duties, instigate and facilitate preservation and development of multilingualism and cultural heritage of national communities traditionally living in the AP of Vojvodina, as well as to use special measures for further promotion of mutual understanding and knowledge of different languages, cultures and confessions in the AP of Vojvodina.

Of particular interest here are art. 20, which prohibits any discrimination, direct or indirect on any grounds, national affiliation, culture or language included, as well as art. 22, which specifies that members of national minorities who are a numerical minority in the total of Vojvodina population enjoy special protection and all rights granted to national minorities and their members by the acts of the Republic of Serbia. And finally, art. 23 confirms that once achieved level of human and minority rights, individual and collective alike, must not be reduced, and that, on the contrary, the AP of Vojvodina can provide for

52 See more: O. Janoš, *Službena upotreba jezika i pisma u AP Vojvodini* (*Official Use of Languages and Scripts in the AP of Vojvodina*), in V. Stanovčić (ed.), *Položaj nacionalnih manjina u Srbiji* (*The Status of National Minorities in Serbia*), Srpska akademija nauka i umetnosti, Belgrade, 2005, pp. 517–527.

53 Službeni list Autonomne Pokrajine Vojvodine (*Official Gazette of the Autonomous Province of Vojvodina*), 17/1991.

54 Službeni glasnik Autonomne Pokrajine Vojvodine (*Official Gazette of the Autonomous Province of Vojvodina*), 17/2009. Also at: www.puma.vojvodina.gov.rs/dokumenti/zakoni/Statut APV 2009.pdf.

additional or more rights, i.e. rise the level of national communities with the smallest share in total of the AP Vojvodina population.

Though the mentioned provisions create necessary preconditions for the protection of national minorities, official use of their languages and scripts included, (clearly stating that in that connection appropriate regulations of the Republic of Serbia are to be applied – which, as already demonstrated, are of rather high quality – and precisely specifying the achieved level of minority protection must not be reduced but only improved), the bnew Statute has a special article entitled "Official Languages and Scripts". The article specifies that in the AP of Vojvodina organs and organizations in official use are: the Serbian language and Cyrillic script, Hungarian, Slovak, Croat, Rumanian and Ruthenian languages and scripts, and that the right to official use of other national community languages is in compliance with law and provincial decree, ratified international treaties, law, and provincial assembly decree.

2. In accord with its competences from the so-called Omnibus Law (2002), the Assembly of the AP of Vojvodina enacted the *Decree on a More Detailed Regulation of Certain Issues of Official Use of National Minority Languages and Scripts in the AP of Vojvodina* (2003)[55] on 15th May 2003. The Decree regulates certain issues regarding the official use of national minority languages and scripts in Vojvodina, including official use of national minority languages and scripts in displaying the names of settlements, other geographic names, names of streets, squares, etc[56].

The Decree provides that where a minority language is in official use, names of settlements and other toponyms are written in the language and in accordance with orthography of that minority, and in line with its traditions.

Article 6 stipulates that where minority languages are in official use, names of settlements and other toponyms, names of streets and squares, names of organs, traffic signs, information and warnings and other public inscriptions have also to be written in the language and in accordance with orthography of that minority, and in line with its traditions. These inscriptions are written after the text in Serbian, below or to the right of it, in the same font and size. Even if national minority language and script are in official use only on a part of a territory of a local self-government unit, these names are to be written in the language and script of a national minority in a settlement or a community unit.

According to the art. 8, para. 1, territory of official use of a national minority language is defined by a local self-government unit's statute. A local self-

55 Službeni list Autonomne PokrajineVojvodine (*Official Gazette of the Autonomous Province of Vojvodina*), 8/2003.

56 See also: art. 1 Decrees.

government unit's statute regulates official use of a national minority language and script on its whole territory only if share of that national minority in its total population, according to the latest census, amounts to 15% (art. 8, para. 2). This solution is, basically, taken from the Law on Protection of Rights and Freedoms of National Minorities (2002), and was discussed earlier in this paper. The solutions regarding the achieved level of rights are also taken from the same Law (art. 8, para. 4).

However, the novelty and further elaboration of the established principles is the solution that, if the language of a national minority is not in use on municipal territory as a whole, municipal statute *may* stipulate its official use in those community units or settlements (i.e. parts of the municipal territory), inhabited by larger number of members of a given national minority (art. 8, para. 5).

Of special interest is the solution that, if the language and script of a national minority are not in official use on the territory of a local self-government unit as a whole, the unit is obliged to introduce them in the official use in a settlement or a community unit on its territory, where live at least 25% of members of a national minority, according to the latest census (art. 8, para. 3).

Article 7 stipulates that traditional names of towns, municipalities and settlements specified by the national council of a given national minority, within three months from the date when this Decree comes into effect. If national council of a given national minority does not specify these names, the Executive Council of the AP of Vojvodina (i.e. government of the Province) will – in co-operation with local self-government units, national minority organizations and experts in linguistics, history and geography of a given national minority – specify them. In each case, the specified names are published in the *Official Gazette of the Autonomous Province of Vojvodina*.

Finally, it is worth mentioning that art. 10 of the Decree stipulates that the Executive Council of the AP of Vojvodina at least once a year submits to the Assembly of the AP of Vojvodina a report on exercise of the right to official use of the national minority languages and scripts. Monitoring of application and implementation of the Decree is among the duties of the provincial body in charge of monitoring the *status* and realization of national minority rights (art. 11).

The Decree also regulates a number of other important issues, such as: providing for funds for effectuation of right to official use of languages and scripts (art. 12), sanctions for decree violations (art. 13), and the like.

3. As for the official use of national minority languages, in toponomastics as in other spheres, of interest here is also the *Decree of the Assembly of the AP of*

Vojvodina on National Communities Council (2010)[57]. It regulates the *status* and structure of National Communities Council, election of its members, decision-making procedures, etc.

Article 11 of the Decree is especially important here. It stipulates that in its discussion of questions and adopting regulations within its scope of activity which are, directly or indirectly, relevant for effectuation of minority community rights, and particularly regulations by which institutions important for preservation and promotion of culture are established, as well as other regulations in the spheres of culture, education, public information and official use of languages and scripts, the Assembly of the AP of Vojvodina must have a beforehand opinion of National Communities Council. A general formula of paragraph 2 of the same article defines quite a broad scope of Council's activities. Namely, it stipulates that the Council discusses and gives its opinions and suggestions in matters relevant for co-existence of the Serbian nation and national minority communities in the AP of Vojvodina. Finally, art. 11, para. 3 specifies that subject to Council's discussion and opinion are annual and other reports of the provincial ombudsman, Government of the AP of Vojvodina and other administrative provincial bodies that are, directly or indirectly, relevant for effectuation of national minority communities rights, and particularly for supporting preservation and promotion of multilingualism, multiculturalism and multiconfessionalism.

On the grounds of art. 14 of the Decree, the Council may request reports from the provincial government, provincial administrative organs or other organization, institution or public service to which the AP of Vojvodina is founder, in matters relevant for protection and effectuation of national minority communities rights.

4. Some other provincial legal acts are also important, among them the Decree *on Distribution of Budget Funds of the Provincial Secretariat of Legislation, Administration and National Minorities for Donations and Transfers to Municipalities in the Autonomous Province of Vojvodina in Which National Minority Language and Script are in Official Use*[58]. It specifies that after public call for applications the Secretariat transfers funds to municipalities where national minority language and script are in official use for co-funding projects related to implementation by municipal or town statute defined official use of languages and scripts, among other for covering costs of boards displaying names of organs, organizations, settlements on roads, streets and squares written

57 www.puma.vojvodina.gov.rs/dokumenti/Odluke/Pso o savetu nacz.pdf.

58 Službeni list Autonomne Pokrajine Vojvodine (*Official Gazette of the Autonomous Province of Vojvodina*), 6/2008.

also in national minority languages in official use in that settlement, municipality or town[59].

2.5 Acts of local self-government units

The legal acts of municipalities and other self-government units, their supreme acts – statutes, in the first place – are of special practical interest, since these acts introduce into official use national minority languages and specify other concrete issues on the territory a unit covers. Still, their solutions must remain within the framework of enacted laws and other regulations of the Republic and Province.

2.6 International obligations

The Republic of Serbia is a party to a number of important multilateral and bilateral international treaties which, at least to a certain degree, directly deal with these issues.

1) Regional Treaties

Serbia is, among others, party to two important treaties concluded under the auspices of the European Union – *The European Charter for Regional or Minority Languages* (1992) and *The Framework Convention for the Protection of National Minorities* (1995)[60]. Both treaties stipulate obligation of member States "to allow and/or encourage ... the use or adoption, if necessary in conjunction with the name in the official language(s), of traditional and correct forms of place-names in regional or minority languages" (art. 10, para. 2g of the European Charter), "endeavour ... that traditional local names, street names and

---

59 More on this: *Informator o radu Pokrajinskog sekretarijata za propise, upravu i nacionalne manjine* (*Information Sheet on Activities of the Provincial Secretariat of Legislation, Administration and National Minorities*), p. 21; www.puma.vojvodina.gov.rs/dokumenti.php?&PHPSESSID=q91gt14chtut23legct0n96.

60 On the grounds of succession, the European Charter for Regional or Minority Languages binds Serbia since 1st June 2005; the Framework Convention for the Protection of National Minorities since 1st September 2001. See: http://conventions.coe/int/Treaty.
It is interesting in this context that the Federal Parliament of the Federal Republic of Yugoslavia enacted an act ratifying The Framework Convention as early as on 3rd December 1998 (Službeni list SR Jugoslavije – Međunarodni ugovori/*Official Gazette of the FR of Yugoslavia – International Treaties*/6/98), but the ratification documents were deposited with the European Council on 11th May 2001.

other topographical indications intended for public are also written in local language, where there is a sufficient demand for such indications" (art. 11, para. 3 of the Framework Convention).

Having in mind that the European Charter leaves certain degree of freedom to the State-parties regarding the obligations undertaken, it is interesting to note that the Republic of Serbia accepted that the respective obligations apply to even ten national minority languages (Albanian, Bosnian, Bulgarian, Croatian, Hungarian, Romanian, Romany, Ruthenian, Slovakian and Ukrainian), with only one reservation. Namely, Serbia limited the meaning of the notion from the art. 1b that "the territory in which the regional language is used" to it "will refer to the areas in which regional and minority languages are in official use in line with the national legislation"[61].

2) Bilateral Agreements

It is also of great importance that the Republic of Serbia is also bound on the grounds of succession by a series of *bilateral agreements* on protection of minority rights signed by the FR of Yugoslavia or the State Union of Serbia and Montenegro. The agreements were signed with Romania, Hungary, Macedonia and Croatia[62].

So, for example, the *Agreement Between the Federal Government of the FR of Yugoslavia and the Rumanian Government on Cooperation in Protection of National Minorities* (2002), among other things, in its art. 3, para. 2 stipulates that the parties to the Agreement will, in line with their international obligations and national legislation, enable their national minorities:

> "Use of their own languages in procedures in local organs, as well as administration and court, and the display of topographic indications, names of places, street names and names of public services in languages and scripts of national minorities wherever it is applicable".

---

61 More about it at: http://www.conventions.coe.int/Treaty/Commun/ListeDeclarations.asp?NT=148&CM=8&DF=10/11/2010&CL=ENGL&VL=1.

62 The Agreement Between the Federal Government of the Federal Republic of Yugoslavia and the Government of Rumania on Co-operation in the Field of Protection of National Minorities (2002), the Agreement Between Serbia and Montenegro and the Republic of Hungary on the Protection of Rights of the Hungarian National Minority Living in Serbia and Montenegro and Serbian National Minority Living in the Republic of Hungary (2003), the Agreement Between Serbia and Montenegro and Macedonia on the Protection of Rights of Serbian and Montenegrin National Minority Living in Macedonia and Macedonian National Minority Living in Serbia and Montenegro (2004), the Agreement Between Serbia and Montenegro and the Republic of Croatia on the Protection of Rights of Serbian and Montenegrin Minority in Croatia and Croatian Minority in Serbia and Montenegro (2004).

Basically, the agreements with Hungary (2003), Macedonia (2004), and Croatia (2004) have the same provisions.

More precisely, art. 5, para. 5 of the *Agreement Between Serbia and Montenegro and the Republic of Hungary on the Protection of the Hungarian National Minority Living in Serbia and Montenegro and the Serbian National Minority Living in the Republic of Hungary* (2003), specifies:

> "In regions where national minorities live in considerable numbers, or places of particular cultral importance for them, parties to the Agreement, in compliance with their legislations, provide for display of settlement names, names of streets and other public objects, as well as topographic data, inscriptions and information in public places, in national minority own language and in accordance to its ortography and grammar rules. National minority members have the right to public display of boards with names of companies, inscirptions and other information of private nature in their own language".

Similarly, art. 3, para. 2 of the *Agreement Between Serbia and Montenegro and Macedonia on the Protection of the Serbian and Montenegrin Nations in Macedonia and the Macedonian National Minority in Serbia and Montenegro* (2004), specifies:

> "Within framework of their legislations, parties to the Agreement, will enable national minority members to use their own language in local administration, before administrative organs and courts, as well as display of topographic inscriptions, names of places, streets and public institutions in minority languages".

Finally, basically the same solution is content of art. 6, para. 2, sub-paras. 7–8 of the *Agreement Between Serbia and Montenegro and the Republic of Croatia on the Protection of the Serbian and Montenegrin Minority in Croatia and the Croatian Minority in Serbia and Montenegro* (2004):

> "Parties to the Agreement bound themselves that in regions where national minority members live, and in compliance with their internal legislation and adopted standards of international law, to provide for official use of national minority language and script, and so in:
>
> (...)
>
> – in use of bilingual forms, inscription boards, seals and marks of state organs, local self-government organs and legal entities with public authority,
> – in marking names of settlements, straeets and squares, public inscriptions in traffic and toponyms".

So, Serbia is bound not only by its own legislation, but also by the relevant international treaties – multilateral and bilateral – that within relevant provisions stipulate the official use of national minority languages, including display of topographic indications, names of places, street names, etc. in these languages.

3. Practice

The fact that a country has a fairly good legislation still does not mean that the relevant social relations are really good enough. In other words, there is always question whether and to what extent those regulations are implemented in practice. On that issue, impartial analysis usually points out both the good and bad examples (positive instances and, on the other hand, some problems). Serbia in this regard is no exception.

3.1 Positive instances

The legal solutions regarding official use of languages in various spheres, including in displaying of names of settlements, geographic and other toponyms, are implemented in practice. In line with the competences provided to municipalities by the Law on Official Use of Languages and Writings to regulate by their statutes which languages will be in official use on their territory, many municipalities have introduced into official use national minority languages and scripts in conjuction with the Serbian language and the Cyrillic script.

Quite understandably (ethnic diversity, positive traditions, etc.) the AP of Vojvodina is leader of this practice. According to the Report of the Provincial Secretariat for Legal Acts, Administration and National Minorities submitted to the Executive Council of the AP of Vojvodina on 13th November 2006 (hereinafter: Report 2006)[63], in 38 of total of 45 municipalities in Vojvodina, in conjuction with Serbian, a national minority language was in official use[64]. Of these 38 in 31 municipalities one or more national minority languages were in official use on whole municipal territory, and in 7 in its parts[65].

In some municipalities a number of languages were in official use: 4 in 4 municipalities (Novi Sad, Zrenjanin, Kovačica and Plandište), 3 in 10 municipalities, and 2 even in even 20.

Only Serbian was in official use in 7 municipalities, *Hungarian* in 27 whole municipal territories and in 4 settlements and 4 community units on territories of

63 Report on Realization of the Right to Official Use of National Minority Languages and Scripts in the AP of Vojvodina, Novi Sad 2006. Available at: http://www.puma.vojvodina.sr.gov.yu/inform/Informacija_slupotreba_jezika_2005.pdf.

64 The table with the overview of the official use of national minority languages and scripts in the AP of Vojvodina (by municipalities and languages), made by the Provincial Secretariat for Legal Acts, Administration and National Minorities, see: http://www.puma.vojvodina.sr.gov.yu/dokumenti/ostalo/sljezik.pdf.

65 *Report (2006)*, *cit.*, p. 4.

other municipalities; *Slovakian* – in 10 whole municipal territories and in 3 settlements on territories of other municipalities; *Rumanian* – in 8 whole municipal territories and 11 community units on territories of other municipalities; *Ruthenian* – in 5 municipalities and 1 settlement; *Croatian* – in 1 municipality and 2 settlements on territories of other municipalities; *Czek* – in 1 municipality[66].

With no further detail these data show that the legal solutions regarding official use of national minority languages (where their members comprise 15% of total population, or when it is a matter of acquired rights), as well as the provisions of the *Decree on a More Detailed Regulation of Certain Issues of Official Use of National Minority Languages and Scripts in the AP of Vojvodina* (2003) regarding introduction of national minority languages in official use in a settlement or community unit (where their members on that territory comprise 25%, according to the latest census)[67] are fully implemented.

In this context the advantages of the protection of acquired rights should be stressed again. Were the principle of acquired rights not introduced, the Hungarian language would have been in official use in only 14 municipalities, Slovakian in 3, Rumanian in 1 only, while Croatian, Ruthenian and Czek would not have been in official use at all. Thus, due to the consequent implementation of the protection of acquired rights, in a number of places official use of a national minority language has been preserved though a very small number of its members (their percentage in total population)[68].

According to the latest data of the Provincial Secretariat of Legal Acts, Administration and National Minorities, published in 2010 and reflecting the state of affairs in 2009[69]: out of total of 45 municipalities in Vojvodina in 39 towns and municipalities one or more national minority languages and scripts were in official use in conjuction with Serbian.

In 31 towns or municipalities one or more national minority languages are in official use at the whole respective territory, and in 8 towns and municipalities only in some settlements. Actually, of total of 45 towns and municipalities in Vojvodina, only Serbian language is in official use in only 6 places – inžija, Irig, Opovo, Pećinci, Ruma and Sremski Karlovci.

---

66 *Ibid.*, pp. 4–5. There is also a detailed list of municipalities and settlements.

67 For more details: *Report (2006)*, *cit.*, pp. 5–6.

68 G. Bašić, K. Crnjanski, *Politička participacija i kulturna autonomija nacionalnih manjina u Srbiji* (*Political Participation and Cultural Autonomy of National Minorities in Serbia*), Belgrade, 2006; p. 101. Accessible at: http://www.fes.org.yu/index.php?str=1121.

69 *Official Use of National Minority Languages and Scripts at territory of the AP of Vojvodina*, Novi Sad, May 2009; www.puma.vojvodina.gov.rs/dokumenti.php?&PHPSESSID=q91gf8tq 14chtut23leget0n96.

This statistics is throughly presented in a document of the Provincial Secretariat of Legal Acts, Administration and National Minorities entitled "*Report on Effectuation of the Right to Official Use of National Minority Languages and Scripts in the AP of Vojvodina*", published in March, 2010, referring to the state of affairs in 2009 (hereinafter: Report 2010)[70].
According to this Report on the territory of the AP of Vojvodina[71]:

- *Hungarian* language and script are in official use on whole territory of 28 towns[72] and municipalities, plus in 8 more settlements[73];
- *Slovakian* language and script are in official use on whole territory of 10 towns[74] and municipalities, plus in 3 more settlements[75];
- *Rumanian* language and script are in official use on whole territory of 9 towns and municipalities[76], and 1 settlement[77];
- *Ruthenian* language and script are in official use on whole territory of 5 towns and municipalities[78], and 1 settlement[79];
- *Croatian* language and script are in official use on whole territory of 1 town (Subotica), and 4 settlements[80];
- *Czech* language and script are in official use in 1 municipality (Bela Crkva);

---

70 *Izveštaj o ostvarivanju prava na službenu upotrebu jezika i pisama nacionalnih manjina u AP Vojvodini* (*Report on Effectuation of the Right to Official Use of National Minority Languages and Scripts in the AP of Vojvodina)*, www.puma.vojvodina.gov.rs/dokumenti/inform/Inf 2009/Izvestaj ostv prava nacm 2009.pdf. The Report was submitted to the government of the Autonomous Province of Vojvodina. It discussed and adopted it at its session on 19th May 2010, and entitled the Provincial Secretariat of legal Acts, Administration and National Minorities to continue its cooperation with other provincial organs, organs and organizations of local self-government units, organizational units of state administration, public enterprises, institutions and services in the field of effectuation of national minority right to official use of national minority languages and scripts. The Secretariat was also charged with certain concrete tasks. See: Government Conclusions No. 090–00750/2010 (to be founded on the same Internet address as the Report, as its attachment).

71 *Izveštaj* (*Report*), *cit.*, pp. 8–9.

72 Ada, Bač, Bačka Topola, Bela Crkva, Bečej, Vrbas, Vršac, Žitište, Zrenjanin, Kanjiža, Kovačica, Kovin, Kula, Mali Iđoš, Nova Crnja, Novi Bečej, Novi Kneževac, Novi Sad, Odžaci, Plandište, Senta, Sečanj, Sombor, Srbobran, Subotica, Temerin, Titel and Čoka.

73 Banatska Topola, Kikinda, Rusko Selo, Sajan, Kupusina, Svilojevo, Vajlovica, Ivanovo.

74 Alibunar, Bač, Bačka Palanka, Bački Petrovac, Zrenjanin, Kovačica, Novi Sad, Odžaci, Plandiđte and Šid.

75 Stara Pazova, Bajša and Lug.

76 Alibunar, Bela Crkva, Vršac, Žitište, Zrenjanin, Kovačica, Kovin, Plandište, Sečanj.

77 Banatsko Novo Selo.

78 Vrbas, Žabalj, Kula, Novi Sad and Šid.

79 Novo Orahovo.

80 Stara Bingula, Bački Breg, Bački Monoštor and Sonta.

- *Bulgarian* language and script are in official use in 1 settlement (Ivanovo in the town of Pančevo);
- *Macedonian* language and script are in official use in 1 settlement (Jabuka in the town of Pančevo).

Total of 5 languages and scripts are in official use in the town of Pančevo and its settlements, 4 languages and scripts are in official use in 6 towns and municipalities, 3 languages and scripts in 13 towns and municipalities, 2 languages and scripts are in official use in 19 towns and municipalities in Vojvodina[81].

Comparison of figures of the 2006 Report with those of the 2010 Report clearly demonstrates that the official use of national minority languages and scripts is far from being reduced; on the contrary, it became even broader. So, in the meantime the official use of national minority languages has been even more persistently effectuated in practice.

The official use of national minority languages in the above cases includes, among others, writing of public inscriptions and names, and thus also the names of settlements and other geographical inscriptions, street and square names, traffic signs, etc. in these languages and scripts.

In doing so, in practice are used traditional names of towns, municipalities and settlements in a national minority language. The lists of these names specified by the Hungarian, Rumanian and Slovakian national councils were published in the Official Gazette of the AP of Vojvodina[82].

So, the National Council of the Hungarian national minority specified traditional names of 263 settlements in 28 municipalities. For example, for the Serbian name for Vojvodina capital – Novi Sad – a Hungarian synonim *Újvidék* was specified; for Serbian Bačka Topola – *Topolya,* for Serbian Bela Crkva – *Fehértemplom*; for Serbian Kanjiža – *Magyarkanizsa*; for Serbian Kovačica – *Antalfalva,* Kovin – *Kevevára*; Mali Iđoš – *Kishegyes*; Novi Bečej – *Törökbecse*; Odžaci – *Hódság,* etc.

The National Council of the Rumanian national minority specified traditional Rumanian names of 38 settlements, and the National Council of the Slovakian national minority the traditional Slovakian names of 30 settlements (2 of which administratively are parts of the city of Beograd)[83].

---

81 *Izveštaj* (*Report*), *cit.*, p. 9.

82 Službeni glasnik Autonomne Pokrajine Vojvodine (*Official Gazette of the Autonomous Province of Vojvodina*), 12/2003 and 13/2003.

83 For example, for Serbian name Banatsko Novo Selo the Rumanian is *Satu Nou*, for Bela Crkva – *Biserica Alba*, for Serbian Dolovo – *Doloave*, for Jankov Most – *Iancaid*, Kovin – *Cuvin,* etc. For Serbian name Bačka Palanka Slovakian is *Bačska Palanka*, for Belo Blatno – *Biele Blato*, for Gložan – *Hložany*, etc.

Since the National Council of the Ruthenian national minority had not specified the list of traditional names of settlements in their language in due time, the Executive Council of the AP of Vojvodina (Vojvodina government) – in compliance with the art. 7 of the *Decree on a More Detailed Regulation of Certain Issues of Official Use of National Minority Languages and Scripts in the AP of Vojvodina* (2003) – did it by its Decree on specification of traditional names of municipalities and settlements in the Ruthenian language in May 2006[84].

Among other interesting data, worth mentioning is that the Provincial Secretariat for Legal Acts, Administration and National Minorities – in compliance with art. 6 of the *Decree on the 2005 AP of Vojvodina Budget*[85], in connection with implementation of the *Decree on a More Detailed Regulation of Certain Issues of Official Use of National Minority Languages and Scripts in the AP of Vojvodina* (2003) – made two public calls for applications for distribution of transfer funds of total of 5 million dinars asking municipalities where a national minority language and script are in official use to apply. The funds were ment as financial support to projects related to the implementation of by municipal or town statutes defined official use of languages and scripts, and in that connection, costs of making and displaying boards with names of organs and organizations, settlements on road direction signs, street and square names written also in national minority languages being in official use in a settlement, municipality or the city of Novi Sad[86]. The same practice continued in the years that followed[87].

Quite understandably, though the AP of Vojvodina leads in this respect, the relevant legal solutions are also implemented in some parts of the so-called Central Serbia (Serbia without provinces). It should be repeated that whether a certain national minority language will be introduced into official use depends upon the percentage of minority population at a given territory (i.e. that the percentage of minority population in the region of Central Serbia is substantially lower than in the AP of Vojvodina).

---

84 Službeni list Autonomne Pokrajine Vojvodine (*Official Gazette of the Autonomous Province of Vojvodina*), 6/2006. Thus, for example, for Bačka Topola was specified Ruthenian name *Бачка Тополя*, for Bela Crkva – *Била Церква*, etc.

85 Službeni list Autonomne Pokrajine Vojvodine (*Official Gazette of the Autonomous Province of Vojvodina*), 32/2004.

86 Informator Pokrajinskog sekretarijata za propise, upravu i nacionalne manjine, 2005–2006, (Information of the Provincial Secretariat of Legal Acts, Administration and National Minorities), Novi Sad, 2006, p. 21, http://www.puma.vojvodina.sr.gov.yu/dokumenti/ostalo/Informator2005-06sr.pdf.

87 For more, see*: Izveštaj 2010* (*Report 2010*), *cit.*, pp. 27–29.

Thus, the *Bosnyak language and script* were introduced in official use in 4 municipalities in which Bosnyaks are either majority or a considerable percentage of total population (Novi Pazar, Tutin, Sjenica, Prijepolje); *Albanian* in 3 municipalities of Southern Serbia (Preševo, Bujanovac i Medveđa)[88]; *Bulgarian* in 2 municipalities (Dimitrovgrad and Bosilegrad – on the Serbian – Bulgarian border), and *Vlack* or *Rumanian* is to be introduced to official use in 4 municipalities (Žagubica, Kučevo, Bor and Boljevac)[89].

As in Vojvodina, in municipalities in Central Serbia where minority language is in official use, topographic signs are also written in the minority language.

Finally, it should be said that the Advisory Committee monitoring implementation of the Framework Convention for the Protection of National Minorities (implementation of art. 11 of the Convention) noted that the Law on Official Use of Languages and Writings of Serbia provides valuable guarantees, and that good practices are present as for display of public topographic signs in local self-goverment units where a minority language is in use[90].

In its Second Opinion on Serbia as of 19th March 2009, the Advisory Committee noted certain positive developments in that field. In that connection the Committee observes that art. 11 of the National Minority Law stipulates that local names, names of streets and other topographic signs have also to be written in national minority languages that are in official use. The Committee praised increase in writing of traditional names and toponyms in minority languages in the province of Vojvodina, and highlighted contribution of some national minority national councils in codification of local names[91].

3.2 Observed problems

However, that good legal solutions are mostly implemented in practice does not mean there are no problems. The latter differ and have different forms, and their manifestations vary in degrees in different regions. The responsible bodies at different levels usually justify their non-implementation of legal solutions with resort to reasons such as unclear provisions (different possible interpretations –

---

88 These municipalities are in Central Serbia, i.e. not in Kosovo and Metohija.

89 G. Bašić, K. Crnjanski, *op. cit.,* pp. 106–107.

90 Advisory Committee on the Framework Convention for the Protection of National Minorities, *Opinion on Serbia and Montenegro,* ACFC/INF/OP/I(2004)002, 27th November 2003, para. 83, http://www.coe.int/t/e/human_rights/minorities/.

91 Advisory Committee on the Framework Convention for the Protection of national Minorities, *Second Opinion on Serbia and Montenegro adopted on 19 March 2009,* §§ 183–184, p. 34; www. coe.int/t/monitor.ng/minorities/3 FCNdcs/Table en.asp#Serbia.

even without obvious reasons), insufficient financial, personnel and other resourses, citizens indifference, and the like.

In some cases the solution that national minority councils specify traditional names of towns, municipalities and settlements in their languages faced the resistance of local population. Thus, in some of the AP of Vojvodina municipalities the decisions of national councils regarding traditional names were wrongly interpreted – i.e. that for their implementation a prior consent of municipality statute is needed. The Provincial Secretariat for Legal Acts, Administration and National Minorities intervened with its interpretation that such specifications are automatically implemented after their coming into effect, and that the official use of a national minority language entails use of names specified by the respective national council, without any further verification[92].

However, the most often were the inappropriate reactions of the majority population, but also misunderstandings between different national minorities arose, even within a single minority. So, for example, traditional Hungarian names of four places (Feketić, Telečka, Debeljača and Kovačica) turned to a subject of a serious debate. A group of Stara Moravica inhabitants, unsatisfied with suggested traditional Hungarian name of their place "*Bácskossuthfalva*", launched initiative the name should be "*Ómoravica*", for it is, as they claimed, more familiar[93].

Despite high quality of legal solutions, the implementation of official use of national minority languages and scripts faced financial problems, and, somewhere, even an active subversion of local authorities.

In this connection it should be noted that some (though isolated) attempts to abandon the official use of a minority language occured. So, there are claims that the Srbobran mayer, despite undisputable legal provisions, tried in various ways to curb the official use of the traditional Hungarian name of that place (*Szenttamast*)[94].

In April 2005, the municipal assembly of Šid adopted the *Decree on Changes and Amendments to the Municipal Statute* by which the official use of Latin alphabet and Slovak and Ruthenian language in the municipality were abandoned. However, when the municipal authorities understood that the Decree

92 *Izveštaj* (*Report*), *cit.*, p. 15.

93 *Ibid.*

94 See more: Savez Vojvođanskih Mađara, (*Union of the Vojvodina Hungarians*), *Aktuelna pitanja u vezi ostvarivanja prava Mađara u Vojvodini* (*Actual Issues in Realization of Hungarian Rights in Vojvodina*), www.VMSZ.org.yu/sh/aktuelno/2005-11-21-htm?id=18 (1st April 2007).

was illegal, its implementation was curbed and it was annuled at the next assembly session[95].

Multiethnic community of Subotica was also faced with certain problems. In 2005, the national council of the Bunyevtsi national minority addressed the Subotica municipal assembly demanding application of affirmative action measures and introduction of their language to official use on territory of Subotica. The responsible municipal bodies did not answer that initiative, though the principle of affirmative action had already been applied in the introduction of Croatian language and script to official use on the territory of Subotica municipality.

In this context, it should be reminded that the *Decree on a More Detailed Regulation of Certain Issues of Official Use of National Minority Languages and Scripts in the AP of Vojvodina* (2003) stipulates that where national minority language and script are not in the official use on the municipal territory as a whole, they will be introduced in the official use in a settlement or a community unit (i.e. specified areas of that municipality), if the percentage of a given national minority in that settlement or community unit is 25%, according to the latest census (art. 8, para. 3). The solution is consequently implemented in majority of instances, but still some municipalities failed (as of the end of 2006) to fulfill this obligation[96].

Even when at the state organs intervention the state of affairs in many places was improved, i.e. their statutes were adjusted to the relevant legislation solutions[97], there are places where it was not done yet. So, despite the explicit provision of the above mentioned art. 8, para. 3 of the *Decree on a More Detailed Regulation of Certain Issues of Official Use of National Minority Languages and Scripts in the AP of Vojvodina* stipulates (2003), Inđija and Irig municipalities have not yet adjusted their statutes to it[98]. In that connection, it is observed that in Inđija municipality's settlement Slankamenski Vinogradi the Slovakian language and script should be introduced to official use since Slovaks are 74.81% of total population; that in the Irig municipality's settlement Dobrodol the Hungarians are 75.59% of total population, and 63.4% in Šatrinci; and that the Croatian language and script should be introduced to official use in

---

95 *Godišnji izveštaj Pokrajinskog ombudsmana za 2005. godinu* (*2005 Report of the Provincial Ombudsman*), p. 20; http://www.ombudsman-apv.org.yu/srpski/dokumenti/izveštaji/2005/index.htm.

96 For particular cases, see: G. Bašić, K. Crnjanski, *op. cit.*, pp. 102–103.

97 Among others, only in 2008 such by Serbian standards big and important places as town of Pančevo, town of Sombor and Vršac municipality adjusted their statutes to the relevant legislation solutions. See more: *Izveštaj 2010 (Report 2010)*, *cit.*, pp. 9–10.

98 *Izveštaj 2010* (*Report 2010*), *cit.*, pp. 9–10.

the Šid municipality's settlement Sot, where Croats make for 40.07% of population[99].

Of course, it should be said again that the issues connected to official use of national minority languages directly influence their official use in displaying of names and settlements and other toponyms.

Most *boards at the entrance to settlements* were set earlier and the diversity (and in most cases, irregularity) in spelling of names is apparent. The majority of boards with settlement names are improperly written – only in Cyrillic or Latin script (exp. "*Нови Сад*" – "*Novi Sad*"), only in Serbian in Cyrillic or Latin script, in national minority language and script only, and the like. More recent boards better fit provisions on official use of languages. A particular problem is that now and then the boards displaying settlement names are repainted (usually with spray colours) – either those in minority or in Serbian language[100].

However, even if the legal solution regarding the display of multilingual boards with settlement names is generally implemented in practice, multilingual *boards with street and square names* happen to be definitely rarer. They are by far scarcer, many being worn-out, more than thirty years old[101]. In many cases of replacement of the old with new boards, inscriptions were only in Serbian and Cyrillic script. The *Decree on Specification of House Numbers, Displaying of House Numbers and Displaying of Settlement, Street and Square Names (2003)* will hopefully contribute to gradual disappearance of the mentioned problems. However, it has been justifiably objected that the term envisaged for replacement of the existing boards displaying settlement, street and square names is too long (ten years), so that so far there are no apparent improvements in practice[102].

So, a general observation still holds that local self-government units and settlements where names of streets and squares are properly written are rare. In some settlements there are no boards with street and square names at all – exp. Lovćenac, Bajša, Vlajkovac, Uljma, Feketić[103]. Moreover, even in the Vojvodina capital Novi Sad no board with street or square name written in all languages in official use is to be found. All the more, even the board at the very road entrance to Novi Sad is not written in compliance with the Novi Sad town statute[104].

---

99 *Ibid.*

100 *Izveštaj 2006* (*Report 2006*), *cit.*, p. 15; *Izveštaj 2010* (*Report 2010*), *cit.*, p.23.

101 J. Oros, *Iskustva vojvođanske vlade sa promocijom različitosti i tolerancije* (*Experiences of the Vojvodina Government in Promotion of Differencies and Tolerance*), in *Promocija različitosti* (*Promotion of Differencies*),Izbor predavanja i diskusija, Seminar, Fruška Gora, 24th–26th February 2006, www.ndnv.org/različitost/seminar2.html.

102 *Izveštaj 2006* (*Report 2006*), *cit.*, p. 15.

103 *Izveštaj 2010* (*Report 2010*), *cit.*, p. 22.

104 *Ibid.*

Though in most instances constitutional and legal solutions are consequently implemented in practice, there, unfortunately, are certain cases of disregarding, even open violation of these norms and principles.

If certain problems obviously arise in Vojvodina, known for its ethnically diverse composition and long tradition of multiculturality and tolerance, it is not surprising that problems are present in Central Serbia. In any case, it should be said that, despite a sufficient number of positive instances, (so far) the exercise of the right to official use of languages has not been implemented in a desirable way in municipalities of Central Serbia, and that their practice is behind the one in the Vojvodina municipalities. Having in mind substantially lower concentration of minority population in Central Serbia, such a situation is partly justifiable.

Still, some inconsistencies are indisputable. So, for example, though the Bosnyak language has been introduced to the official use in other places, in Priboj where Bosnyaks make for more than 15% of total population (thus fulfilling legal condition to have their language in official use), local authorities are so far missing to meet the legal obligation and introduce their language to official use. This is obvious in displaying of public inscriptions, street and square names, names of parts of settlements, names of local and state bodies and services, names of toponyms and traffic signs. And all that despite the fact that the so-called democratic parties, including a Bosnyak one, are in power[105].

Leaving the question whether justified or not[106], objections of some members of the Hungarian national minority should be noted here. Namely, they find the administrative boarders of certain municipalities thus defined that a number of whole settlements with thousands of members of the Hungarian national minority do not make for 15% of total municipal population, and even more so

105 E. Džudžević, *Položaj i ostvarivanje prava sandžačkih Bošnjaka u SCG* (*Position and Effectuation of Sandžak Bosnyaks Rights in SCG*), in V. Stanovčić, *Položaj nacionalnih manjina u Srbiji* (*Position of National Minorities in Serbia*), Srpska akademija nauka i umetnosti, Belgrade, 2007, pp. 481–493. Also available at: http://www.bnv.org.yu/preporucujemo.php?lang=ba&profil=2.

106 With no intention to initiate here any debate with the mentioned claims, it should be noted that herein cited paper was written for conference held in 2005 (though published in 2007), that the positive legislation provides for, and under certain conditions, stipulates as mandatory introduction of a national minority language into official use also at certain parts of a given municipality, and that the solutions are implemented in practice. As it has been already elaborated, there is no need of repetition. In other words, even if the share of Hungarian national minority is not high enough at municipality territory as a whole, official use of its language and script is possible in that parts of municipality where it is.

after the 2002 census. Thereof fears that some rights might gradually fade away, despite the so called acquired rights[107].

And finally, apart from other weaknesses in implementation of relevant regulations in practice (hardly to be avoided), it should be stressed that the Roma – due to their disperse settlements – still retain a specific *status* compared to other national minorities. Though among the most numerous national minorities (108,000 according to the latest census; even 800,000 according to estimations of Roma organization activists)[108], they hardly exceed 15% of total population in any municipality (i.e. legal condition for mandatory introduction of a national minority language and script in official use). And even when they do, the official use of their language is hardly fulfilled in practice, including in displaying of settlement and other topographic names. In fact, so much indicates they are the most vulnerable ethnic groups in Serbia[109].

Despite some tributes, the Advisory Committee for monitoring respect of the Framework Convention for the Protection of National Minorities noted certain weaknesses in the field. In its First Opinion, the Committee underlined that "additional efforts are needed in practice, for example, concerning street inscriptions in parts in considerable numbers inhabited by Rumanians and Croats, respectively"[110].

And in its Second Opinion on Serbia (19th March 2009) too the Advisory Committee made some critical objections. Its general observation was that additional efforts in practice were needed for a full implementation of guarantees provided for by the Framework Convention in connectionto display of traditional names and topographic signs in national minority languages[111]. Among else, the Committee underlined that various problems were reported, such as: resistance of local authorities, frequent wrong spelling of names of places in minority

---

107 *Bozoki Anzal, Neka aktuelna pitanja i problemi položaja Mađara u Vojvodini* (*Some Actual Questions and Problems of the Status of Hungarians in Vojvodina*), in V. Stanovčić, *Položaj nacionalnih manjina u Srbiji* (*Position of National Minorities in Serbia*), Srpska akademija nauka i umetnosti, Belgrade, 2007, p. 535.

108 N. Dobrković (ed.), *Ljudska prava u Srbiji 2006* (*Human Rights in Serbia 2006*), Beogradski centar za ljudska prava, Belgrade, 2007, p. 195.

109 More about *status* of Roma in Serbia: S. Zlatanović, *Pregovaranje o identitetu: Romi koji to i jesu i nisu* (*Negotiating Identity: Roma that are and are not*), in V. Stanovčić (ed.), *Položaj nacionalnih manjina u Srbiji* (*Position of National Minorities in Serbia*), Srpska akademija nauka i umetnosti, Belgrade, 2007, pp. 639–647, and literature quoted there.

110 Advisory Committee on the Framework Convention for the Protection of National Minorities, *Opinion on Serbia and Montenegro*, *cit.*, par. 83, http://www.coe.int/t/e/humanrights/minorities/.

111 Advisory Committee on the Framework Convention for the Protection of National Minorities, *Second Opinion on Serbia adopted on 19 March 2009, cit.*, § 182, p. 33.

languages (in compliance with Serbian and not respective national minority orthography), and writing names of places in Serbian language (in Cyrillic and lating script) instead both in Serbian and the respective national minority language (in compliance with its orthography)[112].

The Committee further noted that, despite plenty of positive examples in Vojvodina, the situation in other parts of Serbia was much less favourable. It was particularly stressed that the practice differed considerably from the accepted legal solutions in the Nothern parts of Serbia with Vlach i.e. Rumanian population, as well as in some Sandžak municipalities inhabited by Bosnyaks. And all that, in spite the fact that population of those national minorities, in both cases, exceeds 15%. Finally, the Committee underlined that so far there were no positive improvements regarding the request of the Bulgarian national minority for change the name of town Dimitrovgrad to a traditional one (Caribord)[113].

In line with these objection, the Committee recommended Serbian authorities to monitor implementation of legal guarantees in connection with display of names of places and topographic signs in minority languages, in consultation with national councils of the respective national minorities, as well as to secure consequent implementation of the guarantees all around Serbia[114].

The Serbian Government in its answer (comment to the Second Opinion of the Advisory Board) objected that, in its opinion, presented findings of the Committee contained an one-sided interpretation which neglects important circumstances the Republic of Serbia had highlighted in its Report. In that connection, it underlined that laws regulating effectuation of particular constitutionally guaranteed rights were valid in the Republic of Serbia as a whole, and that thus, on normative level, were no differences in legal *status* of national minorities in different parts of the State. The Government especially pointed out that the regulations that the AP of Vojvodina adopts are of lower legal power than laws, and that they are adopted on grounds of laws and thereof are incapable to create a legal regime resulting in uneven legal *status* of national minorities in different parts of the State[115].

The Government found appropriate to additionally explain that eventual differences in official use of minority languages did not result exclusively from the existence of political-territorial autonomy at a part of the state territory,

---

112 *Ibid,* § 185, p. 34.

113 *Ibid.,* §186, p. 34.

114 *Ibid.,* § 187, p. 34.

115 Comments of the Government of Serbia on the Second Opinion of the Advisory Committee on the Implementation of the Framework Convention for the Protection of National minorities (received on 30th September 2009), Serbian version, p. 7; www.coe/t/dghl/monitoring/minorities/3 FCNdocs/Table en-asp#Serbia.

because the official use of languages and scripts is partly in competence of local self-government units. In other words, even if there were certain differences in regard to the official use of languages and scripts, such differences might be an outcome of the acquired rights in a particular sphere of social life guaranteed by the Constitution of the Republic of Serbia and the Law on the Protection of Rights and Freedoms of national Minorities; result of high percentage of a national minority members in total population of certain local self-goverment units, or a consequence of different economic capacities of different local self-government units, or different geographic regions[116].

However valid arguments of the Government of Serbia might be, the fact is that relevant regulations of the Republic of Serbia in this domain are not always and everywhere in practice consequently implemented, and that still the improvements are possible.

4. Conclusion

According to the above said, positive Serbian legislation undoubtedly creates solid foundations for the official use of minority languages, including their use in display of names of settlements, geographic signs, street and square names, traffic signs and the like. In this regard, the situation is probably much better than in many other States, including those considered as truly democratic.

The fact that these issues are regulated by the Constitution and other relevant laws and other regulations entail such a conclusion. Besides, the adopted very liberal solutions were elaborated in co-operation with national minority representatives and were well evaluated abroad.

Finally to repeat: toponyms and other respective signs should be written, and where certain conditions are fulfilled *have to be inscribed* (i.e. mandatory) in national minority languages, in line with their traditional names and orthography. Through their national councils the national minorities themselves specify these names in their own language.

However, this does not mean the legal regulation is ideal. In the first place there is a certain inconsistency between relevant laws (fortunately not influencing the practice). These shortcomings were recently mostly eliminated by the latest changes and amendments of the Law on Official Use of Languages and Scripts, and adoption of other relevant regulations. Though these developments were not in focus of this paper, numerous state and other organs are in charge of consequent effectuation of the adopted solutions (various ministries, courts,

116 *Ibid.*

ombudsmen of various levels, national minority national councils, etc.), and unsatisfied parties have at their disposal a lot of processual opportunities – from complaints in an administrative procedure, initiating administrative litigations as well as the other court procedures, including procedure before the Constitutional Court, and addressing relevant international institutions.

Generally speaking, the practice justifiably deserves to be positively evaluated, and that despite certain mistakes, even violations of law herein mentioned. A better understanding of complex circumstances the Serbian society as a whole – majority and minority ethnic groups alike – experienced and still is experiencing is necessary when doing any evaluation. A confirmation to this assumption is that there were certain misunderstandings, even conflicts, not only between majority and minority population, but also between different national minorities, even within the same minority. We ought to believe that such phenomena will fade away with the further democratization of this society and, especially, with the degree to which the tolerance is preserved and improved. We are actually free to say that despite all the weaknesses and inconsistencies, the existing situation is not bad (much better than in many other environments), but it could and should be better. But, for such an improvement, good will of both majority and minority population is indispensable.

Bibliography

Antonić S., *Venecijanska komisija i ćirilica, Nova srpska politička misao* (*The Venice Commission and the Cyrillic Script*), special edition 2/2008.

Bašić G., *Položaj manjina u SR Jugoslaviji od stagnacije ka afirmaciji* (*Status of Minorities in the FR of Yugoslavia: from Stagnation to Affirmation*), in Macura M., Stanovčić V. (eds.), *Položaj manjina u Saveznoj Republici Jugoslaviji*, (*Position of Minorities in the Federal Republic of Yugoslavia*), SANU, Belgrade, 1996.

Bašić G., *Položaj Bošnjaka u Sandžaku* (*Status of Bosnyaks in Sandžak*), Belgrade, 2002.

Bašić G., *Zaštita prava nacionalnih manjina u SRJ prema standardima Okvirne konvencije za zaštitu nacionalnih manjina Saveta Evrope* (*Protection of National Minority Rights According to Standards of the Framework Convention for the Protection of National Minorities of the Council of Europe*), Belgrade, 2002.

Bašić G., Crnjanski K., *Politička participacija i kulturna autonomija nacionalnih manjina u Srbiji* (*Political Participation and Cultural Autonomy of National

Minorities in Serbia), Belgrade, 2006, http://www.fes.org.yu/index.php?str =1121.

Bozoki A., *Neka aktuelna pitanja i problemi položaja Mađara u Vojvodini* (*Some Actual Questions and Problems of the Status of Hungarians in Vojvodina*), in Stanovčić V., *Položaj nacinalnih manjina u Srbiji* (*Position of National Minorities in Serbia*), Srpska akademija nauka i umetnosti, Belgrade, 2007.

Dobrković D. (ed.), *Ljudska prava u Srbiji 2006* (*Human Rights in Serbia 2006*), Beogradski centar za ljudska prava, Belgrade, 2007.

Dobrković D. (ed.), *Ljudska prava u Srbiji 2009* (*Human Rights in Serbia 2009*), Beogradski centar za ljudska prava, Belgrade, 2010.

Džudžević E., *Položaj i ostvarivanje prava sandžačkih Bošnjaka u SCG* (*Position and Effectuation of Sandžak Bosnyaks Rights in the State Union of Serbia and Montenegro*), in Stanovčić V. (ed.), *Položaj nacionalnih manjina u Srbiji* (*Position of National Minorities in Serbia*), Srpska akademija nauka i umetnosti, Belgrade, 2007.

Hok R., *Prilog istoriji pravnog regulisanja upotrebe jezika naroda i narodnosti u Vojvodini* (*A Contribution to the Legal Regulation of Use of Languages of Nations and Nationalities in Vojvodina*), Zbornik radova Pravnog fakulteta u Novom Sadu, vol. 6, Novi Sad, 1972.

Jončić K., *Nacionalne manjine u Jugoslaviji* (*National Minorities in Yugoslavia*), Belgrade, 1962.

Jončić K. (ed.), *Nations and Nationalities of Yugoslavia*, Belgrade, 1974.

Korhec T., *Granice univerzalnosti manjinskih prava – o značaju teritorije i brojčanosti – sa posebnim osvrtom na pravo na službenu upotrebu jezika nacionalnih manjina u Vojvodini* (*Limits of Universality of Minority Rights – On Importance of Territory and Numbers – With Special Emphasis on Official Use of National Minority Languages in Vojvodina*), in Stanovčić V. (ed.), *Položaj nacionalnih manjina u Srbiji* (*Position of Nationaly Minorities in Serbia*), SANU, Belgrade, 2007.

Korhecz T. K., *Službena upotreba jezika i pravna država* (*Official Use of Languages and State of Law*), in *Pravni život*, 14/2007.

Krivokapić B., *The Ethnic Structure of the Federal Republic of Yugoslavia and the Concept of a Minority Community*, in *Yugoslav Law,* 1/1993.

Krivokapić B., *Ethnic Minorities in the Federal Republic of Yugoslavia and Their Rights*, in *Yugoslav Law*, 2–3/1994 and 1/1995.

Krivokapić B., *Neki problemi u vezi sa pravnom uređenošću položaja manjina u SR Jugoslaviji* (*Some Problems Related to Legal Regulation of the Position of National Minorities in the FR of Yugoslavia*), in Macura M., Stanovčić V.

(eds.), *Položaj manjina u Saveznoj Republici Jugoslaviji* (*Position of Minorities in the Federal Republic of Yugoslavia*), SANU, Belgrade, 1996.

Krivokapić B., *Položaj manjina u ustavima donetim na teritoriji bivše SFR Jugoslavije* (*Position of Minorities in Constitutions Adopted in the Region of Former SFR of Yugoslavia*), in *Zbornik Pravnog fakulteta u Nišu*, 1997.

Krivokapić B., *Međunarodni i uporedni standardi u materiji prava etničkih manjina i praksa Jugoslavije* (*International and Comparative Standards in Matters of Ethnic Minority Rights and the Yugoslav Practice*), *Manjine u međunarodnim i dokumentima SR Jugoslavije* (*Minorities in International Documents and Documents of the FR of Yugoslavia*), Belgrade, 1999.

Krivokapić B., *Novo jugoslovensko zakonodavstvo o zaštiti prava i sloboda nacionalnih manjina* (*Recent Yugoslav Legislation on the Protection of National Minority Rights and Freedoms*), in *Zbornik Pravnog fakulteta u Splitu* (*Collections of the Split Faculty of Law*), 3–4/2002.

Krivokapić B., *Problem naziva manjina – nacionalne, etničke ili..?* (*Problem of Naming Minorities: National, Ethnic Or...?*), in *Pravni informator,* 1/2002.

Krivokapić B., *The Federal Law on the Protection of Rights and Freedoms of Minorities (2002) in the light of the standards established by the Framework Convention for the Protection of National Minorities*, in *Yugoslav Law*, 1/2003.

Krivokapić B., *Serbia and Montenegro: The New Legal Framework for the Protection of Ethnic Minorities*, in *Revue québécoise de droit international*, vol. 16.1, 1/2003.

Krivokapić B., *Pojam, vrste i naziv manjina* (*Notion, Kinds and Name of Minorities*), in *Prava čoveka*, 5–6/2003.

Krivokapić B., *A Contribution to the Initiative for New Legislation of the Republic of Serbia Relating to Official Use of Language*, in *Yugoslav Law*, 3/2003.

Krivokapić B., *Službena upotreba jezika u međunarodnom pravu i novijem zakonodavstvu nekih evropskih država* (*Official Use of Languages in International Law and Recent Legislation of Some European States*), Belgrade, 2004.

Krivokapić B., *Službena upotreba jezika u pravu Italije* (*Official Use of Languages in Italian Law*), in *Strani pravni život*, 1/2004.

Krivokapić B., *Službena upotreba jezika u Ruskoj Federaciji* (*Official Use of Languages in the Russian Federation*), in *Strani pravni život*, 2–3/2004.

Krivokapić B., *O nekim problemima službene upotrebe jezika u unutrašnjim porecima država* (*On Some Issues of Official Use of Languages in Internal State Orders*), in *Anali Pravnog fakulteta u Beogradu*, 2/2005.

Krivokapić B., *Protection of Linguistic Minorities and Toponomastics in Serbia*, in de Vergottini G., Piergigli V. (eds.), *La toponomastica in Istria, Fiume e Dalmazia. Profili giuridici*, vol. I, Florence, 2009.

Krivokapić B., *Enciklopedijski rečnik međunarodnog prava i međunarodnih odnosa* (*Encyclopedic Dictionary of International Law and International Relations*), Belgrade, 2010.

Lomansky P., *Službena upotreba jezika i pisama u našem savremenom ustavnom sistemu* (*Official Use of Languages and Scripts in our Current Constitutional Order*), in *Pravo: teorija i praksa*, 9/1999.

Lućić M., *Položaj i prava manjina u Vojvodini* (*Status and Rights of Minorities in Vojvodina*), Novi Sad, 1993.

Milivojević Z., *Jugoslavija i Okvirna konvencija Saveta Evrope za zaštitu nacionalnih manjina* (*Yugoslavia and the Framework Convention for the Protection of National Minorities of the Council of Europe*), in *Međunarodna politika*, 1075/1999.

NACIONALNE MANJINE I PRAVO (*National Minorities and Law*), Helsinške sveske, vol. 15, Belgrade, 2002.

NACIONALNE MANJINE U SR JUGOSLAVIJI (*National Minorities in the FR of Yugoslavia*), Savezno ministarstvo nacionalnih i etničkih zajednica, Belgrade, 2001.

NATIONAL MINORITIES IN YUGOSLAVIA, *Federal Ministry of National and Ethnic Communities*, Belgrade, 2001.

Obradović K., *Položaj nacionalnih manjina na teritoriji nekadašnje SFRJ – pravo, praksa i perspektive* (*Position of National Minorities in Former SFRY – Law, Practice and Perspectives*), in Dimitrijević V., Paunović M. (eds.), *Prava i slobode: međunarodni i jugoslovenski standardi* (*Rights and Freedoms: International and Yugoslav Standards*), Belgrade, 1995.

Oros J., *Službena upotreba jezika i pisama u AP Vojvodini* (*Official Use of Languages and Scripts in Vojvodina*), in Stanovčić V. (ed.), *Položaj nacionalnih manjina u Srbiji* (*Position of National Minorities in Serbia*), SANU, Belgrade, 2007.

OTVORENI PROBLEMI NARODNOSTI U JUGOSLAVIJI (*Open Issues of Nationalities in Yugoslavia*), *Conference in Maribor 5–6.6.1990*, *Pravo: teorija i praksa*, Novi Sad, 1991.

Pajvanćić M., *Prava nacionalnih manjina u ustavnom sistemu Srbije* (*National Minority Rights in Constitutional System of Serbia*), in *Pravna riječ*, 22/2010.

Paunović M., *Nationalities and Minorities in the Yugoslav Federation and Serbia*, in Packer J. & Myntti K. (eds.), *The Protection of Ethnic and Linguistic Minorities in Europe*, Åbo 1997.

Pavlović-Križanić T., *Manjinska prava u SR Jugoslaviji i Republici Srbiji* (*Minority Rights in the FR of Yugoslavia and the Republic of Serbia*), in Samardžić M. (ed.), *Zaštita nacionalnih manjina* (*Protection of National Minorities*), Belgrade, 2002.

PRAVO I PRAVO NA UPOTREBU JEZIKA (*Law and Right to Use of Language*), group of authors, Belgrade, 1990.

Ralić P., *Prava manjina u Srbiji* (*Minority Rights in Serbia*), Belgrade, 1992.

Samardžić M., *Položaj manjina u Vojvodini* (*Position of Minorities in Vojvodina*), Belgrade, 1999.

Samardžić M., *Tranzicija i manjine u Vojvodini* (*Transition and Minorities in Vojvodina*), in Samardžić M. (ed.), *Zaštita nacionalnih manjina* (*Protection of National Minorities*), Belgrade, 2002.

Stojković LJ., Martić M., *Nacionalne manjine u Jugoslaviji* (*National Minorities in Yugoslavia*), Belgrade, 1953.

Turćinović F., *Pogled na relacije prava SRJ i prava EU u sferi zaštite ljudskih prava sa posebnim osvrtom na prava manjina* (*A View of the SFY Legislation Relation to the EU Legislation in Matters of the Protection of Human Rights, With Special Consideration of Minority Rights*), in *collected papers: Usklađivanje prava SR Jugoslavije sa pravom Evropske unije* (*Adjustment of the FR of Yugoslavia Legislation to the European Union Legislation*), Niš, 1999.

Zlatanović S., *Pregovaranje o identitetu: Romi koji to i jesu i nisu* (*Negotiating Identity: Roma that are and are not*), in Stanovčić V. (ed.), *Položaj nacionalnih manjina u Srbiji* (*Position of National Minorities in Serbia*), SANU, Belgrade, 2007.

Linguistic rights and minority toponymy in Romania

Sergiu Constantin

Summary

1. Introduction

This article aims to present in brief the legal framework for the protection of the linguistic rights of national minorities in Romania and to assess its level of implementation through an overview of the State of affairs on the ground. Firstly, we shall examine the most important aspects of the use of minority languages in the educational and judicial systems. Secondly, the research examines the linguistic rights of minorities in relation to public administration, including the issue of place names and bilingual signs.

This concise presentation of the existing legal standards is followed by a rather detailed evaluation of their impact at the level of different minority groups. Based on comprehensive reports and comparative studies, the article shall address both the progress made in the implementation process in recent years and the problems that still need to be resolved. Finally, we shall summarize the main conclusions regarding the linguistic rights of national minorities within the Romanian legal system.

2. National minorities and their linguistic rights: a brief overview of the educational and judicial systems

Romania has twenty officially recognized national minorities, but its legal framework contains no clear legal definition of the concept[1]. The draft law on national minorities recognises them as "constitutive factors" of the Romanian State[2] and enumerates the minority groups that shall benefit under the law[3]. The national minorities are defined as "communities of Romanian citizens living on the territory of Romania from the moment the modern Romanian State was established"[4]. These communities are numerically inferior to the majority population, they have their own "specific ethnic identity expressed by culture, language or religion" and they wish to preserve, express and promote this identity[5]. The European Commission for Democracy Through Law (so-called Venice Commission) expressed concern regarding the list of officially recognized national minorities, which apparently has an exhaustive character[6]. Moreover, the Venice Commission criticised the proposed definition of a national minority because it introduces citizenship as an objective element of the definition, thus leaving minority persons that are not citizens outside the scope of the law. While this may be acceptable when it "concerns political rights and in particular the right for national minorities to be represented in Parliament, the

---

1 One might reasonably speak about a vicious circle: according to art. 7, para. 1 of Law no. 67/2004 for election of the local public administrative authorities and to art. 2, para. 29 of Law no. 35/2008 on the election of Chamber of Deputies and Senate, national minorities are those represented in the Council of National Minorities, a consultative body of the Government. On the other hand, Government Decision no. 589/2001 on the establishment of the Council of National Minorities, stipulates in art. 2 that its members are the organisation of national minorities represented in the Parliament.

2 Art. 2 of the Draft Law on the Status of National Minorities. The document is available in Romanian and English in the Minority Rights Information System (MIRIS) database, at http://www.eurac.edu/miris.

3 According to art. 74, the national minorities in Romania are Albanians, Armenians, Bulgarians, Czechs, Croats, Greeks, Jews, Germans, Italians, Macedonians, Hungarians, Poles, Roma, Lipovean Russians, Ruthenians, Serbs, Slovaks, Tatars, Turks and Ukrainians.

4 This element of the definition is rather vague but it seems "to refer to the moment in history at which Romania was confirmed in its current frontiers. This seems to indicate that the relevant time is 1919, although the creation of modern Romania may be seen as a process rather than a definite event". Venice Commission Opinion no. 345/2005 regarding the Draft Law on the Statute of National Minorities Living in Romania, CDL-AD(2005)026, Strasbourg, 25th October 2005, p. 5. The document is available online at http://www.venice.coe.int/docs/2005/CDL-AD(2005)026-e.pdf (accessed 30th November 2010).

5 Art. 3 of the Draft Law on the Status of National Minorities.

6 Venice Commission Opinion 345/2005, p. 5.

same reasoning is less convincing as regards cultural and educational rights"[7]. The Government sent the draft law on national minorities to the Parliament in 2005. It seems to be blocked in endless debates within various parliamentary commissions due to the lack of political will for its adoption.

The demography[8] and territorial distribution of national minorities reflects their historic background and characteristics. There are minority groups concentrated in certain regions of the country (e.g. Hungarians in Transylvania or Turks and Tatars in Dobrogea). The opposite is true of the Roma: as they used to lead a nomadic life, the minority is consequently scattered across the territory. Some minorities live in rather compact groups in the territorial-administrative units that border their kin-States (e.g. Ukrainians and Serbs), while others have traditionally been settled in the middle of the country (i.e. Saxon Germans and Hungarian Szeklers from Szeklerland)[9]. Jews and Greeks are good examples of small and mostly urban minorities, while a large number of Lipovean Russians[10], for instance, occupy the fishing villages of the Danube Delta. Last but not least, we can speak of diversity inside certain minority groups. For example, unlike most of the Bulgarians, who are Orthodox, the Bulgarian community in Banat is Roman-Catholic. Germans of Banat (also known as Svabi/Swabians/Schwaben) and Germans of Transylvania (the so-called Sasi/Saxons/Sachsen) have different religions, traditions and dialects[11].

---

7 Venice Commission Opinion 345/2005, p. 6.

8 See the statistic data of the last official census (2002) in the Annex.

9 There is no consensus over the origin of Szeklers. According to various theories they are the descendents of Huns or Magyars or Avars. They speak Hungarian but they have also their own specific customs and traditions. Szekleland is a territory in the center of Romania which covers present-day Covasna/Kovászna, Harghita/Hargita and (partially) Mures/Maros counties.

10 Lipovean Russians are believers of old rite of Russian Orthodox Church who left Russia 200 years ago due to religious persecutions. For details see O. Vinteler, *The Community of Lipovean Russians from Romania*, in *Journal for the Studies of Religions and Ideologies*, no. 3, Winter 2002, p. 158. The article is available online at http://www.jsri.ro/old/html%20version/index/no_3/onufrie_vinteler-articol.htm (accessed 30th November 2010).

11 The first Saxon communities in Transylvania are established by the Hungarian kings in XII century. The Swabian settled in Banat in XVIII century when the region was part of the Habsburg empire.

2.1 Education in minority languages

The Constitution guarantees the right of persons belonging to national minorities to learn their mother tongue and to be educated in their own language[12]. The Romanian education system, which ensures the right of persons belonging to national minorities to preserve, develop and express their ethnic, cultural, linguistic and religious identity is based *inter alia* on principles of decentralization and intercultural dialogue[13]. According to the new Law on national education no. 1/2011[14] education is a public service, and it is provided in the Romanian language as well as in the languages of national minorities and in international languages. In each locality, education establishments or study facilities are organised and operate with instruction in the Romanian language and/or, as appropriate, in the languages of national minorities, or teaching is provided to each pupil in his or her mother tongue in the nearest locality enabling this process[15]. Law no. 1/2011 contains an entire section on "Education for persons belonging to national minorities". Article 45 stipulates that persons belonging to national minorities have the right to study and learn in their mother tongue at all levels, types and forms of pre-university education. Depending on local needs, at the request of parents or legal guardians and pursuant to the law, pre-university groups, classes or establishments with instruction in the languages of national minorities are organised[16]. The legal regime in this field is based on the so-called "personal principle", meaning that minority education shall be established at any location in the country in which the minimum number of students as required by law can be ensured. For example, in Bucharest it is possible to study in Hungarian at the primary and secondary levels, although Hungarians represent fewer than 1% of the inhabitants. Pupils who do not have the possibility to study in their mother tongue in their locality of residence shall be reimbursed the cost of transportation to the nearest school with instruction in their mother tongue or receive free accommodation and meals in the boarding school with instruction in their mother tongue[17]. In the pre-university education with instruction in the languages of national minorities, all subjects are studied in

---

12 Art. 32, para. 3 of the Romanian Constitution. The document is available in Romanian and English in the Minority Rights Information System (MIRIS) database at http://www.eurac.edu/miris (accessed 30th November 2010).

13 Art. 3 (e), (g) and (i) of Law no. 1/2011.

14 Law on national education no. 1/2011 of 5th January 2011, published in Official Gazette no. 18 of 10th January 2011.

15 Art. 10, paras. 1 and 2 of Law no. 1/2011.

16 Art. 45, paras. 1 and 2 of Law no. 1/2011.

17 Art. 45, para. 7 of Law no. 1/2011.

the mother tongue, except for the Romanian language and literature course which is taught according to specific syllabi and textbooks elaborated for the respective minorities[18]. The teaching of the subjects "Minority language and literature" and "History and traditions of national minorities" is carried out based on specific syllabi and methodologies developed by teams of experts in the language and culture of the national minority in question. Pupils belonging to national minorities who attend schools with instruction in Romanian or in a language other than their mother tongue are given the opportunity, on request and pursuant to the law, to study their mother tongue and literature, as well as the history and traditions of that national minority, as part of the core curriculum. The syllabi and textbooks for the subject "History and traditions of the national minority" are approved by the Ministry of Education, Research, Youth and Sport (hereinafter MERYS)[19]. In primary and secondary education with instruction in the languages of national minorities, the subjects History and Geography of Romania are taught in those languages according to curricula and textbooks identical to those for classes with instruction in the Romanian language, with the obligation to transcribe and learn the Romanian toponymy and proper names as well. The history curricula and textbooks shall reflect the history and traditions of the national minorities in Romania. In secondary and postsecondary education, in which the subjects and special training modules are taught in minority languages, the specific terminology is also learned in Romanian. In pre-university education, the admission tests and graduation examination tests may be taken in the language in which the subjects have been studied, according to the law[20]. MERYS provides three types of textbooks for pupils belonging to national minorities: (1) textbooks drawn up in the language of instruction which is their mother tongue; (2) textbooks translated from Romanian into minority languages; (3) textbooks imported from kin-States that are approved by MERYS[21]. The language of instruction may be used in internal communication and in communication with the parents of pupils and preschoolers in the case of education in the language of national minorities. In primary education with instruction in the languages of national minorities, the grades are communicated in writing and orally also in the language of instruction[22]. Teachers who teach groups or classes in minority languages must prove their professional competence in the language of the respective national minority. They are entitled to training and improvement skills programmes in the language of instruction in

18 Art. 46, paras. 1 and 2 of Law no. 1/2011.
19 Art. 46, paras. 6 and 7 of Law no. 1/2011.
20 Art. 46, paras. 8, 10, 11 and 12 of Law no. 1/2011.
21 Art. 45, para. 13 of Law no. 1/2011.
22 Art. 45, paras. 14 and 15 of Law no. 1/2011.

Romania or abroad[23]. National minorities have the right to be represented in the management bodies of the education establishments, school inspectorates or equivalent institutions in proportion to the number of classes and in observance of professional competence criteria, according to the law. In schools which also provide instruction in the languages of national minorities, one of the principals shall be a teacher from among such minorities, in observance of professional competence criteria[24]. Law no. 1/2011 also regulates the public and private university level education for national minorities in multicultural and multilingual institutions of higher education or in faculties, departments, lines of studies and teaching groups[25].

With regard to the implementation of these legal provisions, it can be argued that education in the mother tongue is ensured depending on the demographic situation, demands, and needs of the national minorities. The larger the national minority, the greater the chance that members of the minority will take full advantage of the legal framework. Nevertheless, it is often the case that small minorities living in compact groups in certain areas can benefit to a greater extent than can a larger minority scattered all over the country. Regarding pre-university education, Hungarians, Germans, Ukrainians, Serbs, and Slovaks can study in their mother tongue at all levels, from kindergarten through secondary school. Turks and Croats may avail themselves of two secondary schools located in the areas in which most of them live, where instruction takes place partially in their mother tongue. Education in only the mother tongue is established at the primary school level for Czechs and Croats and at the kindergarten level for Bulgarians. Vocational education in the mother tongue is available only for Hungarians. Russian, Polish, Greek, Armenian and Roma pupils are enrolled in schools with instruction in Romanian where, upon request, they can study their mother tongue, history and traditions[26]. At the university level, within the state educational system, it is possible to study several specializations in two minority

23 Art. 45, para. 11 of Law no. 1/2011.

24 Art. 45, paras. 8 and 9 of Law no. 1/2011.

25 Arts. 135 and 227 of Law no. 1/2011. According to art. 363, on the date at which the law entered into force, the following three public higher education institutions receive the *status* of multicultural universities: Babes-Bolyai University of Cluj-Napoca/Kolozsvár, University of Medicine and Pharmacy of Târgu Mureş/Marosvásárhely and University of Theatre Arts of Târgu Mureş/Marosvásárhely.

26 According to the official Statistics of Ministry of Education for the academic year for 2004/2005, available online (in Romanian) at http://www.edu.ro/index.php/articles/c176/ (accessed 30th November 2010). See also the list of secondary schools with tuition in minority language and secondary schools with partial tuition in minority language in the academic year 2005/2006, available online (in Romanian) at http://www.edu.ro/index.php/articles/c113/ (accessed 30th November 2010).

languages (Hungarian and German). At the multicultural Babes-Bolyai University[27] in Cluj-Napoca/Kolozsvár, 15 out of 21 faculties provide both a Romanian and a Hungarian curriculum, while 9 faculties provide both Romanian and German curricula. The Faculty of Reformed Theology and the Faculty of Roman-Catholic Theology provide courses in Hungarian only. Babes-Bolyai University proposes long- and short-term academic studies for 105 specializations in Romanian, 52 in Hungarian and 13 in German[28]. Before the adoption of the new Law on national education no. 1/2011, the primary criticism regarding the Babes-Bolyai University was that Hungarian language education did not enjoy financial autonomy and was not efficiently organized[29]. In fact, one of the central demands of the Hungarian minority since the fall of communism has been the division of Babes-Bolyai University and the establishment of a separate state university with instruction in the Hungarian language[30]. Another specific request in the field of education is the allocation of state financial support to the two private Hungarian language universities set up in Transylvania[31]. These higher education institutions are financed mainly by Hungary, although their students are Romanian citizens who pay taxes in Romania, as does the majority Romanian population, which has access to state subsidized university education in their mother tongue in all specializations. Ethnic Hungarian academics point out that public higher education does not offer instruction in Hungarian for "important subjects like engineering sciences, arts, agriculture, forest science, music and veterinary medicine," and that Hungarians are underrepresented at

---

27 Babes University (with tuition in Romanian) and the Bolyai University (with tuition in Hungarian) were merged by the communist authorities in 1959.

28 Details on the multicultural character of Babes-Bolyai University are published on its website at http://www.ubbcluj.ro/en/despre/misiune/caracter_multicultural.html (accessed 30th November 2010).

29 *Divers Bulletin*, "Young ethnic Hungarians ask for state university in mother tongue", No. 38(234), 23 October 2006. *Divers* is a news bulletin about ethnic minorities living in Romania that is edited every week by the Balkan Investigative Reporting Network, with the financial support of the King Baudouin Foundation, Belgium and Ethnocultural Diversity Resource Center. For details, see http://www.divers.ro/ (accessed 30th November 2010).

30 *Ibid.*

31 In 2001, Sapientia University was established as a private and independent Hungarian-language university with three branch campuses in Transylvania: Cluj-Napoca/Kolozsvár, Târgu Mureş/Marosvásárhely, Miercurea-Ciuc/Csikszereda. In Oradea/Nagyvárad a separate Hungarian language private institution known as the Partium Christian University was established.

university level[32]. It remains to be seen if the implementation of the new Law on national education no. 1/2011 will provide solutions for these problems.

2.2 Use of minority languages in the judicial system

According to the Constitution, and under the terms of the organic law, Romanian citizens belonging to national minorities have the right to express themselves in their mother tongue before the courts of law, but the means of exercising this right "including the use of interpreters or translations, shall be stipulated so as not to hinder the proper administration of justice and not to involve additional expenses to those interested"[33]. According to the Law on Judicial Organization no. 304/2004, if one or more parties demand to express themselves in their mother tongue, the court must ensure, without charge, the use of an interpreter or a certified translator. When all parties demand or agree to express themselves in their mother tongue, the court must ensure the exercise of this right, as well as the proper administration of justice, including the right to an open, public, and adversarial procedure. Nevertheless, the requests and procedural papers are drawn up only in Romanian. The debates held by the parties in their mother tongue are recorded in writing under the court president's dictation, and only in Romanian. The objections raised by the parties with respect to translations and their transcription have to be settled by the court after the end of the debates in the case and recorded in the final document of the proceedings. The interpreter or the translator must sign all the documents that are drafted or transcribed based upon his/her translation[34].

Official information regarding the implementation of legal provisions on the use of the mother tongue in judicial proceedings is not currently available. However, according to the 2004 EU Commission's Report on Romania "after the constitutional revision introducing the right for citizens to use their mother tongue in civil court cases, Hungarian is extensively used in certain areas"[35]. Romanian authorities have recently acknowledged that they have no data on

32 B. Bodo and M. Bakk, "*Minority University Charter*", *paper presented at the Conference on Bi-/Multilingual Universities, 1–3 September 2005*, Helsinki University, Finland, pp. 2–3. The paper is available, at http://www.palmenia.helsinki.fi/congress/bilingual2005/presentations/Bodo.pdf (accessed 30th November 2010).

33 Art. 128, paras. 2 and 3 of the Constitution.

34 Art. 14 of Law no. 304/2004. The document is available online in Minority Rights Information System (MIRIS database) at http://www.eurac.edu/miris (accessed 30th November 2010).

35 Regular Report from the Commission on Romanian's progress towards accession, 6th October 2004, Brussels, p. 30. The document is available online at http://ec.europa.eu/enlargement/archives/pdf/key_documents/2004/rr_ro_2004_en.pdf (accessed 30th November 2010).

where or to what extent these regulations are applied: "There are no relevant statistics in the courts of law concerning the use of the Hungarian language, but it is known from concrete examples that this practice exists, especially in the areas where there is a large concentration of population speaking Hungarian"[36].

3. Public administration, place names and use of minority languages

3.1 Current legal standards

The Romanian Constitution establishes the general principle that in the territorial-administrative units where citizens belonging to a national minority are significantly represented, provision shall be made for the oral and written use of that national minority's language in relations with local public administrative authorities and decentralized public services, under the terms stipulated by the organic law[37]. The Law on Local Public Administration no. 215/2001, as the framework legislation in this field, stipulates that citizens belonging to a national minority who constitute at least 20% of the inhabitants of an administrative-territorial unit, shall enjoy the right to use their mother tongue in their relations with local public administration authorities, under the terms set forth in the Constitution, the present law and in the international treaties ratified by Romania[38]. The legal regime in this field is therefore based on the territorial principle because these linguistic rights can only be enjoyed by persons belonging to national minorities in certain territorial-administrative units (cities, town, municipalities). Law no. 215/2001 was amended by Law no. 286/2006, which states that not only do the local authorities have the obligation to ensure the use of a national minority language in the administrative units where at least 20% of the inhabitants belong to the respective minority, but so do the public institutions that are subordinated to the local authorities and the so called "de-concentrated public services" of the central bodies[39]. Some of the subsequent

36 Romania's Initial Periodical Report on the Implementation of the European Charter for Regional or Minority Languages, MIN-LANG/PR (2010)11, Strasbourg, 26th October 2010, p. 165. The document is available online at http://www.coe.int/t/dg4/education/minlang/Report/PeriodicalReports/RomaniaPR1_en.pdf (accessed 30th November 2010).

37 Art. 120, para. 2 of the Romanian Constitution.

38 Art. 19 of Law on local public administration no. 215/2001 (with subsequent amendments) as republished in the Official Gazette no. 123/2007.

39 De-concentrated state administration exists at the county and local levels. Several ministries maintain their own subordinated administrative entities at the levels of the counties and local

provisions on the rights of national minorities stipulated by Law no. 215/2001 were amended in 2006 as well. Citizens belonging to a national minority enjoy the right to address in their mother tongue, in writing or orally, not only the local public administration authorities and their specialized personnel but also the bodies subordinated to the local councils. They shall be answered both in Romanian and in their mother tongue[40]. As a logical consequence, persons who speak and write the minority language must be employed in public relations posts within the local administration[41]. A similar provision can be found in the Law on the Status of the Public Servant no. 188/1999, which also bans any discrimination between public servants on the basis of ethnic criteria[42]. Article 39, para. 7, and art. 94, para. 8, of Law no. 215/2001 specify that in the territorial-administrative units where the share of citizens belonging to a national minority is at least 20% of the number of inhabitants, they shall enjoy the right to be informed in their mother tongue about the agenda of local or county council sessions. These provisions remained unchanged, as did art. 50, which stipulates that "(...) decisions of a normative character shall be brought to the public knowledge also in the mother tongue of the respective minority, while those of an individual character shall be communicated, only upon request, in the minority language". Under the same condition (that persons belonging to a national minority represent at least 20% of the inhabitants) the local authorities must also ensure inscription, in the respective minority language, of the names of localities and public institutions under their authority, and of public announcements[43]. The version of the Law on Local Public Administration approved in 2001 stipulated that in local or county councils where the councilors belonging to a national minority represent at least one third of the total number, their mother tongue may also be used in council meetings. After the amendment of 2006, the requirement was reduced to at least one fifth of the number of councilors. In such cases, translation into Romanian should be ensured, courtesy

authorities. For example, the Ministry of Finance has general directorates for public finance and financial control at the county level and financial administrations at the level of the local authorities. The Ministry of National Education has education inspectorates, and the Ministry of Health maintains public health directorates.

40 Art. 76, para. 2 of Law on local public administration no. 215/2001 (with subsequent amendments) as republished in the Official Gazette no. 123/2007.

41 Art. 76, para. 3 of Law on local public administration no. 215/2001 (with subsequent amendments) as republished in the Official Gazette no. 123/2007.

42 Art. 25, para. 2 and art. 91 of Law no. 188/1999 (with subsequent amendments) as republished in the Official Gazette no. 251/2004.

43 Art. 76, para. 4 of Law on local public administration no. 215/2001 (with subsequent amendments) as republished in the Official Gazette no. 123/2007.

of the mayor. Nevertheless, in all cases, the documents of the council meetings must be drawn up in the Romanian language[44].

In order to speed up the implementation process, the Government issued Decision no. 1206/2001 on the adoption of application guidelines for the provisions concerning the right of citizens belonging to national minorities to use their mother tongue in local public administration, as stipulated in the Law on Local Public Administration no. 215/2001. This regulation details the rights of national minorities in relations with local authorities. For example, it stipulates that official ceremonies organized by the local public administration authorities shall be performed in Romanian but, in administrative-territorial units in which citizens belonging to a national minority represent at least 20% of the number of inhabitants, the language of the respective minority may be also used. Upon request, marriage ceremonies may be performed in the mother tongue of the persons to be married, provided the matrimonial officer speaks the respective language. Marital documents and certificates must be drawn up exclusively in Romanian[45]. Governmental Decision no. 1206/2001 contains specific provisions regarding the implementation of norms concerning minority languages and toponymy, bilingual signs and the inscription of the names of public institutions[46]. The act contains twenty-three Annexes[47] of minority language names of localities where the local authorities should display bilingual signs. Law no. 340/2004 on the Institution of Prefect gives this government representative in each county the power to take necessary measures to ensure the

---

44 Art. 42, para. 2 of Law on local public administration no. 215/2001 (with subsequent amendments) as republished in the Official Gazette no. 123/2007.

45 Art. 9 of Governmental Decision no. 1206/2001 on the adoption of application Guidelines for the provisions concerning the right of citizens belonging to national minority to use the mother tongue in local public administration, as stipulated in the Law of local public administration no. 215/2001. The document is available online in Minority Rights Information System (MIRIS database) at http://www.eurac.edu/miris (accessed 30th November 2010).

46 Articles 11 and 12 of Governmental Decision no. 1206/2001 stipulate that: "Article 11 – (1) Inscription in the mother tongue of the name of localities in which citizens belonging to national minorities make up a percentage of at least 20% of the number of inhabitants shall be on the same sign, under the Romanian name, with the same characters of the same size and color, as described in Annex 2 hereto. The inscription shall be applied both to entry road signs and to exit road signs. (2) Mayors shall be responsible for the manufacturing of said road signs. The expenses therefore shall rest with the local budgets".
"Article 12 – Inscription in the mother tongue of the name of public institutions under the authority of local or county councils shall be painted on a plate identical in size, type, letter-size and color to the one inscribed in Romanian. The plate shall be placed immediately below the plate with the official denomination in Romanian".

47 Annexes 1/2, 1/4, 1/5, 1/7–1/13, 1/15–1/22 were modified by Governmental Decision no. 1415/2002.

use of minority languages in relations with public administration, according to the law, in the territorial-administrative units where at least 20% of the total number of inhabitants belong to a national minority[48].

On 17th July 1995, Romania signed the European Charter for Regional or Minority Languages (hereinafter "the EChRML"), but it took more than twelve years to incorporate this international convention into the domestic legal system. The Parliament finally adopted a Ratification Law on 24th October 2007, which entered into force on 1st May 2008[49]. According to Romanian law, "minority or regional languages" are the languages of national minorities[50]. These twenty languages are listed in art. 2 of the Ratification Law[51].

Article 4 of the Ratification Law enumerates ten minority languages to which Part II of the EChRML shall be applied[52], while art. 5 specifies both the minority languages to which Romania undertakes to apply Part III of the EChRML and the provisions chosen for each of these languages: Bulgarian, Czech, Croatian, German, Hungarian, Russian, Serbian, Slovak, Turkish and Ukrainian. It is worth noting that Romanian authorities decided not to include the Romani language among those listed in art. 5. According to the 2002 census, Romani is the second largest minority language, and therefore one may reasonably argue that it is unfair to include it on the list of minority languages covered only by Part II of the EChRML, while other minority languages spoken by only a few thousand people benefit the special protection of Part III[53]. It seems that the difficulties foreseen in implementing the EChRML's provisions in the case of Romani language played a significant role in the decision taken by Romanian authorities.

According to the Ratification Law, the State shall allow or encourage local authorities to use these ten minority languages in debates in local councils, to publish their official documents also in these minority languages, and to use and

---

48 Art. 19, para. 1 point (m) of Law no. 340/2004 on the Institution of Prefect.

49 Law Concerning the Ratification of the European Charter for Regional or Minority Languages, no. 282, 24th October 2007, published in Official Gazette No. 752, 6th November 2007. The text of the law is available in Romanian and English in the Minority Rights Information System (MIRIS) database at http://www.eurac.edu/miris (accessed 30th November 2010).

50 Art. 3 of the Ratification Law.

51 Albanian, Armenian, Bulgarian, Czech, Croatian, German, Greek, Italian. Yiddish, Macedonian, Hungarian, Polish, Romani, Russian, Ruthenian, Serbian, Slovak, Tartar, Turkish and Ukrainian, as stipulated in art. 2 of the Ratification Law.

52 Albanian, Armenian, Greek, Italian, Yiddish, Macedonian, Polish, Romani, Ruthenian and Tartar.

53 For details see S. Constantin, *The Romanian Law on Ratification of the European Charter for Regional or Minority Languages*, in *European Yearbook of Minority Issues,* Vol. 6, 2006/7, pp. 575–584.

adopt the traditional and correct forms of place names[54]. All provisions of the EChRML regarding administrative authorities and public services and the use of minority languages shall be applied in the territorial-administrative units where the persons speaking one of the ten minority languages represent at least 20% of the population. Romanian administrative authorities and public services shall ensure that employees who are in contact with the public use the respective minority languages in relations with persons who submit oral or written applications and/or documents in the minority language. Last but not least, every person concerned has the right to use or adopt a family name in the minority language[55].

3.2 Implementation and situation on the ground

A 2005 Shadow Report on the implementation of the Framework Convention for the Protection of National Minorities has concluded that the implementation of the legal provision regarding, *inter alia*, the display of minority languages place names is not homogenous but instead depends on the openness of the local authorities[56].

A second Shadow Report from 2005[57] points out a discrepancy between the Framework Convention for the Protection of National Minorities (FCNM) and the Romanian law no. 215/2001 that allows the local authorities to refuse the display of bilingual street names. Indeed art. 11, para. 3 of the Framework Convention requests the display of "traditional local names, street names and other topographical indications intended for the public," while art. 90, para. 4 of Law no. 215/2001 mentions "the names of localities and public institutions under their authority, and announcements of public interest" but nothing about street names. Despite this inaccuracy in the Romanian law, the Advisory Committee on the FCNM, in its First Cycle Opinion on Romania, welcomed "the fact that the Law on local public administration adopted by the Parliament in early 2001 will authorize, *inter alia*, bilingual street signs in localities where a minority

54 Art. 10, para. 2, d), f), g) of the EChRML.

55 Art. 10, para. 5 of the EChRML.

56 G. Andreescu, *Shadow Report on the Implementation of Framework Convention for the Protection of National Minorities*, Ombudspersons for National Minorities, January 2005, p. 40. The report is available online at http://www.minelres.lv/reports/romania/PDF_Romania_Ombudspersons.pdf (accessed 30th November 2010).

57 *Shadow Report on the Implementation of the Framework Convention for the Protection of National Minorities in Romania,* PRO EUROPA League, 2005. The report is available online at http://www.minelres.lv/reports/romania/PDF_Romania_ProEuropa.pdf (accessed 30th November 2010).

represents over 20% of the population"[58]. It is obvious that the request to display bilingual street names is legitimate despite the fact that it is not expressly mentioned by Law no. 215/2001 because Romania has ratified the FCNM and its provisions became part of domestic legislation. Nevertheless, local and central authorities that replied to several NGO requests regarding this issue considered that the bilingual inscription of street-names would mean "exceeding the legal frame"[59]. It is submitted that at that time such problems occurred in part due to the low level of knowledge within the administration regarding the linguistic rights of national minorities as stipulated by the international instruments ratified by Romania.

In its Second Opinion on Romania, the Advisory Committee on FCNM considers that "Romania has made significant progress in applying article 11, para. 3 of the Framework Convention through the implementation of Law No. 215/2001 on Local Public Administration. (...) In practical terms, it appears that these provisions have been implemented in more than 20 counties, in localities where the conditions required by the law have been met, and also in some cases – according to non-governmental sources – in localities where the 20% requirement has not been reached"[60]. The Advisory Committee also acknowledges the existence of a number of shortcomings in implementation reported by representatives of the national minorities (for example Ukrainians), and recommends that the Romanian authorities pursue their efforts to ensure the display of bilingual place names in the municipalities where a national minority reaches the 20% legal threshold.

---

58 Advisory Committee on the Framework Convention for the Protection of National Minorities, First Opinion on Romania, *ACFC/INF/OP/I(2002)001*, p. 12. The First Opinion was adopted on 6th April 2001 and is available online at http://www.coe.int/minorities (accessed 30th November 2010).

59 Notice no. 9077 of 24th June 2002 to the Prefect of Mures County and Notice no. 3592/RDP/562/Dc of 18th July 2002 of the Ministry of Public Administration) in the *Shadow Report on the Implementation of the Framework Convention for the Protection of National Minorities in Romania*, PRO EUROPA League, 2005, p. 10.

60 Advisory Committee on the Framework Convention for the Protection of National Minorities, Second Opinion on Romania, *ACFC/OP/II(2005)007*, p. 25. The Second Opinion was adopted on 24th November 2005 and is available online at http://www.coe.int/T/E/human_rights/minorities/ (accessed 30th November 2010).

In 2006, the Research Center on Inter-ethnic Relations[61] made public an extensive report[62] on the implementation of the minority rights provisions of Law no. 215/2001. The research team sent a questionnaire to 522 local administrations and registered data regarding 1249 municipalities where the following national minorities are living: Bulgarians, Croats, Czechs, Germans, Greeks, Hungarians, Poles, Russians, Serbs, Slovaks, Tatars, Turks and Ukrainians. The report concludes that all the efforts at the central level are not sufficient to ensure effective implementation of the law because its success depends to a certain extent on the institutional capacity of the minority to influence the process at the local level[63]. Additionally, the data shows that the implementation of existing norms has had a different impact on different national minorities. The following three categories can be identified[64].

- Implementation has had a *significant impact* on Hungarians, Ukrainians, and Croats, as it influences the linguistic rights of more than 2/3 of the persons belonging to these minorities. The reason is that these minority groups are numerous and/or are living in compact groups in certain administrative units where in most cases they represent more than half of the population.
- Implementation has had a *medium impact* on Bulgarians, Czechs, Serbs, and Slovaks, as it influences the linguistic rights of more or less half the persons belonging to these minorities. They are small, and although they may live in compact groups, they represent at least 20% of the population in just few municipalities where the relevant minority provisions of Law no. 215/2001 can be applied.
- Implementation has had a *minimum impact* on Germans, Greeks, Tatars and Turks. Even though these minority groups traditionally live in specific regions (Transylvania and Dobrogea), they are not numerous and in most of the administrative units they do not represent at least 20% of the population. As a

---

61 The Research Centre on Interethnic Relations (CCRIT) is a non-profit organization and its researchers are academics from the Sociology Department of "Babes-Bolyai" University. For further details see http://www.ccrit.ro/index_eng.htm (accessed 30th November 2010).

62 I. Horvát, R. Rat, K. Vitos, *Implementation of Legislation Regarding the Rights of National Minorities in Romania. Linguistic Rights in Public Administration,* Research Center on Inter-ethnic Relations February – March 2006. The project was financed by the Department of Inter-ethnic Relation of the Romanian Government and the report is available online (in Romanian) at http://www.dri.gov.ro/cd-2006/raport_final/raport.doc (accessed 30th November 2010).

63 *Ibid.*, p. 226. For example, if the minority proportion is lower than half of the population in a territorial-administrative unit (but still at least 20% as requested by law), the probability of not having bilingual signs displayed as stipulated by law is higher.

64 *Ibid.,* p. 227.

consequence they cannot benefit from the minority provisions of Law no. 215/2001.

Regarding toponymy in minority languages, the report concludes that in 79.4% of the municipalities that were asked to respond to the questionnaire, the provision on bilingual signs was implemented, while in 6.5% of cases the law was not applied[65]. The names of the public institutions that are subordinated to the local authorities (cultural houses, kindergartens, schools) are bilingual in 2/3 of the above-mentioned municipalities.

The table below[66] shows the number and percentage of administrative units where the legal provisions regarding the use of the mother tongue in relations with local authorities are applied. Only approximately half of the municipalities that answered the questionnaire ensure all the minority rights stipulated in Law no. 215/2001 (see the percentages in bold).

	No. administrative units	% administrative units
Mayor office	293	86.9
Police	154	45.7
Mail office	258	76.6
Civil registration Office	257	76.3
The local council agenda is made public also in minority language	189	**56.1**
Normative decisions are made public also in minority language	171	**507**
Individual answers are sent in minority language	166	**49.3**
Public announcement of general interest in minority language	271	80.4

65 *Ibid.*, p. 225. The authors did not receive any answer from the local authorities of 7% of the municipalities examined. In 7% other cases there is a specific situation (e.g. there are no signs at all or since the last census the municipality merged with another one).

66 *Ibid.*, p. 225.

The research showed clearly that the smaller (but still over 20% of the population) and less territorially concentrated a minority is, the smaller is the chance that the local authorities properly implement the legal provisions regarding the linguistic rights of the respective minority. Where a minority represents a significant part of the population (i.e. over 40%) it is highly probable that people enjoyed at least some of the rights regarding the use of minority languages in relations with the public administration[67] even before the adoption of Law no. 215/2001, therefore the legislation did not drastically change the situation on the ground. On the other hand, in the municipalities with small minority populations (but still over 20%) where the use of minority languages in relations with authorities was rather limited or non-existent before the adoption of Law no. 215/2001, the implementation process has been slower. The paradox is that precisely in these municipalities there is a need for effective implementation of the legal provisions regarding the linguistic rights of minorities. It would represent a real change to the existing situation and an added value for the minority population[68].

In May 2007, the Committee of Ministers of the Council of Europe recommended that Romania "continue to improve the implementation of the national legislation concerning the practice of indicating place names in administrative-territorial units in which people belonging to national minorities represent over 20% of the local population"[69]. The ratification of the EChRML in the same year has reinforced the periodical assessment of the progress in this field. According to Pop[70], the local authorities have the obligation to implement the provisions of Part III of the EChRML in the case of ten selected minority languages, in 341 out of the 2952 territorial-administrative units. Hungarian

67 For example, oral communication in minority language with the local authorities, street and place names, public announcements.

68 I. Horváth, *Evaluarea politicilor lingvistice din România (Assessment of Linguistic Policy in Romania)*, in L. Salat (ed.), *Politici de integrare a minorităţilor naţionale din România. Aspecte legale şi instituţionale într-o perspectivă comparată (Policies of Integration of National Minorities in Romania. Legal and Institutional Aspects in a Comparative Perspective)*, Ethnocultural Diversity Ressource Center, Cluj-Napoca, 2008, p. 210.

69 Resolution CM/ResCMN(2007)8 on the implementation of the Framework Convention for the Protection of National Minorities by Romania, adopted by the Committee of Ministers on 23 May 2007 at the 996th meeting of the Ministers' Deputies. The Resolution is available online at http://www.coe.int/minorities (accessed 30th November 2010).

70 D. Pop, *Autorităţile administrative şi serviciile publice (Administrative Authorities and Public Services)*, in M. Căluşer (ed.), *Carta europeană a limbilor regionale sau minoritare în România. Între norme şi practice (European Charter for Regional or Minority Languages in Romania. Between Norms and Practices)*, Ethnocultural Diversity Ressource Center, Cluj-Napoca, 2009, pp. 63–64.

minority is the only one that amounts for more than 20% of the population at county level, and is the case in six out of the 42 counties. There are only four territorial-administrative units where the EChRML provisions shall be implemented for two minority languages and none in which the special protection would cover three minority languages.

The first assessments of the EChRML's impact confirm the uneven benefit for national minorities due to the fact that the use of minority languages in relations with public administration is guaranteed according to the territorial principle. A 2009 study of on Romania's implementation of the EChRML in the field of administrative authorities and public services reaches similar conclusions to the Research Center on Inter-ethnic Relations' 2006 report of on the implementation of the minority rights provisions of Law no. 215/2001. Among the ten minority groups that enjoy the special protection of Part III of the EChRML, only Croatians, Hungarians and Ukrainians have more than 50% of their population able to exercise their linguistic rights[71]. As shown in the table below, almost 82% of the persons belonging to Croatian minority live in territorial-administrative units where this minority reaches the 20% threshold. At the opposite pole is the German minority, with less than 3% of the population living in such areas. The Croatian minority is small but concentrated mostly in certain rural areas. The German minority is ten times bigger, mostly urban and much more territorially dispersed. Most of the persons belonging to the Ukrainian minority live in the regions that border their kin-State. Ukrainian and German minorities are comparable in terms of size, but more than 65% of the ethnic Ukrainians from Romania live in areas where the local authorities have the obligation to implement the minority provisions of Law no. 215/2001 and the EChRML. The first conclusion is that the size of the minority group matters less than its territorial concentration. Secondly, the present system is more advantageous for minority communities from rural areas where the population is lower[72]. Indeed, in urban centers with large number of inhabitants it is less probable that a minority reaches the 20% threshold. This is true even in the case of the large Hungarian minority concentrated in Transylvania. Almost half of the Hungarians who are not able to exercise their linguistic rights in relations with public administration live in six cities of the region[73]. An example illustrates the paradox very well: 60,287 Hungarians who are residents in the city of Cluj-Napoca (Kolozsvar) do not enjoy the right to use their mother tongue in relations

71 *Ibid.*, p. 66.

72 *Ibid.*, p. 66.

73 Hungarians amount for 18.86 % of the total number of inhabitants in Cluj-Napoca (Kolozsvar), 17.50 % in Zalau (Zilah), 14.83 % in Baia Mare (Nagybanya), 13.01 % in Arad, 8.14 % in Brasov (Brasso) and 7.65 % in Timisoara (Temesvar).

with public administration but 978 Hungarians who live 30 km away in the commune (municipality) of Căianu (Magyarkalyan) benefit from the existing legal framework because they amount to 39.08% of the total population of the commune.

Minority	Minority population in areas A*		Minority population in areas B**		Total minority population	
	No.	%	No.	%	No.	%
Bulgarian	2,950	36.76	5,075	63.24	8,025	100
Czech	1,467	37.22	2,474	62.78	3,941	100
Croatian	5,581	**81.99**	1,226	18.01	6,807	100
German	1,686	2.82	58,078	**97.18**	59,764	100
Hungarian	1,062,417	**74.20**	369,417	25.80	1,431,807	100
Russian	14,878	41.57	20,913	58.43	35,791	100
Serbian	3,847	17.05	18,714	**82.95**	22,561	100
Slovak	7,572	43.96	9,654	56.04	17,226	100
Turkish	1,316	4.10	30,782	**95.90**	32,098	100
Ukrainian	40,308	**65.97**	20,790	34.02	61,098	100
Total	1,139,075	69.13	518,412	30.87	1,679,118	100

* areas A = territorial-administrative units where the minority population accounts for at least 20% of the inhabitants. In these areas, the authorities have the obligation to implement the minority provisions of Law no. 215/2001 and the EChRML.

** areas B = territorial-administrative units where minority population amounts to less than 20% of the inhabitants. The local authorities do not have the obligation to implement the minority provisions of Law no. 215/2001 and the EChRM in these areas.

In 2010, the Romanian Institute for Research on National Minorities published a case study[74] on the implementation of the existing regulations regarding the linguistic rights of minorities in relations with public administration in Harghita (Hargita) County, where 85.36% of the population declared Hungarian

---

74 I. Horváth, I. Veress, K. Vitos, *Utilizarea limbii maghiare în administrația publică locală și în instituțiile deconcentrate din județul Harghita (The Use of Hungarian Language in Local Public Administration and in the De-Concentrated Institution in Harghita County)*, Working Papers in Romanian Minority Studies no. 27/2010, Romanian Institute for Research on National Minorities, Cluj Napoca, 2010.

as their mother tongue in the 2002 census. Of the entire Hungarian population of the county, 94.6% live in territorial-administrative units where they reach the 20% threshold. The study assesses the presence of the Hungarian language at the administrative-institutional level (place names, bilingual signs, official communications etc.) and shows both the level of acceptance of minority languages by the state authorities, as well as when and how the persons belonging to the national minority exercise their linguistic rights. The main conclusion of the research is that the use of the Hungarian language according to the existing norms is ensured in the majority of these territorial-administrative units[75]. However, there are some institutions (e.g. police, mail office) that lack a unitary coherent policy regarding the use of minority languages. It was also observed that the de-concentrated public services of the central bodies are less successful than the local authorities in implementing the law. The socio-linguistic impact analysis shows that the majority of the Hungarian population of the county uses Hungarian in relations with both local authorities and de-concentrated public services[76] but that there is a gap between the levels of oral and written communication. Over 80% of the Hungarian population of the county always or mostly uses Hungarian in oral communication with public authorities. When it comes to written communications, the number drops to slightly over 50 %[77]. However, written communication in Hungarian in Harghita (Hargita) County reaches a surprisingly high level when one takes into account the fact that many local authorities do not have bilingual administrative forms. As a matter of fact, this is a well-known problem, and in recent years the Romanian Institute for Research on National Minorities has developed a specific project that aims to make the necessary bilingual (Romanian-Hungarian) administrative forms available online[78].

It is undoubtedly true that the level of implementation of the legal provisions regarding the linguistic rights of national minorities depends very much on the ethnic structure of the territorial-administrative units. In municipalities where the national minority represents the majority of the local population, it can influence/control the decisions of the local authorities. From this perspective, the role of the central authorities is more important in the areas in which a national minority, although reaching the 20% threshold, is still too small to be able to influence the outcome of the decision making process in the local elected body. In such cases, the Prefect representing the Government in each county is

75 *Ibid.*, p. 97.

76 *Ibid.*, p. 98.

77 *Ibid.*, p. 84–85.

78 For details (in Romanian and Hungarian) see http://www.ispmn.gov.ro/node/formulare-bilingve (accessed 30th November 2010).

expected to take the necessary measures to make sure that, according to existing legislation, minority languages are properly used in public administration.

In October 2010, Romania submitted its Initial Periodical Report on the Implementation of the EChRML to the Council of Europe. According to the Romanian Government, national minorities reach 20% of the total population of "**417** localities – municipalities, cities, communes – in a number of 21 counties"[79]. It is worth noting the data regarding the toponymy because Romanian authorities argue that "there are **469** localities (municipalities, cities, communes) in 21 counties" that also display names in the languages of national minorities[80]. The discrepancy between the numbers is not clearly explained in the country report but it might be the consequence of the proactive attitude of certain local authorities, who have decided to display bilingual place names even though the national minority population amounts to less than 20% in the respective territorial-administrative units. The case of Sibiu (Hermannstadt), a city in Transylvania, is illustrative in this sense. The mayor is an ethnic German, and the city has bilingual place names although, according to the 2002 census, the German inhabitants represent only 1.61% of the total population. Another example is mentioned in the 2010 report of the Romanian Government: "In eight localities in the country, all in Suceava County, there are bilingual inscriptions in Romanian and Polish on the nameplates. The only municipality in the country where the population exceeds the 20% [threshold] is Cacica – 23% Polish population"[81].

As we already mentioned, the Romani language is not covered by the special protection of Part III of the EChRML. However, according to Law no. 215/2001, Roma minority shall enjoy linguistic rights in relations with public administration in territorial-administrative units where it reaches the 20% threshold. As often it happens, the practice looks quite different from the theory. The situation on ground is complicated by the existence of different Romani dialects. A "common Romani language" exists only in school textbooks published in recent years. As a consequence, the local authorities face an unusual challenge when the Roma minority requests bilingual toponymy, street and public institution names. An illustrative example from 2010 is the village of Ticvaniu-Mare, where local authorities and Roma representatives got lost in translation. What is the Romani language word for "Police"? Is it "Jandaria" as the local advisor for Roma issues

---

79 Initial Periodical Report on the Implementation of the European Charter for Regional or Minority Languages in Romania, *MIN-LANG/PR (2010)11*, 26th October 2010, Strasbourg, p. 80. The report is available online at http://www.coe.int/t/dg4/education/minlang/Report/PeriodicalReports/RomaniaPR1_en.pdf (accessed 30th November 2010).

80 *Ibid.*, p. 81.

81 *Ibid.*, p. 57.

argues or “Poralo” as the deputy-mayor insists? Asked to solve the dilemma, a well-known Roma rights activist and philologist, declared that the correct word in Romania language is “Grastarlin”[82]. It seems that the future implementation of linguistic rights in the case of Roma minority depends very much on the evolution of the so-called “common Romani language”.

4. Conclusions

The main features of the Romanian system for minority protection are the extensive legal framework and its slow implementation in certain fields. No one can deny that persons belonging to officially recognized national minorities can rely on specific legal provisions in order to defend their linguistic rights in education, public administration and the judicial system. In the last decade, the use of minority languages in relations with public authorities increased significantly, especially at the local level. The progress is less visible in the de-concentrated public services of the central bodies. Moreover, there is still a clear gap between the existing norms and the reality on the ground. The use of minority languages in the administrative sphere depends very much on the strength of the local minority population. In the territorial-administrative units where a national minority represents the majority of the local population, the situation is better than in the areas in which the respective minority, although reaching the 20% threshold, is still too small to be able to influence the decision making process.

Another important aspect is that the system itself needs further development. Let us remember that a law on the *status* of national minorities has not been approved yet and that the provisions of Part III of the EChRML selected by Romania do not go beyond the standards for the protection of national minorities that already existed in the Romanian legal system. The present situation of small and/or dispersed minorities raises legitimate concerns because the impact of the EChRML’s provisions on these minority languages seems to be insignificant. A rather large proportion of persons belonging to national minorities cannot take advantage of the rights stipulated in the existing legal framework because they amount to less than 20% of the population in the territorial-administrative units where they live. A reduction of the threshold (for example at 10%) would have a clearly positive impact for minorities, but at the moment it is highly improbable

82 V. Popovici, G. Lacatus and D. Alexe, *Roma Language Request Causes Confusion*, WAZ.EUobserver.com, 17th May 2010. The article is available online at http://waz.euobserver.com/887/30078 (accessed 30th November 2010).

that new regulations are going to bring such change. However, it cannot be ruled out that (at least some of the) minority languages will enjoy better protection in the future. For example, it remains to be seen how the issue of Romani language use in relations with public administration will be addressed.

Annex:
Romania – National Census 2002 (excerpts)

Ethnic composition	**ROMANIA**	**%**
Total population	21,680,974	100
Romanians	19,399,597	89.47
Hungarians	1,431,807	6.60
Roma/Gypsy	533,140	2.46
Ukrainians	61,098	0.28
Germans	59,764	0.27
Russian-Lipovans	35,791	0.16
Turks	32, 098	0.14
Tatars	23,935	0.11
Serbians	22,561	0.10
Slovaks	17,226	0.07
Bulgarians	8,025	0.03
Croatians	6,807	0.03
Greeks	6,472	0.02
Jews	5,785	0.02
Czechs	3,941	0.01
Poles	3,559	0.01
Italians	3,288	0.01
Armenians	1,780	*
Macedonian Slavs	695	*
Albanians	477	*

Ruthenians	257	*
Mother tongue	**ROMANIA**	**%**
Total population	21,680,974	100
Romanian	19,736,517	91.03
Hungarian	1,443,970	6.66
Romani/Gypsy language	237,570	1.09
Ukrainian	57,407	0.26
German	44,888	0.20
Russian	29,246	0.13
Turkish	28,115	0.12
Tatar	21,272	0.09
Serbian	20,411	0.09
Slovakian	16,027	0.07
Bulgarian	6,735	0.03
Croatian	6,355	0.02
Greek	4,170	0.01
Yiddish	951	*
Czech	3,381	0.01
Polish	2,690	0.01
Italian	2,531	0.01
Armenian	721	*
Macedonian	482	*
Albanian	469	*
Ruthenian	163	*

Source: Romanian National Institute of Statistics at http://www.insse.ro/cms/files/RPL2002INS/index_rpl2002.htm (accessed 30th November 2010)

Bibliography

Advisory Committee on the Framework Convention for the Protection of National Minorities, *First Opinion on Romania, ACFC/INF/OP/I(2002)001*, Strasbourg, 6th April 2001.

Advisory Committee on the Framework Convention for the Protection of National Minorities, *Second Opinion on Romania, ACFC/OP/II(2005)007*, Strasbourg, 24th November 2005.

Andreescu G., *Shadow Report on the Implementation of Framework Convention for the Protection of National Minorities*, Ombudspersons for National Minorities, January 2005.

Bodo B. and Bakk M., *Minority University Charter, paper presented at the Conference on Bi-/Multilingual Universities*, paper presented at the Conference held at Helsinki University, Finland, 1–3 September 2005.

Constantin S., *The Romanian Law on Ratification of the European Charter for Regional or Minority Languages*, in *European Yearbook of Minority Issues,* Vol. 6 (2006/7).

DIVERS – News bulletin about ethnic minorities living in Romania, edited every week by the Balkan Investigative Reporting Network, with the financial support of the King Baudouin Foundation, Belgium and Ethnocultural Diversity Resource Center.

European Commission for Democracy Through Law, *Opinion no. 345/2005 Regarding the Draft Law on the Statute of National Minorities Living in Romania,* CDL-AD(2005)026, Strasbourg, 25th October 2005.

Horváth I., Rat R., Vitos K., *Implementation of Legislation Regarding the Rights of National Minorities in Romania. Linguistic Rights in Public Administration*, Research Center on Inter-ethnic, Relations February – March 2006.

Horváth I., *Evaluarea politicilor lingvistice din România (The Assessment of Linguistic Policy in Romania)*, in L. Salat (ed.), *Politici de integrare a minorităţilor naţionale din România. Aspecte legale şi instituţionale într-o perspectivă comparată (Policies of integration of National Minorities in Romania. Legal and Institutional Aspects in a Comparative Perspective)*, Ethnocultural Diversity Ressource Center, Cluj-Napoca, 2008.

Horváth I., Veress I., Vitos K., *Utilizarea limbii maghiare în administraţia publică locală şi în instituţiile deconcentrate din judeţul Harghita (The Use of Hungarian Language in Local Public Administration and in De-Concentrated Institutions in Harghita County)*, Working Papers in Romanian Minority Studies, no. 27/2010, Romanian Institute for Research on National Minorities, Cluj Napoca, 2010.

Initial Periodical Report on the Implementation of the European Charter for Regional or Minority Languages, *MIN-LANG/PR (2010)11*, Strasbourg, 26th October 2010.

Regular Report from the Commission on Romanian's Progress Towards Accession, Brussels, 6th October 2004.

Pop D., *Autoritătile administrative şi serviciile publice (Administrative Authorities and Public Services)*, in M. Căluşer (ed.), *Carta europeană a limbilor regionale sau minoritare în România. Între norme şi pratici (European Charter for Regional or Minority Languages in Romania. Between Norms and Practices),* Ethnocultural Diversity Ressource Center, Cluj-Napoca, 2009.

Popovici V., Lacatus G. and Alexe D., *Roma Language Request Causes Confusion*, WAZ.EUobserver.com, 17th May 2010.

Resolution CM/ResCMN(2007)8 on the Implementation of the Framework Convention for the Protection of National Minorities by Romania, adopted by the Committee of Ministers on 23rd May 2007.

Shadow Report on the Implementation of the Framework Convention for the Protection of National Minorities in Romania, PRO EUROPA League, 2005.

Vinteler O., *The Community of Lipovean Russians from Romania*, in *Journal for the Studies of Religions and Ideologies,* no. 3, Winter 2002.

Geographical indications as means of protection of minorities: the situation in Hungary

Orsolya Farkas

Summary

1. Introduction

When a traveller in crossing a settlement can notice that the name of the settlement is indicated also in a language different from the one spoken by the major part of the population in that country he or she realises that the settlement is linked to a specific ethnic group. If in the settlement street names, signs on public offices are indicated in the minority language and there are museums, monuments which bear testimony of the presence of that minority, the traveller will have the impression that the minority group plays an active role in the life of that settlement. If the traveller is curious enough, these signs can serve as a point of departure in order to explore and recompose the social and cultural geography of the settlement and its minority. But the traveller is an outsider, driven by curiosity. For the insiders, for those who recognise themselves as members of this minority, these indications tell much more: they create an environment which confirms the still tangible presence of the group, they contribute to the preservation and promotion of the identity of the community and its members.

The establishment of such an environment requires an active contribution of public authorities. First of all it is necessary to set up a legal framework which creates the institutional and procedural conditions and guarantees providing access to the factual exercise of the right to preserve identity. Secondly, the participation of public authorities is not exhausted by one legislative intervention, but it must have a constant character inasmuch placing sufficient financial resources at disposal in order to ensure that these institutions can function regularly and are managed professionally.

The present paper has in its focal point the Hungarian legal framework regulating the establishment and the use of geographical indications in minority languages. To better understand the role of these indications in the specific national context the paper shortly recalls the historical background which is characterised by the presence and the eventful participation of various ethnic groups. Turning into the present it is spelled out which minority groups are recognised by the legislation in force and some of the institutions playing a key role in the protection of minorities are described. The dimensions of this paper do not give the possibility to design a comprehensive panorama on such protection therefore those institutions are selected which strictly relate to the central issue of this paper. Since the recently set up Government has started ambitious projects on the transformation of public life, some of these projects, which significantly influence the protection of minorities are also mentioned. Subsequently the specific legal norm on the establishment and registration of geographic names is examined. The application of such norm is not problematic, if accompanied by measures which ensure the availability of financial resources for the physical realisation of minority language signs and if civil servants are appropriately trained in order to be able to correctly manage the Register.

It is also suggested that in the evaluation of the role of geographic indications as means of protection some other indicators can be of help. With regard to the particular historical background and to the fact that today in Hungary the numerical presence of minority population is limited, signs and identifications indicating minority related ethnographic museums, commemorative sites, cemeteries play an important role. These sites can contribute to the reconstruction of the historical traditions of minority groups even in cases when for today they are substantially assimilated. How far the legislation is concerned about the minority relevance of the issue could be seen as a more complex and sensitive indicator than place names.

2. Minorities in Hungary's history

When towards the end of 800 the first Hungarian settlers arrived in the basin of the Carpathian mountains they found already various ethnic groups, like Avars, Bulgarian-Turkish, Huns, Slovenes, Slavs, Germans, Jews and others populating the territory. Still in the IX–XIII century the dominant population was composed of the descendents of these groups and not of the descendents of Hungarian settlers[1]. Then, throughout long centuries Hungary could experience major population changes when new ethnic groups arrived either in a spontaneous or in an organised manner. Some of them later gained independence, some others insisted on their belongingness to Hungary. Some of them left Hungary after some time, some others settled down. Some have lived together with Hungarians, some others kept their own groups. The historical presence of various ethnic groups in Hungary is extensively analysed by experts of the subject matter, from the point of view of the present paper it is sufficient to indicate the highly eventful nature of the historical background[2]. Such a background puts on the spotlight the importance of geographical indications in the re-exploration of the presence of various ethnic groups throughout a kind of stratified the history where subsequent events covered with sand the previous ones.

Just two examples should point towards the colourful history of minorities. For example, the group of Kuns arrived in the first half of the XIII century in two waves, both times they felt to be frightened by Tartar troops which were advancing towards Central Europe. Historical documents mention 15 and 40 thousand families respectively. When their prince was killed in 1241 some of the Kuns left Hungary, but after some years they moved back. After the Tartar devastation they received lands from various kings with the aim to settle them down and to create a military force in support of the Hungarian king. According to the reconstructions on the basis of settlement names Kuns were present in the most various parts of Hungary[3]. Later they completely assimilated, but some regional denominations (Kiskunság, Nagykunság) and settlement names (Kiskunfélegyháza, Kunhalom, Kiskunhalas) indicate that traditionally Kuns lived in these areas.

---

1 Gy . Kristó, *Magyarország lélekszáma az Árpád-korban* (*Population of Hungary at the age of the House of Árpád*), in J. Kovacsics (ed.), *Magyarország történeti demográfiája* (*Hungary's historical demography*), Budapest, 1997, p. 40.

2 See e.g. E. Mályusz, *A középkori magyarság település- és nemzetiségpolitikája* (*Settlement and nationality policies of Hungarians in the Middle-Age*), Budapest, 2002; Z. Ács, *Nemzetiségek a történelmi Magyarországon* (*Nationalities in the historical Hungary*), Budapest, 1986.

3 Gy. Kristó, *Nem magyar népek a középkori Magyarországon* (*Non-Hungarian people in Hungary at the Middle-Age*), Budapest, 2003, pp. 219–232.

With the Settlement Agreement of 1867 The Austrian-Hungarian Monarchy was set up, but regarding its ethnic composition it was seen as a particular establishment in the actual Europe. It was different from France or Germany, which were based not only on a specific territorial and economic unit, but also on a common national identity. The Monarchy could also be described around a single economic entity, but it was composed of a large variety of ethnic groups. There were 11 different groups, Austrian-Germans, Hungarians, Czechs, Poles, Croatians, Serbians, Romanians, Ukrainians, Slovaks and Slovenes living in its territory. But any of these had an absolute majority, the largest groups, Austrian-Germans and Hungarians represented at about 20% of the total population each, and more than 50% was divided among 9 groups. However, most of these groups maintained their institutions and identity acquired during the Middle Age and the evolving nationalist movements at times put in danger the existence of the Monarchy itself[4]. Following the Hungarian-Croatian Settlement Agreement of 1868, which attributed to Croatia specific autonomy rights, the zone of Fiume was divided into two parts: the County of Fiume made part of Croatia, whereas the city of Fiume remained part of Hungary. Still today, the popular denomination of the city is Fiume notwithstanding the official Croation version, which calls it Rijeka.

The peace agreements signed at the end of World War I changed the situation drastically. Already in 1917–18 most ethnic groups present in the Monarchy expressed their wish of secession from the Monarchy and subsequently Serbs, Croatians, Romanians, Czechs, Slovaks, Poles and Ruthenians set up their own institutions preparing the way to the establishment of their national state[5]. According to the decision taken at Trianon in 1920, Hungary lost approximately two thirds of its territory. The new geographical construction affected all minorities: Serbs, Croatians, Slovenes and Slovaks became separated from their kin-state, Ruthenians were divided among various States[6]. As consequences of the war itself and the peace agreement, the number of minorities and their proportion in relation to the total population started to diminish[7]. Although the peace agreement obliged the Hungarian Government to guarantee minority rights, in particular linguistic ones, this obligation was respected only to a

4 I. Diószegi, *A Ferenc József-i kor nagyhatalmi politikája* (*Power politics at the age of Franz Joseph*), Budapest, 1987, pp. 6–7.

5 A. Pók, *A magyarországi nemzetiségi kérdésről (1868–1918)* (*About the nationality issue in Hungary (1868–1918)*), in *História*, 4/1982, pp. 19–26.

6 More than 3 million Hungarians remained outside of the new borders as well.

7 Those of not Hungarian mother tongue represented only 7.1% of the population. Source: L. Tilkovszky, *Nemzetiségi politika Magyarországon a 20. században* (*Politics towards nationalities in Hungary in the XX century*), Debrecen, 1998, p. 7.

limited extent. The tense relationship with the neighbouring countries did not improve the situation of minorities either[8].

After the end of World War II the deportation of Germans and the more or less voluntary population exchange with Slovakia further diminished the numerical presence of minorities[9]. It remains troublesome to estimate the size of minority groups for this period of time. The 1949 census contains data relating to this issue, but certainly a substantial number of persons did not declare his or her identity and mother tongue being afraid of negative consequences[10]. The Constitution, adopted in 1949 following the pattern of the Stalinist one, declared the prohibition of discrimination based on the belongingness to minorities and foresaw the right to have mother tongue education and the protection of national culture[11]. On the contrary to the constitutional prescription these obligations were not entirely implemented. Associations of minorities were also set up but they hardly could function using their full potential. The mainstream orientation guiding the treatment of minorities was the one of their automatic assimilation. Political leaders supposed that in 10–15 years minorities would have assimilated in a spontaneous way, partly because their members felt being frightened based on past experience such as deportations and population exchange, partly because of the lack of initiatives to preserve and strengthen their identity[12].

---

8 Gy. Bindorffer, *Nemzetiségi politika Magyarországon Szent István korától a rendszerváltozásig* (*Politics towards nationalities in Hungary from the age of St. Stepen until the change of regime*), in T. Gyulavári, E. Kállai (eds.), *A jövevényektől az államalkotó tényezőkig. A nemzetiségi közösségek múltja és jelene Magyarországon* (*From the incomers to the constituent parts of the State. The past and present of communities of nationalities in Hungary*), Budapest, 2010, pp. 23–25.

9 The various forms of deportations regarded approximately 250.000 Germans and the population exchange affected approximately 50.000 Slovaks. There was an agreement on population exchange between Hungary and Yugoslavia as well, but it involved a considerably lower number of persons. Gy. Bindorffer, *Jövevényektől az államalkotó tényezőig. Nemzetiségek és nemzetiségpolitika Magyarországon 1790-től napjainkig* (*From incomers to constituent part of the State. Nationalities and politics towards them from 1790 till today*), Budapest, 2009 at: http://www.kisebbsegiombudsman.hu/data/files/184992660.pdf, pp. 92–97.

10 The number of Germans, e.g. diminished to 2617 persons in 1949, but increased to 8640 in 1960. Similar tendency can be observed regarding the Slovak minority: 7808 persons in 1949 and 14 340 in 1960. The numerical changes reflect the changes in the political climate when more persons belonging to minorities declared their identity. Statistical source: N. Kovács , L. Szarka (eds.), *Tér és terep. Tanulmányok az etnicitás és az identitás kérdésköréből* (*Space and field. Studies around the question of ethnicity and identity*), Budapest, 2003, p. 240.

11 Art. 49, paras. 2 and 3 of the Law XX of 1949.

12 Gy. Bindorffer, *Nemzetiségi politika Magyarországon Szent István korától a rendszerváltozásig* (*Politics towards nationalities in Hungary from the age of St. Stepen until the change of regime*), in T. Gyulavári, E. Kállai (eds.), *A jövevényektől az államalkotó tényezőkig. A nemzetiségi közösségek múltja és jelene Magyarországon* (*From the incomers to

Against this historical background, at the end of the 1980s the new political elite considered the protection of minorities as a priority issue. The approach which characterised the new initiatives was the one which put in the centre the self-organisation of minorities themselves. To do so it was indispensable to set up a coherent legal and institutional framework. These activities have been started and they were inspired both by national initiatives as well as by obligations deriving from international human rights documents. However, under various aspects completeness is still to be achieved. Some institutions relating to the main focus of this paper will be recalled later, at this point there is another consideration to which attention should be paid. As it was shortly described in the above paragraphs, throughout the history of the Hungarian State various ethnic groups played an important role. Some groups participated in a rather tangible manner influencing high politics as well, whereas some others were less notable. However, all of them added linguistic, cultural and traditional elements to the richness of the population living in this territory. Then in the last century, Trianon, the deportations and the population exchange drastically diminished the numerical presence of minorities. This process was completed by a minority policy which at the best can be described as a negligent one and for the end of the 1990s it resulted a minority population which could hardly be aware of its identity. Most elements of this identity, such as the everyday use of the language, a shared material and intellectual culture, historical traditions, ways of living, celebration of particular events (like marriage), which indicate the belongingness to a specific community seem to be mostly disappeared[13]. A newly constructed institutional framework based on positive discrimination cannot replace the lost elements, at the best it can promote its recovery, but it can establish new forms of participation which demonstrate the belongingness to a certain minority group. To tell the same in different words, as a significant part of the substantial elements defining minority identity have become invisible or are on the way to do so, more formalistic elements came to the forth. These elements are the participation in minority organisations or associations, representation in minority self-governments, membership in groups promoting cultural traditions. These institutions, if they function correctly and are filled with content, can contribute to the enforcement or revitalisation of the substantial elements of minority identity.

---

the constituent parts of the State. The past and present of communities of nationalities in Hungary), *cit.*, p. 31.

13 The loss of these elements is also due to e.g. mixed marriages with members of the majority population or to the use of the majority language in settlements where Hungarians are in majority. Other elements relate to labour related migrations, changes in the economic and social structures, the uniforming effects of modernisation.

3. Minorities today and the legal framework for their protection

3.1 Recognised minorities

The Act on the Rights of National and Ethnic Minorities (Act LXXVII of 1993, hereinafter: the Minority Act) provides the following definition of national and ethnic minorities: those groups which have been lived on the territory of the Republic of Hungary for at least one century, which represent a numerical minority among the population of the country, whose members are Hungarian citizens, who are distinguished from the rest of the population by their own languages, cultures and traditions and at the same time demonstrate a sense of belonging together that is aimed at preserving all of these and at expressing and protecting the interests of their historical communities[14]. Article 61, para. 1 of the Act lists 13 minorities as recognised ones: Armenians, Bulgarians, Croats, Germans, Greeks, Poles, Roma, Romanians, Ruthenians, Serbs, Slovaks, Slovenes, Ukrainians. If a further minority group wants to benefit from the Act it has to prove that it fulfils the requirements of the Act by presenting at least 1000 signatures of those who can exercise electoral rights and belong to that specific group. The President of the Hungarian Academy of Science is called upon to express his opinion[15].

The following table presents in the percentage of the total population and in absolute numbers the various groups on the basis of the 2001 census[16].

At the 2001 census national identity was measured on the basis of four components: minority language as mother tongue, belongingness to the minority group, attachment to the culture and traditions of the minority group, the use of minority language in family, among friends. In the case of various minority groups, like Slovaks, Germans, Gypsies, there were more individuals who indicated to use the minority language in family and among friends, but they did not do so regarding the mother tongue. This situation can be explained by the

---

14 Art. 1, para. 2. The Act is available in English at the Minority Rights Information System (MIRIS) http://miris.eurac.edu/mugs2/index.jsp?TopBarItem=Home.

15 Art. 61, para. 2 of the Act. Recently the Jewish, Russian, Hun and Bunjevci communities made use of that possibility. For different reasons, but any of them obtained official recognition. The Advisory Committee on the Framework Convention of National Minorities made a recommendations to Hungary to make efforts to include the possibility for persons belonging to other groups to enjoy the protection of the Framework Convention and to be covered by the national legislation on minorities (Advisory Committee on the Framework Convention for the Protection of National Minorities, Third Opinion, published 18th March 2010, ACFC/OP/III(2010)001, § 36).

16 Official data from the Hungarian Statistical Office. http://www.nepszamlalas.hu/eng/volumes/24/tartalom.html .The next census is to be held in 2011.

fact that these people still speak the minority language, but the language that they use spontaneously and speak better, which are the characteristics of the mother tongue, is not anymore the minority language, but that of the majority, that is Hungarian[17].

Hungarians	92.3%	9 416 045
Roma /Gipsy	1.9%	190 046
German	0.61%	62 233
Slovak	0.17%	17 692
Croatian	0.15%	15 620
Romanian	0.07%	7 995
Ukrainian	0.04%	5 070
Serbian	0.03%	3 816
Slovene	0.02%	3 040
Polish	0.02%	2 962
Greek	0.02%	2 509
Bulgarian	0.01%	1 358
Ruthenian	0.01%	1 098
Armenian	0.006%	620
Others (non recognised minorities like Jewish, Chinese)	0.15%	16 081

3.2 The protection of minorities

Some cultural, linguistic and educational rights attributed to minorities were declared by the Constitution and other norms before the change of political system, but these norms did not provide for a coherent framework and in most cases their implementation remained troublesome. The Minority Act approved in 1993 gathered in a catalogue the individual and collective rights of minorities,

17 *Népszámlálás, 2001. IV. Nemzeti kötődés – A nemzeti és etnikai kisebbségek adatai* (*Census, 2001. IV. Nationality ties – data on national and ethnic minorities*), Budapest, 2001.

but missed the opportunity to establish or complete the institutional and procedural conditions which could guarantee the exercise of the rights related to political participation in the Parliament and throughout minority self-governments[18]. The Minority Act was amended in 2005 in relation to the establishment and functioning of minority self-government but this institution continues to feed critics. The legal framework provides for the election of the Parliamentary Commissioner for National and Ethnic Minorities (hereinafter Ombudsman) as well. Hungary signed the European Charter for Regional or Minority Languages and the Framework Convention for the Protection of National Minorities (hereinafter mentioned as European Charter and Framework Convention).

Both the Hungarian Constitution (art. 68, para. 1), and the Minority Act (art. 3, para. 1) recognise national minorities as a constituent part of the state. Similarly, both documents, in art. 68, para. 3[19] and in art. 20, para. 1, relatively, recognise the right of minorities to be represented in the Parliament. This issue has been periodically on the political agenda since 1990, but still have to be resolved[20]. Generally there are non ethnic Hungarians among the Members of Parliament (hereinafter: MPs), but they are elected in representation of the mainstream political parties.

The Act LXIII of 1990 inserted a new paragraph into art. 68 of the Constitution stating that national and ethnic minorities can establish local and national level self-governments. The current legal framework is defined by the Act CXIV of 2005 which amended the Minority Act. As neatly spelled out by the at time Ombudsman for National and Ethnic Minorities, Jenő Kaltenbach, the previous legal framework had to be modified in order to limit the possibility to elect the members of minority self-governments to those who effectively belong to minorities. For this purpose the register of voters of minority self-governments

18 A. Magicz, *A kisebbségi önkormányzatok és a kisebbségi választójog* (*Minority self-governments and minority suffrage*), in T. Gyulavári, E. Kállai (eds.), *A jövevényektől az államalkotó tényezőkig. A nemzetiségi közösségek múltja és jelene Magyarországon* (*From the incomers to the constituent parts of the State. The past and present of communities of nationalities in Hungary*), *cit.*, 2010, pp. 205–228.

19 Introduced by the Act XVI of 1990 which foresaw the election of the representatives of minorities by the members of the Parliament. This provision was amended by the Act XL of 1990 in less than 4 months time by the new democratically elected Parliament. The new provision does not specify the methodology of the elections, it simply states the right of national and ethnic minorities to be represented.

20 The most recent concept elaborated by the Ombudsman for national and ethnic minorities. http://www.kisebbsegiombudsman.hu/hir-161-kisebbsegek-parlamenti-kepviseletenek.html.

was introduced[21]. Currently only those persons can participate in the election of local minority self-government who are registered on this list. No one can register on more than one list and the voter has to declare his or her affiliation to a certain minority. Elections of local minority self-government can be organised if there are at least 30 persons registered on the minority voters list and there are at least 4 candidates. Minority self-governments can be elected also at territorial and national level[22]. The local minority self-government is elected directly, whereas territorial and national minority self-governments are elected by the members of local minority governments. Still the current legal framework lacks procedural and institutional guarantees which should ensure that minority self-governments are elected exclusively by the members of those communities which should be represented by these self-governments. In occasion of the elections held both in 2006 and in 2010 minority self-governments were established at settlements where, according to the 2001 census, people belonging to that specific minority were not present[23].

Minority self-governments are the expression of cultural autonomy as it is laid down also in the Preamble of the Minority Act. More precisely it is stated that the establishment of minority self-governments realizes cultural autonomy and the Parliament considers it as one of the main conditions of the specific enforcement of the rights of minorities. The Act attributes to minority self-governments powers mainly in the fields of culture, linguistic rights and education. From the point of view of this article minority self-governments play an important role since it is the local or territorial minority self-government which has to present to the local self-government the request regarding

21 J. Kaltenbach, *Jelentés a 2006. évi települési kisebbségi önkormányzati választásokról* (*Report on the 2006 election of local minority self-governments*), Budapest, 2007 and *Kisebbségi Kézikönyv* (*Minorities' handbook*), 2006, at: http://www.kisebbsegiombudsman.hu/hir-233-kisebbsegi-kezikonyv.html.

22 Territorial self-government can be elected if there are at least 10 local minority self-governments in the county or in the districts of Budapest (art. 14); national minority self-government can be elected if there are at least 4 local minority self-governments (art. 22) of the given minority group. The Act LXII of 2010 diminished the number of the members of minority self-governments. Parallel to this the number of members of local self-governments was also decreased and there are draft proposals to decrease substantially the number of MPs.

23 See the report prepared by the Ombudsman for national and ethnic minorities which analyses the 2010 elections at: http://www.kisebbsegiombudsman.hu/data/files/187663711.pdf. More in details see: A. Magicz, *A kisebbségi önkormányzatok és a kisebbségi választójog* (*Minority self-governments and minority suffrage*) in T. Gyulavári, E. Kállai (eds.), *A jövevényektől az államalkotó tényezőkig. A nemzetiségi közösségek múltja és jelene Magyarországon* (*From the incomers to the constituent parts of the State. The past and present of communities of nationalities in Hungary*), *cit.*, pp. 222–223.

geographical indications and names of public offices written also in minority language.

3.3 Insight to the up to date situation

Following the last parliamentary elections held in the spring of 2010 the Hungarian political situation acquired a particular shape. The coalition which won the elections, FIDESZ Hungarian Civic Union and the Christian Democratic People's Party (KDNP), gained more than 2/3 of the seats in the Parliament. This fact will inevitably have important repercussions on the legislation since such a majority is sufficient to amend also those laws which require a qualified majority of 2/3. Since the new political design very probably will bring important changes into minority policy as well it is worthwhile to mention a few elements[24]. Regarding the composition of the Parliament, it is of interest to note that the Lungo Drom National Roma Advocacy and Civic Union is also member of the leading parliamentary coalition and the President of Lungo Drom was elected as deputy leader of the FIDESZ parliamentary group. There are 3 Roma MPs among FIDESZ MPs and 1 in the new parliamentary group, Politics Can Be Different (LMP). One MP, who is also member of a Croatian Minority Self-Government in a settlement was elected deputy leader of the KDNP parliamentary group. There are some other MPs who belong to minority groups.

The details on the composition of the new Parliament are important since the direct representation of minorities in the Parliament is still unresolved. This omission violates the Constitution and has already been criticised various times by the Council of Europe. The new Parliament modified the Constitution which now states that up to an 13 MPs may be elected for the representation of national minorities[25]. This amendment makes part of a broader project which foresees a complex electoral reform including the substantial decrease of the number of MPs. The direct representation of minorities should become reality in the Parliament formed after the political elections in 2014.

The attribution of a specific role to the leader of Lungo Drom goes beyond the issue of the representation of minorities. The situation of Roma is particularly severe, a substantial part of people belonging to this minority group are subject

24 As notified also towards the Council of Europe in the Comments of the Government of Hungary on the Third Opinion of the Advisory Committee on the Implementation of the Framework Convention for the Protection of National Minorities 17th September 2010, GVT/COM/III(2010)002.

25 The amendment was adopted on 25th May 2010. Published in the Official Journal: MK no. 85, 25th May 2010.

of or frightened by social exclusion and racially motivated actions against them are also on the agenda. To improve living conditions and promote social inclusion of Roma a Ministerial Commissioner was recently appointed: the same President of Lungo Drom who is the deputy leader of the FIDESZ parliamentary group. He is responsible for overseeing and monitoring the implementation of inclusion projects. The involvement of a high representative of the minority group in the decision-making process and in the supervision of the implementation should ensure the sharing of responsibility in the success of the projects designed for the improvement of the situation of this minority group[26].

In the new Government structure the Ministry of Public Administration and Justice is responsible for the coordination of administration matters related to Hungary's national and ethnic minorities. A Junior Minister's Office for Church, Civil Society and Nationality Affairs was set up in the new Ministry. In June 2010, this Office launched a social dialogue involving all interested parties in relation to the revision of the Minority Act considering in particular its operational effectiveness and the role of self-governments. This revision should establish a coherent framework for the political participation of minorities eliminating lacunae and opportunities for abuse.

In April 2011 a completely new Constitution was adopted which will enter into force on 1st January 2012[27]. Contrary to the amendment introduced in May 2010 the new Constitution does not specify the number of MPs who would represent minority communities. It simply states that the participation of minorities in the activities of the Parliament is regulated by a constitutional law (art. 2, para. 2). The 1949 Constitution, as amended, used the word "representtation", whereas the new Basic Law speaks about "participation". It remains to the constitutional law to specify the exact content of "participation"[28].

The Preamble of the new Constitution recognises minorities as parts of the Hungarian political community, as constituent parts of the State. The preservation of the languages and the culture of minorities is taken as a burden. In the section entitled as "Freedom and Responsibility" art. XXIX is dedicated to minorities. It repeats that minorities are recognised as constituent parts of the State and it spells out the right of every Hungarian citizen belonging to a minority community to his/her identity and to the preservation of this identity. This element is a novelty compared to the previous Constitution whereas other

26 Some earlier initiatives indicated similar intention. O. Farkas, *The Roma and Their Integration to the Labour Market: A Comparison between Hungary and Slovakia*, in *European Yearbook of Minority Issues*, vol. 3, 4/2003, Leiden, 2005, pp. 340–342.

27 Published in: MK no. 43, 25th April 2011.

28 According to art. T(4) the adoption and amendment of a constitutional law (*sarkalatos törvény*) requires a 2/3 majority of the votes cast.

rights, such as the right to mother tongue education, the preservation of cultural heritage, the use of minority languages and the use of individual and collective names in minority language were already present in the previous Constitution. Similarly, minority communities may set up local and national self-governments. Capillary regulation concerning minority rights and the election of minority self-governments will be provided by a constitutional law.

Major change will be carried out in the institutional structure regarding the protection of minorities' related rights. According to art. 30, there will be one ombudsman competent for the protection of all fundamental rights with two deputies, one with responsibilities towards future generations and another one to protect the rights of minorities living in Hungary. The Ombudsman and his/her deputies will be elected by the approval of 2/3 of the MPs. Detailed rules will be provided in a further law. This structural shift was sharply criticized by the current Ombudsman arguing that, among others, the deputy responsible for minority issues would not have decisional rights, at the best he can prepare the dossiers and suggest solutions. For the final word the competent person will be the single ombudsman. Such a structure will diminish the effective protection of minorities, as their rights will not be treated any more with particular attention, by a specific ombudsman, but the issue will be placed among all other fundamental rights on equal footing[29].

It would be premature to spell out any evaluation regarding the changes introduced by the new Constitution. As it often happens the written words will be filled with real content throughout their application in the practice, their interpretation by competent bodies and by the enactment of the detailed regulations. It will be interesting to see in which way the newly created framework will substantially change the protection of minorities.

4. Linguistic rights, topographical indications

4.1 The underlying context

The protection of minorities means the establishment of legal and institutional conditions which make possible the preservation of identity of minority groups. Identity can be described according to its various aspects, such as national,

29 Speech of the Ombudsman for national and ethnic minorities at the Parliament relating to the drafting of the new Constitution, 22nd March 2011: http://www.kisebbsegiombudsman.hu/index.php?action=print&item=671

ethnic, cultural, religious, linguistic but also all or some of these elements in combination[30].

The preservation of identity requires positive actions from the side of state authorities. The Framework Convention lays down the requirement that "the Parties undertake to promote the conditions necessary for persons belonging to national minorities to maintain and develop their culture, and to preserve the essential elements of their identity, namely their religion, language, traditions and cultural heritage" (art. 5)[31]. The Explanatory Report attached to the Framework Convention defines religion, language, traditions and cultural heritage as essential elements of the identity of a national minority (§ 43). As far as linguistic rights are concerned, the same Report states that "the use of minority language represents one of the principal means by which such persons can assert and preserve their identity" (§ 63).

The rights relating to the use of minority language, again, is composed of a range of facets, such as its use in contact with public administration and judicial bodies, educational rights, the use of one's name in the form of the minority language, the possibilities to display in minority language topographical indication. Among these elements, with regard to the subject matter of this paper, art. 11 of the Framework Convention spells out specific protection regarding the following issues:

- the right to use one's surname and first names in the minority language and the right to official recognition of them;
- the right to display in minority language signs, inscriptions and other information of private nature visible to the public;
- public authorities shall endeavour to display traditional local names, street names and other topographical indications intended for the public also in the minority language.

This last aspect, which links identity, language rights and the environment where one lives should be examined in details. It should be noted immediately that the Framework Convention does not speak about a right, as it is the case regarding the use of one's name in minority language and the right to display signs of private nature in minority language, but it requires that the States should make efforts to display traditional local names, street names and other topographical indications intended for the public also in the minority language. In addition,

30 The individual and collective dimensions of these rights are discussed by: A. Eide, *Cultural Rights and Minorities: On Human Rights and Group Accomodation*, in K. Hastrup (ed.), *Legal Cultures and Human Rights*, The Hague, 2001, pp. 25–42.

31 http://conventions.coe.int/Treaty/en/Treaties/Html/157.htm.

further conditions are established in art. 11, para. 3: topographical indications in minority language should be shown in areas traditionally inhabited by substantial numbers of persons belonging to a national minority and there should be a sufficient demand for such indications. This formulation makes possible the establishment of numerical thresholds and other conditions in relation to topographical indications and leaves considerable space of manoeuvre for the States. This opportunity influences in a significant manner whether a specific state complies with the obligation laid down in the Framework Convention and to what extent[32].

Concerning the obligation laid down in art. 11, para. 3 of the Framework Convention response can be found in art. 53, para. 1c of the Minority Act. The law specifies that the settlement's local authority must ensure, in accordance with the motivated request of the minority self-government operating at local or at territorial level, that writing appearing on signs in indications of place and street names, public offices and titles of bodies carrying out public services or communications concerning their operation can be read in addition to the Hungarian language text and style, and with the same content and in the same form, in minority language as well. The local authority decides with regard to the motivation of the request within 30 days from the presentation of the demand[33]. By locating the right to minority self-governments to formulate a request for such indications the Hungarian legislator incorporated into the national norm the conditions laid down by the Framework Convention. The conditions regulating the establishment of minority self-governments foresee that only recognised minorities can elect self-governments and recognised minorities are the ones which are defined by art. 1, para. 2 of the Minority Act; furthermore the law establishes thresholds regarding the numerical presence of members of minorities for the election of local self-governments requiring that at least 30 persons are registered on the minority voters' list. The discretionary power left to the local authority on the qualification of the request corresponds to the phrasing of the Framework Convention which requires from the States to

32 See also: T. Malloy, R. Medda-Windischer, E. Lantschner and J. Marko, *Indicators for Assessing the Impact of the FCNM an its State Parties*, Draft Study (EURAC, Bolzano/Bozen, 2008) at: http://www.eurac.edu/en/research/institutes/imr/Documents/FCNM_Index_Study_final_webpage.pdf.

33 The same article regulates that the local government operating in the settlement concerned must ensure, in compliance with the motivated request of the minority self-government that the announcement of decrees and the placing of announcements, besides Hungarian, also take place in minority language. Parallel to this the local government should ensure that documents used during public administration procedures are made available in the minority native language as well.

endeavour the disposition of geographical indications in minority language without assigning an absolute obligation on them.

The scope of the Hungarian law goes beyond the requirements of the Framework Convention inasmuch it previews minority language indications also for public offices and bodies carrying out public services as well as for communications concerning their operation. The city of Battonya made specific efforts to manufacture Hungarian, Romanian and Serbian language signs that indicate the names or relate to the operation of public offices and public service[34]. The settlement is close to the geographical meeting point of Hungary, Romania and Serbia and institutions of the city have built close relationship with partner institutions of the minorities' mother countries. The government support of programmes promoting the use of mother tongues of minorities in public life is also contained in documents of bilateral minority joint committees operated by Romania and Serbia[35].

The Framework Convention limits the requirement towards its state parties to the establishment of favourable conditions in the framework of their legal system. However, the fulfilment of this requirement should include also those guarantees which ensure the adequate implementation of the established rules. These guarantees stand for the availability of financial support e.g. for the physical realisation of minority language signs or for the professional training of civil servants who are in charge of the management of the register of geographical indications.

It should be added that the European Charter, to which Hungary is a contracting party, also makes reference to geographical indications. However, the material scope of art. 10, para. 2g is more limited than that of the provision contained in the Framework Convention, as the European Charter mentions only "the use or adoption, if necessary in conjunction with the name of the official language(s), of traditional and correct forms of *place-names* in regional or minority languages"[36]. The Framework Convention has a larger material scope, it includes street names and other topographical indications as well. The two documents lay down similar formulation with respect to the obligation of the Contracting Parties by requiring to allow or/and encourage the use or adoption of place names in minority or regional language (European Charter), and to endeavour to display topographical indications also in the minority language

---

34 Battonya is called Bătania in Romanian and Батања in Serbian.

35 Third Report submitted by Hungary pursuant to Article 25, Paragrapfh 1 of the Framework Convention for the Protection of National Minorities, 4th June 2009. ACFC/SR/III(2009)007) 92.

36 Emphasis added. The European Charter is available at: http://conventions.coe.int/Treaty/EN/Treaties/Html/148.htm.

(Framework Convention). Therefore, as it was already discussed in relation to the Framework Convention, there is a positive obligation towards public authorities to support the use of such indications in minority language.

The Hungarian Governments submit periodic reports on the implementation of the European Charter and the Framework Convention as the documents themselves so require. The last reports recall the efforts of financial nature made by the Government to supply settlements where minorities are present with bilingual place and street name signs as well as signs at public institutions[37].

4.2 Government Decree 303/2007 (XI.14) on the establishment and registration of Hungarian official geographical names

Already before the approval of the Minority Act in 1993 place names in minority languages were not completely missing. In 1976 the Minority Department of the Central Committee of the MSZMP (Hungarian Socialist Labour Party) prepared a list on place names in minority languages to promote the set up of public signs and collected names of noted personalities representing minority culture and history whose name could be used to denominate streets and institutions[38]. In 1980, in about 180 settlements, for the first time, the name of the settlement appeared in the minority population's native language[39].

The MT[40] Decree 71/1989 (VII.4) on Official Geographical Names in Hungary did not make specific reference to organisations or associations of minorities in listing those elements which had to be taken into consideration when geographical names were established[41]. The list contained indications to the actual name used by the population concerned, the opinions of local social

---

37 Fourth Periodical report presented to the Secretary General of the Council of Europe in accordance with art. 15 of the Charter, 22nd January 2009 (MIN-LANG/PR(2009)1, 65; Third Report submitted by Hungary pursuant to Article 25, Paragraph 1 of the Framework Convention for the Protection of National Minorities (see footnote 31).

38 I. Fehér, *Az utolsó percben. Magyarország nemzetiségei* (*In the last minute. Nationalities in Hungary*), Budapest, 1993, pp. 38–60.

39 First Report submitted by Hungary pursuant to Article 25, Paragraph 1 of the Framework Convention for the Protection of National Minorities, 21st May 1999, ACFC/SR(1999)010; 73.

40 Minisztertanács –Council of Ministers.

41 Although in this period of time the Central Committee of the MSZMP already decided to improve its minority politics. The first drafts of a minority act were laid down and also the institutional framework regarding the representation of minorities was enlarged by setting up a Minority College with advisory capacity next to the Government (Council of Ministers with the at time used denomination). See in details: R. Győri Szabó, *Kisebbségpolitikai rendszerváltás Magyarországon* (*Change of regime in minority politics in Hungary*), Budapest, 1998.

and economic organisations and the local authority, historical traditions, in particular historical research. Geographical names in minority languages could also be established and these denominations were included into the register of Geographical Names.

Regarding the compliance with art. 11, para. 3 of the Framework Convention a major step was taken by the approval of the Government Decree 303/2007 (XI.14) on the establishment and registration of Hungarian official geographical names (in the following mentioned as the Government Decree). It recognises as official geographical names the denominations of settlements and geographical surface names in minority languages as well as historical, traditional geographical names used by national or ethnic minorities. More specifically, the Government Decree establishes the following categories for geographical names:

a) Geographical surface names and denomination of regions of national significance (such as mountains, valleys, basins, geographical, ethnographical or ethnic areas) generally indicated on maps of a scale equal or smaller than 1:200 000;
b) Geographical surface names of local significance (parts of agricultural or silvicultural units, geographical surface names) generally indicated on maps of a scale equal or larger than 1:200 000;
c) Nature reserves;
d) Water names including natural waters (such as rives, lakes), pools and channels and constructions (such as dams);
e) Denominations for the purposes of transport and transposition of information of national significance (such as railway stations, airports, harbours, major bridges, post offices);
f) Denomination of countries;
g) Administrative denominations used for statistical and territorial development purposes by the public administration (such as counties, regions, smaller territorial units);
h) Denomination of settlements;
i) Denomination of a part of a settlement;
j) Denomination of public domains (such as streets, squares, parks, alleys);
k) Denominations used in local public transport.

According to art. 5, para. 4 of the Government Decree, in all the abovementioned categories official geographical names in minority languages can be determined, but with the exception of points *b), d),* and *k)*, (geographical surface names of local significance, water names and denominations used in local public transport) the name in minority language can be established only together with the Hungarian denomination. This division does not exclude, at least in theory, the determination of certain geographical names only in a minority language. This can be the case of the denominations of geographical surface names of local significance and of denominations used in local public transport in areas inhabited traditionally by minority groups. On the contrary the same possibility remains rather improbable concerning the geographical names relating to water. Natural waters, like rivers or lakes occupy such a territory that they are in contact with various communities, therefore it is likely that a Hungarian denomination exists. In the case of artificial constructions related to water the situation is different, since these interventions generally are financed from public resources, it is plausible that a Hungarian denomination, established already in the planning phase of the project prevails.

The same paragraph of the Government Decree provides rules regarding the transcription of minority language geographical names: if the original language uses Latin script, the form of the minority language denomination should respect the grammatical rules of the original language, whereas if the original language uses non-Latin script both the original way of writing and the transcription based on the Hungarian alphabet are considered as official way of writing.

Concerning the determination of official geographic names, the Government Decree requires the taking into consideration of a number of different aspects regarding mainly the traditions and characteristics of the specific area. More specifically it recalls elements as the actual application of denominations by the local population, the opinion of the local public administration and minority self-government, the presence of minorities and linguistic requirements.

The Government Decree contains provisions also with regard to the amendment of geographical names. Among other cases it might happen if the problem of identical denominations cannot be resolved in another way and this identity creates confusion, or if there is an evident change in the use of the denomination. This provision reflects the awareness of the legislator that the use of language evolves in time. At the same time the norm provides a safeguard as well, stating that denominations related to historical traditions cannot be amended. From the point of view of the protection of minorities this provision can be beneficial as far as it can promote the modification of a denomination to a minority language if the conditions in the society so request, but the inserted safeguard can shelter the preservation of a traditional denomination in a minority language even if proposals for amendment so urge.

The Government Decree sets up a Committee on Geographical Names to manage the tasks related to the establishment of geographical names. The Committee is composed of representatives of various Ministers according to their competence[42]. The Minister in charge of the Prime Minister's Office appoints a representative to the Committee who handles the tasks relating to geographical names in minority languages[43]. According to art. 4 of the Government Decree the Committee has the following tasks: it establishes geographical names, it provides expert opinion relating to certain geographical names mainly of local relevance[44], it takes position on the correctness of geographical names. In relation to geographical denominations in minority languages the Committee, if it finds necessary, might ask the opinion of the local or national minority self-government. The Committee, when prepares an expert opinion concerning denominations of local relevance has to take into due consideration traditional names. When street, square or similar public domain names are at stake their denomination should reflect traditions and specific characteristics of the local environment or should be related to persons tied to it. The just mentioned requirements can promote the use of denominations in minority languages or of persons linked to minority groups in settlements where traditionally minority population has been living, even if the number of this population has significantly decreased.

The official geographical denominations are contained in the Register of geographical names including the names determined in minority languages. The data contained in the Register is open to the public.

4.3 Indications relating to elements of cultural heritage: architectural monuments, cemeteries, commemorative signs

In examining the current legal framework on the protection of minorities paying particular attention to place names and other geographical indications as means of protection in the case of Hungary one should bear in mind the following specific elements: Hungary has a rich history with regard to the presence of various ethnic groups in its territory but for today the number of people belonging to minority groups has significantly decreased. Those who identify

42 For example, the Minister responsible for Agriculture and Rural Development appoints a representative to handle the tasks relating to maps of large scale, and to the registration of geographical names; the representative of the Minister of Transport handles the issues relating to transports and infrastructural networks; the representative of the Minister of Defence handles the tasks relating to maps of smaller scale and to issues of military topography. In the Committee the representatives of various state Agencies (like the Statistical Office) and of scientific institutions (like the Hungarian Academy of Science), are also invited.

43 According to the new Government structure set up following the parliamentary elections held in 2010 this competence was shifted to the Ministry of Public Administration and Justice.

44 In such cases the competent authority to take the decision is the local self-government.

themselves as belonging to one of these groups live widely spread in the country, they live together with Hungarians and are entirely integrated[45]. These elements contribute to their automatic assimilation. In such circumstances the preservation of minority identity can be fostered by creating such an environment where tangible elements prove the presence of a minority group. Such elements can be geographical indications, signs on public offices, but also the presence of museums, architectural monuments, traditional houses or farms, commemorative signs and statutes of prominent members of minorities or cemeteries.

Having in mind the specific historical background of minorities living in the contemporary Hungary, a few words should be said about the just mentioned testimonies of the past, which, in most cases can tell more about a minority group that place and street names. Article 16 of the Minority Act lays down that minorities have the right to protect and develop their traditions and language, to preserve and enrich their material and intellectual culture. Minority self-governments can establish institutions to make possible the exercise of these rights, but more often than not they have no sufficient financial resources and expertise. Therefore it remains to local public authorities to make functioning these institutions[46].

Most collections preserving minority culture are of ethnographic nature. They are composed of farms and houses constructed according to particular characteristics specific to certain minority groups and they also present the ways of living mainly in rural, popular environments. Regarding the protection of cultural heritage the applicable law ensures the participation and requires the cooperation, between public authorities and, among others, organisation of minorities, but the same law does not spell out a definition on minority related constructed memorials. This means that the registers do not contain indications regarding the minority group which set up the construction, and consequently currently nobody knows how many minority related constructions make part of the cultural heritage and therefore are protected as such[47].

---

45 Only the Romanian and Slovenian minorities can be linked to a specific geographic area. They live along the borders of Hungary close to their kin-State.

46 Report of E. Kállai, *Ombudsman for National and Ethnic Minorities on the implementation of minorities' cultural rights,* 2010, at: http://www.kisebbsegiombudsman.hu/data/files/165788766.pdf.

47 O. Szabó, V. Vass, Á. Weinbrenner, *A nemzetiségi kulturális jogok vázlata* (*Outline of minorities' cultural rights*), in T. Gyulavári, E. Kállai (eds.), *A jövevényektől az államalkotó tényezőkig. A nemzetiségi közösségek múltja és jelene Magyarországon* (*From the incomers to the constituent parts of the State. The past and present of communities of nationalities in Hungary*), *cit.,* p. 404.

Cemeteries evidently form part of cultural heritage, but currently there is no register which list those cemeteries and graves which are significant for minority groups. It would be a task for the Authority for the Protection of Monuments and for the local government to decide which cemeteries or graves should be protected in particular in those settlements where only cemeteries indicate the late presence of minorities. However, in most settlements there are no financial sources for such activity and public foundations can provide limited support as well[48]. The situation is much similar in the case of statutes, monuments, commemorative signs. There is no data available collecting these elements of cultural goods although they bear testimony of the past of minorities either it was glorious or tragic, they remember of prominent personalities or of determining events in the history of these groups.

The already analysed Government Decree 303/2007 (XI.14) on the establishment and registration of Hungarian official geographical names foresees that the Register of geographical names contains those geographical indications which are not considered as official geographical names, but which are important from the point of view of the use of various maps. Such indications can regard e.g. monuments or museums and the registration is based on the communication of the owner or manager of the institution (art. 6, para. 3). The Register might give indications regarding the elements of cultural heritage of minorities but in any case the Register is exhaustive.

The minority specific indications of the just recalled material elements of cultural heritage might constitute a more sensitive indicator in evaluating the protection of minorities than an investigation limited to place and street names. The completion of the legal framework in view of the preservation of minority specific cultural heritage requires a multifaceted intervention from the legislator The previous paragraphs pointed out some fundamental lacunae of the current Hungarian legislation, such as the need for a definition of constructed memorials relating to minorities or the non-existence of registers in the case of graves, monuments etc. Remedy to such problems could be provided by a horizontal intervention of the legislator which reconsiders all relevant pieces of the legislation such as the one on the establishment and functioning of museums, ethnographic sites, architectural monuments and so on. These norms do not focus on minority related issues therefore a meticulous revision is needed in order to add those elements which can guarantee that specific interests of minorities

48 O. Szabó, V. Vass, Á. Weinbrenner, *A nemzetiségi kulturális jogok vázlata* (*Outline of minorities' cultural rights*), in T. Gyulavári, E. Kállai (eds.), *A jövevényektől az államalkotó tényezőkig. A nemzetiségi közösségek múltja és jelene Magyarországon* (*From the incomers to the constituent parts of the State. The past and present of communities of nationalities in Hungary*), *cit.*, p. 405.

could be protected. A further issue regards the participation of public authorities in ensuring the continuous functioning of the institutions and memorial sites. This requirement goes beyond the setting up of an appropriate legal framework and it concerns the constant availability of financial resources. These financial resources are indispensable not only for the maintenance of these institutions but concerns also the vocational training of those who can provide expertise for their operation. Only if these requirements are respected minorities can exercise their rights to the preservation of their culture and traditions. Compared to these issues the disposal of geographical indications in minority language seems to be a less complex task.

5. Conclusions

This paper reviewed the Hungarian legal framework under the optic of the use of minority language geographic names as means of protection of minorities. In order to put into a context this instrument the obligation deriving from the Framework Convention for the Protection of National Minorities was recalled. It was indicated that the Hungarian legislation goes beyond the requirements laid down in the Convention by making available the same protection to indications relating to public offices, bodies providing public services and communications concerning their operation.

Apart from this positive aspect some critics should also be spelled out. One concern regards the protection of those minorities which are currently not recognised by the Minority Act. This issue was also remembered by the Advisory Committee on the Framework Convention which invited the Hungarian authorities to make efforts to include the possibility for persons belonging to groups other than recognised minorities to enjoy the protection of the Framework Convention and to be covered by the national legislation on minorities[49]. Another concern relates to minority self-governments. These bodies play a central role in the establishment of geographic names in minority language, since they are empowered by the law to present such a request to the local authority. As it was examined in the above paragraphs, in various occasions minority self-governments can express their opinion in relation to indications in minority language. Minority self-governments aim the legitimate representation of minority groups, but the current legislation does not contain those guarantees which can ensure such representation. Remedy to this problem can be provided only by a

49 Advisory Committee on the Framework Convention for the Protection of National Minorities, Third Opinion, published 18th March 2010, *cit.*, §§ 32 and 36.

comprehensive revision of the institutions underpinning the protection of minorities.

The last part of the paper suggests that indications relating to certain elements of cultural heritage of minorities can be used as more sensitive indicators than place names alone to assess the protection provided for minorities by these instruments. Minority specific indications on museums, architectural monuments, cemeteries constitute the meeting point between geographical indications and the preservation of cultural heritage. In the case of Hungary, which has a rich history but whose minorities still have to re-discover themselves after a troublesome period, these indications might give a considerable contribution.

Bibliography

Ács Z., *Nemzetiségek a történelmi Magyarországon* (*Nationalities in the historical Hungary*), Budapest, 1986.

Bindorffer Gy., *Jövevényektől az államalkotó tényezőig. Nemzetiségek és nemzetiségpolitika Magyarországon 1790-től napjainkig* (*From incomers to constituent part of the State. Nationalities and politics towards them from 1790 till today*), Budapest, 2009 at: http://www.kisebbsegiombudsman.hu/data/files/184992660.pdf.

Bindorffer Gy., *Nemzetiségi politika Magyarországon Szent István korától a rendszerváltozásig* (*Politics towards nationalities in Hungary from the age of St. Stepen until the change of regime*), in Gyulavári T., Kállai E. (eds.), *A jövevényektől az államalkotó tényezőkig. A nemzetiségi közösségek múltja és jelene Magyarországon* (*From the incomers to the constituent parts of the State. The past and present of communities of nationalities in Hungary*), Budapest, 2010.

Diószegi I., *A Ferenc József-i kor nagyhatalmi politikája* (*Power politics at the age of Franz Joseph*), Budapest, 1987.

Eide A., *Cultural Rights and Minorities: On Human Rights and Group Accomodation*, in Hastrup K. (ed.), *Legal Cultures and Human Rights*, The Hague, 2001.

Farkas O., *The Roma and Their Integration to the Labour Market: A Comparison between Hungary and Slovakia*, in *European Yearbook of Minority Issues*, vol. 3, 4/2003, Leiden, 2005.

Fehér I., *Az utolsó percben. Magyarország nemzetiségei* (*In the last minute. Nationalities in Hungary*), Budapest, 1993.

Hastrup K. (ed.), *Legal Cultures and Human Rights*, The Hague, 2001.

Győri Szabó R., *Kisebbségpolitikai rendszerváltás Magyarországon* (*Change of regime in minority politics in Hungary*), Budapest, 1998.

Gyulavári T., Kállai E. (eds.), *A jövevényektől az államalkotó tényezőkig. A nemzetiségi közösségek múltja és jelene Magyarországon* (*From the incomers to the constituent parts of the State. The past and present of communities of nationalities in Hungary*), Budapest, 2010.

Kaltenbach J., *Kisebbségi Kézikönyv* (*Minorities' handbook*), 2006, at: http://www.kisebbsegiombudsman.hu/hir-233-kisebbsegi-kezikonyv.html.

Kaltenbach J., *Jelentés a 2006. évi települési kisebbségi önkormányzati választásokról* (*Report on the 2006 election of local minority self-governments*), Budapest, 2007.

Kovács N., Szarka L. (eds.), *Tér és terep. Tanulmányok az etnicitás és az identitás kérdésköréből* (*Space and field. Studies around the question of ethnicity and identity*), Budapest, 2003.

Kovacsics J. (ed.), *Magyarország történeti demográfiája* (*Hungary's historical demography*), Budapest, 1997.

Kristó Gy., *Magyarország lélekszáma az Árpád-korban* (*Population of Hungary at the age of the House of Árpád*), in Kovacsics J. (ed.), *Magyarország történeti demográfiája* (*Hungary's historical demography*), *cit.*

Kristó Gy., *Nem magyar népek a középkori Magyarországon* (*Non-Hungarian people in Hungary at the Middle-Age*), Budapest, 2003.

Magicz A., *A kisebbségi önkormányzatok és a kisebbségi választójog* (*Minority self-governments and minority suffrage*), in Gyulavári T., Kállai E. (eds.), *A jövevényektől az államalkotó tényezőkig. A nemzetiségi közösségek múltja és jelene Magyarországon* (*From the incomers to the constituent parts of the State. The past and present of communities of nationalities in Hungary*), *cit.*

Malloy T., Medda-Windischer R., Lantschner E. and Marko J., *Indicators for Assessing the Impact of the FCNM an its State Parties*, Draft Study (EURAC, Bolzano/Bozen, 2008 at: http://www.eurac.edu/en/research/institutes/imr/Documents/FCNM_Index_Study_final_webpage.pdf.

Mályusz E., *A középkori magyarság település- és nemzetiségpolitikája* (*Settlement and nationality policies of Hungarians in the Middle-Age*), Budapest, 2002.

Nemzeti és Etnikai Kisebbségi Jogok Országgyűlési Biztosa (Parliamentary Commissioner for National and Ethnic Minorities), *A kisebbségek parlamenti képviseletének koncepciója* (*The concept of the Parliamentary representation of minorities*), 2008 at: http://www.kisebbsegiombudsman.hu/hir-161-kisebbsegek-parlamenti-kepviseletenek.html.

Nemzeti és Etnikai Kisebbségi Jogok Országgyűlési Biztosa (Parliamentary Commissioner for National and Ethnic Minorities), *Kisebbségi Kézikönyv*

(*Minorities' handbook*), 2006 at: http://www.kisebbsegiombudsman.hu/hir-233-kisebbsegi-kezikonyv.html.

Nemzeti és Etnikai Kisebbségi Jogok Országgyűlési Biztosa (Parliamentary Commissioner for National and Ethnic Minorities), *Jelentés a 2010 évi települési kisebbségi önkormányzati választásokról* (*Report on the 2010 election of local minority self-governments*), 2010 at: http://www.kisebbsegi ombudsman.hu/data/files/187663711.pdf.

Nemzeti és Etnikai Kisebbségi Jogok Országgyűlési Biztosa (Parliamentary Commissioner for National and Ethnic Minorities), *Jelentés a kisebbségi kulturális jogok érvényesülésének vizsgálatáról* (*Report on the implementation of minorities' cultural rights*), 2010 at: http://www.kisebbsegiombuds man.hu/data/files/165788766.pdf.

Népszámlálás, 2001. IV. Nemzeti kötődés – A nemzeti és etnikai kisebbségek adatai, (*Census, 2001. IV. Nationality ties – data on national and ethnic minorities*), Budapest, 2001.

Szabó O., Vass V., Weinbrenner A., *A nemzetiségi kulturális jogok vázlata* (*Outline of minorities' cultural rights*), in Gyulavári T., Kállai E. (eds.), *A jövevényektől az államalkotó tényezőkig. A nemzetiségi közösségek múltja és jelene Magyarországon* (*From the incomers to the constituent parts of the State. The past and present of communities of nationalities in Hungary*), *cit.*

Pók A., *A magyarországi nemzetiségi kérdésről (1868–1918)* (*About the nationality issue in Hungary (1868–1918)*), in *História*, 4/1982.

Tilkovszky L., *Nemzetiségi politika Magyarországon a 20. században* (*Politics towards nationalities in Hungary in the XX century*), Debrecen, 1998.

Concluding remarks

Valeria Piergigli

Toponomastics is an eminently linguistic discipline that studies the origin, history and meaning of proper names of public places, or places open to the public. However, since the XIX century, the study of place names has not only attracted the interest of linguists and dialectologists but also of experts in other disciplines, such as geographers, archaeologists, topographers, epigraphists, numismatists, palaeographers, philologists, natural scientists and above all historians in a wide range of sectors. Many scientific disciplines can contribute to toponomastic research, not only explaining the origin of place names, but also their transformations in time, and in certain cases their demise, in relation to the events of a population or a community of people that lives or lived in a place in a certain historical period.

With the advent of the modern State, legislation was dedicated to toponomastics, not only meeting the practical need to facilitate communication and rationalise planning, especially in towns, but also giving the choice of place and street names a sense of belonging to the community. These requirements called for appropriate legal and administrative definition.

Today, toponomastics is still not a subject exclusive to scholars and people of culture. It implies choices related to present and future land management and has symbolic cultural and political meaning, especially when a toponym expresses a sense of belonging to minority communities, distinguished from the rest of the population by linguistic and cultural traits, which it is desired to conserve.

The law, beginning with international law, is concerned with toponomastics in various ways and through various institutions. The United Nations have developed progressive interest in the subject since the 1950's, through the institution of a group of experts (UNGEGN) having the task of providing qualified technical assistance for the standardization of geographical names, which is necessary to intensify and simplify international communication in an increasingly interconnected community of States. Even in that period, the UN could not ignore the linguistic and cultural pluralism of many societies, and this pluralism was worthy of protection through regulation of toponomastics. In this regard, UN Resolution no. 4/1967, and in particular Recommendation D that stipulates recognition of linguistic pluralism also in toponyms, is still a legal milestone. As far as the European context is concerned, to these instruments can be added several conventions elaborated within the Council of Europe and regarding protection of minority idioms and their speakers. On ratifying States, these conventions impose various obligations regarding public use of languages different from the official state language, including their use in the denomination of public places. They are the Framework Convention for the Protection of National Minorities and the European Charter for Regional or Minority Languages. These treaties encourage States to take positive actions to express topographic indications in the minority language, as well as in the official language of the State, in the historical territories of minority communities (art. 11, para. 3 Framework Convention, and art. 10, para. 2g European Charter). Although monitoring to ensure implementation of these obligations is relatively ineffective, through periodic reports to the Council of Europe, ratifying States must demonstrate that they are taking steps towards implementation, including restoration of traditional toponomastics. On this regard, the results are not always fully satisfactory.

Among the legal systems considered in this volume, it is noteworthy that certain States long accustomed to situations of internal linguistic and cultural pluralism have not ratified the conventions of the Council of Europe. The Framework Convention has not yet been signed by France and it has been signed, but not ratified, by Belgium. The European Charter has been signed, but not yet ratified, by Italy and France, while Belgium has not even signed it. These attitudes confirm a certain persistent prudence of certain national authorities, which while they cannot ignore the existence of minority situations or linguistic pluralism within their borders, are reluctant to commit themselves internationally to affirmative actions of linguistic and cultural promotion of minorities and their idioms, possibly for fear that such recognition could threaten national integrity.

The diversity in toponomastic legislation in the cases examined in this volume is a result of the different approaches taken to the general regulation of linguistic minorities and regional and minority languages. Indeed, the attitude in the matter of toponomastics varies according to: a) whether or not the law envisages official use, at least locally, of minority idioms, or goes as far as putting them (or some of them) on an equal footing with the official language of the State; b) whether or not the law makes public use of minority languages conditional to a certain percentage of speakers or a minimum number of requests in a given geographical area; c) whether the law chooses to protect minorities on the basis of the personality or territoriality principle: the former does not consider the places of settlement but is based on free choice of the language to use in public relations; the latter draws territorial boundaries to coincide with those of minority languages in order to protect them (and the respective speakers) in well-defined geographical areas; d) whether the law opts for the model of total or integral bilingualism, or for linguistic separation, on the basis of a preference for facilitating contact and cultural integration between the various national components in mixed-language areas, or of the necessity to favour the conservation of a minority group, avoiding its assimilation into an economically and culturally stronger group, respectively. The above criteria may also be mixed within a certain legislation, admitting, for example, the principles of personality and territoriality, bilingualism and linguistic separation, depending on the specific sector (schools, relations with the public administration, the media, toponomastics) in which the measures of protection have to be implemented. It is worth noting that certain plurilingual systems like those of Switzerland and Belgium, as a general rule, are reluctant to qualify the respective idioms as "minority languages" and speakers as "linguistic minorities", since the languages are considered co-official and equal, irrespective of the number of speakers.

One should also not forget that the use of languages in toponomastics is closely linked to the identification of areas: indeed, more than in other sectors, the principle of territoriality for the protection of minority identities is expressed in the determination of place names, for reasons intrinsic to the science of toponomastics. Thus legal regulation of toponomastics depends on the configuration chosen for attributing forms of autonomy to local bodies, according to the well-known models of regional and federal State, and this, however, is dynamically influenced by the processes of devolution currently encountered in many European States in connection with particular identity claims. Moreover, almost everywhere decisions on toponomastics are largely the responsibility of local authorities.

Many elements of differentiation affect the attitude of national authorities towards legal regulation of toponomastics as an instrument of protection of linguistic minorities, irrespective of whether or not these communities qualify as minority communities. There is nevertheless an element of analogy, in some senses unifying, constituted by the fact that *public administrations tend to be amenable to recovering traditional place names* in areas of historical settlement. This willingness emerges from all the regulations (constitutional, legislative and sublegislative; state and local) that the various systems have adopted on the subjects of protection of national and autochthonous minorities' rights, official use of languages and alphabets, local self-government, regional organisation, denominations of towns, streets and squares.

At first glance, this attitude appears positive, especially compared to the diffidence encountered in areas implying recognition of more onerous public uses of minority languages, such as teaching of or in a minority language, relations with administrations and the courts, in which the State has to be able to ensure proper training of personnel in the various sectors and to have financial resources. This is confirmed by the contrast between the generalised ratification of art. 10, para. 2g of the European Charter to ensure recovery of historical toponomastics, and the reservations implied by non ratification of the Charter's various options regarding the right to use a regional or minority language in relations with administrations and public services.

The positive impression given by the fact that States are at least in principle inclined to valorise or at least not oppose restoration of traditional toponomastics, as they are encouraged to do by international agreements and UN recommendations, does not always stand up to scrutiny in practice. Indeed, in many pluralistic and plurilingual contexts, partial and incomplete regulatory measures are often compounded by delays in implementation, making the *laws adopted relatively ineffective*. Unless solved, these problems not only slow down attainment of a major profile for policies of protection of minority languages, but can seriously threaten peaceful coexistence between communities and may even lead to serious conflict between the different social components.

Toponomastics is a more "sensitive" sector than others due to the immediate visual perception it offers of measures taken with regard to cultural identities present in an area. While public administrations seem widely amenable to recovery of historical names, at least on the level of provisions and formal commitment, they tend to assign the right to use traditional toponyms a lower rank in the hierarchy of measures for the protection of minorities. The *apparent favour for restoration of historical toponomastics* can therefore be interpreted as a sign of lack of awareness, even in systems positively disposed to adopting open and liberal linguistic policies, of the highly symbolic value that place names in minority idioms have for linguistic minorities, or conversely, as a sign of awareness of the social impact political decisions in this sector have on intercommunity relations, to the point of discouraging public institutions from adopting real and effective measures of promotion and valorisation. In either case, toponyms end up being considered (and protected) like "cultural goods", underestimating the technical profiles related to their attribution or recovery, and their determination is usually handed over to the competence and discretion of local authorities, who are not always adequately orientated on the subject by special guidelines of state bodies.

In Switzerland, each canton determines the official languages in the various public sectors according to the territoriality principle, assigning the regulation of local toponomastics to municipalities. Similarly, in the United Kingdom, since the start of the devolution of powers at the end of last century, the definition of linguistic policy has been transferred to decentralised institutions in Scotland and Wales, and the denomination of public places, generally bilingual, is the responsibility of local government. A similar situation is found in France: traditionally reluctant to recognise minority situations, the French regulations attribute adoption of bilingual signposting, if any, to local bodies, in the context of a tolerant attitude on behalf of the State, which does not offer any particular incentives for formulating uniform criteria of reference. In Italian law, which protects linguistic minorities according to art. 6 of the Constitution, the regulation of toponomastics, including that of places where minorities live, is delegated to rather incomplete state laws, sometimes dating back to the Fascist period, or to accumulations of sectorial laws, as well as to measures by regional and local authorities. On this regard, different regulations of toponomastics have been implemented by the Northern regions that are granted a special statute of autonomy. In Valle d'Aosta/Vallée d'Aoste, the almost generalised application of French monolingualism in toponomastics has never caused any particular problems of coexistence between the Italian and French-speaking communities of the region. On the other hand, in Trentino-Alto Adige/Südtirol, the activism showed by the legislator in the Province of Trento contrasts with the attempts at regulation by the legislator of the Province of Bolzano, whose fruitless efforts bear witness to the difficulty of legislative reform, which is often the source of social tensions and widespread malcontent, especially in the Italian-speaking population. In Friuli-Venezia Giulia, the regional legislator has proven particularly active in initiatives to increase the promotion of the Slovenian and Friulan languages in various public ambits, even causing a judgement of the Constitutional Court with regard, among other things, to the faculty of local bodies to express geographic names in Friulan only, giving them the connotations of official names.

The question of the joint use of the official language of the State and minority languages (bi/trilingualism) or exclusive use of the latter (monolingualism) in areas where minority groups traditionally live, is tackled and solved differently in the plurilingual systems studied in this volume. While in Italy the choice of one or the other criterion is linked to the presence of international agreements, consolidated traditions or the exclusively local importance of certain toponyms, elsewhere bilingualism prevails. Thus, in Slovenia, place names are indicated in Slovenian and in the minority language Italian or Hungarian; similarly in Croatia, bilingualism or multilingualism prevails and in Romania place names are bilingual in areas where a minority represents over 20% of the population. Also in Hungary, places tend to be indicated in bilingual form, except for strictly local names used in areas traditionally inhabited by minority communities that can only be expressed in the minority language, and geographic names indicated in the minority language are recognised as official place names. Elsewhere, as in Spain, the law does not oppose expression of place names exclusively in the minority idiom in regions where the latter is considered official, whereas in Belgium, topographic indications are given in the language of the region (French or Flemish) and translated into the other language (Flemish or French, respectively), except in municipalities of the German-speaking region where signs are prevalently only in German, and in the bilingual region of Brussels Capital where bilingualism prevails also in toponomastics.

The problematic effectiveness of laws adopted to regulate toponyms in minority languages also emerges clearly in other situations: in the Austrian *land* of Carinthia, the extreme delicacy of choices in this matter continues to fuel political as well as social and territorial conflict, whereas in Styria the existence of an autochthonous minority is even denied. In Belgium, the difficulty of reconciling freedom of language with the territoriality principle, even in toponomastic law, as well as aggravation of linguistic nationalism and cyclic political-institutional crises, are both the causes and consequences of the bi-national character of Belgian society and threaten to break-up the federal State.

Even in contexts in which regulation of the minority phenomenon and traditional toponomastics seems quite satisfactory, improvements are always desirable, especially to reduce incongruence in regulatory measures or implementation. For example, in Spain, reform of the regional statutes will certainly affect regulation of place names when concluded, by virtue of the valorisation of regional particularities of the *Estado autonómico*. In Serbia, appropriately, solutions adopted by local self-government units include the participation of representatives of the national minorities involved, and the same is envisaged by laws in force in Hungary. In Romania, despite the progressive improvement of legislation there is still a clear gap between the existing norms and their implementation; as a consequence, if a national minority represents the majority of the local population within a territorial-administrative unit its situation is better than in the areas in which the respective minority, although reaching the 20% threshold requested by the law, is still too small to be able to influence the decision making process.

Similar considerations can be made for the regulations of Slovenia and Croatia. With the break-up of Yugoslavia, the erection of state borders artificially divided the Italian-speaking autochthonous national minority between these two new States. In the republics of Slovenia and Croatia, protection of minority communities, also through visual bilingualism, seems to have been conscientiously considered in the laws; however, the long road to effectiveness of formally envisaged rights – including those regarding toponomastics – cannot yet be considered complete. Especially in Slovenia, the Constitution of which expressly recognises only the Italian and Hungarian autochthonous ethnic communities (despite their small size), there is no shortage of cases of legal suspension of regulations, which therefore end up being denied in actual fact. On the subject of toponomastics, the practice of introducing invented or Slovenised geographical names has not ceased, despite detailed regulations upholding the rights of the two autochthonous minorities. This amounts to an attack on the heritage of minority historical and cultural values, even though the law envisages the participation of the self-governing communities of local nationality in decisions of municipal councils on attribution and modification of the names of places, streets and buildings.

In conclusion, the positive efforts of national and local legislators to protect the linguistic rights of autochthonous minorities, including restoration of traditional toponomastics, must be recognised. Especially in the countries of Central and Eastern Europe, significant work has been done in the last twenty years to construct a legislative framework to protect the linguistic rights of national minorities. This work was also done to meet the standards of the European Council (Copenhagen, 1993), although at the time those standards only had political efficacy. With the Lisbon Treaty, in force since 1st December 2009, those requirements have assumed a precise legal meaning for the 27 member States of the European Union, who have explicitly adopted the protection of human rights among their founding values, including the rights of minorities, and have pledged to guarantee respect of linguistic, cultural and religious diversity.

However, the long road towards the effectiveness of rights abstractly envisaged has not yet been completely travelled and, in all the systems examined, small or large steps still have to be taken. Above all in systems that recently advanced policies of minority protection, there have been delays, incongruence and contradictions in the phase of implementation, which have caused a gap between the provisions (apparently detailed and generous) and their practical application. Relationships, not always relaxed, between majority and minority in given territories, the small demographic concentration of minority populations, which even when they reach the percentage required for protection rarely reach a majority locally, and alternation between recognition of the multiethnic nature of a State and nationalistic pressures, especially in countries that recently became democratic, are all factors, often interacting, which impede effective application of the measures of protection and promotion of minority identities, sometimes making restoration or maintenance of traditional place names problematical.

In the near future, consolidation of democratic institutions and synergies between national authorities – state and local – and supranational bodies charged with periodic monitoring of the fulfilment of international obligations should help overcome the contradictions and implementation difficulties described above. For the fruition of the measures of protection provided by the legislation, a sense of self-awareness of community identity plays an important role everywhere. Through participation in decision-making processes on behalf of the linguistic communities concerned and attention that political and administrative authorities fulfil their commitments, communities can actively help to prevent, also through the use or rediscovery of traditional toponomastics, the irreversible loss of linguistic and cultural heritage.

Schriften zum internationalen und zum öffentlichen Recht

Herausgegeben von Gilbert Gornig

Band 1 Michael Waldstein: Das Asylgrundrecht im europäischen Kontext. Wege einer europäischen Harmonisierung des Asyl- und Flüchtlingsrechts. 1993.

Band 2 Axel Linneweber: Einführung in das US-amerikanische Verwaltungsrecht. Kompetenzen, Funktionen und Strukturen der „Agencies" im US-amerikanischen Verwaltungsrecht. 1994.

Band 3 Tai-Nam Chi: Das Herrschaftssystem Nordkoreas unter besonderer Berücksichtigung der Wiedervereinigungsproblematik. 1994.

Band 4 Jörg Rösing: Beamtenstatut und Europäische Gemeinschaften. Eine Untersuchung zu den gemeinschaftsrechtlichen Anforderungen an die Freizügigkeit der Arbeitnehmer im Bereich des öffentlichen Dienstes. 1994.

Band 5 Wolfgang Wegel: Presse und Rundfunk im Datenschutzrecht. Zur Regelung des journalistischen Umgangs mit personenbezogenen Daten. 1994.

Band 6 Sven Brandt: Eigentumsschutz in europäischen Völkerrechtsvereinbarungen. EMRK, Europäisches Gemeinschaftsrecht, KSZE – unter Berücksichtigung der historischen Entwicklung. 1995.

Band 7 Alejandro Alvarez: Die verfassunggebende Gewalt des Volkes unter besonderer Berücksichtigung des deutschen und chilenischen Grundgesetzes. 1995.

Band 8 Martin Thies: Zur Situation der gemeindlichen Selbstverwaltung im europäischen Einigungsprozeß. Unter besonderer Berücksichtigung der Vorschriften des EG-Vertrages über staatliche Beihilfen und der EG-Umweltpolitik. 1995.

Band 9 Rolf-Oliver Schwemer: Die Bindung des Gemeinschaftsgesetzgebers an die Grundfreiheiten. 1995.

Band 10 Holger Kremser: „Soft Law" der UNESCO und Grundgesetz. Dargestellt am Beispiel der Mediendeklaration. 1996.

Band 11 Michael Silagi: Staatsuntergang und Staatennachfolge: mit besonderer Berücksichtigung des Endes der DDR. 1996.

Band 12 Reinhard Franke: Der gerichtliche Vergleich im Verwaltungsprozeß. Auch ein Beitrag zum verwaltungsrechtlichen Vertrag. 1996.

Band 13 Christoph Eichhorn: Altlasten im Konkurs. 1996.

Band 14 Dietrich Ostertun: Gewohnheitsrecht in der Europäischen Union. Eine Untersuchung der normativen Geltung und der Funktion von Gewohnheitsrecht im Recht der Europäischen Union. 1996.

Band 15 Ulrike Pieper: Neutralität von Staaten. 1997.

Band 16 Harald Endemann: Kollektive Zwangsmaßnahmen zur Durchsetzung humanitärer Normen. Ein Beitrag zum Recht der humanitären Intervention. 1997.

Band 17 Jochen Anweiler: Die Auslegungsmethoden des Gerichtshofs der Europäischen Gemeinschaften. 1997.

Band 18 Henrik Ahlers: Grenzbereich zwischen Gefahrenabwehr und Strafverfolgung. 1998.

Band 19 Heinrich Hahn: Der italienische Verwaltungsakt im Lichte des Verwaltungsverfahrensgesetzes vom 7. August 1990 (Nr. 241/90). Eine rechtsvergleichende Darstellung. 1998.

Band 20 Christoph Deutsch: Elektromagnetische Strahlung und Öffentliches Recht. 1998.

Band 21 Cordula Fitzpatrick: Künstliche Inseln und Anlagen auf See. Der völkerrechtliche Rahmen für die Errichtung und den Betrieb künstlicher Inseln und Anlagen. 1998.

Band 22 Hans-Tjabert Conring: Korporative Religionsfreiheit in Europa. Eine rechtsvergleichende Betrachtung. Zugleich ein Beitrag zu Art. 9 EMRK. 1998.

Band 23 Jörg Karenfort: Die Hilfsorganisation im bewaffneten Konflikt. Rolle und Status unparteiischer humanitärer Organisationen im humanitären Völkerrecht. 1999.

Band 24 Matthias Schote: Die Rundfunkkompetenz des Bundes als Beispiel bundesstaatlicher Kulturkompetenz in der Bundesrepublik Deutschland. Eine Untersuchung unter besonderer Berücksichtigung natürlicher Kompetenzen und der neueren Entwicklung im Recht der Europäischen Union. 1999.

Band 25 Hermann Rothfuchs: Die traditionellen Personenverkehrsfreiheiten des EG-Vertrages und das Aufenthaltsrecht der Unionsbürger. Eine Gegenüberstellung der vertraglichen Gewährleistungen. 1999.

Band 26 Frank Alpert: Zur Beteiligung am Verwaltungsverfahren nach dem Verwaltungsverfahrensgesetz des Bundes. Die Beteiligtenstellung des § 13 Abs. 1 VwVfG. 1999.

Band 27 Matthias Reichart: Umweltschutz durch völkerrechtliches Strafrecht. 1999.

Band 28 Nikolas von Wrangell: Globalisierungstendenzen im internationalen Luftverkehr. Entwicklung der Regulierung und Liberalisierung unter Berücksichtigung strategischer Allianzen und des Code-Sharing. 1999.

Band 29 Marietta Hovehne: Ein demokratisches Verfahren für die Wahlen zum Europäischen Parlament. Legitimation gemeinschaftlicher Entscheidungsstrukturen im europäischen Integrationsprozeß. 1999.

Band 30 Nina Kaden: Der amerikanische Clean Air Act und das deutsche Luftreinhalterecht. Eine rechtsvergleichende Untersuchung. 1999.

Band 31 Brigitte Daum: Grenzverletzungen und Völkerrecht. Eine Untersuchung der Rechtsfolgen von Grenzverletzungen in der Staatenpraxis und Folgerungen für das Projekt der International Law Commission zur Kodifizierung des Rechts der Staatenverantwortlichkeit. 1999.

Band 32 Andreas Fürst: Die bildungspolitischen Kompetenzen der Europäischen Gemeinschaft. Umfang und Entwicklungsmöglichkeiten. 1999.

Band 33 Gilles Despeux: Die Anwendung des völkerrechtlichen Minderheitenrechts in Frankreich. 1999.

Band 34 Michael Reckhard: Die rechtlichen Rahmenbedingungen der Sanktionierung von Beitragsverweigerung im System der Vereinten Nationen. 1999.

Band 35 Carsten Pagels: Schutz- und förderpflichtrechtliche Aspekte der Religionsfreiheit. Zugleich ein Beitrag zur Auslegung eines speziellen Freiheitsrechts. 1999.

Band 36 Bernhard Mehner: Die grenzüberschreitende Wirkung direktempfangbaren Satellitenfernsehens aus völkerrechtlicher Sicht. 2000.

Band 37 Karl-Josef Ulmen: Pharmakologische Manipulationen (Doping) im Leistungssport der DDR. Eine juristische Untersuchung. 2000.

Band 38 Jochen Starke: Die verfassungsgerichtliche Normenkontrolle durch den Conseil constitutionnel. Zum Kompetenztitel des Art. 61 der französischen Verfassung. 2000.

Band 39 Marco Herzog: Rechtliche Probleme einer Inhaltsbeschränkung im Internet. 2000.

Band 40 Gilles Despeux: Droit de la délimitation maritime. Commentaire de quelques décisions plutoniennes. 2000.

Band 41 Christina Hackel: Der Untergang des Landes Braunschweig und der Anspruch auf Restitution nach der Wiedervereinigung Deutschlands. 2000.

Band 42 Peter Aertker: Europäisches Zulassungsrecht für Industrieanlagen. Die Richtlinie über die integrierte Vermeidung und Verminderung der Umweltverschmutzung und ihre Auswirkungen auf das Anlagenzulassungsrecht der Bundesrepublik Deutschland. 2000.

Band 43 Karsten Bertram: Die Gesetzgebung zur Neuregelung des Grundeigentums in der ersten Phase der Französischen Revolution (bis 1793) und deren Bedeutung für die deutsche Eigentumsdogmatik der Gegenwart. 2000.

Band 44 Ulrike Hartmann: Die Entwicklung im internationalen Umwelthaftungsrecht unter besonderer Berücksichtigung von *erga omnes*-Normen. 2000.

Band 45 Thomas Jesch: Die Wirtschaftsverfassung der Sonderverwaltungsregion Hongkong. Eine Darstellung vor dem Hintergrund der Wiedereingliederung in die Souveränität der Volksrepublik China. 2001.

Band 46 Sven Gottschalkson: Der Ausschluß des Zivilrechtsweges bei Eigentumsverlusten an Immobilien in der ehemaligen DDR. 2002.

Band 47 Gilbert Hanno Gornig / Gilles Despeux: Seeabgrenzungsrecht in der Ostsee. Eine Darstellung des völkerrechtlichen Seeabgrenzungsrechts unter besonderer Berücksichtigung der Praxis der Ostseestaaten. 2002.

Band 48 Andreas Zühlsdorff: Rechtsverordnungsersetzende Verträge unter besonderer Berücksichtigung des Umweltrechts. 2003.

Band 49 Katja Schmitz: Durchgriffswirkung von Maßnahmen der UN und ihrer Sonderorganisationen unter besonderer Berücksichtigung von Resolutionen des UN-Sicherheitsrates – Die Entwicklung supranationaler Strukturen. 2003.

Band 50 Stefanie Rothenberger: Die angemessene Nutzung gemeinschaftlicher Ressourcen am Beispiel von Flüssen und speziellen Ökosystemen. Eine vergleichende Betrachtung zum modernen Verständnis eines klassischen völkerrechtlichen Nutzungsprinzips. 2003.

Band 51 Christoph von Burgsdorff: Die Umsetzung der EG-Datenschutzrichtlinie im nicht-öffentlichen Bereich. Möglichkeit einer zukunftsorientierten Konzeption des Datenschutzes in der Privatwirtschaft unter besonderer Berücksichtigung des BDSG. 2003.

Band 52 Frank Reinhardt: Powerline. Verfassungs-, verwaltungs- und telekommunikationsrechtliche Probleme. 2003.

Band 53 Chie Sato: Immunität Internationaler Organisationen. 2004.

Band 54 Johannes Thoma: EU-Recht und Schranken hoheitlicher Staatstätigkeit. 2004.

Band 55 Wolf Peterhoff: Rechtsansprüche enteigneter Volksgruppen und ihre Durchsetzbarkeit. 2004.

Band 56 Do-Hyub Kim: Das deutsche parlamentarische Regierungssystem als mögliches Modell für Korea. 2004.

Band 57 Alexander Koberg: Die Exilregierung im Völkerrecht. Eine Untersuchung ihrer rechtlichen Klassifikation. 2005.

Band 58 Nils Christian Carstensen: Das Verhältnis des Seerechtsübereinkommens der Vereinten Nationen von 1982 zu fischereirechtlichen Übereinkommen und deren Streitbeilegungsvorschriften. 2005.

Band 59 Oliver Franz: Osttimor und das Recht auf Selbstbestimmung. Eine Untersuchung zur Anwendung des Selbstbestimmungsrechts der Völker am Beispiel Osttimors. 2005.

Band 60 Michael Kadgien: Das Habsburgergesetz. 2005.

Band 61 Felix Wolf: Terrorversicherungen und europäisches Wettbewerbsrecht. Verschiedene Modelle staatlicher Beteiligung an einer Terrorversicherung für Wirtschaftsbetriebe und ihre Vereinbarkeit mit dem europäischen Wettbewerbsrecht. 2005.

Band 62 Heiko Bertelmann: Die Europäisierung des Staatshaftungsrechts. Eine Untersuchung zum Einfluss des Europäischen Gemeinschaftsrechts auf das deutsche Staatshaftungsrecht unter besonderer Berücksichtigung der Haftung für judikatives Unrecht. 2005.

Band 63 Cedric Christian Meyer: Konkretisierung unbestimmter Rechtsbegriffe im deutschen und französischen Anlagenzulassungsrecht. 2005.

Band 64 Philippe Gréciano: Die Gerichtsbarkeit der Europäischen Gemeinschaften. Rechtsprechung und Rechtssprache Europas aus französischer Perspektive. Mit einem Vorwort von Theodor Öhlinger. 2007.

Band 65 Anne-Louise Schümer: Die Stellung des Ministerpräsidenten in den Bundesländern im Vergleich. 2006.

Band 66 Helen Ghebrewebet: Identifying Units of Statehood and Determining International Boundaries. A Revised Look at the Doctrine of *Uti Possidetis* and the Principle of Self-Determination. 2006.

Band 67 Arne Hertel: Beihilfen an kleine und mittlere Unternehmen. 2006.

Band 68 Markus Günther: Europol. Rechtsschutzmöglichkeiten und deren Vereinbarkeit mit nationalen und internationalen Anforderungen. 2006.

Band 69 Christian Wicker: The Concepts of Proportionality and State Crimes in International Law. An Analysis of the Scope of Proportionality in the Right of Self-Defence and in the Regime of International Countermeasures and an Evaluation of the Concept of State Crimes. 2006.

Band 70 Hauke Stöwsand: Zyperns Beitritt zur Europäischen Union. Vom Antrag auf Mitgliedschaft bis zum Protokoll der Beitrittsakte. 2007.

Band 71 Natalie Rowohl: Weltbank und Internationaler Währungsfonds: Ihre Mandate und deren Abgrenzung. Stand und Reformvorschläge. 2007.

Band 72 Ru-Huei Liu: Europäisierung des deutschen Umweltrechts. 2008.

Band 73 Katja Lange: Der Status der Aufständischen im modernen humanitären Völkerrecht. 2007.

Band 74 Tarik El-Shabassy: Die Durchsetzung finanzieller Sanktionen der Europäischen Gemeinschaften gegen ihre Mitgliedstaaten. 2008.

Band 75 Karsten Seifert: Das interamerikanische System zum Schutz der Menschenrechte und seine Reformierung. 2008.

Band 76 Nora Graaff: Staatenverantwortlichkeit. Vom „völkerrechtlichen Verbrechen" zur „schwerwiegenden Verletzung einer zwingenden Völkerrechtsnorm" anhand der ILC-Kodifikationsarbeit. 2008.

Band 77 Aldona Szczeponek: Die Umsetzung des Völkerrechts und des europäischen Gemeinschaftsrechts in Polen. Unter Berücksichtigung verfassungsrechtlicher Lösungen anderer europäischer Staaten. 2008.

Band 78 Christian Friedrich Fonk: Europäische Luftqualitätsziele und nationale Erfüllungsverantwortung. 2009.

Band 79 Christina Prinzhorn: Der Grundsatz des öffentlichen Zugangs zu amtlichen Dokumenten aus der Perspektive des internationalen Rechts. Materiell-rechtliche Vorgaben durch das internationale Recht für Informationszugangsrechte in den nationalen Rechtsordnungen Europas. 2009.

Band 80 Steffen Eicker: Der Deutsch-Herero-Krieg und das Völkerrecht. Die völkerrechtliche Haftung der Bundesrepublik Deutschland für das Vorgehen des Deutschen Reiches gegen die Herero in Deutsch-Südwestafrika im Jahre 1904 und ihre Durchsetzung vor einem nationalen Gericht. 2009.

Band 81 Niels Beisinghoff: Corporations and Human Rights. An Analysis of ATCA Litigation against Corporations. 2009.

Band 82 Gesine Wolf-Zimper: Zielgerichtete Sanktionen des Sicherheitsrates der Vereinten Nationen und effektiver Rechtsschutz. 2009.

Band 83 David Bergius: Die offene Frage des Privateigentums der Vertriebenen im deutsch-polnischen Verhältnis. 2009.

Band 84 Axel Rolf Schneider: Petitionen zum Europäischen Parlament mit Berücksichtigung des Bürgerbeauftragten. 2009.

Band 85 Tobias Nord: Rechtsnachfolge bei zwischenstaatlichen Organisationen. 2010.

Band 86 Marcel Bongard: Emissionshandel und effektiver Rechtsschutz: Ein unvereinbarer Gegensatz? Eine Untersuchung zu den Auswirkungen marktwirtschaftlicher Umweltschutzinstrumente auf den Individualrechtsschutz am Beispiel des Emissionshandelssystems. 2010.

Band 87 Armin Huhn: Amtshaftung im bewaffneten Auslandseinsatz. Anwendbarkeit und Leistungsfähigkeit des Amtshaftungsrechts bei Verletzung des *ius in bello*. 2010.

Band 88 Johannes Mosters: Ethische Beschaffung. Sekundärzwecke im Zeitalter der Globalisierung. 2010.

Band 89 Thomas Herntrich: Thüringen. Von den thüringischen Kleinstaaten nach Zerfall des Alten Reiches bis zum Freistaat Thüringen. Eine völkerrechtliche und verfassungsrechtliche Betrachtung. 2010.

Band 90 Marcelo Antonio Villagrán Abarzúa: Verfassungsrechtliche Grundlagen der Gemeindeverwaltung in Chile. Auch ein Beitrag zur Dezentralisierung und Dekonzentration. 2010.

Band 91 Manfred Hechtl: Die offensive Defensive: Das Recht der präventiven Selbstverteidigung? Lösungsansätze für (scheinbare) Bedrohungen durch einzelne Staaten und internationale Terrornetzwerke. 2011.

Band 92 Christian Grüner: Quantität und Qualität der europäischen Rechtsetzung. 2011.

Band 93 Anna Keller: Der neue Rechtsrahmen für den öffentlichen Rundfunk in Frankreich. 2011.

Band 94 Jörn Eschment: Musterprozesse vor dem Europäischen Gerichtshof für Menschenrechte. Probleme und Perspektiven des Piloturteilsverfahrens. 2011.

Band 95 Marija Dietrich: Staatliches Souveränitätsverständnis im Wandel der gesellschaftspolitischen Strukturen. Eine Perspektive der Europäischen Union nach Inkrafttreten des Vertrags von Lissabon. 2011.

Band 96 Philipp Austermann: Die Anrechnungsbestimmungen im Abgeordnetenrecht des Bundes und der Länder. Eine verfassungsrechtliche und verfassungspolitische Untersuchung unter besonderer Berücksichtigung des Abgeordnetenstatus. 2011.

Band 97 Gilbert Gornig (Hrsg.): Krisengebiete der Welt. Völkerrechtliche und politische Aspekte. 2011.

Band 98 Jörg Brackmann: Genehmigung, Anmeldung und Anzeige gentechnischer Arbeiten und Anlagen. Nach den Änderungen des Gentechnikrechts 2002, 2005 und 2008. 2011.

Band 99 Giuseppe de Vergottini / Valeria Piergigli (eds.): Topographical Names and Protection of Linguistic Minorities. 2011.

Peter Lang · Internationaler Verlag der Wissenschaften

Marcus Galdia

Legal Linguistics

Frankfurt am Main, Berlin, Bern, Bruxelles, New York, Oxford, Wien, 2009.
434 pp.
ISBN 978-3-631-59463-6 · hardback € 80,80*

This book introduces into the problems of Legal Linguistics. It starts with the most fundamental legal-linguistic question, i.e. how law is created and applied with linguistic means. In breaking down this vast question, the book identifies the linguistically relevant aspects of language use, especially its terminology, and scrutinizes the most significant legal-linguistic operations such as the legal argumentation, the legal interpretation, and the legal translation. Based on case analyses, it canvasses the language use strategies that are most instrumental in the developing of professionally convincing legal argumentation, primarily around terminological units. Towards the background of these and other linguistic operations in law, the book reflects upon some practical problems related to the regulation of language use and the emergence of the global law.

Contents: Foundations of Legal Linguistics · Legal Speech Acts and Legal Discourse · Legal Argumentation · Legal Interpretation · Legal Translation · Textuality of Law · Linguistic Aspects of Global Law · Linguistic Rights

Frankfurt am Main · Berlin · Bern · Bruxelles · New York · Oxford · Wien
Distribution: Verlag Peter Lang AG
Moosstr. 1, CH-2542 Pieterlen
Telefax 0041 (0) 32 / 376 17 27

*The €-price includes German tax rate
Prices are subject to change without notice

Homepage http://www.peterlang.de